15 . IV . 15

Second Hand.

STAFFORD
CRIPPS

To Corinne, Helen and Sarah

STAFFORD CRIPPS

A
POLITICAL
LIFE

Simon Burgess

VICTOR GOLLANCZ

LONDON

The right of Simon Burgess to be identified as the
author of this work has been asserted by him in accordance
with the Copyright, Designs and Patents Act, 1988

First published in Great Britain in 1999
by Victor Gollancz
An imprint of Orion Books Ltd
Orion House, 5 Upper St Martin's Lane, London WC2H 9EA

A CIP catalogue record for this book is
available from the British Library

ISBN 0 575 06565 6

Typeset by Selwood Systems, Midsomer Norton
Printed and bound in Great Britain by
Butler & Tanner, Frome and London

CONTENTS

PREFACE

The Rt Hon. Sir Stafford Cripps KC, MP, FRS (1889–1952) was something of a puzzle to the general public, journalists, opponents and associates, friends, his own family and even, at times, to himself. Why should his character and actions be any more explicable to a biographer?

The attempt to explain the mystique of Stafford Cripps, which had become an important part of his political appeal, was first made in two wartime studies: *Cripps – a Portrait and a Prospect* (1942) and Patricia Strauss's *Cripps – Advocate and Rebel* (1943). They were able to give only the barest outline of his early years, although Strauss, seeing him at close quarters throughout the 1930s, provided more of an inside view. Eric Estorick, in his more substantial *Stafford Cripps – a Biography* (1949), had privileged access to many of Cripps's private papers, but the result was uncritically flattering, and unfortunate in its timing (see Chapter 24). The posthumous *The Life of Richard Stafford Cripps* by Colin Cooke, completed with the co-operation of Cripps's devoted widow, Dame Isobel Cripps, was not well received and strangely unreal. A short profile appeared in a book of iconoclastic essays in the early 1960s,[1] Lord Attlee dismissing it because it had been written 'by someone who never knew him'.[2] A new, official, biography was eventually commissioned in 1972, but has been held up by unforeseeable delays. There have been, in the meantime, several monographs covering particular phases of his political activities – leader of the Socialist League in the 1930s, wartime ambassador to the Soviet Union, and wartime emissary to India[3] – but no overall assessment. The more recent portrait, by Chris Bryant, while strong on Cripps's personal side, was too superficial in its coverage of his public activities to make good the deficiency.[4]

Although Cripps was an important figure in the wartime coalition, and one of the 'big five' members of the Attlee governments, his contribution to military victory and economic recovery remained questionable and contentious, the 2 million papers held by Nuffield College (with more retained by the family) shedding little light on this, and the number of surviving witnesses who knew or worked with him rapidly dwindling. His supposedly forbidding personality – 'Austerity Cripps' – though misconstrued, acted as a further difficulty. 'Cripps he has failed to animate,' one novelist wrote of the author of a study of Britain during the Second World War. 'Could one?'[5]

An advantage has, however, followed from this neglect. Since the 1970s, historical appreciation of the war and early post-war years has come of age and been stripped of much of its mythology. This has happened for two main reasons. The public records covering the wartime and post-war period were gradually released under the thirty-year rule, yielding a wealth of new archival material to add to other unpublished papers; and viewpoints about the recent past have been powerfully reshaped by contemporary developments in British politics, bringing about a dramatic shift of perspective. The aims and achievements of the wartime and Attlee governments have, for the first time, been authoritatively documented and radically reinterpreted.

A balanced account and appraisal of the public and political career of Sir Stafford Cripps must take account of these advances in evidence and interpretation. The 'stained-glass' representation of earlier biographers will no longer suffice. Even the most high-minded politicians have to operate in a crowded, three-dimensional reality of human and institutional constraints, the impact they make depending on their effect on others as much as on the satisfying of their own conscience or ambition.

Cripps was hardly a conventional politician. How many other front-rank ministers of modern times have, while still in office and within sight of the premiership, preached the futility of all political action? Supremely self-confident but unskilled in skulduggery, contemptuous of party machines and lacking in any feel for the loyalties of the labour movement, Cripps doubted, as he once confessed, whether he altogether understood politics.[6] The cynical suggest that politicians have no independent existence, springing to life only in a collective setting. The task of the political biographer is to marry what Cripps, from his lonely pinnacle, believed he was doing with the momentous circumstances of national survival that he, his colleagues and his country were obliged to face.

My gratitude must go, firstly, to the late Lady Theresa (Sir Stafford Cripps's third daughter) and Sir Robert Ricketts, and Sara Mason (their daughter), who, learning of my interest, showed kindness and hospitality in talking to me about Sir Stafford Cripps, without associating themselves in any way with the project.

I am also grateful to those who agreed to talk about their often very distant memories of Cripps: Major and the Hon. Mrs Derek Allhusen, George Blaker, Vincent Brome, Sir Max Brown, Walter Carrington, Baroness Castle, Lord Cockfield, Lionel Elvin, the Rt Hon. John Freeman, Wally Jenkins, Julia Mash, the late Dame Alix Meynell, Sir Max Nicolson. Lord Plowden, Cecilia Sebestyien, the late Baroness Seear, Romer Topham and Sir Geoffrey Wilson.

Thanks are also due to Lord Parmoor for showing me, and allowing me to quote from, a copy of the memoir of Theresa Cripps by Alfred Cripps (the first Lord Parmoor); Rachel Cook, Gavin Knight and Joan Barksfield for a tour of Parmoor House and its history; Nicholas Meinertzhagen, for conversations and for reading through an early draft of Chapter 1; the librarians of the Middle Temple Library; Paul Tyler, for his compendious knowledge of the Woolwich Labour Party; Irving Rogers, for generously letting me read his late father's unpublished autobiography, as well as many letters and photographs; the staff of the Bristol Record Office; the Rt Hon. Tony Benn MP, for a tape of Sir Stafford Cripps speaking; Anne, Countess Attlee, for showing me valuable correspondence; Pamela Clark, of the Royal Archives; Mark Barrington-Ward, who copied out important portions of the diary of his father; Mark Pottle, for sending me extracts from the diary of Violet Bonham Carter, by courtesy of her literary executors; the British Library; the Bodleian Library; the National Archives of Canada (Graham Spry papers, thanks to Irene Spry) in Ottawa and the Thomas Fisher Rare Book Library (Alan Jarvis papers) in Toronto; Professor K. O. Morgan, for notes of his interview with the late Lord Trend; Nicholas Owen; Howard B. Gotlieb, director of the Mugar Memorial Library, Boston University, for the post-war diary of Cecil King; Mary Woods, for opening a suitcase and looking inside; Barbara Forbes-Adam, for her letter; David Astor, for answering my enquiry; Peregrine Worsthorne, Alan Watkins, Hugo Young and Anthony Howard, who provided information about old Fleet Street colleagues; Professor George Jones; Philip Ling; Elizabeth Al-Qahdi, for the Strachey papers; Susan Knowles, of the BBC Written Archives Centre; the Mass Observation archive at the University of Sussex; the Staff at the Lambeth Palace Library and Barbara Affolter (née Liechti), for letters, photographs and a scrapbook covering the Crippses' stays at the Bircher-Benner Klinik, Zurich.

To Michael Estorick I incurred a special debt in being allowed to see the working papers used in his late father's biography of Cripps, especially his notes of interviews.

Acknowledgement for allowing me to quote from material is owed to the gracious permission of Her Majesty the Queen; to the Public Record Office for Crown Copyright papers; to the Warden and fellows of Nuffield College (the Cripps papers); to the kind permission of the National Library of Wales (the Thomas Jones archive); to the British Library of Political and Economic Science (the diaries and papers of Beatrice Webb and Hugh Dalton); to the Clerk of Records in the House of Lords Record Office (on behalf of the Beaverbrook Foundation Trust) (the David Lloyd George papers); to Anne, Countess Attlee; to Lord Methuen (the Courtney diary); to Diana Collins; to Mark Barrington-Ward; to Jane, Elizabeth and Eliza Bonham Carter; to the Bristol Record Office and Irving Rogers (Bristol East Labour Party archive); and to Robin Gordon Walker.

To Sean Magee, at Gollancz, I am most grateful for his constancy. Bob Davenport made sense out of much nonsense.

A final salute goes to my parents and to my brother, who heroically joined in the hunt.

1

DAD

My children, God has willed that you should grow in the wild garden of the world, without the tender care of your Mother ... but we can turn together towards the memory of Mother as a source of strength and courage, looking back, not with regret, but with gratitude. You, her children, must show that you have inherited some portion of the noble, unselfish nature, and that in this way you will raise to her the only monument which has an enduring value.

Alfred Cripps, in 1893[1]

'Sir Stafford,' wrote one contemporary of Chancellor Cripps, 'ever since he entered public life, has sincerely and zealously been engaged in breaking the mould in which he was shaped, so that similar types will not again be possible in this country.'[2] The accusation that Stafford Cripps – offspring of a wealthy and landed family, son of an eminent lawyer and peer of the realm, Lord Parmoor, and holder of a knighthood – was motivated by some psychological quirk driving him to do away with his own privileged kind was familiar in the 1930s and 1940s.

He had, it was recalled, denounced the rallying cry of 'King and Country' (a call to which he used to respond), advocated abolishing the House of Lords (in which his father sat), and condemned the failure of the Churches to tackle urgent social issues (though he was a lay Anglican) – all in the name of non-violent social revolution, and with a reckless disregard for respectability which delighted his associates and exasperated the Labour Party's moderate figures. No one else, in Tory eyes, so typified the discord and degeneracy of the British Left in the inter-war years.

In the very different circumstances after 1945, when the incoming Labour Government was confronted with having to restore Britain's economic position, it was Cripps who became most closely identified with export-led austerity and high taxation, eliminating luxury and poverty in pursuit of the greater good of fair shares, even though this was not always popular with the party's own working-class supporters. Cripps epitomised the well-born political puritan, his single-minded dedication to the task, his 'first-class mind brooding on our affairs' – Churchill's phrase – reinforcing the impression of a grim, gentlemanly leveller.

This was not how those closest to Cripps saw him. 'I am afraid people don't understand him,' his wife observed. 'He is trying to introduce moral and spiritual ideas into politics, and this is not easy in these sceptical, self-seeking times.'[3] Admirers of his essentially happy nature compared him to other moral exemplars of profound radicalism and religious conviction of the recent past, disinterestedly preaching personal sacrifice whatever the cost in public esteem, living proof that England could still produce such character. Indeed, because of Lord Parmoor's own Labourite sympathies after the Great War, Cripps embodied a new, baffling hybrid, the hereditary socialist, his beliefs fore-shadowing his own progressive demise.

Such contradictory impulses – common among many early recruits to the liberal Left from the aristocratic and upper middle classes – must be of import-ance in understanding his personality. They assume added significance set against the major upheavals through which Cripps lived and the country passed. By the late 1940s, the contrast between the lost world of late-Victorian Britain and the new egalitarian welfarism was striking. Few individuals entirely dominate their age, but many have found it fitting, at the time and since, to talk of the era of Cripps. The question was current, and has been of continuing interest: how to relate the spartan, self-appointed saviour of the immediate post-war period to the exceptionally favoured circumstances of his background and upbringing?

The Cripps family name, believed to be of Saxon pedigree, can be authentically traced back to the 1500s, and Stafford Cripps grew up fully conscious that he sprang from a long line of country gentlemen of pronounced Christian outlook. A Milo Crispin, who arrived with the Norman Conquest, is recorded in the Domesday Book; though he may not have had children, several gen-erations of Crispes are later found living at Stanlake, and then at Copcott Manor, in the county of Oxford, and in Cirencester, near Gloucester. By the eighteenth century, the main family branch already had a substantial land-owning interest, with established ties to the clergy, the law and local politics. Joseph Cripps (1765–1847) sat as Member of Parliament for Cirencester in an unbroken run of thirty-five years, stretching over ten parliaments. The Crippses were modest representatives of that quintessentially English social stratum, the self-perpetuating squirearchy, uniting religion, community and 'service' – a code word for leadership. Although their antecedents were uncertain, the family had a strong sense of distinguished lineage, enhanced by arranged marriages and matchmaking, spread throughout the pages of *Burke's Landed Gentry*. A hundred adult relatives came to tea at 11 Downing Street in 1949.

This distant ancestry commingled with the more immediate guidance of

Cripps's parents. Charles Alfred Cripps – third son and sixth child of Henry William, a prominent ecclesiastical lawyer, and Blanche Alexander Cripps – had gifts of charm, tact and ability to go with family connections. Following the path of Winchester and New College, Oxford, which his father and grandfather had taken before him, he obtained four first classes and a fellowship (playing football for the university on the winning side in the Association Cup Final of 1874), but, unattracted by academic life, entered the law and was called to the Bar in 1877. The same year, his brother William, a surgeon, married Blanche Potter, one of nine daughters of the entrepreneurial Potter family who lived at Standish House, near Stroud. The Potter sisterhood were, for their day, highly cultured, with a keen social conscience and a mystic strain, inculcated by centuries of churchgoing. At an evening party held by William and Blanche, Alfred Cripps met Theresa Potter, coming away 'restlessly anxious' for her companionship.

Apart from briefly working with Canon Barnett, the founder of Toynbee Hall, Theresa Potter had no vocational training, was socially shy, and did not at first take to the rising barrister. She spent the winter of 1880–1 visiting Italy with her younger sister, Beatrice, but, after an interval, Alfred and she were reacquainted, got engaged, and were married – they were both twenty-nine – in October 1881, the Potters making up for their earlier disapproval of William by acknowledging that the Crippses were 'worthy people, quite as good as we are'.[4] A first son, Seddon, was born in 1883, after which the newly-weds took over the parental seat of Parmoor, in Buckinghamshire. A daughter, Ruth (in 1884), and two more sons, Frederick Heyworth (1885) and Leonard Harrison (1887), subsequently arrived. A fifth child, and fourth boy, Richard Stafford, was born on 24 April 1889, at Elm Park Gardens, their town house off the Fulham Road in west London.[5]

Parmoor stood on a thickly wooded plateau commanding a view across the Chilterns, set among four hundred acres of hillside and farmland close by the village of Frieth. The nearest towns – High Wycombe, Marlow and Henley-on-Thames – were only a few miles distant, but the estate was relatively secluded. An old road from Marlow to Oxford skirted Frieth, but road connections with High Wycombe were rudimentary; a carrier van did not begin operating until 1895. Traversing the neighbourhood was difficult and time-consuming. Though the village had many springs and ponds, drinking water had to be carried up to the house every day. Rainwater was stored in underground tanks in case of fire. There was no electric lighting.[6] The chair-making industry in Wycombe relied on the train link with London, but Buckinghamshire was the last of the Home Counties to develop a rail network.

Once Alfred began building up his legal practice – he took silk in 1890, and was involved in many celebrated cases before the Parliamentary Bar,[7] bringing in as much as 1000 guineas a week – the house was enlarged, decorated by

Theresa. More land was bought, making Parmoor the centre of village life, providing employment for domestic servants, several tenant farmers and a large troop of agricultural labourers. The local church was restored, the cricket club was revived, and flower shows were held on the spacious lawns. Alfred insisted Parmoor should be a working farm, run on business lines; owing to the success of 'the farm in London', as he described his Bar career, they were able to ride out the agricultural depression of the 1890s. A Liberal at university and a friend of prominent Liberals like Asquith and Haldane, he was alarmed by the struggle over Irish Home Rule, and by the exciting of class distinctions whipped up by 'Radical' (Liberal) orators. Together with his elder brother, Arthur, he financed a newspaper, the *South Bucks Standard* – an 'honest', 'earnest' Unionist organ extolling the virtues of the Salisbury administration (in an area of important Conservative allegiance) and missing no opportunity of praising the conscientious owners of Parmoor. Alfred Cripps was an agreeable paternalist, favouring fair dealing and mutual co-operation between masters and workmen, contributing to the life of his estate far more than he took out,[8] certain his labourers were more contented than his own class.[9]

Stafford (the Richard was soon dropped), youngest of the family, became Theresa's favourite. In a diary entry, when Stafford was barely a year old, Alfred noted that 'Baby does not sleep well, but his mother thinks he has too great a brain development, & looks to him as the rising genius among her boys. We have everything to be thankful for & we feel grateful.' The older children were protective towards, but astonished by, the precocious infant.

Theresa had never enjoyed good health, and the labours of childbirth strained her far from robust constitution. Even so, she remained active, organising a technical institute for young girls in Wycombe and accompanying Alfred to public meetings when – with the help of Mary Playne (née Potter) – he was adopted as Conservative candidate for the Stroud division in April 1893. After addressing a gathering of the Women's Unionist Association in Stroud on Thursday 18 May, she returned to their London home on the Monday, bright and well. According to the informed account in the *Stroud News*,

> On the following day, Tuesday, one of her children [Leonard] getting unwell, she nursed him all the week until the Saturday. On that day the child was quite convalescent, and Mrs Cripps went to her home at Parmoor in the afternoon. She seemed perfectly well, and slept as usual during the night, but complained of her throat on Sunday morning. She went for a walk with her husband during the afternoon, and they all dined together at 1 o'clock, as they always did on Sundays. After dinner she went to her room, and her throat became troublesome. Her husband sent for a doctor, but the medical gentleman did not consider it serious, and ordered bathing with hot water. She however became rapidly worse

after 12 o'clock on Sunday night; the doctor was sent for again at 2.30. He arrived about 5, and declared her case to be hopeless. Mr Cripps at once telegraphed to London to his brother, Dr W. Harrison Cripps, but he did not arrive till after Mrs Cripps' death. She died about 10 o'clock on Monday morning. The immediate cause was suffocation, and an attempt at trachaeotomy proved unsuccessful. The throat must have been poisoned in some very virulent manner. She herself believed that she caught the poison in nursing the child in London.[10]

The funeral in Frieth churchyard took place on the Friday, before a large crowd of mourners. As the coffin was borne to the graveside, 'directly behind walked C. A. Cripps with his five motherless little ones, the youngest little boy, only four years old, holding his father's hand. It was indeed a touching sight.' After the blessing, 'all stood in silence while the little children threw in their flowers before their father led them away.'[11]

Theresa's sudden death from diphtheria[12] – 'swift and almost without warning' – was a heavy blow to Alfred, who aged physically as he sought consolation, referring incessantly to his late wife, convinced of her continued existence and spiritual presence.[13] But his personal sadness was tempered by the need to comfort his uncomprehending children. 'I can only tell you a little at a time how Mother loved you,' he wrote from Elm Park Gardens. 'She would have gone through any grief or sorrow if only to help you to be good and kind. She wished you to grow up loving Jesus and you must come to Pater whenever he can help his dear little Stafford.'[14] When Kate Courtney (another Potter sister) visited Parmoor a few weeks later, she found Alfred in a state of 'forced cheerfulness', 'never forgetting or even trying to – only fearing that the memory should fade some day'. The children, all clad in black,

> talk of their mother especially the two youngest who prattle on with apparently light hearts till some special clinging kiss or half fear of being alone showed a full consciousness of their loss. Lennie's will that no one can sleep in mother's room again – little Staff's 'Take me with you Auntie; your voice makes me think of Mother's it's so like hers.'[15]

Theresa, 'knowing how near death may be', had left behind two documents: one to her husband and one setting out her wishes for the future care of the children. Alfred incorporated them into a privately printed memoir. The impact of her parting message was to survive in surprising ways. She hoped her children would continue to grow up mainly in the country and be educated in the same style as their father, living simply and 'without show', trained to be 'undogmatic and unsectarian Christians', looking upon Christ's words 'as the great hope and light to guide mankind to the entrance of a vast spiritual existence' and choosing Christ as 'their sole Hero and Master'. By emphasising the faith their mother had taught them, 'not to bring sadness but to give you strength', Alfred eased the passing, leaving photographs and likenesses of her around the house, turning the memory of her sacrifice into a permanent reminder.[16]

What effect might this tragedy have had on a young, impressionable mind? The consequences of maternal deprivation in early infancy are disputed. Sudden withdrawal of motherly affection is usually extremely distressing, even when a mother substitute is available.[17] A remarkably high proportion of senior public figures have suffered loss or bereavement in early life, being spurred on, it is contended, by the compensatory need for popular acclaim, even though they are often temperamentally highly strung.[18] Adversity can, paradoxically, instil fortitude of character, encouraging the personal myth that one is 'special'. Cripps, coming from his background, would have high expectations as a matter of course, but all the children turned out very differently, and the whole valedictory tenor of piety and edification was not uncommon.[19] The point is what he was able to make of it. With few first-hand memories of his mother to go on, and a lingering feeling that her dying had been needless,[20] the youngster was left only with the words of her last testament, which he treated literally and as a source of inspiration, idealising her memory and internalising her wishes. Almost exactly fifty years after Theresa's death – in the middle of the war against the Axis powers – he openly appealed for a body of people with the 'violent infection' (sic) of Christianity who were prepared to sacrifice everything, including wealth, privilege and even life itself, for the sake of principles in which they believed.[21] 'As a child, as a boy, and as a young man,' a friend later commented, 'it is clear that the standards he set himself in his daily life were those he thought she would have chosen.'[22] The spiritual legacy of his mother and the prompting of his father, allied in time to his own searching intelligence, were both sources from which he derived inner purpose and direction.

The day Stafford was born, a governess, the diminutive Miss Marshall ('Mazelle'), came to Parmoor to care for Ruth. Mazelle took over the rearing of the Crippses. She had formerly been retained by the Schlumberger family in Alsace, and brought an exotic tone to the household. Alfred wanted the children to grow freely, giving them the run of the grounds and the farmyard. Stafford, meanwhile, would be conducted around the estate by Mazelle, 'seated regally in a pony cart'.[23] With Theresa gone, Alfred disliked inviting any of her other sisters; instead, during the summer holidays, when Seddon and Freddie were back from boarding school, the whole party migrated to the Playnes, at Longfords in the Cotswolds. Aunt Mary, Stafford recalled, adopted him, and his relatives, amused by his habit of delivering wise, grown-up pro-nouncements, took to calling him 'Dad' – a nickname which stuck, even with

Cripps senior, whose whole approach was to treat children like adults.[24] The Playnes were influential notables, owning a cloth factory in the seat of the West of England cloth trade. With Alfred standing in the Stroud constituency, Mary was determined to 'get our Charlie in'. When an election was called in July 1895, Cripps campaigned with his eldest sons, dressed in Eton suits, pulled around in a wagonette. 'Dad', already showing resourcefulness, set up a teashop at home, raiding the larder and charging sixpence a head to his father's helpers.[25] Visiting Stroud, he was 'stolen' by the 'naughty Radicals' and hidden in the back room of a public house.[26] Alfred won by five hundred votes.

Aged eight, Stafford was sent to a boarding school, St David's in Reigate, where Seddon and Freddie had also been and which Leonard was still attending. Responding to the competitive environment, he made such progress he began to outshine Lennie, the elder by two years. To obviate any rivalry, his father transferred him to another boys-only establishment at Rottingdean, on the Sussex coast. For the first time he was entirely apart from other family members. Classes were small and discipline was strict, with the specific aim of preparing pupils for the entrance examination to one of the Clarendon public schools. His dutiful letters home, tinged with shyness and isolation, recorded his schoolboy eagerness to excel. The problem was holding him back. Alfred felt that he himself, as a child prodigy, had been pushed too hard, and was concerned to restrain the youngster's inclinations. 'The chief thing to be guarded against', his headmaster agreed, 'is any overpressure – we must not let him make the pace too great – it's difficult to realise he's so young.'[27]

During the long vacations, once the obligatory hour of lessons was out of the way, high spirits prevailed, much time being spent careering about on horseback and in constructing things – a wooden boat, underground houses in the gardens. Father, returning at the weekends, gave them all playful legal briefs, tied up in red string, to encourage lawyerly habits. His younger brother, Leonard subsequently confirmed, 'absorbed the spotlight and began to create a sort of controlling interest in our nursery', often admitting his intention in life was to finish up as Lord Chancellor – the office famously parodied in Gilbert and Sullivan's *Iolanthe*. It was a poignant aspiration.

Despite having (as a recently elected MP) to abandon part of his practice at the Bar, Alfred's own legal career had flourished, and he had many distinguished clients – among them the London County Council and the Great Western Railway Company. He was also a leading figure on the High Church (ritualist) wing of the Church of England, as well as an adviser to the Prince of Wales. In the Conservative parliamentary party his talents were not readily rewarded, however. Crestfallen at being passed over for the office of Solicitor-General in May 1900, he lost Stroud in the general election five months later. Missing his late wife more than ever, he held out high hopes for his children, monitoring their progress with anxiety.

Stafford Cripps entered Winchester College as a Commoner in the 'Short Half' (autumn term) of 1901, a year younger than most of his peers (he was twelve), but overlapping with the final year of Freddie.[28]

Winchester was then at the very start of the headmastership of H. M. Burge, the first non-Wykehamist to hold the post. Burge, just turned forty, was a tall, stooping, saintly Doctor of Divinity, inclined to be sympathetic, and a deft administrator.[29] Though a traditional classicist, he had been lured by the governors on the understanding he would introduce a broader-based curriculum, which the Public Schools Commission was calling for. The learning of Greek and Latin was still regarded as the pre-eminent discipline, but there was a growing fear that Winchester might lose out to other public schools which did more to cater for entry into the professions. Burge's task was to maintain the quality of classical teaching, while allowing pupils the choice of specialising in modern languages or mathematics and science in their final two years. George Moberley, one of Burge's predecessors, had claimed that all classical learning told on a man's character, whereas elementary science was 'unfruitful'.[30] The object of the reform now desired was to give greater importance to subjects of vocational utility, and of curiosity to the brightest students. Burge also presided over a relaxation of some of the more irrational Winchester 'notions' – the codes and conventions of right conduct peculiar to the College, and a torment for the uninitiated[31] – so that, at the time when Cripps joined, far-reaching changes were under way in College life.

Cripps struggled at first, unused to fagging and perturbed by the demanding academic standard, promotions being based on merit and not age. The family's long association with Winchester, and Alfred's involvement (he became a fellow in 1904, and then a governor), are bound to have helped, making it less likely for him to be picked upon. His best grades were in history, but his writing and spelling remained untidy. Until the age of fifteen, Latin and Greek were compulsory. 'I find he is quite good in getting the main point of what he reads,' Burge wrote to Cripps's father, 'but needs a great deal more practice in setting out his point, leading up to it and seeing what follows from it'; nevertheless, 'he is a thoroughly good fellow'.[32]

Cripps's own interests also developed. He made his first trip abroad, as one of a party journeying across Switzerland, taking in Mont Blanc, until they ran out of money. Foreign travel was from then on a regular annual event. He took to bicycling, then, mechanically minded, acquired a motorcycle licence in 1905, when he was sixteen, and learned to drive the family tourer, fascinated by the working of motor cars. Holidays were spent engrossed in projects, often on his own. George Schuster, a friend of Freddie's at Oxford and a frequent visitor to Parmoor for fox-hunting, could not recall seeing him.[33] But he already had an air of self-assurance – punctuated by exuberant outbursts, dressing up for amateur theatricals or going to the Henley Regatta – remarkable to his sister Ruth, who had an abiding memory of how sure of himself he was. Stafford was 'a regular young devil', witnesses say, 'always ordering people about', and 'it was better to accept the inevitable, for he had his way in the end'. Another (unwilling) guest, Kitty Dobbs, had trouble adjusting to the well-regulated household, 'on one occasion kicking my cousin Stafford during the afternoon tea for trying to make me say grace'.[34]

When the chance came to specialise, he chose science, and especially chemistry, stimulated by the prospect of winning the first entrance scholarship in chemistry to Winchester's sister institution (his father's old college, as well as that of his two oldest brothers), New College, Oxford. Scientists were still disadvantaged, but Burge, the science master reported, allowed 'a wide freedom for boys to develop special gifts, so long as they can prove themselves capable of using the privilege'.[35] Laboratory work in the new Science School building appealed to Cripps's practical side; the necessity for logical and abstract thought to his intellect.[36] Critics of Cripps in later years noted his lack of training in the humanities. In fact he loved the 'magnificent humanity' of Browning, whose poems, celebrating moral rather than physical power, were read at evening recitals by his father and his redoubtable uncle, Lord Courtney.[37] But he liked pointing out he was a 'scientific' and not a 'classical' Wykehamist, lamenting the hold the latter enjoyed in official circles compared with those who innovate or produce. Elected a fellow of the Royal Society in 1948, he considered it the greatest compliment ever made to him.[38] It is not easy to group him with that cohort of Victorian and Edwardian Britons supposedly hostile to 'the industrial spirit'. A country child with gumption, he was neither ignorant nor suspicious of rapid technical progress.

In other respects he conformed to the public-school ideal. At seventeen, in the view of one don, J. S. Furley, Cripps was most mature, the head of his house, and, while keeping order, was likeable and respected – if somewhat remote. 'He seemed', his school contemporary the future author and MP A. P. Herbert thought, 'to live on a distant cloud.'[39] Others were envious his father allowed him to entertain at the Royal Hotel. He was House captain of 'Our Game', Winchester's version of football, with distinctive rules and vocabulary. More enthusiastic than skilful, but always wanting to lead, he aspired to the English model of sporting prowess, imperial patriotism and unquestioning religiosity. A character clue can be had from his reading at Winchester – Bagehot's *Physics and Politics*, originally published in 1872, which explained the laws of society in terms of the doctrines of natural selection and inheritance, justifying a biological hierarchy. The remedy for combating the decline of the English stock, for both father and son, was general education for the working classes, paid out of the rates.[40] Though suffering from unexplained illnesses, Cripps had grown into a 'beefy' six-footer, studious (with his mother's dark eyes) and puckish by turns. Villagers knew him as a virile centre half in the Frieth football team.[41]

An interesting sequel provides a further pointer to his attitudes towards the end of his time at Winchester. The cult of 'notions' had come under increasing attack for sanctioning prefectorial tyranny. A glossary of notions, supplying Wykehamists with a dictionary of their own language, had been completed in 1901 'by three Beetleites', one of whom was Cripps's eldest brother Seddon, making it easier for freshers to learn how they were expected to behave. The older the boy, the more the antiquity and eccentricity of the notions was treasured. That this was Cripps's position is evident from an exchange of letters in the College magazine in November 1908, shortly after he had left:

Sir,

In your last issue I notice a letter purporting to legalise dribbling (in College Canvas at any rate). The writer may be perfectly correct as regards College Canvas, but I feel sure that in Fifteens he would not have the rules on his side. In the 1907 edition of the *Rules of Winchester Football* (p. 10) he will find the words: 'The ball must be always kicked as hard as in the umpire's opinion is possible.' How this can permit of dribbling anywhere in the field, whether in the hot [a scrimmage or scrum] or in open play I, for one, cannot understand. It has always been a more or less recognised rule that there should be no kicking in the hot, and indeed the foregoing words, together with the paragraph on 'kneeling and kicking in the hot', would seem to imply this.

Whether or not the umpires in Fifteens will penalise for this offence remains to be seen; but I am sure that dribbling, of any kind whatsoever, must always be a violation of the spirit of 'The Game'.

R. Stafford Cripps[42]

The author of an adjoining letter, differing 'with all due deference to so distinguished a critic as the late captain of Houses', found it 'too ludicrous' to suppose that, if the ball could not be kicked hard, it could not be kicked at all. 'Mr Cripps credits those who are responsible for our written rules with amazing stupidity.'

Cripps took the strictest interpretation of the rules – adding an inevitable appeal to the spirit of 'playing the game' – but the dexterity with which the quarrel was conducted is noteworthy. The complexity of Winchester's notions was designed to promote ingenuity in argument, since it was always open to the agile-minded to triumph in discussion or avoid punishment by mastering the full range of notions.[43] Cripps, without taking any active part in the debating society, clearly imbibed a great deal of Wykehamite self-assertion.

A revised edition of the dictionary of notions, 'dedicated to all past, present and future Wykehamists', appeared in 1910, largely updated by Cripps himself –

three years after he had moved on. This was not the act of someone engaged in revolt against authority. Cripps was an archetypical Edwardian public school-boy, a youthful traditionalist, oddly unconventional with his grounding in science, but fondly attached to what his old college represented, however obscure to the outsider.[44] He had, in short, the accepting outlook of a young man who does not 'see' the assumptions he has been educated with so much as see the world 'through' them, testifying to the success with which they have been transmitted.[45]

Although lagging behind the topmost students in his final year, Cripps comfortably reached VI Book, the highest division (or class), needing the remaining weeks to prepare for the scholarship examination for New College in December 1907, particularly in boning up on the long-abandoned classics. To the delight of family and tutors, he triumphed, winning the scholarship in natural science and earning the highest praise from the examiners, failing to secure full marks only because he forgot the date of Queen Elizabeth's accession.[46] He is 'of *quite* first-rate ability', Burge wrote in congratulation. 'But better than all that, he is a fellow of real high purpose and genuine appreciation – I respect and like him very much.'[47] His scripts were marked by Sir William Ramsay, holder of the chair in chemistry at University College, London, and Ramsay, talent-spotting for his much better-equipped department, poached Cripps to come and do research under him. His father, reluctant to break with family custom, had strong doubts, but Cripps, captivated by Ramsay's renown, was adamant he should go.

Too much has been made of this episode. One story was that Cripps had been awarded the New College scholarship only as a result of his father's influence; an obituarist described the decision to turn his back on it as a 'strange aberration';[48] it has even been implied that Cripps might have learned to mix better had he gone to Oxford as intended. The truth was that he did outstandingly well in the examination and did not take much persuading that he had the makings of a research scientist with one of the country's most distinguished chemists. None of this altered his aim of eventually going into the law.

Having overcome Alfred's reservations, Cripps matriculated at University College, London, early in 1908, staying at the family home in Queen's Gate Gardens (from where Sir Alfred walked to his chambers each weekday), and travelling from there to the Gower Street laboratories. Ramsay had brought together an accomplished team of researchers, many engaged in building upon his discovery of the 'noble' gases, for which he had won the Nobel prize in 1904.[49] He enforced a methodical routine, but trusted students to carry on without constant supervision, only coming in at the critical point 'to see all the fun'.[50] Cripps, completing the junior and intermediate stages of his courses, took to the experimental work with relish. For the 1909–10 session, he was appointed as a demonstrator on the staff.

He had got to know Alfred ('Jack') Egerton (grandson of the 2nd Baron Harlech), who had been at UCL since 1905, had just taken his finals, and was starting work at the Royal Military Academy at Woolwich. Cripps, Egerton soon became aware, was a 'tremendous ragger', always playing practical jokes.[51] Egerton became a firm friend, and was invited to Queen's Gate Gardens and Parmoor, where he joined in the horse-riding, dancing and animated discussions.[52] The atmosphere was of gracious living and unrestrained enjoyment, punctuated by demonstrations of Cripps's own handiwork – though a model plane which he built, hoping to emulate the widely reported first flight of a glider, crashed on take-off. 'Aunt Bo' (Beatrice Webb), welcomed to the 'luxurious comfort' of Parmoor in December 1909, disapprovingly recorded that both Seddon and Stafford looked pasty, overfed and under-exercised:

> Stafford has distinct talent, if not a touch of genius, and would naturally be strenuously ambitious. But the indefinite ease of the life, and the very slight demands made on him, are loosening his moral and intellectual fibre. It is odd that exactly the 'school' that thinks the most terrible struggle against fearful odds is good for the poor, take steps to prevent young persons of their own class from having some kind of struggle – even for the pleasures of life.[53]

'We are all awaiting breathlessly the issue of the great battle,' she added. The 'battle' was over the Liberal 'People's Budget', challenged by the House of Lords. A general election seemed imminent, and Sir Alfred,[54] long since adopted as the Conservative and Unionist candidate for High Wycombe, was preparing for a stiff contest.

Sir Alfred had been asked to stand for the South Buckinghamshire division in 1906, but had not been willing to desert his seat at Stretford, in Manchester (won at a by-election in 1901), and, unable to secure the father, the local Unionists had adopted his oldest son, Seddon, who stood on an 'England first' platform.[55] The South Bucks Standard – 'Cripps's Chronicle' – reminded readers of 'how genially the Parmoor family exercise the old-fashioned graces of their influence, along with a keen regard for all the present-days interests of the daily life of the district';[56] the Liberals pointed out that Seddon Cripps, claiming to be 'Bucks born and bred', [57] was actually delivered at his late mother's home of Standish. Stirred by the fair-trade controversy, South Bucks turned Liberal, ending twenty years of Unionist representation. Sir Alfred's own defeat at Stretford was a further setback. The moment the election was over, the Unionist association in Wycombe set in train a complete overhaul of the local party, with Sir Alfred the designated candidate.

Electioneering in Wycombe was characteristically rowdy. Sir Alfred –

acknowledging real differences to do with the Budget, tariffs, temperance and religious schooling (it was a strongly Nonconformist area; he feared for Anglican teaching in schools) – regretted the highly charged mood. The Liberal, expecting defeat, resorted to personal attacks but could not stem the tide in favour of Cripps – part of a general Unionist swing across southern England. A huge crowd assembled in order to hear the declaration, but, before it could be read out, Cripps was advised to leave by the police. Angry opponents went on the rampage, setting fire to property: the reading of the Riot Act and a violent police baton charge followed.[58] Returning up the hill to Frieth, 'the Squire' was met by excited well-wishers, accompanied by a rendition of 'For he's a jolly good fellow.'[59]

During the campaign, Sir Alfred's youngest son was stationed at the offices of the *South Bucks Standard* – which doubled as the Unionist committee rooms – revelling in the occasion.[60] One day, Isobel Swithinbank, the tall, fair-haired daughter of the chairman of the Denham branch of the local Unionists, came to the offices to help. Cripps saw her, and, although they did not meet, she was invited to a house party at Parmoor by Ruth, and then stayed at Queen's Gate Gardens. She and Stafford corresponded that summer, while apart, and then set off for a skiing holiday in Switzerland with Leonard, Ruth, 'Jack' Egerton and a chaperone. Mutually attracted, they decided to become engaged on the spot. Told to report back and explain themselves, they expressed an overwhelming desire to get married as quickly as possible, 'Dad' 's wilfulness being much apparent.

Isobel's father, concerned about his daughter's 'ultimate happiness', wrote to Sir Alfred – they were old associates – saying that he understood Stafford was considering a career either in business or, with a view to later going into politics, at the Bar. Reassured that Sir Alfred would maintain his son in funds, Swithinbank saw it was obvious the couple would have a 'united income' sufficient to tide them over, in which case a political life might be more suitable. However, 'Isobel', he made clear, 'has been brought up in the country and knows little of town life.'[61]

Since Sir Alfred was hardly without means, Swithinbank's worry needs explaining. The Swithinbanks lived at Denham Court, a sixteenth-century manor house surrounded by a large estate in the heart of Buckinghamshire farming country. Isobel's mother, Amy, was one of two daughters of James Crossley Eno, originator of Eno's Fruit Salts, the sparkling health tonic. Eno – the name is thought to derive from a Huguenot surname, Eneau[62] – had started out in the 1850s as a pharmacist in the port of Newcastle, serving sailors suffering from indigestion and constipation with a concocted powder which produced an effervescent, non-alcoholic drink when mixed with water.[63] Word of the properties of the drink spread to other ports of call, at home and overseas, and business expanded. In 1876 Eno moved to London, converting a one-man operation into a large-scale manufacturing process in New Cross. Eno's Fruit Salts flourished, protected from rival remedies by their registered trademark and secret formula. By the turn of the century, worldwide sales amounted to several thousand gross of bottles a year, with huge profits. Since J. C. Eno's only son, Crossley, had died in his teens, Amy Swithinbank and her sister were the prospective beneficiaries of a substantial fortune.

Isobel's own childhood had been sheltered and largely solitary. Her father, forced to give up soldiering after a serious riding accident, occupied his time as an amateur chemist; he was also active on Buckinghamshire County Council, and owned a 500-ton steam yacht, moored at Cowes. Isobel was introduced at Court, and had her portrait painted by John Charlton RA. Her schooling was markedly religious and sin-denouncing. Awed by Cripps's brains, she could not stand up to him intellectually, but had strong instincts, a compassionate nature and an infinite adaptability to circumstances. His ambitions became hers, as the two of them became wrapped together in an *egoisme à deux*. In time, Lady Eno – Hugh Dalton's snide epithet – gained recognition in her own right, accompanying her husband on his travels and prompting his designs.

Their parents counselled a five-year wait; the youngsters – he was just twenty-two and she twenty – would not agree to delay, and, persistence paying off, were married at St Mary's Church, Denham, in July 1911, uniting 'two of the best-known and esteemed families in South Bucks'.[64] All branches of the Cripps, Potter and Swithinbank clans attended, guests being entertained by an orchestra in a huge marquee in the grounds of Denham Court. Among the wedding gifts of silverware and jewellery (including a silver salver from 'the trades-people of Uxbridge) were £10,000 worth of shares from J. C. Eno, to be held in trust. The couple honeymooned in Ireland.

Marrying early compelled Cripps to settle his intentions. Since Isobel's annuity far outweighed his income as a research scientist, he decided to sit for the Bar, eating his dinners and attending his father's chambers in the Middle Temple. His time at UCL was not wasted. He invented a pyknometer, a device for measuring the density of gases, and was joint author of a paper on 'The Critical Constants and Orthoberic Densities of Xenon', submitted to the Royal Society and read (i.e. tabled) in 1912, the youngest person to attain such an honour. In his final year he was elected president of the Student Union, elegantly furnishing the Union's rooms and raising funds for a sports ground. He had developed an extraordinary personal demeanour, intensely self-absorbed and outwardly imposing. Mortimer Wheeler, archaeologist-to-be, remembered Cripps 'filling any room he entered' with his 'powerful, sombre countenance', his 'quality of presence' comparable for his age only with that of a Wilberforce, an Owen or even a Peel. Cripps, he concluded (forty years on), was 'born on Olympus'.[65]

Against this, he had no first degree,[66] and no immediate prospect of an independent income. In a one-page will made out on the morning of their marriage, he bequeathed everything to Isobel without qualification.[67] He was not, like most of his peers, dogged by the urgent necessity of earning a living; neither, out of self-respect, could he face not being the provider.[68] Settling not far from Frieth and Denham, the young couple had a son, John, born in May of the following year, and a daughter, Diana, in September 1913. Cripps had the advantage of a lucky start, but also much to live up to, entering the shrine to brainpower, masculinity and conservatism – the law – where his father was so influential and his eldest brother, Seddon, was already practising.

A CHEMIST'S WAR

His first duty is to think of himself now, and not to worry over his work,
as he had done his duty equally as if he had become invalided at the
front.

A Ministry of Munitions official to Isobel Cripps in 1917[1]

Of the four Inns of Court, the Inner and Middle Temple are the most ancient;
of the Middle Temple buildings, those in Essex Court are among the oldest. In
the early 1900s, the chambers of Sir Alfred Cripps, at 1 Essex Court, had an
unrivalled eminence. No other advocate had so wide or lucrative a practice.
Whether it was a commercial, compensation or trademark case, and whenever
arbitration involved an unusually large amount or was especially complicated,
Sir Alfred – blessed with a musical voice and a reasoned, persuasive manner –
was the leading counsel. In one ten-year period he reputedly coined over
£100,000, in spite of the long Bar vacations.[2] With thirty years of experience –
'looking like a legal portrait that had stepped from some 18th century frame' –
and with overlapping connections with the royal court, the Church and Parliament, he fully contributed to his father's boast of having four sons in different
walks of life, all at the summit of their chosen field. In an environment where
goodwill counted for much, Stafford Cripps had the inestimable asset of his
family name.

Cripps registered to be called to the Bar in March 1910, attached to the
chambers in Essex Court and, from May 1911 until May 1912, devilling as a
pupil for Arthur Colefax, a junior counsel and expert in patent and trademark
litigation – the one branch of the law combining legal training and a scientific
background.[3]

Patent law was governed by the Patents and Designs Act 1907, passed by
the Liberal government in order to provide greater protection for British
inventions. Patent applications had increased enormously – largely, it was
alleged, because of foreign individuals and companies using them to block
competitors. Particular concern was expressed about the German chemical
industry, manufacturing aniline dye from coal tar by means of a process
invented in but lost to Britain. Patent disputes – concerning the novelty of a

particular invention or the infringement of a patent by 'passing off' – had to go before a special Patent Court. The provisions of the Act made it more difficult to uphold a patent where the relevant chemical process had not yet been got to work properly.[4]

The distinctiveness of patent law dictated the qualities of a successful patent lawyer. It was highly specialised, calling for a grasp of technical processes, skill at cross-examining well-qualified expert witnesses, and an aptitude for conveying the essentials of a complex case to presiding judges, who were often classically educated. It required a special kind of pleading, quite unlike that in theatrical jury cases, where it was not unknown for lawyers to go into court with unopened briefs. Because it was so specialised and because so much was often at stake, the Patent Bar was small in size but extremely well remunerated.

'Master Stafford' served a tranquil apprenticeship, acquainting himself with case law and – in an act of filial dedication – preparing new editions of the family textbooks on the law relating to the Church and clergy and on the principles of the law of compensation. He passed his Bar examinations in December 1912, took part in his first case as a junior to his father and Arthur Colefax (he did not address the court),[5] and was appointed a JP for Buckinghamshire. The grooming was gradual in a briefless first year.

During the conflict over the 'People's Budget', Sir Alfred had been a strong opponent of the Liberal government's 'constitutional wrecking', but was never a diehard. Upset by Asquith's treatment on the floor of the Commons in July 1911 (the week after Stafford's wedding), when the Prime Minister was refused a hearing, he was one of several Unionist MPs who sent a letter of apology.[6] A fastidious loner, rather than a safe party man,[7] he viewed the troubles over Home Rule, labour unrest (there were lockouts in High Wycombe) and the suffragettes with increasing unease, becoming estranged from party colleagues.

Early in 1914, Sir Alfred decided to accept Asquith's invitation to serve on the Judicial Committee of the Privy Council, carrying with it his elevation to the Lords. There was carping at his acceptance of a peerage during the ministry of his opponents, and suggestions that he did so 'in a fit of pique' at having been passed over by his own party.[8] Sir Alfred, adopting the title of Lord Parmoor of Frieth, insisted he could not turn down what was being bestowed by the King, and that he would not abandon his long-held political or Church beliefs.[9] Nevertheless the *South Bucks Standard* – maintained for almost a quarter of a century out of his own pocket – was closed, and he relinquished much of his legal practice. The departure of a leading King's Counsel made available to others the range of his connections. The newly styled Hon. Stafford Cripps reasonably hoped to profit.

Lord Parmoor was spending the summer at Parmoor at the beginning of August 1914 when news reached him of the worsening situation on the Continent. Freddie returned from St Petersburg, travelling back via Germany, where Jack and Ruth Egerton had narrowly avoided arrest. They found their father, alarmed by the rumoured German invasion of Luxembourg, 'in a state of unmitigated gloom'.[10] Both Seddon and Freddie were also against a war. On 4 August, Lord Parmoor led a party up to London, reaching Parliament too late to hear Sir Edward Grey's historic statement that England would honour its obligations and defend Belgian neutrality. War with Germany was declared, and the three eldest sons – notwithstanding their father's misgivings – rushed to the colours, joining up with their territorial regiments. Stafford Cripps, much as he hated the coming of war, felt the country must see it through.[11] Jack Egerton's brother was in the thick of the early fighting, and, after the retreat from Mons in late August, Jack and Stafford made the trip to the front by car to take clothing. Stafford tried enlisting in October, but was rejected by the army as medically unfit.[12] He crossed to France again in October, driving a lorry donated to the Red Cross by J. C. Eno, joining the stores department operating out of the supply depot at Boulogne. The three hundred volunteer chauffeurs, entitled to wear khaki, were an odd assortment, among them a Church of England curate and a music-hall singer. Cripps's duties – shovelling coal and taking it to the forward areas – were heavy, but, as the official Red Cross history noted, the work generally, though 'arduous', was 'cheerfully endured by everyone'.[13]

That November, the German advance having been halted, the weather turned bitterly cold, with heavy snowfalls. Leonard Cripps was wounded in the ankle and taken to hospital in Boulogne, from where Cripps accompanied him back to England. No one believed the temporary stalemate could last. Home on leave at Christmas – when Lord Parmoor was as opposed to the war as ever – 'Stafford', Lady Courtney recorded in her diary, 'says all the Officers coming from the front say the war will be over March or April – but why or *how* he does not report. Seddon hears the same story from army men – opines the men won't & can't stand the strain of the awful trench fighting on either side any longer.'[14]

In fact, military and industrial mobilisation was only just beginning. Cripps carried out his heavy manual labour for several more months, at some cost to his health, and was about to go forward to the Ypres salient for gas work – during the second battle of Ypres (April–May 1915) chlorine gas was used, by the Germans, for the first time – when he was informed by telegram that the newly created Ministry of Munitions desperately needed qualified chemists.

The Ministry of Munitions owed its inception to the first coalition Cabinet of May 1915, and the determination of David Lloyd George, its first minister, to rectify a much publicised shortage of shells and explosives.[15] Front-line demand for ammunition had grown enormously, outstripping what could be supplied by the few private ordnance firms. Lloyd George took the drastic step of erecting several 'national factories' to meet the shortfall. They became the responsibility of the Explosives Supply Department under Lord Moulton, a former Liberal MP and noted patent lawyer, and a fellow Law Lord of Lord Parmoor.[16] The Department obtained the services of an American engineer, K. B. Quinan, manager of the Cape Explosives Company in South Africa, who appointed a team of assistants, including Jack Egerton, and set about designing, building and equipping the new factories. Since the technical staff available to operate these plants was limited, a new class of chemical foremen had to be quickly instructed.

Sir William Ramsay, a vigorous anti-German propagandist,[17] helped through the Royal Society to co-ordinate scientific assistance for producing high explosives. Ramsay had already, in the opening weeks of the war, suggested using aerial bombs filled with prussic acid – an idea turned down by the War Office as being in breach of the Hague Convention. Laboratories were converted to exploring improved methods of making trinitrotoluene (TNT), the main shell-filling explosive. The manufacture of nitric and sulphuric acid depended on imports of sodium nitrate, sulphur and pyrites; stocks of toluene, derived from coal tar, would soon be inadequate; the possibility of combining ammonium nitrate, a synthetic alternative, with TNT had hardly been investigated. Until the output of the national factories was got going, Britain paid for the pre-war neglect of the organic-chemistry industry, and especially the exploitation of synthetic dyestuffs (the substances in explosives and coal-tar dyes being made using the same raw materials and processes), which Germany had taken over and which the 1907 Patent Act had been a belated attempt to counteract.[18] Many of Ramsay's students flocked into government work.

Cripps applied to join the Explosives Supply Department on 16 September, was interviewed, and, with impressive references from Ramsay, Egerton and his father, was taken on as a trainee administrator at the gunpowder factory at Waltham Abbey, north of London.[19] For two months he learned all aspects of the production of gun cotton (a propellant) and tetryl (used in the detonation of TNT), staying in a nearby cottage with Isobel and Mazelle. At the end of November he was sent to Queensferry in North Wales, a 140-acre plant located along the estuary of the River Dee, eight miles from Chester and on the main London-to-Holyhead railway line. Queensferry had been commandeered by the Ministry of Munitions to make propellants for the army, since when it had been extended to double production and attain a weekly output of 200 tons of gun cotton.

Conditions at Queensferry were fearsome.[20] Noxious fumes caused intense irritation to the face and made newcomers choke, until they became habituated. A lungful of the vapour from the chimneys of the nitric-acid stills was deadly; some employees had already been fatally gassed. Women, making up the majority of the unskilled process workers, handled TNT with bare hands, their skin turning bright yellow. Women who fainted were shown 'a judicious lack of sympathy'.[21] Those routinely 'attending' to the equipment were exposed to the danger of spillages and explosions (the boiler houses were placed at least 200 yards apart). Most operatives were – an inspector observed – mainly of the dark-haired Welsh type, unused to shift work or the stringent regulations of 'controlled establishments'. Queensferry had been extended with a huge outlay of resources in a remarkably short time, and yet was under continual pressure from the Ministry to increase output and economise on materials.

Just after Christmas, the superintendent, Colonel Waring, fell ill; in his absence, Cripps, technically still only a junior chemist, found himself assuming the day-to-day running of the entire factory. Over the next ten weeks, he 'practically carried the whole administration on his shoulders',[22] ensuring the production of gun cotton was maintained, dealing with the cost accounts, and supervising the welfare of the 6000-strong workforce. One evening, a Zeppelin in the vicinity, the Holyhead express stopped by the site with its fire doors open, and Cripps, as he used to relate, had to ask the driver to kindly move on. He attempted to do everything, working a sixteen- or twenty-hour day. The physical strain was great, and the extra burden of responsibility made him over-anxious. Unable to relax, he suffered a nervous breakdown. Once Waring returned, Cripps retired to a nursing home in Chester for a complete rest.

His health recovered and he resumed work in July 1916, a local doctor certifying he was not afflicted by any organic disease. Waring, mindful of the lengths Cripps had gone to, asked that Cripps's new promotion to the position of assistant superintendent (promised in January) be retrospectively back-dated. The Treasury refused, and the Finance Branch of the Ministry of Munitions also felt his new appointment and a lump sum in recognition of the responsibilities he had taken on ought to be sufficient, adding grudgingly that 'there don't appear to be circumstances of poverty'.[23] Waring was indignant, feeling Cripps's financial position was immaterial. 'His breakdown was the direct consequence, as I have always felt, of his zeal,' Waring wrote to the Ministry, 'and was one which might have been avoided by another man who put his own personal interests before those of the work at a particularly trying period in the history of H.M. Factory.'[24]

Cripps made no complaint, but continued to demonstrate great administrative flair, knowing what needed doing and the best way to do it, paying close attention to the problems of workers. The productive capacity of Queensferry expanded further, as new plant was added to cope with the manufacturing of tetryl, making it – with Gretna and Oldbury – the largest of the national factories. But it was also the most efficient, according to the Ministry's own account published after the war, without any major labour disturbances or serious breaches of safety (the explosion at the small TNT factory at Silvertown in east London in January 1917 demolished all surrounding buildings, and the sound was heard fifty miles away in Cambridge) – a feat in which Cripps played no small part.[25]

His improved health was only temporary, however. By the summer of 1917 he had broken down again, incapacitated and barely able to walk, and was granted sick leave, moving to a rest home in central London. His doctor confirmed he was 'suffering from Toxic poisoning of the stomach, which has developed as a result of the colitis from which he has been suffering for the last twelve months'[26] – a reference to a disease affecting the mucosa of the large bowel, which Cripps thought he had contracted with the Red Cross in France. Easy to diagnose, it was all but incurable. The aetiology of colitis was unknown, though the attacks of diarrhoea it brought on were not unlike the bacterial infection of amoebic dysentry, rife on the Western Front. The theory that colitis was a psychosomatic disease common to people undergoing an emotional trauma came into currency only in the 1930s; the latest studies indicate the likelihood of an auto-immune disorder.[27] Whatever the exact cause, attacks were irregular, unpredictable and severely debilitating. It would be best, his doctor advised, in view of the climate and conditions at Queensferry, if Cripps did not return; in any event, he needed longer to recover. Isobel, warned he might never be well enough to work again, slowly nursed him back to health.

Briefly, he took up a voluntary desk job – 'not being up to full work I should not, naturally, like to take a paid post'[28] – with the Food Production Department of the Ministry of Agriculture, where Lawrence Weaver, his chief, found him work 'worthy of his gifts and experience'.[29] The two of them got on well, Weaver's interests in architecture and craftsmanship – he had been architectural editor of *Country Life* – appealing to Cripps. Active again, Cripps turned his mind to picking up the pieces of his career. In October 1917, Lord Parmoor put him on the waiting list for membership of the Athenaeum. For the remainder of the war and for some months afterwards, however, he was an invalid, as much a casualty of the conflict as those on active service. For someone who had never worried about his diet, the colitis was a turning-point. It stayed with him for the rest of his life, requiring him to exercise the greatest self-control – he must never lose his temper, doctors urged[30] – and setting him off on an unending search for alternative remedies.

The mystery of Cripps's illness nonetheless supplied a further spur to his self-motivation.

The impact of the war was, for the first few months, largely confined to the families of serving soldiers (the first volunteers only became available in early 1915). Like many of their class, all four Cripps brothers had gone off to serve their country. Lord Parmoor, one of a small band who opposed the war from the outset, was careful to tone down his objections, speaking only of the personal obligation to 'do well and right', even in the face of ridicule.[31]

But, when the Defence of the Realm Act came into force, he attacked the provisions for trial by courts martial and defended the rights of conscientious objectors against the 'overwhelming flood' of militarism.[32] Official censorship went hand in hand with the demagoguery of politicians – principally of Lloyd George, who, Parmoor feared, had most captured the democratic instinct. In late 1917, after the impassioned public appeal of Margaret Hobhouse (the seventh of the Potter sisters), he deplored the stigmatising of those who heeded the call of conscience,[33] associating himself with Lords Landsdowne, Haldane, Morley and Buckmaster in calling in public meetings for a 'just peace', their efforts resulting in a House of Lords debate on a proposed 'League of Nations'.

Courting unpopularity, Parmoor's peace work brought him into touch with a beleaguered circle of anti-war activists – Gilbert Murray, Noel Buxton, Ramsay MacDonald, H. M. Burge (now the Bishop of Southwark, and ministering to the many parents of Wykehamists killed in action) and Marian Ellis, daughter of a Tory MP and devout Quaker, whose twin sister had been imprisoned for distributing leaflets without the approval of the censor. The Churches, instead of denouncing the war, assisted the recruiting drive and justified imposing harsh terms on Germany. Science, directed to the costly demands of destructive modern warfare, should promote the alleviation of suffering and the mitigation of poverty, Parmoor argued.[34] War, he went on (quoting Erasmus), 'has nothing in common with Christ'. Though some – notably Sidney and Beatrice Webb – found Parmoor's conversion to humanitarian progress unconvincing, it was perfectly sincere, and had the important effect of subsequently strengthening the Labour Party, since many of the group either later moved over to Labour or helped form the Party's future leadership.[35] 'Father's work', Jack Egerton recorded of Parmoor in his diary, 'is constructive and ahead of his time; it is based on true Christian principles and it cannot and will not receive, therefore, any commendation from the world in his own time, but we must see that it does from his own family.'[36]

Cripps's father's example brought to life his mother's parting words. Other dissenters were reacting against the older generation who had got England into the war; Cripps followed his father's lead. The war, Parmoor wrote after the Armistice, had been 'demoralising', involving an extension of the spy system – 'in its essence distasteful to all men of honourable understanding' – a maximum of scientifically contrived cruelty, the 'coercive obligation' of conscription, and a 'propagandism' of national hatreds. Force had infiltrated society, with the post-war confrontation of capital and labour an ominous portent.[37] Christians could be patriots and still strive for ideals other than chauvinistic self-interest. The 'unexampled sacrifice' made by all in the war might equally be employed in the task of reconstruction.[38] When Lord Courtney died in May 1918, Stafford Cripps wrote to his widow in praise of his fearless advocacy and self-sacrifice –

everything an Englishmen should prize.[39] They were qualities he saw in his own father, and which he would like to display himself.

Did he have an extra-vivid father identification? His older brothers attested that, as the Benjamin of the family and in his mother's absence, Stafford was open to the greatest paternal influence. Lord Parmoor had courageously stuck by his beliefs, defying vulgar, usually hostile, popular opinion. (At a disorderly meeting chaired by Parmoor in Central Hall, Westminster, Cripps, seated at the back of the hall, heard a member of the audience claim the Cripps surname was a corruption of Krupps, the name of German arms manufacturers.[40]) His conversion went only so far, however. He had shifted his ground and his associates, while continuing to couch his arguments in the moralistic language of the pre-war era. Much of the impetus behind the League of Nations movement derived from the wish for a return to civilised standards.

Recuperating, the younger Cripps had time to dwell on the meaning of the conflict. He envied his brothers and friends who were active while he was disabled; at the same time, he saw the folly and waste of bloodshed; short of the next world – for the attaining of which 'we all yearn' – he ardently hoped some good would emerge out of it. An element of repentance – he had been as heavily implicated in the slaughter as any non-combatant could be – was evident in the 'doubts' which he admitted to.[41] For the first time, he thought through the assumptions he had always taken for granted. His 'awakening', as he was to call it, was not philosophical or political so much as religious and righteous. His faith was essentially simple, but accentuated by ill health, which introduced a note of spartan frugality and gave him an air of high moral intent, even when money-making at the Bar. To say that his physical affliction, and his adaptation to it, was nothing more than a private inconvenience is mistaken. Illness concentrated his disposition, harnessing his exceptional ability and thrusting nature to 'the will of God'.

3

HOLY TRINITY

I suppose all Counsel's arguments suit themselves to circumstances; that is what we are here for; but it would hardly do for Mr Stafford Cripps to invest himself with a white robe in these matters as being immune from such criticisms.

H. P. Macmillan KC, before the Railway Rates Tribunal, 2 February 1926

By the spring of 1919, Cripps had regained enough vigour to return to the Bar, dividing his time between the Law Courts in London, his family and friends in Gloucestershire, and a dedicated interest in the peace-making of the Churches. These were all – law, farming, the Churches – pursuits of a thoroughbred, eager for professional success, social standing and philanthropic works. The problem, Lord Parmoor appreciated, was that the war, though fought to a finish, continued to disrupt the transition to peacetime. Cripps, and not just because of his impaired health, lived with its consequences.

Parmoor dreaded the importing of the wartime spirit of violence into domestic affairs, creating new social conflicts. The relationship between the State, capital and labour had altered, the revival of private industry[1] being counterbalanced by the State regulating public policy to avoid labour unrest. 'Law' and 'policy' increasingly overlapped, and lawyers who could pick their way through the tangles were greatly in demand. Agriculture was as shaken up as industry, chiefly by mechanisation and a shift in private landownership. The major estates disappeared, but those who bought their way in hankered after traditional countryside values. The most pressing danger was international. Since trade – especially food imports – was a priority, hopes rested on a just and durable settlement in Europe that would bring about recovery, and were encouraged by religious groups speaking out against a 'vindictive' peace. It was a matter of profound dismay to find the world was no longer so agreeably ordered; this did not imply that new evils were susceptible to political remedy.

The standard accounts have Cripps gravitating towards public participation in general and the Labour Party in particular as the 1920s wore on and as social divisions became more glaring, and it is true his duties involved him more and more in matters of public moment. But this is to anticipate, misleadingly. In each of his three different pursuits, Cripps spent the greater part of the next few years resisting the claims of political salvation.

Parmoor's chambers were now headed by Arthur Colefax, returning, like Cripps, from the Ministry of Munitions. In Colefax's case, too, the war had been a personal misfortune. German-owned patents – in which he was a specialist – had been opened up in favour of English competitors, even after the ending of hostilities. Married to an energetic wife – the socialite Sibyl – he had to take whatever work came his way. Cripps attended his first hearing with Colefax, which went up to the House of Lords in March 1919, but for the most part he travelled around the Oxford circuit. At the end of the year, however, he appeared again at Colefax's side in a case of direct pecuniary interest.

J. C. Eno, on his death at the age of eighty-seven in 1915, left an estate of £1.6 million, the bulk passing to his two daughters, one of them Isobel's mother. Control of J. C. Eno Ltd was at the same time vested in the trustees of his estate, who saw the opportunity to expand business by registering the rare Eno surname (no relations now bore the name) as a distinctive trademark. The application was heard in December, Colefax, assisted by Cripps, asserting that 'if ever there was a name adapted to distinguish, it is this name'.[2] On the strength of their victory in the new year, the company held an extraordinary general meeting to convert itself into a wholly new firm, enlarging the capital base by issuing £750,000 of ordinary preference shares.[3] Isobel's father became the major shareholder. Fighting off imitations and protecting the secret 'Fruit Salts' formula, about which there was a good deal of secrecy,[4] were vital. The product was, the company's promoters pointed out, one of the country's main pharmaceutical exports, 'which even German research has not wrested from us'.[5] In spite of the 1920 court ruling, when the company asked how best to retain exclusive rights to the 'Fruit Salts' label, Cripps advised that Fruits Salts, being a descriptive term, should only be used as the trademark on Eno's bottles and the 'Eno' brand name never so used – a written opinion known from then on as the 'Eno's bible'.[6]

Cripps was also involved in a critical case dating from before the war. The British authorities were keen to develop a synthetic-dyestuffs industry. A new Patents Act in 1919 imposed restrictions on claims for chemical patents. In the meantime, the British Dyestuffs Corporation was formed under the ubiquitous Lord Moulton, merging two existing firms, British Dyes Ltd and Levinstein Ltd. In 1912, Levinstein's had been challenged by Agfa, a constituent of the German I. G. Farben combine, for infringing a British-granted patent for the manufacture of a leading black dye – a patent Levinstein's now legally owned. The case came before the Court of Appeal in February 1921, with Colefax and Cripps appearing for Agfa. Although the appeal was dismissed, Cripps impressed the court by his lucid account of the supposedly rival specifications, contending that the defendant's process was not just 'equivalent' but 'identical'.[7]

His workload diversified, to include compensation, land acquisition and accident claims with the Great Western Railway. When the telephone in his London flat was disconnected, he wrote indignantly to *The Times* to complain about the officiousness of the Post Office.[8] He grew in self-assurance, lightened by a jaunty prankishness, and started to be seen as a promising patent junior, being admitted to the exclusive Athenaeum with a glittering list of sponsors.[9] Paradoxically it was his part in two protracted, costly and tangled non-patent investigations, taking in a formidable array of legal talent and ample refreshers, which advertised his ability and made his reputation.

A City of London firm, the Duff Development Company, owned some 3,000 square miles of territory in the state of Kelantan on the eastern side of the Malay Peninsula, on which they established rubber plantations. The land was also believed to contain valuable minerals. Formerly Siamese, Kelantan became a British protectorate in 1909. Since the Colonial Office was unwilling to let a private company enjoy such privileges of landownership, the Duff Development Company agreed to waive its exploitation rights under a deed of cancellation in return for a cash payment and the pick of 50,000 acres of agricultural land, as well as associated timber, mining and dredging rights. According to the deed, a railway and/or cart road connecting Singapore with Bangkok would be built by the Government of Kelantan through the Company's concession, enormously increasing its value, but with the final line of the route of the railway to be fixed. Disagreements arising from the deed were to be referred to an arbitrator. In 1913, learning that the railway was likely to skirt the Company's territory, the Company disputed the Government of Kelantan's right to choose a different line of construction. An arbitrator dismissed the complaint, whereupon the Company claimed damages for the non-completion of the railway and adjoining cart road.

In April 1920 the Colonial Secretary appointed an arbitrator, a former colonial judge (in receipt of a Colonial Office pension), to decide whether there had in fact been a breach of contract. The Company had hitherto retained the pugnacious KC William Upjohn, but was now advised by its City solicitors – Drake, Son and Parton – to hire Sir Douglas Hogg and W. J. Jeeves, with the junior help of Stafford Cripps. Bernard Drake was the husband of Barbara ('Bardie') Meinertzhagen, daughter of Georgina Meinertzhagen, a cousin of Stafford's. Cripps was to review the past history of the dispute, analyse the evidence, and establish lines of argument and cross-examination. In an extra twist, the Government of Kelantan countered by employing Upjohn as its legal adviser.

The proceedings lasted five days.[10] Having heard the rival pleadings from Hogg and Upjohn, the arbitrator refused a last-minute plea by Upjohn to frame the award in such a way that it could be appealed against, announcing that there had clearly been a failure to build a railway and road as implied in the terms of the contract and that there would need to be an inquiry to ascertain the nature and amount of damages.

The Government of Kelantan moved for the award to be set aside on the ground that there had been an error in law, maintaining that the arbitrator, misconstruing the deed of cancellation, had not only decided erroneously but had acted wrongly. The motion was heard in the High Court and was refused, whereupon the Government of Kelantan took its case to the Court of Appeal, where it was again rejected, the judges on both occasions rebuking the Government for its conduct. The Colonial Office now suddenly set up the plea that Kelantan was an independent sovereign state, beyond the jurisdiction of the British courts, attempting to kill off the award for damages. The new Colonial Secretary, Winston Churchill – quite cynically, in Cripps's view – wrote to the court to that effect. The court could not challenge this certificate, though remarks were made about the Government of Kelantan's behaviour in initiating litigation and then trying to avoid payment once it had lost. Churchill also informed the Company that Kelantan could not pay and he would not force it to pay. This gave the Government of Kelantan a tactical advantage, but incurred great odium, provoking questions in Parliament and press attacks on the Colonial Office's 'scandalous' dealings.[11]

The Company in turn appealed, with Frederick Maugham KC (replacing Hogg, who had been made Solicitor-General) and Cripps arguing that the court was not bound to accept the Secretary of State's statement since its accuracy was not borne out by the original treaty of 1909. Although the appeal was rejected, the Master of the Rolls, himself accepting the Colonial Secretary's statement as final, added that he would not be sorry if a different decision were ultimately arrived at by a higher court.

The House of Lords began hearing the final appeal of the Government of Kelantan against the arbitrator's award in February 1923, before Lords Cave (the Lord Chancellor), Shaw, Sumner, Trevethin and Parmoor. The Company was now able to argue that the Government of Kelantan could not, having repudiated any liability in the British courts, look to those same courts for an order to set aside the arbitrator's award – an objection recognised as carrying much force. On the fundamental principle, however, it was unanimously found (in a judgement delivered in September 1923) that the arbitrator had acted within his permissible powers and the award should stand.

In June 1924, at the Royal Courts of Justice, the arbitrator opened his inquiry into the nature and amount of damages for which the Government of Kelantan was liable. The proceedings lasted seventy-nine days, spread out over several months, involving a string of witnesses and taking in some 36,000 questions, interrupted by yet another appeal to the House of Lords. The Company, believing the Colonial Office had tried to starve it out of existence, turned down all compromise offers, submitting a total claim for £1,068,298. The Colonial Office was equally intent on ensuring the arbitrator did not succumb to the 'blackmailing' of the Company. The case had also become a battle of wills between opposing counsel.

Upjohn was famously irascible, and Cripps – pernickety and unremitting – irritated him by his 'ingenuity'. It fell to Maugham to carry the main burden of addressing the inquiry, but Cripps, though not often on his feet, would not let his concentration drop, 'never failing' to seize on the slightest inaccuracy in Upjohn's presentation.[12] The Company's case was aided by Cripps's marshalling of the voluminous evidence, enabling them to get the better of some angry exchanges. On one key point, this made a material difference. In February, an order had been drawn up indicating the line the Company alleged the railway was to have taken across its territory, as 'mentioned in the Award of the Arbitrator' and upon which the £1 million claim for damages was based. The inclusion of those words seemed innocuous, until Upjohn – who had been careful to insist the Government of Kelantan always reserved the right to alter the line of the route as it saw fit – belatedly questioned how they had found their way into the original order. Maugham immediately objected:

MR MAUGHAM: I wanted to prevent your suggestion, which I am sure you did not intend, that Mr Cripps slipped it into the Order with some intention of deceiving your side.

MR UPJOHN: Good Lord no! I know Mr Cripps much better than that. I did not know that I made any suggestion that Mr Cripps had done it. I said it was a third party.

MR STAFFORD CRIPPS: You looked at me.

MR UPJOHN: Mr Cripps and I are on such terms that very often one of us will have a joke at the expense of the other. Mr Cripps knows, I say in all sincerity, that I did not in the least impute this to him.[13]

When Cripps cross-examined witnesses put forward by the Government of Kelantan, Upjohn constantly intervened, belittling his efforts. Even so, Cripps scored a notable hit, reducing Samuel Truscott, Professor of Mining at the Royal School of Mines, to speechlessness by referring to his own writings and hammering away at his estimation of mineral deposits in the area. The Colonial Office watched the direction of the inquiry with alarm, observing that the arbitrator was paying greater attention to the Company's arguments.

Upjohn made a last bid by informing the arbitrator that if he made his award a Special Case (explicitly stating his reasons for interpreting the various points of law) the Government of Kelantan would waive its sovereignty and submit to the jurisdiction of the court, reversing its previous position.

The application for a Special Case was heard in June 1925, interrupting the inquiry. Maugham and Cripps entered powerful pleas, insisting the application should not be granted unless and until the Government of Kelantan paid all costs still owing to the Company. At this, Upjohn lost any remaining composure, accusing opposing counsel of tricking him into agreeing to the disputed order:

MR UPJOHN: I assert with firmness and certainty that you cannot get out of my words what Mr Maugham puts into them, and I charge Sir Douglas Hogg, Mr Maugham and Mr Cripps with trying to trap me into an agreement [i.e. the order] well knowing that they were endeavouring to do so.

MR STAFFORD CRIPPS: I think the two names which have been mentioned in connection with mine by Mr Upjohn is a sufficient guarantee that nothing of the sort ever happened.

MR UPJOHN: Their conduct speaks more trumpet tongued than their names.

MR JUSTICE RUSSELL: With that we will adjourn.[14]

The following day, having looked up the papers, Cripps found that he had been the author of the original order, but that it had been drafted along with Upjohn's junior; the offending words had not, he told the court, been added later for the purpose of deceiving. 'At all events,' Upjohn commented, 'memories have not been quite consistent on the other side about this.'

Upjohn's outburst only alienated the judge, who would not consent to making a Special Case on a point of law, leaving matters to the arbitrator and going out of his way to reprimand Upjohn for levelling 'a charge without foundation in substance or in fact'. The Colonial Office refused Upjohn leave to appeal, and he withdrew from the case. The new Colonial Secretary, Leo Amery, took direct control, bringing in another barrister at short notice. Recognising there was no possibility of 'rectifying' the award, he promised the Company he would do everything to facilitate proceedings.

In November 1925 the arbitrator delivered his final verdict: that the Company was entitled to recover the sum of £378,000 from the Government of Kelantan for breach of contract. Even the *Morning Post* considered the actions of the Colonial Office to have been 'open to question'.[15] The award was eventually paid in full, the Company marking its 'strenuous struggle against heavy odds' by inviting counsel to a celebratory dinner. The chairman made a point of writing to Cripps to say how much he appreciated the quality even more than the quantity of the work he had put in. Maugham, normally resentful of Wykehamists,[16] was full of praise. After the case was over, when other solicitors enquired about Cripps's specialities, they were informed by the clerk in his chambers 'that he could do pretty well everything'.[17]

While the Kelantan dispute was being taken from court to court, Cripps's casework with the Great Western Railway had led on to his employment with the London County Council in local-authority compensation and rating cases, and this also bore fruit.

The Railways Act 1921 provided for the setting-up of a Railway Rates Tribunal with powers to fix standardised rates, per mile, for the carriage of goods and fares for passengers on the four amalgamated railway undertakings created by the Act – the London, Midland and Scottish, the London and North-Eastern, the Southern, and the Great Western Railway. The Tribunal was, by statute, a court of inquiry, presided over by a lawyer, but it was a judicial body with administrative functions, authorised to listen to evidence from interested parties and decide on charges that would, 'with efficient and economical working and management', yield sufficient revenue for the companies. Though a retreat from the governmental control of the railways during the war, this was an instance of increased interventionism contrary to the general trend of de-control, leaving the burden of decision to the Tribunal. The magnitude and significance of the Tribunal's remit were understood from the outset.[18]

Among those interested, the London County Council (LCC), encouraging the rehousing of Londoners in purpose-built estates on the outskirts of the capital, served by cheap public transport, wanted to ensure 'the lowest rates which the railway companies can reasonably be asked to afford'. Once the skeleton schedules of charges of the respective railway companies had been compiled, the LCC briefed Cripps to appear before the Tribunal.

He gained an early success before the proceedings of the Tribunal had begun. The railway companies, in submitting outline schedules, considered it impractical to work out a separate schedule for season tickets and workmen's fares – the two classes on which the LCC was building its case. Instructed to make 'the strongest possible representations',[19] Cripps brushed the excuse of the companies aside: 'The Act itself must speak.'[20] Season tickets and workmen's fares were too big a matter of public interest to be left to the discretion of each company. The Tribunal, led by Walter Clode KC (who knew Cripps and had sponsored his application to join the Athenaeum), upheld his contention.

When the Tribunal convened in full session in May 1924, the first of its three stages of work was to determine the 'standard revenue' of each of the amalgamated companies, based on a calculation of the net revenue of the constituent companies in 1913, with adjustments for changes, such as econ-omies following amalgamation, since that date. 'Here', an authority noted, was 'a truly Herculean task' which, once decided, would be unreviewable – explaining the months it took simply to discover the standard revenue.[21] The companies had to prevent holes being picked in their accounting methods to the point that their desired standard revenue would not be obtainable; the traders, passengers and other users, like the LCC and the London Labour Party, set out to demonstrate that the amounts required were less than the companies were claiming, and that the standard revenue should be reduced.

At the first opportunity, Cripps launched into a detailed cross-examination of the accountant of the London, Midland and Scottish Railway – the chief witness for the companies – about his working definitions of 'undertaking', 'value' and a 'work', with which the companies' accounts had been drawn up, questioning the validity of the accountant's assumptions and the adequacy of the information furnished to the Tribunal. The companies had never before exposed their finances to public scrutiny. They were loath to provide ammunition for their critics, and counsel for the Railway Companies' Association, H. P. Macmillan, Lord Advocate in the then Labour government, struck by his learned friend's 'star turn', found his repeated requests exasperating. 'Mr Cripps wants the Minutes of the Directors', he commented wrily. 'I wonder he does not want the directors too!'

The procedure was inevitably time-consuming, and, although an agreed set of working figures for 1913 was eventually arrived at by September, it took a deal between the companies and the traders' and passengers' associations to settle the figures up to the date of fixation of December 1923. Even then, Cripps, unhappy with the paucity of detail about the investment plans of the companies, reserved the LCC's position. The LCC particularly took exception to a £400,000 bonus for amalgamation given to the companies and added to the standard revenue 'for all time', saddling the traders and travellers with a permanent injustice. 'It gives us', Clode said, 'great pleasure to find you before the Tribunal and to hear your valuable criticisms'. Macmillan, too, noted Cripps's ability to proceed independently, driven by 'what he himself is pleased to call his pertinacity, but what we only recognise as zeal'.

The second, no less formidable, stage of the inquiry – beginning in October 1925 – was to establish the estimates of the railway companies' working expenses for the first year of operation. Following further negotiations, the companies put forward a revised set of estimates which allowed for a reduction of their original figures, taking greater account of economies. Delivering the LCC's full submission in January 1926, Cripps again attacked the insufficiency of information substantiating their claim, asking the solicitor to the LCC to serve a subpoena on the Ministry of Transport in order to obtain a breakdown of the £45 million of likely savings which Sir Eric Geddes, introducing the Railways Bill, had spoken of in the House of Commons. The Ministry asserted that the production of official documents would be 'prejudicial to the interests of the public service'.[22] Forced back on to his own devices, Cripps supplied the Tribunal with his own intricately worked out costing of economies, arrears and maintenance, demonstrating that the companies' estimates were inflated by the order of 10 per cent – a clear and forceful contribution for which the Tribunal was 'very much indebted'. Macmillan, responding, felt that in spite of the 'very close texture' of Cripps's argument, it was vague and dialectical. The Tribunal had already been snowed under with tables produced at Cripps's request – all of which, Cripps complained, had been presented to the companies' advantage. The witnesses had tried to satisfy Cripps, but that, Macmillan remarked sardonically, 'is a matter of some difficulty'.

Macmillan, nonetheless, was careful to close ranks with Cripps when newspapers began deprecating the waste of time and money taken up by the Tribunal and singling out the objections of the LCC;[23] such reports, he put on record, were 'most improper' while the matter, exceptional in complexity and importance, was still under consideration.

Delivering judgement in March 1926, the Tribunal accepted the terms of a settlement reached by the companies and traders, adopting in full the suggested deduction of £3 million in savings. In giving this verdict, the Tribunal thanked the assorted interests for the assistance they had received – 'not least counsel for the London County Council'.

The Tribunal then moved on to the final stage: combining the standard revenue and estimated expenditure to arrive at the amount the railway companies would need to raise, and the allocating of this from ordinary fares, season tickets and workmen's fares. Condemning the companies' schedules of fares, the LCC entered a schedule of its own – endorsed admiringly by Alderman Herbert Morrison of the London Labour Party – which, Cripps maintained, more accurately met the statutory requirements incumbent upon the Tribunal. The companies had always had to be mindful of considerations of public policy – Cripps had got as much from Sir Ralph Wedgwood, general manager of the London and North-Eastern Railway Company, who had been on the stand for two weeks, surrounded by a crowd of assistants. Indeed, 'the ability to pay has, historically, always been a more important governing factor than the remunerativeness of the fare'. The distances workmen now had to travel, because of very necessary out-of-town housebuilding, were so much longer, and wages had gone up only as much as the cost of living, so that the Tribunal could not (as the companies were proposing) reasonably fix fares at a relatively greater level than in the pre-war period. According to the LCC's calculations, the maximum most workmen were able to pay happened to coincide with the minimum the companies could afford to charge, which was where the level should be set. It should not be for the railway companies to decide which fares were to be ordinary and which exceptional; this was the very vice the Tribunal was there to prevent.

Summing up, Cripps dismissed the suggestion that his clients were taking a 'political' attitude. The housing and health of the population of London were involved, and, to ensure the continuous availability of cheap train facilities, he asked the Tribunal to accept the LCC's schedule, or at least to lower the rates the companies were putting forward.

Macmillan, defending their schedules, strenuously denied the companies were bound to make a philanthropic contribution to the housing programme of the LCC. After Clode wondered aloud whether the companies had gone sufficiently into the question of workmen's fares, in view of the 'strong case' set out by the LCC, Macmillan was ready to make concessions on the disputed fares, but the offer came too late.

Passing final judgement in December 1926, the Tribunal provisionally fixed the standardised charges, more or less adopting the companies' own estimates, with one exception – that of workmen's fares. In this instance, the companies 'failed to justify their proposed scale', which was 'too high', placing this class of traffic 'permanently at a higher level of charges than other traffic'. The reduction they suggested, though well short of what the LCC recommended, represented a substantial lowering of the original schedules. It was a remarkable tribute to Cripps's almost single-handed efforts to carry the Tribunal with him, and a fitting reward, as railway officials had cause to remember, for 'this singularly able young lawyer', who 'could confound the cleverest of witnesses with his uncanny knack of showing them that he knew more than they did'.[24] The Housing Committee of the LCC, voting his fees, placed on record its appreciation 'of the manner in which the case of the council was throughout presented by Hon. Stafford Cripps KC'.[25] The phrasing was intentional: Cripps had just successfully taken silk – the third consecutive generation in his family to attain that rank and, at the age of thirty-seven, the youngest KC at that time – and had set himself up in his own chambers in Elm Court.

How did he do it? How, in a profession given over to striving, talking shop with the same companions over lunch in the Middle Temple,[26] did he effect so speedy an ascent? It was, in Cripps's case, due not to the possession of exceptional qualities so much as to their heightened combination.

Cripps had good legal connections through his father and family relations, but contacts only provide opening. (His elder brother, Seddon, was unable to make a go of the law, becoming a jovial fox-hunting bursar of Queen's College, Oxford.)

His industriousness was astonishing. He expressed it only tritely, telling a struggling friend (in 1926), 'It is not possible to glide through life without hard work and do well. I know something about life and hard work, and I can assure you that without a real grind to start with you will never get anywhere . . . there is one and one only royal road to success, and that is hard work.'[27] This was no empty platitude. He put in long hours of pre-trial preparation – far more, in the view of one of those who devilled for him, that anyone else on either side.[28] In patent cases, he often made his own models of gadgets to demonstrate in court.

His punishing methods made him a master at organising the trickiest of cases, rapidly digesting the documentation, indexing and cross-referencing it all on sheets of different-coloured paper. He wrote out his pleadings in longhand, but rarely had to refer to them: a freakish eidetic memory enabled him at the shortest notice to cite chapter and verse. Above all, he could switch easily from one case to another without muddle – borne out by his handling of the Kelantan and Railway Rates cases, which ran concurrently throughout 1924–5, in addition to ongoing patent work. 'He once said to me,' Lord Plowden recalled of an occasion in the 1940s:

'If you gave me the papers of any case I have fought in the last twenty years for one hour, I could go into court and fight it again.' Then he paused for a moment and corrected himself, 'No, I would not need the papers.' He said this was no tribute to him, he just had a mind like that. He could put away the facts about a case in a drawer, pointing to his head, and draw it out when needed and it was all there.[29]

Personal fastidiousness played a part. Monastic habits – early rising and cold baths – were common among leaders at the Bar. Cripps developed a quirky, punctilious routine. He was always immaculately tailored, with the standard wing collar. Before appearing in court, he neither ate nor drank, sharpening his wits and sparing his disorderly stomach through abstinence. His one indulgence was heavy smoking, hinting at the constant expending of nervous energy. His infirmity hindered him, but also fired him up (like many scientists and lawyers, he was greedy with time), lending an impression of 'steely purpose'.[30]

His manner in court was polite, logical and emotionless, his speeches being delivered with one further trait – an aura of overpowering sincerity. Cripps would argue a case by intellectually persuading himself of the justice of his plea. Once he had convinced himself, nothing would shake him. Displaying a remarkable grasp of technicalities, he argued as if he was imparting a scientific truth for the benefit of the court. Opposing counsel were out-duelled. Expert witnesses were intimidated. Clients showed their gratitude, but often wished he would smile more. He always, eventually and sometimes controversially, put himself in the position to dominate proceedings. He was conscious of his brainpower, and conscious that others were too.

The whole effect was of idiosyncratic brilliance, indefatigable and unrelenting, and – even in landmark cases mixing legal first principles (what *is* a sovereign state?) and high policy (how are the railways to run themselves?) – fully in keeping with the hard logic and self-sufficient authority of the law as it was conceived and expounded by the later 1920s.[31] Authority, precedent and the strictest construction of the law prevailed, and in specialised cases Cripps was well-nigh invincible. His personal virtues were of the highest order, honed to excess, setting impossibly lofty standards that nothing human could satisfy.

The Cotswolds were Cripps country. During his convalescence, Stafford and Isobel were living at Minchinhampton, near where he had spent many boyhood summer holidays. A third daughter, Theresa, was born in 1919. Not long afterwards, they saw an advertisement for an old moated grange on the edge of the village of Filkins (population 402), lying in the Hampton Hundreds not far from the Oxfordshire–Gloucestershire border. They bought it, going there against doctor's orders, and gradually restored the property. For the next two decades, Goodfellows was the centre of home life – a place of work, in the short weekends when Cripps returned from London, and a rural retreat.

The manor house, constructed out of Cotswold stone, was seventeenth century, with many original features.[32] Cripps rebuilt the hedgerows, planted yew trees, and grew vegetables. The village itself was almost entirely agricultural, mainly cultivating cereals. There was a fine parish church, and a war memorial dedicated by Burge, now Bishop of Oxford.[33] Burge brought Cripps on to the board of Radley School (though John Cripps went to Winchester). The location was convenient for the Oxford circuit, as well as for legal work with the Corporation of Bristol. The ancestral associations and the sense of space were appealing.

Cripps was always quite clear that the possession of property was a title *and* a resource. With the manor house went a farm and some two hundred acres of farmland, though the land was actually owned by Isobel.[34] The tenants' rights were bought up, stock and horses were paid for, and a bailiff was taken on. Cripps threw himself into every aspect of a farming operation. In mid-1920, the coalition government attempted to bring security to farmers by guaranteeing prices and establishing a minimum wage. Within months, prices fell steeply. Cripps was 'knocked sideways' by the decision to repeal the provisions, a betrayal keenly resented in country communities.

High costs had the beneficial effect of stimulating the use of traditional materials, of which (now Sir) Lawrence Weaver, Cripps's old chief at the Food Production Department, was an advocate. The Weavers stayed at Goodfellows, where Cripps and Weaver took up bookbinding, which afforded some 'peace of mind' in their scanty leisure time.[35] They also started up Ashtead Potteries to employ disabled ex-servicemen, selling its wares in a West End shop, Peter Potter Ltd. Weaver was director-general of the United Kingdom exhibits at the British Empire Exhibition at Wembley in 1925, before going into business, taking a seat on the board of Eno's. Both tried to preserve what the countryside was losing, Cripps 'rearing a pedigree flock of sheep, weaving scarves for his children on an old handloom, and working in a carpenter's shop'.[36] In April 1927, the journalist J. W. Robertson Scott started *The Countryman*, a quarterly devoted to rural life, with money Cripps helped provide.[37]

Into this crowded life Cripps managed to fit one other role – that of earnest young world-saver.

Publication of Stafford's new edition of his father's textbook had been held over by the war, and further delayed by the passing of the Church Enabling Act

1919, which entailed much rewriting. Cripps gained more than a grounding in ecclesiastical law. By the time *Cripps on Church and Clergy* came out – dedicated to Lord Parmoor, ' as a token of affectionate regard' – the new House of Laity of the National Assembly of the Church of England was in existence and Parmoor unanimously elected as its first chairman.

Parmoor, while a strong opponent of religious intolerance, held firmly to the established unity of Church and State; equally, he conceived the rule of law, which he administered as a Lord of Appeal, to be a practical expression of Christian principles. Under the impact of the late war, and the subsequent founding of the League of Nations, he had adopted an increasingly inter-nationalist outlook, chiefly through the non-sectarian World Alliance for the Promotion of International Understanding through the Churches.

The World Alliance, established by Scandinavian clerics, endeavoured to enlist the Christian Churches in promoting fellowship and peace between nations. It worked to rally the Churches in helping to avoid any further recourse to war in the settling of disputes, seeing itself as the 'spiritual ally' of the League of Nations, backing up the rule of law (in the shape of the Covenant of the League) with the sanctity of Christian morality. Ultimately, the Alliance sought to alter human nature by 'the exercise of divine power'.

British supporters of the Alliance were mainly drawn from the ranks of religious worthies, but included many Lib–Lab figures cut off from the Liberal Party by the war and disillusioned by the first years of peace. Lord and Lady Parmoor were its principal sponsors, joined by Lord Robert Cecil, the lawyer and former Liberal MP Willoughby Dickinson, and the Bishop of Winchester. It had (in July 1921) four thousand loosely associated members, bonded by the belief that other nations looked to Britain for moral guidance, that God had laid upon them an immense responsibility towards the rest of mankind. The third post-war conference of the Alliance, attended by representatives from twenty-five countries – former friends, enemies and neutrals – was held in Copenhagen in August 1922, and the Archbishop of Canterbury, president of the Alliance, sent the Bishop of Oxford, H. M. Burge, as his personal emissary. Stafford – acting treasurer of the Alliance's British Council – and Isobel Cripps, the youngsters of the party, accompanied the British delegation.

Cripps's relations with Burge took on a more mature character. Burge pri-vately 'dreaded' having to attend yet another international conference of 'frothy utterances'.[38] Once there, however, he displayed 'a growing enthusiasm' for the purposeful approach of the various national delegations. The issues the conference tackled – the rights of religious minorities, and disarmament – were contentious. A heated discussion of the latter led to proceedings being adjourned. Burge demonstrated his mettle by gathering the delegations together informally over breakfast. When the conference restarted, the head of the French delegation publicly shook hands with his German counterpart, to general applause.[39] Burge was won over and, to Cripps's delight, returned to England 'fired with the great possibilities of the movement' and determined 'to do his utmost to make the British Council a real centre of inspiration to the Christian communities in this country'.[40]

The inspiration behind the Alliance chimed with the temper of the times. The League of Nations attracted many who were committed to the objectives of liberal internationalism, however imperfectly enshrined in the Treaty of Versailles. The special feature of the Alliance was that it was ecumenical and undoctrinaire, over and above all other considerations. It was not a-political but supra-political, as Cripps, commenting on the outcome of Copenhagen, spelled out:

> This Conference must be regarded as the most important effort ever made by the combined Churches of the world to exercise their power to overcome the hatred, enmity, and prejudice which has played, and is now playing, so terrible a part in separating and estranging all the nations of the world. Two paths now lie before the world – the one the way of the politican, leading by intrigue and diplomacy to misunderstandings, envies, hatreds and fresh wars; the other way of Christ, leading by love and self-sacrifice to mutual understanding, goodwill, brotherhood and peace. Every Christian must realise his own responsibility in helping to raise the standard of international relationships from the political to the high moral standard, and he must realise, too, that this effort brooks no delay. If the Churches of Christ do not now take this opportunity, not only will the cause of Christianity suffer, but the world will sink into a state of chaos and barbarism.[41]

The contrast between murky politics and Christian purity – which could hardly have been put in starker terms – derived from Burge's teachings. War had broken out in 1914 despite all the comforting assurances of statesmen, jurists and free-traders that war was unthinkable; their reasoning had been 'scattered to the winds'.[42] The only foundation for peaceful existence was offered by 'the Christianising of international relations'. If, as Cripps believed, evil was the fault of wicked people who knew quite well what they were doing, the sole answer was to inculcate more elevated virtues, applying them in both private and public life. People had given up everything for their nation during the war. Would they be prepared to do the same for Christ? Was their love of Christ the stronger?[43] Burge was convinced: 'It seems to me that the man with a religious motive in dealing with social problems always wins in the end – provided he is not a prig.'[44]

At a dinner given by Cripps at the Conservative Club in London, the suggestion was made that the British Council of the World Alliance be reconstituted to widen its representation. In September a team of devotees spent two days at the Bishop of Oxford's residence at Cuddesdon, preparing a report recommending a permanent British Council. A further group met at Parmoor just before Christmastide to draw up a practical scheme. Gwendoline Hill, Burge's secretary, was appointed to oversee the Council's London secretariat. They were not, the editors of *Goodwill* cautioned, 'inaugurating the millennium'. Burge reassured the impatient Cripps that he too was anxious the progress they were making should not be impeded, and was disheartened by the attitude of Lambeth Palace, 'which seemed to treat [the Alliance] as one of a number of benevolent societies'.[45] That was no reason to despair, since the Alliance still carried the best hope of gathering all sporadic independent efforts into one all-embracing 'national institution'.

By May 1923, representatives of six different denominations from England and Wales (bar the Roman Catholic Church) came forward to serve on the new British Council. Burge, Parmoor and Cripps were among twenty Anglicans chosen by the Archbishop of Canterbury. Staying on as treasurer of the group, Cripps was also elected to the Oxford Diocesan Conference of the National Assembly. Burge, as the Council's first president, drummed home the constructive intentions 'of those who profess the religion of Christ', not just in avoiding war but in bringing about an abiding peace. Cripps offered a prize at Winchester College for the best essay on 'Arbitration in the 19th century'. The winner, eighteen-year-old Hugh Gaitskell, collected his award from Cripps in a taxi rushing from the Law Courts to Paddington Station. Cripps 'told the dissatisfied schoolboy that the world's ills could be remedied only by a union of the Christian churches'.[46]

Through the Alliance and other activities, Lord Parmoor established contacts with some of the leaders of the Labour Party, and Parmoor was transformed into a semi-political haven for progressive causes.[47] Officially Parmoor remained a Unionist peer. When the general election of November 1923 deprived the Prime Minister, Stanley Baldwin, of a Conservative majority, the King invited Labour to form a minority ministry. Ramsay MacDonald, the Labour Party leader, wrote to Parmoor to ask if he was willing to serve. Parmoor consulted Burge (who modestly could not think why). Burge advised him that Labour was more likely than the other parties to put international relations on the right basis, and that his own role in furthering such a policy would be 'unique'.[48] But he must stick to the government and not resign when things were not done in the way he wanted. 'That is his besetting difficulty.'[49] Parmoor accepted, looking forward to 'a new foreign policy' which substituted 'friendliness' for 'the war spirit'. In January 1924 he was appointed Lord President of the Council with special responsibility for the League of Nations, becoming – aged seventy-one – the first ex-Conservative MP, knighted by a Liberal prime minister, to sit in a Labour cabinet. Sidney Webb took on the presidency of the

Board of Trade. 'What a joke it is, your father and he in the Cabinet together,' Beatrice Webb informed Stafford.[50]

Parmoor had a hand in two of the main foreign policy moves of MacDonald's premiership – *de jure* recognition of the Soviet Union and the drafting by the League of Nations Assembly of the Geneva Protocol, signatories agreeing to submit all disputes to international arbitration, paving the way for the admission of Germany to the League and the holding of a general disarmament conference. His special responsibility for the League meant that relations with Foreign Office officials were choppy, and – with Charles Trevelyan (President of the Board of Education), another advocate of open diplomacy – he was a well-known opponent of the infant security services. Before MacDonald could ratify the Protocol, he was defeated in the confidence debate over the Campbell case,[51] precipitating a general election. The botched handling of the Zinoviev letter, near the end of the campaign, split the Cabinet down the middle, Parmoor indignantly maintaining the letter had been forged to discredit Labour.[52] As a last act, following electoral defeat in October 1924, a small Cabinet committee, including Parmoor, published a three-paragraph report explaining they could not (without the original) determine the authenticity of the letter, after which the first Labour government resigned. It was a measure of the antipathy generated by Parmoor's political involvements that he was voted off the Oxford Diocesan Conference, allegedly because of associating with the Labour government.[53]

In 1925, the British Council of the World Alliance, just when it was busily encouraging support for the Protocol, suffered a setback. Only a couple of months before the Alliance's conference in Stockholm, Burge fell victim to pneumonia and suddenly died. Cripps had enlisted Burge for the Alliance. In the thick of his heaviest litigation, he paid tribute to his old headmaster and friend. What did he want Burge most to be remembered for? His charm, courtesy, human sympathy, his unstinting effort and his 'great inspiration' to the Christian community. 'Above all', Cripps reflected:

he was insistent that no mere moral or economic force could suffice to bring about peace or goodwill: all these, based in the last resort upon questions of expediency, were bound to fail. One force and one only was strong enough to overcome the hatreds and misunderstandings of the world, and that was the divine force of Christian understanding and love.[54]

Such nobility of sentiment was not universal. To advanced liberals, Burge was very much a political, increasingly Labour-friendly animal, imagining everyone in England was converted to the League. He looked at life from a rarefied point of view, evident in his hostility to every suggested reform of Church ceremonial. He worked for a change of heart, rather than a fundamental change in the structure of society.[55] Hard-headed Conservatives bridled at the cant of 'international harmony' from those 'craving for peace', sensing an 'immense pretension' in the grandiose aspirations of the League. Such criticism hurt Cripps but did not deflect him. He did not flaunt his Christianity: Goodfellows was outwardly pagan. He was always ready to expound his views, without caring to rationalise them. His faith was simple, its 'truth' unencumbered by theological disputation. 'I always thought that his trouble was that he *would* apply his own standards to everyone else', a pupil in his chambers commented.[56] From Parmoor and Burge he gained the uplifting certainty that comes from believing. It was 'our bounden duty' – the duty of all Churchmen and Englishmen intolerant of comfort-loving atheism – he intoned, to be 'doing our Master's work'.

With Burge's passing, several difficulties arose. Partly these had to do with the Alliance's identity. The British delegation to the Stockholm conference submitted a paper on the subject of secret diplomacy – State papers covering the outbreak of the Great War had gradually been made public – but Willoughby Dickinson, the new British head, was at pains to fend off charges that the Alliance was leading the Churches away from pure religion into the devious paths of policy – though he would welcome, he said, 'instilling a little Christianity into the minds of our politicians'. Cripps, recalling the announcement of the Armistice and 'the deep sense of relief and gratitude that the horrors of war had been brought to an end', contrasted that mood with the more recent resurgence of animosities and the ebbing of religious sentiment.[57] Uprooted by the war, the weeds of materialism were growing again, on the Continent as well as in Britain, 'choking the flowers of religion'. The Conference on Politics, Economics and Citizenship (COPEC) had been endeavouring to reconcile capital and labour on Christian lines, only for the general strike of May 1926 to break out and the government then being deaf to appeals by the Archbishop of Canterbury and other Church leaders to resume negotiations. Both interests – the welfare of the community and the standard of living of the workers – 'come home to us', Parmoor pleaded. Cripps himself found the government's attitude unforgiveable. When the miners stayed out indefinitely, he collected money for miners' families.

The Alliance's second difficulty was finance. Cripps launched an appeal for £10,000, directed at the City of London and endorsed by the editor of *The Spectator*, by the author and capitalist Ernest Benn, and by Sir Henry Lunn, the tour operator and long-time adherent of the nebulous cause of Church unification.[58] Working with Count Frederick van den Heuvel, commercial director of Eno's and a business associate of Freddie Cripps, he set up fund-raising meetings of 'the greatest importance for the future of the Alliance'.[59] Whenever such approaches failed, Cripps made up the balance. In 1926–7 he stumped up £344 – by far the largest contribution, without which the British Council secretariat could not have kept afloat.

The greatest difficulty was the one over which the Alliance had least control – events. Britain's refusal (in March 1925) to ratify the Geneva Protocol ruined what, for Parmoor, represented 'a triumph of international co-operation for peace'.[60] Diplomatic relations with the Soviet Union were broken off. On top of all this, the Conservatives insisted on making foreign policy a party issue, branding Labour as unpatriotic. Cripps, promoted to the Executive Committee of the British Council, joined a deputation to 10 Downing Street, reaffirming the Alliance's belief in the living idea of international friendship which could prosper only through the worldwide promotion of Christian teaching.[61]

Hopeful signs emerged with the Locarno Pact and the Kellogg–Briand Pact, renouncing war as an instrument of national policy. But neither compensated for the inability of the League of Nations to build a movement for peace constructed upon 'the application to political matters of the principles of the Christian Gospel'. Even the younger generation – less inculcated with nationalist animosities – were, as Cripps observed, organising in non-Christian groups.

It was the way of politics which was foundering, not Christian feeling for the 'wider love of humanity'. That this was so was clear from the Alliance's ultimate ends. The Alliance was not pacifist, although some individual congregations (such as the Quakers) were. Its doctrine was anti-war idealism, springing from the conviction that deep-rooted conflicts, finding an outlet in political argument and diplomatic formulae, had to be banished by enlightened understanding. The Covenant of the League might have to be invoked, necessitating (Lord Parmoor reluctantly recognised[62]) the use of force to restrain aggression. Even clerics had to agree that the League 'exalts war; it would make the final war a veritable "Holy War" '.[63] The last sanction, however, was not coercion by the League. It was the religion of Christ, 'the Prince of Peace'. 'This world is not enough,' Stafford was fond of saying; 'we must have a religious purpose.'[64]

4

GOING OVER

I asked Cripps once how he – scion of an old landed family and reputedly
earning £30,000 a year as a leader at the Bar – had turned Socialist.
Promptly and simply he answered: 'Because of my religion.'

T. Evans, Daily Express, *20 October 1950*

What does the practising Christian who is personally prospering do in a society which plainly is not?

For Cripps, endowed with a keen sense of social responsibility, his professional and private happiness was increasingly at odds with the disappointments of the World Alliance. One cannot, he professed, 'leave it to others'. The Churches might preach that the love of God was stronger than the love of one's country, but this had a fading appeal, crowded out by more vivid social attractions. It was for him a short step from the cause of international peace to the demand for equality nearer home. Burge had an inkling something was 'profoundly amiss' with the Britain of the 1920s, and that benevolence and loving kindness would not be enough;[1] the leadership of the Labour Party, 'heady in their talk' and as yet 'undisciplined', at least had 'faith'. Impelled by superior selflessness, Cripps was by no means the first, was indeed a latecomer to join the party of progress. What he symbolised, as a front-rank lawyer, farm owner and churchman, was what traditionalists found hardest to take: the pillar of the community gone wrong, the 'humbug' who is conservative in everything except his politics.

His practice at the Patent Bar was certainly blooming. Patent applications had shot up again, several hundreds coming from the German I. G. Farben dyestuffs company alone. Fearing a German stranglehold on the dye industry, Imperial Chemical Industries (successor to the British Dyestuffs Corporation) asked Cripps, one of the small handful of chemical barristers, for his opinion. He advised selecting an almost certainly invalid patent as a test case; victory would free up the whole range of dye colours covered by I. G.'s applications. Cripps took the view that the Law Officer's judgement had been wrong in the case of patent 199771 (the naphthol type of dye, fast to light and washing), because of prior general knowledge and lack of subject matter, and the petition for revocation was presented in September 1928.[2] After hearing the submissions, Mr Justice Maugham – now raised to the Bench – accepted all the propositions Cripps put forward, disposing of the new range of patents I. G. had introduced. 'The case will probably cost the I. G. about £30,000, ICI's solicitor recorded, 'and the effect is to make very nearly the whole of the Selection patents which were taken out by the I. G. subsequently to those the subject of the proceedings, clearly invalid, and consequently the whole Naphthol AS field of dyes is now open to us.'[3] In addition to his large fee, ICI gave Cripps a gold cigarette case.[4] Other prominent clients followed, deferring to *him*. New work placed a heavy load on the juniors in his chambers, who – while not slave-driven – were expected to work hard. Cripps, however, always made the final decision on the handling of a case by himself, confident about both interpreting the law and, as every good patent lawyer can, shaping it. In *Sharpe and Dohme* v. *Boots* he formulated a test of the 'obviousness' of a patent which, though later discarded, was widely cited. A colleague at the Bar believed Cripps had 'beyond doubt one of the finest brains in the country'.[5]

Parliamentary Bar litigation, involving private legislation brought by local authorities and private companies, modified his outlook the most. Cripps had put up such a strong fight for the LCC before the Railway Rates Tribunal that Alderman Morrison employed him to represent the Labour-controlled metropolitan boroughs opposing an LCC bill to co-ordinate passenger transport in London. Hearings of the committee stage in the House of Commons began in March 1929, with a general election expected. Though the Conservative government made clear that any pending bills would carry over into the new parliament, the objectors – 'ably represented' by Cripps – held up the bill, harrying the chairman of the LCC, Sir John Gatti, and forcing several amendments. Private-bill legislation was normally non-contentious, and Morrison realised that Cripps's advocacy was more than occupational. 'When I told him that he ought to be publicly with us as I knew he was in spirit, he replied: "I don't want to enter politics. I am more interested in the Church." '[6] Morrison, looking out for promising recruits, sensed some uncertainty.

Cripps was unequipped for political life. On the other hand, from scraps of surviving evidence, he was plainly being headhunted by assorted patrons for a party which had 'faith' but was wanting in figures of calibre. We know from another source that Lord Haldane – elder statesman in the first Labour government, who died in 1928 – named five lawyers, including Cripps, whose legal services he wished to obtain for the party.[7] D. N. Pritt, who took silk with Cripps on the same day in 1927, had already been approached by MacDonald – Arthur Henderson, national secretary of the Labour Party, having felt that Pritt's leftism would conciliate the militants and his status as a silk assuage the snobs.[8] The Bar was a traditional gateway to politics, but associating with Labour was different. Becoming Solicitor-General in 1924, Patrick Hastings earned suspicion, contempt and 'even hatred from those whom I used to consider old-time friends'.[9] William Jowitt, elected as a Liberal in May 1929 before joining the MacDonald government as Attorney-General and changing party, provoked 'bitter controversy', losing all but one of his juniors.[10] On the formation of the Haldane Society in 1929 by a group of Labour lawyers, Lord Sankey, the Lord Chancellor, intimated that members could expect favoured advancement. High-earning barristers tempted to join could not, however, be sure of retaining the goodwill of clients or of making good the loss of income.

Estimates of Cripps's income were exaggerated; that his wife was an heiress was less widely known. Isobel's father had been unwell for some time; eventually he set off on a long voyage to the Americas and died at sea in March 1928. Cripps, one of his executors, was responsible for disposing of his joint controlling stake in J. C. Eno's.[11] Since for 'family reasons' the Swithinbanks did not wish to retain control, Cripps negotiated the buying out of the company by its Canadian branch, for a price reputedly in excess of £1.5 million.[12]

That autumn, Cripps abandoned part-time farming, buying a larger town house near Hyde Park, keeping Goodfellows for weekends and holidays. His interest in the village did not flag. Witney Rural District Council was thinking of building new cottages in Filkins, using modern brick. Unable to persuade it to construct the cottages in harmony with neighbouring houses, he offered to top up the difference in cost if local materials were used, providing his own architect and buying up stone quarries. Much as he glorified the countryside, he was aware of current predicaments. Agriculture should be efficient, but low wages and poor marketing meant there could be no improvements in productivity for some time to come. Nor, in existing conditions, could private landowners afford to invest. 'It will pay the State to be benevolent if the State is landlord, not otherwise,' he had decided. 'I see no reason why a start should not be made. Nationalization of all unbuilt-on land should be undertaken.'[13]

Just before the election, in May 1929, of a second, minority, Labour government, Morrison approached Lord Parmoor, telling him it was 'one of my ambitions to see Stafford Cripps in the Labour party'. Parmoor suggested Morrison should write directly. The latter promptly applauded Cripps for his 'magnificent fight' over the London Transport Bill, said he appreciated the professional considerations which arose, but asked Cripps to let him know if and when he might like to join Labour's ranks – adding 'of course I greatly respect your own scrupulousness in not intending to join until you are quite clear in your own mind that you accept our principles and our policy'.[14] Cripps, giving a donation to the London Labour Party's election fund, nonplussed Morrison by broaching the question of rural housing, with which Morrison – a Londoner – admitted he was 'not intimately familiar'.[15]

Pritt provides a further character clue – Cripps's anxieties about the established Church. He remembers bumping into Cripps some time after he himself had joined Labour, and being informed by Cripps that he was thinking of joining too 'but as a member of the Church of England he would require some assurance from the leaders of the Party as to their attitude to proposals for the disestablishment of the Church of England before he would be prepared to do so'.[16] The parliamentary battle over the revised Prayer Book in 1928, in which Lord Parmoor figured, weighed in his thoughts. 'Cripps wanted the [Church] Assembly to champion the oppressed classes; instead it discussed for several days the inclusion of King Charles in the Church's Calendar.'[17] Anglican proselytisers for the Labour Party like R. H. Tawney supplied a persuasive rationale for treating progressive politics as a Christian 'calling'.

Whatever the reasoning, it was Herbert Morrison's persistence, as Isobel underlined to Morrison's biographers, which 'made all the difference,'[18] securing for Cripps the offer of the candidacy in Morrison's home base of Woolwich. Woolwich was a pioneering local Labour Party, uniquely combining both West Woolwich and East Woolwich parliamentary constituencies.[19] It had been among the first to bring in individual party membership, long before the model rules of 1918. The Woolwich Arsenal and Dockyard, employing some seven thousand workers, gave the strongly unionised local labour force a self-contained character. In the 1925 local elections, Labour won with a clean sweep. The local party secretary, William Barefoot, one of nature's organisers, had fought West Woolwich at the last three general elections, coming within 332 votes of the Unionist MP, Sir Kingsley Wood. Barefoot was only too ready to stand aside. West Woolwich was winnable, Morrison (by now MP for Hackney South and Minister of Transport) explained to Cripps, but Cripps still had doubts, asking for more time before allowing his name to go forward,[20] his father preferring 'a proper London constituency'.[21] Eventually, although safer offers were made, Cripps informed Barefoot 'I want to win my seat.'[22]

Cripps's reception in the Labour Party was aided by his morale-boosting defence of the new Labour MP for Plymouth Drake, J. J. Moses, against charges of bribery and corrupt practice. A prominent benefactor in the constituency had supposedly used his influence with a boys club to influence the voting of the boys' parents in favour of Moses, who was also accused of improper use of licensed taxicabs and an incomplete return of his election expenses. Lodging of a petition disputing the validity of an election was rare; this was the first the Party had faced. The case was heard before a specially constituted court in Plymouth in October 1929. Election law was tangled, and the two judges admitted they were 'at sea'. Cripps, mastering the case in front of him and not just sticking to his brief, persuaded the court that nothing in the behaviour of Moses could be said to amount to corrupt treating. The judges concurred, dismissing the petition – their voices 'drowned by the roars of cheering from outside'.[23] G. R. Shepherd, Labour's national agent, was lost in admiration: 'It is not too much to say that the success [sic] of the Petition largely rested on your shoulders.'[24] Cripps brushed aside any payment.

Lawyers consorting with the Labour Party risked ostracism by other members of the Bar. Cripps's achievement did not endear him to every Labour activist either. In early November the Executive Committee of the Woolwich Labour Party, after questioning Cripps, invited him to fight West Woolwich at the next election, it having been put about that the party higher-ups 'wanted him in'. Though he had no trade union sponsor, he won the support of two union wards, the Engineers and the Wheelwrights, before the Transport and General Workers' Union branch dug in its heels, suggesting a local councillor, Alderman Berry, instead. One long-standing union man, H. T. Green, despite never having seen Cripps in the flesh, did not like what he heard:

Dear Bearfoot [sic],

I have today received on behalf of Woolwich 4 Bch AEU your communication re: the Honbl R Cripps K.C. The contents astonishes me. When I reflect on the old days of the Woolwich Labour Party and the glorious record of Will Crooks to think that it has sunk so low as to lick the boots of that class which it has always denounced as 'capitalist' I am stupified. I think your communication is a back handed slap at the whole of the working class organisations in the Borough. It bears out what most of us, who still remain clear headed, have contended that 3 New Road [headquarters of the Woolwich party] and the General Council are dominated by middle class opinion & ideas and for years have drifted right away from working class thought. Personally if this candidature materialises I shall do what I can in my power to keep the Hon: Cripps out of West Woolwich even if it may mean the retention of the present Conservative candidate.

Of course this letter is not a reflection of Woolwich 4 Bch AEU but a personal communication.[25]

A requirement that candidates could not be adopted unless they had at least twelve months' membership had never been enforced, but the fact that Cripps had only recently joined the Party – in Woolwich – fuelled antagonism. By the day of the General Council meeting, however, no one else had come forward. Cripps was endorsed without disagreement, the Party accepting financial responsibility in full, and the selection of Cripps – son of Lord Parmoor, 'brilliant young lawyer and a powerful orator'[26] – was released to local newspapers.

The candidate was introduced at a public meeting at Woolwich Town Hall in February 1930, supported by Morrison, Barefoot and the Labour MP for East Woolwich, Harry Snell, the occasion being marked by Communist Party hecklers. Morrison made much of Cripps's 'honesty and sincerity'; Cripps was 'the type of man we ought to have in the Labour Party today'; people of the 'respectable' classes were steadily coming over to Labour, which needed those with 'capabilities for administration and technical knowledge'. Cripps, speaking evenly, admitted belonging to the most Tory profession in the world – but, he continued, a large number of lawyers were and would be turning towards the party which was now 'the only place for a rational man to be'. Extolling the idealism and larger outlook of the new Labour government and praising its policy of disarmament, he devoted the bulk of his speech to unemployment – 'an evil which no one in this world, or the next, can cure in a day'. The government was taking steps in the short term to alleviate suffering and provide temporary work, which the Lord Privy Seal, Jimmy Thomas – 'a hero' who was unfairly being picked on – was promoting, aided by Morrison's railway- and road-building schemes. Slum clearance was another priority. He had been around, and been appalled by, some of the worst slums in London while engaged by the LCC. Tackling this would provide many more jobs. 'I don't believe in safety first [Baldwin's rallying cry]; I believe you have got to take risks.' But a permanent solution would come only once business and industry – including the financial institutions – were reorganised on the basis of social control. For this to happen, the voters had to return a majority Labour government. Until then, Labour was carrying out schemes that should have been started years ago, treating unemployment as a human problem awaiting more fundamental change.[27] At the end of his speech, the *Kentish Independent* commented, Cripps – having dealt firmly with interruptions – was 'cheered to the echo'.

It was Cripps's measured courtroom delivery transposed to the public platform – articulate and intellectual, but with the intellectuality of one who, while knowing a good deal about its subject matter was still a novice in politics. (Morrison, only a year older than Cripps, already had twenty years of politicking behind him.) Like most privileged adherents to the Party in the 1920s, he had largely received a warm welcome. Unlike most others, he had actually succeeded at something – quite spectacularly – before entering. Morrison's biblical dig – Cripps 'is not merely rising; he has risen' – rang true. That he was uncontaminated by political society was one of his assets. He did not convert himself into a socialist; he *developed* into one.[28] His chilly intellectual egoism was to be an enduring trait. When party colleagues began staying at Goodfellows, they were surprised by Cripps dressing for dinner and then packing everyone off early to bed. Cripps was unmoved, insisting this was what he 'always had done, and to change my habits would have implied that I was "playing down" to other people. I came into this party as I am, and I stay that way.'[29]

The MacDonald government had no working majority in Parliament, was under attack from critics within, and stayed in office only with Liberal backing.

If an election were forced, Labour was certain to be defeated. On the central issue of unemployment, the argument for a much larger programme of public works raged across the Cabinet table. In the Commons and in West Woolwich, Kingsley Wood was an effective adversary, highlighting the introduction of short time at the Arsenal, the doubling of the jobless in the borough, and impending rate increases under the Labour council. Cripps, making the rounds with Isobel, could only call for patience. No other government had attempted so much. But, whatever the party, it was the fundamental beliefs it enshrined that counted. In Labour's case, the interests of the individual were subordinated to the needs of the nation, unswayed by press panic or Tory promises. 'What was the duty of the people of Nottingham?' he asked, after a Conservative by-election victory on promises made to the lace industry, in June 1930. 'It was not to consider their own interests to the exclusion of the whole. If it was "hang public policy, we want to be safeguarded", that was the wrong attitude in party politics.'[30] The admonishing tone was authentically puritan, not proletarian. The Labour Party, pure in motive, had to persuade members of all classes of the attractions of a new social system rather than showing what they could get out of it.

Cripps readied himself to do battle with Sir Kingsley Wood. The Fates 'decreed otherwise'.[31]

On 6 October, the Solicitor-General, Sir James Melville, informed the Prime Minister of the recurrence of an old war injury which made it 'absolutely imperative' he give up his post.[32] Melville wrote again on the 11th, his doctors instructing him to resign his office 'now and at once'. One among many of MacDonald's problems was brought to a head – 'no reserve of Labour Law Officers' (there were four barristers on the Labour benches in the Commons, and only one KC). The recently pledged amendment of the Trade Union and Trade Disputes Act 1927 would require skilled piloting through Parliament. Moreover, MacDonald hoped to offer the viceroyalty of India to the Attorney-General, Sir William Jowitt. Pritt recalls being sent for by Jowitt earlier that same year and being told that if he were prepared to stand for Parliament as a Labour candidate Jowitt would make sure he became the next Solicitor-General. Pritt expressed interest, but guessed there would be strong backing for Cripps, who had 'considerable ability' as well as his father and an uncle (Lord Passfield) in the Cabinet. 'There will certainly be pressure for Cripps,' Jowitt agreed, 'but I shall resist it. The decision is, in fact, in my hands, and you can rely on it that I shall appoint you.' Pritt heard no more, until the announcement of Melville's resignation and the appointment of Cripps in his stead. Some time later, when Pritt met Jowitt again, Jowitt surprised him by repeating his earlier offer, adding, 'It was *I* who appointed Cripps; don't believe any of the stories told about any fights over his appointment. I insisted on Cripps, and I appointed him . . .'[33] What had gone on?

MacDonald's instinct was to do what he had tried the year before and entice the Liberal Norman Birkett (a KC) into following Jowitt into the Labour Party, making him Solicitor-General. Birkett had at that time refused point blank, telling reporters 'he could not change his politics in twenty-five minutes'.[34] He was urged to reconsider. Cripps was an obvious alternative, but his complete lack of parliamentary experience told against him. Morrison and Parmoor spoke up for him. The Webbs, contrary to rumours of Fabian leverage, had no involvement. The stoutest advocate of Cripps was Cripps himself. In the middle of the 1935 general election, Cripps was to accuse his (MacDonaldite) National Labour opponent, Archibald Church, of putting it about 'that I went to Ramsay MacDonald in 1931 [sic] and asked him to appoint me Solicitor-General. There is only one person who could give currency to such a lie. It is entirely and absolutely false.'[35] There is tenuous proof of it in MacDonald's diary, however.[36] When Birkett eventually rebuffed MacDonald, the way was clear for Cripps. The only consistent element in Jowitt's statements to Pritt, before and after Cripps' appointment, is that Jowitt was anxious to show that the final decision had been in his keeping. Law Officers' appointments being nominally at the discretion of the Crown, the Solicitor-Generalship carrying with it an automatic knighthood, MacDonald's private secretary wrote to the King on 20 October, commending Cripps as 'in every way the most suitable person to succeed', subject to the agreement of His Majesty. The King replied the same day, 'very glad to approve of Mr Cripps'.[37] 'Thank you for your enquiry,' MacDonald could now let Morrison know. 'He is to be made the Solicitor-General, and I should like to get him in [to Parliament] as quickly as possible.'[38] Morrison revealed the secret at a public meeting on the 24th, after which Cripps assured the audience that the Government intended to repeal the Trade Disputes Act for good. His leap to prominence caught many newspapers unawares, and they variously got his name, age and education wrong. They were on safer ground in describing him as the youngest son of the Cabinet's oldest member, filling the very post denied to his father thirty years before.

· 'Congratulations,' his junior Lionel Heald proclaimed. 'From all accounts it is the best "win" you have yet had, which is saying a great deal!' 'You must be the first of our contemporaries at Winchester to hold high office,' a school friend wrote. His doctor was thrilled – 'It is a very great feather in your cap to have got there, as I am sure everyone will agree, who knows how much ill health you have had to fight against. It would have disheartened most people.' 'I travelled North a few weeks ago with a Law Lord,' another barrister confided, 'and he told me you would be Lord Chancellor before many years had passed.'[39]

Replying to H. P. (Lord) Macmillan, Cripps attributed his 'incursion' into politics 'entirely' to Macmillan's example (which they had talked over several times) of disinterested pubic service, having made up his mind 'to do my share of work besides earn money'.[40] But not all approved his crossing a professional and social divide. 'Just a line of congratulation, and though I don't like your associates one bit, I hope you may be able to prevent them from bankrupting us all!'[41]

'Monday Oct 27th. Buck Pal,' George V entered in his diary. 'Cold & Dull, drizzle in the evening. Saw Bigge & Wigram. Receivd Mr S. Cripps (the new Solicitor Genr) & knighted him.'[42] 'What', he inquired of his new Law Officer, 'do you belong to that lot for?'[43]

5

BRISTOL EAST

And now Stafford Cripps enters the political arena as Solicitor-General
and the winner, by a large majority, of the Bristol seat. Stafford is a
convinced Christian, of the Sankey brand; tall, good-looking, pleasant
voice, an essentially modest and well-mannered man; but a first-rate
advocate in receipt of a large income. He is the only one of the 155
nephews and nieces who might become a big figure in public life. His
one handicap is poor health.

Beatrice Webb, diary, 19 January 1931[1]

The government had its new Solicitor-General, plunged into the official inquiry
into the causes of the R101 airship disaster, where he impressed with his 'boyish'
prowess and knowledge of aerodynamics.[2] The Solicitor-General now had to
be found a seat – urgently. There is much historical instruction and irony in
the way that Cripps – scourge of the Labour Party machine in years to come –
was pushed into place by Transport House.

Almost at once, a vacancy occurred in Whitechapel, on the death of the
sitting Labour MP Harry Gosling, a founder member of the Transport and
General Workers' Union. The value to the party of having Cripps in the House
of Commons to help carry through the Trade Disputes Bill was a strong
card there. Press reports hinted, however, that a rich lawyer would be an
incongruous choice in such a poor neighbourhood, and that the TGWU
favoured one of its own veterans. 'There is a strong objection locally to H.Q.
imposing a candidate, and Mr Henderson knows that he must move cir-
cumspectly.'[3] Once the outcry over the government's recent White Paper on
Palestine (suspending further Jewish immigration to the Holy Land) had
gained ground, the chances of the nephew of the new Secretary for the Colonies – Sidney Webb, now Lord Passfield – being safely elected in a Jewish-
populated area looked slim.

Cripps, in any case, had to give his full attention to his new post as one
of the three principal legal advisers to the Crown, the government and the
departments of State, watching – between times – the deliberations of the
House of Commons from the gallery, while fulfilling a round of public engage-

ments. Replying to the toast at the Lord Mayor's Banquet, he glowingly acclaimed the activities of the merchants and bankers of the first city of the Empire, asking them to appreciate that, if the working of the law seemed antiquated, it was because the legal profession wanted to preserve the valued traditions handed down from the past. That said, he sympathised with the promised inquiry into the law, especially over delays in litigation. He was not a political mercenary, nor the prisoner of his profession, one who knew him well intimated; 'when the time comes for that spring-cleaning of our legal system which is so long overdue, I believe that we can count securely on his full support'.[4] Cripps was amazed to find how understaffed and overworked the Law Officer's Department was, not to mention by the persistence of outdated customs, such as that a Law Officer should lead for the Crown in Inland Revenue and in poison murder cases – the latter a convention which, with Jowitt's consent, he refused to abide by.[5]

'Reluctantly' he gave up the treasurership of the World Alliance; the Council conveyed its gratitude for the invaluable help which, 'in spite of a busy life, busier than that of most men', he had put in over several years.[6] 'It is a great thing that we shall have you in Parliament where you will render good service,' Lord Dickinson wrote to tell him. 'I fear the World Alliance will suffer by it: but do not forget it altogether.'[7] To add to the blow, Gwen Hill, secretary of the British Council, went with him as his private secretary.

In early December, the Labour MP for Bristol East, Walter Baker, died following an operation. This time Henderson did not hold back. Another aspirant, Leah Manning, a headmistress and president of the National Union of Teachers, believed the seat was promised to her, with her union ready to contribute to the upkeep of the local party.[8] Henderson peremptorily ordered her to stand down. She refused. An old friend from Cambridge days, Hugh Dalton, Labour MP for Bishop Auckland and under-secretary to Henderson at the Foreign Office, softened her up, telling her 'Uncle Arthur' wanted the seat for Cripps, making it a loyalty test. Heartbroken, she gave way, at which Dalton, with 'cunning', only then promised her the next vacancy. (Manning fought and won the East Islington by-election in March 1931.)

Baker had been sponsored by the Union of Post Office Workers. The Union, for a second time, consented to waive any prior claim. In haste, after the local agent had been squared beforehand, a meeting of the Bristol East Divisional Labour Party was held on Saturday 15 December at its headquarters over a converted shop in Redfield. The Executive Committee met first, with the area organiser as well as the national organiser, G. R. Shepherd.[9] Shepherd presented the Executive with a short list of one, emphasising the urgency of the situation and that Cripps was needed in the Commons, pressing committee members to endorse him. One influential member, Councillor 'Harry' Hennessy, expressed astonishment that Cripps was in the building before they had even considered the matter. Cripps then addressed the meeting, speaking as someone who belonged to an old Gloucestershire family, who, through legal work, was familiar with the Bristol docks, and who had joined the Labour Party as a result of the ideals contained in the *Labour and the Nation* policy statement of 1928. Cripps, it was made clear, would bear the expenses of the by-election and provide a further £300 a year for the upkeep of the Party.

Even after a resolution was moved to recommend his candidacy, there were complaints that the Committee was being rushed into a decision, without the chance for other local organisations to make nominations. Eventually, however, his name was forwarded, going before the 120 delegates of the full General Council convened immediately afterwards, during which time Cripps had to sweat it out.[10] Shepherd again spoke first. 'I urge the local party, nay, I implore you to accept him.'[11] A handful, led by Hennessy, claimed the rules were being used to force upon them such a raw recruit. Bristol East, Hennessy maintained, was proudly working class and should be represented by one of its own, a worker and not an intellectual.[12] Another delegate demanded 'a real Socialist candidate, not like some of our present MPs'. All the same, a majority warmed to the idea of a titled representative who would hold government office once elected. Cripps was invited to speak, and ably fielded questions; then, after two hours, his candidacy was unanimously carried. Bristol East was praised for doing the right thing – putting the national party before local sympathies[13] – but it had taken all of Henderson's formidable authority to bring about Cripps's adoption.

The city of Bristol, a Liberal stronghold right up to Edwardian times, had also been an early centre of Labour and radical politics, nurtured by propagandist open-air meetings, Clarion cycling clubs and Nonconformist chapel-going.[14] Bristol Trades Council, along with the Bristol Socialist Society and the local branch of the Independent Labour Party, had been instrumental in securing the first independent representatives of Labour on the city council. Many Labour and trade union leaders – including Ben Tillett and Ernest Bevin – first rose to prominence in and around the Bristol area. Up until 1914, however, Labour was only a vocal minority on the Liberal-dominated council, though it was increasingly militant.

Bristol East was a miniature model of the apparently irresistible electoral replacement of the Liberals by Labour. A predominantly working-class area with a high concentration of coal mining, heavy industry and manual trades, as well as an ICI branch at Netham, it had been the only division in Bristol to be contested by Labour before the war, and had undergone the wholesale unionising of labour in several large factories (Fry's, Will's) during wartime.[15] In 1918 the seat was held by a Coalition Liberal, and again, with only a slim majority over Labour, in 1922. Walter Baker had finally taken Bristol East in 1923 (Bristol North falling to Labour at the same election), holding it in a straight fight with the Liberals in 1924 and 1929, boosting the majority to over 11,000. The East End of Bristol was especially affected by the slump, scarred by factory closures, unemployment and poor housing, the St Philip's ward being one of its worst slums. Roughly 10 per cent of all families fell below the standard of minimum needs, even with the modest prosperity of the later 1930s.[16] In the shifting sands of three-party politics, Bristol East stood out as one of Labour's safest seats.

As Cripps discovered, the local party caucus was active, vibrant – and ardently 'Red'. The young full-time agent, Herbert Rogers, had been among the handful in at its inception in May 1918; dedicated, unselfish, a conscientious objector and formidably cantankerous, he was happy to work with local Communists (until CP members were excluded from the Labour Party in 1925) and, during the general strike, was a passionate believer in worker's control. After the passing of the Trade Disputes Act in 1927, which deprived the union of a political fund, Rogers – a tireless organiser – had no choice but to rely on membership dues, subdividing the constituency street by street, aided by an army of canvassers and collectors, pushing membership well above the two thousand mark. The Act, as Rogers demonstrated, reacted on its authors.[17] Once Cripps was selected, he was asked to provide the increased sum of £400 a year, still leaving the constituency to collect as much again through fundraising. Although he thought this 'a little bit on the high side', Cripps did not want 'to enter into any controversy with the local association'.[18] Rogers spent the Christmas break working out a plan of campaign for a candidate who had never before fought an election.

Labour's opponents sprang two surprises. The Liberals adopted Walter Baker, a stalwart standing on the Lloyd George ticket but sharing the same name as the late MP. The Liberal was free to attack on unemployment, knowing Cripps would be unable to retaliate because of the Labour government's reliance on Liberal MPs for sustaining it in office. At the last moment, a 23-year-old Conservative also came forward – the Tories had not contested Bristol East since 1910 – creating a three-cornered contest, splitting the anti-government vote. Over the next fortnight many of the government's leading figures were brought in to bolster the Solicitor-General. Cripps propounded the 'full Socialist programme' of social control for the common good, but also – since it bore on the Trade Disputes legislation – protection of the right to strike. Challenged by Sir John Inskip (the former Attorney-General and MP for Bristol Central) that this meant the Law Officers of the Crown ranging themselves behind the Trades Union Congress, Jowitt advised Cripps to reply on the stump rather than in cold print,[19] which he did, decrying the 'mass of ignorance' on the issue and reminding Inskip the Law Officers were bound to act 'without party bias'. 'See that trade unionists have fair treatment that is what they want and this they are entitled to,' Parmoor telegrammed.[20]

Unlike the other parties, Labour had the priceless advantage of a grass-roots organisation. On polling day, 16 January, on a reduced turnout, Cripps triumphed, winning the same share of the vote as Baker had in 1929, the Conservative pushing the Liberal into third place. The new MP for Bristol East, 'hatless and a little dishevelled,'[21] was carried shoulder high into the street for a torchlight procession. Cripps thanked Rogers, saying he was gratified to know Isobel and he had been among friends; Rogers pledged his complete future loyalty. To MacDonald, Cripps reported afterwards:

My Dear Prime Minister,

Thank you very much for your kind telegram of congratulations.

The result was good I think considering how tremendously popular Walter Baker was and how little I was known.

They had no use for the Liberal on unemployment plans at all and as he fought solely on that he got decisively turned down. He got a good many of our votes by the confusion over the name.

The Tories got – I should think – 1–2 thousand of our votes by promising safeguarding to all the local industries, or rather suggesting that they would probably have it.

We made the Trade Disputes Bill a direct issue and that undoubtedly helped us.

I hope the result may make the Liberals more amenable![22]

Parliament reassembled on 20 January, Cripps, watched by his father, being introduced to the Commons by the Chief Whip and the Attorney-General. Elected at the first attempt, his seat 'ready made', he had, having lifted a knighthood on the way, moved straight on to the front bench – 'gifts of fortune'[23] offered, coincidentally, as another rich, hitherto favoured, convert was talking his way out of the party. Sir Oswald Mosley's memorandum proposing an overhaul of the system of government and a 'scientific' attack on unemployment, Cripps stated during the by-election, was 'dictatorial'.[24] The parliamentary machine was inadequate, as the Party generally accepted. But if anything was to be done in the life of the current parliament it was 'essential' to make the best use of existing institutions. Mosley's venture with the break-away New Party was even more disturbing, neutralised only by the strictest loyalty. 'Nobody ought to sacrifice his freedom of thought, but if the Labour party, as a party, decides on a certain course of action, whether it is right or wrong, I support it, and unless every Member of Parliament does that government will become impossible.'[25]

6

1931

Cripps explained he had become a teetotaller to protest against heavy drinking in the House of Commons. He was particularly upset by the 'most demoralising' spectacle of rich Conservative members plying their working class colleagues of the Labour party with alcohol.[1]

'The House of Commons', a long-standing denizen once wrote, 'is notoriously a jealous mistress.'[2] It envies those who enter it with an already established reputation, still more the fortunate few who go straight in at the top. Cripps had done both. He made his maiden speech from the dispatch box during the debate on the Solicitors' (Clients' Accounts) Bill, professing how respectful he was of parliamentary traditions. For a stripling lawyer-politician, his diffidence was well received, albeit fleetingly. Within days, he had run into trouble, not only with the party opposite, but with the government's own followers ranged on the benches behind him.

Governing without a majority, the MacDonald government kept its legislative life going by the crudest of high-level deals. Labour was committed by promises made to the TUC to repeal or at the very least amend the contentious provisions of the Trade Union and Trade Disputes of 1927, which curtailed sympathetic strikes and prohibited any industrial action designed to 'coerce' the State or to cause 'hardship' to the community. Of all the trade unions' demands, restoring of the position before the 1927 Act had the highest priority. Earlier setbacks in establishing union immunities had mostly occurred as a result of judicial decisions; the Act of 1927 was the first in which Parliament had 'taken an active part in fettering the rights of Labour'.[3] Furthermore, although party leaders were aware of the damaging stigma of the strike weapon, the bitterness aroused by the collapse of the general strike had not yet subsided. Party–union relations were dogged by mutual suspicion. With the government bound to legislate, the Liberal Party, alternately wooed and insulted, would support the Bill at its second reading – leaving its hands free at the committee stage – only in return for legislation to reform the electoral system. Without

Liberal acquiescence the Bill was certain to be defeated and the government forced to resign.

MacDonald and Henderson, after some havering, bought the Liberals off. The snag was the Liberals would not accept the complete repeal of the Act, wanting to retain Clause 1, prohibiting 'political' strike action. Jowitt and Cripps, having at last got the Prime Minister's authority, met the TUC General Council to agree to concessions to the Liberal viewpoint. Reluctantly (Bevin – general secretary of the TGWU – was already angered by the slightest imputation of 'coercive' trade unionism), the TUC decided to go along with the arrangement, and Jowitt was instructed by MacDonald to draft an 'innocuous' clause preventing strike action with an avowed political or revolutionary object.[4] The text of the Trade Disputes and Trade Unions (Amendment) Bill was issued in mid-December. Simultaneously, the outline of a bill to introduce the Alternative Vote was hurriedly drawn up by the Home Secretary.

What was left obscure – what the Conservatives had tried to pin Cripps down about during the Bristol by-election – was whether the new Trade Disputes Bill would legalise the kind of nationwide general strike which had taken place in 1926, which the 1927 Act had specifically been brought in to make unlawful: whether, in law, another general strike would be legally possible.[5] The restrictions on the right to strike of the 1927 Act were to be relaxed, but the illegality or otherwise of a trade dispute was to be determined by the High Court. Jowitt, leading off for the government on the first day of debate, on 22 January, declined to reply to Sir John Simon's leading question, deftly explaining that the new Bill legalised nothing which was illegal before 1927, but was merely returning the position to the *status quo ante*. After MacDonald announced that the Bill, instead of being dealt with on the floor of the House, was to be sent upstairs to a standing committee, lawyers on the Opposition side probed mercilessly, making capital from the all too evident split in Liberal Party ranks. By the third and closing day, an answer could no longer be avoided. The General Council of the TUC, expressing 'a certain apprehension' about what ministers would say, primed trade union MPs to be ready to put across the TUC attitude.[6] Immediately after a boisterous speech by Churchill, portraying MacDonald as 'the boneless wonder', the House passed 'with proper decorum' to the new Solicitor-General.[7]

Sticking closely to his longhand notes, Cripps charged the old government with having gone much further than was necessary in curbing trade union activity. There was a difference between purely 'industrial' and purely 'political' strikes; it all depended on where the line was drawn. Casting aside lawyerly circumlocution, he then came to the crux. Opinions differed, he said, about whether the general strike was legal under the old law, but since it had clearly been in furtherance of the miner's lockout this (to Labour cheers) made it so. 'There is no doubt in anyone's mind that the general strike would have been illegal under the Act of 1927,' he went on. In his opinion, coming to the present Bill, the general strike of 1926 would be illegal under its provisions too, since a court looking at the substance of the case would probably find the strike's 'primary object' was not purely industrial – an observation which Jowitt, seated alongside Cripps, visibly assented to.

This 'startling assertion', the parliamentary correspondent of the *Daily Telegraph* noted, was listened to in silent amazement by the trade unionists, 'staggered' to find that – if Cripps was right in what he was saying – 'they have been buying a pig in a poke'.[8]

Cripps finished his statement by commending the Bill for its balancing of 'the removal of the sense of injustice' with safeguards against 'the usurpation of power by any class'.

While Liberal members took Cripps's view to be 'authoritative', Jack Bromley (of the National Union of Railwaymen), speaking for the TUC, and Ben Tillett, a dockers' leader, both strongly objected, Bromley openly threatening that, whatever the legal position, the General Council of the TUC would in the same circumstances act in exactly the same way as it had in 1926. 'Jimmy' Thomas, Secretary of State for the Dominions, winding up for the government, also refused to be influenced, as he put it, by any legal argument. The government having applied the closure, the Bill passed its second reading by the unexpectedly large majority of 27, the bulk of the Liberal Party abstaining and only seven following Simon into the 'No' lobby. Chronically fatigued, MacDonald was relieved and delighted, writing in his diary of the 'firm lashing attack by JHT & including a splendid speech by the Solicitor-General'.[9]

Cripps had not committed anyone apart from himself, and had been able to give an honest reply, knowing that the courts pay no heed to parliamentary debate; tactically, too, the Liberals, on whose abstentions the government was counting, were reassured. The drawback was his alienating of the TUC, already disturbed about the rough treatment in store for the Bill at the committee stage. Arthur Hayday, president of the TUC and MP for Nottingham West, chose his words carefully when addressing a meeting in his constituency:

> The Solicitor-General's view that the General Strike is buried by the new bill is certainly not shared by the Trades Union Congress. They will not endorse any bill that sets out to declare the 1926 stoppage illegal.
>
> We of the TUC say that if we thought that the first clause of the present bill would have declared illegal that which we have always said was legal, we would have refused to subscribe to it. We don't believe it. That is one man's opinion.[10]

The Prime Minister tried to mend fences by asserting that the general strike had been not a political but an industrial strike, which the new Bill ought not to make illegal. The Conservative Party chairman, Neville Chamberlain, instantly fired off an open letter, asking to know if MacDonald agreed or disagreed with Cripps's statement in the House. MacDonald neatly got over this by observing that, if one took Cripps's view of the nature of the general strike then he would indeed be right, but that he (MacDonald) did not agree as to its nature. A further letter from Chamberlain, highlighting again the inconsistency between the Prime Minister and a junior Law Officer, brought from MacDonald the rejoinder that, whatever either of them might think, it was entirely a matter for the courts.[11] 'If', the Morning Post commented, 'the Liberals are satisfied they must ignore the Prime Minister's view, if the TUC is satisfied it must ignore the Solicitor-General's view. If both are satisfied they must wish to be deceived.'[12]

Everything depended on whether the Liberals still loyal to Lloyd George would feel free to water down the Bill in committee. On 26 February four Liberal amendments were published, including one outlawing strikes detrimental to the 'health and safety of the community' – a much broader Clause 1 than even that in the 1927 Act. Supported by the Conservatives, the standing committee carried the proposed amendment by 37 votes to 31. At this point the patience of the TUC ran out. The new amendment was 'totally unacceptable', Walter Citrine, the TUC general secretary, wrote to MacDonald. The Liberal Party's actions were tantamount to 'a declaration of war' on the trade union movement. Unless the Liberals withdrew the offending clause, the TUC would have done with the Bill, daring the Liberals to do their worst.[13]

The Cabinet, in MacDonald's absence, instructed Jowitt to play for time, spinning out discussions with the aim of getting the Opposition to reveal their attitude more fully. On 3 March, in a moment of high emotion, Cripps denounced the Liberal attempt to introduce provisions that were normally part of emergency powers, effectively driving starving strikers back to work. With MacDonald unwilling to make the Bill a matter of confidence, Jowitt announced its withdrawal. The Liberals then claimed the amendment had been drafted by none other than Jowitt. The TUC General Council asked the Prime Minister for an explanation. Newspapers accused 'the subtle Attorney' of entering into a conspiracy with the Liberals to trick the TUC. Jowitt called the report 'a pack of lies'. Citrine, comparing MacDonald's mind to a bale of hay, reiterated the original union position that they would be content only when the Act was fully repealed.

The loss of the Trade Disputes Bill did not, in the end, threaten the survival of the government. Even so, the recriminations over the Bill brought the political and industrial wings of the labour movement close to breaking point. This was to have important repercussions that summer. The Liberal Party had put paid to the Bill, but not before the 'unfortunate' (Bevin's word) actions of senior ministers, and a single-sentence pronouncement from a stiff-necked young Solicitor-General, possessor of a prized parliamentary seat, had cut the ground from under the TUC.

Kingsley Wood, in one last sally, elicited through a parliamentary question the size of the salaries and fees owing to the Law Officers, mocking this manifestation of 'Socialism in Our Time'. In fact, Jowitt and Cripps volunteered a reduction of £10,000 in their joint fees in return for a reorganisation of the Law Officer's Department.[14]

The arithmetic of minority government made for long hours. Cripps, however, already had views about the deficiencies in parliamentary procedure. He was one of only three ministers – with George Lansbury and Major Clem Attlee, who had taken over from Mosley as Chancellor of the Duchy of Lancaster – who joined in discussions at Easton Lodge, in Essex, of the new Society for Socialist Inquiry and Propaganda (SSIP) which, working with the New Fabian Research Bureau (NFRB), the Oxford academic G. D. H. Cole and Ernest Bevin had got off the ground at the end of 1930 to generate fresh ideas for future policy. Pritt and Cripps bankrolled its early activities. The merits of bills were not usually to blame for parliamentary problems, in Cripps's opinion;[15] the difficulty lay in pushing them through. Round-table examinations of a piece of legislation, as had happened with the Trade Disputes Bill, led only to delaying tactics. The Lords (Lord Parmoor was leader of the Labour peers), having thrown out the Education Bill in February, should be replaced by a new second chamber, reorganised into committees without the power to decide principles. After one House of Commons dinner, Beatrice Webb approvingly noted the high moral tone of the reformers, 'amateurish but free of the assumed evils of political life – disinterested, public spirited and amazingly free from corruption and vice'.[16] Her nephew, in public, was soon straying outside his technical brief. 'When you hear of the spread of Communism or had it suggested that people in this country were going towards Stalin, I only wonder why they have not gone. If I had lived in the state I have seen some living in, I would have been an out-and-out Communist.' 'We must see to it', he said in March, that the Labour Party is going to 'wipe aside the opposition of the House of Lords' and then carry through the wishes of the majority of workers.[17]

Abandonment of the Trade Disputes Bill was survivable; defeat of the Finance Bill would finish the government off. In February, Philip Snowden, Chancellor of the Exchequer, had issued a stern warning about the state of the country's finances, mentioning the need for 'disagreeable measures' to combat a danger 'which no one party can solve'. An operation for prostate trouble put him out of action for much of March and most of April, so that even MacDonald had little idea what measures his Chancellor had in mind. The one known item was a plan to incorporate into the Finance Bill an entirely new scheme for the taxation of land values – an old favourite of Snowden's, recalling

Lloyd George's Budget of 1909. Like the Trade Disputes Bill, land taxation was politically symbolic, but without having much of a bearing on the immediate economic evil of rising unemployment.

During Snowden's absence, the groundwork for the tax was prepared by the Financial Secretary to the Treasury, Frederick Pethick-Lawrence, in co-operation with Cripps – who among his many talents was well versed in conveyancing law – the two of them being assisted by the Inland Revenue.[18] The principle behind the tax – securing to the community the value of any improvements in developed and undeveloped land brought about by redevelopment – was entirely laudable, and had non-socialist support. The difficulty was whether the tax could be made to operate. The Liberals, as Cripps appreciated, would need placating.[19] Still, a tax on land was a long-held Liberal Party aim, and one, moreover, which had been advocated in the Liberal election pamphlet, *We Can Conquer Unemployment.*

Announcing the tax in outline on 4 May, the week after a subdued Budget speech, Snowden adopted a special resolution for incorporating the scheme into the Finance Bill. In its final form, the tax was, even to officials, 'hideously complicated'.[20] It entailed a two-stage valuation of all units of land, followed by the imposition of a site-value tax (as if the land were not built on) on the owners of all land, to the tune of 1d in the pound on the full market value, beginning in the financial year 1933–4. Agricultural land used solely for cultivation, and sites owned by local councils, the railways and Churches (though not all Church lands), was exempt. Snowden took the polemical line that the land belonged to the people – thus uniting, as the press crowed, every duke, parson and golfer across the Isles against him. Taxing the land in the way proposed was, for the Conservative Party, arbitrary and iniquitous, but Lloyd George gave his unqualified approval, promising to support the measure through all its legislative stages.

Snowden, still not fully recovered, asked Cripps to help see it through the Commons, thanking him for the 'very valuable work' he had already put in.[21] The upshot was that Cripps, Pethick-Lawrence and William Graham, the President of the Board of Trade, were the ministers in charge of the passage of the Finance Bill. From the opening sparring, when he was given the job of winding-up the debate on the resolution, the Solicitor-General emerged as the land tax's ablest exponent, calling it a matter of 'common justice' that those owning land who have benefited from public spending should pay some acknowledgement to the community for the benefit they have gained.

Though he had private reservations about parliamentary practice, Cripps's 'brilliant advocacy' of successive clauses 'confounded' Tory opposers.[22] Once the Conservatives had declined to agree a timetable for debate, the government was forced to consider the unusual step of guillotining discussion of the Bill during the committee stage on the floor of the House (something which had not occurred since 1914), when the opportunity for spoiling amendments would arise. With Liberal blessing, however, the Bill was safe, passing its second reading by 270 votes to 230, even with the imposition of a three-line Conservative whip. Cripps denied that the tax would only stimulate an explosion of speculative land use along roads and railways. 'Sir', an objector from Burford wrote to the *New Statesman*, 'The Solicitor-General has shown his love and care for the beauty of the countryside by himself building delightful cottages in Oxfordshire. Surely he will not be party to a Land Tax without taking care it does nothing to encourage 'ribbon-development'?[23]

After Whitsuntide, many Liberal MPs returned with new objections, inflaming divisions in the party between the Lloyd George and Simonite wings. The tax was discovered to be a form of 'double taxation', because land value already entered into the assessment for income tax under Schedule A. A Liberal amendment was drawn up, remedying this defect by converting the tax into a mere duty on undeveloped land. MacDonald and Cripps were ready to accept; Snowden, angered by the Liberal *volte-face*, would not. Word was put about that the Chancellor would rather withdraw the land tax altogether than allow it to be emasculated. As the day of the vote approached, Snowden gambled on flushing the Liberals out, convinced that they would not force a decision fatal, should an election follow, to their own existence.

The contrast between the obdurate Chancellor and the deft Solicitor-General was underlined on 11 May, when, after resisting an amendment calling for further exemptions, Cripps agreed to reconsider the matter in time for the report stage. It was too much for Josiah Wedgwood, an old land-taxer from his Liberal days. Giving up on the scheme, he wrote bitterly to Snowden. 'Last night, moved thereto by Inskip, Cripps consented to consider the omission of tithe from both "cultivation" & land value,' so hiding the Churches' share in land and spoiling the valuation. 'I feel certain that it was Cripps clericalism & MacDonald's presence that did the trick.'[24]

Labour and the Liberals had brought the crisis upon themselves; the responsibility fell to Cripps – still only a junior-ranking minister, but with an untiring grasp of the subtleties of the legislation, his speeches a pleasing mixture of 'grace' and 'force'[25] – to extricate them. 'If anyone can save [the land tax] from extinction,' the Bristol *Evening World* commented admiringly, 'Sir Stafford is the man.'[26] Over the weekend of 13–14 June, he stayed up in town, trying to find a formula that would satisfy the Liberal leaders.[27] According to Henderson, the Labour Party was in no fit shape to do electoral battle. MacDonald, writing to Snowden on the Saturday morning, expressed his dismay at the 'disturbing' prospect which would arise when the Liberal amendment came up for discussion. The parliamentary party, he said, 'will be furious with us if we were to throw in our hand next week. The issue is not regarded by the great bulk of our Members as being big enough.'[28]

On the Sunday, consulting with the senior Liberal Sir Herbert Samuel at Samuel's house, where MacDonald and Lloyd George later joined them, Cripps came up with a 'promising expedient': the rate of levy could be graduated according to the degree of development of the site. The tax yield would be much smaller, but would cease to exert a double burden. In the jumpy atmosphere, the Liberals withdrew their amendment, replacing it with Cripps's sliding-scale alternative.[29]

Would the Chancellor accept? Snowden gave the initial impression of grudgingly considering it. The moment the Liberal leaders arrived, however, his old obstinacy returned, and he exchanged bitter comments with Lloyd George, who stormed out of the room. Later the Liberals reaffirmed their support for the Cripps compromise, after which the Chancellor 'silent coldly & critically examined whispering with Graham and Cripps. Would say nothing. Meeting adjourned.'[30] For the rest of the day an increasingly fraught Cabinet was kept in suspense by a Chancellor who refused to be 'humiliated' by Liberal machinations. He finally decided to give his decision in the morning. To cap it all, while a large number of Scottish Labour MPs were journeying down on the Scotch express, the government was caught out in committee by a minor Conservative amendment to do with the assessment of the land-values tax, which Cripps, the government already yielding on other exemptions, also had to allow.

MacDonald made 'one last appeal' to his Chancellor, warning of the 'electoral debacle' facing the party if the land tax were lost. He, Snowden, should put his personal feelings to one side, accept the scheme as it now stood, and claim it as a victory – 'as indeed it is'. 'Do not destroy – as far as it can be destroyed – the work of our life-time.'[31] The letter 'turned the scales'.[32] The Cabinet met at 10 a.m. and heard Snowden accept the Liberal amendment – the only known occasion he climbed down under Cabinet pressure.[33] In a farcical final act, before a crowded House fully expecting the demise of the government, the Speaker ruled the Liberal amendment out of order.

It is a moot point who had got the better of the bargain. Snowden rounded off the third reading of the Finance Bill by lambasting the cowardice of the Lloyd George Liberals and Simon's contingent, the latter (enticed by a Conservative offer of a free run in their own seats) having just relinquished the Liberal whip. From that point, Liberal leaders would treat with Labour only through Graham or the good-humoured Cripps. But, as Simon – dumbfounded by Cripps in one passage of arms – graciously observed, there was no doubting the effectiveness of the 'iron fist' of the Chancellor concealed in the 'velvet glove' of the Solicitor-General, the latter 'ingenious enough', thought Chamberlain, 'to justify almost anything'. Snowden could derive some comfort from the outcome. Although 'unwarrantable concessions' had been given, the cardinal principle of the land tax was intact, and future parliaments could build upon it. This was Cripps's view too. In later years, the impost could always be increased – not excluding the eventual nationalisation of land, which remained party policy. A *Punch* cartoonist had Lord Parmoor beaming with pride, father awarding son with first prize.

In Bristol, Cripps followed up his success – the greatest triumph of any minister in the government, according to the *Yorkshire Post* – with another attack on the Lords, which, watching over the government 'like a big pelican, will have to disappear'. An election 'may come on you like a thief in the night'. As for the problem of war debts, worrying Western governments and banks, so far as Great Britain was concerned 'the only way lies in debasing our coinage'.[34] Visiting slum dwellings in North Kensington afflicted by a high rate of infant mortality, he called them 'the best picture of hell that could be imagined'.[35]

Exhausted by the demanding debut of coping with two major bills, but flushed with plaudits, he departed for a rest cure at a clinic in Baden-Baden, suffering from his intestinal complaint and, while there, an attack of septi-caemia from a nasal infection (leaving his nose a permanently purple colour), collecting himself for when Parliament reassembled after the summer recess.

Thus stricken, Cripps followed developments at home only from the news-papers, until his father and stepmother (Marian Ellis, whom Parmoor had married in 1919) reached Baden-Baden on 23 August, bringing word that the Cabinet was deeply divided over a programme of economies in public spending needed to reduce the budget deficit and restore financial confidence in sterling, which – even before publication of the report of the May Committee, warning of a severely unbalanced budget[36] – was coming under great strain.

Parmoor, facing an operation, had had his resignation in the hands of the Prime Minister for several months; round-the-clock Cabinet meetings had sapped his remaining strength. All the same, he was among a group of ministers holding out against a revenue tariff or – as one of the suggested prerequisites of a loan to be raised by American banks – a cut in unemployment benefit, insisting the deficit be made up by 'an additional charge apportioned on the better-to-do members of the community'. As Parmoor later related in his autobiography, MacDonald at this stage was already in touch with Opposition leaders. The 'dole' issue was put to the Cabinet the day after Parmoor had departed, when, after an emotional address by the Prime Minister, ministers decided by a slender majority of 11 to 9 to recommend a 10 per cent reduction in benefit. Unable to continue in office without a united Cabinet, MacDonald had no alternative but to go to the Palace and resign. With the Bank of England's foreign credits almost exhausted, an audience of the King and the main party leaders was fixed for the morrow.

The surprise the next day was not the dissolution of Parliament or a general election – Cripps's 'thief in the night' – but the immediate reappearance of MacDonald as Prime Minister of a 'National' coalition, a government of persons rather than parties, formed for the purpose of meeting the present emergency, after which it would disband. Snowden, Thomas and Sankey joined MacDonald along with leading Conservatives and Liberals to make up the new Cabinet team.

On the morning of 26 August, an urgent telegram arrived for Cripps: "HOPE YOU PROGRESSING STOP WOULD YOU LIKE TO GO ON – RAMSAY MACDONALD." Cripps cabled to say he was returning to England straight away – a message MacDonald took as indicating his acceptance of the offer. That evening, the Bristol *Evening World* stated that Cripps 'may remain Solicitor-General'. Bristol Borough Labour Party met to give its endorsement of those members opposing the policy of the National government, but Herbert Rogers could only tell reporters he knew nothing of Cripps's intentions.[37]

MacDonald's invitation to 'go on' put Cripps in a quandary. Before the recess, he had – the whole government had – voted for the Anomalies Bill, brought into clamp down on dole abuses; but he was hostile to drastic cuts. He was not averse to the idea of a temporary union of the parties, provided the object in view was to get over the immediate emergency.

When he arrived back in London late on 27 August, the position was still not at all clear cut, though the animosity among Labour Party colleagues was already apparent. MacDonald, Cripps learned, had asked all the Law Officers to stay on, and there was a strong feeling they should stick together without presuming to judge the politics of the situation. In legal circles, Cripps was expected to continue to serve. MacDonald had discouraged other junior ministers from staying with him, since to do so would mean their political death through 'blacklegging' by the Labour Party machine – especially after the release of the party manifesto, on the 27th, denouncing the new coalition. (Parmoor, it was not forgotten, had ratted twice: on the Conservatives and on the Liberals.) Some – Parmoor included – refused office, though Morrison, still close to Cripps, did so only after much hesitation, his respect for the Prime Minister greatly increased. MacDonald, on a more personal level, had done much to give Cripps his start. Talking with first Snowden and then Henderson, Cripps 'could hardly believe that they were giving accounts of the same crisis'. Jowitt – against all his inclinations, according to Cripps – had decided to stick by MacDonald, just as MacDonald had stuck by him in 1929. This did not spare him from a second bout of vilification. The one person who strongly pressed Cripps to remain was Sankey. He sent for Cripps on the morning of 28 August, and lectured him for an hour in a censorious fashion, explaining how the country was in immediate peril and how they must not yield to the trade unions. When Cripps replied that he intended to reject MacDonald's offer, Sankey dismissed him with the words 'Then that ends our friendship.'

At a historic meeting of the Parliamentary Labour Party that afternoon, MacDonald did not appear, leaving Sankey and Malcolm MacDonald, the Prime Minister's son, to justify the course he had taken. On a show of hands, calculated to intimidate waverers, Labour MPs voted solidly to go over into opposition to the coalition, electing Henderson (who was most unwilling) their new leader, and J. R. Clynes and Graham his deputies. Feelings were very mixed, however. Ben Tillett for one, after announcing to the gathering that 'the class war is here', privately wrote to MacDonald denouncing the hysteria of some critics. Cripps also found the atmosphere and sentiments of the meeting 'alarming', particularly the excitable talk – crudely led by Dalton – about a 'banker's ramp' having done Labour down. 'Hard thinking' was needed to devise a new financial programme. The SSIP and the NFRB, he hoped, would make a constructive start right away. Cripps was not one of the ultras, bent on closing the door to MacDonald's staying in the party. Worn out by non-stop interviewing, he retired to bed, but his conciliatory views were forwarded by John Cripps to the two thousand of his constituents brought by buses on an outing to Goodfellows on the Saturday. He deprecated 'hasty judgements of those Labour ministers who have conscientiously felt it their duty to continue in the National Government', he said. Theirs was 'a most difficult position'. Even if they had made 'a profound mistake', 'it is no reason for us to forget the very great services which they have rendered our party'. In an accompanying gesture, he gave up all of the fees still owing to him, telling the Treasury to 'put it towards the cuts'.

The radicalising impact of August 1931 upon the Labour Party and the wider labour movement has often been spoken of, usually unfavourably. Recent research shows just how swift the response – one writer calls it a 'stampede' to the left – actually was. A sizeable minority of the Cabinet had been prepared to countenance some though not all of the economies by Snowden, before pulling back from the brink. *Labour's Call to Action*, while denying the reality of the financial crisis, had at least spelled out specific measures, such as the mobilising of foreign investments, which would not penalise the poor or the unemployed. The new policy committee of the PLP, meeting from early September onwards, effectively captured the initiative, replacing the 27 August manifesto with a raft of grandiose schemes. It was what Cripps among others had been calling for, urging on Graham that it was vital for the party to 'divorce' itself from its past, throwing off the attitude of compromise and half-hearted slogans with 'a slap-up Socialist policy' for dealing with the whole economic and financial set-up.

Although Margaret Cole (one of their number) argued that the prime movers in the SSIP were insulated from the violent shock of MacDonald's betrayal because they had long since given up hope,[38] an earlier biographer, Eric Estorick, concedes that Cripps was 'profoundly stirred' by the episode. He felt sad for Jowitt, but otherwise there was no remorse. Cripps, who had no background in economics, now entered on a crash course in economic theory, as if he was getting up another legal brief. An older head, Graham, who was an economist, might have curbed Cripps's fervour. But Graham took the separation badly, 'almost as if he had been some dumb animal suddenly struck', as Cripps put it, by Snowden's incomprehensible departure.[39] Some tentative contacts were made with sympathisers in the City, through the financial journalist on the *New Statesman*, Nicholas Davenport. Henderson also saw J. M. Keynes, leading light on the Macmillan Committee. Keynes, however, scoffed at the idea of a banker's conspiracy, convicting the banking community of stupidity more than malice.[40] This ran counter to Labour's accusations of financial sabotage, which swept along even Morrison and Pethick-Lawrence, not to mention Cripps, who now sat on Labour's Policy Committee, adopting a much more openly political role. Outsiders took note. Lloyd George's chief of staff, Colonel Tweed, reported at the end of August that the Labour leadership was in difficulties, since Henderson was elderly 'and the only other possible leader is Cripps, who probably will be a Prime Minister some day but at present is too new to parliamentary life to be seriously considered'.[41]

Cripps reached some rash conclusions about MacDonald's behaviour. Lord Parmoor applauded his son's bravery in standing by his party, but it was Beatrice Webb, denouncing MacDonald, Snowden and Thomas, who had referred to a letter from MacDonald to her husband the previous July in which he talked of future moves 'which may surprise you'. Jowitt told Cripps of Thomas making preparations for a National government. Cripps, moreover, got hold of the idea that MacDonald had been outmanoeuvred by the King, who, once Baldwin flatly refused to form a government, obliged him to put himself at the head of a coalition – a version Cripps soon retailed to two sceptical ex-ministers, Morrison, staying at Goodfellows in the first week of September, and Dalton. The 'definite knowledge' which Cripps got from the Webbs he passed on to others, this in turn finding its way to Beatrice, who thus met herself coming back. Sidney Webb then reproduced the same version of events in a famous article in the *Political Quarterly* in 1932 – an account that Parmoor, taking the daring view for a lawyer that MacDonald had acted unconstitutionally, accepted 'without question'.[42] As a result, as Bassett pointed out in his historical defence of MacDonald,[43] Cripps was one of the main conduits for the melodramatic myth of 1931, which had MacDonald plotting to form the National government some time in advance, in combination with the King, the Tories and the bankers. Beatrice Webb, in her later years, often lamented how little influence she and her husband had over their headstrong nephew. However, it is evident with the events surrounding the fall of the second Labour government that they played on his over-agitated imagination.

The view formed with blinding clarity in Cripps's own mind that the crisis was not an alibi for failure, but an opportunity to banish old policies along with the old leaders and go forward with a thoroughgoing policy of reconstruction – ready to be put into operation if and when an election came.

Facing former colleagues for the first time across the floor of the House of Commons on 8 September, MacDonald opened a debate on a motion to bring in a Supplementary Budget, introducing the disputed economy measures side by side with increases in taxation. He referred to the breathing space which the coalition had given the country, without which sterling would have been driven off the gold standard, with an inevitable collapse of the currency. Henderson made a moderate retort, but, in an unusual step, referred to discussions in Cabinet and Cabinet committees before the breakup of the government, locking horns with MacDonald over what cuts had or had not been accepted. From other contributions, however, it soon became obvious that the Labour Opposition was vulnerable to a double attack: from the new government side for having ducked the test of democratic leadership, and from the Independent Labour Party and other dissidents for its lack of resolution. The coalition secured a comfortable victory, by 309 to 249, a dozen Labour MPs voting with the government and a further five abstaining. Snowden proceeded to bring in his supplementary measures, in the teeth of ill-tempered accusations and counter-accusations – above all, about whether or not and up until what point the 'Henderson' party in the former Cabinet had committed itself to exploring the cuts now being presented to the House.

On 15 September, following the imposition of pay reductions on State employees, a mutiny of naval ratings broke out in the Atlantic Fleet, moored at Invergordon on the Clyde. The withdrawal of foreign funds from the City of London, slowed by the forming of the coalition, picked up again. On the 20th, Britain went off the gold standard. This gifted to the Opposition a knock-down argument – the MacDonald coalition, brought into being to 'save the pound', had failed in its overriding objective. However, after Henderson had advised his supporters during the Gold Standard (Amendment) Bill debate not to oppose, 112 Labour Party backbenchers defiantly voted against when the House divided.

For the third reading of the National Economy Bill, on 29 September, Cripps was put up to reply for the Opposition. He laid into his former chiefs, maintaining that the cuts brought in with fantastic scaremongering to restore confidence and defend sterling had now lost their point. He extracted from Chamberlain, the new Minister of Health, the injurious admission that the coalition had not been under any 'moral obligation' to accept the conditions for a loan that was to be raised by foreign creditors. And he put up a minimum defence of the outgoing Labour government, in so far as it had, in its brief existence, at least acted as a bulwark preventing any decline in working-class living standards. With the Labour government out of power, the way was open for 'panic measures dictated by financiers'. It was, his party asserted, only by bringing the industrial and financial machine under public control, starting with the nationalisation of the banks – a proposal at the forefront of party discussions – that the problem could be surmounted.

This speech of the new Cripps delighted his own side. It was 'well conned', and Cripps was 'unruffled' by interruptions and 'apt in retort'.[44] His soapbox style drew amazement from MPs opposite. Had not the honourable gentleman himself wasted many weeks on the land-values tax, while the country was 'approaching Niagara'? Had not the government of which he was a junior member collectively agreed to at least a substantial part of the economies? Did he really believe that the government had been brought down by a machiavellian conspiracy of financiers? Holford Knight, a barrister and one of the small band who had left Labour to go with MacDonald, jumped at the spectacle, correctly noting that it was Cripps's first recorded parliamentary excursion into political waters. 'He continually denounced the capitalist system. This fine blossom of the capitalist system, who has been rocked and dandled into a legislator!' Far from offering a radical remedy for economic ills, Cripps had, the Tory MP Robert Boothby observed, fallen back on the flimsiest kind of Victorian-age sentimental socialism.

Cripps – 'able', 'pious', without personal vanity, and forming, with Isobel, a devoted couple, 'moving among the younger men with ease and modesty' – was confirmed as a leading figure in Henderson's team by his first appearance at a Labour Party conference, in Scarborough one week later.[45] As one of ten ex-ministers, each of them presenting a policy resolution forwarded by the National Executive Committee, he moved a motion pledging the Party to reverse the contested 10 per cent reduction in unemployment benefit. The programme taken overall, though toned down after consultations with Bevin and Citrine, bore the signs of drafting by the academic and activist Harold Laski, who was telling his associates that 'I stay with the Left of Labour and, if necessary, I go to the extreme Left.'[46] Henderson was more circumspect, but could contrive only a fragile unity. Party discipline was already shaky, forcing the conference to require all candidates to act in harmony with the standing orders of the PLP. Among the sharp policy disagreements, monetary policy was central. In the original wording of the official proposer, Pethick-Lawrence, the Party intended bringing the banking and credit system under 'public control'. Frank Wise, the financial brains of the ILP and an adviser to Centrosoyus (the Soviet co-operative wholesale organisation), attempted to get the terms altered, to specify nationalisation (and not just control), including the taking over of the Bank of England and the joint-stock banks. In a rumbling intervention, Bevin told delegates not to quibble over words, since everyone understood that what they were all after was ownership, which was best obtained by socialising credit. To Bevin's astonishment, Wise dropped the amendment without pressing it to a vote, because of an 'assurance' he said he had received from the platform.

Speaking to his own motion, Cripps told delegates to jettison the idea that large-scale, long-term unemployment could be solved by 'patching up' cures. In a ringing phrase, he controverted Sidney Webb's famous dictum of the 1920s. 'It is not now a question of the "inevitability of gradualness". The one thing that is not inevitable now is gradualness.' Moments after Cripps had sat down, Henderson rose to announce that he had just heard Parliament was to be dissolved and a general election would be held on Tuesday 27 October.

Conceived as a way of maintaining a policy – the gold-standard parity of sterling – which it had been compelled to abandon, the MacDonald coalition appealed to the country for a 'free hand' transcending party or sectional differences. MacDonald's followers maintained the decision to go to the country was an essential means to national solvency. The Opposition saw nothing but an anti-socialist electoral alliance, trading on 'bastard patriotism', aimed at crushing the Labour Party. Pitting the 'bankers' against 'the people' provided Labour with a ready-to-hand electioneering platform.[47]

Quickly off the mark, on his way back to London Cripps stopped off in East Hull to support the Labour candidate. Since capitalism was breaking down, he told a well-attended meeting, the Labour Party had the first real chance it had ever had to put into practice the reorganising of the social system. Labour had prepared 'a complete scheme ready for when they got back into power', involving 'taking over' the Bank of England and 'dealing with' the joint-stock banks. They would not go back on to the gold standard; other ways would be found to put at the government's disposal the country's foreign investments. When they had controlled finance, they would have half-controlled industry, which – sooner or later – had got to be run so that the benefit went to the country and not to the credit of private individuals.[48] Pre-empting the release of the Party's election manifesto by twenty-four hours, his remarks made up a small item on the front page of most of the national dailies.

Coalitionists worked up a storm of condemnation. The Scarborough con-ference had been inconclusive about the banks, while the manifesto did not go into details. What could Cripps mean? If the Labour Party had 'a complete scheme', Simon demanded, 'let us see it'.[49] Cripps, in league with Graham, was planning to mobilise foreign securities. What did that mean too? Were they not 'geese smashing the golden eggs'? With such wild and ruinous projects, the moment Henderson crossed the threshold of Downing Street sterling would 'tumble headlong', said the economist R. H. Brand. Walton Newbold, a former Communist MP campaigning for 'Jimmy' Thomas in Derby, asked Cripps to tell everyone what he had in mind – adding that, having mixed in the company of the current Labour leadership, he was quite certain 'Uncle Arthur' would not be able to restrain those of his younger associates from 'rampaging round the country in the name of the organised workers'.[50]

Wise, springing to Cripps's defence but disparaged as a 'Muscovite', explained that his was the scheme which Cripps had referred to, and which had been incorporated in the manifesto, *Labour and the Nation*. This admission only fuelled a remarkable radio broadcast by Snowden (standing down at the election), who rounded on his former allies. Having abandoned office in August, they had proved themselves to be 'wholly unfitted to be trusted with responsibility', he insisted. Theirs was 'the most fantastic and impracticable programme ever put before the electors', meant to be implemented, he supposed, by a joint committee of the Labour Party and the Trades Union Council. 'This is not Socialism – it is Bolshevism run mad.' In a syndicated article, he upbraided Graham and Cripps – 'Labour's little Lenins', whom he had tried to teach the rudiments of finance to but found unteachable – for aggravating the country's difficulties by spreading fear and undermining confidence.[51]

His own seat in Bristol East 'quite safe'[52] (initially it seemed he might even be re-elected unopposed), Cripps made flying visits to other parts of the West Country and South Wales, determined not go be cowed. At Swansea he vowed that, so long as there were people who could go out at night and drink champagne at fashionable hotels, 'the surtax is not high enough'. At Cardiff he challenged the coalition's monopolising of the Union flag. On 19 October, visiting the dockside division of Plymouth Devonport, he said 'the trouble in the Navy served the government right'. The *Morning Post* exploded, denouncing the 'discreditable' avidity of the ex-Solicitor-General – 'a British gentleman', who, to serve a party end, 'has dug up what was decently buried, for all the world like a dog with a stinking bone, and who has fouled his unsavoury morsel in the act of resurrecting it'.[53] The learned counsel knew full well, the paper added, that his present colleagues were the ones who had decided on the very same economies before shamelessly quitting their posts. It was a canard difficult to dispose of, even among Labour supporters. The fact was, Cripps informed a Bristol trade unionist,

> no decision about cuts was ever come to by the Labour Cabinet and the whole responsibility of the present cuts rests entirely upon the shoulders of the National Government. As Arthur Henderson has repeatedly said, he and others refused to come to any decision at all until they had the complete scheme for balancing the budget before them, and this was never submitted.[54]

Labour's campaign launch in Bristol was accompanied by fresh allegations. The main speaker, Lansbury, indignantly replied to Snowden's broadcast. Cripps again advocated State control of the banks, telling the crowd 'it is in your hands'. Later, responding to a charge of running away, he retorted sharply that those who followed Henderson had not broken the pledges they had given to the electorate in 1929. Presented with the threat of savers withdrawing their money should the Labour Party get back, he said a strike of capital seemed to him just as 'Bolshevik' as a strike by labour. In Gloucester on the 21st, he called Snowden a turncoat and his speech a tissue of falsehoods. 'If Mr Snowden knew in February last that the country was on the verge of bankruptcy, why did he not make provision for avoiding bankruptcy in his budget in April?'[55]

A National candidate in Bristol East – a retired London accountant, J. M. Spreull – was adopted only at a late hour, holding his first public meeting on 19 October, eight days before polling. He was unable to obtain a hearing, and the meeting broke up in uproar. Cripps had to appeal to supporters to refrain from bullying. Nor would he allow blasphemy. Posters appeared around the constituency telling voters to 'Let Cripps Carry your X'; the day after, the 'Carry' was pasted over with a 'Have', Cripps having intended to drop out unless they were altered.

As polling day approached, other means of influence were exerted. The local press mocked 'Sir Oracle'. A well-known vicar and leading socialist in Bristol East declared for the National government.[56] The Barton Hill Silk Mills – large local employers before the mills had closed – were rumoured to be reopening, provided the coalition were returned; on the eve of voting, smoke belched from their chimney stacks. In the closing days, Labour was blamed for having raided Post Office savings to bolster the Unemployment Insurance Fund – an assertion Snowden artfully affirmed. Even so, although Spreull outspent Cripps in an effort to make up lost ground, the Bristol East Labour Party's final canvass returns still had their candidate some six thousand votes in front.[57]

Spared a devastating upset, Cripps hung on – by just 429 votes, National candidates carrying off the four other Bristol seats in contests against Labour by convincing majorities. Referring to Cripps's 'escape', the Evening Times believed Spreull's narrow defeat – by 19,006 to 19,435 – was the surprise of the night; had he begun earlier, Bristol East might have gone National too. Across southern England, Labour candidates were routed. Cripps remained the only Labour MP representing a constituency south of the river Thames. Further north, Henderson (in Burnley), Hayday, Clynes, Graham and Bevin were all beaten, the Labour vote holding up only in the East End of London and the South Wales and Yorkshire coalfields. Among other ministers, only the veteran Lansbury and Attlee survived. The Labour Party in Parliament – a generational cohort of its leaders wiped out by the exodus of August and the verdict of the electorate – was reduced to a rump of fifty-two MPs.

Hard-pressed by legal cases, Cripps could snatch only a few days rest at Goodfellows, bewildered by the election result. He looked to Henderson for reassurance:

I expect our experience of the dishonesty and lying of the other side was the same as yours. This, coupled with the Post Office Savings stunt and intimidation of a wholesale kind by employers is what brought us down in Bristol.

But what is our little band to do in the House of Commons shorn of all its leaders? It seems to me that we have got to think very hard as to our best policy to pursue in the House so as to preserve our position in the country, where those who fought for us form a solid and determined nucleus whose spirits must be kept up. Unfortunately many of those who have got back will be of the excitable, tub-thumping nature which will not help us in the House and will make the tail almost as big as the dog!

I do hope that you will be well enough to come South and take charge of things before we have to do anything in the House. I feel we so desperately need your wise advice and experience.[58]

Henderson, even out of the Commons, was certain to stay on as national leader. Not a few wanted Cripps to assume the chairmanship of the PLP. 'Apparently the choice for leadership in the Commons will lie between you and Lansbury,' Lord Marley, Labour's Chief Whip in the Lords, told him. Lansbury, he went on, 'lovable as he is, yet is too old and too woolly', as well as being compromised by membership of the late Labour Cabinet. 'I feel we want a keen legal mind, flexible and quick-thinking.'[59] If the proposal was made, he hoped Cripps would allow his name to go forward. Susan Lawrence, an NEC elder, expected great things from Lansbury and him working in tandem.[60] The *New Statesman* agreed that Cripps would be the best leader.[61] Cripps was not tempted. Lansbury was already one of his best friends, and a 'great pleasure' to work with. He meant to put in a full parliamentary attendance, using his large income to finance himself and to some extent the Party. Had he pushed himself forward, there would certainly have been resistance. Cripps had antagonised many in the trade unions (who recalled his role over the Trade Disputes Bill) by his talk at the outset of the election about nationalising the banks – an issue which, Transport House believed, clearly lost the Party votes.[62] The Cripps who had so expertly steered the land-values tax through Parliament had spouted 'irresponsible' comments on the stump; he had kept his own seat, but others had gone under. There was well-timed muttering about middle-class lawyers ensconced in the upper reaches of the party. At the first meeting of the new PLP, Henderson arranged places in advance by notifying Lansbury and Attlee they would be standing as chairman and deputy leader of the PLP. Cripps was away in court. He was, however, the possible next leader-in-line. 'Trained from infancy' but unaffected, he was well equipped intellectually and had 'the requisite staying power', *Reynold's News* indicated – 'although his natural shyness means that other people may have to "run" him'.[63]

The assembling of the new parliament, with coalition MPs spilling over on to most of the Opposition side of the House, was effectively the concluding round of the election. Lansbury led for the Opposition in the Debate on the Address, but Cripps moved a lengthy amendment, claiming that, since the National government had no proposals of its own, the Opposition – so recently misrepresented – would do its job for it. Drawing on a memorandum by Graham, Cripps took planning as his theme and public control as his remedy. Goaded by MPs on the other side, he had nothing to apologise for. *He* had always been against the cuts, having 'objected to them from the moment I first heard of them'. Taxation of land values was 'a feeble effort by the late Chancellor of the Exchequer, who has now turned out to be a Tory'. New MPs hoping for prompt action should, he went on, be warned of the Prime Minister's artistry in avoiding the issue by carefully planned inquiries. Thomas, seated at MacDonald's side, rejoindered that it was hardly becoming for those ignorant of the labour movement until a few months ago to sneer at Snowden, adding that the Labour Party was advancing the same policies which the electors had only just resoundingly rejected. Cripps thought MacDonald was frightened by his intellectuality. MacDonald's discomfort stemmed instead no less from private unease than from the tragedy that had befallen his old party. 'Individually they are as a rule good fellows, but the political company in which I find myself gets increasingly distasteful. I cannot live in it. Opposite is a spiteful & small minded crowd of graceless late colleagues, those who expected and asked for most being now the meanest, like Sir Stafford Cripps.'[64]

7

RED SQUIRE

I do not want to see the Labour Party go back on the swing of the
pendulum. I would rather wait until a firm foundation has been laid in
the brains of the people in this country for a true Socialist programme.

Cripps, November 1934 [1]

The rout of October 1931, even more than the 'betrayal' of August, was a
defining moment in the short life of the Labour Party and labour movement.
Out of defeat, different factions drew different, in many respects opposing,
lessons.

The strong version – of which an unrepentant Cripps, taking his cue from
leftists like G. D. H. Cole and Laski, emerged as the most conspicuous advocate – treated the election as the logical outcome of the party's experiences in
office, and of the whole MacDonaldite outlook in the party. The last Labour
government, hampered by habits of cautious reform and windy perorations,
had, with the onset of economic distress, handicapped itself by its own conservatism. The cuts, for want of an alternative strategy, were unavoidable. The
Party was rescued only at the very last moment by Henderson waking up to
the danger and leading the loyalists out of the Cabinet. In no time, however,
the election was upon them. Labour's natural supporters were unfamiliar with
the proposals for nationalising the banks as part of the planned co-ordination
of industry, and were swamped by scare stories. Even so, those policies
remained relevant, the country being endangered by 'some sort of catastrophe'.
Mood mattered more than manifestos. Defeat could be celebrated, since, with
almost 6.5 million votes to build on, the next election would provide a clear
choice between the parties of capitalism and the party of socialism. Cole,
analysing the causes of the setback, put the case for converting Labour into a
vehicle for realising great principles:

The Labour Party, if it has any meaning at all, stands for socialism. If it does
not, of what use is it? Old liberalism was a better instrument of moderate reform
than Labour is ever likely to be. The Labour Party has value and potentiality
only if it means and stands for something radically different. And if it does, it

ought not to go vote-catching on terms negating this purpose, but remain in Opposition until it can really get the support of the electors behind it on its own terms ... Can Labour do these things? ... I do not know; I only hope. But I do know that if it fails in this, it fails altogether.[2]

The milder view, beginning from similar assumptions, was more markedly influenced by trade union thinking. The union hierarchy also criticised Mac-Donald's remoteness, attributing most of the government's difficulties to lack of consultation, but they did so because of the disregard of majority decisions agreed upon by the party conference. The unions, like the Left, wanted to plan the economy and revive trade, but few believed that the economic system was about to disintegrate. High ideals had to come second to problems requiring immediate action – like unemployment. It was damaging to advertise fears of capitalist sabotage in advance. The industrial and political wings of the labour movement must co-operate more closely, remembering the primary purpose of the Party's creation. For the unions, as for the Left, Labour was a class party, but a party needing to pay heed to the financial backing, voting strength and economic interests of trade unionism, as had been historically intended.

This disagreement was ideological, to do with competing views about the fundamental nature of the Party; it was a dispute about internal power and who was to exercise it; and it was an increasingly personalised contest among individuals with stark differences of style and temperament. Throughout the 1930s, the persisting conflict as to what the Party should be about overlapped with conflict about how it should be organised and who should lead it.

Tensions between the parliamentary and extra-parliamentary arms sprang up almost at once, contributing to Lansbury's misgivings about his accidental elevation to the chairmanship of the PLP. Avuncular, mutton-chopped, lampooned as a woolly sentimentalist, he had (as former editor of the *Daily Herald* and champion of 'Poplarism', a campaign against high rates being levied on the poorer London boroughs) a proud left-wing past and was, though over seventy, a surprisingly energetic, though frustrated, First Commissioner of Works in 1929–31. In August, he had unhesitatingly followed Henderson. He had oppositional indignation in abundance, suited to the Party's predicament – MacDonald, watching from the other side of the House, still saw in him the hoarse, brawling East End vestryman – but his old rebelliousness undermined him when it came to upholding the PLP's standing orders, and five members of the ILP split off to form a separate party. Maintaining an 'ever-open door' for the shrunken contingent of Labour MPs, he sought to emphasise how their faith was 'unshaken' by recent disasters and how much could be got from exposing the humbug of the National case. With Attlee and Cripps as his principal lieutenants, he led a 'united brotherhood'.

Lansbury's friendship with Cripps was political and, exceptionally for Westminster, personal; with a gulf of thirty years in age and just as wide in background, it was scarcely one of equals. Cripps was Lansbury's disciple, deserving of guidance. Lansbury acted as another father substitute, as Burge had done in the 1920s. They had in common Anglican affinities, also unusual in Labour circles, as well as a love of the English countryside. Despite coming from a political family, however, Cripps lacked a political credo, which Lansbury, beyond declaring that 'whoever fights Socialism fights God'[3], could not supply. The double strain of court appearances during the day and the Commons in the evenings left little opportunity to put this right.

Cripps's ideas were an amalgam of piety and planning. He preached revivalism, coloured by assertive declarations of socialist intent, his opinions – unconventional for his profession – curiously offset by the cold, unemotional delivery of the smartly attired lawyer. 'I saw Uncle Arthur [Henderson] yesterday,' Lansbury wrote to Cripps towards the end of 1931. 'I found him a bit upset with the sort of forward policy we aim at, he talked of miners and others demanding something to go on with and not being content to wait for Socialism.' Henderson was not to be blamed, Lansbury reasoned; his generation had spent their lives doing small things while advocating big changes. 'You must make him see the movement he has done so much to foster will perish if once again it gets lost in the morass of gradualism.'[4] But even Lansbury, conscious of his own zealotry, worried that Cripps's cleverness was apt to run away with him. Cripps wanted to revolutionise the machinery of government and Parliament to give democracy 'fuller and quicker power' – not, he tried to reassure Lansbury, 'for a group of extremists but for the people as a whole'.

As the sole member of the existing PLP sitting on the National Executive, Lansbury quickly became aware of the growing rift with Transport House. He tried luring Lloyd George into the Party as a counterweight. Rivalry also surfaced with colleagues now out of the Commons who depended on constituency support to stay on the NEC. Dalton, back lecturing at the London School of Economics, having sung Cripps's praises in the autumn, completely changed his tune. Morrison told the Webbs that Cripps was being 'spoilt' by too swift an ascent. Cripps dismissed his recruiter to the party as 'reactionary'.[5] Graham, for whom Cripps found a job with a firm of City stockbrokers, was much more level-headed. He, too, intended to recapture a seat and re-establish himself as the party's leading economic spokesman. But he died of pneumonia in January 1932, and Cripps had no one else to turn to. The collapse of the gold standard gave rise to a vogue for quack blueprints for currency reform, sweeping Cripps off his feet. He spoke to the SSIP on the topic of Silvio Gesell's theory of 'disappearing money'. Though he 'did not pretend to any knowledge of economics', it seemed to him to offer a means of 'getting rid of the money curse'.[6] Others were less credulous. He fared better tied to his brief in parliamentary debate, forcible but clear and orderly, with the 'readiness' of the professional pleader.[7] He easily took offence, however. Churchill talked of a 'loathsome speech' by the ex-Solicitor-General, whereupon Cripps' mouth 'sagged at one corner, the unfailing sign that his personal feelings have been touched'.[8]

Lansbury endeavoured to bring Cripps on, but self-doubt hindered him. In conversation he confessed he sometimes felt like giving up and joining the Communists. Cripps retorted that, were Lansbury to go wrong, he would 'lose faith in everybody'.[9] Editing the *Daily Herald*, Lansbury had struggled with youthful Communists on his staff – 'wild colts' agitating for 'implacable class war'.[10] One was William Mellor, a founding member of the Communist Party of Great Britain (CPGB) and, after quitting in 1921, a powerful propagandist (succeeding Lansbury in the editor's chair), as well as 'a most formidable heckler'.[11] Through G. D. H. Cole and the SSIP, Mellor met Cripps. Claiming capitalism would not tolerate a future socialist government, he was soon harrying Cripps into adopting a more resolute stance on public ownership and not just control of industry. When the ILP broke from Labour in June 1932, a dissident group led by Frank Wise and H. N. Brailsford proposed amalgamating with the SSIP to create a new socialist society. Cole was doubtful, Lansbury very much opposed. Negotiations opened, however, hastened by the wish to secure the affiliation of the resulting Socialist League to the Labour Party in time for the Party's annual conference at Leicester in October. Bevin was also unenthusiastic, especially when the ILP group insisted that Wise and not he must chair the new body. Wise was known to be difficult. Bevin both disliked and distrusted Mellor. Cripps acted as go-between, reconciling Bevin to the arrangement. Even so, Cripps was sensitive to Transport House opinion, knowing 'the ghost of disaffiliation' loomed over the League unless it made it clear that it supported 'a single, strong Labour Party' and would remain within it 'at all costs', concentrating purely on propaganda.[12] Above all, he was adamant it should not rival the official party. As the financial mainstay of the fledgling League, Cripps, with Attlee, was appointed to the League's National Council.

Cripps was hopeful of an 'advanced spirit' at Leicester, provided the appropriate diagnosis was made. Expedients to 'make capitalism tolerable' had got them nowhere. Only a complete change of the economic system would suffice. The courage and the will to do this could come only from an upsurge of idealism, to compensate for the vital but dulling effect of organisation.[13] They were bound to arouse the hostility of finance and industry, which had realistically to be recognised in advance. That was why, he concluded, Labour should never again accept office as a minority government. The disillusionment of 1929–31 ran too deep; the risk of revolution was far too real.[14]

His suspicion of left-wing antics inflamed, Bevin was further enraged by the proceedings at Leicester. Charles Trevelyan, setting the tone, pleaded for a 'full Socialist policy'. Henderson, replying, for once was unable to hold the attention of delegates, and Trevelyan's motion passed without even a card vote.[15] In the debate on banking and finance, the Socialist League, in its first showing, engineered a narrowly agreed reaffirmation of the Scarborough pledge to nationalise the Bank of England, amended to take in the joint-stock banks, moved by Wise and lobbied for by Mellor, who used his contacts with the National Union of Railwaymen to swing the NUR block vote.[16] Bevin, amid shouting, bluntly explained the difference between a theoretical person and the practical trade union official. Cripps spoke from the floor, insisting that if they rejected the amendment they would be going back on everything agreed at Scarborough. Pethick-Lawrence vainly reminded conference of the vote-losing Post Office lie.

The outcome highlighted mounting unease about the direction the Party was taking. Attlee and Cripps, in touch with Cole, Dalton grumbled, 'sit in Lansbury's room at the House all day and all night and continually influence the old man. With none of these are Uncle's relations close or cordial'.[17] Cripps wanted Henderson to retire as party leader. Chided by Pethick-Lawrence for his dogmatism over the Wise amendment, Cripps cautiously answered, 'I hope I shall always keep an open mind, capable of being convinced in these matters ... but you must have an open mind too.'[18] In practice he went to the limits of the sayable. If Labour did not intend bringing in socialism when it next came into office, he told a meeting in Orpington, 'I shall have no further use for it.'[19] It was no good doing things by halves, he said in Hampstead in December – there had to be a revolution by constitutional means, though he sometimes thought a bloody one might be necessary, or else they would have to adapt the parliamentary machine with a half-dictatorship. (The Director of Public Prosecutions examined press reports of his statement.) Accused by Randolph Churchill (son of Winston) of Communist sympathies, he argued he had been inaccurately reported. 'I can assure you that I am not at all worried by the heresy hunt which no doubt will continue!' he informed one correspondent.[20] A political project, tempered by virtuous ambition, was taking shape. Beatrice Webb, sharply observing her uninstructed, highly strung nephew, captured the heroism. 'The fate of the Labour party in the next decade seems likely to be settled according to whether Stafford possesses or does not possess the intellect and will to build up a more sincere Socialist party – a far more difficult task than any other leader has had for the last 100 years in Great Britain.'[21]

The Socialist League began as a small, loosely organised propaganda body, devoted to 'the achievement of the Socialist Commonwealth in this country, within a world-wide system of Socialism'.[22] The driving belief was that capitalism – the liberal economic order – was collapsing but that socialism could not triumph until socialist teaching was more widely disseminated. Socialism required 'the making of socialists'. The fate of the late Labour government had demonstrated the power of economic interests to overthrow an elected administration. On the continent, the challenge of socialism had been met by extremist takeovers; in Britain the same result was obtained by the device of a National coalition. The menacing rise of fascism in the rest of Europe – Hitler became the German Chancellor in January 1933 – and the formation of the Mosley-led British Union of Fascists, instilled an urgency into the League's activities that its grandiose aims did not provide. Gripped by a sense of impending calamity, the League gambled on the future, prophesying revolution without claiming to advocate it.

Why, in that most difficult of decades to comprehend, did the possibility of approaching doom seem so plausible? For the convinced socialist, the question was nonsensical: socialism, prophesying the crisis and collapse of capitalism, was self-evidently true. Current explanations about the vogue for left-wing ideas – that many leftists were reacting against their bourgeois upbringing or derived emotional satisfaction from the drama of commitment – were therefore beside the point. The revolt against capitalism, the fellow-travelling John Strachey observed, 'is real, is objectively determined, and has nothing to do with the personal flaws and faults of any of those members of the intelligentsia who support it'.[23] The evidence, as R. H. Tawney, an early Socialist Leaguer held, lay in the facts of a system 'on the slide'. Cole, arguing that the world economy was closer to collapse than ever before, went the whole hog, suggesting 'smashing it now, though you and I will hardly enjoy it'.[24]

Economic discontent was already widespread, among those in insecure white-collar jobs as well as the unemployed. Left-wingers sought to capitalise, or to thwart others who tried to do so. When rioting broke out in Bristol, Cripps, anxious to counteract Communist influence, pointed out that if the government gave way it would show that force pays, while 'we who are urging the workers to be constitutional' would be left without a leg to stand on. The effectiveness of the League stemmed from its existence, calling for 'continual vigilance and rebuttal'[25] from ruling elements in the labour movement. That the League expressed the desire to hurry the coming breakdown – 'the greater the demands the workers made to maintain their standard of living, the shorter the life of capitalism' – only added to the hostility it aroused.

The League organised a series of lectures in the spring of 1933. The second, by Cripps, examined what he understood to be the central issue of the Labour Party's mission – 'can socialism come by constitutional means?' It was a class analysis of the most clinical kind (Cripps did not read widely), imagining the advent of a socialist government, the opposition it was likely to meet, and the measures it should take to ensure a socialist programme was carried out. 'Counter-socialist activities', he predicted, would begin before a future Labour government had even taken over. In that case, the Party should enter office only if it had majority support in the country and a working majority in Parliament. The first step would be to bring in an Emergency Powers Bill. If the Lords objected, the Crown would be asked to create a decisive number of new socialist peers. If this were refused, the government could continue in office regardless, provoking a capitalist uprising which the army would have to quell. Resigning and forcing a second election on the issue of obstruction by the Lords was a better alternative. Should this stalemate result in a threatened right-wing dictatorship, the socialist government must assume dictatorial power until yet another election could be held, even if this meant prolonging Parliament for a further term. Once a mandate for socialism was obtained, they could establish 'general protective control' over the economy and finance, adapting antiquated parliamentary procedures for the purpose. The Lords would be abolished, time-wasting debate would be curtailed, and statutory changes would be made through Orders in Council – effectively rule by decree, beyond the reach of the courts. All of this, he acknowledged, involved 'an uphill fight'. He thought it possible to make the changes constitutionally, though this was not certain since everything turned 'upon the action not only of the socialists but the capitalists too'.[26]

Cole ('nor can we put limits to the degree of dictatorial power we may have to assume'), Wise ('freedom of speech is not one of the eternal verities'), Mellor and Attlee all spoke in much the same vein, the lectures combining to form a powerful current of maximalist politics, with Cripps and Attlee – occupying places in the upper ranks of the parliamentary party – the most prominent figures. They were already pushing for a stronger line in party policy, putting before the NEC a joint paper on the necessity of nationalising the joint-stock banks at the first opportunity.

Press attacks – *The Times* heralded 'the revival of the class war in all its intolerance, crudity and bigotry' – had been expected. The response from Transport House was more ticklish. In March 1933, the reconstituted National Joint Council (NJC) dismissed a Communist proposal for a united front against fascism, denounced fascism and communism even-handedly, and rebuked those in the Party toying with dictatorship. In April, Bevin upbraided Lansbury for wanting to attend a Socialist League rally without clearance from the NJC, adding that he looked 'to the parliamentary leaders to help preserve unity of action. Our job in the unions is difficult enough.'[27] Henderson criticised people 'in our own movement' who had come 'dangerously near to denying the possibility of establishing socialism by democratic means'. His remedy was 'obedience'. The *Daily Herald* gave Cripps space to reply. Dictatorial methods were, he agreed, highly objectionable. But a dictatorship of the Left was at least preferable to one of the Right, by making the workers the masters of their own destiny. The aim was to use the power of the State to carry through the people's will, as the best way of preserving (not destroying) democracy, before 'a regime of Hitlerism' took hold.[28]

Cripps's contrasting reactions to the German Reichstag fire (in February

1933) and to the arrest in the Soviet Union of six employees of the Metropolitan-Vickers Electrical Company showed his partiality. He assisted Pritt in establishing a 'Commission of Inquiry' into the Nazi allegation that the Reichstag had been set alight by Communists. In the Metro-Vick case, however, after weathering several minutes of uproar in the House of Commons, he said he saw no right in international law to intervene in Soviet internal affairs. It made no sense to him to pile up ill-feeling, or to stigmatise the Soviet Union as a 'petty tyranny'. After reading the transcript of their trial, he said it was impossible to be sure the men were innocent.[29] His sympathy with the Soviet Union was well known, though not – one careful student has commented[30] – at all easy to summarise. Cripps was willing to brave ridicule – by praising Soviet religious freedom, for example – but did not join the Fabian fact-finding trip to the Soviet Union in 1932. The Russians 'had done a great thing for civilisation', though he 'did not agree with every step they had taken'.[31]

It was less pro-Sovietism than applying the doctrine of class struggle to international imperialism that made him begin to give up on the League of Nations. Without the League's involvement over the Japanese invasion of Manchuria, he believed in late 1932, things would have been a thousand times worse. When a Japanese threat to Russia emerged, he grew alarmed by the ring of hostile states forming up against the Russians. The League could no longer be trusted, and the obligations of the Covenant 'we must consider ... as no longer binding'. The way to prevent future conflict was through a general strike, which would stop 'war hysteria sweeping away the commonsense of the people'.[32] His sudden preference, as Noel Buxton charged,[33] for 'international anarchy' in place of 'international organisation' was striking.

As for co-operation with the Communist Party, the Socialist League had tried but failed to get the NEC to consider 'united action'. Cripps was bound by the outcome. Strachey sounded him out in April 1933. 'You will appreciate', Cripps wrote back, 'that however much I may personally desire an approchement between the various working class movements in this country, I must remain perfectly loyal to the decisions of my own Party Executive.'[34] At the separate conference of the Socialist League in June, a resolution favouring united action with the CPGB and the ILP was defeated.

Pulling more than his weight in the House and in weekend speeches (he volunteered for far-flung engagements, able to pay the cost of travel), Cripps soon broadened his range of targets, dismantling old allegiances. The Churches had abandoned their role of aiding the disadvantaged. Christianity was finished – on this, Tawney and he, introduced by the Webbs, were agreed. Law was organised oppression, its only function being to uphold the existing order. Laski found him 'eager for law reform on a much wider scale', despite the entrenched conservatism of Bench and Bar.[35] All institutions were assessed by whether they were part of or opposed to the system of ruling-class supremacy.

Anyone – wealthy barristers included – who had no share of economic power counted as working class.[36]

'Cripps', Dalton recorded in May 1933 after visiting him in his chambers, 'is a problem.' Lacking political judgement, he entertained the most fantastic ideas, seeing fascism everywhere, simplifying everything into a clash of 'capitalists' and 'workers'. Dalton left satisfied that Cripps was unstable, his actions destabilising for the Party. 'The man is a dangerous political lunatic.' It was a duty, he resolved, to prevent Cripps from holding any influential position in the Party.[37]

From this moment, there was a concerted effort by Transport House to bring the PLP leadership to heel, given impetus by Cripps's election (following Wise) to the chairmanship of the Socialist League. Lansbury, while exasperated by Cripps's impatience, wanted Cripps eventually to succeed him. When Lansbury told Henderson this, the latter said that, if that were to happen, 'I would feel that all I had worked for had gone for nothing.'[38] For Henderson, Cripps had become an obsession, his 'all or nothing' approach being politically disastrous. Dalton and Morrison (suspecting the parliamentary leaders were trying to block their return to Parliament) prevailed upon Henderson to go back to the Commons and take back the leadership, to subordinate the PLP to the wider party. The intrigue was fuelled by grumbling from trade union leaders about Lansbury and threats about union funding of the Party.

What was Cripps up to? One judgement – the judgement of Walter Citrine, TUC general secretary – was that the Socialist League was aiming at dictatorship. Preaching that the accomplishment of socialism required the exercise of dictatorial power was wild talk, Citrine declared, which 'placed a weapon in the hands of our enemies'. He confronted the leaders of the League at a private meeting in July 1933, detailing 'the tendency to dictatorship' in many of their pronouncements and charging them with bringing about the very prospect – a fascist Britain – they purportedly opposed.[39] Might not the National government – citing Cripps in its defence – choose to stay on indefinitely? In that event, an independent trade union movement was unlikely to survive. By foreseeing a financial crisis when Labour next came to power, they were senselessly alarming people already scared out of their wits in 1931. Citrine realised that the spokesmen of the League were sincere, but was baffled that a man of Cripps's legal eminence 'could utter such irresponsible drivel'.[40] *The Times* carried a story that Henderson, in the lead-up to the October party conference in Hastings, had patched up a temporary truce. Cripps, denying the claim that he approved of dictatorship as 'wholly inaccurate', promised the League would 'naturally accept' whatever decisions conference came to.[41]

Publication of the League's lectures by Gollancz fanned the flames of controversy. *The Times* was in the forefront again, accusing Cripps of willing the means of dictatorship while trying to avoid responsibility for the ends, of playing on 'a distinction without a difference'. The League, according to Tories, was exploiting the danger of a revolutionary civil war, however much it expressed a horror of it.[42] Cripps complained he was being misrepresented in order to frighten the electorate. Unless the procedures of Parliament were speeded up, the Party was courting disaster with an 'inevitable' violent takeover, 'either from the extreme Conservatives or the Communists'. The Party had to understand what it was up against. He, for one, was ready to use the full sovereign power of Parliament – overriding the Commons, the Lords and the judges – to give effect to a popular socialist mandate.[43]

Those wanting to win back a seat in the Commons detected method in Cripps's madness. Cripps, it was conjectured, did not believe the Labour Party was fit for an early return to power – indeed, did not want it to return until it had the right policy and the right leader. In the meantime he was free to antagonise – doing his opponents' work for him, Lloyd George observed – confident the National government would bring itself down. The way would then be clear for a fully socialist programme. Lansbury doubted that Labour would ever command a parliamentary majority. Cripps was of the opinion that, if it ever did, it would have one and only one chance to initiate a fundamental changeover:

> There are some people who think I want a dictatorship. It is the last thing in the world that I want. I don't think there is a man in the world who is fit to be a dictator in this country or in any other. The change I want in the economic system must be brought about by democratic means, and not by bloody revolution.[44]

What *was* Cripps up to? Dalton picked out Cripps's half-crazed lack of judgement, normally a terminal political failing. Cripps, however, whatever Dalton thought, was fanatically straight, idolised by activists and contemptuous of the self-serving timidity of the party machine. Moreover, he did not covet the highest office. 'Stafford does not want the eventual leadership, he knows he is the wrong man and George will gladly retire; but it would be fatal to have Henderson back again.'[45] His lifestyle hardly suited the vocation of would-be revolutionary. He lived simply at Goodfellows, but had a large retinue of servants, builders and a chauffeur, costing several thousand pounds a year, on top of the expense of London. He had always been 'a little God', explained Barbara Drake, never having had to submit his will to others or to recognise his own limitations.

The Socialist League submitted a raft of amendments to the main conference report on 'Socialism and the Condition of the People', specifying a rapid transition to socialism and openly setting itself up as an alternative source of policy. Bevin issued a warning. The unions financed the party, making it possible for members of the middle class to hold positions of authority, but the 'new intelligentsia' were annoyed that Labour did not change its course as often as they changed theirs. The day before the Hastings conference opened, he told Cripps he was so disgruntled with the political wing (the candidacy for the forthcoming by-election in Clay Cross had gone to Henderson, ahead of the TGWU nominee) that his union might secede from the party altogether, with other unions following.

In the event, the NEC backtracked. The League, with Cripps agreeing, happily toned down its own approach. Moving a four-point amendment, Cripps said he shared the demand for 'absolute unity of purpose', asserting only that if the Party really meant what it proclaimed then they had to be clear how to go about converting the capitalist into a socialist system. Since the Executive was apparently prepared to take a further look at the League's proposals, he withdrew the amendment. Lansbury then came forward as the 'spokesman' for the NEC, explaining he had been 'asked to say' that the matter would be discussed further and the Executive would report back at the following year's conference.

The face-saving angered many delegates. 'Manny' Shinwell was astounded that the confusion was to carry on for another twelve months. Bevin poked fun at the spectacle of the League – advocates of a 'rapid transition' – asking for more time to consider how they were going to do it. Attlee and Wise tried to demonstrate the realism behind the League's proposals. But the most effective contribution was from the MP Herbert Lees-Smith. Regretting that Cripps had not had it out with the conference, he showed how, should a constitutional conflict arise, the resulting election would turn not on 'Labour versus the Banks' or 'Labour versus Capital' but on 'Labour versus the King' – a clash that would set the Party back fifty years. For the Party to even think of occupying office without an election was 'fantastic'.

The inconclusive outcome did Cripps the greater harm. Loyalty to the movement was compared with the League's loyalty to (ever shifting) 'ideas'. Snubbing Cripps was quite unfair, according to Lansbury, as 'he is speaking all over the place for us and works like a slave'.[46] It was left to supporters to point out that Cripps and Attlee had *stayed* with the party in 1931, when Mosley and MacDonald had fled, and that the strategy of the League – its original propagandising role now forgotten – was to press for the full socialist programme within the party fold.

The Socialist League could at least draw some encouragement on foreign affairs – Henderson's central preoccupation (he was chairman of the World Disarmament Conference in Geneva). Trevelyan, making it on to the NEC, moved a resolution committing the Party to resistance to war, including the declaration of a general strike on the outbreak of a conflict. Dalton, for the Executive, let it pass unopposed, not wishing to antagonise the conference moments before a statement by Henderson, who gave an exposition of the League of Nations' policy of collective security backed up by economic sanctions and 'other powers'. Cripps enthusiastically suggested the speech be published in full.

At this unsettled hour, Germany announced its withdrawal from the Disarmament Conference, leaving the League of Nations one week later. What little the British government had done, Cripps indicated, had been such 'as to make the gods laugh'. The only way to prevent the government from breaking its pledges was to call a general strike, 'compelling' the trade unions to draw up plans for that 'great resistance'. To Citrine, it was yet another scarcely credible outburst. Condemning resort to the strike weapon, he chided those who shuffled off responsibility by sheltering behind the unions.

When the Commons debated disarmament, Cripps, working closely with Henderson and Philip Noel-Baker, still stood by the Covenant of the League of Nations, which bound Britain to support it 'with economic boycott and with armed forces if necessary'. In truth, Opposition policy was disorientated, but Cripps hoped his party would move towards a 'collective peace system', uniting against aggressor nations, although because of recent developments 'a number of people are now definitely talking of abandoning the League as a hopeless and dangerous weapon'.[47]

A chance circumstance now intervened. Lansbury, opening a party bazaar in Gainsborough on 9 December, slipped on a step in the dark and fell heavily, fracturing his thigh. The bone was badly set, so that when he was brought back to London by ambulance it had to be rebroken and reset. His life was in immediate danger; in any case, he would be out of action for many months.

The Crippses were 'absolutely devastated'. Cripps felt 'quite lost' when he next took his seat on the Opposition front bench, telling Lansbury in a scribbled note that 'Ernie' and others had been to the House to see 'Clem'. Attlee, Lansbury's deputy, temporarily filled his leader's shoes. Journalists had already been trailing Cripps. An attentive photographer snapped him leaving Westminster after an all-night sitting on the morning of 15 December. Cripps, it was assumed, would shortly be 'trying on Lansbury's crown'.

Apprehensions about Cripps becoming leader were fanned by his appointment with Pritt as counsel for the plaintiffs in the case brought by the organiser of the National Unemployed Workers' Movement (NUWM), claiming damages for 'trespass, conversion and detinue of documents' against the chief commissioner of the Metropolitan Police, Lord Trenchard.[48] Cripps turned the courtroom deliberations into a State trial, attacking the 'extraordinary proposition' that there was a common-law right enabling the police to search without a warrant. The plaintiffs were self-proclaimed Communists, the NUWM a Communist 'front' under surveillance by the Special Branch.

Arrangements for replacing Lansbury were about to be settled, with Attlee remaining as acting party leader. That he did so was due to the magnanimity of Cripps. Attlee did not have sufficient income, apart from his £400 MP's salary, to take on the extra workload for an indeterminate period. If he had to lead in the House, his only other source of income – journalism – would become impossible, anything he wrote being treated as official. He was already some £500 short and thinking of moving to a smaller house. The Party in Parliament was 'quite resolved' Henderson must not supersede Lansbury. Reflecting over Christmas 1933, Attlee let Cripps know what he had decided:

> I think the only thing for me to do is to resign my position as temporary leader and for you to take over. It is an awkward time because of the position of Henderson but as he is still occupied with his Conference he will not be available. The only other likely person will be Arthur Greenwood but his disability [whisky] seems to be getting worse and I do not think that the Party would stand for him. I doubt if the Party would want anyone but yourself. Personally I think that you are the man who ought to be leading the Party and if G. L. should not return you would be the one to take his place. It would I think be disastrous if the lead were to slip back to Transport House.[49]

'To quote J. H. T[homas].,' Attlee signed off, 'I am in an ell of an ole and this is the only way that I can see to get out of it.'

Cripps replied the same day. Lansbury might not come back before October, in which case he – Attlee – ought to be paid as the full-time Leader of the Opposition. Cripps could not possibly be leader himself; that would 'never' be right, particularly while he was running the Socialist League in conflict with the NEC. Instead, he could use his considerable 'earning power' to the Party's advantage. Since Lansbury was already paid out of party funds, Cripps suggested donating £500 to the Party to cover Attlee, which, Cripps said, he could easily recoup by skipping party meetings to stay in court.[50] Expressing his wish they could go on serving together, he wrote in similar terms to Lansbury, enclosing a cheque.

This candid exchange testifies to the closeness of the parliamentary triumvirate of Lansbury, Attlee and Cripps, and their severance from party headquarters. The transaction had two major consequences. By fixing a salary for Attlee, they prevented the succession passing to Transport House by default. Attlee held the fort in Lansbury's absence. Had he not done so, he might not have become leader himself in 1935. Cripps, in the meantime, was free to press the argument about the Party's ultimate aims all the way to the next conference, hoping to prod the NEC into a policy of 'militant Socialism',[51] even if it ended up splitting the Party in two and even at the expense of electoral support.

Cripps made his next speech at a small meeting in Nottingham on 6 January. His theme was 'War and Fascism'. He connected the dangers of international economic rivalry to the risk of a British-style 'country gentleman' fascism which would benevolently suppress working-class opinion. He did not personally believe in private armies, 'but if the Fascists started a private army it might be for the Socialist and Communist parties to do the same'. When a Labour government came to power, it would have to act rapidly, taking control of the land and capital. Answering questions, he had 'no doubt that we shall have to overcome opposition from Buckingham Palace and other places as well'.

Although Cripps did not occupy any official post in the Labour Party, and the likelihood of his becoming leader was 'not imminent',[52] his comments created a sensation, the row not being stilled by his explaining he had been referring not to the Crown but to 'Court circles and officials and other people who surround the King'. Government politicians lined up to denounce the foolish outburst of a 'frightened political child' who was, in the words of Snowden, carrying on like a 'mock dictator'. The King, informed of the speech, was rattled. 'What does he mean by saying that Buckingham Palace is not me? Who else is there, I should like to know? Does he mean the footmen?'[53]

Cripps clearly had in mind the 'betrayal' of 1931 – the founding myth of the Socialist League. Lansbury, a republican, excluded from the 1924 Labour government by royal veto, regarded royal power as unimportant.[54] At Hastings, Lees-Smith had scored a telling hit by arguing that the only possible outcome of the Socialist League's plan of action was a hopeless battle with the King. Laski took up the challenge in the *New Clarion*: 'The country must be made aware of what is involved in a policy intended to prevent a future Labour Government from implementing its victory at the polls. We must make our position plain without delay; and, not least, we must make it equally plain in Buckingham Palace as in Downing Street.'[55] Cole was critical of oversimplistic sloganising. Laski, by contrast, felt Cripps had grasped the essential need for a drastic attack on existing institutions, with a long and arduous struggle to convert opinion beforehand, shelving the prospect of early office. Cynics grew weary of the dreary egotism of the Cripps family.[56] Cripps affected amusement at 'the hare which had been set running', impervious to the disapproval of high society. 'Lunched with Lady Colefax,' wrote Robert Bruce-Lockhart, diarist on the *Evening Standard*, shortly after the uproar. 'Sat next to an old Colefax [Sir Arthur] who is very keen on fishing. He tells me that Stafford Cripps was in his chambers. He is not an ambitious careerist, but really believes all he says. He has money and will have more – his wife's mother is an Eno of Fruit Salt fame!'[57]

The Cripps bogey was largely the doing of the Rothermere press. Lord Rothermere used the 'hysterical' Cripps as a pretext for swinging the *Daily Mail* into backing Mosley's British Union of Fascists, publicising the switch ('Hurrah for the Blackshirts!') in the issue of 15 January 1934. Mosley's followers began barracking Cripps's meetings, calling for 'hands off Buckingham Palace'. An attempt was made to daub yellow paint over his name at the entrance to his chambers. He received a death threat from 'A Member' of the BUF.[58] It was put about, on the basis of anecdotal information in Beatrice Webb's autobiography, that Cripps was half-Jewish.[59]

But the twinning of Cripps *with* Mosley as opposites conspiring to subvert British democracy seemed even more well founded. Both were well-off Wyke-hamists; both were readily typecast as fraudulent 'supermen'; both despised a political order petrifying into obsolescence, from which they hoped the masses were ready to desert. Baldwin, MacDonald's second in command, denounced the enemies within, warning of loss of traditional liberties entailed by the revolutionary programmes of Cripps and Mosley and portraying the National government as the only bulwark against alien influences.[60] 'The word "intelligentsia" has as little to do with intelligence as the word "gent" has to do with gentleman,' he commented.[61]

Cripps having gone back to London, Isobel wrote to Lansbury about the unfairness of it all, the press lying in wait like 'vultures' for her husband.[62] Lansbury advised Cripps not to say anything more. Interviewed from his hospital bed, he would not be drawn on the 'Buckingham Palace' speech. No one had raised the question of the leadership with him, and if he were fully to recover he would resume it again.[63]

Bevin travelled to Bristol to bring the 'comedy' to an end. Admitting to a 'strong admiration' for 'my friend Cripps', he pressed him not to lead the party 'up the garden path':

We have had Mosley, the ILP and MacDonald. They have all gone. I would say to all the middle-class gentlemen who come into our ranks that, in every crisis the working class have had to face, the one solid, courageous section which has not been moved has been the trade union movement. I would rather go a little slower than go off on a tangent on this or that theory.[64]

The Bristol *Evening World* – part of Rothermere's stable – advertised a challenge to Cripps to resign his seat and contest a by-election from a newly formed 'United British Party', which did not consider Cripps 'the right sort of man to represent a working-class constituency'.[65] The *World* handed in the challenge at his chambers. Cripps laughed it off. 'Both the Bristol papers are full of this business,' his agent wrote. 'East Bristol will know that they have a representative.'[66]

A Constitutional Sub-Committee of the NEC had been created to consider the Socialist League's far-reaching constitutional proposals. Cripps was requested to appear before it. Dalton, Cripps's antagonist-in-chief, has left a vivid account:

Cripps seems quite unable to see the argument that he is damaging the party electorally. It is all 'misreporting', or picking sentences out of their context. He has become very vain and seems to think only he and his cronies know what Socialism is or how it should be preached. His gaffes cover an immense range – Buckingham Palace – League of Nations – 'compelling' Unions to declare a General Strike – prolonging Parliament beyond five years, unless ... 'seize land, finance and industry' (without compensation?) – Emergency Powers Bill in one day, giving 'all necessary powers' ...

I make a violent – perhaps too violent – speech asking that this stream of oratorical ineptitudes should now cease, or some of us who are very reluctant to enter on public controversy with other members of the party, will come to the limits of our tolerance. It is the *number* of these gaffes which is so appalling. Our candidates are being stabbed in the back and pushed on to the defensive. Tory H.Q. regard him as their greatest electoral asset. Many of the speeches are simply incompetent presentation of a good case. But remarks on General Strike are most improper for a member of the professional classes, who couldn't deliver his own section of the working class on the battlefield.[67]

Attlee and Laski spoke up for Cripps, prepared to leave the Executive if it were to single out individual transgressors. Cripps dared the NEC to name him, Lansbury's assurance convincing him that the NEC would make itself a laughing stock by ducking out of a quarrel.[68] By 18 votes to 4, the Executive voted to release a statement reiterating the Party's adherence to parliamentary democracy and repudiating individual expressions at variance with democratic tenets. Seeing the mild censure, Cripps felt his best course was to 'leave it alone'. Isobel busily sent off copies of an article by a local reverend – including one to Cripps's anxious father – extolling the talents of a man divinely commissioned 'to apply Christian ethics on a scale never before attempted'.[69]

The real casualty was Henderson. He argued against issuing any rebuke. But he was also unhappy about the preparation of detailed policies on which subcommittees of the Executive were working. Overruled, he lost control of the direction of the Party, eventually relinquishing the post of national secretary. Differences in outlook among the younger politicians consequently became more clear-cut. Attlee defended Cripps: 'you could not find a more loyal, sincere and unselfish colleague'.[70] Dalton and Morrison, however – the latter achieving majority Labour control of the London County Council in the local elections of March 1934 – helped formulate an unmelodramatic party programme, rejecting the 'crisis' methods of Socialist Leaguers and finding a ready ally in Citrine.

This emerging reappraisal of party policy, suggesting ways of improving the functioning of capitalist industry alongside the goal of transforming it, blunted the force of the Crippsite refusal to take office until a majority of the electorate was won over to full socialism. Moderates took a grip on the policy-making discussions of the NEC and the National Joint Council (renamed the National Council of Labour), laying out a more intellectually vigorous set of policies which did not rely on overt doctrines of class struggle or capitalist collapse. With the backing of the largest unions, the architects of the policy review were confident of winning the argument that had been postponed at Hastings.[71]

Cripps and Mellor were equally determined to force a once-and-for-all vote on whether the Party definitely meant to bring about a decisive shift of economic power. 'He is collecting his forces,' Beatrice Webb noted at the start of May 1934; he was displaying the fervour of 'a fanatic, but with a fanaticism of an eager novice' who was still an 'amateur' at the political game, and all too fallible. Should he head leftward (like the Webbs) towards Soviet Communism, she guessed, he would either be premier or end up in prison.[72]

Cripps drafted a policy pamphlet – Forward to Socialism – to indicate to the labour movement how the Socialist League would have it approach its tasks, advancing a scheme for the radical reform of the machinery of government, a five-year plan of socialisation, and an alliance with Soviet Russia. This was put to the League's conference in May. Introducing it, Cripps laid into the pro-moters of incipient gradualism, arguing that the 'general tempo' of policy mattered more than detailed steps – an approach which several branches disliked for being 'old fashioned'. A resolution on a 'united front' of the Labour Party with other working-class organisations proved even more divisive. Cripps high-handedly passed the resolution without allowing any discussion. The conference over, Cripps was trailed once more by the newspapers, Bea-verbrook's Express dubbing him the 'Red Squire' of Filkins and, more absurdly, 'the apostle of Socialism in Our Time enforced by machine guns'.

To shape party policy, Cripps had also to try to alter the composition of the NEC, on which Trevelyan and Susan Lawrence were the only League sup-porters. Cripps was nominated for a place on the Executive in June. Gwen Hill, his personal secretary, asked Aneurin Bevan, MP for Ebbw Vale, for the names of secretaries of the miners' lodges. After a talk with another Welsh Labour MP, she thought better of it. 'He pointed out', she told Herbert Rogers, 'that it might well do more harm than good, as it will be likely to alienate the Executive if they came to hear that the Lodges had been circularised, and it would in any case rather detract from Sir Stafford's prestige as people would be sure to imagine that he was behind the effort himself, and knew all about it.'

The official party document, For Socialism and Peace, came out in September, summarising a policy of socialism-by-stages through the reorganisation, control and ownership of finance and industry, to be effected by a speeding up of parliamentary democracy. The League tabled no fewer than eighty-six separate amendments, effectively asking the conference 'to disown the Executive and the Trade Union Congress on almost every major point of policy'.[73] After some give and take, the League's proposals were slimmed down to four main heads: emergency powers, socialisation, compensation, and war and peace.

On the first day of the Southport conference, the Executive offered a way out: if the League did not press its amendment, the NEC promised to consider a hypothetical challenge from the House of Lords, should the Lords attempt to reject the legislation of a Labour government. Cripps claimed a victory of sorts, though he had avoided a vote.

On the second day, Cripps and Mellor put the case for getting the Party to say explicitly how a Labour government proposed to proceed once in power. They were answered in a teasing speech by Morrison, who thought the League's proposals for pure socialism were impossibly general. Recalling that Cripps – whom he had had 'something to do with bringing into the Party' – had helped him with the compensation clause of his London Passenger Transport Bill in 1931, Morrison called a card vote, crushing the League by 2,146,000 votes to 206,000. On the question of compensation following nationalisation, Morrison – winding up again – emphasised the fact that, in formulating policy, 'we have to consider not only what we want; we have to consider what we can persuade the country to accept'. The amendment was lost by an even larger margin.

As for the Party's approach to war and peace, the entry of the Soviet Union into the 'capitalist' League of Nations, in September 1934, cut the ground from under any alliance of socialist states. If an aggressor nation broke the peace, the British government – the party document recommended – deserved positive support, even in the use of military force by the League of Nations. Attlee, admitting he had once been a unilateral disarmer, insisted they could not wash their hands of comrades in authoritarian regimes like Germany and Italy, where a general strike was impossible. Lansbury, well enough to address delegates, refused to do so, or to qualify his pacifism. On this amendment too, the League went down to defeat, by 1,519,000 votes to 673,000.

To cap it all, Cripps, with Attlee, won a seat on the NEC – the person the Executive had come close to repudiating in January was now captured by the machine, as union leaders intended. 'When a man is a nuisance the best way to make him behave properly is to burden him with responsibility.'[74] 'Stafford had muddled things,' Susan Lawrence remarked, 'and had been deliberately put on the Executive to muzzle him as they were trying to muzzle her.' It was 'a pretty sticky body', he confessed after attending his first NEC meeting, its insistence on collective responsibility being 'entirely wrong'.[75] For Socialism and Peace has often been described as the most radical programme the Labour Party had up to that time produced. Cripps was unimpressed, sensing 'a definite lurch to Liberalism', distinguished by 'temporising' reforms. Under the constitution, furthermore, the whole field of policy could not be reopened by conference for another three years. But this was not a reason for quitting the Party. The first essential, he told the *Herald*, was 'absolute unity'.[76] Straight after the conference, the CPGB and the ILP renewed the offer of united action, which the Labour Party summarily dismissed. Responding to Strachey about co-operating in anti-fascist activity, Cripps did not budge:

> As you know my views differ greatly from the rest of the Executive, with possibly one or two exceptions, but I still feel convinced that the only effective thing to do is to try to stir up the party from inside, and it is quite idle to hope that a great mass of the party will ever combine with outside Left Wing organisations: the fear of disruption is too great.[77]

Wearing his barrister's garb, Cripps gave a brilliant demonstration of how to fight trade union battles. After a gas explosion at Gresford Colliery, near Wrexham, took the lives of 265 miners, the government hurriedly established a court of inquiry. The Mineworkers' Federation normally conducted its own cases, but, although the Federation sent a representative, the North Wales Miners' Association also appointed Cripps, who acted without payment. The inquiry was a golden opportunity of proving that the pursuit of profits had jeopardised safety in the pit, endorsing the argument for taking the mines out of private enterprise. Cripps had extreme difficulty persuading miners, who feared victimisation, to give evidence; he ended up pledging that if any victimising took place he would raise the matter on the floor of the House of Commons. His junior, Geoffrey Wilson, rejigged the figures for air-flow ventilation, putting them up in graphic rather than in columnar form, revealing a steady deterioration in conditions. Cripps so severely interrogated the colliery managers that opposing counsel, Hartley Shawcross, protested to the inspector about his cross-examining methods.[78] After thirty sittings – the longest mining investigation of its kind – the inquiry closed under a weight of evidence about cost-cutting economies and breaches of safety regulations. His remarkable handling of the inquiry, and of ensuing compensation cases, gave Cripps a 'revered' name with miners.[79]

Cripps also got embroiled in another public row. The President of the Board of Trade, Walter Runciman, warned bank investors of 'the principles of Sir Stafford Cripps'. Labelling Runciman the true inventor of the Post Office ramp in 1931, Cripps said a Labour government would act quickly against those 'threatening financial sabotage and inciting others to it'. Before the Oxford University Labour Club he went further: 'I cannot imagine the Labour Party coming into power without a first-rate financial crisis.' The caution of the NEC, looking into measures to combat financial panic, was knocked for six. To Morrison, Cripps maintained that everything turned on the price they were willing to pay for peaceful change. Morrison was only half-persuaded. 'The moral I suppose is that you are a moderate and, in the long run, that may prove to be right,' he wrote.[80] This time, the Executive formally dissociated itself from Cripps remarks, denying that a financial crisis was 'inevitable'. Personal dislikes ran deep, but Jim Middleton, the new party secretary, hoped to overcome them by 'more rubbing of shoulders between Cripps, Morrison, Citrine, and Bevin'.[81] Cripps himself intended fighting under the Labour banner for as long as he was allowed. The best way to counteract a financial crisis, he persisted – 'an enemy only to his friends'[82] – was for a Labour government immediately to take over the joint-stock banks, flushing out the Lords. When the NEC and TUC met to examine proposals for reforming parliamentary procedure, however, Citrine, Cripps and a surprised Dalton saw eye to eye, Citrine believing in being over-prepared for any eventuality. The odd man out was 'poor old Lansbury', shocked that they might 'destroy the spirit of Parliament'.[83]

Foreign policy disagreements were not so easily squared. The Southport statement on war and peace still contained traces of ambiguity, 'war resistance' co-existing with support for the League of Nations. This ambiguity was reflected by the respective leaders of the PLP, now facing three ways – Lansbury consistently pacifist, Attlee newly embracing collective security through the League but not ready to vote for increased spending by the government on defence, and Cripps denouncing all wars as 'capitalist' wars. In February 1935, following publication of the government's White Paper on defence, Attlee spoke first on a motion of censure and Cripps wound up. Attlee stuck to safe ground, condemning the pointless piling up of arms. Baldwin, 'telling the truth to democracy' in a bewitching intervention, cautioned against the sway of sentiment. Cripps alluded to Baldwin's frankness, observing that 'some people seem to think that I am too frank'. He bemoaned the government's abandoning of the League of Nations, stretching back to the outbreak of the Sino-Japanese dispute in 1931–3. Pressed by Tories, he indicated that the League ought to have explored every option, including economic sanctions and 'armaments if necessary' – an admission that the 'Peace Party' would have gone to war with Japan that had the House gasping. One historian, analysing what the Labour Party said at the time of the Manchurian crisis rather than after it was over, has characterised Cripps's claim as 'retrospective fantasy'.[84] Baldwin exploited the opening, accusing Cripps of wanting 'security on the cheap'.

In the House of Commons in late May, with the Labour Party opposing the increased estimates for the RAF, Cripps loyally espoused the party line on use of the League of Nations as the instrument for combating aggression; hours later, at the Socialist League conference, in order to quell suggestions that they should throw themselves behind the League of Nations now that the Soviet Union had joined, he was declaring that 'under no circumstances will we assist in war waged under capitalist will for capitalist ends'.

He drew temporary deliverance from his dilemma by fastening on to the

Royal Jubilee celebrations for George V in June, siding with 'the many who feel depressed and dismayed by the Jubilee ballyhoo', and attracting more press criticism. Rogers, informing him that the poorest parts of his constituency had led the way in street celebrations, conveyed the local party's worries.

At the E[xecutive] C[ommittee] meeting last evening we had under consideration further arrangements for the General Election. Some of our members are getting particularly jumpy arising out of the misrepresentations [sic], and they have instructed me to write to you to request that you do not accept too many outside engagements to take you away from the Division during the Campaign. They feel that we shall have to fight very hard, and we cannot afford to take too many risks.[85]

By coincidence, the results of a 'Peace Ballot' sponsored by the League of Nations Union were announced at the very moment that Italian troops began massing on the borders of Abyssinia, setting the League of Nations a demanding diplomatic test.

The longer Lansbury remained as leader, the more he felt uncomfortably tied to an 'intolerable' policy in favour of collective action by the League. He communicated the Party's view to the Foreign Secretary in late August, but, as he told colleagues, he could not personally support it and if it came to war he would resign at once. Cripps, by contrast, was arranging a series of nationwide meetings, urging 'mass resistance to war'. This begged the question of exactly how that resistance was to be made good. By arming (eventually, by a Labour government) or by disarming? By trusting the National government or by attacking it?

Mellor, Laski and Bevan tried to stiffen the support of Labour's left wing for the League of Nations. The Soviet ambassador, Ivan Maisky, admiring Cripps but recognising the 'muddle' in his thinking, canvassed him in the same sense.[86] Cripps held back, professing – he said to his aunt – to find the Soviet Union's turn to the League 'rather amusing'. Gathering at Margate before the Trade Union Congress, the National Council of Labour decided to uphold the authority of the League, backing the threat of sanctions to restrain Italy. 'Cripps', in Dalton's version, 'came only for the first day. He made a most perfunctory speech, opposing sanctions and what must, he said, become an imperialist war. He spoke, it was quite obvious, not to persuade but only for the record.'[87] When the matter was voted on, he did not appear. Lansbury, Bevin later swore, voted in favour of sanctions.[88] Citrine thereupon made clear to Lansbury that it was his duty to deliver the Party's message to Congress, asking delegates 'not to let George Lansbury down' by rejecting military sanctions.

The Foreign Secretary Sir Samuel Hoare's speech before the League of

Nations Assembly on 11 September – committing Britain to 'collective resistance to all acts of unprovoked aggression' – revived faith in the League, uniting the parties. Morrison delivered the Labour Party's unqualified approval, congratulating the government on its tardy conversion. But, at the anti-war conference he addressed on 14 September, Cripps refused to support the Margate policy, insisting 'the economic seeds of war would remain'. A union secretary recalled what Cripps had said in the Commons in March about imposing sanctions against Japan, accusing him, to cheering and booing, of a *volte-face*. Cripps could only weakly reply that he had been trying to discover whether the National government was prepared to operate economic sanctions.[89] An ambiguous Socialist League resolution only just scraped home. At other similar conferences around the country, the view that sanctions were 'imperialist' ran into similar difficulties.

According to the League's secretary, J. T. Murphy, had Cripps come out strongly in favour of sanctions, he would have swept the Labour Party. Instead, after conferring further with Lansbury, he fired off a letter to the NEC, tendering his immediate resignation from the Executive and citing his divergence of view from the official party position. Even Mellor had not known Cripps was about to jump. Dalton was merciless:

> During the present Parliament he has on a number of occasions, and indeed only a few months ago, expounded the party's foreign policy with lucidity and with every appearance of sincerity and understanding. A fortnight ago, for the first time since his election to the party executive, he expressed a different view, and proposed that this country should stand impotently aside in the crisis, violate its treaty obligations under the Covenant of the League of Nations, and signal 'all clear' to Mussolini in his aggression. Such a policy, in effect, though not, of course, in intention, is pro-Fascist and pro-war.[90]

Cripps, Dalton told Kingsley Martin, editor of the *New Statesman*, was 'naive, often to the point of sheer imbecility ... but now he must be argued with and answered', branded as a 'quick change artist'.[91] Cripps was equally forthright. Dalton, being run by Transport House, 'looks upon this as an opportunity of getting rid of a rival!'[92] As for Abyssinia, Italy would make a show of force and the League a show of sanctions, followed by the partitioning of the country. Germany would then make new frontier demands in Europe. Hence his 'rebellious' resignation, to illustrate 'where I stood'. If there had to be sanctions, they had to be 'working class sanctions', designed to dislodge Baldwin. This left the Socialist League in utter confusion – Mellor wanted to attack Lansbury too – but Cripps cared only for the demoralisation of Labour, completely controlled by the right wing with the aim, if Dalton had his way (Cripps thought), of driving left wingers 'right out of the party'.

All the conflicts about power, policy and personality agitating the Party since 1931 were spectacularly argued out at Labour's annual conference, in the Brighton Dome, in October 1935. Throughout the two-day foreign-policy debate, an invasion of Abyssinia likely at any moment, 'at every table in the crowded lounge and conference corridors, delegates were talking about sanctions, and what *kind* of sanctions'.[93]

The issue, Dalton argued in recommending the use of 'all necessary measures' to stop Italy, was that of 'standing firmly' by the policy the Party had recently reaffirmed in Parliament, when it had been defended by both Lansbury and – he read out the extracts – Cripps. Were they really to turn their back on the League just now, when the government, after shameful neglect, was making a 'death-bed repentance'? Cripps turned Dalton's argument upside down: what mattered was not what Britain as a country should do, but 'who is in control of our actions'. For his part, he could never forget the sordid excuses of 1914, which he had foolishly believed. If they supported sanctions, they would be condemning the workers to military action, 'without power of control or recall'. 'I have been accused of changing my views,' he went on. 'I have changed them, because events have satisfied me that now the League of Nations, with three major powers outside, has become nothing but the tool of the satiated imperialist powers.' He had put the Party's policy in the Commons for as long as he had felt able. His great regret was not realising much earlier the dangers towards which they were heading. Labour was not in government, and ought not to try to act through the 'capitalist and imperialist' government which was.

A succession of speakers came to the rostrum, pulling Cripps to pieces. John Marchbank, general secretary of the National Union of Railwaymen, argued that those unwilling to observe the decisions of conference should 'get out'. A Labour MP, John Wilmot, felt that the party had no right to 'pass the buck' to the trade unions. In the afternoon, Mellor, attacking the 'Robber's Charter' – the Treaty of Versailles – insisted that 'our enemy is at home'. Dismissing Mellor's 'black-and-white categories', Attlee denied that the labour movement was being lined up behind the National government; the government, after the four years in which he had been putting the Party's position in the House, was only now falling in with what Labour had been demanding all along.

It was then the turn of Lansbury, who was greeted by a prolonged ovation. He explained the impossible position he was in, his personal belief – 'force is no remedy' – having never altered. 'It may very well be that in the carrying out of your policy I shall be in your way.' God intended people to live peaceably. According to his son-in-law and biographer, 'he had rarely spoken as movingly'.[94]

Lansbury gave way to Bevin, as a hailstorm began beating down on the roof of the Dome. In a savage assault, Bevin turned his fury on Lansbury and Cripps, shattering their arguments. 'It is placing the Executive and the Movement in an absolutely wrong position to be hawking your conscience round from body to body asking to be told what you ought to do with it.' The Party, he went on amid interruptions, had been betrayed. People had talked on the platform about 'destroying capitalism'. The middle classes and the lawyers – this looking at where Cripps was sitting – have not done too badly under capitalism. Those opposed to the resolution should actually be calling for withdrawal from the League of Nations. 'You cannot be in and out at the same time, not if you are honest.' Cripps had turned up at Margate, spoken briefly and then departed, playing to the gallery. The General Council of the TUC felt let down. In the last few years they had patiently revived the National Council of Labour to ensure that a future Labour government 'would not be left as before with no policy'. He finished with a final angry swipe at Cripps:

> And who am I to let my personality protrude as compared to this great move-ment? Who is any man on that platform? I do sincerely ask this Conference to appreciate the Trade Unionist's position. Sir Stafford Cripps said there would be no split. He has done his best (Voices, 'No, No'). Oh, yes. Let me call attention to what has happened. He was elected a member of the Executive last year. I know nothing of what has happened in the Executive, but it is a most unusual thing to resign just prior to a Conference. If there was no intention to cast doubt upon it, he cast reflection upon the rest of us who took responsibility when he was not present. It was cowardly to stab us in the back as he did by resigning and not going through. If he felt that the matter ought to have been reconsidered, why didn't they call the body together again? Why didn't they call us into consultation? The great crime of Ramsay MacDonald was that he never called in his Party, and the crime of these people is that they have gone out, they have sown discord at the very moment when they could have called the body together again to consider whether or not there ought to be something done. We were left to get the news in the morning papers.
>
> I ask any Trade Unionist: Have you ever found it in your own Union? Have we ever treated one another like that?[95]

Lansbury tearfully made to reply, but was cut off by the chairman. Cripps, Morrison noticed, hardly seemed upset. If one went in for politics, Cripps told his Socialist League ally in the next seat, one had to expect rough knocks.[96]

The conference ended for the day, and the debate resumed in a calmer atmosphere on the following morning. Morrison set out to please everyone, endorsing sanctions but asking for tolerance from the majority as well as the minority, irritating only Bevin. On a card vote, the resolution was over-whelmingly carried. Five days later, Lansbury resigned as party leader, the PLP executive installing Attlee as his interim replacement.

Was there a plot to remove Lansbury and drive Cripps out? Labour's foreign-policy aims had for too long been at cross-purposes and could not survive the test of reality. Did this test also imply sidelining Lansbury and Cripps? Francis Williams (though not in his 'life' of Bevin) asserted that Lansbury, wanting his favourite disciple to be his successor, left the unions little choice but to 'destroy' him first – that Lansbury 'handed them the opportunity' at Brighton.[97] Press reports of the Brighton debate mention unnamed trade unionists bent on banishing Cripps. By resigning from the NEC before Brighton, however, Cripps, it was generally felt, had 'done for himself as possible leader' (A. V. Alexander), had 'cooked his own goose' (Dalton), throwing all his efforts away in a self-destructive gesture.

Was his crime, then, to have ended up on the losing side? Was his 'class pacifism' ultimately as futile as Lansbury's 'ethical pacifism'?[98] Charges of inconstancy, coming on top of the ill health of Isobel, clearly took their toll, doing him lasting damage. If, however, the indictment is that he overlooked the merits of policy (deterring Mussolini) in order to play politics, the reckoning is more uncertain. It is as valid to suppose he was playing politics in order to obtain the correct policy – saving the Party, that is, from rushing into the arms of the National government. Cripps, characteristically, thought he knew better. Deciding to resign also from the PLP Executive, he admitted, 'it is not as if I can regard this as a minor matter. I believe it is a long step upon the slippery slope which may lead the Party to destruction.' Already, after Italy had invaded Abyssinia, he detected signs of a realisation 'that the view which I took at Brighton was the right one'. By the time he wrote those words, Baldwin, brandishing his 'sham' sanctions, had resolved to 'dish' the Opposition, and a general election – set for 14 November – was upon them.

Baldwin's appeal to the people in October–November 1935 was twin-pronged: 'wholehearted' support for a League of Nations policy of collective security, allied to rearming to 'repair the gaps' in Britain's defences. He hoped for a mandate based on personal trust. National candidates were able to set against this the disorganised, leaderless state of the main Opposition party.

The Labour Party stuck to a pro-League policy too, but tied to a demand for all-round disarmament and the disbanding of air forces. Cripps, though he spoke far and wide, held fast to his anti-war credentials, avoiding controversy – Bevin visited Bristol without incident – by harping on the National government's 'dishonesty'. He distributed gramophone records of his speeches, couched in an Old Testament tone, castigating equally the race for 'greater armaments' and shameful 'luxury', revealing that he met many capitalists who paid him 'fantastic sums' as a lawyer, convincing him of the necessity for a workers' government.[99] He predicted a deal would be made with Mussolini – 'when the election was over. That is why we are having a quick one.'

His 'National Labour' opponent in Bristol East, Archibald Church (a Mac-Donaldite MP in 1931) fought hard to puncture the 'insufferable arrogance' of the sitting MP, who 'is unable to accept the sincerity of anyone else but himself'. The local Labour Party coined the slogan 'Don't be a traitor to your class – vote Cripps.' Church, who came from humble origins, asked what Cripps could conceivably know about the working classes. In his election literature, Cripps was shown side by side with Lansbury – two 'apostles of peace'. Church said Cripps had forgotten to mention that he had been the superintendent of a munitions factory in the Great War. Cripps countered that his experience at Queensferry was 'one of the reasons for becoming so ardent a pacifist' [sic]. On the eve of polling, Church made his last throw, putting it about that he and not Cripps was the official Labour Party candidate. Denouncing him as a Labour renegade, Cripps called on voters to send Church from Bristol with 'the biggest hiding he has ever had'.

The early betting on election night was that Cripps had been defeated. In fact he polled 22,009 votes to Church's 15,126 (on a slightly lower turnout than in 1931), pushing his majority up to almost 7,000. In the rest of Bristol, Labour acquired one other seat, Bristol South. Nationally, however, the total of 108 Labour gains did nothing more than dent Baldwin's parliamentary majority, more than ever Conservative in composition.

In the subsequent inquest, Cripps blamed the hesitant, reforming programme of the Party – inadequate for maximising working-class support – for which the whole leadership was at fault. Morrison, one of several prominent figures returning to the house – including Clynes, Dalton and Shinwell – dismissed adopting a narrow, class-centred appeal, ramming home his message that the Party would not win elections if it went about shouting of a financial crisis. Cripps wished only to retire to the 'silence and obscurity' of the back benches; Morrison, with Dalton canvassing on his behalf, was a contender for leader. Ironically, therefore, Morrison was Cripps's first choice, since Greenwood was too lax and Attlee had 'no personality!' The PLP met on 26 November – Cripps and Pritt (the latter also elected), the two KCs in the Party, arriving in their gowns. In the second round of voting, Attlee benefited from a transfer of votes from Greenwood's backers and convincingly won the run-off against Morrison. While Major Attlee assembled his team to face the new Parliament, Lansbury and Cripps quietly took up exile together in the seats 'below the gangway'.[100]

8

REJECT

I assert, and I do not believe any one can seriously deny the proposition, that alone and with a policy of 'pure socialism' the Labour Party cannot gain an absolute majority at the next election.

Cripps, in the New Statesman, *March 1939*

For the briefest interlude, in the few short years leading up to the flashpoint Labour Party conference in 1935, an avowedly left-wing Christian socialist, Sir Stafford Cripps, commanded a hearing and used it to propagate anti-capitalist protest. Warning of sabotage, social uprising and the clash of arms, it was not long before he was being singled out – on all sides – as an oddball impostor, a crankish barrister betraying the good sense of the working people he claimed to speak for, his ideas as unorthodox as his appearance was orthodox. Not the least of his maddening attributes was that he gave no sign of pretending. The 'problem' of Cripps was settled, in the short term, only by a brutal public denunciation.

Was this what foiled Cripps? Bevin, after Lansbury was accorded an emotional farewell, ruthlessly expressed what was the majority view, imposed by the party's union paymasters. But the Labour Party's impact, when the general election came, was blunted by the resilience of the British economy, which had a far greater effect in marginalising discontent. Cripps was not a revolutionist, though he enjoyed ribbing his playboy brother and charmed Keynes by his contempt for conventional economics, hatred of bankers and belief in deficit financing on a grand scale.[1] He was convinced he was living in a decaying society, the 'museum piece' of parliamentary democracy. The Left, if it was in earnest, had to persuade the party and the voters that there was no alternative but to go 'the whole hog', calculating that an extreme policy would win more support than a cautious one. Labour was vanquished and there was no 'first-class financial crisis'. Nor, thanks to Baldwin – 'an extremely pleasant and attractive gentleman', Cripps acknowledged, 'but as clever as a cartload of monkeys'[2] – was there a genteel collapse. The National government, Cripps was willing to concede,[3] had, by its own lights, done well, borrowing to rearm and stimulating economic recovery.

From this point on, his simplicity of utterance and honesty of outlook were turned in a new direction. Cripps, expostulated one Labourite, was 'at it again'. Before Abyssinia, he had concentrated almost exclusively on possible upheavals likely to accompany any attempt to introduce socialism by democratic means; after it, he switched to the disrupting effect of foreign dangers, which – hard on the heels of the Hoare–Laval fiasco[4] – loomed increasingly large. Before, he had pursued a long-haul strategy for the Labour Party, as the one vehicle of political change; thereafter he improvised short cuts in conjunction with other 'progressive elements' climbing on the anti-National government bandwagon. Before, he had been an outlandish class warrior; now he was a 'devoted missionary', looking to the menace of war to achieve the revolution blocked in time of peace.

The cluster of attitudes adopted by the British Left in the later 1930s – strongly tainted by Russophilia – have not worn well. To many, they look wrong-headed, even stupefying, their pro-Soviet treachery inexcusable. The culpability of Cripps – oblivious to patriotic feeling, approving only of 'a war worth fighting', judging that, of the two evils of British imperialism and German militarism, the latter was the lesser[5] – seems to stand out. It is the 'social patriots' within the Labour Party who are credited with waking up the Party to the need for national defence, just as they devised a practical programme of reform eventuating in the legislation of the 1945 Labour government. There are limits, however, to rewriting contemporary history. All attempts to topple the National government came to naught. As long as foreign policy remained in the hands of 'the Old Gang', suspicion of the Soviet Union was a motivating fear. Some may contend the Labour Party's success after 1945 sprang from its more far-sighted thinkers of the 1930s. But it took the military disasters of 1939–40 to discredit Chamberlain and usher in the wartime social transformation that gave Labour its chance.

In early 1936, Cripps reached two decisions: to transform the Socialist League into a fully constituted party within the Party, expanding its membership even at the expense of local Labour parties, and to create a weekly socialist newspaper, which he had discussed with Strachey and the publisher and 'tireless dynamo'[6] Victor Gollancz.[7] Their meeting resulted in the launching of two publishing ventures of the era: the Left Book Club and The Tribune, which was set up using a trust fund under the direction of Cripps, with Mellor as editor. Until The Tribune could begin publication, Cripps kept his own counsel, boycotted by the Daily Herald and Transport House. 'Stafford is keeping quiet,' Morrison mentioned to the Webbs. 'I sometimes talk to him, but I feel that I do not know what he is thinking or what line he intends to take.' As Beatrice Webb knew, he was 'preparing an assault on the capitalist stronghold with his scratch body of followers, "a senseless adventure", Morrison thinks'.[8]

Party and paper required a policy, which Cripps proceeded to provide. Shortly after Brighton, the Communist Party reapplied for affiliation to the Labour Party, only to be rejected again. Once the CP declared its willingness to band together in an anti-fascist alliance in defence of peace and democracy, this was enough to persuade Cripps that the CP's application should be supported. Writing in *The Socialist* news-sheet in March 1936, he pointed to the benefits of a 'progressive' or popular front, as had been formed in France and Spain. But if Labour was to be an effective instrument, not just of democratic defence but of socialist change, it must combine with other working-class parties or organisations – he mentioned the CP and the ILP. Endorsing the 'unity of the Left', the National Council of the Socialist League, off its own back, initiated talks with representatives of the CP. The official party stiffly informed the League that the Communists, trying to join a party whose principles they did not share, were engaging in a 'new deviation' for tactical ends.[9]

Adopting the united front went hand in hand with 'total opposition' to the National government, which the Labour Party's support for a League of Nations policy had compromised. Abyssinia was lost. Hitler re-entered the Rhineland. Baldwin's 'false pledges' were 'misleading' the country about Britain's own defences. The danger of the labour movement being enlisted in a war in defence of imperialist interests made it imperative for the workers to 'take control of their own government'. If there was to be a war against fascism, the most Cripps was prepared to consider was a conditional offer by Labour to back the National government – providing the conditions were impossible to fulfill.

The nationalist uprising in Republican Spain in July 1936 further polarised opinion. Abyssinia was colonial, Spain European. Mounting evidence that Italy and Germany were supplying the rebel nationalist side raised the danger not only of a Spanish class war, but a wider European war between fascism and Bolshevism. Confronted by 'contending fascisms', the answer was a united Left. The Socialist League resolved to outlaw 'class collaboration', urging 'the closest possible relationship of all working class forces'. The lone dissentient – the secretary, J. T. Murphy – resigned from his post, warning that a united front would wreck the League, the CP simply manipulating the League as a stepping stone into the Labour party.[10]

On the eve of Labour's annual conference in Edinburgh in October, Cripps picked his moment to deliver some typically breathtaking pronouncements, intent on unsettling party frontbenchers who, he considered, were only too eager to present themselves as a safe choice whenever the electorate wanted a change of personnel but not of fundamental orientation. Answering those recommending conditional support for rearmament, Cripps proposed making 'every possible effort' to stop the National government recruiting for the armed forces, so forcing it into conscription. 'Don't let us be made fools of by another slogan like "save democracy" or "curb Prussian militarism" ... I think it is likely if Great Britain were conquered by Germany that Socialism would be suppressed, though that is not certain. Don't forget that Ludendorff sent Lenin into Russia and that Germany entertained the Irish rebels during the war.'[11] If Britain was pushed into war, he argued in Leeds on 1 October, he 'devoutly hoped' the workers would revolt. 'I hope that the present government can be made to understand that that will happen. It will be a very healthy thought for them to have at the back of their mind.'[12]

The Brighton conference had lived up to the ideal, the movement making up its mind on the issue of the hour. Edinburgh offered only equivocation. The unions, Laski complained, 'turned down all and every suggestion for the united front' and made the foreign-policy debates 'the worst mess since 1931'.[13] 'Everybody grumbling,' Dalton noted in his diary. 'Trouble with the constituency parties, Co-ops, Spain, armaments.' Bevin had never felt more disillusioned. It was all Attlee could do, in his first conference as full leader, to hold the Party together around a contradictory stance, though he found the outcome 'pretty rotten'.[14]

Spain was the principal cause. In deference to French Socialist fears, the Executive stood by non-intervention by outside powers – 'a very bad second best' in the words of Greenwood. In a stirring intervention, Bevan ridiculed having an arms embargo while the rebels were being supplied by the fascist powers. Bevin and he traded insults. No sooner was the resolution on non-intervention carried – by a majority of 3 to 1 – than (the next day) the platform gave ground after an eloquent speech from a Spanish delegate, La Pasionara, sending Attlee and Greenwood back to London to ask the Prime Minister to examine breaches of the embargo.

The international debate was equally unsatisfactory. Dalton, who earlier in the year had tried and failed to get the PLP to stop opposing the defence estimates, argued that, in a world where all other countries were increasing their armed forces, a Labour government would have to increase arms too. Morrison balanced the force of Dalton's contribution, insisting Labour would still be free to oppose rearmament under the National government. Cripps was incredulous. 'For the sake of honesty', he asked conference for 'a clear statement one way or another'. For once, Bevin had some sympathy – Morrison's speech, he said, was 'one of the worst pieces of tight-rope walking' he had ever encountered at a conference. If they had to rearm, he, unlike Cripps, was prepared to face it, because the first thing 'victorious fascism' wiped out were the trade unions. Attlee promised the National government would not be given a blank cheque, reserving the right of the PLP to decide how it proposed to vote on the issue in the Commons, the resolution being passed by 1,738,000 votes to 657,000.

The conference, in Mellor's view, had been 'cheated of its right' to know what it was deciding.[15] The voting down of resolutions on the affiliation of the CP and the formation of a united front underlined the continuing ability of the party and union leaders to fend off unwelcome proposals, irritating constituency delegates. Before the conference was over, the nucleus of the League – now including George Strauss, another (wealthy) protégé of Morrison's – had met to synchronise publication of the first issue of *The Tribune* with a full-dress unity campaign. Deliberately going against conference decisions banning joint activity with the CP, they risked expulsion, particularly now that Dalton was party chairman.

Cripps, chancing his arm, spoke on the same platform as Communists in Strauss's constituency of North Lambeth. He travelled next to Stockport, as a by-election in nearby Preston entered its final stages. He repeated his hope that the government would resort to conscription, enabling the workers to protest *en masse*. That way, they would have the government beaten. Questioned about Labour's attitude to rearmament and to a German attack, he said the Opposition should withhold its support, since working-class interests were hardly identical with those of British imperialism. Moreover, 'if Germany should defeat Great Britain in a capitalist war, I do not believe it would be at all a disaster for the working classes. It would be a disaster for the profit makers, but not necessarily for the working classes.' The losers in 1918 had not suffered more than the winners. In fact, the real victors were the Russians, who had overthrown tsarism and established a worker's state.

Citrine was unable to understand how anyone with education and the power of control of speech could say such a thing.[16] 'Sir Stafford regards military defeat at Nazi hands as one method of getting what he wants, and so he opposes British armaments because they might prevent that defeat,' the editor of the *Daily Herald* spelt out. 'Heaven help the Labour Party if this sort of thing continues to be said from a Labour platform.'[17] Union leaders, upset by sniping from a new committee of constituency parties (of which Cripps was chairman) demanded that persistent offenders be 'brought to heel'. Cripps contested the accuracy of the version of his speech which appeared in the *Manchester Guardian*, claiming he had referred to the defeat of 'British imperialism' – but the shorthand notes of the paper's reporter did not bear him out.[18]

Pritt took soundings in the parliamentary party. 'The poisonous attitude of Dalton is held by practically no one,' he told Cripps. Greenwood, without attacking Cripps, thought it was enough to say emphatically that his view was not that of the official party. As for those closest to Cripps, 'the general attitude of the left-wing to you is warm affection and hope for leadership'.[19]

Examining the press reports, Dalton received an 'evasive' reply from Cripps. The NEC convened – Cripps being too busy at the Law Courts to attend – and, although one or two wanted to expel him 'without further ado',[20] issued a rebuke 'unanimously' dissociating itself from and 'categorically' repudiating his views. Cripps, invited to see the Executive to clear up 'misunderstandings', demurred – judged in his absence, they could consider the future in his absence too.[21] He meant to 'disregard the attacks as they only recoil on those who make them', thinking it best to leave well alone, 'unless on this occasion they screw up their courage to put me out of the Party, which they may do'.

In print, Cripps felt 'bound to state' his view that, if British imperialism could not be brought down by their own efforts (an 'infinitely better' solution), it must happen by 'foreign aggression'. Imperialist rivalry had been replaced by the 'international class struggle'. The greatest danger was of capitalist powers combining against working-class ones, principally the Soviet Union. He did not refer to Germany. Only a few days later, Germany and Japan agreed an anti-Comintern pact.

The Stockport row had not completely died down when the abdication crisis broke. Cripps, whose closest friend at the Bar was Walter Monckton, the King's adviser, was consulted about the legal implications of Edward VIII marrying a commoner and staying on the throne. Many in the Labour Party wanted to allow 'the democratic King' to marry whomsoever he pleased, hoping to capitalise on Baldwin's embarrassment. Attlee, however, had privately pledged not to take office if the government fell. If the King married, Cripps informed Monckton, his wife would automatically become Queen, meaning the King was bound to accept ministerial advice about whom he could and could not marry.[22] If he refused to give up the contemplated marriage, Cripps said in public on 5 December, he had to abdicate. 'It is most unlikely that he would find any alternative government.'[23] Had the lady in question been a member of the English aristocracy, he could not resist adding, the government might have viewed things differently. The King, according to the *New Socialist*, was being badgered out by a government which did not take kindly to his advanced opinions. In his 'Buckingham Palace' phase, Cripps had treated the monarchy as one of the main props of the capitalist State. In late 1936, the danger to the throne was a distraction.

To initiate a unity campaign, talks between the Communist Party, the Independent Labour Party and the Socialist League took place in Cripps's chambers shortly after Edinburgh. Cripps and Mellor had to try to ally with both parties, but were authorised to unite with the CP even without the ILP.

Recent infighting made for bitterness and distrust. Harry Pollitt and R. Palme Dutt, the CP representatives, believed Fenner Brockway of the ILP was an MI5 informer.[24] James Maxton, accompanying Brockway, remembered the last time the ILP had become 'fatally entangled' with the CP.[25] Mellor was a seasoned disrupter. It was also unclear how organisational unity might be achieved, and around what programme. The CP was only too anxious to affiliate to the Labour Party, working towards a popular front of anti-national-government forces, aligned to the Soviet Union's 'fight for peace'. The ILP, on the other hand, would agree to reapply to join Labour only if it could continue to advocate a policy of revolutionary socialism (which it thought the CP had shed), based around a 'proletarian worker's party'. The CP and the ILP, in fact, were considering entering a united front for diametrically opposing reasons – the CP to facilitate a popular front, the ILP to prevent one.[26]

The talks were kept going only by the transparent desire of Cripps to seal an agreement. He was ignorant of doctrinal niceties – Brockway saw he was lost during the discussions about rival left-wing factions in Spain, 'impatient' with controversies about democracy and revolution, and unconcerned about the Moscow trials, arguing they were an internal matter for the Soviet Union. He relied on Mellor to put the League's case, smoothing over differences by skilful drafting.[27] Pollitt admired him as 'the only clean man in the whole of that bunch', appreciating the way he got people who had abused each other in the past to work together.[28] In the ILP's view, Pollitt plainly set out to woo his impressionable comrade.

A united-front agreement finally emerged, with the objective of unifying all sections of the working-class movement within the ranks of the Labour Party and the trade unions in 'the common struggle against fascism, reaction and war'. Attached to this central objective were a further number of limited aims – abolition of the means test, a national plan for the distressed areas, a modest scheme of nationalisation – to be secured by the return of a Labour government. The unity campaign was to take precedence over the separate interests of the three organisations.

The CP obtained the two things it wanted: a back door into the Labour Party and advocacy of an alliance with the Soviet Union, which the others would 'abstain' from criticising. To bring the ILP in too, as well as to satisfy the Socialist League, Cripps drew up two addenda, leaving both organisations free to oppose rearmament so long as there was a National government and permitting the ILP to affiliate to Labour only after the 'democratisation' of that party.[29]

This final proviso – 'democratisation' – sheds light on what Cripps was endeavouring to pull off. The Edinburgh debates had done for the left-wing minority, but the official leadership derived no comfort from what had transpired. The Executive was widely felt to be 'unrepresentative' and conference decisions 'undemocratic', which encouraged demands for a revised party constitution and greater power for constituency parties. Union leaders scented a left-wing conspiracy. As has been shown in a scholarly rediscovery of the Constituency Parties Association, Cripps's reluctant connection with the grass-roots movement was a mixed blessing.[30] There was considerable overlap in aims, however, between the embryonic unity campaign for 'galvanising' the labour movement – flooding it with committed socialists – and constituency activists wishing to establish that the Labour Party rightfully belonged to its members.

Mellor tried to harry the Scottish Socialist Party into the unity campaign in December. The CP, the ILP and the Socialist League had reached an accord, he told the SSP council, 'the ILP giving more guarantees than asked for, even to the extent of agreeing to become once more affiliated to the Labour Party when the Party was democratised by the Socialist League'. The SSP – which had been quarrelling bitterly with the ILP – was enjoined to 'come in or be wiped out'. Mellor stressed 'how necessary it was to keep this matter secret as any leakage would mean that Bevin would smash them one by one before they were ready to launch their joint action'.[31]

The pilot issue of The Tribune appeared with a print run of 55,000 on 1 January 1937, disseminating the gospel of 'working class unity'. The National government, the paper proclaimed, was the original united front – the united front of capitalism, formed in 1931 – which held on to power by exploiting the disunity of the Left. By putting aside factional disputes, a militant spirit could revive the socialism that had been the 'living principle' of the movement. 'The Labour movement must choose. It has come now to the turning point of its history.'[32]

That weekend, Socialist League members were presented with a unity agreement which, at the last moment, they could only accept or reject. Many took strong exception, unhappy about 'arm-twisting'. Some called for the resignation of the entire National Council. Cripps gave an assurance that, since Labour's head office was 'trembling at the knees', disaffiliation of the League was unlikely to follow, though the NEC had sent out an edict on party loyalty reminding members of its 'full disciplinary powers'.[33] Challenged, he tied endorsement of the unity deal to a vote of confidence in the Council.[34] By 56 votes to 38, with 23 abstentions, the united front was carried, accompanied by protests that the League had turned its back on working exclusively with and through the Labour Party. While, as Dalton and Bevin had been planning, the leaders of various parts of the movement were gathering on the Isle of Wight to put Cripps on the spot – 'Do you want us to win? What are you playing at?' – the man himself was in London, 'cock-a-hoop' at the League's decision.

Pinning everything on the unity campaign, Cripps – turning away much legal work – Mellor and G. R. Mitchison, signed the unity manifesto on behalf of the League on 18 January. 'The United Front of the Working Class to fight Fascism and War' kicked off at a huge demonstration at the Free Trade Hall in Manchester, addressed by Cripps (quoting William Blake's 'Jerusalem'), Pollitt and Maxton, and attracting a long list of sponsors. The chairman of the Socialist League, the publisher of The Tribune and the champion of the unity seemed set on realising one of David Low's cartoon prophecies for 1937 – Cripps 'expelled from the Labour Party for being a socialist'.

The NEC reacted promptly, the Herald already reproaching those who imagined they were furthering the interests of the Party by being disloyal to it.

On 24 January, establishing it had the authority to act without right of appeal, the Executive disaffiliated the Socialist League for its open defiance of official policy. Attlee and Morrison, favouring delay, were outvoted.

This was only the first step: the expulsion of individuals still remained. The NEC, however, did not wish to damage the London County Council election campaign, where Morrison's London Labour Party was defending its majority. The CP had been active in the capital, supporting Labour candidates whether welcomed or not, giving rise to acrimonious exchanges. Cripps gloried in the suspense, confessing he might be making his last speech as a party member (on 19 February, in Oxford) and that he was 'hanging by the skin of my teeth' (21 February, in Glasgow);[35] fellow unity speakers were taken aback by his frugal eating and first-class carriage.[36] Attlee, for one, was increasingly dismissive of 'heretics seeking martyrdom'. Cripps 'is driving himself out', Bevin told Cole.[37] In Bristol, the Borough Labour Party was besieged by complaints from Bevin's TGWU about Communist infiltration, the attempted unity campaign causing much 'ill-feeling', though the Bristol East party had taken the trouble to express its 'complete confidence' in its MP.[38] 'Friction is widespread, I am glad to say,' Cripps responded, 'and is considerably waking up the movement.'[39]

A dazzling contribution at the close of the Commons debate on the Gresford Colliery disaster won Cripps a reprieve. When the NEC met the following day, it decided to shelve any further action, the parliamentary party being well aware it could not afford to dispense with the services of one of its foremost debaters. Strauss, however, was stripped by Morrison of his chairmanship of two important LCC committees.

Undaunted, Cripps took note of two significant steps by the party: the publication of an *Immediate Programme* of 'constructive' proposals for 'social-ism and social amelioration', and the PLP's decision to vote to reduce the defence estimates rather than oppose them outright. This last was 'all wrong', putting the arms machine under the control of their 'class opponents',[40] though it had Bevin's powerful endorsement ('Hitler can only now be stopped by rearming and fighting'). With exquisite timing, Cripps addressed a unity meeting at Eastleigh in Hampshire, site of the test airfield for the Supermarine Spitfire fighter plane, which was being built in the locality.[41] 'Money cannot make armaments', he announced:

Armaments can only be made by the skill of the British working class, and it is the British working class who would be called upon to use them. Today you have the most glorious opportunity that the workers have ever had if you will only use the necessity of capitalism in order to get power yourselves. The capitalists are in your hands. Refuse to make munitions, refuse to make arma-ments and they are helpless. They would have to hand the control of the country over to you.[42]

It was a carefully worded provocation, coming only a month after the preparation of a secret defence report to the Foreign Secretary that Germany, by May 1937, would have 800 long-range bombers to Britain's 48.[43]

Tory MPs demanded Cripps be prosecuted for incitement to strike. The right-wing press described his comments as an abuse of public privilege, for which he should be 'dealt with'. Partridge, in *Punch*, drew Cripps on a soapbox in his KC's gown, angrily shaking his fists, while the sky filled with airplanes of 'foreign menace'. His exhorting of workers to refuse to make munitions – to leave the country defenceless – was the height of his inter-war infamy.[44]

Leading trade unionists were outraged. Industries engaged in the rearmament programme had been plagued by unofficial stoppages. Calls to strike weakened the leadership's grip on the rank and file, already loosened by the united front agitation. Trade-union anti-Communists on the NEC attacked Cripps for 'talking without thinking', arguing for the sternest measures. 'Cripps must go'.

Dalton, in public, talked tough. Malcontents must stop 'creating dissension'; otherwise 'we shall go forward without them'. At the NEC, he prodded a majority – Attlee and Morrison again wanted to put things off – into a clever *démarche*. Having disaffiliated the Socialist League in January, the Executive decreed membership of the League to be 'incompatible' with membership of the Party, debarring League members from 1 June, putting the onus on Cripps and his followers to choose their allegiance.

The CP argued that the League should voluntarily disband, looking to reverse the NEC decision at the next conference. To the 'great surprise' of Maxton and Brockway, Cripps agreed.[45] The bulk of the National Council of the League, led by Mellor, maintained it would be better to remain in being until the conference and dissolve only if it were defeated. Cripps's sudden switch caught many unawares, and for the first time the Bristol East party was no longer solidly behind him. He tried consoling Rogers. 'I should personally have preferred, as I told you, the closing down of the League, but when one is working with a number of people one cannot be too autocratic!' His finances were stretched by extra commitments (*The Tribune* was running at a heavy loss), although when the *News Chronicle* suggested the League might fold because he was unprepared to finance it indefinitely he reprimanded the editor for his 'bad taste' in discussing his private financial affairs. He denied having contributed the sum of £1,000 to the League during the past year, nor had he contributed to unity-campaign funds.[46] Dalton weighed in, describing the League as 'a rich man's toy'. In any event, Cripps expected to lose the Labour whip in June, then becoming an independent MP.

The League met to settle its future. Cripps was reconciled to a dignified scuttle. Though Mellor still wanted the League to make a fight of it, both were hamstrung by Cripps's 'deceiving' assurance given in January that it would never come to such a choice.[47] Delegates were told the success of the unity campaign depended on the League folding, eliminating the single left-wing organisation in the Labour Party. With unanimous agreement to break up, Cripps dressed up the end of the League as an act undertaken for the sake of the movement.[48]

To co-ordinate continuing unity activity, a National Unity Campaign Committee was established. It lasted all of three weeks, until the NEC announced that members of the Labour Party appearing on a platform with the CP or the ILP would automatically be expelled. For the second time, Cripps presided over a humiliating climbdown. When Lionel Elvin, a member of the Socialist League Executive, expressed amazement that the Committee had buckled at the first threat from Transport House, Cripps was unconvincing:

> It is a little difficult to explain the entire situation. The Labour Party members of the Unity Committee were divided at first in their views. George Strauss, William Mellor and I were anxious to carry on, but the Communist Party were insistent on taking the line now taken, and were supported by Harold Laski and Dick Mitchison, and after Harry Pollitt's speech at the Communist Party Congress, although not impossible, it was difficult to proceed, added to increasing friction over Spain between the Independent Labour Party and the Communist Party.[49]

Did the Communist Party 'deliberately wreck the Socialist League', as Brockway surmised?

The ILP claimed 'it was on the advice of the CP that the Socialist League was dissolved. It was on the advice of the CP that the joint meetings between Labour unity supporters, the ILP and the CP were stopped.' Pollitt's comrade Willie Gallagher, however, in his *The Chosen Few* (1940), pinned the guilt for suspending joint activities on Cripps alone.[50] The fragmentary evidence in Cripps's own papers lends substance to the critics of his shortcomings. His imagination fired by the idea of unity, he bounced the League into agreeing with the campaign, with little regard for the reservations of those who felt they were being presented with a *fait accompli*. Forced to retreat by the NEC, he showed an alarming willingness to finish with the League, scattering its modest membership. He wildly hoped that 'unity' would sweep the labour movement; all it did was antagonise the Labour Party's existing MPs, candidates and constituencies in those areas where it was most active. Pollitt guilefully got the headstrong Cripps to commit himself to a hazardous cause, the upshot of which was that the Socialist League destroyed itself 'in a quixotic attempt to create unity between the Labour Party and the Communist Party'.[51]

Maisky called on the Webbs the day after the Socialist League voted to dissolve, 'cross-questioning us', Beatrice wrote, 'about Stafford's staying power if he were confronted with a revolutionary situation – would he not back down? Stafford says things without considering the consequences – and when the consequence occurs, in an unpleasant fashion, he does not always *stick to his guns*', a reflection 'of his queer immaturity of conduct and also of the company he keeps'.[52] Unity had inhibited him from censuring the Soviet regime. Absence of coverage of the trials of old Bolsheviks showed *The Tribune*'s 'blind spot', according to Michael Foot, a young contributor.[53] The Leaguer H. N. Brailsford – condemning the Soviet Union as 'a terror based on lies' – was a lone exception. Cripps said little, preferring to maintain a judicious silence. But he professed to believe, and possibly even did, that Britain was in imminent peril unless it reorganised on virtually Communist lines, lining up with countries 'taking the path of human progress'.

The annual conference, in Bournemouth in October, provided one remaining chance to contest the issue of unity. It also allowed Cripps, Mellor and Strauss to test opinion by putting their names forward for the proposed new constituency-chosen places on the NEC. Cripps, however, denied that an organised slate was being run by the Left, 'deploring any attempt to influence votes, whether in the public house bar, the hotel corridor or the conference hall', standing himself on his 'known views'.[54]

Cripps moved and Laski seconded that the section of its report justifying the NEC's actions towards the Socialist League and the united front should be referred back to the Executive. Cripps defended the right of party minorities to try to convert the majority, holding that the Executive had reacted harshly only because it feared the Party would change course in 'an unwanted direction'. The platform insisted it was not possible to be inside a party on one's own terms. The president of the Lancashire Mineworkers' Federation, John McGurk, sneered at Cripps, 'a rich man with rich pals around him', who would be found where Mosley was before long. Morrison, summing up, was in no doubt that a united front would split the Party 'from top to bottom'. He begged his 'friends' to 'drop it'. By 1,730,000 to 373,000, the referring-back motion was lost.

This time, moreover, the Party and the movement's attitude to rearmament was unequivocally in favour. The view Dalton had fought for – persuading the PLP to abstain on the defence estimates and ridiculing the Left's 'Arms for Spain' but not 'Arms for Britain' – won hands down, with Bevin's backing. In the summer, Cripps had said the switch by the PLP put paid to the Party's electability and 'should not be allowed to stand'. He thought, he told intimates, that Morrison was 'really with us, but won't come out into the open so long as he feels Bevin would take the chance to bump him off'.[55] By October, all opposition to rearming had been fragmented by the quarrel about unity and the demise of the League, very much of Cripps's own doing.

Conversely, two unitarians, Laski and Cripps, as well as Pritt, found their way on to the Executive in the new, enlarged constituency section which the conference unexpectedly endorsed. Analysis of the voting threw up the fact that two-thirds of constituency-party delegates voted against the attempt to refer back the NEC report but more than half gave their votes to Laski and Cripps.[56]

Was Cripps prepared to knuckle down? Bevin explained that the rebels were being given their chance – in Cripps's case a second chance – to make an 'honest' contribution.[57] The president of the Mineworkers' Federation, Ebby Edwards, wrote to Cripps to apologise for McGurk's outburst. In response, Cripps praised the 'new spirit' in the Party. He wound up the nine-month unity campaign, stepped down from the presidency of the Committee of Constituency Labour Parties, and submitted a large donation to the Labour Party. His rehabilitation was confirmed when he was elected as one of twelve backbenchers in the 'A' team of the PLP, devised to assist Labour's front bench.

Doubling up one of the largest practices at the Bar, much of it in landmark cases, his parliamentary and extra-parliamentary exertions exerted a heavy toll on his health, and he had to spend the turn of the year cancelling all engagements. His adopted vegetarian diet brought some relief from his stomach disorder, supplemented by nature cures and the occult 'natural healing' theories of a Hungarian eccentric, Edmond Szekely. But this was more than counteracted by a restless inability to unwind, his anxiety to 'save civilisation' – accounting for his histrionic politics, detractors said – and his being worn down by the exhaustion of time, money and disappointed hopes.

The historiography of appeasement is complicated by the wide disparity between the course of contemporary political debate in the late 1930s and the subsequently available official archives. It suffers from the further difficulty that many historical accounts of the period have been written backwards – to justify attitudes, revise reputations, or apply moral instruction.

A case in point is the stages by which the Labour Party became aware of the nature of the threat posed by Hitler's Germany and knew how that threat should be met, if not fought. The toughening up of Labour policy – initiated by Bevin and imposed on the Party with more (Dalton) or less (Attlee, Morrison, Greenwood) agreement by the leadership in the Commons – is a well-varnished tale, the shine brought fully back to it in Pimlott's insightful biography of Dalton. That many across the party continued to harbour muddled and fluctuating sentiments, concealed by virulent attacks on Baldwin and Chamberlain, was typified by the chopping and changing of Cripps, who, in the space of less than two years – with all the earnestness he could summon – executed several somersaults, consistent only in his beseeching the Party to throw off its inferiority complex. 'The Dissenters', the repudiators of power-politics, 'blamed their political opponents for the catastrophe of 1939'; but 'they themselves contributed to it' by being unable to offer a clear-cut, convincing policy in its place.[58]

Cripps willingly agreed that his foreign-policy prescription for international peace – a confederation of socialist states – was 'utopian'. It was simply the only alternative he could visualise to the 'imperialist' League of Nations practice of trying 'to superimpose political peace on economic war'.[59] The National government had got the British public to accept what it otherwise would not have accepted by going ahead with rearmament under the 'camouflage' of collective security. How was war-mindedness to be allayed? 'Reaction in Germany and revolution in Russia have both been marked by excesses which no normal human being could do other than loathe.' His indictment against Chamberlain, Prime Minister upon Baldwin's retirement in May 1937, was that he first courted and then encouraged fascist aggression, as a bulwark against Soviet Bolshevism and as a means of diverting Hitler from Britain's overseas empire.

The Crippses knew Germany and had many anti-Nazi friends, among them Adam von Trott zu Solz, whom John Cripps had met at Balliol College, Oxford. Cripps helped many European refugees to resettle in Britain. In Lansbury's time as leader, the PLP was careful not to confuse the Party's criticisms of the Versailles Treaty with sympathy for Nazi grievances. The muted Labour response to German re-entry into the Rhineland, combined with Cripps's reckless comments about the results of a German 'conquest' of Britain, wiped away much goodwill.

In November 1937, at the unofficial invitation of Goering, Lord Halifax, the Lord President, visited Germany, where he talked with Hitler about 'possible changes in the European order'. Cripps charged Halifax with offering Hitler a 'free hand' in south-eastern Europe provided he would not touch the British colonies for five years. 'We are heading either for war or Great Britain becoming a fascist country.'[60] If the National government were to successfully seek re-election some time in 1938, he did not think British democracy would survive.

This was a neatly executed change of front. Cripps had not, in the early 1930s, meant to do away with democratic institutions: it was just that he attached greater importance to introducing socialism. The prospect of the National government extending into a further, third, term of office – flaunting the battle cry of 'God, King and Country' – shifted his whole emphasis, with some urgency, to the safeguarding of British democracy. References to the holy of holies, 'working-class power', gradually faded, giving way to the appeal to humanitarian instincts.

In the *Herald*, he recommended an immediate peace conference before and not after the fighting, between those democratic nations ready to settle their economic problems peaceably, with Britain giving a lead by offering to pool its colonial resources. Eventually those co-operating would move on to a basis of common defence, creating a stronger League of Nations and deterring militaristic designs.[61] Berlin newspapers denounced him as 'a bootlegger of Soviet morals'.[62]

Germany's annexation of Austria in March 1938 threw him into fresh, caustic, denunciations. By dealing with the dictators, Chamberlain had gravitated into 'the fascist orbit', egged on by 'the Cliveden set' (those frequenting the family seat of Lord and Lady Astor), the people 'who would like to see Great Britain a fascist state'.[63] He did not care what form it took, but he wanted a government representative of 'the common people', who were humanity's hope.[64] Ideas of cross-party collaboration revived. But Cripps was careful not to commit himself while the Labour Party had yet to work out where it stood. To John Gollan, secretary of the Young Communist League, he replied that

> it is no good trying to force unity work just at the moment, as unfortunately quite a lot of our people have been seriously upset by the Russian trials [of Bukharin, Rykov and others, charged with 'Trotskyite' espionage and wrecking], with a consequent reaction against communism. However, I hope the matter of the general consideration of anti-fascist forces may be considered in the next few days and until after that consideration I cannot say anything further. Please keep this confidential.[65]

By the end of March, a 'united peace alliance' was being widely touted, for the Labour Party to team up not only with the CP and the ILP but also with the Liberal Party and others, including Tory dissidents – a popular front under another name. Left-wingers who had hotly opposed collaboration with non-socialists only a few months beforehand began to take notice. The NEC released a new circular on party loyalty, again ruling out a united or popular front.[66] The Tribune was quick to tack to the prevailing wind, however, calling for a conference to explore the idea of the 'Peace Front', uniting 'everybody to the left of Chamberlain'. Cripps got hold of a story that aircraft workers in Bristol were painting swastikas on newly-made planes bound for Germany. Writing in The Tribune, he was even more insistent, arguing – with the total conviction he had previously deployed on the other side of the case – that the fascist danger surely merited abandoning working-class control for the time being. To overthrow Chamberlain they had to unify all shades of progressive opinion and all classes, emphasising self-defence but making concessions to moderate opinion on domestic reform.[67] The editor of Reynold's News was delighted to announce that 'no less an authority than Sir Stafford Cripps, a member of Labour's NEC, casts honest doubt upon the prospect that, in a general election as to time and issues by Mr Chamberlain, Labour alone and unaided can dislodge the National government'.[68] At an assembly of popular-fronters on 23 April, Cripps urged an escape from 'the mere traditional methods of party politics'. He did not mean to commit the unions, 'but if they can and will support us, we will stand behind them'. One hundred and twenty local Labour parties declared themselves in favour of an alliance.

In a short Commons speech on the air estimates on 9 May, he finally spoke up for rearmament with 'full speed and vigour', even under the reviled National government. Kingsley Wood, the Air Minister, delighted in Cripps's conversion to rearming by 'capitalists'. He looked as if he was falling in with Labour policy, years too late. In reality, it was the prerequisite for a popular front, which Labour – 'all at sixes and sevens' and unable to seize the opening, Laski heard from Cripps[69] – was letting slip. His public insults were directed with bitterness at Chamberlain ('a Birmingham manufacturer') and Halifax, his future plans by reactivated contempt for the inadequacies of his own party.

On 14 May the NEC gave its verdict on the popular front, and on the table-turning of Cripps, once its antagonist from the left, now assailing it from somewhere to the right. The insurgents – Cripps, Laski, Pritt and Ellen Wilkinson, a *Tribune* board member – were outvoted, one report claimed by the chairman's casting vote. In a further circular, a popular front was comprehensively dismissed as politically unsound, electorally disadvantageous, and governmentally impossible. But the door was left ajar to allow for 'an internal crisis in the Conservative party'. Cripps complained about the document's one-sidedness.

Dogged by colitis and suffering from strain, Cripps planned to take a long break in Jamaica, leaving in July. He had one piece of unfinished business.

The Tribune, with sales hovering around the uneconomic 30,000 mark, had adjusted – Mellor rather grudgingly – to the 'Peace Front' strategy. Cripps did not propose 'to pay many thousands a year to run a paper which is not in harmony – broadly – with my views'.[70] It was decided to harness *The Tribune* to the commercial resources of the Left Book Club, giving Gollancz a seat on the board and the LBC a centrefold to publicise its offerings. The popular front – Gollancz had supported one since the start of the LBC – would be the paper's policy. Gollancz, Strachey and Laski, the three book selectors, stipulated, however, that Mellor would have to go.

Shortly before leaving on holiday, Cripps – disregarding eight years of political association – summoned Mellor to a brief interview to tell him he must give up the editorial chair, which, with 'typical insensitivity',[71] he offered to Foot, Mellor's assistant, implying that if Foot turned the job down the paper would close. Loyal to Mellor, Foot declined, agreeing only to hold the fort until Cripps found an alternative.[72] Cripps had no intention of losing control of the paper to Gollancz, but the eventual new editor was H. J. Hartshorn, formerly of the *Sunday Mirror* and a covert member of the CP, illustrating Cripps's credulity (he gushingly described Strachey's *Why You Should be a Socialist* as 'unanswerable' and 'the best material for conversion ever brought out'[73]).

Brailsford was saddened. 'The Socialist left is allowing itself to be driven from all its strategical positions by the Communist Party. With great subtlety it drove the Socialist League to suicide and now it is capturing *The Tribune*.'[74]

The Crippses and their two youngest daughters set sail for Jamaica in late July. After an absence of over two months, unaware of developments in Europe and 'thoroughly rested' – though Cripps was unable to refrain from involving himself in Jamaican politics, telling the inaugural meeting of the People's National Party to demand self-government – they were on their way back across the Atlantic in September when they learned of renewed anxieties about war, Chamberlain's flight to Munich, and the reaching of an agreement with Hitler. Cripps's 'very great relief' mingled with apprehension that it made another war 'all the more certain'.[75]

Parliament was recalled. The Labour Party, in the House and in the *Herald*, had given the Prime Minister a 'Good Luck' send-off. When the terms of the Munich agreement for the carving up of Czechoslovakia sunk in, the Opposition condemned it as a shameful surrender – 'one of the greatest diplomatic defeats that this country and France have ever sustained'. Cripps, called to speak on the third day of debate, accused the government of never having believed in collective security and of never having had any constructive policy for peace, staving off war by sacrificing the national interests of other countries. What he did not, what his party could not, say was whether Labour would really be prepared to guarantee Czechoslovakia's existing frontiers from armed attack. *The Times*, excelling in partisan distortion, identified his 'apparent recantation of complete pacifism'.[76] Intense pressure was applied by the government whips to ensure the motion supporting the agreement was comfortably carried, whittling down the abstainers to some thirty dissidents grouped around Anthony Eden, Leo Amery and Churchill.

On the stump, Cripps was bolder. Munich was 'the final stage in what had been a long drawn out tragedy'. Chamberlain was celebrating the agreement by telling the country that rearmament must be accelerated, because 'British foreign policy now hung upon the word of Hitler'. Cripps wanted Britain 'strongly armed'. But had Hitler been confronted by a firm democratic alliance – a reference to Chamberlain's ignoring of the Soviet Union – he would never have tried to impose his will. 'I would have taken the chance of it, anyway,' so Cripps said.[77]

What was to be done? Labour might band together with anti-Government Tories, fomenting a parliamentary breakaway. Cripps excitably sounded out Dalton, of all people. The popular front was 'dead'. But by itself the Labour Party had no chance of removing Chamberlain. They should draw up a programme for rebuilding collective security – soft-pedalling socialism – which Attlee, Morrison and Dalton should put to Tory rebels. When Dalton broached it, he was confident the rest of the labour movement could be persuaded.

Simultaneously, could not Attlee be toppled and replaced by Morrison, who had greater drive? Dalton said shunting Attlee aside was out of the question, but undertook to explore the possibilities. Nothing came of it. The Tory dissidents – Churchill aside – were reluctant to break cover.[78]

A clutch of by-election protests raised new hopes. At Oxford, in October, the master of Balliol College, A. D. Lindsay, standing as an 'Independent Progressive', ran the Conservative candidate close after the Labour Party withdrew from the contest. In marginal Dartford in the first week of November, the seat was actually taken by Labour, the Party accosted by the Tories for wanting war. The most spectacular fight came at Bridgwater, a largely rural constituency in Somerset, which turned into the proving ground for an *ad hoc* popular front. Two prominent locals – Richard Acland, Liberal MP for Barnstaple and landowner, and Cresswell Webb, vicar of Oare and Left Book Club subscriber, invited the journalist and broadcaster Vernon Bartlett to stand under the 'Independent Progressive' label. Bartlett consented, providing he had the backing of the local Liberal and Labour parties. Once the local Labour Party, going against Transport House (and on Cripps's advice), refused to put up a candidate, the way was clear. Thirty-nine Labour MPs – one-quarter of the PLP – sent a letter of support. Cripps dispatched a 'very useful cheque', loaning his private car and his election agent, although his personal services were 'politely declined',[79] 'lest he should say something that would frighten away hesitant Conservatives'.[80] Rogers, along with several other agents, took the organisation of the campaign in hand, drafting in helpers from Bristol. The high turnout (84 per cent) contributed to a strong anti-Government swing (7.6 per cent), sufficient to carry Bartlett to victory, stimulated, if not decided, by the salience of the Munich issue. (The day before, in a contest in industrial Walsall, the National vote held up much better.)

The national Labour Party refused to be swayed, fearing a revival of the popular-front commotion. Bevin, antagonised by the letter sent to Bartlett by Labour MPs, threw trade union support for the Labour Party into doubt again. The NEC, reprimanding Cripps for 'interfering' at Bridgwater, would only admit to examining a range of electoral options, without compromising the full socialist programme or the sovereign independence of the Party. The refusal to work with other 'oppositional elements' was one which Cripps, Bevan and others would ordinarily have endorsed. The defeat of Chamberlain, however, was a 'desperate urgency', Cripps wrote in *The Tribune* – of higher priority even than the 'purity of socialist doctrine'.[81] Deprived of an annual conference – it had been moved back to May 1939 – the life had gone out of the party organisation at the very time it was most needed. 'In my view at the moment,' Cripps told Labour's national agent, 'the Party is being completely killed by the dead hand at the administrative centre.'[82] A Labour area organiser for Surrey (where Labour did not hold a single seat), having read *The Tribune*, guessed what was coming next – a signal for the popular front. In reply to his letter, Cripps argued they must take 'every conceivable step'. He had been all over the country and seen the 'tragic state' of the Party, damaged by 'heresy hunting and weak leadership, which of course go together'.[83] The riposte he got was to the point. The claim of heresy hunting was 'cant', the talk of 'fighting fascism' and 'revitalising the labour movement' just 'pitiful flapdoodle'. As for Cripps's claim to be sincere, 'No one disputes it. Chamberlain is every bit as sincere too. Sincerity is as likely to accompany stupidity as any other quality, and in fact has nothing whatever to do with the case.' Cripps claimed the democratic right to change party policy. This was 'a cover for conduct more closely akin to treason'. As for the condition of the Party, 'the doses of your remedy have accentuated the disease'.[84] 'Dear Kneeshaw', Cripps frostily retorted, 'Thanks very much for your lecture, which does not seem to be very helpful.'[85]

Having waged 'one effort after another' to make his ideas the ideas of his party, in January 1939 Cripps mounted the last, most audacious, of his individualistic assaults on the party hierarchy. On 9 January he forwarded a copy of a 5000-word memorandum to Middleton, the general secretary of the Labour Party, and to every member of the NEC, urging on them the idea of a popular or democratic front – 'a National Opposition to the National Government' – for their 'most urgent consideration', before the chance was closed off by a general election.

Public opinion, he began, was sympathetic to 'some form of combined opposition'. Their overriding aim was to defeat the National government, but they had frankly to admit that the Labour Party was unlikely to be strong enough to beat the government single-handedly. This led him to a short-term, emergency tactic to mobilise extra support, for which the Labour Party should form the nucleus. 'I should certainly not desire', he observed,

> to encourage the Party to any combination with other non-socialist elements in normal political times. I have in the past always strenuously opposed such an idea. But the present times are not normal, indeed they are absolutely unprecedented in their seriousness for democratic and working-class institutions of every kind. In such times it is impossible to overlook the fact that a too rigid adherence to Party discipline and to traditional Party tactics may amount to losing the substance of working-class freedom and democracy for the shadow of maintaining a particular type of organisation which is, as a mere machine, in itself of no value.

He proposed a minimum programme – protecting democratic rights, tackling unemployment, national planning – for the lifetime of a single parliament, the Labour Party temporarily sacrificing socialist principle in order to unify moderate opinion – a programme, he commented, beyond the capability or inclination of a purely Labour government. Labour should declare its willingness to negotiate with other opposition parties and groups, including the Liberals, the ILP and the CP (but not 'reactionary imperialists', i.e. Tory dissidents). Nothing else could save the Party or the people of Britain from 'disaster'. Learning his lesson from the previous May, when all discussion of popular fronts was stamped out, he reserved the right – should the NEC not see its way to accepting its principles at an 'immediate meeting' – to circulate his memorandum to the movement with the object of gaining support.

A horrified Dalton, who had not given up all hope of cultivating Conservative dissidents, tried to talk 'Crazy Cripps' out of it. Unable to speak freely, because Lady Cripps sat knitting throughout, he could make no impression. Cripps, uncompromisingly self-righteous, was dismissive of most of his colleagues and deaf to the argument that he was hurting the Party. 'He seemed almost to welcome the prospect of expulsion, as a martyr's crown.'[86]

Cripps had little expectation his memorandum would be accepted forthwith and *in toto*. He bargained on panicking the Executive into looking again at a popular front by threatening to appeal over its head to the wider party. The NEC agreed to his 'peremptory demand', not wishing to give him an excuse for acting precipitately. Meeting on (Friday) 13 January, Cripps was asked at the outset what he meant by asserting the right to circulate the memorandum if it were rejected. One or two members of the Executive protested at such 'disloyal' behaviour, but nothing further was said. Instead, insulted by the challenge to the authority and ethos of the Party, the NEC confronted the memorandum and its author head on. Attlee was more than reluctant to 'run counter' to conference decisions, preferring to stick by a clear-cut programme of socialism. Morrison could not see how electoral deals could be practicable. Several trade unionists spoke up for what Chamberlain had done at Munich. Dalton followed, condemning those 'seeking personal popularity at the expense of party unity'. Cripps spurned a final injunction not to plunge the movement into yet another 'useless and disturbing controversy', after which the memorandum was put to the vote and rejected by 17 votes to 3. As the meeting ended, Cripps remarked to Pritt, 'I shall take this to the Party.' Pritt advised him to think it over. Cripps replied, 'I have thought it over, and I shall move at once.' He then stepped outside Transport House, borrowed a coin from a waiting journalist, and telephoned his secretary, giving the order to post off the offending memorandum to all Labour MPs, candidates, local Labour parties and other affiliated organisations, but not to the press or any non-party members.[87]

It is impossible to exaggerate the indignation Cripps unleashed, reopening the issue of a progressive alliance precisely when the Party was quietly encouraging greater elasticity by either Labour or the Liberals standing aside in certain seats. His intervention spiked the Executive's guns, jeopardising any likelihood of throwing Chamberlain out. By telling the Party it could not win unaided and ought to be prepared to give up its cherished principles, he was gifting 'certain' victory to the National government. For many, Cripps's manoeuvre was the final straw, the culminating moment – the Party 'neither able to do with him nor without him'[88] – in his erratic odyssey.

On 18 January the NEC reassembled for a second meeting. Cripps could not attend, owing to an urgent legal consultation with the Midland Bank. After much plain speaking about his conduct and a demand from at least one member for his immediate expulsion, the decision was taken – at Morrison's bidding – to refer the matter to the Organisation Sub-Committee (on which Cripps sat) for a report. Heartened by the first signs of grass roots' support – among trade unionists only Will Lawther of the Miners lent his backing – Cripps twitted the Daily Herald for favouring an undiluted socialist programme and needled 'purists' who saw no point in having a Labour government if it did not go all out. He had, he thought, committed no crime and had no wish to form another party. All he desired was for Labour to provide the leadership the country was looking for, not by conceding its basic beliefs but by preserving democratic society, on which any possibility of socialism depended.

The editor of the Herald, Francis Williams, on the morning the NEC again reconvened, gave him his answers. The 'agile' Cripps could not understand that the Herald 'opposes an alliance with Communism because we believe in democracy and an alliance with Liberalism because we believe in Socialism. That perhaps is because his own loyalty to both principles is intermittent'. Cripps had considerable talents, employed only spasmodically in loyal service but more consistently to 'overthrow' party decisions, and was launching a freshly disruptive campaign which, it must be clear to him, could only split the movement.[89] 'This is the best day's work you have ever done for the Labour Movement,' Bevin wrote to Williams in congratulation. 'Cripps will destroy everything we've given our lives to build.'[90]

By that stage, Cripps had received the Organisation Sub-Committee report, drafted in the form of a charge sheet of misdemeanours. He read through the document in disbelief, peppering his copy with outraged remarks. Citing the Labour Party constitution on the objects of the Party and the conditions of membership, it made clear the NEC possessed the authority to declare a member ineligible in cases of wide divergence from the programme, principles and policy of the Party, which the attempt to 'operate' a popular front con-travened. Cripps, it continued, had been largely responsible for series of campaigns seeking to change the Party's objects, first in a left-wing and then in a right-wing direction, covering so wide a territory that 'it is impossible to believe that he still adheres to the terms on which he holds membership'. It cited the rival activities of the Socialist League ('Why not?'), his resignation from the NEC at the time of the Abyssinian crisis ('Why not?') and the unity campaign ('Socialism!'), but also a string of 'irresponsible speeches' ('No!') from as early as 1932, exhaustively listed in an appendix, which had presented Labour's opponents with opportunities for unwarranted attack. Since the Bournemouth truce of 1937, the NEC had still had to devote itself to issues largely stirred up by Cripps ('What?'), including the peace alliance of March 1938, the Bridgwater by-election, his public defeatism and its discouraging effect on Party workers ('Then why do they ask me to go and speak everywhere?'), and his new memorandum, circulated without warning to the Party outside in a deliberately prepared campaign from the offices of *The Tribune* ('Complete lie'), displaying 'an indifference to the welfare of the Labour Party and a demand for a degree of liberty incompatible with loyal membership'. In view of past campaigns 'calculated' to weaken the Party and give aid to its opponents, the wide departure from the Party's aims and objects, and the present organised effort to change the Party's direction and leadership ('Not a scrap of evidence of this'), Cripps was required to reaffirm his allegiance and withdraw his memorandum, failing which he would cease to be a member.

At the outset of the NEC meeting, the chairman, George Dallas, asked Cripps whether he was prepared to conform to the recommendations of the report. Cripps bluntly declined, denying any intention to split or undermine the Party, and pointing to the tireless contribution he had made over the last eight years, including speaking at several meetings a week until his health forced him to cut down. Correcting false quotations, he argued that episodes before the 1937 conference were irrelevant as he had been voted on to the NEC with the full endorsement of all the constituency parties. 'It will be with great regret that I shall part from my colleagues but with the most profound conviction that I have taken the right course.'

Repeated attempts were made to have him reconsider. He suggested one compromise – a popular front only in the two hundred or more admittedly hopeless constituencies – but would not withdraw the memorandum 'as it would mean nothing and not be honest'.[91] Dalton – astounded by the 'slipshod', 'grotesquely defeatist' assumptions of the memorandum, expressive of 'the political judgement of a flea' – finally posed three questions, which he imagined any capable lawyer would know how to get round. Did he think continuing the campaign would strengthen or weaken Chamberlain? Did he believe he had any chance of carrying the party conference? And when would the campaign reach finality? Cripps – jutting out his lower lip and chin in martyred defiance[92] – did not think he was strengthening Chamberlain, believed he could persuade the conference, but could not say when the campaign would end, whereupon W. A. Robinson, general secretary of the Distributive Workers' Union, moved his expulsion, which was agreed by 18 votes to 1 (Ellen Wilkinson was Cripps's only supporter; Pritt was ill).

Politicians try to win in different ways. Dalton and Morrison, adept at manipulating the party machine, had been cultivating other parties out of the public eye, 'the less said the more done'. Cripps's grandstanding undermined these efforts from within. But he exulted in his isolation, the victim, his Bristol East party concluded, of a 'hostile caucus'.[93] His expulsion only confirmed what he had long suspected. He had given the Party the one chance it realistically had to win power. The Party had chosen not to take it, preferring to fool people into voting for Labour by hiding behind 'the full socialist programme' (which the Party only half-believed in), when in actual fact it was scared stiff of taking on the responsibilities of office. 'Are they afraid of power?' he wanted to know,[94] 'threatening them with their greatest terror – to become the government themselves'.[95] Cripps, to his colleagues, was an impossible maverick, of great ability and extreme instability – the rebuke levelled at all the rejects of the 1930s. An offer to Cripps from Dalton – relayed by Ellen Wilkinson – of a special conference, provided he would abide by its verdict, was 'brushed aside'.[96] Once he had declared his intention of bringing his expulsion before the party conference in Southport in May (the Party permitting), they were, Dalton recognised, in 'a fight to the finish'.

The Chartist-style 'Petition' campaign was Cripps's personalised vehicle for publicising a popular front – minus, this time, the Communist Party or the ILP. Over half a million copies of a pamphlet 'petitioning the British people' were printed, enjoining voters to 'unite to win'. 'The country may not trust the Government, but neither does it rally to the Opposition.' But, as Bridgwater showed, when Labour made common cause with the Liberals by avoiding a three-cornered contest, victory was possible. The Labour Party was asked to postpone socialism, so that Labour and the Liberals could march together on an agreed programme. A national committee was set up, enlisting Bevan, Strauss, Gollancz and the Coles, with local volunteer committees to collect signatures by a door-to-door canvass, to be completed no later than 28 May, the day before the Southport conference was starting.

The 'Petition' was publicly launched in Newcastle at the beginning of February, when Cripps called on 'the parties of progress' to put aside their differences to save democracy. Although he wished for reinstatement, he did not care 'a pin' for his personal position. He won the signatures of Trevelyan and Lawther, and gained the support of the *Manchester Guardian*, the liberal *News Chronicle* and the Communist *Daily Worker*, but lost his two backers on the NEC (Pritt pulled out on the orders of the CPGB). The Liberal leader, Archibald Sinclair – 'One thing keeps the Government in power. The Labour party' – promised to co-operate.[97]

The Labour Party published two documents detailing the Executive's charges against Cripps, dragging up past indiscretions and accusing him of trying to turn the Labour Party into a Liberal party. Bevin, rivalling Dalton in Crippsophobia, and widely thought to have brought about the purging of Cripps, ensured the unions held steady. Morrison lashed out at the use of 'big money' to buy support, refusing a private talk with Cripps.[98] Even Attlee, with a lingering affection for Cripps, said the 'swing over' in his views demonstrated he was too unreliable – 'in a few months he may ask us all to change again ...' Labour candidates backing the 'Petition' were not recognised by Transport House. Cripps, Dalton told Jowitt (who had rejoined the Party), 'is the hell of a nuisance', but not 'much more'. He was confident Cripps's expulsion would be approved at Southport and the popular front rejected. 'Since he has challenged us, he must be defeated, and law and order re-established in the Party. That, I think, is the general view.'[99]

The Party did its best to tie the merits of the popular front to the petulance and insubordination of Cripps, caricaturing his personal politics and belittling the impact of his 'Petition', though a quarter of a million signatures were reportedly garnered.[100] When the campaign spread to Scotland, Labour's Scottish secretary repudiated those individuals – Maxton, Mosley and now Cripps – who put themselves above the Party, taking 'the high road to fascism'.[101] Cripps was struck by 'the personal bitterness and vindictiveness with which they [the NEC] are attempting to cloud the political issue', explaining it by the bankruptcy of their arguments.[102] He did, however, provide cause for concern, melodramatically appearing at Earls Court on 12 March in a darkened hall to the sound of rolling drums, four spotlights trained on 'the Leader'.[103]

Actually, as Colonel Tweed told the onlooking Lloyd George, the 'Petition' campaign was flagging, with Gollancz and the Coles urging Cripps to call it off. Bevan and Strauss, on the other hand, felt there was nothing to lose by continuing – they were also expelled from the Labour Party shortly afterwards. Cripps himself was 'pretty miserable', but shirking a decision one way or the other. The campaign, relying on £5000 of Isobel's money, was just not properly financed or organised. 'Like so many orators, Cripps believes in the illusory magic of great public meetings, without comprehending in the slightest that a movement does not evolve by spontaneous combustion,' Tweed reported.[104] Dalton, shadowing Cripps, saw this at first hand when he went up to Hull at the end of March. He sat at the back of the City Hall while Cripps spoke at length to a large crowd, sowing 'suspicion and mistrust of the Party, and its leaders in parliament and on the N[ational] E[xecutive], in the minds of his hearers', but largely listened to in silence.

German occupation of the rest of Czechoslovakia in mid-March jolted the government into a unilateral territorial guarantee to Poland and – after many denials – the introduction of compulsory military service. Rumours of an all-party government resurfaced. In a flash, Cripps turned right round again. In the 'grave new situation', with Chamberlain about to drop appeasement and call for 'national unity', Cripps wrote to Middleton proposing an 'accommodation' aimed at maximising opposition to Chamberlain. The Executive took no action. Catching the Speaker's eye in the foreign-affairs debate in the Commons on 3 April, Cripps reverted to his former argument that the Labour Party had no business lending the government its support. The guarantee to Poland was simply laying the ground for another Munich. The 'Petition' campaign modestly titled the reprint of his speech *One Man Speaks for the People*. When the bill for military service was brought in, he demanded the conscription of wealth, 'democratised' fighting services, and an alliance with Russia. He alarmed a Fabian Society conference, however, by advocating resistance to all war preparations, adopting the line that Hitler's defeat would destroy fascism but strengthen British imperialism – this 'delivered with the cold ruthlessness of a hanging judge'.[105]

Stranded between Government and Opposition, Cripps, always influenced by the company he kept, developed closer links with Liberals. His popular-front proposals were all short-term items of moderate reform attractive to the Liberal Party. Many Liberals, he discovered, 'were more advanced than some members of the Labour party'.[106] He had traversed the early 1930s highlighting the futility of socialist half-measures. Did the popular-front programme suppose the capitalist economy was, after all, reformable?

Keynes, searching for a political middle way, thought so. He told Violet Bonham Carter (Asquith's daughter) he intended signing the 'Petition', instructing Cripps it was 'very important not to split existing parties but to capture them',[107] though he would have been happier if Morrison and other Labour moderates supported it too. For opposite reasons, the younger economists in the Labour Party – Dalton was their mentor – also thought so, mocking the popular front's deletion of socialism in favour of 'ameliorative' social-service measures which skirted round the strategic question of economic power and State socialism.

What of Cripps's own liberal-left affinities? It is unlikely he stopped to consider the implications. He presented his proposals as a condensation of Labour's *Immediate Programme*, referring to nationalisation by the softer term 'national control'. While resolutely claiming to remain a socialist (as did Bevan and Strauss), he dismissed 'abstract socialism', wanting to stem the anti-democratic tide by 'preserving the decencies' (of free speech) and relying on superior 'moral strength'. His belief that the party-political divide was outdated was music to the ears of other centrists. In the autobiographical essay he wrote for a Liberal symposium edited by Acland, he admitted he was gladdened by the wide measure of agreement among progressives about the 'unobjectionable' proposals of the 'Petition', evident from his bulging postbag.[108] He took 'fiendish delight' in inveigling Lloyd George into shaking hands with Pollitt on a public platform.[109] Cripps, too, was blown about by the buffeting of the approach of war, which was his prime consideration. But it is arguable the popular front – complete with its enlightened plan for plenty and its premature Keynesianism – was an early signpost on the road to eventual electoral victory in 1945.[110]

Cripps combined the 'Petition' campaign with a full working day. One common-law case, for which he did not receive a penny, was for the appellant in *Radcliffe* v. *Ribble Motor Services Limited* before the House of Lords in February 1939, which, according to the appellant's solicitor, 'if it [did] not swept away altogether the odious doctrine of common employment, very nearly did so, and in any case circumscribed it within very narrow limits for the future'.[111] Another, *Westminster Bank* v. *Liverpool Marine Insurance Company Limited*, heard before the Commercial Bar in May, was unrivalled in the number of counsel employed and the complexity of claims and counter-claims. Facing two friends, Walter Monckton and Sir Patrick Hastings, Cripps delivered an opening statement which took up five days and would have gone on into the next week had an out-of-court settlement not been reached. Monckton praised Cripps for his 'conspicuous fairness', Hastings for 'his absolute fairness, but of course from one point of view'. For this one case, Cripps is said to have grossed £10,000.

It was in his capacity as a masterly pleader – pleading for his political life – that Cripps hoped to win his way back into the Labour Party at Southport. Unsure of the constitutionality of allowing Cripps to address the conference in person, the NEC asked him if the party rules provided for such an eventuality. He suggested the solution was to suspend standing orders. The Conference Arrangements Committee decided not to allow him to speak. Opening the conference on 29 May, Dallas put it to a card vote. By the narrowest of majorities, Cripps – but not the other expellees – was granted a hearing. He did not, however, have free rein. He was limited to the technicality of his expulsion in January; the issue of the popular front was to be debated on a subsequent day. The 'Petition' and the signatures he had amassed could not, therefore, be presented. Cripps showed Bevan and Strauss the text of what he proposed to say. Both felt the tone was wrong – that conference was an emotional body and would not appreciate a disquisition on democratic rights. Cripps answered that it was too late to change.[112]

Cripps took the stage to a crescendo of cheering and booing. Reading from his fifteen-page script, he explained he would be speaking only for himself and would not enter into any argument about the rights and wrongs of the popular-front policy. Why had he been expelled? So far as he could ascertain, the sole reason was because he had circulated his memorandum. He claimed he was justified in doing everything in his power to convert his colleagues to his way of thinking. If the conference shared his idea of democracy in the Party, he asked it to reverse the NEC's decision and vote for his and his fellow expellees' reinstatement.

His time up, standing orders were reimposed and Dalton rose to reply. 'Nobody has been expelled for expressing an opinion,' he asserted. Cripps was expelled for refusing to give an undertaking reaffirming his allegiance to the Party or to withdraw his memorandum. The disturbances in the Party before Bournemouth could not be disregarded, but in any case Cripps had been brought on to the Executive on the 'understanding' that disruptive campaigns would cease. Minorities had to submit to majority decisions. If the NEC had not done what it did, demoralisation would have spread throughout Labour's ranks.

Hennessy, of the Bristol East party, and Dudley Collard, from the Haldane Society of Labour Lawyers, spoke in defence of Cripps, pointing to the principle of free speech and the 'flimsy' grounds of his expulsion – was he to be hounded out in 1939 for things he had said in 1932? This left time for two highly effective rejoinders. The first, from a former MP, Ralph Morley, contained praise for Cripps's evident sincerity and debating skill, but came back to the essential fact that the Party could not – no organisation could – tolerate individuals unwilling to adhere to its principles and constitution. The final contribution was a roasting from George Brown, a local party delegate, who complained that the Party had spent 'nine blasted months in a pre-election year just doing nothing else but argue the toss about Cripps'.

Conference endorsed the NEC report by 2,100,000 votes to 402,000. Fewer than half the constituency parties, and only the Distributive Workers' Union, sided with Cripps. By three o'clock his fate was sealed and he departed from the gallery of the hall, commenting that 'it is quite clear that the party does not want me back, and I shall be the last person to try to force my way back',[113] walking up and down the windy seafront 'terribly upset'.[114]

Bevan and Strauss were all for reapplying for membership on the spot. Within twenty-four hours, all five of the expelled had applied to be allowed back in, ready to sign any undertaking, Cripps reasoning that he had always said he would abide by the final word of the conference. The Executive was in no hurry to act. Cripps left Southport, not even staying for the debate on the popular front. At the earliest opportunity the 'Petition' campaign was disbanded as no longer 'practicable',[115] drawing a line under a decade of political agitation, leaving Cripps with no option but to 'sit back a bit and watch what happens'.[116]

What happened was a sharp scuffle over the leadership. Attlee was unwell with prostate trouble during and after Southport, confining him to a clinic. In the Sunday Referee, Ellen Wilkinson contributed a short article about Cripps, 'a restless intellect' longing for the 'regeneration of mankind' who was happiest directing campaigns. She absolved him of personal ambition, and revealed that when Lansbury fractured his thigh in 1933 Cripps had persuaded Attlee to assume the leadership of the PLP instead. 'Life would be simpler for the Labour Party if Cripps were a mere careerist, preferring the fat fees of the Bar, as some enemies assert,' she wrote. 'Nothing is more untrue'. His drawback was 'a fatal lack of understanding' of industrial life and working-class culture. He would, however, make a magnificent lieutenant to Morrison, the one person capable of standing up to Chamberlain, acting in tandem with Dalton and Greenwood.[117] She followed with a second, unsigned, article, eulogising Morrison and criticising Attlee's ineffectuality. Bevin and Citrine – Dalton believed – also favoured the right change of leader. The Greenwood camp, however, was seething with Wilkinson, and, when the PLP met, Morrison had to deny any foreknowledge of the articles. A motion of confidence in the convalescing Attlee was carried *nem con.*

Partyless, though retaining the backing of Bristol East, Cripps saw with clarity that party politics in the normal sense was 'discredited' and 'useless' for the time being, the threat of war never having been nearer. He had done all he could to get the Labour Party to see sense, risking his own neck, without reward. The country, so ill served by its leaders, would have to endure 'some tragic upheaval' before they might all emerge again 'into the light'.[118]

A polemical bestseller of the Dunkirk summer of 1940, co-written by former *Tribune* contributor Michael Foot and rush-released by Gollancz, pilloried the 'guilty men' of the National government who had been entrusted with the nation's defences throughout the 1930s. The argument was tendentious, but the demonising of political opponents was widespread. Had not Cripps, troublesome standard-bearer of leftist causes, much to answer for?

Tories, cherishing Cripps as a godsend, thought him dangerously absurd, a self-proclaimed 'anti-fascist' who, at various times, had welcomed conquest by a foreign power, tried to hinder recruiting, and urged those engaged in vital weapons production to down tools – the last an incident the Air Minister, Viscount Swinton, had not forgotten nor forgiven long after retiring.[119] Charming and courteous in conversation, Cripps, to his Tory detractors, disgraced his education, rank and riches by hypocritically identifying with 'the workers'.

The popular front having fizzled out like other campaigning failures, his other critics were among a large body of Labourites – MPs who admired his parliamentary performances but could not tolerate his waywardness; union chiefs resentful of his pulling power; even other left-wingers, aghast at his impulsive bungling. Fellow Labour MPs were to cite Cripps as one reason why the city of Bristol was unprepared for the heavy wartime air raids.[120] The surprise was that he had survived for so long on sufferance, that he had not been banished from the Party earlier than he actually was.

'He is in reality a youngster in politics,' a sharp-eyed parliamentarian wrote of Labour's outcast. 'Before his body became so lean and ascetic he looked almost callow and immature.'[121] The King's Counsel, it turned out, was verdant green, mischievous were he not so engagingly trusting, an 'easy touch' for phoneys.[122] 'When a Communist with a long record of scheming and intrigue against Labour assured him that henceforth he intended to be a friend and a brother, the good Stafford took him at his word.'[123] Unfortunately, possessing an unequalled breadth of knowledge, no one else exuded such an air of infallibility. During its years of opposition, Labour fell back on the convenient argument that in foreign affairs everything had gone awry after 1931. Cripps nurtured his own version, maintaining that the National government would no longer be in power if the Party had listened to his many warnings. No weight of adverse votes would persuade him otherwise. Of all the wasted opportunities, none seemed so calamitous to him as the ignoring of Soviet Russia.

Cripps's pro-Sovietism was still, in 1939, wholly intact. He referred to the forced industrialisation of Russia as 'one of the greatest marvels of the world'.[124] The Soviet Union was also an important element in the popular-front idea, the keystone of an anti-Nazi coalition, until Stalin, wearying of the obstacles put in the way of a Western alliance, had indicated (even before the fall of Czechoslovakia) his unwillingness to repay the 'warmongers' in the West who were relying on him 'to pull the chestnuts out of the fire for them'.[125] Distressed that the government was throwing away any chance of influencing Soviet actions, Cripps set about lobbying ministers. He wrote to Halifax of his concern, based on word from his German informant, Adam von Trott, about negotiations between Russia and Germany, carrying the ominous threat of German troops being released to turn westward.[126] He tried enlisting Baldwin, before approaching Churchill, urging him publicly to state his readiness to join the government, hoping Chamberlain would have to yield. A disheartened Churchill 'pointed out that but for Chamberlain's switch on foreign policy after Prague's occupation the Popular Front movement would have swept the country' and Cripps 'gathered he would have supported it'.[127] Bordering on despair, Cripps finally advocated an 'all-in government' excluding only Chamberlain and Simon, the last remaining way to demonstrate 'a united nation ready to defend ourselves'.

That July and August, the Crippses took off for a cruise around the Mediterranean, aware of increasing international tension. When Parliament was recalled in late August, he fought the urge to return, feeling he had done all he humanly could. Within days, he changed his mind and rushed back. The announcement of the German–Soviet non-aggression pact 'shocked' him, though he recognised – Maisky later recorded – 'it was inevitable and legitimate in the situation created by the Anglo-French sabotaging of tripartite negotiations'[128] – a spin on events that Maisky assiduously wished on friendly newspapers. The Communist Party, meeting to consider the pact, accepted it as a means of buying time for the Soviet Union, but rebels, led by Pollitt (whom Cripps still wanted in an alternative popular-front government, led by Lloyd George[129]) refused to abide by the new anti-war line, recanted, and were then sacked. Cripps saluted Pollitt for standing up for his views ('whatever they were') and assured him of his deep friendship.[130]

Once Germany invaded Poland and Soviet troops occupied the western half of Polish territory, Cripps's defence of Russia – which had acted for its 'self-protection' and because it saw more likelihood of sympathetic ideological change in fascist Germany than in imperialist Britain – was so convoluted he had to let Bevan rewrite it for publication.[131] The only course still open, Cripps assumed, was to admit the mistake of guaranteeing Poland's integrity and immediately rectify this by a special agreement with Soviet Russia, prising it apart from Germany. To this end a trade agreement represented the best hope. Informally, he helped with new anti-profiteering legislation for the Board of Trade, but only after a request to Chamberlain asking to serve 'in any capacity' had come to naught.[132]

War prompted several changes in his professional and private life. He terminated his practice at the Bar, pressing Monckton to do the same. Since Goodfellows depended on his income for its upkeep, this had to go too, being given to Bristol City Council as a centre for evacuated children. His secretary, Gwen Hill, was dispensed with. He was busy winding up his affairs, he informed his father at the beginning of September, fully conscious of the protracted struggle that lay ahead 'before aggressive Fascism is stopped.'

At this late hour, Cripps, in alignment with Lloyd George, the *New Statesman* and assorted individuals on the centre-left, saw little sense in fighting if it resulted only in another Versailles. Nor did he preclude negotiations with 'the German people', freed from Hitlerism. In October 1939, after Hitler dangled peace proposals before the British, cryptically referring to a German secret weapon, Cripps did not dismiss them out of hand, given the alternative of 'the destruction of all the values of civilisation'. He wanted a clear declaration of war aims and an international conference of the major powers, upsetting the Tory benches by 'illegitimately' using the war situation to 'foist his ideas upon the rest of us'. 'The key to the whole question lies in Russia, which alone of the countries which are at present neutral [*sic*] has the power to influence Germany by her threats.' He was ready, he said, to support a compromise peace for a 'new world', including Britain withdrawing from India and handing over its colonies to an international trust. Lloyd George, when Cripps appealed to him, ducked out, arguing it was impossible to obtain a hearing so long as Hitler possessed his secret surprise.[133]

Estranged from his *Tribune* allies, Cripps completely refused to accept the conditions required for rejoining Labour which reached him in September – an expression of regret, amounting to a confession of wrongdoing, and an undertaking to refrain from campaigning against party policy. His actions, he believed, were 'more than ever justified'. Had the progressive parties combined in the spring, they would not now be in such a 'ghastly position'.[134] Bevan was readmitted in December, followed by Strauss. Cripps, urging the trumping of the German peace offer with comprehensive proposals to set alight world opinion (between the covers of an increasingly Stalinist *Tribune*), retained his virtuous independence, unwilling to bow to Labour's 'muzzling order' and adamant nothing could be done 'with the crowd that are there now'. Their hostile attitude towards Soviet Russia in particular was 'asking for the most awful trouble'.[135] The longer he stayed out, he informed Laski, the more use he could be for cause and country.

The 'key' was Russia. Cripps was not soft on Russia but hard, brooking no disagreement. When one reader took against *The Tribune*'s condoning of Soviet policy, Cripps did not want to argue, except to suggest 'there is a great deal to be said in support of the line that they have taken'.[136] Three months later, he was making a flying visit to Moscow. Within six months, he was the accredited British ambassador to the Soviet Union. Within eighteen months the Soviet Union had been invaded by Germany, and Cripps was toasting an Anglo-Soviet treaty of alliance in the Kremlin.

9

GLOBETROTTING

Nothing except trying to think and work out some method by which
we may get a better and saner world after the tragedy is over.
Cripps, asked by The Countryman *what were his plans for the first winter*
of the war[1]

Like many unlikely comebacks, Cripps's began with a going away. If war had
not come, he had anticipated a general election in which the Labour Party
might end up with only fifty seats. Had Labour put up an official candidate in
Bristol East, his own seat would have been in jeopardy. In that event, he had
planned a tour of the 'rising nations' in Asia, travelling to India to visit Pandit
Nehru (a friend, and one of the leaders of the Congress Party), China and the
Soviet Union. After war was declared and his offer to serve the government
was rejected, he decided to set off all the same.

He saw it as a way of widening his outlook and, though he would be 'without
standing', exploring possibilities. He had an unshakeable belief that the Nazi–
Soviet pact was unnatural; that, in spite of all the difficulties, it was important
to remain on speaking terms with the Russians. Churchill, brought into the
Cabinet by Chamberlain, at the Admiralty, expected the Soviet Union – pursuing 'a cold policy of self-interest' – to break with Germany at any moment.
Cripps became the 'architect' of rapprochement behind the scenes, liaising
with Maisky and persuading Halifax to send out a trade mission to Russia,
which he could accompany as legal adviser[2] – an idea aborted by Russian
incursion into Finland at the end of November.

Russia's attack coincided with increasing unrest in India, brought into the
war by viceregal command. Proposals for an Indian federation had lapsed. The
Hindu Congress Party was pressing to be an equal partner in the central
government. The Viceroy, the Marquess of Linlithgow, refused to go beyond a
commitment to eventual self-governing dominion status for India. Cripps,
badgering Halifax (a former viceroy himself) about India too, suggested greater
self-government during the war as well as a constituent assembly, a surer way
of inviting 'the whole-hearted co-operation of the Indian people in our effort
to establish democracy and freedom in the world'.[3] Writing to Nehru of his

hope that an 'arrangement might just be come to', he occupied the last few days of November in drawing up a paper to show to Sir Findlater Stewart, the Permanent Under-Secretary of State for India, who, though he thought Cripps 'scrupulously straight', withheld official approval.[4] The most Cripps obtained was a promise to give the scheme serious consideration if Indians approved of it.

Cripps asked Robert Boothby, Tory MP and Churchill acolyte, to join his tour, Boothby's exuberance providing an antidote to his own 'pietas'. Boothby turned him down, doubting he could withstand the rigours of a mule ride down the Burma Pass into China. Instead, Cripps took a junior in his chambers, Geoffrey Wilson, well to the left and one of Cripps's hero-worshippers. Cripps made it plain he was travelling in a purely personal capacity and not as an 'emissary';[5] even so, he hoped that as an unofficial intermediary he could more easily build bridges. He reassured his Bristol East party that his visit was in no way connected with the National government.

Before leaving, he had *The Tribune* to attend to. Advertising had dried up and circulation was down to 9000. In a parting leader, he reacted to the Soviet conflict in Finland by asking readers to 'Put Yourselves in Russia's Place'. The attack on Finland, however, created an 'open breach', detaching the Communist Party from left-wing liberals and shaking Cripps's faith.[6] Under Hartshorn's editorship *The Tribune* took a rigid Soviet line, endorsing the Comintern policy of 'revolutionary defeatism', to the point that Palme Dutt wrote a *Tribune* article telling subscribers to cease reading the paper.[7] While Cripps was away, Hartshorn was pushed out by Bevan and Strauss.

Cripps left London with Wilson on 30 November 1939, travelling by boat and train to Naples, where they caught an airliner, arriving in Karachi on 7 December. The next three weeks were spent in a daily round of discussions – with Nehru, with Mohamed Jinnah, the Muslim leader, in Bombay, and with the Viceroy in Calcutta. Cripps presented his outline scheme to all the principals, collecting their views about the mechanics of Indian independence, keeping copious notes from which to draft the basis of a longer-term settlement.

The visit 'heightened Cripps' awareness of the urgency of the Indian problem';[8] it also brought him up against the intractability of Anglo-India. Jinnah, seeing Cripps being 'shepherded around' by Congress, was anxious only to establish himself as the unique voice of Muslim interests. As long as Jinnah fomented unrest, Nehru complained, he would not meet him. Cripps put his ideas for a loose federation of provinces to Gandhi, sitting shoeless in his mud hut, impressed by the 'extreme simplicity'. Gandhi pronounced it an 'acceptable' basis for negotiation, but indicated the next step was up to the British. Stewart, back in London, did not mince his words: Cripps was 'guilty of wishful thinking to the point of crookedness', pretending, Stewart thought (falsely), to have official backing.

From India, Cripps and Wilson set off for China at the end of December, making their way to Rangoon before continuing by train and car along the main Burma road into China. Just across the border, they inspected an American-sponsored aircraft factory, before flying to Chungking (the temporary capital) in Generalissimo Chiang Kai-Shek's private airplane, meeting his government and studying the Chinese war effort against the Japanese. Cripps was impressed by some industrial co-operatives he was shown. In fact he was given a 'fantasy picture' of the Kuomintang, which he readily accepted.[9] He wrote long documents about transport organisation, submitting them to Chiang Kai-Shek, who asked him to become his industrial supremo.

While staying in Chungking, Cripps expressed interest in visiting Sinkiang, the most westerly Chinese province, rumoured to be under Soviet control. The Soviet ambassador, learning from Maisky that Cripps was 'a friend of the Soviet Union' but one puzzled by the Finnish war, promised to see whether Cripps could fly on from there to Moscow – a 3000-mile round trip – to see 'one of those in authority'. This was arranged, probably because of a mistaken Soviet belief that Cripps, semi-officially, might help in heading off a British intervention on the side of the Finns.

Having arrived by plane in Urumchi, the Sinkiang capital, Cripps and Wilson waited for three days, escorted by armed guards. When the weather cleared, they flew on to Alma Ata, on the Soviet border, joining a Soviet plane which ferried them to Moscow, staying for a day and a half.

The climax of their rushed visit was a two-hour interview in the Kremlin with the Soviet Foreign Minister, Vyacheslav Molotov. The British ambassador had been recalled to London after the Soviet attack on Finland. Cripps told Molotov he understood the 'defensive' nature of the non-aggression pact with Germany and of the incursion in Finland. He was not, however, aware how seriously Anglo-Soviet relations had deteriorated. When Molotov urged him to return quickly to London to help repair them, Cripps explained he would not be reaching home until the end of April. He wanted instead to know about the Soviet attitude to India, China and Japan, about which Molotov was less forthcoming. In a note of his conversation for Halifax, Cripps felt he had heard enough to hope for a 'gradual separation' of the Soviet Union from Germany. Foreign Office officials were sceptical, reluctant to be tempted by Soviet feelers, characterising Cripps – whose turning up in the Soviet Union was 'most untimely' – as a 'willing tool' of the Russians.[10]

Bad weather hindered the return to Chungking, obliging Cripps and Wilson to switch from the plane to a car, arriving back exhausted and several days late. Although Chiang Kai-Shek renewed his offer for Cripps to become his adviser, they soon departed for Hong Kong, Shanghai and Japan, where Cripps called on the Japanese Foreign Minister. Flying back to Hong Kong, they island-hopped across the Pacific, arriving in the United States at the end of March.

Cripps made his way from the west to the east coast, talking with prominent Americans, raising money in aid of the Chinese co-operatives, and meeting the press – all the time warning that if the Soviet Union was isolated by the West it would turn to Germany for closer economic, perhaps even military, co-operation.

They did not set sail for Gibraltar until 12 April, hearing on the way back of the German extension of the war to Norway and, alarmingly (they were travelling on an Italian boat), the Italian declaration of war on Britain. Separating from Wilson on arriving at Naples, Cripps got back to England in time for his fifty-first birthday, after an arduous circumnavigation of over 45,000 miles, circling the war zone and visiting fourteen countries in five months.

He hoped, Cripps told the infirm Lansbury, he had developed 'a capacity to learn' from his travels.[11] Lionel Fielden (Lord Parmoor's private secretary when he was Lord President) had met Cripps in India and found him 'enormously improved', being both humbler and more willing to listen to contrary views. Cripps also thought he had been able to make use of his freedom of action, pointing him, he anticipated, in the direction of 'Eastern affairs', his personal diplomacy having revealed 'a chink of light' in India and China and – above all – in the Soviet Union.[12]

10

LEFT SPEAKING TO LEFT

I entirely appreciate your feeling of frustration from which I also
suffered at many moments, but I always remember what your Turkish
colleague, Haidar Aktay, said to me when I first arrived in Moscow that
an Ambassador's job was a very extraordinary one in that for five years
he might appear to be doing nothing and then in five minutes he might
alter the whole of international relationships.

Cripps to A. Clark-Kerr, his successor as ambassador in Moscow, 12 June 1942 [1]

The displacement of Chamberlain in May 1940, rather than the landslide
election victory of the Labour Party in 1945, is now seen as the defining moment
in modern British history, a '1931 in reverse', when power passed into the hands
of a new regime.[2] The war, in this interpretation, was a 'people's war', but one
engineered by Parliament, which, with the country on the brink of national
extinction, turned against the politicians in office, creating a governing consensus lasting throughout the war and long into the post-war period. Paradoxically, it was a 'spontaneous eruption' that neither the government nor
Opposition parties expected.[3] Cripps, ejected from the Labour Party, did not
foresee the removal of Chamberlain, had only a minor effect on his downfall,
and was as unhappy with the new administration as with the old.

The Britain he returned to was in the throes of upheaval, but a Britain in
which, to his intense frustration, nothing had changed. After a curious lull, the
war had flared up again and British forces had seen action in (and been
evacuated from) Norway, without the government providing any indication of
what the country was fighting for. Its policy towards Russia, China and India,
Cripps observed, was unaltered. The offer to revive trade talks with Russia
had gathered dust. The Labour Party, for its part, was strongly opposed to
negotiations with the Soviet Union. Bevan and Strauss, controlling *The
Tribune*, told Cripps there was little chance of ousting Chamberlain and were
unable to devise a distinctive left-wing attitude.[4]

To meet the 'rising storm' with an alternative, Cripps composed an anonym-
ous letter listing a proposed new government, envisaging Lloyd George as

prime minister, with himself as putative Chancellor of the Exchequer. *The Times* would not publish it unless it was signed so he breakfasted with Esmond Harmsworth, proprietor of the *Daily Mail*, and the letter -'by a British politician' – duly appeared on the front page of the *Mail* on 6 May 1940.[5] By that time, Halifax was the preferred prime minister (if he was enabled to sit and speak in the Commons) and Attlee Chancellor, bolstered by a quartet – Churchill, Morrison, Eden and Lloyd George – of ministers without portfolio, to inspire people with 'the will and capacity to win the war'.[6]

A two-day debate on Norway and the wider handling of the war began on 7 May. Chamberlain made a poor speech and was strongly attacked by two Conservative MPs, Sir Roger Keyes and Leo Amery, encouraging Attlee and Sinclair to hope for a small-scale Tory rebellion. On the second day Morrison rose to announce the Labour Party would be forcing a division, provoking an angry appeal from Chamberlain to his 'friends' in the House. A string of 'venomous' speeches followed,[7] one of them by Cripps, reporting American opinion on the desirability of a change of government and declaring Chamberlain 'unfit to carry on' – 'a closely reasoned attack', in the view of one member of the Eden group[8]. Churchill, begetter of the Norway fiasco, adopted a belligerent defence in winding up, but when it came to the vote the government majority was greatly reduced by Tory abstentions. On 10 May, German forces crossed into the Low Countries. Chamberlain, whom Labour refused to serve under, gave way to Churchill, and a national coalition was formed with enthusiastic support from the Opposition benches.

Cripps was out on a limb. The new government contained many 'Munichites'. Posts had been apportioned according to party strength, not ability. Labour's leaders were swallowed up in a reactionary administration, when what Parliament needed most was a 'real' Opposition. To Labour jeers, he asked the Speaker to look into changes to parliamentary procedure to facilitate this. The only MP he could interest was Pritt, also now an independent after his expulsion (for vindicating the Soviet invasion of Finland) in March.[9] A war government was in office, but manned by all the wrong people – Cripps as unattracted by the Labour Party 'Old Gang' as by the Tory 'Old Gang' – fighting for all the wrong reasons.

Halifax, exempted from Cripps's carping, had several overseas appointments to make. Attlee, in Cabinet, suggested sending 'an important figure' to the Soviet Union. Cripps offered to go out as a special envoy. He had the valuable support of R. A. Butler – Halifax's deputy, who had shielded Cripps from Foreign Office scorn when he had seen Molotov in January.

Dalton, as luck would have it, was installed at the Ministry of Economic Warfare (MEW), with a direct say in any Soviet trade talks, in view of Soviet circumvention of the economic blockade on Germany. Dalton questioned Cripps's 'suitability' – he was awkward, a lone wolf with poor judgement whom he (Dalton) had had to have put out of the Labour Party, though he had not seen much of him since. He tried quashing the idea.[10] The Prime Minister, however, reacted favourably, though he had time for only the briefest of words with Halifax before the matter came up at Cabinet. After other names were mentioned, Dalton relented ('We will try and make it go, but if it goes wrong, don't blame me'). Cripps was selected, with a remit to 'create better relations'.

By sending him with 'full liberty', Halifax hoped Cripps's known sympathies would show the desire for Anglo-Soviet relations to take a turn for the better. Churchill wrote in his memoirs he had not realised the Soviet antipathy towards left-wing non-Communists. Attlee did not 'kid' himself 'our left winger would have any more influence on Uncle Joe than a right winger'[11] – but this was plainly the wish. Dalton, warming to the idea of removing Cripps for good, saw Maisky, commending Cripps for the very reason that 'in quieter days' he had been expelled by Labour. Dalton added that trade talks were liable to spill over into political issues. 'I am not unhopeful', Butler minuted, 'that Sir Stafford Cripps will produce results.' Sir Alexander Cadogan, Permanent Under-Secretary at the Foreign Office (FO), did not hide his unease: 'He is an excellent lawyer and very nimble debater in Parliament but he has not yet won his spurs in diplomacy. Enthusiastic individuals like Sir Stafford Cripps ... think they can swing a country.' 'I do not think Sir Stafford Cripps thinks he can "swing" the Soviet Union,' Butler replied. 'In fact I know he is under few illusions, though his active brain may conceivably find contacts which will not be unhelpful.'[12]

Other officials shared Cadogan's worries. Cripps might be regarded by the Russians as a gentleman 'renegade' who could not possibly enjoy the full confidence of His Majesty's Government. It was important he should not be able to overstep the mark, as Labour members of the Cabinet were inclined to suspect he might. When the trade departments asked for more 'flexibility', the FO mocked the remote possibility of the Soviet Union changing sides.

The Soviet government initially refused to accept a special envoy, insisting on a full ambassador and making fools of the British government, as Cadogan had guessed they would. Halifax – using the argument that the Russians were in the mood for a 'friendly gesture' which might improve the chances of the trade mission – got the War Cabinet to agree at short notice on 27 May. The end result of this upgrading was to grant Cripps an extraordinary degree of latitude at an especially perilous moment. Waiting in the British Embassy in Athens, *en route* to the Soviet Union, he clustered with Geoffrey Wilson -also appointed to Moscow – around the ambassador's radio, listening to BBC reports of the evacuation of the beaches at Dunkirk.

Circumstances fortified his belief that it was given to him to put right a legacy of mutual mistrust. He had not forgotten his reservations about the Churchill government. His one condition of acceptance – apart from the right to retain his membership of the House of Commons – had been that his appointment should reflect 'a genuine desire to treat Russia as a friendly neutral'.[13] Churchill was too busy to see him before he left, but sent a stirring note, grateful that Cripps had undertaken 'this most difficult and delicate task at so critical a juncture' – 'no one could do it better'.[14]

After a hair-raising flight over Macedonia (his plane was struck by lightning, turning completely on its back[15]), the new ambassador landed at Moscow airport on 12 June, welcomed by the embassy staff and a Soviet representative.

The early signs were deceptive. Molotov sent his calling card. Two days later Cripps made his first official courtesy call. He impressed on Molotov the usefulness of a Balkan bloc to deter Germany. Molotov was far more interested in the collapse of the French front. Cripps had to state firmly that France would not be suing for peace and Britain was prepared to endure long hardships until it emerged victorious. The Soviet reaction to events in the West had been to extend Russia's control over the Baltic states (envisaged in the secret protocol to the Nazi–Soviet pact, which came to light only in 1948). At the same time, the Soviets denied any tension in their relations with Germany. When Cripps raised the trade issue, he was, Sir Orme Sargent (Deputy Under-Secretary at the FO) noted, kept waiting 'on the doormat'. To overcome the impasse, Butler proposed a personal message from Churchill to Stalin, enabling Cripps on the strength of it to see Stalin three weeks later on 1 July – Stalin's first meeting with a foreign ambassador since the signing of the Nazi–Soviet pact in August 1939.

Churchill warned Stalin of the danger to the Soviet Union as well as Britain of German hegemony in Europe, stressing the desirability of a common policy of self-protection and investing Cripps with authority to discuss it in full. He made no reference to a new Europe. In a 'severely frank' talk lasting just under three hours, Stalin informed Cripps that Hitler was unlikely to establish domination in Europe without command of the seas. He turned a deaf ear to the suggestion of taking the lead in the Balkans. Russia would abide by its agreement with Germany on the supply and exchange of materials, avoiding open conflict. If Britain fell, however, Cripps gathered, Stalin expected to have to face a German attack in 1941. Churchill's failure to visualise a new 'equilibrium' in Europe after the destruction of the old one appeared to be a major stumbling block.

The views of the ambassador and the FO were already diverging. Halifax, rejecting the peace talk of Hitler, employed such outdated sentiments that Cripps, unable to see any Soviet officials and feeling the situation was set in stone, wanted to resign on the spot and return home. He was told to stay put. 'And damned good for him!' Cadogan burst out.[16] In a speech on 1 August, in which Molotov pointed to the fundamental common interest of Russia and Germany, all he would say about the arrival of Cripps was that it 'does possibly reflect a desire to improve relations with the Soviet Union'.[17]

With Maisky's intervention, Cripps was allowed to see Molotov again, but came away with the impression the Soviet–German alliance was far too 'firm to be shaken *for the present*' (emphasis in the original). This did not exclude all possibility of change, provided Britain was ready to choose whether to let things plod along or, as he favoured, go for broke, giving up everything – sacrificing the Baltic states, releasing Baltic assets held in London, and pushing hard for a non-aggression pact of its own with the Soviet Union. The FO united in its hostility. Use of the term 'non-aggression' was inadvisable. It was 'folly' to imagine Britain could purchase Soviet goodwill. Most damning of all, Cripps was seen to be in the 'odd' position of those critics of the appeasing of Hitler who were now all in favour of appeasing Stalin, who was 'quite as hard-boiled a dictator'. Halifax, doubting the value of one-sided concessions, would only contemplate recognising the Soviet *de facto* 'absorption' of the Baltic states. Cripps was informed by the Cabinet he should make no attempt to negotiate.

His exasperation at the 'semi-docile' British attitude was unrelieved by the oppressive surroundings. The Embassy was in an 'appalling' state, dilapidated and understaffed. Cripps did not speak or read Russian, but brushed up his rusty French. Starved of company until Isobel arrived in October, he acquired an Airedale, which he took on long walks around Moscow accompanied by his police guard. His only contacts were with other members of the diplomatic community, who found it equally difficult to obtain reliable information. Anxious to remain alert, he had working in his favour only the lingering Russian fear that Britain might one day line up with Germany.

He tried nevertheless to maintain an unprejudiced view of Soviet life, angered by the anti-Soviet 'hymn of hate' whenever Englishmen or Russian *émigrés* gathered.[18] Russia had the 'most grave defects', starting with its physical circumstances and its people. They were bad organisers and devastatingly neglectful of business, but the organisation of agriculture on the scale required would defeat any government. There were 'Asiatic' cruelties, grisly purges and a war atmosphere; but there had been in tsarist times too. Shortages and waste abounded, but much output went on export. Stalin was attempting by a tremendous effort to stimulate an industrial revolution, progressing step by step, even though his methods of dictatorship were highly repellent. But Cripps's charitable observations provided little assistance in fathoming the mind of a man like Anastas Mikoyan, the Soviet Minister of Trade. Butler asked his FO officials for a book they could recommend about Russia. Fitzroy Maclean, who knew Russia intimately, drew a blank. 'I can only suggest a visit to the USSR. I understand that Sir Stafford Cripps is finding his most instructive.'[19]

In September and October, events turned decisively. Japan joined in a tripartite agreement with Germany and Italy, aimed at partitioning the British Empire. A German threat to the Balkans was creating instability, making the allegiance of Turkey, hitherto neutral, all the more important. Cripps saw one last fading opportunity of driving a wedge between Russia and Germany, requiring 'something really bold and imaginative'. He proposed a sweeping promise to Russia, temporarily recognising the part of Poland under Soviet control (the Poland Britain had gone to war for in 1939), a benevolent non-aggression treaty, and the guarantee of full participation in post-war arrangements along with the United States. He backed this up with a letter to the Foreign Secretary stressing the difficulties of righting twenty years of Anglo-Soviet distrust. Halifax did not reply for several weeks, giving Cripps something of a free hand. He swiftly drafted an outline offer and placed it before Molotov, Halifax simply informing the Cabinet of the approach.

Either it was too late, Cripps subsequently concluded, or the offer was not big enough to offset the expediency of the Soviet agreement with Germany. Earlier in October, Stalin had sent word to Joachim von Ribbentrop, the German Foreign Minister. Molotov was invited to Berlin to see Hitler to concert their 'long-range policy'. News of Molotov's trip took Cripps aback, and he protested vigorously to Andrei Vyshinsky, Molotov's deputy, adding that the British offer would not stay on the table indefinitely. Tuning into the BBC, he heard the terms of his confidential proposal read out. The best excuse the FO could give was that publication rebutted left-wing claims in Britain that no effort was being made to win the Soviet Union round.

The episode revived his view that, with his own personal position suffering, he ought to head for home. Gwen Hill, his former secretary, indicated that Cripps was being told to sit tight 'because a good many of the Government people think it is an excellent thing that he should be out of the way'.[20] He felt the same, writing to Monckton that his ineffectiveness was due to what had drawn Russia and Germany together, both of them wanting to have done with the rotten civilisation that Britain still blindly clung to. It was a revolutionary war in which Britain was on the wrong side, the past – 'at the moment'. If changes were to be made, they had to be introduced while the war was on; victory would only reinforce old ways, making democratic reform all the more unlikely.[21]

All the same, Cripps was surprised to find that other countries assumed Britain's intentions were calculated. This, had he but known it, was greatly to his benefit. From the time he had landed in Moscow, his mere presence in Russia had irritated Hitler. The German ambassador, Schulenberg, cabled at the end of May to say there were no grounds for apprehension – Soviet policy was unchanged. After Cripps met Stalin on 1 July, Molotov (on Stalin's instructions) handed to Schulenberg a résumé of what was said, emphasising that Stalin did not see any danger of Germany wanting to engulf Europe.[22]

Cripps also told the Balkan ambassadors what had transpired. The Greek minister reported to Athens, where a German agent in the Greek foreign ministry passed the information on to Berlin. Italy intercepted messages from the Yugoslav ambassador about anti-German comments made by Molotov, seeming to show Cripps – who was received when Schulenberg was fobbed off – making inroads. He had apparently forecast that the Russians would be fighting on the allied side within a year.[23] The meddling of a half-breed, drawing-room Bolshevik with special access to the Kremlin excited Hitler's paranoia.[24] Hitler, according to Liddell-Hart, the military historian,

> puzzled by the way the British did not seem to realise their hopeless position ... looked to Russia for the explanation. Over and over again as the months went on he said, to Jodl [chief of staff of the German armed forces] and others, that Britain must be hoping for Russian intervention, or she would have given in. Already there must be some secret agreement. The despatch of Sir Stafford Cripps to Moscow, and his conversations with Stalin, were confirmation of it. Germany must strike soon, or she would be strangled.[25]

Hitler's fears were not allayed by Molotov's visit, which brought stiff Soviet terms for agreeing to join the three-power pact of Germany, Italy and Japan. Believing the only reason Britain kept going was because it was working to embroil Russia in a war with Germany, Hitler abandoned the military defeat of Britain, switching to the threat from the East. By December 1940, preparations began for the overthrow of Soviet Russia, set for May 1941. On this fateful decision the Second World War was lost and won.

Thinking the chances of a German–Soviet falling out were receding, Cripps went into reverse. Vyshinsky had orally turned down his October offer, but Cripps had taken this as a personal opinion. Upset by Molotov's visit, he decided to stop running after the Soviet government, beginning by with-drawing the earlier proposals for a trade agreement. Since Britain was in a position of weakness, and his own reputation had been dented by the FO leak, he was determined to demonstrate that Britain was not to be 'trifled with'.

His about-turn alarmed FO officials. Cripps, it was feared, was letting his feelings colour his appreciation of Soviet intentions. Nothing should be done to break off relations in an abrupt manner. Eden, who became the new Foreign Secretary in December, was particularly concerned that such a rupture might give the misleading impression that he (Eden) was adopting a tougher attitude. Cripps – not as close to Eden as to Halifax – held fire, induced to try to draw out the Russians. He sent Eden a paper setting out a series of constructive war aims, asking for it to be circulated among progressive Tories in the admin-istration. It was a mark of his growing esteem, however, that he was being tipped to return home and take up a major ministry as a counterweight to

Bevin, the Minister of Labour. Churchill himself continued to believe Cripps and the Soviet Union – 'a lunatic in a country of lunatics'[26] – were well suited.

For six weeks Cripps saw no Soviet officials, exchanging only notes, inadvertently encouraging the idea that he was losing faith. There were even German-inspired rumours of his imminent recall. A new trade agreement, concluded in January 1941, suggested that German and Soviet political closeness persisted, notwithstanding Cripps's cardinal conviction of their 'fundamental hostility'. Holding himself back, the war of nerves told on his health. But it also produced a larger misfortune. His plain speaking with the Soviet government had shown his sincerity. Suddenly going cold, he undid his earlier work, reawakening Soviet suspicion and contributing to Soviet misconceptions in the approaching spring and summer.

The freeze thawed only after Eden lectured Maisky about Cripps being ill-treated. Molotov called Cripps to the Kremlin on 1 February, talking of 'considerable hopes' they had originally placed in him. He went on to definitely reject the October offer. Cripps misread the import of his comments, trying to interest a 'bored' Molotov in arrangements for post-war collaboration. Reporting to London, he recommended withdrawal of the trade proposals, the original purpose of his mission. More dangerously, with Vyshinsky he touched on the ultimate temptation for Britain in a drawn-out conflict of coming to 'some arrangement' with Germany for restoring western Europe to its former status, giving Germany freedom to seek to expand eastward. 'Cripps', one historian has curtly commented, 'had no authority from London to make this statement.'[27]

Deterioration in German–Soviet ties began over the Balkans. Germany began a troop build-up in Romania, with the intention of moving into Bulgaria to counteract British activity in Greece. Bulgaria succumbed, allowing German troops to flood in. For the moment, Yugoslavia resisted German threats. Eden, visiting Ankara, hoped to enlist Turkey on the Greek side in the event of a German attack. Cripps flew to Istanbul by a Soviet plane put at his disposal, taking the night train to Ankara to confer with the Foreign Secretary. Cripps was all for renewing his offer of recognition of Soviet control of the Baltic states and unblocking their assets. Brokered by Cripps, a Soviet–Turkish declaration of understanding was rapidly agreed, even though British officials were unimpressed. At the end of March, Prince Paul of Yugoslavia caved in to German pressure, before being toppled by a Yugoslav army coup. Cripps pressed Eden a second time, demanding fresh instructions. The reaction of Cadogan was to try to temper Cripps's 'imprudence', wishing him to stick to the policy of 'reserve'. When Yugoslavia and the Soviet Union signed a non-aggression pact on 5 April, Cripps was again insisting the Foreign Office must act quickly to encourage the Soviets. By 13 April, Yugoslavia had been overrun by Germany. The next few weeks, Cripps thought, would be crucial. Germany was likely to present Russia with new extreme demands and tell it if it did not submit the alternative would be war. But the Soviet government had given no indication it was about to be more forthcoming, as the Foreign Office kept reminding him.

The fault, Cripps had to accept, did not lie on the British side; it was the 'fault or fear' – with 2 million German troops on its borders – of the Soviets.[28] What could tip the balance in Britain's favour? Churchill, at the end of March, thought he had it. His famous warning telegram to Stalin, unaccountably held up by Cripps, became a prize exhibit when Churchill refought his battles in his multi-volume account of the Second World War.

The Prime Minister (writing after the war[29]) read with 'relief' and 'excitement' an intelligence report from 'one of our most trusted sources' about the movement and counter-movement of German armoured divisions on the railway line from Romania to Poland. As soon as Prince Paul of Yugoslavia capitulated, the tank divisions, originally on their way south to Yugoslavia, were ordered northward to Cracow in Poland; after the army coup in Belgrade, they were immediately sent back to Bucharest. To Churchill, this single incident 'illuminated the whole Eastern scene like a lightning flash', revealing that Hitler, once Yugoslavia was in the bag, moved troops up to the Russian frontier, only to cancel the command in order to support the invasion of Yugoslavia and subsequently Greece – postponing what must mean an inevitable assault on Russia. Not having communicated with Stalin since June 1940, Churchill composed a short personal message to the Soviet leader on 3 April, intending to arrest his attention and alert him to the danger, which Cripps was to deliver personally.

I have sure information from a trusted agent that when the Germans thought they had got Yugoslavia in the net – that is to say, after March 20 – they began to move three out of five Panzer divisions from Roumania to Southern Poland. The moment they heard of the Serbian revolution this movement was countermanded. Your Excellency will readily appreciate the significance of these facts.[30]

Eden, in accompanying comments, suggested Cripps might add that Germany obviously intended to attack the Soviet Union sooner or later and it would be in the Soviet interest to put 'every spoke in the German wheel' in the Balkans.

Nothing was heard from Cripps until 12 April, when he explained he had only just submitted a long letter of his own to Vyshinsky arguing the case for active Soviet measures. Were he to also convey the Prime Minister's short message, with its indication of a German attack which the Soviet leadership was quite well aware of, the only probable effect would be to weaken the impact already made by his own letter – an objection Eden agreed had some force.

'Vexed' at the inexplicable delay, Churchill twice told Eden -on 16 and 18 April – of his surprise that its delivery should be 'resisted' by Ambassador Cripps, who was not alive to the 'exceptional' military significance of the facts it contained. Only on 19 April, after the fall of Yugoslavia and the virtual German occupation of Greece, was the message finally given by Cripps to Vyshinsky, who four days later told Cripps it had reached Stalin.

Churchill ended his historical account on a sombre note: 'I cannot form any final judgement upon whether my message, if delivered with all the promptness and ceremony prescribed, would have altered the course of events. Nevertheless I still regret that my instructions were not carried out effectively.'[31]

Cripps's obstinacy and effrontery – words Churchill used in October 1941[32] – still linger in the half-light of history. Churchill's volume covering the period was completed in 1950, shortly after he and Cripps had clashed over the devaluation of the pound. In the official history of the Second World War published in 1964, the authors remarked that 'Mr Churchill's design was unhappily frustrated by the egoism of the Ambassador', who was unwilling to mar the effect of one of his own messages, passing on the contents of the telegram only after its immediate value had been squandered.[33] Cripps's actions were 'inexcusable'. A more fully documented account by Woodward in 1970 printed the exchanges Churchill had left out, showing how active Cripps had been in April, but was critical of his disobedience, endorsing Churchill's view that it was Cripps's plain 'duty', without discussion, to pass the telegram on, irrespective of whether he believed it would be welcome to the Soviet government or not.[34] The more recent history of British intelligence in the Second World War, noting Churchill's indignation, was less scathing. The fact that this account disclosed for the first time that Churchill's warning derived from two remarkably precise German air force 'Ultra' decrypts – which Cripps knew nothing about – strongly bore out the Prime Minister's side of the argument.[35] The Churchillian critique of Cripps's costly error was faithfully followed in most other studies. It was only with the re-evaluation of Cripps's mission to Moscow by Gorodetsky in 1985 that the full diplomatic background was filled in.[36] The fragmentary evidence from Soviet archives which has since seen the light puts Churchill's telegram of early April in the wider context of why Stalin failed to act on this and the many other warning messages.

Cripps, under his own steam, had already been conducting an approach to the Soviet government, while waiting for further instructions. Like Churchill, he had been predicting a war between Germany and Russia ever since the fall of France. In June 1940 he told Molotov the British believed Germany would turn east if France collapsed. In July the Germans got wind of Cripps's view of an inevitable war between Germany and Russia, and that he believed Hitler would act that autumn or the following spring.[37] In January 1941 Cripps was certain of Germany attacking Russia 'not later than the end of June'. Arriving back in Moscow from Ankara in late February, he announced his 'firm conviction' to an off-the-record press conference, and was rumoured to have told Vyshinsky that Germany would turn on Russia after defeating Yugoslavia, Greece and Turkey – the source of his 'reliable' information apparently the American ambassador or Swedish minister in Moscow. In the last week of March, appealing for a Cabinet decision, he thought the weight of indications of German intentions might justify reopening talks with the Soviet government.

By then, Churchill had been shown the evidence of the 'Ultra' decrypts. When Cripps's appeal came before the Cabinet, Churchill did not give a clear lead. In the judgement of his military advisers, the Germans were massing troops on their eastern front to intimidate the Soviets. Eden decided any attempt to open talks again would be unwise. Churchill, who had up to then been largely uninvolved in policy towards Russia, suddenly (in Martin Gilbert's phrase) took a 'calculated risk', firing off the message so pregnant with military significance.

The missing element in Churchill's version was Cripps's replies, explaining he had only just passed on what Prince Paul had been told by Hitler, of a German invasion of the Soviet Union, and that to see Stalin – whom he had met only the once – was 'out of the question'. Churchill agreed that Cripps could see Molotov instead, but a second telegram from Cripps, crossing with one from Churchill, told of his preference for letting things stand, as events were moving in Britain's direction.[38] If he communicated Churchill's message, Cripps was sure Stalin would regard him only as a troublemaker, his 'planted' message a British 'provokatsiya', which was indeed how Vyshinsky took it.[39] 'In London', Cripps confessed to a journalist after the German attack,

> they had no idea what difficulties I was up against here. They did not want to realise that not only Stalin, but even Molotov avoided me like grim death; for several months before the war, Vyshinsky was my only contact, and a highly unsatisfactory one at that. Stalin, I can tell you, did not want to have anything to do with Churchill, so alarmed was he lest the Germans found out. And Molotov was no better.[40]

These exchanges provide a fuller picture; it is still incomplete. Cripps glossed over the 'difficulties' which were of his own creation. He had given plenty of speculative warnings of a German attack. What – chronically indiscreet – he had also done was accompany them with disturbing hints that, if the Russians did not budge, the attractiveness to Britain of a separate peace with Germany would grow, allowing Britain to back out of the conflict and leave Russia at the mercy of Hitler. Without FO permission, he had intimated this to Vyshinsky in October. He reverted to the possibility in a memorandum to Vyshinksy in

February. He made a similar claim at a confidential press briefing on 6 March, stating Hitler might sue for peace if he were allowed to seize the USSR and, if Britain's situation were to deteriorate, influential circles in Britain and the United States which wanted the USSR's destruction might pressure the British government to accept Hitler's proposals – a comment which reached Stalin's ears on 11 June.[41] Finally, in his long letter to Vyshinsky on 12 April (which he gave precedence to ahead of Churchill's message), he incautiously revived the possibility of a British 'arrangement' with Germany to end the war, wanting to know whether the Soviet government intended to improve relations with Britain or leave them on a 'wholly negative basis'. It is no wonder this irritated, Maisky said, the Soviet government, the principal effect of both Cripps's and Churchill's warnings being to encourage the Soviets disastrously to discount any chance of a German onslaught.[42]

It also accounts for the high anxiety of the Soviet authorities about the sensational flight to Scotland of Hitler's deputy, Rudolf Hess, on the night of 10 May 1941, carrying with him, as the BBC shortly reported, unspecified peace proposals. On all the essential points – whether Hess was acting on his own initiative, whether he warned of an impending German attack on Russia, and whether he hoped to stir up an anti-Churchill peace party – there is continuing controversy, even after more than half a century. The only certainty is that Stalin, who double-crossed the West in August 1939, believed the British were preparing to negotiate with Germany and was encouraged in this by incoming reports from Soviet posts abroad. Maisky cabled that a 'struggle' was going on inside the British government between those wanting a fight to the finish and a peace faction of former 'Clivedenites' who were more interested in fighting Russian Bolshevism than in prosecuting a war with Germany. Belief in the existence of this 'other Britain' had inspired a German attempt to kidnap the Duke of Windsor in Portugal, a plot confounded by Churchill's emissary, Walter Monckton (recently made the head of the Press and Censorship Bureau of the Ministry of Information), who may have told Cripps of it.

Cripps, from the best of motives, fanned Soviet suspicions of a separate peace, fed by his dislike of 'Munichite' Foreign Office civil servants. The American ambassador in Moscow had to assure his British counterpart that Churchill was made of sterner stuff. Even so, Cripps suggested using any disclosures by Hess to increase Soviet fears that Russia would be left to face Germany alone unless it acted in the face of German preparations to attack – a course which the FO, claiming Cripps was jumping to conclusions, ruled out as far too dangerous.

By an unknown route, the German Foreign Ministry got hold of the substance of Cripps's letters to Vyshinsky. Cripps, Schulenberg was told, had declared that German occupation of the Balkans presented 'a direct threat to the security of the Soviet Union'; if the Soviet Union did not take the initiative, it would eventually be 'compelled to meet the whole impact of German power'.[43] Two days later, on 24 April, the German naval attaché in Moscow noted that, according to the Italian Embassy, Cripps had predicted 22 June as the date of outbreak of war between Germany and Russia – a rumour, the attaché added, which was 'manifestly absurd'.[44] The message was inscribed in the German naval diary for the same day, with an accompanying exclamation mark.[45] In conversation with Hitler on 28 April, Schulenberg strove – unsuccessfully – to persuade him the British were not pulling the strings, pointing out that Cripps was still being ignored by Molotov, who remained fully committed to the Axis powers. Stalin, he ventured, had already shown a willingness to increase supplies of transported grain to Germany. But he could not shake the Führer's fixed view of British involvement in the uprising in Yugoslavia, and its poisoning of the diplomatic wells.[46]

This was not the estimation of British influence taken by Cripps or by the government in London. Ostensibly to obtain Cripps's advice about an understanding with Russia and Turkey, he was recalled from Moscow for 'consultations' on 2 June. An underlying reason may have been to bring him to heel. He made his way home via Sweden, 'a beaten man', expecting never to return to Russia.[47] With all the signs of an increased German build-up, Russia, he feared, would go to any lengths with Germany, short of demobilising, to avoid a conflict.[48] At a Cabinet meeting, Churchill and Eden (talked into it by Cripps) persuaded their colleagues to support a promise of collaboration with Russia should war break out. The Webbs saw Cripps the day afterwards. 'Stafford *on the whole*', Aunt Bo recorded, 'is in favour of the survival of Soviet Communism', and thought if Stalin could reach a compromise peace without the entry of Germany into the Ukraine 'he had better do so'. Churchill he found a 'splendid' war leader, but a firm believer in the domestic *status quo*. For the Labour leadership Cripps had complete contempt. He was 'disinclined' to rejoin the party, even at the behest of his Bristol East comrades. As to the prospect of radical changes, he told Rogers, it was not possible to expect people wholly engaged in defending Britain to think much about the future. All that was possible for the time being was for those who did appreciate the need for change to 'hold themselves ready' until the occasion arose, as it must do after or at the close of the war.[49]

The Russians interpreted his withdrawal as a hostile act, this view being reinforced by British press reports (digested and distorted by Maisky) of a worsening in German–Soviet relations. The result was a breach of diplomatic protocol. In a TASS communiqué of 14 June, handed by Molotov to Schulenberg, Cripps was singled out. 'Even before the return of the English Ambassador Cripps to London', but especially after his return, it ran, there had been widespread rumours of 'an impending war between the USSR and Germany in the English and foreign press'. They were 'a clumsy propaganda manoeuvre of the forces arrayed against the Soviet Union and Germany, which are interested in a spread and intensification of the war'. Germany was not making increasing demands, stories of a German attack were without foundation, and both sides were continuing to abide by the terms of the non-aggression pact. Stalin threw out an offer of new talks, incensed by the flood of indiscretions from the British, 'the mere forecast of the storm seeming [to Stalin] to bring the storm nearer'.[50]

A heavy responsibility fell on Maisky, whose memoirs – as Gorodetsky has demonstrated – are quite misleading about the month of June 1941. During the Khrushchev era, heralded by Khrushchev's 'secret speech' in 1956, strong emphasis was placed on blunders by Stalin in ignoring the warnings of Churchill and Cripps.[51] Maisky was the person who furnished the evidence for the trumped-up complaints (against Cripps) in the TASS communiqué, which the Soviets used to probe German intentions. It was Maisky too who brushed to one side any possibility of improved Anglo-Soviet collaboration. What he said in his long telegram of 18 June is still unclear, but it seems he had taken fright. Khrushchev credited Maisky with forwarding another explicit warning from the offended Cripps, which Maisky appeared to think had more to it than the aim of stirring up trouble: 'As of now Cripps is deeply convinced of the inevitability of armed conflict between Germany and the USSR which will begin not later than the middle of June. According to Cripps, the Germans have at present concentrated 147 divisions (including air force and service units) along the Soviet borders ...'[52] In Cripps's words, Russia's inability to organise condemned it to military defeat, and Maisky could not convince him otherwise.[53] On the morning of Saturday 21 June, Cripps burst in on Maisky at the Soviet Embassy, telling him the British had reliable information of a German attack on the following day, or at the very latest on the 29 June, adding 'You know that Hitler always attacks on Sundays.'[54]

At daybreak the following morning, while German forces were already crossing on a wide front into Soviet territory, Schulenberg presented Molotov with the German declaration of hostilities, accusing the Soviet Union of violating the terms of the non-aggression pact, 'carrying Bolshevism further into Europe'. The recent activities of Ambassador Cripps for 'still closer political and military collaboration' with England was one of several further pretexts. Since the Soviet Union was about to attack Germany from the rear, the Führer had ordered Germany 'to oppose this threat with all the means at their disposal'. Hitler's own declaration spoke of plotting by Britain's ambassador, one of the 'Jewish Anglo-Saxon warmongers'.[55]

The moment of truth had arrived, but only after Cripps, summoned back from his post, had given up any hope of altering Soviet opinion. The success of his failure was reward enough. 'Barbarossa' was not his doing. Hitler ordained the conflict. Russia entered the war only because it was attacked. The

German–Russian war would have occurred anyway, Cripps or no Cripps. But he was the 'messenger of disruption',[56] the scapegoat shot at by both combatants. This is the origin of the myth that Cripps brought the Soviet Union into the war on the British side – because the Germans and the Russians did him the honour of saying so.

Even before the German onslaught, the argument about what form of collaboration to offer the Soviet Union, given Britain's involvement – and reliance on American aid – in other theatres of war, was bound up with how long it was thought the Soviets could last out. Wanting an open-ended commitment to the Soviet cause, Cripps supposedly brought about 'the conversion of the War Cabinet and of Dill [chief of the Imperial General Staff] and the soldiers'.[57] In reality the military, opposed in any case to a 'repugnant' Soviet alliance, anticipated a rapid Soviet collapse. Cripps had no expertise, and could go only by the unanimous view of the Chiefs of Staff that the Germans might reach Moscow within six weeks. The phrase that Germany would cut through the Soviet troops 'like a (hot) knife through butter' was not his, though others attributed it to him.[58] Churchill's broadcast on the evening of 22 June, putting his anti-Communism behind him and pledging 'whatever help we can to Russia and the Russian people', owed more to the prevailing trend of wariness than to any last-minute contributions from Eden, Beaverbrook or Cripps, who were all at Chequers at various times during the day. It remained for Cripps, bearing the brunt of good-natured jibes about Communism by Churchill, and sent on his way by a Privy Counsellorship and an encomium from the Prime Minister on the floor of the Commons – even the *Daily Express* praised his hard life of 'sacrifice' and 'service'[59] – to make his way back to Moscow and turn Churchill's ambiguous offer of assistance into a fully functioning alliance. He departed on 26 June. Four days later, his father, Lord Parmoor – then in his eighty-ninth year – passed away.

Cripps reached Moscow on 27 June, bringing with him a small military mission. The reception he was accorded 'surpassed his expectations'.[60] Information about the course of the battle was hard to come by, but German troops were reportedly advancing into Latvia, Lithuania and Belorussia. The Soviet government's attitude was entirely transformed. Meeting a businesslike Molotov twice in one day, Cripps was pressed for a full-scale political agreement. Responding cautiously, since he was unable to commit himself, Cripps reminded the Soviet Foreign Minister of his rejection of an earlier political offer (in October 1940), suggesting it was important to establish a new basis of trust. The British still had serious doubts about whether the Soviet Union would put up much of a fight, beyond bringing a breathing space to Britain. Originally sceptical, Cripps gradually came round to the view that if the Russians could hold out until winter closed in – with all the practical aid

Britain could spare – it might prove the turning point of the war.

In a personal letter to Stalin on 7 July, Churchill expressed his admiration for the 'spirited resistance' and 'bravery' of the Russian soldiers and people, undertaking to do everything to help them that time, geography and Britain's resources permitted. Stalin, only now recovering from a 'paralysing shock',[61] cut through the preliminaries by proposing an Anglo-Soviet declaration of principle providing for 'mutual help', without specifying quantity or quality, and a commitment from both parties not to conclude a separate peace. This second condition reflected a constant Soviet fear, particularly after the Hess episode, though Cripps did not blame the Russians on this score 'as we have tried to make them so [afraid] in the past'. (Volkogonov – Stalin's biographer – on the other hand, recounts a story of Stalin and Molotov, in early July, trying to contact Hitler through the Bulgarian ambassador with the object of offering to surrender territory in return for a peace deal.)[62] Cripps drew up a draft treaty which was speedily endorsed by both Roosevelt and the British Cabinet, and the signing of the Anglo-Soviet pact for joint action in the war against Germany took place in an ante-room of the Kremlin on 12 July. Cripps dropped his vow of abstinence to toast the occasion with a glass of Russian champagne.

At Britain's insistence, the pact was not a treaty; Russia was referred to as a 'co-belligerent', not an 'ally'. But the domestic political impact of the alignment was not lost on Cripps, since Stalin had been urging a second front against Hitler in the west. The 'fullest use' should be made of the pact to 'whip up' the feeling of the workers, while showing how much co-operation the British government had already been able to achieve, he advised Monckton. Everything must be done – by Bevan, Zilliacus and others, bypassing Transport House – 'to stop the CP cashing in'.[63]

Temporising at first, Cripps, supported by the head of the military mission, Major Noel Mason-Macfarlane, quickly came out in favour of giving the greatest material help Britain could manage, in spite of Soviet reticence about revealing Russian military plans. Behaving as if the British expected the new Russian front to collapse could only have a deleterious effect. Churchill's emotional messages were no substitute, Eden observed, for actual military assistance. By the end of June, Soviet representatives submitted to the British and American governments an inventory of requirements, to be supplied by Arctic convoy. Cripps – for the first time subjected to German air raids on Moscow – proposed a top-flight conference to explore requirements and exchange information, putting it to Harry Hopkins, Roosevelt's emissary, on 31 July. Hopkins made the idea his own, presenting it to Roosevelt and Churchill at their summit in Placentia Bay, Newfoundland, in August.

The pace of the German advance – occupying half the Ukraine and reaching the gates of Leningrad – impelled Stalin to strengthen his demands, berating Cripps for the failure to open a diversionary front in France or the Balkans.

Cripps urged on Churchill 'a superhuman effort', without which 'the game is up'. Cripps hoped to lead the conference delegation, shifting policy in a more favourable Soviet direction. To this end, he made a sudden decision to return to London. Churchill halted him in his tracks, tartly replying that, if by 'super-human' Cripps meant superior to Britain's physical limitations, then 'these attributes are denied to us'. A large contingent of fighter aircraft was on its way, in addition to deliveries of munitions, equipment and raw materials. Churchill sympathised with Cripps's having to watch the agony of Russia at close quarters, but he had larger considerations to bear in mind, including the theatre of operations in the Mediterranean and the Middle East.

The appointment of Lord Beaverbrook, Minister of Supply, to head the delegation cut off Cripps's route home. Isobel, who had stayed in Britain, was obliged to cultivate his supporters for him, assuming a more overt political role as a 'mother confessor'. Informed by Cripps of his wish to return, Eden tried to discourage him, arguing that his departure at such a critical time would create misunderstanding. Besides which, Churchill instructed him to say, there were no vacancies in the government. Cripps disavowed any wish for another job – 'that sort of attitude is not my form' – but made it clear he was not prepared to exclude himself from politics for the sake of a diplomatic career. Both Labour and Conservative members of the Cabinet, mindful of the pro-Soviet appeal the ambassador could tap, had every wish for him to be made to stay put. Labour loyalists, knowing all about his past antics, were not wel-coming. 'If the Labour party is to apologise to Sir Stafford Cripps,' a Transport House officer commented, 'surely Sir Stafford Cripps should apologise to the British people.'[64]

The Anglo-American supply mission, headed by Beaverbrook and Averell Harriman, reached Archangel at the end of September. Cripps went out of his way to prepare the ground, giving Beaverbrook his own account of 'living in a vacuum' without accurate information or a readiness on the part of the Soviets to open up. As far as he could tell, food was short but there had been no general evacuation of the capital. The Russian forces, however, were fighting 'magnificently': 'Before I left London I said that I thought according to the best information that one could gather as to the state of the Russian army the Germans would get to Moscow in five to six weeks. I am glad to have been proved completely wrong.'[65] Beaverbrook, who left Cripps's papers unread, chose to stay at the Hotel National rather than the British Embassy. Cripps was not shown the telegram traffic from London (Churchill put special stress on keeping 'Ultra' secure). On the first day, 28 September, the ambassadors were excluded from the conversation Beaverbrook and Harriman had with Stalin. When Beaverbrook semi-seriously suggested to Cripps that they should form a political alliance back in Britain, Cripps said he did not think they could work together, repelled as he was by Beaverbrook's capacity 'to lie like a trooper for his country'. Cripps complained that Beaverbrook, because he had no wish to bargain with the Soviets – or raise contentious issues like the Polish problem – 'took all the cards out of my hands',[66] ordering him about (Dalton heard with relish) like an errand boy.

Cripps received only a garbled account of the fifteen hours of talks with Stalin. To his amazement, he did not obtain fuller details until one month later, from London. He acknowledged Beaverbrook's achievement in agreeing a quota system of long-term supplies to the Soviet Union, but pointed out to Eden it was wrong to say all Soviet demands had been satisfied. His brush with Beaverbrook, and the malign influence he felt Beaverbrook was having on Churchill, reinforced Cripps's doubts about the commitment of Churchill's coalition.

Convinced Churchill did not want the closest collaboration with Russia, and feeling his usefulness was at an end – aside from acting as a 'post-box' – Cripps repeated his wish to fly home at once. Eden tried to mollify the fickle ambassador, talking of his superb service.[67] Two days later, the front only seventy miles from Moscow, the Embassy was frantically evacuated, the staff setting off by train for Kazan, 500 miles to the east, and then Kuibyshev, where, amid 'an indescribable jam of bodies and luggage', Cripps bumped into Walter Citrine and a TUC delegation. In further telegrams to Churchill, he challenged his strategic priorities, arguing that Britain seemed to be carrying on 'two relatively unrelated wars' instead of concentrating on a combined effort. He agreed that Stalin's request for the dispatch of twenty-five to thirty British divisions was a physical absurdity, but 'they [the Russians] are now obsessed with the idea that we are prepared to fight to the last drop of Russian blood as Germans suggest in their propaganda'. Churchill, increasingly unhappy with Beaverbrook's misrepresenting of the supply mission, sensed the political danger of a difficult subordinate, 'evidently' (he told Eden) 'preparing his case against us'.[68]

Shunted off to Kuibyshev, and allowed to see only Molotov, who complained the British had still not replied to the Russian request for British troops, Cripps felt even more isolated. He told Citrine he believed the front would hold. 'The Russians had such a capacity for suffering that they would endure where other nations would give in.'[69] Forbidden to return to Moscow, he went to the extent of drafting a note to Stalin instead, virtually siding with the Soviet against the British government, in the belief it might prod Churchill into letting him go. Monckton, arriving in Kuibyshev to co-ordinate information policy with the Russians, managed to dissuade Cripps from sending it.

Churchill's difficulty was dealing with a disunited Cabinet, while resisting too many concessions to the Soviet view. Stalin had been demanding that Britain also declare war on Hungary, Romania and Finland, and Eden was sympathetic both to this and to discussions about post-war relations. Beaverbrook, 'the victim of the furies' and on the point of resignation, made a strong bid to lead the public call for a 'Second Front'.[70] If Cripps were to return too, championing the Soviet cause, the Prime Minister would find himself in an extremely exposed position. The way to 'keep Cripps quiet' was provided by Eden, who proposed that he himself journey to the Soviet Union to reassure Stalin of the British desire for a sincere collaboration. Stalin, in a broadcast to mark the anniversary of the Russian revolution, had attributed Russia's plight to the absence of a second front; in a brusque reply to Churchill, he implied a continuing lack of confidence. When Cripps saw this, it bore out 'everything' he had been saying about British half-heartedness. His task as 'ambassador extraordinary' was at an end, as there was 'nothing more that I can do'.

Churchill composed a remarkable remonstrance, warning Cripps against the folly on which he seemed set. Abandoning his post when the battle for Moscow was hanging in the balance would not be understood even by his friends. Churchill's own government had never been stronger, and he was ready to face any 'political opposition' Cripps might mount, though he would do so regretfully. Cripps could expect no help from the Soviet government if he made a public row. It would be 'a most unequal struggle which could only injure the interests to which you are attached'. By the time Cabinet discussed the matter, this attempt to scare Cripps off was swapped, for a more moderately toned message. Soon afterwards, Eden's visit was announced.

The upsurge in public support for the Soviet Union was the vital factor. Since June, several 'aid for Russia' campaigns had sprung up. Progressive churchmen proclaimed a Russian 'holy war'. John Moore-Brabazon, Minister of Aircraft Production, was sacked for saying he hoped Russia and Germany would annihilate each other. Since British troops were in the field only in North Africa, the government was vulnerable to charges it was not making an all-out effort. Beaverbrook agitated for a second front. Cripps, a more authentic man of the Left, clearly intended to turn the issue into an evangelical crusade. Hitler's Germany had been the making of Churchill, lifting him into office and power. What might Stalin's Russia do for Cripps?

In its simple form, the question was never put. The day Eden set sail for Russia, 7 December, the American fleet in Pearl Harbor was subjected to a surprise Japanese air attack, bringing the United States – whom Germany also declared war on – into the conflict. Churchill immediately rushed off to see Roosevelt, with the result that when Eden reached Moscow, with little new to offer, he had Cripps bearing down upon him and the Prime Minister out of reach. Eden and Cripps, between them, ironed out a draft agreement renouncing territorial aggression and pledging a fight to the finish of German military power, Eden then allowing Cripps to sit in on his discussions with Stalin. Russian insistence on recognition of the Soviet Union's 1941 frontiers (when its very capital was in grave danger of capture) was, however, ruled out, at long distance, by Churchill, who would make no hard-and-fast commitments without American consent. Stalin relenting, the visitors were treated to a drunken Kremlin banquet. But Eden had brought with him the news that Cripps was at long last free to take his leave of the Soviet Union.

The Soviet dictatorship, Cripps concluded on his departure, had saved British democracy, though he was not thanked for having clung so long to the hopeless belief that Germany and Russia would eventually be separated. On his way through Moscow, he saw Molotov and Vyshinsky, but not Stalin. There was no diplomatic send-off and no official to bid farewell when he left by boat from Murmansk. The whole arrangement, he thought – without bitterness – was calculated to show he was 'in disgrace' or that Anglo-Soviet relations were 'not good'.[71]

THE ASTRAKHAN CAP

He bore himself as though he had a message to deliver.
Churchill, in his war memoirs, speaking of Cripps's return from Moscow[1]

His intimate friends tell me he thinks he is the Messiah.
Averell Harriman on Cripps, in early 1942[2]

The curious politics of wartime Britain – connecting the high-level activity of the Churchill coalition to the subterranean swings in public morale – threw up many strange phenomena. With the extraordinary elevating of Cripps, coming back from his eighteen-month posting in the Soviet Union, the home front embraced a new, somewhat bemused, popular hero.

Sailing home by the Arctic convoy route, Cripps landed in the Firth of Cromarty on 23 January 1942, pausing to hear news of a Russian counter-offensive before Moscow and Leningrad. He reached Euston station that same evening, met by Isobel and a party of journalists and photographers. Sporting an astrakhan cap, he stood blinking before the flashlights, the personification of the Soviet alliance.

Recent Russian victories aside, the new year had been one of uninterrupted gloom for the government. Churchill, just back from his trip to see Roosevelt, badly needed to shore up his authority. To this end, he took two steps: a vote of confidence from the Commons, and the creation of a Ministry of Production to take overall responsibility for every aspect of war production. This required reconstructing the Cabinet – only the second full-scale reshuffle since May 1940. Churchill, as he told Eden, much preferred a Cabinet of 'obedient mug-wumps' to one full of 'awkward freaks'.[3] But Cripps was too valuable an asso-ciate – and too incalculable an adversary – to be allowed to set himself up in opposition. The head-to-head contest with Cripps, the 'fist in his face'[4] which Churchill had contemplated in the autumn, was forgotten. Over lunch on 25 January, he offered Cripps the post of Minister of Supply – outside the War Cabinet – about to be vacated by Beaverbrook, who, as the new production overlord, would become his immediate superior. Cripps asked for time to think it over. He saw Maisky and R. Barrington-Ward, editor of *The Times*, which strongly favoured the government bringing Cripps on board. Cripps told the latter his joining was 'in the perspective', and Barrington-Ward, learning of what was making Cripps hesitate, told him the Prime Minister could not be expected to forgo 'his stimulants, to wit, his Beaverbrook'.[5] Later, Cripps dined with Beaverbrook, who, at Churchill's bidding, did his 'utmost' to persuade Cripps to accept, explaining he could 'write his own ticket'.[6]

Away from England (apart from two short intervals) for more than two years, Cripps had hardly had the chance to get his bearings. He sought out a most unlikely ally – Bevin, Minister of Labour. Bevin, on past record and in his present position, had it in his hands to nullify Cripps. Isobel's efforts paid off. Before her husband's arrival, she reported some success in rebuilding links with 'the T.U. side and E.B.' Cripps's own band of disciples, grouped in the 1941 Committee – advocates of a 'new Britain'[7] – urged him to get Bevin to 'vouch' for him. Cripps made a 'beeline' for Bevin,[8] admiring his 'guts' and 'drive'. The pending reshuffle brought them to combine. Bevin, determined that Beaverbrook's new powers should not include control over the supply of labour, worked on Cripps, 'turning him against Beaverbrook' (in Dalton's secondhand account). Cripps having all but accepted Churchill's offer, Bevin told him to take it only if it meant a seat in the War Cabinet. Another counsellor was Thomas Jones, contact man of the great and the good, lured back from his Welsh retreat by Isobel and by David Astor, son of the proprietor of *The Observer* and a member of the 1941 Committee. As a result, on top of a War Cabinet ranking, Cripps asked for guarantees from Churchill of freedom from encroachment by the Ministry of Production, as well as the right to override private interests in obtaining raw materials. Cripps also saw Bevan and Strauss, who were using the revamped *Tribune* to conduct an attack on Churchill's war strategy (Cripps publicly disclaimed any further responsibility for *Tribune*.) Both warned him against entering the coalition. Cripps was now minded to turn the offer down, but uncertain whether to thus take a temporary break. Egged on by Bevan, Cripps stayed away from the confidence debate, making sure his letter of refusal arrived at No. 10 just before the critical Commons vote. Adopting the role of 'friendly critic', he declined the post of Supply, but left open his availability for other special tasks which might arise – such as India.

Needing time to reflect – he would not go back to the Bar (his chambers and all his books had been 'blown to billy ho' in an air raid in October 1940) – he withdrew to his new home, Frith Hill, in Gloucestershire, lauding the Soviet war effort and the economy which made the Russians 'the only people who have been able to meet the blitz tactics of Hitler with success'.

Any power he might have to do good, he stated in his letter to Churchill, stemmed directly from the expectations of the public, whom he did not wish to disappoint. The thousands of letters he received expressed popular acclaim for 'a man sent by God'.[9] After the *Daily Herald* claimed he had been 'asking an unreasonably high price' for entering the government,[10] Cripps scolded the editor over the telephone for trying to drive him out of public life again. 'We are all of us naturally missionaries for those causes in which we believe,' he told *Life* magazine in answering twenty questions about the Soviet Union.

Leaving the next move 'up to Mr Churchill', Cripps played his Russian ace on 9 February, giving his first public speech in Bristol. He said he had warned the government about the Nazi–Soviet pact before it was signed in 1939. Stalin had genuinely wanted an alliance with Britain and France, but the opportunity was missed. The sole means now of defeating Germany was the Soviet army, given 'every aid and help'. He repeated the substance of the speech in the fifteen-minute 'Postscript' slot (made famous by J. B. Priestley) on the radio, contrasting the harsh Russian and the relatively safe British conditions. The two countries were seemingly fighting unrelated wars, though it was 'a single war' made indivisible by common suffering. He felt 'a lack of urgency' in Britain, cluttered up by old conceptions, outmoded party politics and private economic concerns. Total war demanded a total effort. Anyone holding back because of personal interest was given short shrift in Russia. 'Are your hardships and sacrifices comparable to those of the Soviet citizens who are fighting your battle just as you are fighting their battle?'[11]

The broadcast, homely and restrained, had an electrifying effect. Nine out of every ten of a sample who heard it said they approved of his sentiments ('full of sense', the country was 'not doing enough', it would 'shake some people up'), the highest approval rating ever recorded. Cripps was unknown, but there was a growing demand for bringing him into the government and even into the War Cabinet, the first 'progressive' alternative to the Prime Minister since Churchill took office. The broadcast had a further effect: it enraged another accomplished radio performer – the Prime Minister.

'How', other politicians wondered about his splash of publicity, 'does he do it?'[12] The impact of what he had to say was helped by its timeliness. In the Western Desert, Benghazi had just fallen to Rommel. In the Far East, Japanese troops in Burma were advancing on Singapore. Nearer home, two German prize battleships escaped up the English Channel, avoiding serious damage. It seemed to be a war Britain was losing. Cripps carefully avoided alluding to current military setbacks, leaving his audience to draw the inference.

His overnight popularity was enhanced by his idealised public image. In the pre-opinion-poll age, the public mood was largely unanalysable. In wartime, morale was closely monitored. Mass Observation, a private survey organisation, made a special study of Cripps.[13] It found the message he imparted was aided by how little he was personally known. He had spoken with straight-forwardness and evident sincerity, in stark contrast to the overflamboyance of Churchill or standard ministerial statements. Cripps stood for himself, independent and unattached, compared with the old parties and the usual faces. Above all, he was resplendent with success; the rest of the political class was tarnished by disasters. In all of this, Cripps – the ill-fitting maverick thrown out of the Labour Party and banished to the Soviet Union – was exceptionally fortunate. All his handicaps became advantages. All his 'snakes' turned into 'ladders'.

These findings must be treated with care. Systematic polling was still in its infancy. Mass Observation mostly used unpaid amateurs. Many of those questioned showed a distinct lack of political interest, being unable or unwilling to offer unprompted opinions. The preconceptions of Mass Observation – of a Britain moving leftward – strongly shaped its results.

Cripps was popularly associated with Russia, but other than this, he was without liabilities. Few (only 1 in 30) recalled his inter-war behaviour. A small number remembered he had been expelled from the Labour Party, without being able to say why. The public – as opposed to the parliamentary – impression was of a new man, without an incriminating past, the focal point for only half-formulated ideas of progressive reform that lay behind his celebrating of 'the common people'. This provides a large part of the explanation of the transmuting of the Cripps of the 1930s into the Cripps of the 1940s. His return from Russia in the spring of 1942 can justly be described as a resurrection.

The immediate effect was his supplanting of Beaverbrook. Cripps, a distraught Beaverbrook reminded colleagues, had predicted Russia would fall in a matter of weeks. Cripps, when Russia kept in the war, had wanted to 'bargain' with the Soviet government about supplying matériel, which Beaverbrook had overridden. Cripps, unlike he, had not got on with Stalin or been trusted by his ministers. His journalists were unable to dispel the legend.[14] Cripps had 'brought Russia in on Britain's side';[15] he was the architect of a closer relationship with Russia, the man who had 'never recanted'. The world had changed, not he. But Kingsley Martin, editor of the *New Statesman*, expected further debunking.

> Now that he has apparently decided not to play in with the present Cabinet, a subtle press campaign is practically certain. It is true that he was very isolated in Moscow; that was inevitable in view of Moscow's policy for the first two years of the war. It is also true that the strength of Russia's resistance was a pleasant surprise to him. But he was more right than most people.[16]

Cripps tried to be realistic about Russia, given the wartime imperatives. This realism did not escape censure. The illusions of the inter-war Right (about Germany) were shattered in 1939. To many observers the illusions of the Left, which, though shaken by the Nazi–Soviet pact, revived in 1941 with the return of the Soviet Union to the anti-fascist camp, were equally sinful. But the condoning of the pact, the make-believe that Russia was neutral up until it was attacked, the readiness to recognise its 1941 borders, were all things Cripps conceded to Russia. The assuaging of Stalin, no less than the appeasing of Hitler, was tantamount to conniving at Soviet expansionism, except that the 'men of Munich' were now to be found on the Left.[17]

Although evidence is patchy, Cripps seems to have met this argument in three ways. Barbara Drake confirmed that his stay in Russia made him realise that revolution left an aftermath of brutality. He appreciated the sense of social and economic democracy, but felt keenly Russian intolerance, crudeness, suspicion and indulgence.[18] Another witness, Mervyn Stockwood, a vicar in his constituency, said Cripps visited Bristol East to speak in St Matthew's Hall – he gives the date as May 1941, but it was probably1942 – to deliver an uncomfortable lecture on the excesses of Stalinism: 15 million political prisoners and a dictator betraying socialism in a regime indistinguishable from Hitler's Germany.[19] Asked if the abuses were remediable, he said it all depended on 'whether or not you believe in the triumph of the human spirit. I do, but it may take five hundred years'.

It was pointless, therefore, applying Western standards. Soviet actions would be governed by a ruthless regard for Soviet interests, as anyone who had dealt with Stalin or Molotov, as he had, could see. He shocked liberal friends by denying Soviet foreign policy need have any ethical basis.[20]

What was left was the brute fact of Soviet power, and its future extension. If the Soviet Union were to overcome Germany, it would end up in Berlin, able to dictate terms by force. Had the British been more forthright, they could have made the most of the weakness of the Soviet Union when – in July 1941 – the Russians would have accepted any conditions.[21] The only basis for future association was 'friendly co-operation', starting with Soviet frontier demands, he advised the Polish government-in-exile.

Cripps addressed a large meeting of parliamentarians in one of the committee rooms of the Commons. Labour's hierarchy kept away, but the lobbies hummed with talk of MPs 'lining up' behind him. So soon after the capitulation of Singapore to the Japanese on 15 February, the conviction grew even among Commonwealth representatives that Cripps was needed in office. The Australians, virtually defenceless, were particularly in a frenzy.[22] Chatting with Stanley Bruce, the Australian High Commissioner, Cripps indicated he was willing to 'lend a hand' only if the War Cabinet was reconstituted, not to balance the parties but bring in the right personnel. Beaverbrook was a 'menace', Churchill, a tired-out warhorse.[23] The whole war machine had to be reorganised. Cripps, Bruce reported to his superiors, was the first person he had come across who could stand up to and influence Churchill.[24] At the same time Bruce attempted to turn Eden and Attlee – both members of the War Cabinet – against Churchill.[25]

Stuart, the Chief Whip, alerted Churchill to the danger. 'We must', Churchill replied, 'enlarge the bait'. He saw Cripps again on 17 February, offering him a seat in the War Cabinet and the dual non-departmental posts of Lord Privy Seal and Leader of the House of Commons. To 'accommodate' Cripps, Attlee moved aside, taking the honorific title of Deputy Prime Minister. Beaverbrook, after a brief reign as Minister of Production, was dropped altogether, as were Greenwood and Wood. The changes, fought over for days, were more extensive than expected, but still left Churchill (controversially) in charge of Defence. Labour's hostility to the non-party people's champion was uninhibited. Attlee tried to prevent Churchill from taking the 'unreliable' Cripps in. 'Having excommunicated Cripps in the peace,' Beaverbrook wryly commented, '[Attlee] is not going to make him assistant Pope in the war.'[26] Eden too was upset, believing the Prime Minister had offered the leadership of the House to him. The compact between Churchill and Cripps was, however, far-reaching. Churchill, sobbing, appealed to Cripps for them to pull the country through.[27] Cripps, installed in offices at 11 Downing Street, understood they were to run the war in unison, 'quietly confident' that through Churchill he and Eden could drive the government machine.[28] The Prime Minister, for his part, knew how to handle the pretender. 'Well, did you make your peace with Buckingham Palace?' he quipped after Cripps had been to see the King.[29] 'He is talented, he is sincere and above all he is lucky,' a Tory MP wrote of Cripps's remarkable ascent, 'but he is in a powerful but difficult position.'[30]

Identifying a 'restiveness' in public opinion, the new Leader of the House – 'erect and distinguished'[31] – delivered his first Commons speech on 25 February, promising to convey the concerns of MPs to the War Cabinet and vice versa. 'I saw Aneurin Bevan standing below the bar watching Cripps as if he were a fallen angel,' Chuter Ede wrote that night in his diary. 'Cripps, Bevan and Strauss were expelled together from the Labour party. Bevan and Strauss made their peace; Cripps remained obdurate. Today Cripps leads the House of Commons; Strauss is his PPS [Parliamentary Private Secretary] and Bevan stands below the bar!!'[32] Cripps reeled off a number of bracing measures marking the changeover to the fullest of war efforts, among them an over-hauling of the machinery of government, the elimination of selfish personal extravagance, and a restriction on sporting activities. 'No person can be allowed to stand in the way of efficiency or swiftness of production.' A true picture of the war would be given to the British public. Preparations for post-war reconstruction were to continue. Constancy of purpose was the keynote: 'The circumstances are very grave, and the Government are convinced that it is the wish of the people in this country to meet this grave situation with all the seriousness and austerity that it undoubtedly demands.'

'War austerity' had been talked of ever since rationing had been introduced. What was new was the way this exhortation chimed with the high thinking and modest living the Crippses now practised, occupying only a two-room apartment in Whitehall Court, subsisting on £5 a week, with Cripps seen eating his frugal breakfast in a Lyons' Corner House alongside other office workers. It also fitted in with his anti-materialistic streak, though Isobel was anxious he should not be cast as a killjoy, nor that the 'Hallelujah Chorus' of adulation should sour his working relationship with the Prime Minister.[33]

Cripps's entry into the highest reaches of the government came about by impressing the urgency of the situation upon the public, the press and the politicians. The Prime Minister had to give way, yielding to Cripps a share in the making of the war and the peace. All the unfavourable contrasts Cripps had drawn were with the 'gallant' Soviet Union, German propagandists promptly labelling him 'Stalin's Viceroy'. The first test of his new partnership with Churchill was not, however, over the central direction of the war or the Anglo-Soviet alliance, but about India, imminently endangered by the Japanese.

THE OFFER

I told Nehru that if they accepted my terms *I* should be such a
Tremendous Figure in England that *I* could do everything.
                    Cripps to Lionel Fielden of the Observer *in April 1942*[1]

By March 1942, the war, in its thirtieth month, was finely balanced. The worst
of the Blitz had been weathered. The Soviet Union and the United States had
been forced into the fight, allied with Britain. Each extension of the war,
however, made greater demands on the resources of Britain's highly exposed
empire. Supplying Russia hampered the provisioning of the Far East. Singapore
surrendered to the Japanese, and Burma was quickly overrun. With the Pacific
and the Indian oceans wide open to Japanese naval power, the whole of the
Indian subcontinent looked to be in peril.

To rally India to its own defence, the British government reconsidered
courting nationalist feeling by promises of self-government. In August 1940 a
proposal was made by the Secretary of State for India, Leo Amery, holding out
future dominion status for India in return for co-operation in the war. It was
roundly rejected by all communities – Hindu, Muslim and Sikh. The most
Amery conceded was reconstituting the Viceroy's Executive Council to allow
for an Indian majority, without granting Indians the right to frame a new
constitution.

Pressure for a commitment to immediate dominionhood – from Indian
leaders, but also from Labour members of the Cabinet, and even from Roosevelt – obliged an unwilling Churchill to set up an India Committee of the
Cabinet, charged with devising a fresh constitutional advance. Attlee took the
chair, with Amery, Sir John Anderson (Chancellor of the Exchequer), Sir John
Simon (all three with Indian experience) and Cripps the other prominent
members. The Viceroy, Lord Linlithgow, had only just complained that mag-
nifying the constitutional issue would lose India and the war for them. The
division was not between implacable diehards and enlightened reformers.
Attlee, fearing a 'brown oligarchy', wanted to save India for the Empire. Amery,
who had been on the other side from Churchill over the India Act of 1935,
was shedding his imperialist cast of mind. Cripps had doubts about putting

responsibility for defence into Indian hands – a step too far in wartime. The common assumption of the Committee was that Britain's long-term ties with India would remain unbroken.

Cripps had often been mentioned as a special envoy to India. Before he joined the War Cabinet, the Labour Party encouraged suggestions he be sent out to reach a settlement. ('It would save so much bother', a Transport House official was quoted as saying. 'We can admire him from afar.'[2]) He was, more-over, on record as an advocate of Indian independence. With Cripps on the Committee, Amery drew up an initial declaration of aims, envisaging full dominion status after the war, the election of a constituent assembly, and (if it wished) a separate state for the Muslim minority, inviting Indians to participate in the 'counsels of their country'. Cripps's insistence that the Viceroy be replaced was omitted. To go even that far, Cripps assured a supporter of independence, there had been '*enormous* struggles'.[3]

The draft declaration was seen by the War Cabinet and the Cabinet for the first time on 3 March, to general acceptance. It then went before a larger assembly of the full Cabinet and most junior ministers, bringing in (Cripps noted) 'reactionary Tories'. Churchill failed to provide a satisfactory explanation of the background to the declaration. Discouraged, Cripps considered resignation. Faced with the Prime Minister's decision to hold back the declaration for some weeks, he fell back on the sending of an emissary, offering to go out and put the declaration across himself. Churchill leaped at the offer. 'It was', Churchill told Amery, 'just because Cripps was of the left that it would be much easier for him to carry through what is essentially a pro-Moslem and reasonably Conservative policy.'[4]

The declaration made a definite statement of future intent – post-war Indian self-government – but was hazy about obtaining Indian participation in the interim. Cripps, Amery established, was departing with a specific scheme, 'otherwise it would be said he was going out to negotiate'. On the other hand, the plan was not cut and dried, leaving Cripps to 'square the circle' by negotiation, permitting the Viceroy to bring more Indians on to the Executive so long as this was consistent with the requirements of defence and good government.[5] Whatever the outcome, it would have to come back to the War Cabinet for final approval.

Announcing the decision to a surprised Commons on 11 March, the Prime Minister spoke of a just and final settlement, whereby Cripps would 'strive to procure' the Indian parties' 'assent' to the declaration. Cripps's removal on an impossible errand delighted the Conservative back benches. The Left were dismayed that, once again, he was being called in to repair the derelictions of the 1930s.

To what extent was the Cripps 'offer' made in good faith? Even where the archives are so abundant (the official history of the Cripps mission runs to 900 pages[6]), it is unwise to be categorical. Many saw the offer from start to finish as an elaborate hoax which was never meant to pave the way for independence, its sole purpose being to quieten foreign, largely American, criticism.[7] The timing of the offer, ahead of the advancing Japanese, aroused cynicism. This does not do justice to the actualities. The offer was a gamble involving risks for the British either way, succeed or fail. The one course the India Committee ruled out was to do nothing. Both Churchill and Cripps, Amery sardonically observed, 'got the bit between their teeth' without either of them fully realising where they were heading. Halifax, translated to the Washington Embassy, put to the King the danger of misunderstandings. 'I have always liked Stafford Cripps and, as Your Majesty says, he comes in with a large opportunity. He has of course never had responsibility in Government and looks like having a pretty hard job to start off with in the shape of India. The ignorance of people here about India is quite portentous.'[8] The viceregal circle held similar views about the politicians back in London.

Cripps sincerely believed in a free India. The declaration was largely of his making, and he had suggested going to India of his own volition. For him, 'lightning swoops' had their uses in politics. Isobel informed others she had always known her husband would have to make the attempt. Had he been Prime Minister, he would have delivered a broadcast 'lifting the whole of India to its feet'. He was dazzled by the prospect of a settlement which would ensure the future independence of India. It was a manifestation, *The Observer* wrote approvingly, of his 'suicidal honesty'.[9]

Cripps had a further reason to be confident. Churchill's statement to Parliament talked of Cripps procuring the necessary measure of assent. But the impression Churchill gave him before he left was of a more flexible task, expressing high hopes of a good result (forbidding any public discussion in Britain in the meantime which might prejudice Cripps's efforts) and intimating, in Cripps's opinion, 'that he, Cripps, could make such concessions as might in his discretion be necessary in order to effect a settlement'.[10]

Cripps and his entourage – Graham Spry, David Owen and Frank Turnbull[11] – landed at New Delhi on 23 March. The door to the airplane stuck fast – an ominous portent. Japanese bombing raids on Calcutta had been continuing. It was said that Subhas Chandra Bose, a Congress rebel whose whereabouts were unclear, was, with German and Japanese backing, recruiting an Indian National Army to drive out the British.[12] German radio was doing its best to discredit the mission.[13] But, aside from Gandhi's campaign of non-co-operation, there was no general sense of war urgency. On top of all this, the Viceroy was wary of a representative of the War Cabinet and 'friend of India' descending on the subcontinent to solve the problems of centuries in a couple of weeks.

During their first talk, Linlithgow – melancholic and shrewd, a viceroy who had never seen an Indian rupee[14] – made known his anxieties. Cripps's arrival short-circuited his own scheme of political reform. Though he did not question Cripps's public spiritedness – few politicians would embark on such a risky venture – he recognised that Cripps was quite capable, if things went against him, of cabling home for greater latitude, undermining viceregal authority. Unacquainted with Cripps's instructions but not wishing to appear obstructive, he gave his endorsement to the *de facto* promise of dominion status for India after the war. When Cripps showed him his suggested arrangement, under clause (e) of the declaration, for a reformed executive made up entirely – save for Archibald Wavell, the Commander-in-Chief – of Indian representatives, the Viceroy passed it back, saying, 'That's my affair.'[15] 'He insisted', Cripps commented in his report of their meeting, 'that so far as the transitional stage was concerned the implementation of paragraph (e) should be done by him as Governor-General.'

Cripps, however, was unwilling for the moment to divulge the contents of the declaration to the existing executive. It was only after protests that he did so, to be confronted with some very close questioning about clause (e). Linlithgow, checking with Amery, received the reply that the War Cabinet was prepared for any or all of the positions on the Executive to be offered to Indian leaders should this prove essential – subject to the agreement of His Excellency and the Commander-in-Chief.[16] Talking the matter over with H. V. Hodson, the then Reforms Commissioner of the Government of India, Cripps was much more emphatic. 'You must realise that the Cabinet has quite made up its mind that India shall have everything in the way of *de facto* Dominion Status and complete Indianisation of the Executive Council except for defence.'[17]

Cripps had come invested with what he took to be the full authority of His Majesty's Government, whatever the reservations of the Viceroy and his Executive, able to use his powers of advocacy and exposition to stretch the terms of the declaration as far as they could go. If he could broker a deal, turning the Executive into a quasi-Cabinet, he was certain Linlithgow would have to go along with it. He had heard enough to know the principal battle was not over pledges for the future but over the arrangements for the immediate 'critical period'.

His first visitor was A. K. Azad, (Muslim) president of the Indian National Congress. Cripps, despite Linlithgow's opposition, put his proposal for a reformed executive to Azad, explaining that the Viceroy would function as a constitutional monarch, normally accepting the advice of the Executive/Cabinet. Azad gained the clear idea that the Viceroy's power of veto would lapse. In return he told Cripps that Congress, accepting that the British must control preparations for war, wanted the 'appearance' of an Indian Defence Minister. Jinnah, leader of the Muslim League, who Cripps saw later that afternoon, was even more forthcoming, gladdened that the declaration already envisaged the right of non-accession of any province to the new All-India Union. He, too, understood Cripps to say that the Viceroy would treat the executive as an effective Cabinet.

Encouraged, Cripps asked Churchill's consent for publication of the declaration. His evening meeting with the Viceroy was also encouraging. Linlithgow said he was willing to 'take big risks' and 'pay the big price' by way of the Executive Council, provided Cripps could secure the co-operation of all sides, without 'stealing His Excellency's cheese to bait his own trap'.[18]

While Cripps was planning the presentation of the declaration, Gandhi arrived by invitation. Cripps ignored custom by escorting him from his car. Their meeting was less hopeful. Disclaiming any official connection with Congress, Gandhi leafed through a copy of the declaration. He then told Cripps that, if that was all that the offer amounted to, 'I would advise you to take the next plane home.' Gandhi objected to the possibility of a separate Pakistan. Nor was he able to recall having blessed Cripps's 1939 plan, which closely approximated to the current offer. It was only much later, as Cripps was going to bed, that he heard of Gandhi's withering dismissal of the declaration as 'a post-dated cheque on a failing bank', implying that Indians should look to Japan for their liberation.

The day before the declaration was to be publicised, Cripps saw C. Rajagopalachari, the secretary of the Indian National Congress,[19] who urged on him that an Indian Defence Minister would make all the difference, demonstrating the irreversibility of Britain's offer, which might just – with Nehru's decisive backing – carry the Working Committee of the Congress, in spite of Gandhi. Together they revised clause (e), placing the organising of the defence of India in the first instance upon the Government of India, leaving full responsibility for the prosecution of the war with the British. Cripps dispatched the modified version to Churchill, who telegraphed his approval.

Cripps's command performance before two hundred journalists on 29 March 'was the greatest case of his career and he pleaded it magnificently'. He read out the proposal which the British government was prepared to make if it met 'with a sufficiently general and favourable reception', but asked Indians to rely ultimately on his good word. Some journalists broke into heckling,[20] but he asked for common courtesy. Whenever a critical query was raised, he was ready, exhibiting 'quicksilver geniality'.[21] India was being given the chance to govern itself like any other dominion, framing its own constitution and looking after its own frontiers and finances. States wishing to stay out of the Union could form a separate union of their own. But in the meantime it was impossible for Britain to cede the defence of India. The scheme stood as a whole. It was for Cripps alone to judge if there was an adequate degree of acceptance. 'I never saw him hesitate and he knew that every word he said would be reported all over the world and that the British government would be held to it.'[22] For the first time, 'the agent of the British government had quietly signed away the title deeds of the old British Raj'.[23]

On the thorniest issue, dividing up the defence portfolio, his candour may have been excessive. He made, the Viceroy's son suggests, a curious remark: 'You cannot change the constitution. All you can do is change the conventions of the constitution. You can turn the Executive Council into a cabinet.' This 'rash and irresponsible suggestion' – baiting the trap with the Viceroy's cheese – had not been cleared with Linlithgow.[24] Cripps had added that it would be dishonest to say an Indian Defence Minister would be responsible for the defence of India, but he had hinted enough to indicate a quasi-defence post was for the taking. The point was crucial: if the Viceroy could no longer override the Executive, he would not – at some later date, once the war was over – be able to block the promise of post-war freedom.

While Congress examined the implications of the declaration, Cripps was not at all optimistic, going over in his mind the possible ways of reconciling the Congressional demand for the defence portfolio with the integrity of Britain's defence of India. Without a magic formula he would be 'finished'. Gandhi, he felt sure, would stop at nothing to thwart any compromise. Predicting the probable rejection of the declaration by Congress and a 'resort to suppression' by the Government of India, he cabled to Churchill for authority to create a full Indian minister of defence, intending to discuss this with Wavell, returning shortly from Burma. Soon afterwards, he learned of the Working Committee of Congress vote, by 7 to 5, against acceptance of the declaration. The Committee insisted on the establishment of 'a truly National government' and demanded the constitutional changes required to bring this about. From what Cripps gleaned, however, the nub of their objections – 'It is the present that counts' – was the refusal to transfer the defence portfolio.

Cheered by the 'general approval' for 'our great offer', Churchill stiffened. Before the War Cabinet and the India Committee, he warned that an Indianised executive might order the recall of Indian troops from the Middle East. Amery, apprehensive of an open break, tried to tone down his hostility. What emerged was acceptance of the idea of an Indian appointee with defence responsibilities but an insistence that the War Cabinet should be told before any new commitments were given. Conveying this decision, Churchill reminded Cripps the declaration was a commonly agreed 'final position'. This coincided with the starting up of private cables from the Viceroy and Wavell (not shown to Cripps) critical of the treatment of the existing Executive, the handling of the talks, and the misleading suggestion about 'cabinet government', demonstrating to London that Cripps had not won the Viceroy's confidence.[25]

Colonel Louis Johnson, the personal representative of Roosevelt, arrived in Delhi at the head of an American supply mission.[26] At Cripps's written request, Johnson became an intermediary. Cripps outlined three options – refuse all concessions, introduce an Indian Defence Minister subservient to the Commander-in-Chief, or divide the defence portfolio between a War Ministry and a Minister for the Co-ordination of Defence. Cripps favoured the second of these, but – he informed Johnson – expected Linlithgow and Wavell would oppose both of the last two options, in which case the offer was 'doomed'.[27] India, in that event, would at best retreat into neutralism. Within twenty-four hours of arriving, Johnson had urgently contacted Roosevelt, asking him to intercede with Churchill before it was too late.

In fact, on 5 April, Linlithgow and Wavell agreed to support the third choice, cabling London to that effect. But, because Linlithgow was kept in the dark about Cripps's original instructions, his fears grew. He dispatched a further telegram to Churchill – Isobel's host at Chequers – demanding it be made crystal clear that the constitutional position of the Executive Council and in particular the 'overriding' powers of the Viceroy would remain unchanged.[28] Cripps had presumptuously assumed that the Viceroy, by developing the conventions, would be able to act *as if* the Executive Council had been turned into a collective Cabinet. The Viceroy successfully prevailed on Cripps to exclude any reference to a future 'Cabinet', substituting instead the phrase 'National Government'. Their discussion was not aided by the comments of 'an Indian politician' (Nehru) that the only question was who was to be 'boss' and that all defence responsibilities should be placed in Indian hands, nor by news of heavy shipping losses inflicted by a Japanese fleet in the Indian Ocean.

The War Cabinet, guided by the India Committee, replied on 6 April. Cripps was authorised to pursue an Indian defence portfolio, so long as the Commander-in-Chief's position was safeguarded. The special powers of the Viceroy must, however, be preserved. 'There should be no misunderstanding between you and the Indian political leaders on this point.'

Cripps was now able to put the revised offer to Azad and Nehru, though Nehru doubted he would be able to talk the Working Committee of Congress round, evidently hoping Roosevelt might 'squeeze' the British into further concessions. The obstacle was not Nehru, however, but Gandhi. Cripps had his own solution to the Mahatma. 'I'm sure I could out-fast him and bring him to terms. He would call begging me to take a sip of orange juice and be ready to sign the proposals. That would rouse the Indian people!'[29]

Instead, he made a final appeal to Nehru, telling him 'the moment for supreme courage' had come. Prompted by Johnson, he reworked the Indian defence portfolio option, 'dressing the doll up another way'. The old proposal had been to create a new Indian Defence Minister, invested with all those powers the Commander-in-Chief could safely relinquish. Reworked, the Defence Minister would retain all functions not explicitly transferred to the War Ministry, meeting what Congress was asking for. Wavell was antagonistic when Johnson put this to him, but eventually gave in. Linlithgow preferred reverting back to defining what the specific functions of the new Ministry of Defence would be.

Johnson gave the new draft to Nehru on 8 April. Nehru's response was to ask if they could return to the prior position of a listing of functions to be handed over to the Commander-in-Chief's War Department. This was accepted, and copies were handed to Nehru (again), Linlithgow and Wavell. At their regular evening meeting, however, Linlithgow vented his reservations, objecting that disputes over the allocation of functions should be referred back to London. When Cripps told him the Cripps–Johnson formula had already gone out to Congress, Linlithgow blew up. Johnson appeared, claiming a settlement was in sight. All the animosity between the Viceroy and Cripps came to the surface. Cripps could only argue lamely that the revised formula had been seen by one of the Viceroy's staff, but he was unshaken. The Viceroy, he told aides, 'is becoming a bloody nuisance. He thinks that because he has been shown everything courteously, he must decide everything. I am going ahead – why the bloody hell should he hold up everything between HMG and the parties?'[30] Privately he began considering who should be acting Viceroy 'if there is to be a change'.

The Viceroy set out his grievances in a lengthy telegraph to Amery. Cripps had exceeded his instructions. He (Linlithgow) could not, however, run the risk of letting Congress drive a wedge between Britain and the United States, and would therefore agree to the revised formula. But he hoped Amery understood his injured feelings. Amery realised the nature of the agreement that Cripps, with the intrusion of Colonel Johnson, was closing in on. Cripps was asked to explain exactly what had been offered to Congress and how far acceptance of the offer depended on the defence formula. Churchill, before the War Cabinet convened, demanded the separate approval of Linlithgow and Wavell. He followed with a second cable, explaining (on the strength of a talk with Harry Hopkins, Roosevelt's special adviser) that Colonel Johnson was not empowered to involve himself in any matters outside the narrow confines of his technical mission. This attitude was backed up by the War Cabinet, relayed to Cripps later that same day, rebuking him for going behind the Viceroy's back and asking for a clear account of where his discussions now stood, deeming it essential that he bring the talks back to the Cabinet's original scheme.

Cripps, explaining and re-explaining the terms to Congress and insisting he must have their definite answer by the next day, took the new twist badly. Realising the Viceroy had been sending cables without telling him, 'it means', Cripps commented, 'I can no longer trust him'.[31] His instructions rescinded, 'all my government is "ganging up" on me'. With a satisfactory settlement within reach, Cripps, in some embarrassment, had to inform Johnson he could not now make any change whatsoever to the original declaration without

Churchill's approval, and that Churchill would consent only to changes explicitly agreed to by the Viceroy and the Commander-in-Chief.[32] Johnson told an incredulous Cripps he had learned from Wavell that the British did not intend defending India from the Japanese anyway.[33] Cripps indignantly cabled to Churchill, certain he had stayed within the four corners of the declaration but offering to hand the matter over to someone else: 'Unless I am trusted I cannot carry on with the task.'

In their final talks with Cripps, Nehru and Azad noted the way Cripps skirted round the question of viceregal authority. They had been given to understand the Viceroy would act as nothing more than a constitutional figurehead. Cripps now seemed to be drawing back, as the War Cabinet's telegram required him to. Before, he had spoken of a 'National Government'. Suddenly he could give no assurances about the conventions the Viceroy would try to operate. To Congress, his efforts to explain this away[34] – an accusation he strongly denied – was a betrayal, 'the whole structure' he had built up, as Nehru told Johnson, having no foundations. Opponents of the offer grabbed the opportunity to move the rejection of the revised scheme, which was enough to tilt the Working Committee of Congress against acceptance. A telephone call from Gandhi, intercepted by the Government of India, carried the day. Azad's final letter of rejection expressed disillusion that 'the new picture you placed before us was really not very different from the old', since the Viceroy would continue to exercise all his old powers. Once Congress had declared its opposition, the Muslim League publicly followed suit.

Any hope of salvaging the talks was killed off by the War Cabinet repudiating any right of Cripps to negotiate or for there to be any convention limiting the Viceroy, Churchill ticking him off by cable for being drawn into positions 'far different' from any the Cabinet had approved at the outset. 'You have done everything in human power,' the Prime Minister reassured him. 'You must not feel unduly discouraged by the result. The effect throughout Britain and in the United States has been wholly beneficial.'[35] With that, he danced a jig around the Cabinet room.[36]

Although he felt robbed by the late intervention of his colleagues, Cripps latched on to the objections of Congress – and the influence of Gandhi – as 'the real cause of the breakdown of the negotiations'.[37] Their rejection had been on the widest ground and not solely on the defence issue. The original declaration had embodied a genuine offer of freedom to India, he explained in a farewell broadcast. Past distrust, however, remained too strong for present agreement. Large-scale constitutional changes of the kind Congress had sprung on him were 'practically impossible' in time of war. 'Congress wanted all or nothing – they could not get all, so they got nothing.' The draft declaration was withdrawn, he said, and the position reverted to the one before he came out. A tired, empty-handed Lord Privy Seal and his party flew out of New Delhi on 12 April, three weeks after arriving.

Roosevelt, learning from Johnson that Churchill had caused the deadlock, made a belated attempt to postpone Cripps's departure, but this brought only a long bout of cursing from the Prime Minister. After calming down, he sent his reply. Cripps had already left and all the explanations had been published. The issue simply could not be reopened all over again. 'Anything like a serious difference between you and me would break my heart . . .'

To nationalist Indians, Cripps's behaviour was utterly mystifying. Why had he, an avowed ally of Indian freedom, acted as the 'Devil's Advocate' of British imperialism, unless it was to bestow upon the British government a much needed propaganda victory? He was too wooden and insensitive, Nehru thought, his take-it-or-leave-it approach far too dogmatic for Indian tastes.[38]

American opinion – though not all shared Johnson's views – was persuaded there was no mystery. While Cripps had been in earnest, the Indian problem crying out for a swift settlement, his government had never expected or wanted him to succeed, 'torpedoing' his offer at the vital moment. Cripps, Johnson affirmed to the State Department, admitted it was possible that Churchill had sent him to India with the deliberate intention of destroying his political future.[39]

Failure was a bitter pill. In the House of Commons (Churchill was not in his seat) and the War Cabinet, Churchill at first tried to avoid a discussion, there being 'no particular point'[40] – Cripps maintained the official fiction that Congress, encouraged by Gandhi's wrecking, had blocked an agreement. When a backbencher suggested that his instructions had been the limiting factor, he vigorously shook his head. His personal standing was not harmed. The failure, *The Times* argued, would have been not to have made the attempt.[41] He locked away the knowledge that too many people both in India and at home – Gandhi and the Congress Party, unready for responsibility, the Viceroy, sending him packing, Churchill, hiding his joy behind mock solicitousness, even Attlee, silently praying for a break between Churchill and Cripps[42] – wished him to trip up.

He left India offering to take the blame if it would help in uniting the country in its resistance to Japan. He had done his duty, with the best offer he could extract out of the coalition, even if this put him – a party of one – at variance with friends and supporters. What he was not prepared to do was defend a policy in which he had no share. It brought home to him that, on defence policy as much as on wider government policy, he must 'stay close to Winston',[43] inducing him to make the right decisions.[44]

13
===

TAR

If Torch fails, we are all sunk.

Eden to Cripps, October 1942[1]

Throughout the weeks and months of heavy losses in South-East Asia, a dispirited Churchill – often found with his head in his hands, complaining of the immense burden he had to endure – fell back on a dogged refrain. The war was his war, winnable only in his way. His command of the military machine was the only guarantee of final victory. This central contention Cripps – the newest (with Oliver Lyttleton, Minister of Production) of the seven members of the War Cabinet – had the temerity to contest. If the Prime Minister could win the war by his mercurial methods, then he, Cripps, 'really had no use'.[2]

Stuck with Cripps, Churchill worked off his irritation by poking fun at his spartan holiness, unsure whether Cripps, who had gone to the brink of his brief in India, would stick by him. Cripps's anomalous status helped. He was a Leader without a party, welcome to the Conservatives (the Commons still dominated by the Conservative intake of the 1935 election) because he was so unwelcome to Labour. The richest of ironies was that Cripps soon had his hands full shielding the Prime Minister from parliamentary criticisms of one-man government with which Cripps largely agreed.

Nevertheless, Cripps, displaying 'an intense interest in the whole running of the machine',[3] yearned for changes.

He pushed in the first instance for a redirecting of the conduct of the war. The Prime Minister had been magnificent, but had shouldered an impossible load, taking too many operational decisions on impulse. It was Cripps, in his maiden speech as Leader of the House in February, who revealed that the policy of 'area' bombing of enemy cities was 'coming under review' – a giveaway which incensed the new Commander-in-Chief of Bomber Command, Air Marshal Arthur Harris.[4] In March, stopping off in Cairo on the way to India, Cripps sided with General Auchinleck in ruling out – because of tank short-ages – any resumption of the offensive in the Western Desert before May, infuriating Churchill.[5] More disturbingly, he took seriously the German peace feelers reaching him from Dr Visser 't Hooft (of the World Council of

173

Churches), who gave him a memorandum from Adam von Trott. Cripps showed the document to Churchill. Churchill insisted on 'absolute silence'.[6] Cripps subsequently told 't Hooft he could encourage von Trott, but only on the basis of Germany's defeat.[7]

Cripps widened his scope by recommending a complete overhauling of the machinery of government, another 'Haldane' (after the inquiry of 1918), suggesting a new war directorate, under a single Minister for War, to supercede the Chiefs of Staff Committee, and a drastic reduction in the number of inter-departmental committees.

He connected a more effective prosecution of the war with plans for the post-war world, the war a 'forcing-house' for change. Churchill was loath to look too far ahead, lest this detract from the priority of victory. He disliked the idea of 'misery first' that Cripps had initiated, made up of 'fussy restrictions' which were 'too often inculcated by people who are glad to see war-weariness spread as a prelude to surrender'.[8] Nevertheless Cripps got his way with a range of measures across Whitehall departments to prohibit pleasure motoring, luxury clothing and entertainments. The war, he broadcast, was condemning all the old inequalities of wealth and class, fostering a new sense of comradeship, a spirit the country must 'coolly and scientifically' apply to the tasks of recon-struction – an 'uncompromisingly and radically Socialist' speech, Harold Nic-olson wrote, 'not wholly in harmony with the party truce'.[9]

The influence of this levelling outlook was shortly demonstrated. Dalton, moved to the Board of Trade in the February reshuffle, came forward with contentious proposals to increase fuel production and decrease fuel con-sumption, adopting a scheme (by Sir William Beveridge) of domestic fuel rationing. Conservative MPs hated the points system rationing involved; they hated still more an associated idea to requisition the mines, a stepping-stone to full-scale State control. Dalton watched Cripps's comeback with some envy, expecting the bubble soon to burst. But Cripps was his willing ally over coal, restive enough to make of it a first-class 'show-down'. After Dalton had addressed the Conservative 1922 Committee, Cripps sent his second PPS, the Tory Gerald Palmer (of the biscuit manufacturers), to gauge the Committee's opinion.[10] He then used the Tory divisions to quash an alternative rationing scheme which would, he claimed, encourage a black market in coal. Officers of the 1922 only just stopped short of reprimanding Palmer for divulging confidential party discussions.[11] Dalton went on to push for a larger reorgan-isation of the coal industry, designed to be more attractive to the coal owners. On this, too, Cripps was prepared to 'go out', teaming up with Dalton, Attlee and Bevin – the latter suspecting the Leader of the House was already looking for an excuse to split from the government.

In the event, in the one Conservative parliamentary revolt of the war, a compromise was reached, with reorganisation of the Mines Department and postponement of rationing. It brought Cripps into touch with Tory reformers, however. At a Fabian gathering, he defended the electoral truce, did not want to press for fundamental changes during the war, and argued for a post-war National Progressive Government[12] to consist of centre-ground politicians from the non-trade union wing of the Labour Party and advanced Conservatives. Had Cripps been 'nobbled'? Orwell asked. Any credible challenger to Churchill needed Tory backers. It said much for Cripps's ingenuousness that, only a little while after tangling with the 1922 Committee, he was giving dinners to Labour, Liberal and Conservative MPs. At one of these 'in honour' of Cripps at the Savoy, attended by an amused R. A. Butler (by now Minister of Education), Cripps – feeding on one small omelette and two bowls of salad – astonished the assembly by wanting a wartime general election, envisaging a joint government of Lyttleton, Eden and himself, Churchill having been pushed aside once victory was secured because he did not understand the home-front problems of unemployment and housing.[13] Another young Tory, David Eccles, thought Cripps 'admirable' and not at all demented.[14] Bevin, on the other hand, attending a meeting with flattering Conservatives a little while afterwards, exclaimed he was too wily an old dog to be fooled: 'I am not Stafford Cripps!'[15]

During the times when Churchill was away, Cripps endeavoured to make headway revamping the government machine. Whenever Churchill was at his most unreasonable, Cripps could always find a further reason for staying put: Beaverbrook. Cripps judged his influence over the Prime Minister by one criterion – the more he saw of Churchill, the less effect Beaverbrook could have. It was personal – Cripps thought the Beaver a Svengali figure – but also to do with policy. Beaverbrook represented high profits, private control and amorality. He was playing a 'deep game', exploiting the second front, about which Cripps was losing interest, denigrating Cripps in his newspapers. Any hope Churchill might have of bringing Beaverbrook back came up against the combined blocking of Cripps, Bevin and Attlee.

For the time being, Cripps's prestige as an out-of-the-ordinary member of the government remained high (he read all the Mass Observation reports). Fellow MPs had a keener appreciation of his deficiencies. He was always clear and precise, but lectured the House, insensitive to its changing mood, mixing poorly in the corridors and hardly entering the Smoking Room. He was not 'formidable', did not carry votes in his pocket. Following a free vote on the Sunday opening of theatres, Shinwell, a prominent critic of the Government, claimed government MPs had been dragooned into the 'Aye' lobby; Cripps's denial was 'poppycock'. Bevan, in the thick of a fierce anti-Churchill campaign in *The Tribune*, lodged the same complaint. Cripps struggled to justify the holding of secret sessions, insisting that matters like shipping losses (which were enormous) could not be debated publicly. So long as the war continued to go badly, he was branded by association.

Discontent peaked after the shock capture by Rommel of the garrison of Tobruk on 20 June, prompting the tabling of a vote of censure on 'the central direction of the war'. Cripps summarised the reasons for the disturbance of opinion in the Commons and the country in time for Churchill's reply, after the Prime Minister's return from Washington. The angry reaction to the news from Libya and the victory of an 'independent' (an employee of Beaverbrook's *Express*) in the Maldon by-election, Cripps considered, were not aimed at Churchill personally but stemmed from a generalised feeling that something was wrong with 'those in authority' which needed righting without delay. He listed six points common to 'seriously thinking people'. The reports from Cairo had been consistently over-optimistic. Better generals were necessary, with an aptitude for mechanised warfare (Cunningham, outmanoeuvred by Rommel in late 1941, had never handled armoured forces before). British weaponry (Beaverbrook's tanks) was inferior. Not enough use was made of scientific advances. Contrary to claims, British air superiority had been ineffective. This led on to wider doubts about the supreme military command.[16]

The movers of the motion weakened their own case by contradictory arguments. The inexperienced Lyttleton, however, who was put up for the government at the end of the first day, performed poorly, reflecting badly on Cripps, who had picked him.[17] Churchill, on 2 July, robustly turned the debate into a vote of censure of his critics, the House dividing to defeat the motion by a crushing 475 votes to 25. From his attitude, it was apparent to Cripps that the Prime Minister had little intention of mending his ways. A few days later, taking tea with rebel Labour MPs, Cripps told them of his dissatisfaction. He did not think the government would last much longer, nor did he intend staying in it.[18]

Before 'clarifying' the situation, Cripps invited Thomas Jones to see him about what 'may have very great consequences – in one way or another'.[19] Cripps was thinking of presenting the Prime Minister with a blueprint for a higher professional war directorate (an idea obtained from Liddell-Hart, the military strategist, through David Owen), freed from departmental or service loyalties, accompanied by a morale-raising campaign demonstrating what Britain was fighting for. If Churchill did not agree to it, he would resign. 'TJ', pitying the innocent Cripps, supported handing in the proposal but advised against threatening resignation. Through other intermediaries, Cripps tried to discover who else would join him. Malcolm MacDonald, High Commissioner for Canada, was surprised to be called to Cripps's office and asked in strictest confidence whether he thought others might be ready to replace Churchill with Cripps himself (MacDonald did not pursue the suggestion).[20] Up to ten ministers were believed to be in favour. The editor of *The Times* was asked if he would pledge his paper to Cripps. Barrington-Ward, protecting his independence, did not think Cripps would get anywhere by acting alone.[21] In the end Cripps sent off his memorandum to Churchill, who took it with him on his trip to the Middle East, the Afrika Korps knocking on the door of Alexandria and his premiership tottering.[22] 'Here we are', Churchill told the troops, 'surrounded by sand, not a blade of grass or a drop of water – how Cripps would love it.'[23]

One more military reverse, 'TJ' reckoned, and Churchill would go. Anxious to avoid Eden, the Labour MP Ivor Thomas told him, most Conservatives would look elsewhere. Since a majority of the Labour Party preferred Cripps to Attlee, this would carry Cripps to the top.[24] His ascendancy was 'inevitable'. The whole world, Isobel remarked, had suddenly come within their orbit, their 'band of supporters' mounting. This took only slight account of how far her husband's stock had fallen on the Left. Cripps, Strauss's secretary told his aunt, was deep down a conservative. Beatrice Webb carried the critique further. He was self-centred, never consulted others, and only ever promoted his own policy, which was constantly changing. He was hostile to Soviet communism. Listening to an account of an evening with the Cripps family, in which Cripps discussed picking the right moment to resign (while ensuring he did not let 'the Beaver' in at the head of a 'Peace Party'), Dalton pored over every detail of the Lord Privy Seal's 'nauseating', 'egoising', 'farrago of nonsense'.[25]

Churchill's riposte to Cripps's memorandum, composed after the failed cross-Channel raid on Dieppe, was a flat negative.[26] He did not think morale was as bad as Cripps suggested, so that one 'should not be swayed by passing gusts of public or parliamentary feeling'. As for the scheme for a war directorate, it was 'unhelpful'. The guiding principle of military leadership was that plans were formulated by those responsible for executing them. 'Any clever person can make plans for winning the war if he has not to carry them out.' The prospect of 'a disembodied Brain's Trust browsing about among our secrets' was unattractive. Relations between the services had never been so smooth, so he saw no reason to withdraw his confidence from them. Cripps's recipe was nothing more than 'a planner's playground'. Cripps was unassuaged. 'The man simply won't listen to evidence.'[27] 'Winston', he confided to Maisky, 'thinks I am a dreamer and a utopian, but I am firmly convinced that my plan is the shortest road to victory.'[28] The Cabinet consented to set up an investigation into the machinery of government (Cripps's earlier notion), but even this was to be carried out internally. Churchill was no less scornful. 'Nature is harmonious, not architectonic.' Such 'speculative' distraction was the rightful province of 'persons of leisure'.[29]

This snubbing convinced Cripps that he could not go on if his advice was not going to be heeded. He explained his troubles to a variety of listeners.[30] In the five months since his Indian mission, Churchill typically dealt directly with ministers, or in the Defence Committee, where the real work was straightened out. Cripps had asked to join it three times, to no avail. Beaverbrook was seeing

Churchill again regularly. Short of a revolution, the only alternative was 'some sort of compromise national unity' in home policy, the chance for fundamental change having passed by in 1940. Bevin and Citrine wanted to preserve trade union bargaining with employers. People were being 'bribed' to work harder with capitalist incentives. The Labour Party, however, 'would not touch [Cripps] with a bargepole'.

In spite of a publicity ban, his personal following remained considerable – Mass Observation recorded a steady 70 per cent popularity – but this was bound to wane. He could not wait until the next catastrophe struck. His advisers – Beveridge and the *Times* leader-writer E. H. Carr – both urged him to resign. All of the Cabinet was unhappy with Churchill's methods, but none of them would go to the point of departing – Eden least of all. Cripps's only course seemed to be to 'go out' with a fanfare, using his resignation speech to establish an alternative policy. Trapped in the government, there was no other way. 'He mustn't get so covered with tar that it won't melt off,' as Isobel put it.[31] 'Cripps is not, I think, without political ambition,' Barrington-Ward judged – 'in fact I'm sure he isn't – but ambition of a praiseworthy kind and answerable to conscience.'[32]

The difficulty of his position was highlighted by a row in the Commons on the day (8 September) the House returned after the recess. He had set aside two days of debate to review the progress of the war. Before the Prime Minister had come to the end of his opening speech recounting his visit to Moscow to see Stalin, members began trickling out of the chamber. When Attlee rose to speak, it was all but deserted, even though there were some three hundred MPs in the precincts of Westminster. Cripps had criticised the attendance record of MPs on a previous occasion. Bringing proceedings to a premature close, he admonished those members who could not wait for their luncheon for not taking their duties as seriously as soldiers at the front. Shinwell wanted to know what right the Leader of the House had to make such comments, however much he might not be concerned about meals himself. At the War Cabinet, Churchill teased Cripps with inciting MPs, whereas he valued their 'silent support'. Cripps could only point to the damage done to the prestige of Parliament, observing it was 'a mistake to assume all criticism is necessarily captious or hostile'.[33]

The House adjourning, Cripps went off for a week's break, returning to hand in a personal letter to the Prime Minister, communicating his anxiety that he did not enjoy Churchill's 'full confidence'. He was no longer relied upon for help, felt out of touch on matters about which they should concert, and feared he was sacrificing his whole future to a 'shadow' existence.[34] In a later note, he again went over all his complaints about the persistence of slackness and apathy, reflected ultimately in the production effort. Too much decision-making was 'hand-to-mouth'. The War Cabinet only 'hurriedly' met to consider crises, and could not be said to be 'conducting' the war at all. No one man could manage both the strategy of the war and the provision of resources effectively. And, even if the present machinery was right, the personnel was wanting. The Chief of the Naval Staff, Admiral Pound, was 'past his best'. He urged Churchill to make changes. The public had to be given some hope for the future. The 'inducements' so far made – in the form of increased pay or larger profits – were entirely financial, whereas Cripps wished to stress 'service' and 'sacrifice'. 'The reward should be what we are fighting for and not what people can get now.' He recalled Churchill telling him that if he (Churchill) was to run the war, he must win it his way. But Cripps was 'compelled' to press for the adoption of views which, he was certain, were 'essential' for the success of the war effort.

Churchill inclined at first to letting Cripps go. Eden talked him out of it. Instead, Churchill replied by expressing his surprise, having believed their relations were 'most cordial' and their conversations 'stimulating'. About the conduct of the war, however, he was unmoved. Another person would no doubt do things differently. Nor did he appreciate Cripps's less than generous comments about Admiral Pound or the work of the Admiralty. With complete optimism about the impending operations in the Western Desert, he viewed the future with undiminished firmness of purpose, asking Cripps to curb his 'uneasiness' and endure the waiting too.

While this exchange was taking place, Cripps endeavoured to encourage a 'spiritual incentive' by speaking to the Industrial Christian Fellowship at the Royal Albert Hall on 26 September, flanked by the Archbishops of Canterbury and York. He followed up with a broadcast sermon. The message was identical. The institutionalised Churches had failed to provide leadership for the poor and oppressed, too easily accepting 'society-as-it-is'. Bold teaching of Christian principles would, if rigorously applied, create a demand for far-reaching social and economic changes. Slums were 'an insult to God'. Religious truths were necessarily progressive. The Churches had a social responsibility, just as politics needed Christianising. Temple, the new Archbishop of Canterbury, hoped to bind together a national clerical coalition, converting business to Christian ethics. The Prime Minister's son, the MP Randolph Churchill was not thankful, disliking the spectacle of the Archbishop's politicking as much as the Lord Privy Seal's heavenly uplift. Cripps wanted the Church of England to be disestablished and disendowed – a step even Temple baulked at.

Isobel, explaining that the position with the PM was 'more unsatisfactory than ever', posted an SOS to Thomas Jones asking if he could come to London again at short notice as her husband was expecting shortly to have an interview with Churchill. Kept waiting two nights running, Cripps was finally summoned out of bed to see Churchill at 11 p.m. – a late hour which put some ministers at a disadvantage, but which Cripps liked, 'for it was then that you really got down into his mind'.[35] The first hour was friendly but firm, Churchill attacking Cripps for upsetting his government, telling him if he resigned he would disappear without trace. Cripps insisted he could not continue to serve if he was not fully consulted, either as a member of the War Cabinet or as Leader of the House. Churchill repeated he had to be allowed to run the war in the way he considered best, demanding an answer from Cripps, one way or another, within the next twenty-four hours. On that note, at 2.30 a.m., they parted.

Eden's published diary indicates that Churchill was clearly 'up in arms', convinced Cripps's actions were part of a wider conspiracy – which included Eden and Attlee – to establish a 'government of national salvation'.[36] Churchill spluttered with rage (in the version of his faithful Minister of Information, Brendan Bracken[37]) at the hardihood of Cripps, who had come to inform him of his 'dissatisfaction', and who he felt like having arrested.

The following night – lamenting that 'I never seem able to team up with anyone'[38] – Cripps was ready to resign, thinking several moves ahead.[39] Called again by Downing Street, he was sheepishly met – Churchill's doing – by Eden and Attlee, who 'begged' him to think again, considering the damaging effect his resignation would have abroad and on the armed forces.[40] If he were to go at that most critical moment, Attlee told him, he would never be forgiven. He was offered alternative (technical) posts, either co-ordinating supply in Washington or as Minister of Aircraft Production, but outside the War Cabinet. Their efforts allayed Churchill's suspicions that they were engaged in 'a deep-laid plot'.

When Churchill confronted Cripps at midday on 2 October, he was all smiles, impressed by Cripps's willingness to change jobs and reassured that Cripps's griping was a genuine personal difficulty of an honest patriot. He pressed Cripps to delay his resignation until after the launching of Torch (the American landings in North Africa). Cripps saw Eden, who told him to think only of the national need – though Cripps tried tempting him by saying they 'should all get on much better without W. anyway'. On 3 October he drafted a reply. Unconvinced that changes to the directing of the war were 'unnecessary', he emphasised his wish not to disturb morale or unity in advance of the operations in the Western Desert. 'When the time arrives', however, 'I will revert to this matter.'

There was never any question the Prime Minister would not prevail. In the 'oppressive pause' before El Alamein, Churchill doubled the stakes, obliging Cripps to stay his hand. Cripps was hardly a consummate politician. There was no conspiracy as such. Eden would not commit himself. Many of the criticisms Cripps made about the prosecuting of the war were echoed by other ministers, and have been endorsed by historians. Allied strategy, once the wartime apparatus of Anglo-American collaboration had been established by the middle of 1942, succeeded in spite of Churchill, not because of him.[41] Cripps had prospered only because of bad times. Doubtless he thought he would be prime minister sooner or later. Isobel, according to 'TJ', talked as though she were already ensconced at No. 10. At the key moment, Cripps was unable to resist the appeal to behave honourably. To show his gratitude, Churchill began circulating confidential military information to the War Cabinet and took Cripps off to review the Fleet at Scapa Flow. Cadogan oozed mandarin disdain. 'How unprincipled these politicians are. When it suits their political book, they put their "conscience" before the national interest.' Even 'TJ', who had advised Cripps to wait, was perplexed. 'Cripps is a curious mixture of earnest Christian and ambitious politician. I suppose he has so strong a sense of mission that he does not see how it strikes others as climbing and cant.'[42]

Did Cripps err in rivalling Churchill over the Prime Minister's handling of the war, instead of tying his fortunes to the coming prospects of post-war reform?[43] Winning the war was the present, make-or-break danger, Cripps reasoned. Government and country could not stand another military catastrophe. Churchill would survive, bolstered by victory, or he would 'crash'. Either way, the course of the conflict – having to take the offensive – would become harder, not easier. Sustaining domestic morale was important, and not just by giving the population a distant prospect. Part of Cripps's case was that periodic slumps in morale were adversely affecting the productive effort, impairing fighting ability. He had as many qualms about offering a future reconstruction bounty as he did about giving money rewards while the war was on. Churchill, for his part, was deliberately avoiding specific pledges.

In mid-October, it transpired that some ministers wanted to 'temporise' over the publication of a report by Beveridge recommending an all-inclusive social-security scheme. Beveridge was being leaned on to divide the scheme into five-year stages, but was refusing to trim. Cripps invited Cecil King, a director of the *Daily Mirror*, to Whitehall Court on 'a matter of great importance'. He filled him in on the general contents of the report, telling him to push it 'with all vigour'. King, not knowing of the forthcoming battle in the Desert, was baffled by Cripps's anxious state,[44] but rushed back through the blackout with his scoop, throwing the *Mirror* behind Beveridge's report and warning it must not be 'pigeon-holed' indefinitely.[45] Calling on the Webbs, Cripps spoke confidently of waging war with maximum effort, but professed a belief in the projects of Keynes and Beveridge, 'both of whom were going "left"', adding that Beveridge's 'great work' was being held up by Cabinet colleagues because it was too revolutionary.[46] Bracken was already informing Churchill that some of Beveridge's friends were 'playing politics' with the report, and that Beveridge should be prevented from leaking it.[47]

Montgomery's decisive breakthrough at El Alamein, forcing Rommel's armies to turn in disorderly retreat, unloosened an outpouring of national celebration. Cripps, touring factories in the North, hailed 'a glorious victory

for our arms in the new Libyan campaign'.[48] The Anglo-American Torch landings in Morocco and Algeria threatened the Axis troops from the rear. The
Prime Minister, flushed, called Cripps to account. Cripps took a week's holiday,
promising to talk on his return.[49]

In the Debate on the Address of the new session on 17 November, Cripps,
steering close to the coalition line of avoiding commitments to post-war legislation about which there was no agreement, set out the tempo of future
advance, arguing the government would proceed without controversy, Right
and Left advancing together. It was his swansong as Leader of the House.
Churchill, receiving (again, in Bracken's account) an apology from Cripps,
magnanimously offered him the Ministry of Aircraft Production, with the
deputy chairmanship of the newly constituted Anti-U-Boat Warfare Committee thrown in. He could also 'carry on with his Christian Socialist addresses'.
After talking the position over with Thomas Jones and Jan Christian Smuts,
the South African Prime Minister – who both encouraged him to take a grip
on the U-boat war – and his younger entourage, who saw his heart was not in
resignation, he decided to accept. He did not doubt Churchill wanted to remove
a 'nuisance'. Were he to refuse, however, Churchill might confront him with
resignation – 'an unfortunate moment for Cripps but excellent for the PM'.[50]
In his new post he could make a real contribution to the war he thought was
being so badly mishandled. But it removed him from the realm of domestic
policy, which was to dominate discussion after the turn of the year. Hearing of
his decision, Churchill was overcome by Cripps's noble act.[51] The newspapers,
having little to go on, presumed Cripps had been demoted, moved to a post
where his 'pronounced individuality' would be of greater use.[52] Gallingly, he
was replaced in the War Cabinet by Herbert Morrison, the Home Secretary.

Rejoicing at the turning of the tide in the Middle East was attended in some
quarters by gloating at the puncturing of the myth of Cripps, the undeserving
beneficiary of an exaggerated wave of public acclaim, now 'soured by British
victories'. Ever since India, Churchill had humoured Cripps, shackling him
with difficult assignments but denying him the substance of power. Realising
the impossibility of fundamentally altering the wartime state or economy,
Cripps looked for the chance to cut loose. The right issue never arose. In the
end, his 'differentness' counted against him. He lost his bearings. His ideas
were unformed ('He did not really know why he was a socialist', Elvin has
said[53]); he had no organisational backing and no high-level advisers. His popularity slowly drained away.[54] He was left with an elevated self-belief (for which
Churchill's was more than a match) that he was his country's saviour. 'A man
without party is peculiarly dependent on popular esteem. If he loses that, he
loses everything.'[55] Cripps, a friend remarked, 'hanged himself'.[56]

1 Parmoor
(*Lord Parmoor*)

2 'Dad' with his
father and sister (*Lord
Parmoor*)

3 The Queensferry
munitions factory in
mid-1915 (*Flintshire
Record Office*)

4 Labour's bashful victor in Bristol East, January 1931 (*Illustrated London News*)

5 The next leader? Cripps – George Lansbury had just been hospitalized with a broken thigh – setting off from the Commons for his chambers on the morning of 15th December 1933, after an all-night sitting of the House (*Hulton Getty*)

COUNSEL AGAINST THE DEFENCE

Sir Stafford Cripps, K.C. (*Ex-Law Officer of the Crown, at Eastleigh, March 14*). "TO-DAY YOU HAVE THE MOST GLORIOUS OPPORTUNITY THAT THE WORKERS HAVE EVER HAD . . . REFUSE TO MAKE MUNITIONS, REFUSE TO MAKE ARMAMENTS."

6   Partridge on Cripps, barrister-politician and enemy within – Punch magazine, March 1937 (*Punch*)

TRAPEZE TRAGEDY ?

—*Copyright*

11 1945: eating
(*Hulton Getty*)

12 1945: praying
(*Hulton Getty*)

13 18 August 1947. A cigar-smoking Cripps, summoned back from holiday because of the convertibility crisis, arrives in Downing Street. Moments later he was (unsuccessfully) urging Bevin, the Foreign Secretary, to 'take over' from Attlee (*Popperfoto*)

14 The two colossi: Cripps and Bevin (*Hulton Getty*)

15 'Now I must tell you why . . .' Justifying the devaluation of the pound to the press in September 1949, flanked by Harold Wilson (*Hulton Getty*)

14

MAP

'We are fighting this war for our lives. The old ways were good ways –
decent ways'.

'Wars always lead to change.' *Cripps conversing with Churchill, January 1943*[1]

Cripps went to the Ministry of Aircraft Production (MAP) in the guise of
prime-ministerial troubleshooter. 'I was asked to do a job which was said to
be necessary and urgent,' he let a perplexed backbench National Liberal know,
'and I felt it my duty to accept it regardless of my position in the War Cabinet.'[2]
Beaverbrook's crash fighter programme of the summer of 1940 had long since
given way to the Air Ministry's 'clarion call' for heavy bombers, but the MAP's
output was falling far short of service demands, undermining Bomber Command's saturation bombing of Germany's industrial centres. The U-boat battle
in the Atlantic, relying heavily on aerial detection, and also partly within the
MAP's area of competence, was equally momentous. That pursuit of the
bombing offensive cut across the war at sea added to the magnitude of the
task.

With his scientific education and fervent drive, Cripps turned the Ministry
round. His first proper office made him into a battle-hardened minister. But
the unintended consequence was just as far-reaching. The Ministry was the
most statist in Whitehall. Out of his experience a distinctively Crippsian
outlook emerged – the overriding importance of greater productivity, aided
by beneficent bureaucratic control, in a setting of national self-denial – that
preoccupied him for the remainder of his public life.

His temperament and aptitudes were well suited to the enormous scope and
scale of the MAP's responsibilities. The Ministry's role was not to run the
aircraft-manufacturing business. Its task was, as Cripps conceived it, to administer the industry in a way that would maximise output. In 1942–3 that function
was vital. The failure to expand production of heavy bombers represented the
greatest danger to Britain's war strategy.[3] For this reason, MAP was by far the
largest claimant on all factors of production – above all, on the supply of
labour. The government, the principal paymaster, underwrote the costs. It was

an archetypal instance of the dovetailing of private enterprise and public power.

To supplement the existing small number of pre-war professional plane-makers, the Ministry had constructed a much larger network of 'shadow' factories – often automobile firms – operating on an agency basis. Both the specialist companies and the 'shadow' factories subcontracted their work to thousands of engineering outfits, across the whole range of light metals, armaments, equipment and instruments, so that the Ministry reached into the smallest business concerns. MAP was not only the country's largest single employer of labour, but also industry's biggest customer, wielding commensurate penalties. Firms which continually failed to come up to requirements were often taken over and restructured to improve their capacity.

The Ministry, therefore, operated at the crossover between rival service arms, competing departments of State and outside economic interests, spearhead of the only means (before the Allied invasion of Europe) of directly inflicting damage on German soil. There is still no academic consensus about the extent of mobilisation of the British war economy relative to that of the other belligerents. But there is no doubt the coalition believed in MAP's war-winning potential.

The standing of the Ministry was unhappily offset by its recent history of unfulfilled production targets. Ever since Beaverbrook's unorthodox reign, the number of finished airplanes had steadily risen without ever attaining the set total output or the specified range of types, and modifications in new marks added to time-consuming hold-ups. The RAF and the Fleet Air Arm could never be certain of the number of planes they were likely to receive. With courage, Cripps put in place a 'realistic' minimum programme compiled by the MAP's statistician, John Jewkes, which, although a revision downward of the previous target, at least represented the output that the Ministry was prepared to guarantee. The perennial difficulty in drawing up a plan was how to arrive at an accurate assessment of possible output without relying on what individual firms told the Ministry's overseers. Putting it bluntly, said David Owen, there was a good deal of hard lying.[4] Cripps did not subscribe to the 'carrot' or incentive approach, but started with a yardstick of efficient management rather than accept some degree of inefficiency in advance. Better firms would respond when they saw every chance of exceeding their totals; the less productive would be set a target beyond their current output level but not beyond their capacity. The final targets the Ministry would 'insist on', he promised Churchill. 'I can assure you that both I and all my staff will do our utmost to improve upon the figures.'[5]

The intention was to encourage 'realistic' programme-making. This is not to say the process was entirely rational: uncertainties were intrinsic to it.[6] The sheer mechanics of preparation usually meant a programme was obsolete before it was even issued, and necessarily subject to 'continuous adjustment'.

The placing of tenders was hazardous, owing much to accident (Merlin engines, earmarked for Mosquitos, could luckily be fitted to the later Spitfire models). No common standard of the relative efficiency of different firms was ever devised. Whether or not the monthly production returns were good or bad was 'largely fortuitous'. The Ministry was nevertheless obliged to plan its way ahead, allocating resources so as to determine the pattern of future output.

Many in the MAP expected the new Minister would be inflexible and intolerant. He quickly disabused them. He called together the senior staff, urging them to use their own initiative rather than come directly to him. Whenever possible, they should telephone instead of using up yet more paper.[7] He instituted morning meetings with the Permanent Secretary, Sir Archibald Rowlands, the Chief Executive, Air Marshal Sir Wilfred Freeman, and the head of the Production Efficiency Board, Sir Charles Bruce-Gardner (the pre-war chairman of the British Society of Aircraft Manufacturers), to identify delays and recommend action. His 'lightning mind' was immediately appreciated. He rapidly digested the contents of a brief and consulted without fuss, always with a view to a constructive answer. However heavy the paperwork, he returned all his files the next day, annotated in red ink. It was a 'pleasure' to be briefing 'the best Counsel in the cabinet'. In committee, he was 'keenly penetrating, acutely analytical, economically selective', his warm, human side hidden.[8] Like all leading barristers, he cut himself off from the feelings of others, arguing with precision and turning pale when he could not get a point accepted. If he defeated colleagues in discussion, he mistakenly thought he had persuaded them. Conversely, he gave way with good grace, provided a concession did not involve any sacrifice of principle. In the 'closed' politics of committees and conferences he was a logician, 'evoking superlatives' from the Prime Minister for his handling of the Anti-U-boat Warfare Committee.[9]

Each weekend he set off on an inspection tour of MAP factories, to put across the Ministry's policy to the management and workforce, his wife accompanying him with a brown cardboard box containing their vegetarian meals. On the train or in flight, he passed the journey working on his papers. He liked astounding his hosts with his intimate understanding of aerodynamics. The assistants he brought in – Owen, Spry, Norman Luker (his speech-writer) and favourites like Anne Shaw, an expert in motion study from Metro-Vickers – as much as the regular officials, noted his unselfishness, a 'religion' to him. His only earthly vice was tobacco, enveloping his wood-panelled office at Millbank in a fug of cigarette and pipe smoke from first thing in the morning. Freeman – 'no respecter of persons' – was soon saying he could not wish to serve under a better master.[10]

Manufacturers were horrified by Cripps's appointment. To his distress, reprints of Partridge's *Punch* cartoon ('refuse to make munitions') were cir-culated by one industrialist.[11] Firms he visited suspected he was looking for excuses to nationalise them. He idealised working men, addressing them as 'Comrades', which 'stank of Russia'.[12] He believed in extending the system of Joint Production Committees which united management and workers in tackling obstacles in the way of faster production (the Minister could not meet the trade unions directly). One outspoken manager told the press he felt like 'shooting the swine'.[13] When Cripps proposed to renew Orders in Council granting him powers to bring in new directors to a firm, he was reminded in the Commons that the move 'would be treated in certain quarters as another step in an attack upon management'.[14] Compulsory acquisition of Short Brothers under Defence Regulation 18 – the Minister arrived at a day's notice, ignored the managers, and put in a controller[15] – forcing the company to switch production from Stirlings to Lancasters, demonstrated his intent.

In late February 1943, an unsigned memorandum emanating from within the industry was forwarded to the Prime Minister by Conservative MPs. Titled 'Probable Fall in Aircraft Production', it accused Cripps of undermining management, encouraging subversive labour relations, and lowering morale – a deterioration for which the MAP bore the entire responsibility.[16] 'The machinations of the Minister are forcing politics to become the first thought of executives.' Churchill passed a copy to Cripps. Cripps attributed it to a group of self-made autocrats with antiquated attitudes whom he had mentioned to the Prime Minister some weeks before. Joint Production Committees were, he added, government policy. 'I do not propose to alter my methods or my policy and I am perfectly prepared to be judged by the results which they produce.' The production figures for March bore him out, with total output exceeding the programmed target (the only month it ever did so), but he was not complacent. 'We do not allow ourselves a pat on the back,' he minuted to Lyttleton, Minister of Production. 'A particularly good week may only be the result of, or prelude to, a particularly bad one.'[17] Speaking to the 1922 Committee of Conservative backbenchers, he said he regarded private industry as being 'on trial'.

Caution was justified. The Ministry was riddled with corruption; the industry was dogged by managerial squabbles; there was confusion between pay and piece rates and also a rash of petty stoppages – much the legacy of Beaverbrook's 'ramp'. Indeed, Cripps believed Beaverbrook was directly implicated in some unofficial strikes. But the main shortcomings were structural – Cripps instanced the poor managerial state of many firms as well as the need for trade unions to exert more control over their members.

Difficulties were compounded by the slow reaction to emergency work. The Atlantic U-boat war, directed by the high-powered Anti-U-Boat Warfare Committee, was one example.[18] Once the Admiralty had made its case, Cripps pushed the idea of VLR (Very Long Range) aircraft, only for delays to arise in the conversion of fuel tanks on American Liberators.[19] This in turn hampered the Allied ability to close the 'blind' gap in the mid-Atlantic or to harass

German submarines in the Bay of Biscay. In the absence of Naval 'Ultra' (Shark) until March 1943, shipping losses mounted alarmingly.[20] When Wellingtons were finally equipped with ASV (anti surface vessel) radar, subsequently modified to incorporate the H2S target location device, the conflict was transformed by Coastal Command and the loss of tonnage was dramatically cut.[21]

There were also clashes of scientific opinion about the aerial threat from the enemy. In mid-1943, intelligence leads indicated the Germans might be developing a pilotless rocket at a test site at Peenemünde on the Baltic coast. Lord Lindemann, Churchill's scientific adviser, believed the story was a hoax. R. V. Jones, whose job was to anticipate German scientific advances, struggled to persuade ministers of the reality of the danger. Cripps, he saw, 'seemed to be more activated than anyone else, wanting Peenemünde attacked at once'.[22] Cripps argued the point in a Cabinet paper, submitting this every day for a fortnight until others were won over.[23] The eventual raid delayed the rocket programme long enough to prevent the launching of V1 flying bombs on London until after D-Day. Churchill then charged him with conducting an inquiry into pilotless aircraft, in which, however, he became more sceptical about the evidence.[24]

After the Italian armistice in September 1943, aircraft output slackened off, reflecting to Cripps's dismay, a widespread attitude that 'the war was as good as won'.[25] Total production of fighters and bombers had gradually increased, measured by numbers, structure weight and structure weight per man hour, but the MAP's programme had to be 'realistically' lowered again. Output eventually hit a peak in the first quarter of 1944, when the labour force was at its largest (1.8 million) but by that stage a general scaling down of munitions production was already under way. The Minister still used his interventionist foresight. He bought out Power Jets Ltd, the Whittle jet-engine company, maintaining it was in the public interest that the government should have a defence establishment of its own, grinningly explaining how he had discovered a 'painless' way to nationalise private enterprise by purchasing all the equity shares.[26] Whittle, who made the first approach to Cripps, later 'bitterly regretted' having done so.[27] One biographer of Barnes Wallis argues that Cripps denied the designer of the bouncing bomb a knighthood because Wallis had worked on the private-enterprise airship R100.[28]

It is commonplace to talk of Labour ministers in the wartime coalition forming a solid phalanx, dominating the home front and gaining in stature and patriotic credit, the policy of the Party conveniently adjusted by the stresses of war.[29] Cripps, nominally an independent, is usually regarded – in the way Dalton said Beveridge was not – as 'one of us'. In several respects, this is inaccurate.

For one thing, fitful relations between Labour ministers militated against any close co-ordination, let alone with Cripps. Bevin, who had found all the available labour Cripps had preferentially asked for, grumbled when the MAP could not usefully absorb it all.[30] Dalton continued to take pleasure in Cripps's crackpot fantasies. Morrison was the only figure Cripps had any affinity with. When Morrison released Mosley from jail in 1943, Cripps defended his decision. Attlee, judging by later utterances, thought the war had led Cripps to a more 'balanced' view. Cripps sent him a progressive speech of his, which included the pointed observation he had no party 'not because I sought the desert, but because I was driven into it'.[31]

The return of Beaverbrook to the government confirmed their collective weakness. In July 1942, the Bevin–Attlee–Cripps trio had been powerful enough to shut him out, Cripps refusing to serve in a government with Beaverbrook. In September 1943 Churchill could get his way. Cripps – 'shuddering' at the mere mention of the Beaver[32] – would have liked to 'walk'.[33] On the other hand, he had been urging the aircraft workforce to extra effort; it would look like a dereliction of duty if he were to depart. He contented himself by sending a letter of protest to Churchill about the 'undesirability' of the new appointment, though making it plain he wished to continue in his present post. It was not usual, Churchill responded, for a prime minister to consult his colleagues about Cabinet-making.[34] To rub it in, Beaverbrook was given the post of Lord Privy Seal, with responsibility for civil aviation.

Cripps's independence was accentuated by a further inconvenience, apt to be overlooked. While he had been without the Labour whip for four years, mixing with Acland's Common Wealth party and various Liberals, the Bristol East Labour Party had fallen into a chaotic condition. Its offices had been requisitioned, the agent, Herbert Rogers, was away on war work, and it had fallen to Hennessy to keep up appearances. Hennessy was adamant Cripps should rejoin the Labour Party at the earliest opportunity.

In February 1943, a by-election took place in Bristol Central, following the death of the Conservative MP. His widow, standing in his stead, wrote to Cripps asking for a message of ministerial support. Cripps side-stepped the request by asserting his 'independence', which forced him to refrain from playing any part in an electoral contest outside his own constituency. Breaking the terms of the electoral truce, however, ten leading members of the Bristol East party, joined by Mervyn Stockwood, now secretary of the local Common Wealth party branch, decided to assist the 'Independent Labour' candidacy of Jennie Lee (wife of Aneurin Bevan). For their pains they were reported to the borough party and found themselves not simply suspended but – like their Member – expelled forthwith. Waving aside objections, Transport House reorganised the Bristol East division, disbanding the existing 'rebel' General Council and forming a new one. Some but not all of the ten retracted and returned to the Party.

The formation of a local official party, and the likelihood of an official candidate (C. E. M. Joad, the well-known philosopher and broadcaster, was mentioned), clouded the atmosphere. As late as the spring of 1944, Greenwood had spoken to a meeting of both Labour camps explaining why the new party intended opposing Cripps at the next general election, with the aim – as Rogers described it – 'of driving you out of the constituency'.[35] At a rally in September, Hennessy, who had gone over to the new party, criticised Cripps personally, calling him a political 'chameleon' who had gone cold on the question of old-age pensions. The local MP still had a spellbinding effect on local audiences, however, causing Stockwood to think Cripps could hold the seat on his estimable merits alone. 'Had anyone else given the lengthy address on industry I am quite sure the audience would have left, but because it was Stafford they listened wide-eyed and open-mouthed and said it was quite wonderful!'[36]

The reference to industry raises the last, in many ways most important difference separating Cripps from his erstwhile Labour colleagues. Cripps prided himself on his far-sightedness, free of 'party shackles'. The lessons of wartime seemed to Attlee to show how strongly the Labour Party's assumptions were gaining general acceptance, helping to 'refine' the party programme of the 1930s. This largely trade unionist outlook, which Cripps had attacked for being too moderate (in his united-front days) and too uncompromising (after he had switched to a popular front) was hardly likely to appeal to him after he had witnessed the bleak condition of wartime industry. Going round factory floors and workshops, the evidence hit him with revelatory force.

The outdated practices of the aircraft establishment – supposedly at the forefront of technical change – gave him all the insights he needed. An industry insider, Roy Fedden, became Cripps's special adviser, as well as chairing the Aircraft Advisory Committee. Cripps called him in on his first morning and said he had heard Fedden was a 'stormy petrel' but was prepared to trust him. He sent Fedden on a three-month tour of the United States to examine the latest in aviation construction. Fedden was awestruck by the colossal size of American companies, their organisation and staffing, their investment in research, and their production-line methods, all of which he detailed in his final report. Cripps – 'a clear thinking man of vision' with 'a keen appreciation of post-war dangers ahead' – gave Fedden 'inspirational support', trumpeting his report as 'the greatest single volume that has ever been written about a single industry'.[37] British aircraft manufacturers read it with disbelief, the majority refusing to accept they had anything to learn from 'unsuitable' American techniques, branding the report 'Fedden's folly'.

To Cripps, with a grasp of technical problems rare in the top levels of Whitehall,[38] the conclusions were inescapable. Understanding how rapidly Britain was being left behind, he argued for the recruiting of a corps of highly qualified engineers, deploring the snobbish respect for the humanist scholar in the great schools and universities. Scientific strength gave Britain the edge.[39]

He proposed setting up a technological institute, which the industry lobbied actively against (the Cranfield Institute was eventually set up in 1946). 'I hope you aren't leading me up the garden path,' Cripps remarked to Fedden. 'They say you are, but I believe you.'[40]

Party politics, beginning to stir, Cripps saw as a hindrance rather than a help. The parties were too sectional and too conservative. In the circumstances they would face after the war, no 'ism' should be allowed to interfere. The war had amply illustrated that they had to approach problems by the practical test of judging by results. The 'amazing' record of wartime production pointed to the lesson. Capital and labour had forged a 'partnership' built on team spirit and mutual respect. There could be no going back to the bitter industrial relations of the inter-war years. The nation owed a debt of gratitude to management, though many firms were run on archaic, unprofessional lines. The unions, on their side, had at one time been solely concerned with obtaining the most for their members; now they participated fully in the Joint Production Committees, extending democracy into the workplace. Bevin had assured the unions that, in the war effort, labour would not be taken advantage of. In return, it was incumbent upon them not to exploit their new-found influence.[41]

Greater use had to be made of the application of science, with large numbers of scientists and technicians being educated and trained. Britain had to discover how best to rebuild and re-equip industry, paying attention to 'human' and not just mechanical problems of the productive process.[42] The State would have to step in. It was not a matter of absolutes: of total nationalisation or completely free markets. Control counted for more than ownership. The State could organise investment industry by industry, accompanied by international bulk purchasing and State trading. It would be up to the private sector to 'justify its continuance', not letting the country down by failing to modernise. Every factory was a 'national asset'. But there was no reason to prop up 'dying' industries. A new public service would see to it that government and market operated for the good of the whole, carrying over the wartime thrust of 'planning' and 'enterprise' into the post-war era.

The war, which revealed what needed doing, also magnified the enormity of the challenge lying ahead. In the cause of total conflict, Britain had achieved the 'almost impossible', but at the expense (unlike in the 1914–18 war) of its overseas investments and overseas markets. For Britain to re-establish its standing, let alone improve upon its standard of living, the British would have to make a 'prodigious' effort, the recapturing of manufacturing and trade necessitating – on Dalton's Board of Trade calculation – an increase of 25 per cent on the export level of 1938. This would be made all the more daunting by the promises of Beveridge about post-war spending on welfare, to which the coalition was committing itself. That was why the contribution of a fully employed economy was so cardinal if Britain was even to begin to tackle the predicament.[43]

On welfare, Cripps certainly wavered. He purposely stayed away from Cabinet when the Beveridge Report was considered, identifying with Labourites who were displeased by the government's lukewarm attitude, but he was whipped into voting for it in February 1943. He said he wanted to get away from the 'can't afford' mentality. The Beveridge Report, Cripps told Thomas Jones, was 'masterly', but 'financially staggering', even for a country used to talking in terms of hundreds of millions of pounds.[44] The added burden put an even greater premium on exporting. He could see no alternative but a deliberately induced, though temporary, reduction in domestic consumption. For all these reasons, it seemed to him that Britain – notwithstanding the prevalence of reaction and war-weariness – was on the eve of the most difficult economic period in its history.[45]

How was the necessary supreme effort to be accomplished? What motive was there to substitute for the spur of common dangers? Employers would not be able to use the fear of unemployment any more. Unauthorised strikers in wartime were – he had been saying – 'saboteurs'.[46] The war again provided an answer of sorts. How was the war being won? Not by allowing the free play of the market, the libertinism of monopoly, or individual selfish greed – characteristics he equated with private property. The critics of wartime regulation were quite wrong. Government had not enslaved. It had brought the country to the brink of victory. Only the government could have organised the logistics of war and secured the moral authority to enforce sacrifice, creating an altruistically inspired, State-centred egalitarianism.[47]

The underpinning of the active State could not be anything other than that of Christian teaching, the doctrine of fair shares furnishing the soundest basis for right conduct. The huge advance in the destructiveness of weapons of war reinforced the importance of moral restraint. In an after-dinner lecture – 'God is my Co-Pilot' – to Bomber Command at High Wycombe, organised by John Collins, the RAF chaplain, Cripps offended senior ranks by preaching they should send their men on a bombing mission only when they were certain it was morally as well as militarily defensible (Dresden had recently been fire-bombed).[48] Coming from the Minister of Aircraft Production, this led to an ugly argument. One officer asked whether Cripps's lack of sympathy for the air offensive against Germany explained his unsuccessful, delay-ridden tenure at MAP.[49] He had nothing to reproach himself for on that score. 'Your MAP leadership', Bruce-Gardner congratulated him, 'means that the Fighting Services are being supplied with all the Planes necessary, both in quantity and quality.'[50] Cripps then (in January 1945) irritated Churchill by publicly suggesting treating a defeated Germany with clemency. His misgivings must have been greatly aggravated by the secret development of atomic fission. When, that spring, he wanted to find out more, he was 'warned off'.[51] One lunchtime, he shared with Amery and other ministers his apprehension that British scientists 'were very near the point of splitting the atom in a fashion which would result in a similar process taking place for a hundred miles around the initial point and destroying all lives in that area'.[52] The war had stimulated a leap in invention with which morality had not been able to keep pace. Material advances required moral curbs, if all sense of civilised values was not to be lost. However vital the need for peacetime industrial regeneration, it must be spiritually controlled.

Cripps's speeches in the later part of the war conveyed, in summary form, the credo of the progressive-minded technocrat, impatient with party politics and eager to convert issues of principle into matters of balance, religiously sanctifying the command economy. It fitted with the non-party opinions of liberal industrialists like Samuel Courtauld, Howard Fergusson and Harry McGowan (of ICI), as well as overlapping with Beveridge and Keynes. 'Keynes is full of splendid plans for the future and he is your man,' 'TJ' informed the Crippses. It was the furthest Cripps went in eschewing all ideological attachments other than that of 'progress', contending that expertise alone could solve problems grown stubborn with the years. Cripps wants 'a coalition of the left', Barrington-Ward noted in October 1944. 'He is sure we are in for a very tough time after the war.'[53]

Cripps's diagnosis and remedy are germane to the long-standing quarrel about British economic decline. Rejecting dispassionate analysis, Correlli Barnett has become the principal decrier of the wartime socialist generation, arguing that intellectuals and opinion-formers created the demand for a better society but neglected the far more critical problem of economic viability. Instead of enjoying the afterglow of broad social advance, the country ought to have been made to confront economic realities. The political class failed to provide leadership, condemning Britain in the longer term to decades of economic stagnation.[54]

Although critical of many other left-wing prophets and publicists, Barnett acknowledges that Cripps did not shirk the issue, calling him astute and 'oddly realistic', before passing on. The long wait for an authorised, fully documented biography of Cripps has not helped to give a full picture, for it is through Cripps that the battle of production has largely to be recounted. As far as wartime circumstances allowed, Cripps spoke out, trying to show that the triumphs of the war would count for nothing if the country did not prepare in time for peace. Cripps was not a 'declinist'. He thought the country could and would recover. But his warnings of root-and-branch industrial change instantly locate us in the milieu of the real Keynes – the Keynes cautioning that Britain would be confronted at the war's end by a precarious struggle for national solvency.

Where Cripps can fairly be faulted is over the kind of prescriptions he endorsed, spawned by the 'illusion' of centralised planning. Cripps, said Jewkes (who devised the MAP programmes) 'never wearie[d] of describing the success of planning during the war at the Ministry of Aircraft Production'[55] – a performance that Barnett closely investigated. Inquiries conducted during the war uncovered a long list of defects – poor quality management, inadequately organised production lines, 'slackness' related to wildcat strikes and union privileges, and brilliant scientific innovation squandered by lack of flexibility. The 'new' aircraft industry, in fact (Barnett maintains) exhibited the same shortcomings as 'older' staple industries. Dramatic increases in output were achieved simply by throwing extra labour and extra tools at the problem, with little attempt to organise production more effectively. The artificially stimulated war economy was used to glorify centrally determined rationing and allocation. Administrators sounded radical, but in fact they were radical only in wanting to hold on to the changes introduced under wartime duress.[56] Cripps had the foresight to appreciate the importance of reviving industrial society – that much is granted – but he wrongheadedly imagined that the peacetime priority for exports could be met not by releasing market forces but by ministers running monolithic departments in Whitehall.

It is a strange 'audit' which is all debit and no credit. It was widely recognised there were deep-seated structural problems. Measures of efficiency did matter. But nobody was really interested in the weight of aircraft produced, only in their fighting power.[57] Strategic bombing did not actually do *enough* damage to make a material difference to victory.[58] The promises of post-war reform cannot be reduced to the yearnings of one man's ego (Beveridge's). Welfare provision was not grafted on afterwards, but grew up during the war, in the course of employing large squads of labour. As the MAP's regional controller for Scotland observed in 1945, quoting one aviation worker, the industry – with its rest pauses, maternity provision, canteens and psychological testing – was 'welfaring its workers to death'.[59]

Such an audit is also – by arguing what *ought* to have been done – profoundly unhistorical. Few people after 1945 seriously contemplated a free-market option or a 'Bismarckian' superstate. The dominant view was one formed by the politicians, permanent civil servants and temporary 'irregulars' – the civilian administrators, like Cripps, sleeping below the Ministry to escape the thudding of the 'mini-Blitz'. The interventionist State, forged by war, was to be the 'tutelary deity', with the departments of government using the knowledge, contacts and influence they had acquired to reorganise and revitalise British industry.[60] Capital and labour were reconciled. Society was disciplined by consent and social solidarity. Whatever the eventual party or political alignment – and Cripps, still ribbed by Churchill ('I drink the brandy, you get the red nose'), did not want the wartime coalition to go on – the contest would turn on a fight to control that administrative machinery and give it stronger political direction. That contest it was for the electorate to pronounce upon.

GESTAPO

It is a sore temptation to recall a rather dubious argument used in the
course of the election campaign by Sir Stafford Cripps. The economic
nation, he said, must be organised and run like an army.

French journalist Bertrand de Jouvenel, in 1949 [1]

Cripps grew with the responsibilities of office, winning the confidence of his
department and the aircraft industry, and gaining Churchill's trust. Warning
of hard times to come and the necessity for economic and spiritual revival, he
was 'busily building a post-war platform'.[2] What he lacked was any kind of
political base. Aside from answering regular parliamentary questions about
the work of his department, he did not speak once in the House from November
1942 until January 1945, when the Commons discussed civil aviation. In votes,
he was classed as 'independent Labour'. At various points, he had flirted
with Acland's Common Wealth party and the Liberals before settling for the
'progressive unity' of all left-wing parties, harking back to the popular front.
Conversing with Attlee in July 1944, he said he meant to maintain his independence until the war had been won, unable to predict his future direction.[3]
If Labour officially withdrew from the coalition – as was increasingly likely –
he knew he would have to rejoin, 'if they will have me'.[4]

The stumbling block was not just Cripps himself but Bristol East, where the
'rebel' party was still at daggers drawn with the newly established official
one. Even Rogers, informing Cripps that constituency sentiment had moved
decidedly leftward, feared a divided Labour vote would cost Cripps his seat.
Cripps made the first move, calling a meeting of the General Council in
October 1944, securing its backing to approach the national party on the
explicit understanding that they should all go back together or not at all.[5]
Returning to London, he saw Attlee again, who was anxious to make it easy
for Cripps. R. T. Windle, the assistant national agent, and Ted Rees, the regional
organiser, were present. They explained that Cripps was free to join on the
spot, provided he signed an undertaking. Cripps refused and stalked out of the
room, leaving Windle and Rees to face Attlee's annoyance. Some days later, it
was announced that Cripps was to be opposed in Bristol East by an official

Labour candidate. Only at this stage, as Dalton gleefully noted years later,[6] did Cripps hasten back down to Bristol to see the borough and divisional parties, amazing Rees by signing on the dotted line. Rogers warned him the story was going around that he had deserted the local party.[7]

A final settlement was not easy to reach. The 'rebels' were invited to reapply for membership of the Bristol East party, so long as the 'rebel' organisation – which occupied party HQ – folded up. Some two hundred did so. They were readmitted, but not before the new party had held its annual general meeting and voted in its officers. Rogers believed they were being punished for their recalcitrant left-wingery. The difficulty was resolved only in February, when the readmission of the last 'rebels' and the sitting MP was formally approved – in Cripps's case after almost six years.

For many senior party colleagues, Cripps remained a questionable asset. Bevin and Dalton, listening to him around the Cabinet table opposing national control of the light-metal industry, asked aloud how he would like to defend his view before the Party's conference. In the Commons he advocated a 'mixed' (public and private) peacetime aviation industry, provoking Labour heckling. Greenwood, acting leader of the PLP, was still intensely suspicious of Cripps (who had effected his removal from the Government in February 1942). Greenwood told Pritt the Party would hold Cripps to the straight and narrow because Transport House had copies of his pessimistic dispatches from the Soviet Union, which they could use to embarrass him.[8] Only Morrison, 'rejoicing' at the new recruit, seemed welcoming. Cripps reciprocated, telling some of Morrison's lieutenants that he would willingly serve under him in a Labour government, but that Attlee, his vanity puffed up by standing in for Churchill when the Prime Minister was often abroad, would not go quietly.[9]

Cripps's thinking brought back to life a wider scepticism about the capacity of the Labour Party to win an election outright. Many party and union people were unhappy about Attlee's leadership. The Party, ambushed by activists at its 1944 conference, had committed itself to a wide measure of public ownership – to Morrison's chagrin. Within the coalition, Labour ministers busily pushed common coalition policies through in the little time they believed they had left, as Cripps did in formulating a revised offer to India with Amery.

When Labour's conference met again in May 1945, three weeks after VE Day, the NEC decided the Party should withdraw from the coalition – against the judgement of Attlee, who wanted to continue until the end of the war with Japan. There was a historic parallel. Conference had taken the Party into the coalition in May 1940; now it was endorsing the decision to pull out. The vote, however, was an expression of grass-roots optimism about the forthcoming election which many leaders – excepting Morrison – did not share. Discussing the projected party manifesto, *Let Us Face the Future*, Cripps took the stand (for the first time since 1939) to loud applause and, being Cripps, dispelled all falsehoods. Observing that the mood of Blackpool was more congenial than it had been at Southport, he went on to warn about underestimating the difficulties of implementing a national plan for industry, an immensely technical task for which no preparations had been made. There would be 'no easy Utopia'.[10] The effect, in no more than half a dozen sentences, was to apply the coldest of douches. 'He advanced amid rapturous shouts. He retired in silence.'[11]

Disappointed by Labour's decision not to carry on in office for a further six months, Churchill plumped for a quick election, forming a temporary, largely Conservative, caretaker government in the run-up to election day, 5 July. Churchill hoped Bevin might consent to stay on. Cripps had only just trooped in and out of an audience with the King, barely exchanging a word, before Churchill was inviting him to hold a post – an offer Cripps cautiously declined.[12]

Casting around for an anti-socialist theme to establish his 'National' credentials, Churchill clutched at the suggestion that Labour's pulling out of the coalition was evidence that the parliamentary party was dictated to by an outside body, the NEC. He made this the centrepiece of his first election broadcast. For good measure, a Labour government, he continued, would have to fall back upon 'some form of Gestapo', however humanely introduced in the first instance, deriving from the Party's 'abject worship of the state'.[13] Often attributed to Beaverbrook, the idea was Churchill's own work, as John Colville, who retrieved the typed draft of the speech from the wastepaper basket, has shown.[14] Churchill's sole regret was not referring to the Soviet NKVD instead.[15] Beaverbrook's *Daily Express*, taking its cue, carried daily extracts from the Socialist League publications of the early 1930s about the use of emergency powers to strike 'a decisive blow at capitalism', and dug up Partridge's cartoon of a tub-thumping Cripps. Other Conservative candidates joined in, warning of socialist 'snoopers', and drawing a comparison between the blackshirts of Mosley and the redshirts of Cripps. Isaac Pitman, the Tory candidate in Bath, recalled Cripps's opposition to rearmament, denouncing him as 'unstable' and 'intimidatory'.[16] The whole far-fetched attempt was to create the impression of an alien party with designs on a police state, the ordering about to be done by Cripps and 'Gauleiter Laski'.

Attlee surpassed himself, delivering an effective rejoinder to Churchill's 'lurid travesty of Labour policy'. Cripps, advocating 'Honest Politics', occupied the high moral ground. Before setting off on a nationwide tour by car, averaging four speeches a day, he sent word to Rogers emphasising they should see to it 'that our standard of behaviour sets an example of honesty and decency'. Despite lapses in the past, 'we in the Labour Party pride ourselves that our programme is honest and straightforward and that we do not have to resort to tricks and subterfuges'.[17]

He was 'profoundly sorry' that the man who had been such a great war leader should stoop to 'vicious' muck-raking.[18] 'We don't want to control the people,' he explained (the trade unions would not tolerate direction of labour), 'but to control all those things – materials, finance, factories and prices – which contributed to production.'[19] These methods had helped win the war. Did it not make sense to retain them in peacetime, when the challenge was going to be still more formidable?[20] Industrial efficiency, he said in his own radio message, was going to be of paramount importance, and in this the State had to play a directing role. The other way was a return to the catch-as-catch-can of private ownership, which the tragedy of unemployment and war had exposed. Nationalisation was not the issue: the trouble was private enterprise, relying upon 'the selfish acquisitive motive' which is 'anti-Christian'. 'One cannot live by one faith on Sunday and by another during the six days of the week.'[21] Since the rest of Europe had swung left, there ought to be a socialist Britain. As for the Soviet Union, the re-election of a 'frightened' Conservative government would only revive Anglo-Soviet rivalry. To a correspondent critical of Soviet tyranny, he countered, 'I believe I know the truth about Russia as well as anyone, and although there are features in Soviet life and methods which I dislike I have an immense admiration for this achievement.'[22] His election literature carried a photograph of him signing the 1941 treaty in the Kremlin, Stalin looking on. According to Rogers, the Labour and Communist parties in Bristol East campaigned 'hand in glove'.

These twin aspects, the strong State at home and socialist alliances abroad – the fruits of his wartime career – coupled with 'disgust' at Tory electioneering,[23] formed the basis of the probity and clarity ('you just couldn't disbelieve him'[24]) of his potent appeal, offering voters a choice between morality and immorality.[25]

The count was held over for three weeks so that the services' vote could be collected. An exhausted Cripps spent the much needed interval gardening. He attended Bristol Town Hall for the result on 26 July and was returned by a greatly increased majority in a straight contest with a local Conservative, polling 27,975 votes to 10,073. Labour's victory in three of the other four seats in Bristol 'surprised us as much as it staggered our opponents', Ted Rees told local reporters.[26] Since it was raining, Cripps abandoned a tour of honour and withdrew to Mervyn Stockwood's study, in the company of Rogers, to listen to the other results.

There are many accounts of the events in Bevin's room at Transport House that day. Stockwood provides the point of view from Bristol.[27] By lunchtime on 26 July, after a number of dramatic Conservative defeats, it was already certain the Labour Party would have its first-ever numerical majority in the new parliament. As the afternoon wore on, the size of that majority went on growing. Many of those intent on removing Attlee, like Laski, had expected Labour to increase its parliamentary strength, but not that it would win.[28] Morrison was due to dine with Cripps on 31 July, to discuss the position before

Parliament reassembled. The magnitude of the Conservative reversal was such, however, that Churchill, rather than wait until the House reconvened, went to Buckingham Palace straight away to tender his resignation. Attlee was summoned.

Attlee, with Bevin, Morrison and Morgan Phillips (secretary of the Party), was at Transport House. Morrison left them to answer a telephone call from Cripps, who put it to him there ought by rights to be a re-election of all the officers of the PLP, including the leader. Morrison agreed, the fact that Attlee was leader of the old parliamentary party not necessarily meaning he would be leader under the new intake.[29] While Morrison was gone, Bevin urged Attlee to go to the Palace, telling him he could leave Morrison to him. By promptly seeing the King and agreeing to form a government, Attlee pre-empted the plotting. Morrison vainly tried to muster support before the Party's victory rally, but Attlee was received with acclamation, before flying off with Bevin to the Potsdam conference. It was Churchill, Cripps told Stockwood, who chose who was to be his successor as prime minister, not the Parliamentary Labour Party.[30]

For those who had endured the trauma of 1931 – Cripps's political baptism – the wait for the return of a majority Labour government had been long and often despairing. The war, Cripps had no doubt, had given the Party its opportunity. This did not necessarily invalidate the left-wing polemics of the 1930s, but the war had transformed everything. The State had vastly extended. A new body of reformers filled many public posts. 'He thought the changed attitude of the civil service remarkable'[31] (Sir Harold Scott, his Permanent Secretary from October 1943 was 'very progressive under the civil service crust', Isobel enthused), the military too. The 'citizen army' of the country – Cripps had lectured Lord Woolton, the Minister of Food, about the valuable work of the Army Education Bureau – looked to the prospect of an economically revived Britain.[32] The 'machinery of democracy' had registered a mandate for 'social transformation', though he had no time to dwell on it. 'It's a great show & now the hard work really starts.'[33]

16

POST-WAR

We can save or wreck our country by what we do and how we do it over the next few years.

Cripps to the staff of the Board of Trade in August 1945[1]

Attlee's parting act before flying back to Potsdam was to fill the main offices in the new government. Bevin accompanied him as Foreign Secretary, having been switched at the last moment with Dalton, now destined for the Treasury. Morrison was Lord President of the Council. Cripps was to go to the Board of Trade, Dalton's old department, where he would be sixth in order of Cabinet precedence. Trade was the post Cripps had asked for.[2] But he made oversight of the Economic and Statistical Section of the Cabinet Office a condition of taking it on.[3] Freeman, who had stepped down from MAP in January 1945, sent his warmest greetings. 'I am very glad you have taken the Board of Trade. It is a job after your own heart and difficult enough to satisfy even you'.[4]

Broadcasting to America on 30 July, Cripps sought to calm transatlantic surprise at the election outcome, describing Labour's programme as 'limited', bringing into public ownership (with full compensation) some of the more important industries, combining State control and private enterprise to plan Britain's national resources over the five-year term.[5] (Laski, on 31 July on CBS, criticised American capitalism, claiming Labour was carrying on where Roosevelt's New Deal had stopped.) The feature the BBC controller found off-putting about the Minister was his brown plaited sandals.[6]

Though the war in the Far East was expected to last anything up to eighteen more months, the task before the Board of Trade was of the first magnitude: to put in hand the conversion of war industry to a peacetime footing and to launch an all-out export drive. From a largely subordinate inter-war role, Trade had been thrust into the limelight by Dalton, who enlarged the department's regulatory function into one of purposive direction, the President of the Board becoming the Chancellor of the Exchequer's *alter ego*.[7] Cripps meant to continue this, reorganising his staff to cope with the wide range of responsibilities, spanning everything from international trade, industrial strategy and the location of industry to fixing price controls and issuing clothing coupons. Sir John

Henry Woods ('John Henry') came over from the Ministry of Production (which was being phased out) to be the new Permanent Secretary.

Barrington-Ward, calling on Cripps – who was seeing new people every quarter of an hour – discovered him 'well-placed in an office which will evoke his remarkable brain power rather than his emotions'.[8] Helped by the renewal of extensive powers in the Supplies and Services Act, Cripps had already sent out a directive to his department, quoting from *Let Us Face The Future* to justify the 'constructive supervision' of private industry. None of the industries with which they were concerned, he made clear, were to be nationalised (nationalisation of iron and steel he did 'not at present contemplate'). Their job was to devise a plan to 'guide' and where necessary 'compel' private enterprise to contribute to 'the revival of national well-being', utilising the controlled productive resources of the country to boost exports and relieve the home market.[9]

The vagueness of Labour policy and its relative neglect of private industry gave him considerable latitude. Industry feared the worst, but his officials had similar misgivings. Woods, feeling Cripps had not taken time to reflect, sat on the directive for several weeks. Charles Bruce-Gardner, reunited with Cripps, told friends he would stay on to advise about industrial reconversion until the Minister did something he strongly disagreed with, and then return to the private sector.[10] *The Tribune*, now edited by the newly elected Labour MP Michael Foot, carried the information that senior Board of Trade civil servants had agreed among themselves to make a stand against the Minister 'should he try to experiment on too bold and novel a line'.[11]

The government had barely got into its stride when two atomic bombs were dropped on Japan. Cripps was rung up by an agitated John Collins. 'What can I do?' he responded. 'The Cabinet was not consulted, only Attlee was informed, the decision was taken solely by the Americans.'[12] To resign, as Collins suggested, would be an empty gesture. Five days later, Japan surrendered, Attlee announcing the news in a midnight radio address. Cripps was still at the ministry, boggling at the implications. 'There is wild jubilation proceeding tonight over the final end of the war,' he scribbled to Felix Frankfurter, a member of the US Supreme Court. 'So far as we are concerned it has raised a hundred new and urgent difficulties and it is hard to see how we can arrive at any solution of some of them. A good many seem to fall to my particular lot!'[13]

Circumstances obliged the government to act as it must, not do as it pleased. Lend-Lease was abruptly suspended by President Truman (Roosevelt had died in April), ending wartime Mutual Aid. A substantial loan from the United States and Canada to tide Britain over seemed unavoidable.[14] Keynes, a key figure in designing an institutional framework for the post-war international economy, trusted to American generosity. It was not thought likely the United States would tie any financial assistance to British commercial policy or the future of the sterling bloc. At a meeting on 23 August, attended by Attlee, Bevin, Dalton, Cripps and Pethick-Lawrence (Secretary of State for India), Keynes recommended aiming for a grant-in-aid of some $4 to $5 billion, though such a high sum might be unattainable. A line of credit, carrying interest and conditions of repayment, was beyond Britain's capacity. Cripps favoured a grant too, but the negotiating team left without any Board of Trade representative.

In the very different atmosphere in Washington, any hope of separating financial from commercial considerations soon vanished. Fred Vinson, the US Treasury Secretary, insisted that discussions about commercial policy must precede any financial agreement. To Cripps's disquiet, Percivale Liesching, Second Secretary at the Board of Trade, had to take a Board of Trade team over to join Keynes. Because the two sides needed only to reach certain under-standings, the negotiations speeded up, helped by British 'sweeteners'.[15] On the central point for the Board of Trade – that Imperial Preference, the system by which imports from outside the British Empire were discriminated against, would be reduced only in return for worldwide tariff concessions, so that Britain could 'export to the full' – Cripps was content.[16] The final financial deal, a loan of $3.75 billion at 4 per cent interest and a commitment to the free convertibility of sterling into other currencies (one year after Senate ratification of the loan), was, however, harsh. Dalton was ready to back out altogether, provoked by an American attempt to force reductions in Imperial Preference as well. Bevin, Dalton and Cripps held firm to get the terms of the loan through a querulous Cabinet.

Putting the deal to the Commons, playing second fiddle to Dalton, Cripps denied that commercial concessions – selling out the Commonwealth, accord-ing to opponents – had been bargained away in exchange for the loan. But the government's defence was unimpressive, splitting its own ranks. One of Cripps's two Lancashire PPSs, Barbara Castle (once of the Socialist League), went to him to say in all conscience she could not vote for it. 'Then your conscience is wrong,' he declared, 'swamping' her with his overpowering intel-lect. She still disobeyed the three-line whip.[17] As Dalton and he both realised, the loan agreement would only afford a breathing-space. The seller's market might not last much longer than two years, leaving little time to re-establish an external balance of payments.

Exports were to be encouraged by 'planning' of the nation's resources. But what kind of planning? Most inter-war thinking concentrated on how to combat the slump conditions of unemployment, not the suppressed demand of 1945. The ministers principally concerned with the economy tended to define planning departmentally.[18] Morrison, charged with co-ordinating domestic (including economic) policy, fought off Cripps's bid to absorb the Economic Section and the Central Statistical Office into the Board of Trade.[19] His own main interest was in legislating for nationalisation. For Dalton, planning meant control over fiscal, investment and employment policy, overshadowed by the adverse balance of trade, but a concern for budget secrecy restricted his openness. Cripps, with his contempt for half measures, wanted to go furthest. Choosing between competing needs and allocating physical resources of men and materials had 'proved its worth' during wartime, he argued. He advocated working out a national five-year plan, apportioning resources between consumer goods, the export trade and capital goods, listing the most important commodities under each broad heading. He wanted a large central staff for the purpose, made up of economists and statisticians.[20] Despite Morrison's disapproval, an official steering committee was created, serviced by the Treasury, to prepare the outline of a central plan for submission to senior ministers.

Cripps was delighted, but Woods, representing the Board of Trade on the committee, was worried about publicity. The idea of planning, he noted, was under 'pretty hot attack', putting off even moderate industrialists. Presentation needed careful thought. 'The government cannot possibly pre-announce its opinion that a slump is coming.'[21] The possibility of a repeat of the post-war downturn of 1918–21 made planning more difficult, but all the more imperative. Controls existed to counteract shortages – that much Morrison conceded. With the Lord President's Committee telling departments wishing to retain a control that they had to prove the need for its retention, Cripps reconsidered. Controls were not perfect instruments, but he had no desire to initiate a general relaxation, because they were vital in influencing the pattern of demand and guiding the direction of production.[22] To his regret, the government 'had not yet formulated a plan for the employment of the national resources and could not hope to do so for several months to come'.[23] Altering the pattern of employment might be 'politically impossible' unless it was part of a publicly understood general plan. As a result, the first Economic Survey did not go beyond a simple statement of existing resources in relation to existing commitments, though Cripps – 'already the dynamic planner', according to one of Morrison's aides – suggested many amendments for the final document, which were all accepted by Morrison without comment.[24]

This did not prevent the Conservatives from claiming the country was suffocating under a blanket of controls. In a censure debate in December 1945, Churchill mocked 'ethereal beings' like Cripps, who by their 'sustained exertions' contribute more and take less out of the common pot than most. The President of the Board of Trade ought to rid himself of the idea 'that it is within the power or thought of any human being at the present to regulate in detail the entire movement and process by which our 48,000,000 people can earn their daily bread'. Cripps, cheered on, believed he had been accused of every kind of harshness, including forcing housewives to go short. He remained 'an incurable optimist', subject to the one requirement that the country mount a tremendous and sustained productive effort. Compared to this, redistributing wealth was only a secondary consideration (an early sign that the party took from him what it would not stand from anyone else). But when he said in the Commons in February 1946 that it was 'right and proper that we plan and, having a plan, that we should try to carry out the plan', no plan as yet existed, having been stymied by divided authority among ministers.

Organising the cotton industry was one pressing priority. The outgoing minister, Oliver Lyttleton, had left a handover note, directing him to the nub of the problem about increasing the output of cotton goods by drawing labour into the spinning section, where pay and working conditions lagged. Cripps saw Sir Raymond Streat, head of the Cotton Board, who was struck by his 'brisk determination'. Three weeks later he unveiled to Streat his pet idea of establishing working parties in particular export industries, under a neutral chairman and an equal number of employers and trade unionists, to investigate and submit recommendations. Cotton, though a special case, featured along with the pottery, wool, boot and shoe, hosiery and furniture trades. Cripps favoured persuasion but did not exclude compulsion, aware that many cotton manufacturers did not want to modernise and saw no need when they could sell everything they could make.[25] The object of the working parties was for the State – the nearest thing to an impartial 'judge' – to ensure employers and employees did not 'gang up' against the consumer.[26]

Securing the approval of Sir Clive Baillieu (president of the Federation of British Industry (FBI)) and Sir Walter Citrine (still TUC general secretary), Cripps edged the scheme through Cabinet only with the greatest difficulty, agreeing to add independent experts to each working party and stressing the government's right to step in if industries did not show willing.[27] Streat wanted to wait and see, but Cripps was not prepared to go back to the Cabinet all over again with a different scheme. The most he could offer Streat was a seat on the cotton working party as one of the independent nominees. Streat, he said, believed in education and progress by consent, whereas 'The condition of England required drastic measures. His party had been elected to do things and do them quickly.'[28] Asking Sir George Schuster to be chairman of the working party on cotton, Cripps 'made it clear' he would not accept any plan which left Streat in control.[29]

After the first batch of working parties was announced, Woods, conveying to Cripps the views of departmental heads, suggested 'hastening a little slowly'. They had obtained only the 'acquiescence' of industry, and ought to see how the first working parties shaped up. Cripps was unstoppable. Pushing for a second wave of parties, he wanted to set up twenty or thirty in all, covering the whole exporting field by the same stage the following year, anxious that time was running out before British industry was exposed to the full force of foreign competition again.[30]

Embracing controversy, he readily acquainted industry with unpleasant decisions. In October, to howls of 'Tripe!', he told the Society of Motor Manufacturers they should set aside half their cars for export, wondering aloud whether the motor industry existed to support Great Britain or vice versa.[31] The chairman of the Wholesale Textile Association informed him that people had had enough of 'the drab existence of the past six years'; Cripps refuted the notion that exports were sent abroad to titillate foreigners.[32] He saw no point in a 'glorious fling' if the country ended up bankrupt.[33] Hard on the heels of this, and overriding official advice, he kicked up a storm by closing the Liverpool Cotton Exchange, on the doctrinaire grounds that it 'created speculation'.

Did the role of 'wicked uncle' – his words[34] – bother him? His unkindest critics, playing on the unpopularity of vexatious controls, suggested he took pleasure in 'starving' home consumers. Cripps valued self-denial and was not above occasionally reproaching others for eating too much.[35] His 'dearest wish' was the early release of more consumer goods, but until the country was in external balance 'austerity standards' would persist.[36] By late 1945, ministerial colleagues who had to enforce his restrictions – Morrison was well to the fore – were chiding him with overdoing the concentration on exports, putting him under 'continuous pressure' to release more goods for the home market.[37]

Ellis Smith, his Parliamentary Secretary and MP for Stoke, heart of the pottery industry, urged an increased home supply too. People were worse off than they had been throughout the war and becoming increasingly 'restive', he argued.[38] Smith, once full of admiration for his minister, suffered several 'stings' thereafter. He found out that George Blaker, Cripps's private secretary, was educated at Eton, and demanded his dismissal. (Purging Whitehall was popular in left-wing constituency parties.) Cripps replied that it was not a good idea, and that anyway he himself had been to Winchester.[39] Smith floundered on the floor of the House, rescued by his officials. Eventually Cripps's patience snapped. Smith was called to No. 10 and told by Attlee he would have to go. In a 28-word letter of resignation, he referred to unspecified 'differences' with the President of the Board of Trade.[40] Smith was the first casualty of the Attlee government.

The saddling of Cripps with the 'austerity' tag, which he was unable to shake off, owed much to his looking the part – grey, gaunt and unsmiling – even though the idea was 'a press phoney'.[41] Plunged in post-electoral gloom, Tories capitalised. Lord Woolton, the Conservative Party chairman, taxed him with practising austerity like a religious cult, ignorant of the joys of life.[42] 'You don't know how happy a nature he really has,' Attlee observed.[43] The only way to salvation was through higher production, especially if the US Senate were to reject the loan agreement. Climbing export figures gave Cripps all the sustenance he needed. 'I am certain our "unpopular" policy has been right and all the vilification well worth while,' he told Woods.[44] Bruce-Gardner realised the almost frightening resolution of his minister to stay the course. 'If you do that you will have a revolution on your hands,' he forewarned. 'What does it matter?' Cripps responded. 'It's what the country will be like in fifty years that counts.'[45]

THE AWARD

One thing is absolutely certain. We can't leave this country without a
settlement of some kind. If we did there would be bloodshed and chaos
within a few weeks.

Cripps in India, to his wife, April 1946[1]

Vocal opponents of 'too much austerity' had grounds for maintaining that the
export drive was denying a greater variety of goods to the domestic market.
They had further cause for complaint about sending emergency foodstuffs to
Europe and famine-struck Asia. One recipient was the British zone in Germany.
Cripps, while arguing it would be wrong to jeopardise Britain's livelihood by
helping the Germans, insisted Britain had no alternative but to assist countries
to which it was morally committed. Nonetheless, Dalton – searching for economies – and Cripps looked forward to a time when overseas responsibilities
might be cut back, releasing some of the 2 million soldiers (one-eighth of the
total labour force) tied up in the armed forces. The Prime Minister was an
unexpected ally. In an extraordinary note to Bevin, he advocated disengaging
from the Middle East, putting 'a wide glacis of desert and Arabs between
ourselves and the Russians', Dalton noted approvingly.[2] The major uncertainty
was the Indian subcontinent.

For the third time, India beckoned Cripps. The difference was a Labour
government firmly in power, pledged to speed India to complete independence,
hoping a single, sovereign India would act even more closely – because voluntarily – with the mother country. On the other hand, the circumstances of
Anglo-India were entirely altered. India was now a creditor nation, holding
£1,100 million in sterling balances run up in London. Anglo-Indian trade,
flourishing between the wars, had dwindled to a negligible level. The prestige
of British administration had been shaken by the famine in Bengal (the result
of a scorched-earth retreat) in 1943. Wavell, successor as viceroy to Linlithgow,
doubted he had the troops to quell serious civil disorder. On all counts –
financial, economic and strategic – the case for early British withdrawal was
compelling. Recent historians have tended to look past Labour's pious declarations about granting freedom to India, as if they were of little account.

Cripps's expressions of 'loving kindness' were genuinely felt. It was just that idealism and realism, for once, fearfully coincided.

The emancipation of India – 'our duty and our debt' – transcended all other obligations. The Empire was, in progressive circles, a great wrong. In the 1930s Cripps had called for its 'liquidation'. After the offer of 1942, he participated fully in the decision to detain the leaders of the 'Quit India' movement. India was not an election issue; Cripps was one of the very few to refer to it. It fell to Labour to act with imagination. An imperial possession of such size had never before been transformed into a self-governing democracy. He did not claim a deep understanding of the East, but had a partiality making him more pro-Indian, and pro-Congress, than many Indians. Attlee and Pethick-Lawrence, the only other members of the Cabinet with a knowledge of India (Bevin did not sit on the India Committee) had to check him from rushing his fences. By the spring of 1946, urgency was paramount.

Nehru, reopening contact, told him he had been hurt by the things said and done during the war, but Cripps's presence in the government gave him renewed hope. Cripps forwarded a copy of Nehru's letter to Pethick-Lawrence, 'not for circulation in your Dept!!'[3] This time, Gandhi trusted there was a determination by the British to 'do the right thing'.[4] They convinced Cripps there was still sufficient faith in British -and his – intentions to make an attempt worthwhile. 'We have just *got* to get something decided', he wrote to the (Australian) governor of Bengal, 'and I think if we maintain an absolute fairness of outlook and no selfishness in it, we may get through alright.'[5]

The postponed elections to the central and provincial legislatures passed off peacefully during the winter of 1945–6, but polarised the country along communal lines, strengthening the hand of the Muslim League. Reviving the rejected 1942 offer would open up the matter of how to go about partitioning India – 'the provincial option' – in the new, immensely more complicated, circumstances. The Cabinet decided to send out a three-man delegation led by Pethick-Lawrence, to include Cripps and A. V. Alexander, Secretary of State for Defence, giving them full liberty to seek an agreement on a new constitutional structure for Indian self-government, with the power to act without reference back to London. Cripps's role was to supply ideas. His thinking already encompassed a new quasi-federal structure, retaining an all-India Union. Believing Gandhi had dished his 1942 offer, his intention was to draw the Mahatma into negotiations, directly or indirectly, to stop him from pulling the rug from under him again. To this end, Cripps took with him – apart from Blaker – two assistants, Majors Billy Short and Woodrow Wyatt, the latter a Labour MP. Otherwise the mission had only a skeleton staff, minimising the India Office's influence. Telling friends he was 'not unhopeful', Cripps was confident of a definite outcome one way or the other, possibly in the form of a British award – 'a recommendation to the Indian people' – to break the deadlock. Working overtime at the Board of Trade, he crammed in several weeks' work, cutting every meal in order to leave his department with enough to do in the month or two he expected to be gone. Before departing on 19 March, the mission was entertained to lunch at Buckingham Palace. India was not mentioned, until they were saying goodbye, when the King, the Emperor of India, wished them 'a nice journey'.[6]

Publication of the *Transfer of Power* series of official documents,[7] supplemented by Wavell's journal and several detailed histories, has established the tribulations of the mission as an historical episode in the endgame of empire, viewed with cool, often ironical, detachment. A reading of Cripps's daily letters home to Isobel shows how much he regarded it as a personal test of endurance. The animateur of the team, he needed constantly to fortify his resolve, to confirm Pethick-Lawrence's observation that those who suffer would be saved. It was his anxiety to 'do right by India', combined with some hard-headed grilling of the assorted Indian parties, that led to his determination not to leave India once again without a settlement. The India Office held no fears for him. 'Quite frankly,' Wyatt was told, 'it doesn't matter what they say because *I* am running this party. Let them talk away about constitutional and parliamentary control but it won't have any result. *We* are really doing the negotiations and keeping them out of it.'[8]

After stopping overnight at Tunis and Baghdad, Cripps and Pethick-Lawrence arrived at Karachi on 23 March, reaching New Delhi the next day, when Alexander, travelling on a separate flight, also arrived. At Cripps's behest, they spent only two days in the grandeur of Viceregal House before moving to offices in the grounds, provided with a teleprinter to communicate with London. In contrast with the tension of 1942, their welcome was hospitable, particularly in the Indian press, encouraging Cripps to believe they had won half the battle, that the dividing line was no longer between Britain and India but among Indians themselves. Wavell was not so easily placated. In their first meetings, the mission had persuaded him – or so Cripps believed – they were not about to 'pull a fast one'. But Wavell had vivid memories of Cripps's last visit.

Over the succeeding weeks the mission consulted with an enormously wide range of Indian opinion, beginning with the Viceroy's Executive Council, the provincial governors and the main political leaders. Jinnah, insisting on the principle of a sovereign, economically viable Pakistan, was reasonable and not averse to meeting with Gandhi. To Gandhi, Cripps sent word through the Mahatma's young emissary, Sudhir Ghosh, asking if he would become 'personal adviser' to the mission. He then went to Gandhi's quarters, arriving in the middle of a prayer meeting. Recalling the events of 1942, he said he had always ascribed the rejection by Congress of his offer to Gandhi's influence. Gandhi contended that all he had done was to advise Congress not to settle. Gandhi was willing to talk with Jinnah – though, as Cripps recognised, he was no child at negotiation. The aim was to knock away some of the obstacles to a united India that Jinnah had been erecting. The mission cross-questioned three Muslim League representatives about this on 2 April, sending them away full of doubts. On the Congress side, Maulana Azad (the president) was forthcoming, but worried about getting too far ahead of his colleagues. Gandhi created a flap by requesting certain 'proofs of sincerity' from the mission, involving the repeal of the salt tax, the release of remaining detainees, and the dismissal of 'undesirables'. On 4 April Cripps spoke with Nehru, who thought an agreement most unlikely because of the obduracy of Jinnah, in which case the mission would have to impose an award.

He again saw Jinnah, who refused to be tied down, waiting – Cripps surmised – for him to make an offer so that Jinnah could dismiss it and demand more. The unofficial contacts of Short with the Sikhs and Wyatt with the Muslims (Blaker was seeing a joint group of the Muslim League and Congress) were equally frustrating, and their 'underhand' nature upset Wavell, who was already disconcerted by the deference shown towards Gandhi.[9] Cripps was haunted by the consequences for 400 million people of failure, of upheaval in the streets if no agreement were found.

Making no progress, he tried a different approach, putting on the table two alternative constitutional schemes he had been sketching out – one a loosely federated all-Indian Union with a large Pakistan, the other a partitioned India with a truncated Pakistan. Jinnah still would not commit himself, even about what he might give up. When Cripps pointed out by taking this attitude he was throwing the mission into the arms of Congress, the most Jinnah would agree to was meeting with Gandhi or Nehru. Gandhi urged Cripps to decide on a scheme that the great majority would support, rather than a compromise unpopular with everyone. Nehru saw no use in meeting Jinnah. There is evidence that at some stage Cripps confidentially showed Congress a draft award. With some relief, the mission decamped to the cooling heights of Kashmir.

Undeterred, the mission reverted back to a federal structure, entailing an all-India Union for defence and foreign affairs and two tiers of provinces grouped by majority. Azad broke cover, suggesting Congress might be ready to talk with the Muslim League. For the moment, however, he did not want Cripps to tell Gandhi or Nehru of this. After haggling with Jinnah, Cripps managed to get him to write a letter inviting the League to meet representatives of Congress, choosing the elevated location of Simla. If the talks came to nothing, Cripps made it clear, the mission would issue an award. Gandhi, discovering Azad's action, had to be reassured by Cripps that there was no intention to deceive.

Having reached this point, the Simla conference began in a roundabout way by discussing a Union by implication, without arguing the merits of such an eventuality. With only the slightest chance of an agreement, the mission used the exchanges as a guide to what kind of workable award rival camps might accept. In the event, the talks – one session lasted nine hours – developed. The Muslim League dropped a number of objections, while the Congress hardliner Vallabhai Patel contributed constructively. Even so, Cripps persisted in thinking their 'only hope' was to coax Gandhi into endorsing an agreement – above all in the arrangements for an interim government (to fill the gap until independence), which Wavell was handling. Each time either side broke off, the members of the mission were able to narrow down the points of contention, without breaching the essential formula of a Union grouped by provinces. Eventually, on 9 May, the conference adjourned, Jinnah and Nehru incredibly needing only to agree about the appointment of an 'umpire' to adjudicate on all disputed questions, the mission holding its breath. It was not to be. Jinnah, once the conference resumed, objected to an arbiter if it meant putting the partitioning of India – the fundamental point upon which the League would not compromise – to arbitration, and the whole package unravelled. Accepting defeat, the mission called the Simla talks to a close.

After seven weeks of efforts at enabling an agreement to emerge from among the Indian communities, but convinced that different tactics would not have got them as far (Wavell thought Cripps's fraternising with the Congress camp 'all wrong'[10]), the mission returned to a scorching Delhi to frame the final details of its award for transferring power. Originating from a ten-page draft in Cripps's own hand, the provisions of the statement had been gone through time and again, its author unwilling to delegate or leave anything to chance. The final wording embodied a concrete scheme for reconciling a united and partitioned India. Since the main Indian political parties had failed to reach agreement, the mission envisaged an interim administration until a new constitution had been drawn up. They intended a three-tier structure – a top-level Union, an intermediate grouping of autonomous provinces (Hindu and Muslim), and a bottom layer of provincial governments and states. To give effect to this basic form, they suggested a constitution-making body, made up of representatives elected by the provinces or forwarded by the states, which could advance only by common agreement. Once the constitution had come into force, any province would then be free to opt out of the grouping in which it had been placed. The constitution would be reconsidered after the expiry of ten years. India would become not just a Commonwealth dominion (the 1942 terms) but fully independent. The award stood 'as a whole'.

As R. J. Moore notes, the document was drafted and redrafted steadily in the direction of a two-nation India. On this, a split in the mission, and between the mission and the normally uncommunicative Viceroy, came close. Pethick-Lawrence and Cripps argued for an overriding 'accommodation' with Congress – with the League if at all possible; if not, without. What Cripps would not countenance was parting from Congress. The Viceroy and Alexander took the view that they should under no circumstances yield to the demands of Congress, even if this meant cutting all contact. If the mission gave way to Congress, Wavell said he would not be prepared to carry on. Alexander threatened to 'bring his ships home'. It was only by taking an absolutely firm line that the mission was able to beat off an attempt by Attlee and the Cabinet to strengthen references to India remaining in the Commonwealth.

The award was broadcast on 16 May – the date was chosen by an official astrologer – inviting comments from the principal parties. Gandhi, first to respond, sought satisfaction on a number of 'pernickety' snags, wanting to know whether each party would be honour bound to make the award work, and whether the terms of the award itself might be altered by the sovereign constitution-making body, which otherwise would not be sovereign. The Muslim League said it would not be replying before 15 June, later brought forward by one week. Just when Cripps was congratulating himself on keeping Gandhi involved at each stage, the Mahatma raised 'embarrassing' difficulties about the grouping of provinces, distorting the answers Cripps and Pethick-Lawrence gave him, effectively returning to a (Congress-dominated) independent Indian government before the drafting of a constitution. Taken aback, Wavell and Alexander, in Cripps's words, 'went off the deep end', demanding the mission should see the able, unscrupulous, 'malignant' Gandhi all together or not at all, stirring in Cripps the fear of losing him.

Round-the-clock exertions sapped Cripps's stamina. In Simla, unacclimatised, he fainted after walking back from visiting Gandhi. On 21 May he collapsed with dysentry, exacerbated by overwork, and was confined to hospital. In the few days when the mission was trying to weigh up reactions to the award, its driving force was incapacitated, meeting no one and seeing no papers. Alexander, with some justice, attributed his infirmity to the shock of Gandhi's turnabout.

In his weakened state, and without telling the rest of the mission, he composed a 'very private and confidential' letter to Gandhi, 'pouring out his heart', the culmination of his efforts – his 'fixation'[11] – to prevail upon the Mahatma. The obstacles in the way of a reasonable statement, Cripps acknowledged, were rooted in 'the experiences of the last century'.[12] But the mission and the main parties had already made such progress that it would be a 'purposeless tragedy' if they did not progress further. 'The key to the whole matter is surely *Trust*.' If the people of India believed in their destiny of complete independence, the intervening period could be of little consequence. If, however, that basic trust was missing, nothing written on paper could convince anyone to see it as other than a trap perpetuating British power. The only way to succeed was in a spirit of full and frank co-operation. The moment for this supreme act of faith on all sides had arrived. 'I am certain that there is no other basis for a non-violent transition – which will truly be the greatest event in World history – than trust and co-operation. I also believe that you, my dear friend, can do more in this direction than any other man in the world.'

Receiving Cripps's 'touching' letter, Gandhi conceded that the award 'demands and commands trust'.[13] But, like everything emanating from the British, it created *dis*trust, being open to all sorts of interpretation which made him question whether a satisfactory interim government or constituent assembly would ever be formed. Having said that, if Cripps wanted any further assistance, he should not hesitate to send a messenger. Cripps's original letter was enclosed.

It took a full fortnight, until 3 June, before Cripps was up and about, ready to make the most of the remaining few days the mission was allotting itself before leaving in the middle of the month. In his absence, Wavell's quiet diplomacy had had some effect. The Working Committee of Congress was known to be in two minds about the award, a growing number seeing virtue in its emphatic repudiation of a two-state solution, which they could seal by joining an interim government. The Muslim League, deploring the rejection of a sovereign Pakistan, drew comfort from the compulsory grouping of prov-inces, implying the right of secession, provided they obtained parity of representation in whatever interim coalition was formed. Once the issue of parity reared up, Gandhi, from a position of strength, did his utmost to spoil a consensus. This brought Ghosh, his emissary, and Agatha Harrison (of the India Conciliation Group) to the mission in a state of 'great perturbation', appealing to Cripps as the one person on whom all hopes rested – at the moment when, as he wryly observed, his colleagues took the view that his earlier clandestine talks with Gandhi had got them all into trouble and he ought not to see anyone from either side. Though it irked him that they could not appreciate the value of informal approaches, the darkening position – the Chiefs of Staff in the UK were preparing to reinforce India with no less than five divisions – stimulated a 'definite cheerfulness', arising from 'inner help' and the aid of Isobel, who had just arrived.

Assuring both sides that they would get parity in fact if they did not insist on the principle, the Viceroy helped to smooth over the altercation, though the nearer they got to an agreement the more exacting the conditions became, the whole process hanging by a slender thread. On 16 June, Wavell published the lists of nominees from Jinnah and Nehru for the proposed interim government, which would – Jinnah had asked for clarification – go ahead whether or not both sides signed up to it. The signs were, however, that Congress was on the point of acceptance.

The humid climate made waiting unbearable, and Gandhi, dominating the proceedings of Congress, made it all the more trying. A note from him was brought to Cripps by Ghosh, referring to 'the storm that is brewing within you', the result – Gandhi asserted – of attempting to reconcile the incompatible.[14] The mission should have the courage to choose, trusting that Congress would treat the Muslims fairly, as he had argued from the start. The best thing would be for Cripps to take his 'poor wife' with him and go back to England, burying themselves in private life. Cripps laughed off the 'ridiculous' letter; he would never give way to his desire to return home unless he was sure he had left nothing undone. Fretful as he was, Pethick-Lawrence and Alexander refused to let him go and see Gandhi alone, in case 'I let them down!'

Gandhi stirred the pot still further by complaining that the mission could not claim to be the final interpreter of its award, and objecting to any idea of an interim government being formed by the Viceroy, forcing Nehru, tired and isolated, to give in. He followed this by another exasperating 'stunt', nominating Azad (a Muslim) to the interim government, knowing full well this would antagonise Jinnah.

After Rajagopalachari had informed Cripps of the struggle within the Working Committee of Congress, the Committee eventually turned Gandhi down. Divorcing Gandhi from the rest of Congress had, Cripps felt, become 'almost inevitable', though it made a nonsense of his earlier tactics. On 20 June, Congress, standing on its head, reversed its decision and rejected the award, the tenacity of 'the Old Man' wearing his opponents out. Cripps got permission to confront Gandhi in person, 'pleading' with him to reconsider. But Cripps's arguments cut no ice. All he could do was press Congress to declare its position, after which the Muslim League would give its own response, neither side wishing to incur the odium of precipitating the breakdown.

An unintended situation suddenly arose. The Muslim League, withholding its opinion on the formation of an interim government, had, on 6 June, accepted the longer-term scheme for constitutional change, a position from which it never wavered. Congress, shifting daily, if not hourly, looked certain to reject both. In this circumstance, the Viceroy was bound by an earlier commitment to go ahead with implementing his interim scheme,[15] which would mean asking the Muslim League to form a government with representatives of the minorities. The effect, Wavell said, would be 'fatal'. Cripps was all for allowing Jinnah the attempt, calculating that he would refuse or fail to make a go of it, opening the door to Congress. He threatened to resign if this was not done.[16] Yet the mission could hardly withdraw the award of 16 May and return to square one again.

Hitherto, the award and the interim government had hung together, Cripps having categorically assured Wavell that Congress would never accept one and not the other. The attraction to Congress of actually accepting the award began to grow, if – the mission was pressed on the point – doing so would mean scrapping the contentious features (such as parity of representation) of the interim government, recovering the ground that Congress had lost to Jinnah. Cripps professed to be as 'startled' by this move as his colleagues. Wavell was immediately on his guard, believing it quite possible Cripps had put the idea in the heads of the Working Committee of Congress. Gandhi still took some convincing, even by Patel, and Cripps only now came round to regretting the hope he had pinned on Gandhi. Twice the mission had been on the point of an agreement. Twice Gandhi had intervened to block one, carrying on in a most 'devastating' manner.

In a last conciliatory move, Pethick-Lawrence and Cripps gave Gandhi to understand that delegates to the proposed constituent assembly need not, as previously stipulated, remain in their respective groupings while drawing up a constitution – a dishonest assurance, angering Wavell,[17] but enough to entice Congress into accepting the longer-term proposals, qualified by its own inter-pretation of the meaning of the award, posing as the defenders of a united India. When Wavell queried this, Cripps astonished him by saying that the award in itself had no statutory force. By a down-to-earth trade-off, the mission – or rather Pethick-Lawrence and Cripps (Alexander was ashamed and appalled) – salvaged the pretence of a commitment from both sides to future constitutional change, obscuring the nature of the deal with fine phrases.

Wavell, believing Cripps had planned the outcome all along, was left with no option but to establish a caretaker administration made up of officials, until a constituent assembly could be convened. Jinnah, deprived of his reward, denounced the mission in a vitriolic public attack, insisting the acceptance by Congress was insincere. Pethick-Lawrence tactlessly argued that the Muslim League's decision of 6 June had been equally bogus. A full settlement had proved elusive, but the last-gasp deal enabled the mission to leave Delhi claim-ing that the making of an Indian constitution could now begin, Cripps adding enigmatically that there was much more that could be said. The farewell (Cripps did not say goodbye to the Viceroy), behind the smiles, exposed the crippling effect of their three-month trial – Pethick-Lawrence was 'tottering and tremulous', and Cripps, 'broken in health if not in spirit ... was so ema-ciated that his clothes hung loosely on him as though they were draping a skeleton'.[18]

The homecomers were unable to prevent their mission from being written off as a valiant failure – an impression which gained ground throughout the summer, when, to the fury of the Viceroy, Congress made plain it did not have the slightest intention of honouring its acceptance of the proposals. Cripps maintained in the House of Commons that India was now fully persuaded of British sincerity. Pethick-Lawrence's biographer (and family friend) repeated the assertion.[19] In a shortened Commons debate, the Opposition were too wholly concerned by what was being given away to contest it. Was the mission guilty of wishful thinking? Could different methods have led to a different result?

Wavell certainly thought so. Cripps – the 'directing genius' of the mission – had too blatantly favoured Congress and too openly pandered to Gandhi, who had constantly outsmarted him. Wavell considered Cripps's style of personal diplomacy especially destructive, his methods duplicitous, his judgements of Nehru, Gandhi and Jinnah all faulty. He quoted Cripps's own comment about him – 'the trouble about Wavell is that he is no politician' – as self-incriminating. Wavell agreed that the award was the best that could be proposed, and a tribute to Cripps's drafting skills. But if the mission had issued an unequivocal statement and imposed it, instead of seeking refuge in ambiguities, Congress and the Muslim League would have had to co-operate. It is a persuasive indictment, fuelled by animus, but one to which posterity, in the light of the achievement of another envoy, Lord Mountbatten, in 1947, has lent support.[20]

It does not follow that the mission was one more false climax, to go with the offer of 1942 and Wavell's Simla conference of 1945. For one thing, the mission stiffened Cripps in his belief that the right and only way forward was to get the Indians to overcome their communal divisions and determine their own future. It was not for the British to decree how India should or should not be governed. If the British could facilitate a peaceful handing over, this would be both morally and politically preferable. Imposing a settlement would not win Indian confidence. The mission could not have simply abdicated responsibility to Congress, washing its hands of any further involvement. Cripps assumed the rationality of those he was dealing with. Gandhi left him dumbfounded, a leader (Cripps) who knew all the answers meeting another leader who knew all sorts of different answers.[21] He barely disguised his view that a separate Muslim state was irrational. If reason alone had been enough, 'Cripps would have cracked it.'[22] Instead, he ended up banging his head in self-consuming frustration.

The other upshot was that Cripps set his sights on removing Wavell, who lacked the 'suppleness' to knit the leaders of the two communities together. Gandhi's policy was delaying, not accelerating, independence. Wavell's 'defeatism' was equally abhorrent, even if there was something to be said for 'the provincial option' (i.e. Pakistan).[23] The moment he returned to Britain, Cripps took up his quest for a replacement for Wavell – Mountbatten, the Supreme Commander in South-East Asia, had occurred to him even while he was still in India – and for a *casus belli* to swing the Cabinet against the Viceroy.[24]

TELLING THE PEOPLE

The war has been won, but the price has not yet been paid.
Cripps, opening the British Industries' Fair, May 1947

The Crippses returned to the relative cool of London and a rising tide of discontent about continuing shortages, rationing and restrictions, threatening to put paid to Cripps's plans to 'go a bit slow I fear for some months if I am to get fit and strong'. Public understanding of the economic position in 1945 had been ill-informed. Disillusionment soon set in. 'Are these hardships really necessary?' the economist Roy Harrod asked.

The Board of Trade was the core ministry, the nearest equivalent to the wartime Ministry of Production, equipped with an array of physical controls but without first call on resources – or, equally importantly, the overriding motivation of military victory. Cripps's self-appointed role was to provide the rationale for hard work by appealing to a moral imperative ahead of material incentives. The State was to do what the market by itself would not, organising – planning – a more efficient and just society. The Board of Trade had to have regard for consumer needs, which, at least in the immediate term, needed restraining. To meet the administrative undertaking, the department doubled in size and extent to just over 15,000 – six times higher than in the inter-war years. Even this expansion was not enough to keep pace with a growing volume of public complaints about coupons, permits and licences, running, by the middle of 1946, at the rate of 900,000 letters a month. The result was an imposing bureaucratic sprawl, 10 per cent of the total civil service, increasingly difficult to co-ordinate and – notwithstanding the 'luminous mind' and 'incredible' industriousness of its President[1] – barely 'administerable'.[2]

While Cripps was away and once he was back, the Cabinet aired its grievances. A group, led by Dalton, pioneer of regional policy, wanted to know why quicker progress had not been made in establishing new factories in the designated Development Areas, where several ministers held seats. Others tried to force a decision to release more supplies to mining areas, to stimulate coal production. Bevan, Minister of Housing, had set in train an overambitious housebuilding programme, for which the timber did not exist – a trade deal with the Soviet Union was stalled. Shinwell, the Minister of Fuel and Power, began advocating an increase in the petrol ration. Cripps applied a simple benchmark, objecting to any proposal which did not clearly contribute to, or detracted from, the 'essential' expanding of the export trade. Resenting being told what was in the country's and the government's best interests, colleagues found it damnably difficult to get the better of him in argument. He was never dogmatic. In June, before his return, bread rationing was introduced for the first time (starting in July). When the new Minister of Food, Strachey, tried to reverse the decision, Morrison, Bevin and Cripps all supported him, but were outnumbered. Cripps was not inflicting his own private miseries on his countrymen. It was only what circumstances allowed. No amount of juggling of supplies for home and overseas could turn a shortage into a surplus. He radiated spartan fortitude, however, rising early, dining frugally (off silver), cultivating a rigid self-control which the trade-union element in the Party found repellent. People would work harder, it was argued, if only they were given something to buy. Cripps persisted in thinking that that would lead only to 'chasing our tail'; the vicious circle had to be broken by boosting output.[3] He shared Attlee's desire to ease consumer shortages, but it was 'not possible to relax restrictions more quickly than we are in fact doing'.[4]

By the autumn of 1946, the first four working-party reports had been completed. Some from the second wave were expected shortly. The recommendations for reorganisation were broadly similar. Both equipment and attitudes were obsolete and inefficient. Easy profits made companies resistant to modernising. The wartime sense of partnership was fading. In the cotton industry, the report actually argued in favour of compulsory amalgamation. Cripps was persuaded by Woods and by John Belcher (his new Parliamentary Secretary) to 'leave it to Streat', who, he was assured, had the requisite drive to bring in changes. Cripps was reluctant to have the threat of nationalisation hanging in the air. But the demarcation of departmental responsibilities did not help. It was only in the spring of 1946 that the Department of Overseas Trade, charged with export promotion, was incorporated into the Board of Trade. Engineering was dealt with not by the Board of Trade but the sponsoring Minister of Supply, though officials at Supply began bypassing their own minister and dealing with Cripps directly.[5]

Government policy appeared to him to be based on misplaced priorities. Labour's first year was one of legislative enactment, funding family allowances and national insurance and preparing the ground for a national health service. Important as these were, he thought they should come second to industrial recovery. He had every reason to worry that the lion's share of the American loan (ratified in July by the US Senate) would go on current spending instead of on capital investment. And, while he was a fervent advocate of nationalising the basic utilities, the productive heart of industry – joining in singing 'The

Red Flag' when the Mines Bill passed its second reading[6] – one could not nationalise a vital trade like cotton in the middle of an export crisis.[7] (He had foreseen this in October 1944.) The export industries – not coal, civil aviation or gas – were, according to Alec Cairncross, who served under Cripps in the Board of Trade, the real 'commanding heights' of the post-war economy.

There were also weaknesses in decision-making. Too great a load was being carried by too small a nucleus of weary senior ministers; there were too many committees and subcommittees they had to attend; far too many minor matters were passed up to the full Cabinet for discussion.[8] Worst of all, there was no direction from the top. Bevin was wholly immersed in the Foreign Office. Morrison, claiming to exercise a co-ordinating role, succeeded only in 'interfering', as Dalton also attested. Both Morrison and Cripps 'in their confidential moments groaned over the utter inadequacy of Attlee as PM'.[9]

One contemporary account has Cripps biding his time. In truth, he was run down, finding it difficult to put his work to one side. He swore by the Alexander technique – 'the secret of a well co-ordinated physical and mental life' – but had not, as he put it, mastered the art of relaxation. After his statement to the Commons on India, he went off for the August recess to the Bircher-Benner Klinik in Zurich, officially suffering from overwork and overstrain. The clinic propagated the doctrine of natural healing, correcting 'internal disturbances' by sunlight, fresh air, hydrotherapy and diet, paying particular attention to serving uncooked vegetable food, supplemented by the Bircher-Benner muesli. By the end of the month he had recuperated enough to write to Attlee, letting him know he had 'at last broken the insomnia' and felt fit to resume work in early September.[10] Speculation about a Cabinet reshuffle started up, with Cripps tipped to move to a new job, possibly as a roving ambassador. Asked whether he would shortly be leaving the Board of Trade, he took pleasure in remarking that, while some of the press were anxious he should do so, 'I am afraid they are not going to be satisfied.'[11]

The idea that Cripps was excluded from foreign and defence policy had substance. Foreign policy was a closed book, the broad lines being settled between Attlee and Bevin. Cripps had more reason than most to object. In the 1945 election, he had championed friendship with the Soviet Union. During the debate on the American loan, when anti-American sentiment surfaced among left-wingers, Cripps had reassured waverers that Britain was still free to trade with any third countries it chose. Deteriorating relations with Russia, given prominence in Churchill's 'iron curtain' Fulton speech in February 1946, baffled Bevin, who was at a loss to explain why the Russians were behaving unreasonably. Defending himself at the party conference, he referred to the efforts of the Board of Trade to secure a Soviet trade agreement, Cripps even offering to fly to Moscow if it would help to wrap one up. Backbench unrest resulted in an Amendment to the Address in November 1946, calling for a 'democratic socialist alternative to an otherwise inevitable conflict between American capitalism and Soviet communism'.

What Cripps minded most were the external constraints on domestic policy, stifling economic recovery. Increasingly costly overseas commitments, greatly adding to the economic burden, brought Cripps into closer accord with Dalton, the Chancellor.

Three controversies in the autumn of 1946 underscored their emerging alliance. In October, the Cabinet approved bringing in a system of national service. This single decision, when demobilisation was still far from complete, aggravated the existing labour shortage. Dalton and Cripps were overruled. In the same month, in a small *ad hoc* Cabinet committee bolstered by the late arrival of the Foreign Secretary, it was decided to proceed with developing the production of uranium 235, a necessary element in the manufacture of an atomic bomb. Again, Dalton and Cripps protested about the huge expense of the project.[12] They favoured internationalising nuclear information under United Nations auspices. (Attlee subsequently formed another committee which took the decision in principle to construct a bomb, explaining much later that some of his colleagues 'were not fit to be trusted with secrets of this kind'.) The third issue of contention arose over Cripps's attempts to resuscitate a Soviet trade deal, to obtain timber and grain. Bevin instructed Cripps not to be unduly 'tough' in reaching terms. A trade delegation left in August, after Cripps had proposed an inducement to the Soviet Trade Mission in London of twenty Rolls-Royce jet engines. A Cabinet committee objected, until Cripps appealed directly to the Prime Minister, who sided with Cripps, arguing that since the engines had been taken off the secret list their sale could not be blocked.[13] Bevin was aghast. He had only just been talking with James Byrnes, the US Secretary of State, who had 'reacted very strongly'. For Cripps, Russia was and would be a valuable market for British exports, especially once the worldwide upturn had passed.

Exports reached and passed their pre-war level by May 1946, reaching 111 per cent of the pre-war figure in the last quarter of the year, while imports were held down to two-thirds of the volume of 1938. According to Board of Trade projections, world trade in manufactured goods would recover by 1950 and might be 50 per cent higher by 1955.[14] Dalton exuberantly announced to Parliament that the export drive had 'succeeded beyond expectation'. Cripps adapted this message for the opening session of the International Trade Organisation (ITO). British exports had risen spectacularly, but total exports were still nowhere near the set target of 75 per cent above pre-war. Export earnings, moreover, were very uneven, creating what Cripps christened a 'double' balance-of-payments problem – a total (though declining) trade deficit as well as a hard-currency deficit, heightened by a world dollar shortage. Departmental policy had been to encourage exports in bulk, without caring too much about their destination. In any case, the government had entered into a commitment not to ration dollars by discriminating against imports from the dollar area. Favouring non-dollar countries would breach the doctrine of multilateral trading. Whenever the question of attempting to alter the flow of foreign trade came up, it was strongly resisted, particularly by the Ministry of Food. Before the ITO, Cripps spoke up for economic sovereignty, long-term commodity agreements and the safeguarding of full employment as an international object-ive, leading the opposition to any general tariff reductions. In the meantime, Dalton's import programme for 1946–7 was bleak. The country was using up the American loan – falling in real value because of rising US prices – far too quickly; unless remedial action was taken, they would be faced with 'highly unpleasant decisions' in 1948 or 1949; for that reason, there could be no relaxing of the export drive.

This simple fact – that in a dollar-scarce international economy exports could not be created or directed at will but relied on management and labour in the exporting trades themselves – had a significant impact on the eventual shape of Board of Trade industrial policy.

The Industrial Organisation Bill translated into legislative form some of the main working-party recommendations, conferring on ministers the power to establish a permanent 'development council' in selected industries and provide grants to assist in modernisation and raising productivity. The councils were to be tripartite, advisory and experimental, representing a new conception of industrial democracy. But, as one civil servant warned, 'the President will find this Bill will prove a good deal more controversial than he at present imagines'.[15]

Industrialists upset by the 'torrent' of denigration from the government, were suspicious of enabling powers and dreaded 'a new despotism'.[16] The FBI disliked having a uniform framework imposed on industry. Cripps's prime concern was the attainment of maximum industrial efficiency and the maximum contribution to the national economy. If this could be achieved by voluntary co-operation, 'no one would be better pleased than himself'. He gave his word that no council would be foisted on unwilling industries.

Development councils, it was agreed, would not impinge upon the trade-union concerns of wages or conditions of work. But inter-war habits con-ditioned by the trade cycle – fear of lay-offs, go-slow restrictionism – died hard. Additionally, it was difficult to find enough qualified employees to sit on the councils. Cripps referred to this dearth in a speech in his constituency, commenting that 'until there has been more experience by the workers of the managerial side of industry, I think it would be almost impossible to have worker-controlled industry in Britain, even if it were on the whole desirable'. Uproar ensued. He subsequently tried to elaborate, insisting 'it is no use misrepresenting the facts in order to appear pleasant'.[17] Very few workers were trained in running industry. It was for the unions to educate their own people.

Exercised by the row, Isobel and he arranged two private dinners with leading trade unionists, laying on non-alcoholic punch.

Cripps's attitude puzzled his local party. Land nationalisation – like worker's control, another favourite of activists – Cripps dismissed in conversation on the (lawyer's) grounds that it would be impossible to trace all the title deeds. What had happened to the red-hot Cripps of 1945?

The provisions of the Industrial Organisation Bill were certainly a retreat from wartime thinking. The coalition had been on the point of creating Industrial Boards with the power to impose compulsory amalgamations as a catalyst for industry-wide change. Even when it came to the cotton industry, which had just voted to bring in a reduced, 45-hour, week without prior discussion with the government, Cripps relied on the benefits of voluntary co-operation. Since the buoyant cotton market removed the need to compete, the only way to squeeze firms was to restrict their profit margins. Streat had agreed to remain in charge of the new Cotton Board only provided there would be no legislative compulsion to force amalgamations. Cripps was content to hold himself in reserve, so that if private enterprise did not redeploy (enforcing redundancies) the government would step in, invoking the powers to do it. 'I like the semi-sick Stafford so much more than the unmoderated Stafford of 1945,' Streat confided.[18]

As chairman of the National Production Advisory Council for Industry (NPACI), the main forum for supervising the private sector, in sponsoring the British Institute of Management and in his relations with the Board of Trade's raw-material controllers, most of whom had extremely close industry links, Cripps was one of the few Labour ministers who took the trouble to seek out continuing consultation. However wide the disagreements, Cripps would listen. It followed that Cripps, skilful in small-group meetings,[19] exercised the right to talk others round. 'Businessmen and business in general showed a great willingness to co-operate with Cripps,' the Secretary to the Cabinet, Sir Edward Bridges recalled; 'this was the foundation for his achievement.'[20] Without goodwill, the objectives behind the Industrial Organisation Bill would be negated. Commending the Bill to a sceptical Parliamentary Labour Party, he said it signalled both 'a recognition that the industries will not be nationalised and an alternative to nationalisation'.

More to the point, Cripps dare not risk antagonising private industry in the middle of the crucial drive for exports. Resources – including scarce labour – had to be moved from contracting trades to expanding ones, though there might be temporary job losses. Exporters were given a greater ration of limited materials, though it caused resentment. On his same visit to Bristol, he had been 'appalled' by the amount of ignorance about the reasons for the country's straitened circumstances. Bruce-Gardner added that it was not confined to the general public but was equally prevalent among industrialists, some of whom saw nothing wrong in circumventing controls. A Prosperity Campaign was one attempt to improve public understanding.

Partnership was supposed to lead to planning. Although French planners took up the development-council model, the idea involved little planning of industry as such. Cripps, briefed by two economists, Austen Robinson and Richard Kahn, was ironing out the basics of a longer-term plan, pushing the horizon back by four or five years.[21] He had no flair for economics. He was unable to see how the distributive trades performed a productive economic function, citing the example of a commodity costing £6 to make being retailed for £29, all of the middlemen's additions being legal. He thought the working man craved 'respect', not higher wages. His aim was for a 25 per cent increase in productivity per head above the pre-war figure – 'pitching our sights pretty high', observed one official, 'and will take a damned long time to achieve', added another. Woods was blunter still about the Minister's clever foolishness – 'What a wonderful mind that man has. What a pity when he talks out of the top of it.'[22]

Time for rectifying the economy was running out. 'Cripps sees this clearly,' Dalton entered in his diary for 29 November, 'but few of the others do. In agreement with me, he and I are both making public speeches about this, and privately I am trying to frighten my colleagues about it.' Cripps was the first, *The Economist* spotted, to plead with and threaten industry. Britain, he told an FBI conference, was living largely on the American and a smaller Canadian loan.[23] These loans were rapidly being 'eaten up', with nothing to replace them. The end of the seller's market fast approaching, they would soon be confronted by sharp external competition. Unless they maintained and increased exports, especially to dollar countries, the country would 'come a cropper', requiring 'drastic action' in order to carry on. Woods, addressing the same conference, argued that the only alternative to a lower standard of living would be to export a large part of the population. 'I am not Father Christmas,' the President of the Board of Trade owned up. Clothes rationing might have to go on for many years to come. Harassed by irate consumers, 'I am tempted', he replied, 'to address your enquiries to the workpeople and managements of Yorkshire and Lancashire.'[24]

The need to economise and to cut back on overloaded foreign commitments combined powerfully to undermine the British presence in India, but economic imperatives did not bring a solution there any nearer. The constituent assembly for which the Cabinet mission had laboured was boycotted by Jinnah, the Muslim League's 'Day of Action' on 16 August 1946 leading to chaotic rioting and loss of life in many cities. Three months passed before Jinnah decided to participate in the new interim government, hitherto dominated by an intransigent Congress Party. Wavell, deprived of a clear line of policy from

London, substituted for political change a 'breakdown plan' of full-scale military evacuation from southern India, apprehensive the British could not hold on for more than another eighteen months but convincing the Prime Minister he was out of his depth.[25] In December, the Indian leaders attended a conference in London. Wavell defended his plan before the Cabinet. In these discussions, Cripps was 'much the best man', keen and incisive, exploiting the Viceroy's defensiveness as the pretext for pushing him aside.

Attlee's new choice was Lord Louis Mountbatten, who had impressed Attlee by his part in returning civilian government to Burma. At the decisive interview in Downing Street on 18 December (Wavell was still in London, but 'discourteously' treated), Attlee and Cripps offered him *carte blanche*. He – by his account – asked for plenipotentiary powers. After a long pause, Cripps gave his consent. Cripps then 'bouleversed' him by suggesting he accompany him as a member of his staff. Mountbatten, who had no wish to become the figurehead for a third version of the Cripps offer, parried the idea by proposing Cripps move to the India Office as Secretary of State, where he could act as Mountbatten's 'rear link' with the government.[26] It is an indicator of the importance Cripps attached to the Indian issue that, though 'staggered' by the idea, he was ready to switch offices. One of Mountbatten's conditions was the announcement of a fixed date by which the British intended to withdraw from India. The irony was later not lost on Wavell, who had suggested it to the Cabinet and had met with violent opposition. Attlee now embraced a deadline as the only credible way of effecting an orderly transfer of power, obliging the Indian parties to grasp the nettle of responsibility – all the while keeping India in the Commonwealth, a point which Cripps had been ready to drop but which Mountbatten, again, had insisted on.

Overwhelmed by an immense range of other dilemmas competing for attention, the Cabinet was thinking not of India but of coal, the problem of problems.

The fuel crisis which broke out over the winter of 1946–7, intensified by unusually long and severe cold weather in the new year, set the Attlee government its first serious test of competence. The crisis was badly mismanaged. The consequences of a minor shortfall in coal supplies were calamitous. Industry shut down across the country, unemployment surged above 2 million, there were many weeks of lost production, and – because the crisis coincided with the vesting date for the nationalisation of the mines – Labour's claim to be planning the economy was severely undermined.

The shock of the fuel crisis did, however, alter the government's order of battle. With Shinwell under a cloud and Morrison indisposed, Cripps was called upon to concoct a rescue plan, rising before dawn to marshall his red boxes. National survival had to become its central preoccupation, he insisted, if the government was not to fall altogether. This enabled him to clinch his case for the introduction of proper machinery for economic planning, and to put the economic facts squarely before the general public. Organisational improvements formed the backdrop to manoeuvrings in the succeeding months to install a more 'dynamic' prime minister.

The setback Cripps had always feared most was an interruption in coal supplies and the dislocation of industry that would ensue. The country had got through the winter of 1945–6 only by a narrow margin. In the spring and summer of 1946, James Meade (head of the Economic Section) and Douglas Jay (Attlee's personal assistant) were already warning of trouble ahead. Speaking at a fuel conference in October, Cripps explained that a coal shortage would be 'the gravest thing for our future national preservation ... it is touch and go whether we shall get through the winter without some hold-up, either of domestic or industrial supplies'.[27] Shinwell, closing the same conference, was defiant. In spite of a 'phenomenal' rise in the demand for electricity, Cripps argued for a voluntary cut in consumption of 10 per cent, confident the present labour force was of sufficient size to make up the gap, given 'encouragement' and not 'criticism'. In Cabinet, he demanded the imposition of cuts, put off until after Christmas. He stole the headlines by incautiously joking that every-one knew there was going to be a coal crisis except the Minister for Fuel and Power.

Shortly afterwards Cripps received a panicky representation from Shinwell, anxious about widespread disruption, belatedly adopting a planned restriction of coal consumption. Cripps told Attlee, 'I at once agreed to immediate action.'[28] A scheme was drawn up by the Ministry of Fuel and Power and the Board of Trade and put before the NPACI, which unanimously concurred with percentage cuts in national coal. To Cripps's amazement, Shinwell then backtracked, sticking by voluntary rationing at the Lord President's Com-mittee, with the result that, when the issue went to the Cabinet on 19 November, Shinwell distanced himself from the 'apprehensions' of his own officials, sug-gesting instead cutting factory-gate deliveries, which had the advantage to him of not requiring a public announcement. Cripps, reporting Shinwell's behaviour to the Prime Minister, maintained that a planned reduction in allocations was 'essential'. Cutting deliveries was 'inequitable and unpre-dictable'. Industry had to know on what basis it would be operating in the coming weeks. Other ministers agreed, but Shinwell got away with a com-promise of Morrison's, Shinwell blaming Cripps for the large rise in the use of electrical goods.[29] Given a second hearing, the Cabinet stuck with the voluntary fuel-economy plan, to begin on 1 January 1947. Cripps wrote to Shinwell to congratulate him on being the 'first home' with the nationalisation of coal and wishing him luck in the 'strenuous' task ahead.[30]

The Cabinet met again to consider the fuel position on 7 January. Many of the bottlenecks inhibiting the transit of coal had been overcome, but this was not enough to correct the brute shortfall of 300,000 tons of coal out of a basic requirement of approximately 1.5 million tons per week. Shinwell, finally caving in, abandoned the fight and gave way to Cripps, whose recommendations occupied the rest of the Cabinet's deliberations.[31] Shinwell's way with figures, Cripps commented to Jay, was to 'sweep them off the table';[32] Cripps worshipped them. He proposed a hefty 40–50 per cent cut in fuel allocations, pooling the surplus into regional fighting reserves. The plan was 'realistic' – akin to the wartime MAP programmes – because deliveries would more closely correspond to allocations. Remarkably, the Cabinet opted for the higher figure, without going so far as to restrict electricity consumption. The Cripps measures came into force only on 20 January, quickly followed by the first reports of short-term working in the Midlands and the North-West. Heavy snowfalls followed. As a case study of the fuel fiasco notes, the crisis preceded the bad weather, but was enormously magnified by it.

Ministers went on the offensive. Cripps stole the show with a 'Cassandra utterance' in Bradford – hub of the Yorkshire textile trade – to the effect that the country could pull through so long as enough labour could be found to raise production. If not, he predicted even greater austerity. The pity was 'the apparent failure of so many people to realise the seriousness of the situation', which he 'could not overstress'.[33] The closing in of the weather did his work for him. Snow turned to blizzards and then frost. Problems in transporting coal reappeared. Snowdrifts impeded roads and railways. Ships serving the east-coast collieries were confined to port. Factory closures spread. At a special meeting of the NPACI, the FBI director-general, Norman Kipping, stayed on his feet to castigate the government for failing to foresee the coal shortage, reducing the trade-union representatives to 'dispirited silence'.[34]

On 6 February, Shinwell announced that the fuel shortage was already 'on the mend', hoping the recommendation of the Central Electricity Board (CEB) – shutting down all power to industry and partly suspending household supplies – need not be resorted to. The next day he was back before the Cabinet to explain that the CEB scheme had to be implemented as soon as possible – 'a complete thunderclap' according to Dalton. He then told the Commons, to a torrent of attacks. The Ministry of Fuel and Power's statistics were shown up as wholly wrong, invalidating Cripps's plan, while Cripps was asking officials where all the 'coal' had gone to.[35] Fuel provision was taken over by a revamped Fuel Committee, chaired by Attlee, assisted by Shinwell's able junior, Hugh Gaitskell.

The newspapers were full of finger-pointing.[36] Shinwell and Cripps were said to be 'at loggerheads', Shinwell outraged at carrying the can. The *Daily Mirror*, briefed at the Ministry of Fuel and Power, acquitted Shinwell, claiming he had been done down by Dalton and Cripps. In *The Observer*, Cripps earned high praise, the intrigues and innuendoes serving little purpose now he had taken up the burden.

> He may not be the most beloved of Ministers, but anybody who had been in touch with industry knows that he is one of the outstanding successes of the government. The public may grumble as it sips its arrowroot, but it has the good sense to realise that Sir Stafford at least has the courage and integrity to pursue an unpopular policy if he is convinced that it is for the good of the country.[37]

'My dear Mannie', Cripps wrote sympathetically to Shinwell, assuring him the rest of the Cabinet were ready to share 'both the responsibilities and the kicks'.[38] The magnanimous tone did not last. Not long afterwards, Dalton and Cripps were telling Attlee it was high time Shinwell went – a view, Cripps felt, held universally by the rest of the government, industry and the country.[39]

Thawing of the snow led to widespread flooding, extending the damage into March, delaying economic recovery and costing the country, in the Board of Trade guesstimate, some £200 million in forfeited exports – 2 per cent of the gross national product.[40] Had the vigilant Cripps been at the Ministry of Fuel and Power, Cairncross concludes, the fuel crisis probably would never have occurred.[41]

Missing the public-relations touch of Morrison (released from hospital, he went to recuperate in the south of France, staying away until the end of April), Attlee devolved responsibility for economic planning – with 'special oversight' of government publicity – on to the President of the Board of Trade.

Cripps had coveted the planning portfolio since July 1945. In the eighteen months that had elapsed, the economic problem – 'cushioned' by the American loan – had grown in magnitude. It was inconceivable to him that the economy could restructure through unplanned enterprise. Recovery had to be State-directed. With so much new economic and welfare spending, the difficulty lay in enforcing priorities. In ministerial discussions about the Economic Survey for 1947, to be published for the first time, the central theme was of 'the great and increasing gap between resources and requirements', the result of a government 'trying to do too many things'.[42] Morrison, blocked (by Dalton) from incorporating the investment programmes of the new publicly owned industries in the annual budget, relied on his economic adviser, Max Nicholson, to come up with 'planning for expansion'. Cripps could think only of the impending disaster if public expenditure were not contained.

Filling in for Morrison, he presented the Economic Survey to the Cabinet on 16 January. There was, he observed, no escaping the truth that the economy was 'overburdened'. He proposed an interdependent set of measures affecting future programmes – postponing raising of the school-leaving age, cutting the housing budget, conscripting women – which offered a 'reasonable prospect' of averting the worst. Reassembling twice, ministers dug in their heels, several arguing it was too late to make changes, which should be held over until 1948. In that case, Cripps answered, there was no point publishing the Survey disclosing such a serious situation if the document did not include the necessary steps to remedy it.[43] Dalton concentrated his fire on the defence programme. Alexander's final offer was a 5 per cent cut, which Dalton instantly accepted, sending round a long letter to Attlee warning that the government was 'drifting, in a state of semi-animation, towards the rapids'. The coal muddle was symptomatic. Hilary Marquand, head of the Overseas Department of the Board of Trade, put the point succinctly to his chief. Every minister had known coal stocks were running down. 'Everybody hoped *his* programme would get by. Nobody pointed out that *all* programmes could not possibly get by.'[44] Ministers eventually agreed to publish an unaltered Survey, Cripps contributing both the introduction (under Attlee's name) and a discourse on economic planning in a democracy. He got Attlee to make Marquand Paymaster-General in charge of co-ordinating policy, Marquand's place going to the 31-year-old Harold Wilson.

Spending ministers, objecting to cuts, also took exception to the moral suasion Cripps applied. His ascetism was 'infecting' the government's standing. Greater austerities would break the public spirit. If they carried on, Bevin prophesied, they would soon have a housewives' revolt to contend with.[45] The President of the Board of Trade waxed evangelical. Free markets – little better than black markets – offended against the intellect as well as against any sense of economic justice. Vegetable price 'ramps' and 'rigging' of coal distribution to merchants, both rife in Bristol, were scandalous anti-social lapses.[46] He nonplussed a group of trade unionists who were pressing for higher wages with a homily on practising restraint – 'that is the beauty of self-rule; its rewards accrue in heaven'.[47] Stories circulated of how little sleep he took. A member of the Council of Industrial Design came upon Cripps

> at his desk in a greatcoat with a large scarf over his shoulders and knitted gloves which made his fingers stick out at odd angles. I think he also had a hat on. The room was icy and was faintly lighted by a candle stuck on a plate. In a somewhat hollow voice he gave me his usual greeting, 'How are you, my dear fellow?'[48]

Mass Observation commented on the 'cold admiration' many people expressed, his association with austerity forming 'the basis of almost all opinions of him'.[49]

Presenting the Economic Survey to the Commons on 10 March, Cripps provided a lucid economic summary of the previous year-and-a-half and set out how, in the coming year, the government proposed bringing the economy into balance, reducing the armed forces and raising exports. Because there were insufficient resources to do all it wanted, a policy of restriction must persist:

> The government have constantly emphasised that fact and we have been criti-cised for too much austerity, for diverting goods from the home market for export, for not allowing more home consumption of this or that other extrava-gant thing that was considered desirable. I believe that anyone who reads the White Paper will now agree that the policy pursued was the right one; indeed, judging by some current Press and other criticism, our mistake has been that we have been too easy going.

The blow delivered by the coal shortage had forced the abandonment of the export target of 175 per cent of the pre-war figure, lowered to the new level of 140 per cent by the end of 1947. For the first time, stress was laid on securing the co-operation of industry. The trade unions would have to play a fuller part. Higher wages were justified only by increased output.

Cripps also announced a further change, strengthening the inter-depart-mental planning machinery through the creation of a small Economic Planning Board, run by a chief planning officer supported by mini-planners within each department, to advise upon and co-ordinate government policy. This, according to the testimony of those involved, marked the real onset of admin-istrative planning, as distinct from the mere continuation of wartime instru-ments. For whatever reason, whether Treasury obstruction or (for Bridges) the reluctance of many ministers, the need for formal planning had not been recognised. The fuel crisis was the catalyst.

It was a lengthy statement, devoid of flashing phrases. In it, however, Cripps inserted a significant reminder. The Opposition charged the government with failing to anticipate the economic storm. Cripps's conscience was clear; he had warned of the magnitude of the coming task during the 1945 election, having been 'rather more cautious than his colleagues in the promises he made'.[50]

Cripps, a Tory backbencher remarked, 'has been evolving a long way in recent months', in contrast to the over-optimism of Dalton – 'there is no financial crisis, there will be no financial crisis' – Morrison and Shinwell. *The Times* – noting the omission of any reference to rising prices in the Survey – compared Cripps's worries about inflationary pressure with the Chancellor's still being exercised by the evils of deflation.[51] Cripps had referred to 'the prospect of over-full employment', a hideous notion to Dalton. The shift was significant. Fear of unemployment was giving way to the danger of an inflationary spiral. Apprehensiveness about a slump in demand faded before the reality of an overheating economy, driven by the new bargaining power of labour.

The precariousness of the position took hold of him. In a vibrant broadcast,

Field Marshal Montgomery called for leaders to dominate events rather than a leader who lets events dominate him. Attlee was due to follow the next evening. Cripps volunteered his thoughts. The Prime Minister should not assume that his listeners understood the national extremity. In his experience, the 'great difficulty' was that so few did. Attlee must hit the right level of simplicity, not too far above the heads of members of the House of Lords, as if he were amicably explaining things to the charwoman. The public were demanding leadership. The Prime Minister's broadcast was 'crucial to the future position of the government'.[52] Attlee was unoffended – invoking 'team spirit' and the miners' need for 'reinforcements' – but it was a first warning of discontent.

Cripps began a fortnightly series of press conferences, part of an educational campaign to tell the public with posters and films that 'we work or want'.[53] Critics accused the government of concealing the truth. The government's own research showed that fully one-half of the adult population still had to learn the basic message that the country needed exports to pay for imports.[54] A majority (55 per cent to 40 per cent) valued security more than self-striving.[55] Cripps intended to explain rather than exhort, believing 'people respond to facts'. At the same time, a new agency, the Economic Information Unit (EIU), was set up alongside the Economic Planning Board (though under the Lord President). The accent on goodwill, determination and resource bore the stamp of wartime, the Unit levelling its appeal on the assumption of a 'civilised, unified community'.[56] Morrison's press performances had been relaxed; Cripps, mastering the facts and figures, stepped commandingly into his shoes.

In early April, after Morrison's return and the naming of Edwin Plowden (Cripps's choice) as planner-in-chief, another idea began to be floated – the demand for Bevin, back from talks in Moscow, to become 'home front' overlord. Cripps shrugged the stories off, but was the probable inspirer.[57] Dalton's diary confirms it. Dalton looked up to find Cripps rushing into his office in 'great excitement', pressing for Bevin, who was the only one capable of talking to the trade unions 'like an uncle'. He had already suggested it to Attlee. 'Unless we can get our planning right, we shall be sunk,' he told Dalton. Morrison was not up to it.[58] Bevin, fitter in health, had no desire to give up the Foreign Office. 'The Labour party has many Prima Donnas. I'm one of them. Nothing would be more disastrous to the Movement if I, or any of the other Prima Donnas, were to become Premier. We should all be at each other's throats from morning to night. The only possible man is Attlee.'[59]

Boxed in by overcommitments, the Chancellor – predicting the American loan would be exhausted by February 1948 – urged further cutbacks. Truman was notified that Britain could no longer afford to send aid to Greece and Turkey. After a parliamentary putsch, the length of national service was trimmed from eighteen to twelve months, accepted by Montgomery on the basis of a general troop withdrawal from India, an eventuality which Mount-batten's departure for India (at the end of March) brought closer. With few ways of directing exports to hard-currency areas, and the ITO talks on tariff reductions stalled (the USA blamed Cripps for holding out over Imperial Preference[60]), attention turned to the swollen import programme. On 21 March a sleepless Dalton told the Cabinet they were recklessly racing through the dollar credit, dicing with 'catastrophe'. In May, he repeated himself, counting on the support of Cripps. With an import deficit of £700 million, they simply had to make larger cuts in projected food, tobacco and film imports. A total cut of £80 million was 'unavoidable'. Strachey, Minister of Food, put up a stiff fight, bringing in an official nutritionist to demonstrate that, if the cut were made, the national diet would be 'physiologically inadequate' for those who could not supplement their rations. Dalton was livid when he discovered Strachey was allowing unauthorised imports. Ultimately, £50 million in food cuts was settled on.

One reason ministers were prepared to gamble arose from a speech in early June by the US Secretary of State, General George Marshall, hinting at a barely formulated plan of American aid to Britain and Europe. Bevin grabbed at the 'lifeline', organising a European response and arranging for Will Clayton, the US Secretary of State for Economic Affairs, to come to London. Cripps refused to be waylaid, telling Woods they must not to allow the possibility of aid to influence their thinking. He put more importance on the prospects of Russian trade to help correct the general trade imbalance. A provisional trade agree-ment with Poland was signed in April. The Board of Trade had not given up on a similar deal with Russia, for which Wilson was angling. Cripps, spotting a useful bargaining counter with Washington, mentioned it to Roger Makins, Deputy Under-Secretary at the Foreign Office. Makins told Bevin, who – the sale of jet engines still rankling – was soon denouncing Cripps as 'halfway to Moscow'.

Without further American aid, what was the alternative? The Treasury drew up a contingency plan.[61] The commitments of the 1945 loan would have to be thrown aside, abandoning non-discrimination in order violently to redirect exports to the Americas. Britain would have to hog non-dollar supplies within a new sterling bloc. They would have to press ahead with a 'famine' food programme, and the conscription of labour into agriculture. All moral and legal obligations would be set aside, in as complete and total a mobilisation as that of 1940. This translated into an Dunkirk-style appeal.[62]

Cripps was boldest in spelling out that the country was in 'economic danger'. The essence of the problem was the mismatching of the vast productive power of the United States and the ailing European and Commonwealth nations. Britain, the point of exchange between the dollar and non-dollar systems, was bearing the burden of the international dollar shortage, expressed through the sterling–dollar rate. The battle of the balance of payments meant that the survival of Britain as 'a great power' was at stake.[63] Propaganda from organisations like the vociferous Housewives' League was 'vicious' and 'unpatriotic'. The country had to 'discipline' itself, however 'painful'. The sole remedy was co-operation from both sides of industry to bring about recovery 'by our own efforts and, if need be, by our own abstinence'. The latest cuts would only delay the inevitable exhaustion of the loan. General Marshall's offer, containing the 'seeds' of the solution the world was wanting, had to be carefully considered. But meanwhile the country had to pay its way, even by reducing the standard of living still further. 'If we don't, he remarked apocalyptically, 'in a very short time we shall be bankrupt and without resources, and we shall then be compelled to go without on a frightful scale – a starvation scale -or else go as beggars to our rich friends and accept whatever conditions they may impose on us.'[64]

19

CLEM

I owe it all to this band of brothers.

Attlee, in January 1947, on the occasion of his twenty-fifth
wedding anniversary

So many 'big decisions' were concentrating on August, Isobel wrote in mid-July 1947, adding parenthetically, 'S. cannot go on at this pace.'[1]

The calls made upon the President of the Board of Trade were unrelenting. With hardly a respite after coping with the fuel crisis, the Economic Survey, and India and Burma, he was all but overwhelmed by the interlocking of the dollar shortage, the liberalising of international trade, and the framing of American assistance. Britain could not go on affording the (mainly dollar) imports of raw materials it needed to build up a larger export trade with which to pay for imports. Stopping over in London at the end of June, Will Clayton told the inner Cabinet of five that the US administration visualised a European plan for recovery, in which Britain would fully participate. Bevin wanted Britain treated as a special partner in any programme, unwilling to give away 'the little bit of dignity we have left.'[2] Cripps chipped in, 'If you want to rehabilitate Europe the [UK] market must be rehabilitated. The dollar drain is coming through the UK.' Dalton scotched any suggestion of changing the commitment to free convertibility of the pound – just three weeks away – though lamenting ('it was our fault') that the timetable of the 1945 loan was 'so wrong'.

Cripps adopted a strong stand at the ITO in Geneva. The Americans asked for a pledge from the British to cut tariffs by an agreed annual percentage. Cripps offered a smaller cut. When it was pointed out that the British reduction was scarcely proportional to the American one, he amazed his counterparts by twice inviting them to lower their own offer. The US delegation concluded that the British, while praising the ITO, were dead set on manipulating the negotiations as a lever with the USA in their pursuit of further dollar aid. Clayton, from Cripps's viewpoint, was blackmailing him into dismantling the sterling area. Isobel took heart that 'world understanding' was growing of what her husband was trying to do.

Relating the mundane production drive to the cultivation of higher 'spiritual strength' took some doing, but Cripps did not stint in his speaking engagements. Overcoming Britain's industrial difficulties would enable the country to rise above materialistic concerns, demonstrating the supremacy of the religious over the political. Politics were corrupting. All past revolutions, however idealistic in origin, had been failures, carrying the ineradicable taint of selfishness and pride, he explained in an American periodical.[3] People were of this world, but, because of original sin, were prevented from achieving their ideals. In his outlook, simplicity was certainty. 'If our conscience is satisfied, we need not fear the criticism of others.'

The paradox of the impersonal, strait-laced Cripps subordinating himself to God's divine love was not lost on close associates. John Collins, who had tried involving Cripps in a Church reform movement in 1945, only for Cripps to back out, made a stab at explaining him for a profile writer:

I don't think there is any particular thing which I can tell you about Stafford, except perhaps to point out two small things. Firstly, that what people sometimes call his 'changeableness' (or more rudely, his habit of letting people down), is in fact due to his honesty; his thought is largely in practical terms and when he comes to the conclusion that he has made a mistake he changes his front out of a sense of obligation to do so. Secondly, he is a man with whom it is difficult to get beyond a certain stage in personal relationships because of his fear of any false emotions. I will add that he is an absolutely dead sincere Christian. He is inclined to think lightly of dogma because he suspects that the clergy who are keenest on dogma generally do least about practical Christianity.[4]

Bluntly, he could not mix. 'He tried to be companionable', one private secretary felt, 'without ever quite managing it'.[5] He was, said Laski, in May 1947, 'superb at things but no good, as always, at persons'.[6] He treated his friends like his documents.[7] Conversely he was taken in by some curious acquaintances – the latest the Italian *émigré* and film producer Filippo del Giudice, retained by J. Arthur Rank, to whom the Board of Trade was giving every encouragement. Cripps and Bevin were frequent guests at del Giudice's home, the dinner table adorned with good food and drink. One weekend the Crippses had the loan of del Giudice's river boat. Cripps, the vegetarian teetotaller, was prepared to make any allowances. 'You can't judge Filippo like normal people,' he maintained. 'Creative artists are different.'[8]

That Cripps kept himself to himself, happy for a bolt-hole from the physical strain of office, was of political moment. The bad blood between the topmost leaders of the 'people's party' clouded their working relationship – and kept Attlee in No. 10. Lord Winster, briefly Minister for Civil Aviation, described to a Labour MP how things operated from the inside. The government was run by four bosses. 'Each controlled certain ministries and appointments. With the exception of Cripps, the other three bosses intrigued hard against each other.'[9] Cripps's belief that only he matched up to the urgency of the times was swelled by observing the disintegration of the government.

Once the pound was convertible into dollars, the loan disappeared before the government's disbelieving eyes. A coal strike in Yorkshire sapped overseas confidence. In the late evening of 30 July, the Prime Minister called together Bevin, Dalton, Morrison and Cripps to discuss the Chancellor's hurried proposals to stop the drain – food cutbacks and a 'stop buying' campaign, as well as, for the umpteenth time, large reductions in military spending. Bevin, touted in recent weeks as an emergency PM, broke into a 'drunken monologue'. Morrison, tetchy about defending his scheme for the public supervision – rather than complete nationalisation – of the iron and steel industry, left in disgust. The Cabinet decided to ask Parliament for emergency powers to direct labour into undermanned industries, but Morrison's hybrid scheme was caught up in deadlock. Dalton alarmed the edgy Attlee by saying he would resign if he did not have his way. Cripps pledged himself (to Dalton) to do so too, intending the two of them to team up with Bevan, Minister of Health and the foremost advocate of public ownership of iron and steel. Cripps then had to race off to Paris to see Clayton, notifying him that, with Britain about to run out of dollars, it was free to adopt any measures necessary to obtain the essentials of life and would not agree to having its freedom of action limited '*in any way*'.[10]

Through Isobel's tea parties, Cripps had links with some of the *Keep Left* group of Labour backbenchers, whose pamphlet argued for a Minister of Economic Affairs to embark on 'real' planning. One hundred Labour MPs signed a motion calling for the creation of a national planning commission. An unsigned letter in the *New Statesman* (actually from a government whip) demanded the removal of incompetent ministers. A deputation went to see the Prime Minister. Dalton was in the Commons Smoking Room, 'fortifying himself'. Moves to hoist Bevin to the premiership had petered out.[11] Attlee, Cripps determined, had to be persuaded to give way – even though Bevin, Morrison and Dalton would never agree on a successor. Removing a prime minister in peacetime was hazardous. How was the change to be made?

Cripps could safely confide in his wife. She was warm-hearted, lived simply, and was politically unsophisticated, until she began to take on a more prominent public role after her husband's return from Russia in 1942, leading the fund-raising for aid to China. She shared his sense of vision, and they discussed everything together. 'As you know,' Cripps told Ghosh, 'I have a high opinion of her and I should find it difficult to get on without her help or advice.'[12] Stafford, she felt, was incapable of a self-interested act. He was upright, whereas Morrison was crude and not always straight. As for Dalton – another schemer –

she never understood why her husband thought of using him to get Attlee out.[13] Dalton's diary is the window giving on to the blow-by-blow intrigues of the summer of 1947. Cripps's movements can be traced only by his wife's letter-writing.

Attlee's shakiness was evident in the 'State of the Nation' debate in the Commons on 6 August, when he brought in an Emergency Powers Bill and detailed some £200 million of 'adjustments' in spending, the barest minimum to forestall resignations. Dalton too was 'ill at ease'. At Cabinet, sensing danger, the Prime Minister bowed to majority opinion and ditched Morrison's iron and steel halfway house, leaving Morrison stranded and embittered. On 7 August, watched from the gallery by his wife, Cripps – thumping the dispatch box – for once caught the mood of the House, offering 'no immediate prospect of relief' but drawing on the 'deep spirit of Christian faith' with which they might move mountains, emerging on to 'that serene, fertile plain of prosperity which we shall travel in happiness as a result of our efforts'. Having 'roused the drooping spirits of his own side',[14] he went directly back to his office and reopened his boxes.[15] It was considered 'the speech of a lifetime' in which he 'pulled out everything he knew by sheer eloquence and passionate sincerity and – but for one insensitive interruption near the end by a Labour MP – finished on the crest of a wave with a thunderous ovation'.[16] 'Sir Stafford Cripps', the *Sunday Express* had it, 'has become so reasonable, so restrained and so well-intentioned, that he is now regarded as being above politics, which raises him to a splendid but isolated summit.'[17]

Attlee broadcast on 10 August – 'I have a heavy responsibility upon me, but so have you too' – before attending a 'superheated' meeting of the PLP to consider iron and steel. Morrison, under an attack orchestrated by Bevan, was given a rough ride. In confused surroundings, a motion rebuffing the critics was narrowly carried, Attlee in effect surviving by four votes. The *Daily Mail* referred to a 'report' that Attlee had been ready to hand in his seals of office.[18] Cripps, who stayed away from the PLP meeting, frantically sent an urgent message to Bevan and his wife, Jennie Lee, to come round. Instead of one of Lady Isobel's 'high-minded teas', they found that 'Stafford was in a highly emotional mood. It was a matter of life-and-death importance to get rid of Attlee. Bevin should take his place and he, Stafford, would take responsibility for the Treasury.' Lee continues, 'It was clear that Cripps thought it would be a still better plan if he himself became Prime Minister; but first Bevin was to be asked. Both these men, with Herbert Morrison, Hugh Dalton and others, had had tentative exchanges of views.' Bevan courteously refused even to think it over, averse to 'palace revolutions'.[19]

On or about 12 August, an unidentified informant approached the political correspondent of the *Daily Mail*, planting the story that Attlee would be retiring in September 'for reasons of health', his place to be taken by Bevin. Morrison's chances were discounted. Dalton was tipped to go to the Foreign Office and Cripps to become Chancellor. Was the informant Isobel?

Dalton, noting Cripps's absence from the PLP meeting, believed he had already gone off on holiday. Jennie Lee's account shows he was still in London on the day – 13 August – the House rose. The Cabinet placings were virtually identical with those Cripps had roughed out, particularly making Bevan the new Minister of Supply to push through the nationalisation of iron and steel.

Giving evidence of the Royal Commission on the Press in April 1948, the proprietors of the *Mail* were questioned about the story. The correspondent, it was stated, had come by the information after 'personal conversations' with some of the ministers mentioned, 'and further evidence of friends of theirs who had confirmed it'. On the central claim that Attlee was about to be replaced by Bevin, the journalist had told his doubting editor that he would stake his name on it.[20] In the handed-down folklore of the *Mail*, he had got hold of a 'beat' by his own sleuthing.[21]

Dalton was settling into his vacation when he was called on by Bridges and Wilfred Eady, Second Secretary at the Treasury, bringing news that the dollar drain was insupportable and that suspension of the convertibility of sterling, six weeks after coming into operation, could not be delayed. The Bank of England had expected the outflow of dollars to subside by the end of August. In fact it had gone on accelerating, quickened by capital flight. Morrison, acting Prime Minister, summoned the Cabinet back to London. Cripps flew up from Devon and arrived at 2 p.m., tanned and smoking a cigar. He spoke first with Dalton in 11 Downing Street. Favouring suspension, Cripps confessed to him that, unless the Cabinet took the tough measures required, he would leave the government. Together they went to see Bevin, staying out of sight of the crowd. Once at the Foreign Office, Cripps – though he thought Bevin had an 'inhibition' about dealing with him – made an approach to Bevin to 'take over' from Attlee. Bevin 'resisted'.[22] An alternative version has Dalton and Cripps putting it to the Foreign Secretary that the country was in an economic mess and needed him to be PM. 'Ernie told them, "if the country is in a mess, it is you buggers who are responsible. Why don't you go away and clear it up?" '[23] The 'inhibition' becomes clear: Bevin had learned in the 1930s that Cripps always jumped ship whenever the going got rough.

When the Cabinet met, Dalton delivered the figures. The rate of the dollar drain had risen sharply in July, averaging $115 million a week. By the end of that month the reserves were down to $1,000 million (£250 million). In the five days up to 15 August alone, drawings totalled $175.9 million. The rate was simply unsustainable (though subsequent statistical revisions have suggested the drain was not as rapid as thought at the time). After months of unheeded warnings, Cabinet sobered up. Suspension of convertibility was agreed to without dissent. An intensification of the spending 'adjustments' was unavoidable.

The *Daily Mail*, after sitting on its scoop for several days, carried it on the front page on 20 August, convinced by the financial crisis that the new prime minister would face 'a variety of the most vital decisions ever to face a government in modern times'.[24] Morrison, at a news conference, said he had checked the truth of the *Mail*'s claim with Attlee: 'I only saw it in one newspaper and as far as I am concerned the story doesn't know what it is talking about.'[25] Cripps in the meantime was seeing Clayton again, explaining to him that any elimination of Imperial Preference was 'politically impossible'.[26] Attlee, after seeming to wobble, returned to his holiday, refusing to be hustled into panicky measures, saying the government's decisions would be announced 'in due course'.

The timing of the moves to displace the Prime Minister had added poignancy in what was Attlee's hour of triumph. At midnight on 15 August, India and a separate Pakistan gained their independence from Britain, engineered by the joint endeavours of Mountbatten and the Prime Minister. Mountbatten had gone out with instructions to consult about handing over power to a united India. In short time he realised the country would have to be partitioned. Congress agreed, provided the end date for transferring power was brought forward from mid-1948 to mid-1947. With the co-operation of the Opposition, comforted by the wish of the Muslim League and of Congress to take up membership of the Commonwealth, the Indian (Independence) Bill passed through Parliament in a fortnight. Cripps's contribution was 'largely unsung'.[27] The celebrations were blighted for him by the hostility of Nehru. Ghosh, dining with the Crippses in London on 16 August, found Cripps 'almost in tears', aggrieved Nehru had not sent a telegram of reply to his congratulations. If Nehru had only trusted him more, Cripps maintained, 'India would never have been divided into two sovereign states.'[28] Nehru later made amends, writing affectionately in October. Bevin, an opponent of Indian independence until very late on, steadied the ship at the TUC, applauding the quickness of 'that little man' (Attlee) in effecting Indian self-government – an act which, were the government to accomplish nothing else, would alone justify it. Cripps regarded the fulfilling of Indian freedom as a fitting moment for Attlee to make way.

Cripps tried a different approach. Isobel got in touch with Thomas Jones, seeking his counsel again.[29] Jones travelled up to London on 28 August. 'I came up this morning at the bidding of the Crippses who were eager for a talk,' he told the journalist Violet Markham. Jones listened to Cripps recounting the government's – and his – economic woes:

Stafford had tried hard last May to persuade the Cabinet to do then what it is now forced to do. He was opposed particularly by Ernest Bevin. It is clear that he & Bevin do not accord easily. Bevin naturally thinks first & last of the foreign aspects of every problem. Cripps' strength is that he is straight, sincere, able & has the confidence of industrialists, masters & men. Bevin has backing in the Country but *not* with the Parliamentary Party. He is loyal to the PM, more so than to the rest of the Cabinet. Herbert Morrison's gifts are political not economic. Dalton much better at Finance than at Industry. Aneurin B has made a v.g. Minister of Health & has taken a very firm line on the nationalization of Steel. He has 'Welsh' outbursts in Cabinet & says things with more heat than light, sometimes. These are the major figures.

The Prime Minister has some valuable virtues which hold the team together. He is a good chairman but has no initiative or drive. Nor can he &/or wife apparently do anything to cement the Cabinet. S has been twice to Chequers & met nobody there outside the family. Nor do ministers meet socially in London. They lack a Beatrice Webb, or hostesses like the older Parties had in excess. In a crisis of this type when decisions are taken which affect numerous departments the PM takes no executive responsibility for their performance or coordination – nor does anybody else. The Planning Board is new. The Home Affairs Committee meets & deals with routine rather than with crisis affairs. No major Minister likes to approach the PM and point out this serious lack, lest he should be suspected of wanting the PM's place...

Herbert Morrison's health forbids him the top place. Bevin says he could not take it but probably would – apparently he drinks not much, but the little he does quickly loosens his tongue & instead of getting down to business he tells stories. So, said C, it was at a recent dinner party with Douglas [the US ambassador] & Clayton present.[30]

Jones could make no suggestion, but Isobel conveyed her thanks, even though they had not reached any conclusions – 'We are apt to think this is necessary!'[31]

Until Attlee returned, Morrison took control, exhibiting much of his old authority. He made renewed attempts to wrest back Plowden's Central Economic Planning Staff (CEPS), which Bridges had put under the Cabinet Office. The early days of the CEPS were not fruitful ones. Plowden insisted on obtaining 'assurances of co-operation' from the Treasury and the Lord President's Office.[32] He thought the CEPS was being hindered in carrying out its remit – to ensure the effective implementation of Cabinet decisions – by Morrison, who did not have the requisite co-ordinating qualities. Plowden was 'sufficiently frustrated' after only one month at his post to ask to see Cripps. 'As usual,' Plowden comments, 'Cripps listened sympathetically to my case but then urged me to be patient for a while as "things are going to change".'[33]

For Cripps, working flat out on an export plan, it was the final proof of disarray. He decided to force the issue, proposing that Dalton, Morrison and he present an all-or-nothing ultimatum to the Prime Minister, urging him in the interests of country and government to give way to Bevin. He meant to threaten resignation and a press conference to show he was in earnest. What possessed him? He plainly thought Attlee did not measure up to surmounting the crisis, but would not budge. Coming from him (Cripps), he imagined Attlee would regard his actions as wholly disinterested. Whether Attlee stayed or went, Cripps was convinced the government could not last anyway.

To have any chance of the plan working, the three ministers had to pounce on an unsuspecting Attlee. On the night of 4 September that advantage was lost when a caller from the Lord President's Office informed the Press Association that the President of the Board of Trade was holding an important press conference on the economic situation at 9.30 p.m. at 11 Downing Street. Fleet Street descended on Downing Street, only to find the buildings in complete darkness and the staff unaware of any conference.[34] Attlee, who took *The Times*, will have read about the hoax over breakfast.

That morning, Cripps accosted Dalton in his office.[35] Attlee *must* be shifted at once, or they were 'sunk'. There was no leadership, no grip or decision. Morrison was out of his depth, feeding out of the hand of Nicholson. Because of this, Plowden was 'in despair'. Morrison, Cripps believed, knew he could not manage his job, as well as not being in good health. Cripps told Dalton of his idea for the three of them to go on a 'pilgrimage' to Attlee to 'tell' him he ought to resign in favour of Bevin. Attlee would have to assent, and at a PLP meeting they would move and second Bevin's election and the deed would be done. Cripps proposed putting the idea to Morrison that evening, sure he could browbeat him into it. Dalton cagily agreed to take part if Morrison would, feeling the three of them would form 'a decisive group'. Cripps added that he was toying with resigning alone, on the grounds that Attlee was no use in the crisis. Dalton recommended choosing a specific issue. Cripps thought he would have reason enough if his export plan was not approved by the Cabinet the following week. Dalton was amused to see that Cripps had already drawn up a new government – Bevin PM and effectively Minister of Production, Cripps his Chief of Staff, and Dalton the Foreign Secretary, to shout across the table at Molotov. Attlee would become Chancellor, with an official residence – 'not too bad a fate' for a man with no money. Morrison would remain Deputy PM and Leader of the House. Shinwell, finally, would be shunted off.

Cripps dined with Morrison at 7 p.m. At 10 p.m. he was back, announcing failure. As Dalton had expected, Morrison would not serve under Bevin, and was adamant *he* should be PM. 'He had charged Cripps with putting a pistol at his head.' Dalton agreed to speak to Morrison himself. Morrison was distraught. He readily accepted that Attlee was no good now, had never led the party and showed no gratitude to those who helped him – a reference to Attlee's abandoning of Morrison over iron and steel. If he were number two to Bevin, 'a strange mixture of genius and stupidity', he did not trust Bevin not to 'knife' him. As for the headstrong Cripps, he never wanted to hear the other point of view. Morrison wanted to be PM because he genuinely thought he could do the job better than anyone else. Insinuations about his health were designed to discredit him. The PLP had to be treated fairly, and whatever the result he would abide by it. But Bevin wanted the prize given to him on a plate.

Dalton and Cripps met up again on the Monday, agreeing there was no point in pressing Morrison. Dalton reiterated it was wiser to resign on grounds of policy rather than personality. Cripps expressed his irritation at the way decisions were not being executed but were 'whittled away' or referred back to committees of officials. 'There was no drive at the centre.' Bevin at the helm would send for ministers individually and settle problems on the spot. He meant to go ahead and confront Attlee on the Tuesday evening. If Attlee took it reasonably, Cripps was prepared to wait until the change could be made. If, however, he was 'tempery', Cripps would insist on resigning, publicising the need for a major reconstruction of the government and nominating Bevin. In the ensuing commotion, Bevin might be prevailed upon to stand. If Attlee were to remain, the government might 'stagger on' briefly and then 'collapse'.

That morning a letter arrived for Cripps from Morrison.[36] In it, Morrison referred to Cripps's proposal to approach Attlee, which he understood had the support of Bevin and Dalton, and to the 'vital' support Cripps wanted from Morrison himself. Bevin was to assume 'dictatorial' powers. Morrison, reflecting on the idea, could not be a party to it. Firstly, it bore a remarkable resemblance to suggestions aired in the *Daily Mail*, which Morrison had had to deny. Secondly, it took no account of the rights of the PLP, which could not be presented with a 'frame-up'. If and when Attlee resigned, there should be an open contest in which all those standing would loyally agree to serve under the others, just as Morrison had done after Attlee defeated him in 1935. As a postscript, he hoped, if Cripps insisted on adding political difficulties to their economic ones, it could all await his own return from holiday.

The lawyer in Cripps took over. He wrote a 'personal and confidential' reply, putting Morrison right.[37] He had not said he had consulted Bevin, and had not spoken of overriding powers. He was prepared to do any or no job, anxious only to assist. 'You agreed', he deftly went on, 'that the present Prime Minister ought to go and someone with more grip should take his place but you indicated that you thought you had the necessary qualifications.' He took exception to the mention of press stories, though he appreciated Morrison was not intending to be 'personally offensive'. The rights of the PLP were protected, but, since 'substantial agreement' was likely, no difficulties were likely to arise. He would proceed with his plan, content whichever of their views was best for the country would win out. As Cripps put it to Dalton, if Morrison was tempted to publish his letter of exculpation, he (Morrison) would have to release Cripps's reply too, disclosing to the world the extent of his ambitions. Morrison, acknowledging their recollections did not tally, got in one last dig, 'earnestly' urging Cripps not to resign at such a bad moment, when people 'might think he was running away at a moment of stress and taking the all too easy course of getting out'.[38]

Much depended on the reception to Cripps's export plan, to be publicly unveiled on 12 September. An inter-departmental committee had worked out export targets for particular industries and particular products.[39] The statistical underpinning of the Economic Survey had been 'falsified by events', the date to achieve total export target of 140 per cent of the 1938 volume slipping still further to the middle of 1948. The committee's task was to provide ministers with a complete picture of the steps they might take; it was for ministers, the committee judged, 'to decide whether and to what extent these sacrifices can be faced'. By June, a list had been compiled covering 150 commodities. Industry itself was pressing for definite targets to aim for. Exports were far harder to control than imports, and critics were contemptuous of the Board's 'arithmetical exercise'; Cripps believed the plan was all that stood between the country and a downward descent into economic depression.[40]

The plan went to Cabinet on 9 September. Industry was to be given a 'practicable task', provided there were 'drastic limitations' upon manpower and materials (including consumer goods) for the home market. The fuel and power demands of the exporting industries would have to be met in full. The plan could be 'wrecked' by a shortage of steel. Textiles would suffer, forcing a reduction in the clothes ration for 1948. Starkly declared, the export trade must come first.

Ministers protested that production was already hampered by existing shortages. The plan, Morrison pointed out, made no mention of the capacity of overseas markets to absorb extra exports, nor of methods to ensure they went to the most profitable destinations. Bevan was apprehensive that endorsement of the plan would prejudice future investment. Cripps brought them back to the point that it was what industry was calling for. The decision went his way, being given freedom to launch the plan on the self-contradictory basis that increased production must go towards meeting the new export targets and easing domestic shortages.[41]

Acceptance of the plan made it all but impossible for Cripps to resign. Nevertheless, he remained set on seeing Attlee that evening – not to threaten resignation, but with the object of persuading him to see sense. Morrison, talking to Dalton, was hoping Cripps would not now do anything hasty. Dalton remained non-committal, inwardly contrasting Cripps's 'courage' and 'audacity' with Morrison's failing nerve.

The 'pilgrimage' of the three had fallen apart, riven by colliding egos, leaving Cripps to tackle the Prime Minister single-handedly. He approached the challenge in a redemptionist mood, certain that Attlee would acquit him of any self-seeking and that audacity would pay off. If they got their planning machinery in order, they would be saving themselves and saving the cause of democratic socialism.

He made his way to see Attlee after dinner. Dalton's account of what Cripps told him is the fullest that exists:

S.C. comes in at 10.30, after a long talk with C.R.A. The latter has been most reasonable, has taken no offence, & has discussed a wide range of possible appointments. S.C. had begun by saying that he thought E.B. should be PM & Min of Production, I go to the F.O. & C.R.A. to the Treasury. C.R.A. said he had no head for these financial questions, E.B. didn't want to leave the F.O., the Party wouldn't have him as leader and he and H.M. would never get on in close proximity in the same Cabinet. After some further talk, C.R.A. said to S.C. 'Why don't you take on the job, & become Minister of Production?' And he proposed further a small Ctee of senior Ministers – our present inner Cabinet of 5 + C. Addison [of the Commonwealth Relations Office] – to be publicly announced, & to take much detail out of the Cab. A number of other Cab. changes were also discussed, but I don't list these here, as they are obviously still very provisional. S.C. said he has asked for time to think about this new proposal. He said that he had never thought of this particular change, but that he felt rather a dirty dog vis-a-vis H.M. In effect, he was pinching most of H.M.'s job, & H.M. would think that this had been a deep laid plot from the start. I said that, for the time being, I thought it would be a very great improvement. Other shifts might come later, in the course of a few months, eg. E.B. might feel quite different after the November Confce of Foreign Ministers. We left it that he would not refuse without speaking to me again.[42]

Attlee's unruffled reaction – the way he adroitly 'bought Cripps off' – is celebrated. The full text of Dalton's diary entry, and other circumstantial evidence, gives ground for a second look. Attlee was forewarned, by the swirling rumours and also by Morrison, who had instructed his PPS, Patrick Gordon Walker, to make sure his exchange of letters with Cripps reached Attlee through the Chief Whip, William Whiteley. Nothing is said in Dalton's rendition about the (apocryphal) phone call Attlee is supposed to have made in Cripps's presence to Bevin, and Bevin's rasping dismissal of plots. On the other hand, in his review of Dalton's autobiographical volume dealing with the post-war years, Attlee had a slightly different recollection. 'I am amused at Dalton's story of the efforts to throw me out,' he commented in the *Evening Standard* in 1962:

I do not know if his account entirely corresponds with that of others. I did not know much about it myself. All I knew was that Stafford Cripps came to see me and told me that he and Dalton, and I think Morrison, thought I had better give way to somebody else – preferably Bevin. I went off at once and saw Bevin, and Bevin at once quashed the conspiracy.[43]

On this reading, Attlee saw Bevin only afterwards, and it was Bevin's bullying, not Attlee's guile, which put a stop to the putsch. Finally, although Attlee's offer to Cripps was a masterstroke, Cripps only undertook to consider it. Pimlott is correct in describing Cripps calling on Dalton again somewhat 'sheepishly'. This is corroborated in Isobel's own correspondence. The opening moves had been taken only after a great deal of 'self-examination', she wrote. Stafford had been intending to place *others* in the leading positions, with no thought of his own fortunes.[44] No wonder Shinwell, gunning for Cripps, dubbed him 'the immaculate deception'.

One further document is illuminating – a note from Gordon Walker to Morrison of 23 September, confirming he had, as instructed, shown the Morrison–Cripps letters to the Chief Whip:

The Chief Whip told the PM about C.'s ideas of resignation, which is said to have shocked the PM. The PM then saw C. who himself said in the middle of the conversation that he thought Bevin ought to and would agree to take his place.

The PM asked the Chief Whip to see B, who denied that C. had ever talked to him at all about the matter and said he wanted no change and would serve under the PM. When the PM told this to C., C. is said to have been disconcerted.

Meanwhile C. had asked the PM to put him in charge of the whole economic front. The PM promised to think this over. C. has also proposed that Harold Wilson should be at the Board of Trade, which would make it into a subordinate department under C.

Another piece of news that Maurice [Webb, chairman of the PLP] gave me was that the original story in the Daily Mail came from a source very close to Lady C. Of this Maurice was quite positive. The Daily Mail was not flying a kite but putting out a story that it believed to be true.[45]

This version – though it may be slanted to spare Attlee – confirms the role of Isobel and seems to attribute to Cripps the idea of his becoming economic supremo.

What passed between Attlee and Cripps about Dalton? This Cripps did not divulge. The short-lived attempt at convertibility was disastrous. Dalton was highly critical of his advisers in the Treasury and the Bank of England, and it is apparent that Attlee blamed the Chancellor for having put so much reliance on his official advice. For some while the Prime Minister had been having doubts about financial policy, sending minutes to Cripps for a second opinion.[46] By suspending convertibility, the government was repudiating the terms of the 1945 loan. Cripps had already angered the USA by his 'callous disregard' of the commitment – also entered into in 1945 – to eliminate Imperial Preference.[47] An important, though implied, element in the strengthening of the planning machinery earlier in the year, and in Attlee's idea of re-creating a 'Ministry of Production', was to integrate the semi-detached Treasury into the planning system. If Morrison was to be the main victim, Dalton's wings were also meant to be clipped. It was a symbolic reversal of his and Cripps's roles in the 1930s – Dalton, the pragmatist of the inter-war years, now condemned for his profligate tenure, while Cripps, the former *enfant terrible*, gained respectability.

Cripps imparted his export plan to two thousand industrialists and trade unionists at Central Hall, Westminster, driving 'one more nail into the coffin of complacency'.[48] The export effort would become 'the first charge upon production'. Each industry had a production target, and raw materials and labour were to be reallocated to help with the targets' attainment. To show its resolve, the government was exploring slashing capital expenditure by £200 million – a firm figure Cripps had insisted his department furnish him with. Companies which could not find markets overseas would be prevented from releasing goods on to the home market. Industrial conscription was not being considered, 'unless it is proved that there is no other way out'.[49] Baillieu of the FBI, welcoming Cripps's 'courageous' plan, said he hoped the Budget and welfare spending would all be made to conform in the same realistic way to the general pattern of productive resources.

At a later press conference, in a radio broadcast and in speeches in the North and Scotland, Cripps underlined 'the extreme urgency of the present need'.[50] Once the dollars ran out, Britain would simply have to stop buying. It was not safe to count on American aid, which, if it came, would be only a 'windfall'. Britain was not – contrary to hysterical newspaper reporting – being turned into a concentration camp.[51] He begged the cotton industry to stump up the extra 12 per cent in output of cloth being demanded of it under the plan. For all the emphasis on joint co-operation from both sides of industry, the tempting resort to compulsion lay behind his every word. 'If they won't or don't do it,' he told Streat, 'they must be made to.'[52] The consequence of still greater stringency, Cripps readily admitted, was to make it 'even more profitable to be dishonest'. The tighter the State control, the greater the premium on black-market activities. To this extent, government policy might be counter-productive. The more it encouraged the production of essentials, the bigger the risk of resources being diverted into the production of lucrative luxury goods. The more the government relied on promoting fair shares, the larger the temptation to disobey the law. By pushing social solidarity to the limit, the official advent of austerity was fraught with moral dangers.

Attlee had offered Cripps a 'super-ministry' with a wide field of responsibility. But for the time being, *The Observer* noted, the big five were 'staying where they were', while Attlee – prevaricating – embarked on a wider reconstruction of his administration, the most extensive since Labour's coming to power. Dalton and Cripps resumed their campaign to move Shinwell from Fuel and Power and promote Bevan to the Ministry of Supply. Informed by Attlee of impending changes, Morrison took it surprisingly well, though he cautioned against granting Cripps the power to give directions to other ministers. Attlee sent a second, conciliatory, letter to Morrison, naming Cripps as the newly titled Minister of Economic Affairs, detailing the extensive range of functions Morrison would still be performing, and proposing a new, single committee of six to be in charge of economic policy-making, on which Morrison would sit. The middle-ranking appointments were more troublesome. Cripps, gratified by Morrison's 'compliance', was disappointed Bevan turned down the Ministry of Supply. Morrison was vehemently opposed. 'It is, I suggest, important not even to appear to reward intrigue and disloyalty or to appear to manifest fear,' he replied to the Prime Minister. As for the proposed Ministry of Economic Affairs, he wanted it made known there was to be no erosion in his own authority. 'He tried to protect his public status but easily gave up his empire,'[53] disturbing friends in the Party and the movement.

News of Cripps's assignment was rushed out on 29 September, in advance of other Cabinet changes. Cripps was to give 'undivided attention' to assisting the Prime Minister in the closer integration of internal and external economic policy. The CEPS, the EIU and the Economic Section were to come under his direct command, along with a small, hand-picked staff. In the associated reshuffle, the production departments under him were to be filled by colleagues he could rely on. Cripps had earned promotion, *The Times* judged, setting him up in 'a power house of policy and decision' the government had been 'so lamentably lacking for so long'.[54] But Cripps did not imagine the changes would stop there, or that Attlee – greeted by cries of 'Down with Austerity' in Nottingham – had beaten him off. 'I don't believe the present set-up will be final as the main move must sometime be made if we are to survive as a Govt.'[55]

20

SIX WEEKS

We have been trying to do too much. The trouble is that there is so much to do.

Cripps at a conference of the London Labour Party, 19 October 1947

The office of Minister for Economic Affairs (MEA) was an administrative improvisation, built to the specifications of its singular occupant. The post was a personal appointment, assigning to Cripps a couple of empty rooms in the Cabinet Office, equipped only with desks and – the popular joke – blotting paper to grow the watercress he lived on.[1] He selected a corps of officials, transferring his three private secretaries from the Board of Trade, reuniting with George Blaker, and plucking Leslie Rowan from the Prime Minister's private office to become – aged only thirty-nine – the MEA's Permanent Secretary. The Central Economic Planning Staff, the Economic Information Unit and the Economic Section of the Cabinet Office were to serve him, while he retained his chairmanship of the NPACI. He made Hilary Marquand his principal assistant.

The small set-up belied the 'rather large' responsibilities – in tackling which, Cripps emphasised, there was 'not a day or a week to be lost'.[2] His job was 'economic co-ordination', not enforcement, knitting the planning machinery together rather than attempting to duplicate the work of departments. Before the coal and convertibility crises, economic planning, such as it was, had been inter-departmental, hindered by the division of authority. The Lord President's Committee degenerated into a forum for open-ended debate.[3] With the MEA, economic co-ordination would be administered full-time, by a leading Cabinet member. The Prime Minister's guidance left no doubt as to the increased scope handed to Cripps, handling both domestic and overseas economic policy, ending the cutting in two of the economy. The new Minister, 'sharing' duties with the Chancellor, was given the task of devising measures to bring about a balance of payments, and the jurisdiction to see those measures were followed up.[4] Finally, it fell to him to frame 'a general economic plan'.[5] The new Economic Policy Committee was to 'reconcile' policies, overseeing the work of a Production Committee (chaired by Cripps) and an Overseas Negotiations Committee (chaired by Rowan). Cripps, at his insistence, stood at the head of a group of subordinate departments, filled with his nominees. 'Cripps has now got three young men whom he seems to trust in the Board of Trade, Supply and Fuel and Power,' Robert Hall (the new head of the Economic Section) wrote. 'Marquand is to take the allocating committees so it won't be for lack of power if Cripps fails – he has all the key posts.'[6]

In politics, power shared is power contested. How well would the system of dual control exercised by the MEA and the Treasury work out? Bridges had been instrumental in divesting the Lord Presidency of its economic portfolio, discreetly favouring Cripps. The Office of the MEA, on the other hand, could potentially act as a counterweight to Treasury influence. There were reservations in both directions. Treasury doctrine held that external policy exerted a harmful stranglehold over domestic finance. Critics of the Treasury dismissed its splitting up of financial from economic policy as old-fashioned. Disputes were inescapable, but the close personal bond between Dalton and Cripps overcame any initial territorial feuding. Asked about the order of batting, Cripps replied unequivocally 'the Chancellor goes in first'.

The redistribution of powers heralded a redirection of economic strategy. Planning was to be accelerated – and not just planning but 'a' plan, consistent with a free society. It was inaction that carried 'the totalitarian menace'.[7] The government had been 'giving priority to too many things'.[8] Structural adjustment of the economy meant directing resources to some sectors and denying them to others, of which the £200 million postponement in capital expenditure was a foretaste. More controls were needed, not fewer.[9] It was as if, a perceptive commentator concluded, Cripps and the rest of the Cabinet were living in different worlds.[10] Most of Labour's election programme belonged to the inter-war period. Cripps was addressing post-war questions of productivity, exports and the trade balance. He was the original export-led growth man. With the coming of the MEA, his personal policy was elevated into a permanent principle of the government.

The first sign of the new line was Dalton's decision to have an autumn Budget in November. At the urging of Cripps, a commitment was made to submit a regular report to the Cabinet about the economic position. The CEPS was asked to bring forward the Economic Survey for 1948 to December, at the same time preparing a longer-term projection covering the years from 1948 to 1952. Cripps, in a short burst of speeches, recommended women not to wear long cotton skirts ('the New Look'), warned of dearer tobacco, and confirmed that the 75 per cent duty on American films would continue.

At a special gathering of the big five at Chequers, Dalton outlined his Budget proposals, chiefly concentrating on the £200 million of cuts in the investment programme and reductions in dollar imports. The proposals, jointly placed before the Cabinet by the Chancellor and the Minister of Economic Affairs, had a hot reception.[11] Strachey was exercised by the delay that the cut in food imports would impose on improvement in diet. Bevan, already unhappy about the recording of Cabinet decisions, denied he had accepted any curtailment of housebuilding, fighting to maintain a target of 180,000 new starts. Dalton and Cripps – settling for total cuts of £175 million – won hands down, fortified by the argument that the public was expecting disagreeable news. This did not prevent Strachey and Bevan from trying to reopen the issue at a later Cabinet, when Cripps politely invoked 'economic necessity'. The Left was partly pacified by a measure to curb the House of Lords, clearing the way to nationalising iron and steel in the 1948–9 session.

Leading off in the Debate on the Address on 23 October, Cripps had the awkward task of setting out the new package of measures and of explaining why, given the events of August, nothing had been done earlier. Conservatives kept their powder dry for the Chancellor, allowing Cripps a free run. Government spending had to be contained. The greatest effort was to be made to break into dollar markets. Simultaneously the government intended expanding colonial resources. The imperative aim was to bring Britain into a position of economic independence by the end of 1948, and in the best shape to qualify for whatever American aid might be forthcoming. He rounded off a largely dry-as-dust recital with an impassioned peroration, composed 'after much thought and communing with his wife',[12] appealing for divine intervention and urging upon the country the 'supporting strength' of a deep draught of Christian faith.

Alan Lennox-Boyd, for the Conservatives, regretting the speech had come two years too late, proclaimed that the hopes of the country rested on Cripps's success. It was, others asserted, a devastating exposure of his own colleagues. Headline writers, reduced to 'Cripps-sized rations', took up the refrain. 'Given 'the task of extricating us from a crisis that is largely of Mr Dalton's making,'[13] Cripps had 'dwarfed' the rest of the front bench by his Churchillian rallying call – 'the speech of an Englishman to his fellow countrymen'.[14] The *Sunday Express* nominated him for the premiership. His popularity soared, the *Daily Worker* grousing about the adulation of the colic-stricken Minister. Shinwell, now at the War Office, thought Cripps was clearing the ground for a coalition.[15] Cripps was quite clear the economies were the only possible alternative to the 'absolutely last resort' of savage deflation.[16] The one note of discord came from the FBI, which, antagonistic to the increasing regimentation of industry, wanted a total cut of £450 million and accused Cripps of not being austere enough.

The urgent redeployment of resources was necessary to bring about economic viability. 'This is a real start in central planning' was Dalton's comment.[17] What did this mean? Subsequent verdicts have been severe, typified by David Marquand (son of the Minister), who has suggested that, 'though the Attlee government wanted to plan, they did not know what to plan, how to plan it or how to create the machinery to put the plan into effect'.[18] A background document by the CEPS, which Cripps put his name to, provides a glimpse of 'the framework of planning' within which he was working.[19]

In general terms, the author stated, while aiming to employ resources as fully and expand them as rapidly as possible, less essential supplies would have to be restricted if vital supplies were to be maintained. 'We cannot live without food. We cannot pay for that food without exports. We cannot make those exports without raw materials. Planning attempts to secure that those first claims are met at the least cost to other desirable but less essential claims.' In seeking stability, it was not sufficient to establish the desirable levels of output. The point was to 'influence' those levels, by direct or indirect means. Three main methods were identified: the planning of imports, of investment and of consumption. Because of Britain's dependence on foreign trade, hard-and-fast planning was impossible. That said, much progress had been made with each method. The import programme for 1948 had been settled, taking a large step in the direction of closing the dollar gap. The export plan, combined with import substitution and new sources of colonial supply, reinforced that trend. The Cabinet had also largely endorsed the new investment programme, fixed at approximately 17 per cent of the national income. Greater investment could be had only at the expense of living standards, for which a Budget surplus would be required. Finally, minimum consumption standards had to be maintained, but the provision of essential goods should determine production plans. The remaining task was to decide on the permissible level of domestic expenditure if inflationary pressure was to be avoided.

Stage I was to improve supplies to industry and build up exports; Stage II was to re-equip industry, and especially the export industries; and Stage III to increase exports to the point where home demands could be met on top of exporting. The bulk of Stage III would have to wait until Stage I produced results, even if this involved 'temporary hardship or inconvenience'.

In the longer term, three broad planning principles were to apply: the maximising of consumer satisfaction; the impossibility, in far from normal circumstances, of complete consumer freedom; and the undesirability of setting production targets across industry, since public demand should be the ultimate guide.

The paper had several defining features. Primacy was given to exporting. To do this, domestic demand had to be held back using both physical (rationing) and fiscal (budgetary) restraints, giving policy a strong anti-inflationary slant. The key shortage was materials rather than manpower. Central planning was not, however, meant to replace the price mechanism. The country, in Cripps's moralistic language, had to be persuaded to work out its own salvation, circumscribed by what was democratically acceptable. 'My dear Hugh, do not worry. We can persuade them to stand for anything,' Cripps told Gaitskell, the new Minister of Fuel and Power.[20] The CEPS, notwithstanding the progress it could report, was under no illusions. 'Their problems are identical to ours,' Austin Robinson minuted after seeing a Czechoslovak delegation, 'but it is quite clear they have had no more success in solving them than we have had.'[21]

Of all the democratic limitations, determining wage levels was the most difficult and – for a Labour government – divisive. Cripps had watched the upward movement of wages and prices with growing alarm. At the Board of Trade he had regularly complained about having to sign unjustifiable orders for price rises. He tolerated wage increases if they were intended to attract labour into undermanned industries or were the consequence of a rise in productivity. When, in May 1947, he said people would have to do without wage rises for the present, he was loudly rebuked by the general secretary of the Transport and General Workers' Union, Arthur Deakin.[22] Cripps repeated himself in November, insisting the country could not afford higher profits or higher wages in its present predicament. He took it as axiomatic that planning should include controlled increases in wages and salaries.

From the very beginning of the government, the Minister of Labour, George Isaacs, had strongly resisted the idea of a wages policy, arguing it was inadvisable to interfere in trade-union pay bargaining. At the Board of Trade, Cripps had been only one voice among several. Installed as co-ordinating minister, he denounced the practice of wage increases in one factory or industry setting a norm for increases for other workers. In a written submission to the Cabinet, he argued for a 'positive' policy of wage relations consonant with the national interest, adjudicated by a central appeals tribunal, urging colleagues to accept the implications for wages of a policy of economic planning.

The issue came to Cabinet on 13 November, the morning after Dalton's autumn statement, in which he had (austerely) raised taxes and budgeted for an overall surplus. Tempers boiled over. Isaacs, talking to his own paper, claimed Cripps's approach would undermine the unions and damage existing arbitration procedures. Furthermore, there was no way of actually enforcing wage limitations. Cripps had the calm support of Morrison, who suggested they ought to leave the decision to the TUC. As the argument dragged on, Bevin flew into a fury, accusing Cripps of 'leading us down the road to fascism'.[23] Attlee left it for the Cabinet to reconsider, adding that until then nothing should be said to the TUC when they met the General Council again in four days' time.

The Cabinet adjourned, Cripps shortly going off to see the Chancellor. As he arrived, Dalton emerged with Morrison and the Chief Whip, whereupon they all made their way back to the Cabinet room to see the Prime Minister. In the few moments before entering the Chamber of the Commons to deliver his Budget the previous afternoon, Dalton had happened to pass on a quick summary of his proposals to a journalist waiting in the lobby. The journalist telephoned the summary to his paper, and the stop-press news was on the streets minutes before Dalton reached the part of his speech relating to tax changes. A Tory MP had lodged a Private Notice Question about it, startling Dalton, who had entirely forgotten about the incident.

Dalton realised he must make a 'full and frank confession', and was duty bound to resign. Morrison felt he was the only one who wanted to spare the 'ghastly'-looking Dalton. The five of them parted, Dalton to the House to apologise. The Opposition gave every indication of letting the matter drop; nevertheless, Dalton, haunted by the fear of constant taunts he could not keep financial secrets, decided he had to go. Attlee, 'hating' to have to do it, accepted his resignation. Cripps – said to have made mileage out of his high principles and to have strongly pressed Attlee to let Dalton go[24] – was appointed in his stead, doubling up as Chancellor of the Exchequer and Minister of Economic Affairs. By 10 p.m. the announcement was made by the BBC.

Francis Williams, the Prime Minister's press secretary, reports seeing Morrison and Bevin, who expressed their regrets about Dalton. Cripps, avoiding any reference to his late colleague, was already looking ahead.[25] That evening, he presided over a dinner for the production ministers in a room at the House of Commons, not mentioning his elevation but showing no remorse for Dalton's 'serious' difficulty. He reserved his emotions for the ex-Chancellor. 'I feel quite inadequate to follow you and I can say from the bottom of my heart that I have never been sadder than I am this morning over the Party and the prospects.'[26]

It was last move in 'the dance of Cabinet intrigue'.[27] Cripps – fifty-eight but in fragile health and under immense stress, praying every night to God for inspiration[28] – stepped forward to hold the front, acutely conscious of how his predecessor had buckled under the load. 'It is a pretty tough assignment and I hope I shall be able to survive it!'[29]

CHANCELLOR

All that now stands between us and disaster is the gold reserves of the
Sterling Area.

Cripps, at a press conference on 7 February 1948

The incoming Chancellor possessed a wider range of responsibilities than any
previous incumbent of the Exchequer. Served by the specialist staff of the
CEPS, the Economic Section and the EIU, as well as the home and overseas
divisions of the Treasury, Cripps brought together for the first time the Treasury's traditional financial concerns of the currency and credit with the embryonic function of economic forecasting and planning. To reinforce his control,
he continued to exercise suzerainty over the production ministries, having
conferred on him unparalleled power to 'direct the national economy'.[1] By a
mishap, the Treasury was restored to its inter-war pre-eminence, enlarged to
accommodate the new task of economic management. In his first day in office,
Cripps set an immediate example, rising even earlier for his cold bath, forgoing
his usual morning walk around St James's Park, and eating lunch at his desk.
A confederate stood 'in awe and humble admiration at the volume of work
and detail which you crowd into your daily round'.[2]

Few other Chancellors have inherited such a daunting position. The night-
mare – collapse of the pound, a starvation diet, a general election – had been
averted. The cuts of August and November, driven through by Dalton and
Cripps, had not, however, begun to bite, since they largely entailed reductions
in future expenditure. Import savings were not as substantial as expected. The
Treasury, Bridges had told the old Chancellor, was powerless to affect capital
flows, though one of the new changes was to plug the gaps in the dollar cordon.
Dollars were still draining away – more so, according to one later Treasury
calculation,[3] in the fourth quarter of the year than at the time of convertibility.
The balance of payments had dramatically deteriorated. In view of the uncertainty of American help, Britain's fundamental economic survival remained
the all-dominating preoccupation. It might be objected that the circumstances
of the summer of 1945 were more sombre. Against that, many of Cripps's own

advisers regarded the period from 1945 to 1947 as wasted years, the lessons of which were only belatedly being learned.[4]

Although the redirection of economic policy was evident in Dalton's time, many expected a new style. Dalton, in the caricature, heeded the call of popularity; Cripps was ruled by his conscience. Dalton, temperamentally, was an inflationist; Cripps a deflationist. Dalton had found the money to pay for Labour's welfare programme. The Crippsian credo warned of a country devouring the seedcorn. The distinction was overdrawn. Cripps, as much as Dalton, believed in budget deficits, should the need to stimulate the economy arise.[5] The problem was not conquering unemployment but the opposite one of containing inflation. For this, Budget surpluses were required, and Dalton had been the first to procure one.

Cripps decided to pilot Dalton's supplementary Budget through the House unchanged. He could not have faced a more testing audience: the Opposition was invigorated by recent local-election results, and many on the Labour side were unhappy at the manner of Dalton's departure. Having only a weekend to prepare, he was forced into an early defence of the new proposals, speaking last on 17 November. Osbert Peake (chairman of the Public Accounts Committee) offered him God's blessing, but cautioned it would be Cripps's fault and not the fault of Providence if he failed. Cripps referred to the loss of Dalton, 'the best and most co-operative of colleagues', who, by his leaving, had upheld 'the highest standards of conduct'.[6] As to Dalton's proposals, they were interim ones, aimed at easing inflationary tendencies – 'disinflating' the economy in the terminology of *The Economist* – until such time as ministers could estimate the size of the inflationary gap between demand and resources. The closing of the gap required a public-spirited effort, through increased production and self-restraint. The government, for its part, was committed to investment cuts, but spending on the social services, housing and food subsidies was safeguarded. The enemies of Dalton's policy of cheap money were also disappointed. Cripps would not be raising interest rates. 'We prefer' physical controls, backed up by the good sense of investors, he said. All Dalton's tax increases would stand. Lord Cockfield – then head of the statistical department of the Inland Revenue – remembers watching from the official gallery, the Chancellor badgered by Tory MPs bent on 'cutting his throat', and Cripps standing his ground, growing redder and redder as he replied manfully to every point.[7]

The critical hour fully justified shock tactics. Everything should be done to diminish the 'menacing' dollar shortage. Productivity was still increasing, but so too were costs and wages, wiping out any improvement. There was a very real danger of 'inflationary disaster'. The country being driven back on to a policy of self-preservation.[8] To maintain 'sound' money, Cripps had to curb some of the unrealistic demands of the Cabinet, especially about housing.[9] It was for him to reassert the government's authority, rebuild economic confidence, and re-establish the country's economic independence, insulating it from further harrowing external blows. To this end, the machinery of government would need to take a tighter grip on investment and imports, developing lines of communication reaching right down to the factory floor in 'a supreme productive effort'.

His whole strategy hinged on 'a strong and stable pound'. The solidarity of the Sterling Area – one-half of the world's trade and payments was conducted in sterling – had been the saving grace of the events of 1947. As banker to the Sterling Area, Britain had an obligation Cripps was not prepared to neglect, not even in return for American assistance. On the contrary, the intention was to expand colonial trade, reinforcing the non-dollar world.[10] With the gradual appearance of a buyer's market, however, some British goods began to look overpriced. To carry conviction, the Chancellor had to be prepared to make an unqualified commitment to the existing dollar value of $4.03 to the pound (set in September 1939) and to reiterate that commitment on every occasion. He scolded two Conservative MPs who had referred to the overseas trade in 'cheap sterling' – below the officially fixed rate – for threatening the stability of the pound and 'disconcerting our own people'. Nevertheless, demanding an 'honest' currency from the honest Chancellor was to set a snare into which Cripps might one day fall.

In January 1948, hearing that the French government proposed to devalue the franc against the dollar but allow other currencies to fluctuate, he flew across to Paris, reproaching the French for allowing 'air' into their economy with 'untoward consequences' – for the British – of sterling trading at a different dollar value in Paris from in London. Seeking American support, he wrote to John Snyder, the US Secretary of the Treasury in succession to Vinson, assuring him he saw 'no reason at present to contemplate devaluation'. Aside from one or two products, the UK's export drive was not being affected by the exchange rate. Lowering the value of sterling would introduce confusion in trade relations 'over a very wide area', as well as knocking confidence at home.[11] Questioned in the Commons, he said altering the rate was 'neither necessary nor desirable'. Having to pay more for imports and receiving less for exports would be a disaster. To him, the claims of finance and manufacturing were not in conflict. A strong pound was also good for industry. Orthodoxy and planning harmonised. He took the precaution at the same time, however, of asking for a war book on devaluation to be prepared in the Treasury.[12]

The priority given to economic recovery and reconversion precluded any lifting of 'meagre' living standards but involved diverting finished goods to foreign markets. More importantly it required shifting economic resources into the 'balance of payments' sectors where they would have greatest effect. This was what Cripps meant by getting industry to accept – or be made to conform to – the national plan. Since resources were already overstretched, how was this to be done? Manpower budgeting had been originally applied, adjusted to the release of labour from the armed forces, but it was a 'sticky' method and had not resulted in a desirable redistribution. The introduction of even a mild direction of labour, in August 1947, sparked off a spectacular row. The distorting impact of inflation, itself a symptom of the maldistribution of resources, was impeding the movement of labour into trades where it was most needed. A rational wages policy of incentives and disincentives had been haggled over since 1945, though it flew in the face of union attitudes.

Ministers had never gone beyond public appeals for restraint, before rapidly backtracking. Whenever a statutory wages policy – Cripps's contrivance – was discussed in the presence of Bevin, 'the hair bristled on [his] spine'.[13] Attlee, Isaacs and Bevin saw the TUC General Council on 17 November. The Foreign Secretary explained they were working at great speed 'examining everything', adamant that if they had to tackle another bout of inflation they would be beaten. Could not the unions work out a voluntary pay policy? he asked. The TUC's on-the-spot response was to ask for more definite guarantees about food subsidies, taxation and price control, and to explore whether pay could be tied to company profits. Bevin pledged they would all be looked into. Cripps, reading the transcript of the talk, saw the way ahead. 'Some pretty extensive promises have been given by the Foreign Secretary,' he minuted Bridges and Plowden. 'We must see that they are implemented.'[14]

After some weeks of examination, the Cabinet consented to the issuing of a White Paper, *A Statement on Personal Incomes, Costs and Prices*, calling for voluntary stabilisation through 'the willing co-operation of both workers and employers in combatting inflation'. The draft – largely Cripps's work – was presented to the Commons by Attlee on 4 February. He spoke of the 'inappropriateness' of any general increase in wages in prevailing conditions. The paper had less to say about prices and profits, though a ceiling on prices had been promulgated. Significantly the government had not consulted the TUC General Council in advance, on the grounds that Parliament had the right to be informed first. Cripps had been prepared to put the proposals to the TUC, not to elicit approval but to ensure the TUC would not oppose them. Meeting the Council a few days before, he had pushed a copy of the White Paper across the table and abruptly disappeared from the room, leaving Isaacs to face the music.[15] It was the Minister of Labour's show, Cripps excused himself to Attlee, 'as he conducted proceedings!!'

The reaction of the PLP was not promising. Some twenty MPs, rounded up by Ellis Smith, wanted the document immediately withdrawn. The larger Trade Union group of Labour MPs, in a rare instance of organised discontent, supported the White Paper but suggested more emphasis on limiting profits. Dalton noted a 'commotion' among backbenchers, who thought Cripps too aloof and feared what he was up to and whom he was in touch with. Conversing with Dalton, Bevin sounded unenthusiastic, claiming the White Paper would only make higher wage claims and unofficial stoppages *more* likely. Even so, he agreed to accompany Attlee and Cripps when they went to see a TUC deputation.

The TUC complained it had been presented with a *fait accompli*. Ministers stood by the document, which they understood the TUC did not really object to. The government was not suggesting a wage freeze; it simply wanted to put a stop to automatic wage increases. Tewson, the TUC general secretary, asked the Chancellor if he could take some steps to create the right psychological climate. Cripps, without prejudicing his Budget, did say he would be approaching the FBI, urging concessions from all sections of the community and inviting industry to consider price and cost controls, which he could then take into account in his Budget. 'As the person responsible for the economic life of the country, unless something of this sort can be arranged we are done for.'

Aware of unrest in the Party, Cripps gave a strong anti-profiteering angle to his Commons speech on 12 February. He sat down to total silence. Left-wingers attacked the pegging of wages, alleging working people were being asked to make all the sacrifices. Cripps was embarrassed by the contribution of a Tory MP, who drew attention to the *de facto* depreciation of the pound – Australian wheat and Argentine meat were being 'marked up' – which the Chancellor must know would thwart the export drive if left unattended. Wyatt, coming to Cripps's aid, pointed to the sting in the tail of the Chancellor's comments, implying action on profits if the response of the FBI was not satisfactory.

Trade-union opinion appeared to harden against the White Paper, fomenting rumours that Cripps was planning to bring in immediate legislation to enforce a standstill. Pressed by the FBI, leading firms agreed to a freeze on dividends. When ministers saw the TUC General Council again on 23 March, just before the TUC conference on the White Paper, Cripps and Bevin spoke with one voice. The country had 'not got the means' to allow a general wage increase. If they were not careful, they were going to have 'another smash'. They were trying to insulate themselves by building up sterling trade as far as possible, appealing to the commonsense of people 'to save us from a desperate situation.' If all went well, they might be in the clear sometime in 1949.[16]

On 25 March, guided by the General Council and assisted by the agreement of scores of major companies not to raise dividends whatever their level of profits, the TUC voted to endorse the White Paper, albeit with two of the largest six unions – the Engineers and the Distributive Workers – siding with the minority. The exemptions the TUC included were extremely wide, however, and a number of wage settlements had been rushed through to beat the deadline. The real test – capping wage inflation in conditions of full employment (in early 1948 fewer than 300,000 people were out of work) – had still to be met.

In Middlemas's formulation, the Labour government was being given a 'second chance'.[17] Austerity and autarchy followed from the ending of the 'fool's paradise' (Bevin's expression to the TUC). The government had to reorientate halfway through its term of office, owing much to the clear-sightedness of the Chancellor, who cared only for pulling the country back from the verge of financial havoc. One can question the accuracy of the government's appreciation of the prosaic 'political realities' within which it had to operate. It would be wrong to dismiss them as unimportant.[18]

Cripps's greatest virtue was his unsparing dedication to Britain's economic renaissance. Putting in three hours' work before breakfast, he always arrived in Great George Street by 8.45 a.m., all his papers read and annotated.[19] His vegetarianism and his Slippery Elm laxative, he argued, gave him the stamina to keep long hours. His appetite was unspoiled. Staying at Balmoral, he polished off the week's ration of eggs in one omelette, in front of the scowling royal family.[20] He allowed himself few private distractions. A patron of the National Trust discovered he was a lover of the arts but had only ever been to the opera once (in Moscow) and 'hates private ownership of everything', giving all his possessions away.[21] Far from tortured, he radiated 'inner poise'. He was a very precise person, without restlessness, though never 'off guard'. 'His is the most strictly regulated personal life in the Cabinet.'[22] Having given up so much himself, he assumed the right to expect the most from his compatriots. 'Perhaps too', Gaitskell mused, 'it is something to do with the martyr complex – at least this is what Evan [Durbin, Parliamentary Secretary in the Ministry of Works] says.'[23]

He was, in addition, the intellectual equal of his civil servants. He was not an economist, and knew less about economics than the public imagined. On the other hand, he was open to advice in a way Dalton had never been, leading to a scramble for his ear. A 'layman', he compensated by surrounding himself with a multitude of different opinions, breaking each point down until he had thoroughly mastered it.[24] Officials had only to go over an issue once for him to commit it to his formidable memory. Above all, he had formed the conscious conviction that financial and economic policy had to go together, revolutionising Treasury practice.[25] He was in this sense a modern Chancellor, but one with a pronounced, high-Victorian moral code.

He carried his methods into his Budget-making. He wanted the Budget debate to include discussion of the Economic Survey, he insisted on revising the national accounts to make it clear the Budget was not just a revenue-raising operation, and he had to make good the promises associated with the White Paper.

Dalton's surplus had been only just enough to ensure that the revenue collected defrayed government spending of every kind. Hall and Plowden both pressed the Chancellor to aim for a further Budget surplus to withdraw additional spending power from the economy, of the order of £350 million on top of the expected £300 million from 1947–8. Further increases were to fall on beer, tobacco and betting, but at the same time Cripps gradually worked into his calculations several tax concessions, lifting income-tax allowances and reducing purchase tax on certain items, all but offsetting the larger revenue. In spite of Cripps's reputation as 'Old Incorruptible', he was simply standing guard over surpluses generated by maintaining his predecessors' tax changes.[26]

The most contentious measure, however, was a capital levy, concerning which the Chancellor was under 'extraordinarily strong political pressure'. Douglas Jay, in the new post of Economic Secretary, worked on officials when the Budget Committee retired to the seclusion of Roffey Park, a rehabilitation centre in Sussex. The Treasury was hostile. Cripps still favoured some kind of charge on investment income, on a one-off basis – for its 'psychological' impact. He showed an outline of his thinking to Attlee, Morrison and Bevin at Chequers.

It was not until the composition of the final draft of the Budget speech that Plowden made a special representation. Over Easter, looking again at the total balance of the Budget, Plowden agreed that the tax remissions which had been added in were wholly justified, but worried that the investment levy, falling on the better off, was unmatched by any equivalent impost on the rest of the community. Unless the Chancellor was prepared to soften the thresholds, he might forfeit the hard-earned confidence of British business:

> During the last six months you have done what no other man in the country could have done, and this is to secure the general support of industry and commerce for a Labour government. This is a priceless asset and one without which there is no hope of surmounting our economic problems . . .
>
> The Budget as it now stands runs the risk of jeopardising one of the most important economic assets that the country has, namely the support that you personally have from both sides of industry.[27]

Plowden's appeal did the trick, Cripps consenting to lift the scales of the levy. Plowden's prime concern since he had taken up his post had been to avoid adding to the burdens of industry. His counsel increasingly influenced the Chancellor. 'Stafford has saved the country from a complete debacle and Plowden has been his chief adviser in all this,' Hall wrote in March.[28]

The final form of the Budget was affected by one last favourable development – the signing into law by the US Congress of the European Co-operation Act, on 3 April, for the provision of bilateral aid to Western Europe, under the European Recovery Programme (ERP). At Cripps's and Bevin's joint insistence, the Economic Survey for 1948 envisaged – failing Marshall Aid – the drastic reorganisation of the British economy. Cripps had frankly explained his 'constant anxiety' to Snyder in March, estimating that even with ERP money there would be continual pressure on the UK's gold and dollar reserves for as far ahead as he could see, and which he very much doubted that Britain – guardian of the stability of sterling – could withstand.

It was a Budget of surprises, and one which did little to 'answer the riddle of Sir Stafford'. The Chancellor commended it to the House as the first 'planning' Budget, taking account of the economic state of the country as a whole. He stressed the external difficulties, and his 'deep and genuine gratitude' towards the United States for the recent vote of Congress. He then announced his intention of budgeting for a larger surplus, of £658 million, glancing as he said this at a beaming Dalton. He detailed the purchase-tax increases, compensated by income-tax reliefs, leaving a modest surplus of £11 million, the whole of the 'real' surplus to come from the continuing tax yield from Dalton's changes in his two Budgets of 1947. Defence, social services and food-subsidy spending would not be cut. After the declarations by industry, he ruled out (to shouts of dismay) a statutory profits tax or dividend limitation, but turned to his one-off 'special contribution' levied on all investment income in excess of £2,000. At 5.15 p.m., the lecture over, 'factual and faultlessly delivered from neat little packets of notes', he snapped the Budget case shut.

The Budget had something in it to annoy everybody. One hundred Labour MPs delivered a written protest about the increases on beer and tobacco. Dalton, in an unhelpful speech, argued for further purchase-tax exemptions. A TUC delegation paid a call on No. 11. The Opposition parties condemned the special contribution as a 'political tax' and a sop to the Labour rank and file. Cripps showed his irritation only once, when the Tory backbencher Ralph Assheton stated that if Britain was driven to devalue the pound it would be precisely because of the high-taxing, high-spending policies being pursued. 'Nothing could be more fallacious,' Cripps answered, bearing in mind they were already exporting to the maximum and devaluation – the 'extreme folly' which he had 'no intention whatever' of perpetrating – could only make exports more expensive. Told he would just have to do it, Cripps was contemptuous. 'That is just the sort of propaganda our enemies abroad are longing for.'

In the ensuing weeks, as the Finance Bill wound its way through the House, Cripps, wondering whether he had been excessively restrictive, relaxed purchase tax on a wider range of items. By the time of the third reading, he banished any deflationary fears, promising further 'discomforts and hardships' if need be. But he showed unexpected leniency. Marquand, the new Minister of Pensions, put to Cabinet in July an increase in war pensions, without preparing a fallback position. He was astounded by the Chancellor's ready agreement, over and above what he was asking for.[29] Cripps's advisers were impressed by his unwillingness to be knocked off course, but had to protect him politically. Fred Lee, his parliamentary factotum, had to point out that if Cripps did not give the keynote economic speech at the Labour Party conference, a resentful Dalton probably would instead. In the end Cripps obtained the personal word of Shinwell, the conference chairman, that if Dalton made any unfavourable references the chair would give him ample time to reply.[30]

The Budget 'judgement', indeed his economic strategy in its entirety, were religiously inspired. He continued to preach the need for industrial modernisation, for 'modern methods' in production. For good measure he issued further denials of devaluation – five in fewer than fifteen weeks from January – warning against the idea of changing the terms of trade as a way of meeting the country's difficulties, which had to be surmounted by personal courage, productive activity and high-minded faith. The ordinary criterion of political efficacy is not whether what is said is true or false but whether it is functional. Cripps regarded these criteria as inseparable. The source of his certainty was 'the full armour of God'.[31] Economic ills were not economic in origin, he told the Church of England's Lambeth Conference, but 'the outcome of a profound moral disturbance in the world'. It took some time to realise it, Jay has attested, but Cripps really believed his decisions were 'directly dictated' by the Almighty.[32] His sermons were as simple as he made them sound, the national plan a microcosm of the Divine Plan.

Christian Action – a non-political campaign for Christian unity in Western Europe, the brainchild of Canon Collins, with Sir Stafford Cripps and Lord Halifax as its founding patrons – was a timely accompaniment to Bevin's crystallising project of Western Union. While the British Chancellor of the Exchequer was loftily cautioning European Christian Democrats against mixing Christianity with national power politics, the British Foreign Secretary was feeling his way towards the five-power Brussels Pact. The London Conference of Foreign Ministers in December 1947 convinced Bevin that Russia wanted only to tighten its hold over Eastern Europe. A Communist coup in Czechoslovakia and – in March – the onset of the Soviet blockade of Berlin confirmed him in this. If Europe was to successfully reconstruct, Western leaders had first to guarantee its security.

The partnership of Bevin, entering his most constructive phase, and Cripps, conscious that economic independence could come only through (temporary) dollar dependency, was to be pivotal. Lop-sided historical accounts of the Attlee government glorify the early reforming burst. Bevin's role in creating a new Europe, as the final volume of Alan Bullock's biography of Bevin sets out, was magisterial. Cripps's part was second only to Bevin's. Both were more highly regarded by the public than by their party. Both struggled to make the purpose of their policies understood. In restoring Britain's external and internal vitality, the health of both of them was ruined.[33]

In the new Cabinet dispensation, policy proceeded on twin tracks. Bevin's hand in the TUC wage accord was exactly the intervention Cripps had hoped for from a Bevin premiership if Attlee had been ejected. The growing inter-relationship of diplomacy with international economic policy provided wider grounds for co-operation. But there were plenty of opportunities – over and above Bevin's hostility to embalmed intellectuals who lacked the human touch – for departmental friction. Cripps, as soon as he became Chancellor, questioned the size of the defence budget, as well as calling for a review of the decision to give top priority to atomic-energy research, arguing the money for its industrial (though not military) development would be better spent on the exporting industries.[34] On the essential European questions, the Foreign Office, so long as Bevin was Foreign Secretary, remained the lead department. Their relations were so 'cordial', however, that the Treasury was given great scope on the economic side of the European 'leap in the dark'.[35] The economic ministries looked to the Chancellor to reinstate their primacy, while Attlee acted 'like a Chairman mediating between his Directors – Bevin and Cripps'.[36]

The passing of the US European Co-operation Act led to the creation of two institutions: the European Co-operation Administration (ECA) in Washington, and the Organisation for European Economic Co-operation (OEEC) in Paris. The latter was responsible for uniting the national requirements of the sixteen participating nations of the ERP into a single submission. In September 1947, when Bevin and Cripps (still at the Board of Trade) had gone to Paris to endorse the preliminary European report to the US government, Cripps even then had said he could not sign, as it involved an infraction of sovereignty.[37] It took Oliver Franks, the British chairman, two hours of hard arguing to get him to withdraw his objection. This did not dispose of the British preference for bilateral discussion with the United States. The means by which aid was to be disbursed, and on what terms, was still outstanding. In deference to British views, the OEEC machinery was only consultative, leaving it at the London end for officials, grouped under 'Otto' Clarke of the Overseas Finance Division of the Treasury, to make recommendations to ministers.

In January 1948 the Cabinet agreed to co-operating with other European governments, with the object of making Europe economically self-supporting. But how far could and should Britain allow European organisations to evolve? There was some US sympathy with British sensitivity about its gold and dollar reserves – Cripps's 'last bastion'.[38] Most American officials were alive, however, to the British wish to cramp the work of the OEEC. The Americans did not hide their desire for the closer economic integration of Europe, even into a protectionist customs union. The British Treasury was alarmed to hear of

Bevin expressing 'misgivings' about the Sterling Area. Reluctantly, a position paper was prepared, elaborating the commercial and 'paternalistic' advantages of sterling trade. When the Cabinet reconfirmed its January decision in March, Bevin and Cripps jointly advocated reconciling the wider goal of trade liberalisation with a 'modified' European economy that might, in time, turn into a single 'economic entity'. Linking the Sterling Area to any European payments system need not create any inconsistency. Britain could 'look both ways'. But Cripps was at pains to stress how decisive a step it would be, 'for good and for all'.[39]

Initialling the Letter of Intent for eligibility to receive transfer payments from the USA, Cripps denied that ceding control of the Sterling Area was a condition of receiving aid. Responding to rumours in America and Canada, he again categorically rejected any intention to devalue the pound; all such reports were 'entirely false'. Abandoning the Sterling Area, the *New York Times* was informed by a government spokesman, would mean the UK 'committing national suicide'.[40] Within the Treasury, only Clarke entertained the contrary view that devaluation was desirable – because they were 'swimming against the stream' of the price mechanism, striving to make people do what hurt their financial interest. If something had to give, Cripps wanted it to be the import programme, requesting the authority to automatically adjust dollar imports to do no more than maintain the existing level of home consumption, since it was 'better to receive as little as is necessary' of ERP funds.

The draft copy of the Economic Co-operation Agreement between the USA and European countries, circulated in early June, contained several disagreeable provisions. Article I gave the US government the right to call into question almost any aspect of Britain's domestic financial policy. Article III talked of balanced budgets as a condition of aid. Article V imposed additional ITO obligations. Article X gave the United States the contractual right to put pressure on the UK to alter the dollar–sterling exchange rate, which would be 'exceedingly dangerous', with, the Chancellor went on, 'disastrous' consequences, harm having already been done by irresponsible discussion on the other side of the Atlantic. To do without aid, on the other hand, was unthinkable, entailing breadline rationing and 1.5 million unemployed (a forecast blurted out by Bevan in public). There were repeated, anxious sittings of the Economic Policy Committee and the Cabinet.

Bevin, about to go away for a short break, had little confidence the Chancellor would remain steady. He had, he recalled, stopped Cripps from haring after an adverse Soviet trade deal in 1947. He now heard that Cripps and Wilson wanted to head to Washington – a presidential election was only four months away – to dispute the terms of the Agreement. Bevin got Attlee to place on record his full support for the Foreign Secretary, ensuring 'nothing hasty' was done to knock away any of the pillars of foreign policy – ERP, Western Union, the American military commitment to Europe – he had diligently constructed.[41]

Attlee and Cripps, in the end, passed on the UK's 'strong objections' to the US ambassador, Lew Douglas, quite ready to risk isolation rather than accept a document which all the other participating states had assented to. Of all the breaking points, the suggestion that Britain would not be free to stabilise its own currency at the rate of exchange of its own choosing was the most unacceptable. The *démarche* worked, the UK being allowed to prevail over the USA 'on those points which she felt were vital to her well-being'.[42] At a late hour, the Americans backed off, eliminating or toning down the offending articles, the State Department concerned not to lend substance to Russian accusations of dictation. Attlee led the expressions of 'gratitude' to Cripps when the Cabinet next met. Douglas, in the US press, was reportedly 'disgusted' that nothing had been done to lower trade barriers or encourage currency convertibility in return for American taxpayers' money.

On 5 July, taking the Commons through the Agreement in his best didactic style, Cripps made much play with the absence of troublesome conditions attaching to ERP aid, his 'simple' and 'dignified' handling defusing any threat of anti-American controversy. Indeed, there was a remarkable turnaround in Labour opinion, with only twelve Labour MPs voting against, though the Conservatives officially abstained. On the exchange rate, he was able to maintain (amid interruptions) that the British remained 'masters in our own house'.

The organisational logistics of aid were also ironed out. Cripps claimed the right to include the sterling deficits of other Sterling Area countries in Britain's general balance-of-payments account. The Americans would agree only if the dominions stumped up 'substantial' additional aid for Britain. When the final division of aid for 1948–9 was agreed to, Cripps found the British share 'unexpectedly satisfactory'. But the USA was increasingly irritated by the UK dragging its feet over the OEEC. An attempt to get round Cripps by approaching Bevin met with anger from the Foreign Secretary. For the meantime, Britain undertook to prepare a comprehensive four-year programme setting out the stages by which the UK aimed to attain economic viability. One further initiative – 'we must justify our use of aid', Cripps vowed – was to employ the provision of ERP dollars to improve production. In talks in Paris with Paul Hoffman, head of the ECA, he proposed establishing an Anglo-American Council on Productivity (AACP), made up of industry and union representatives who would investigate methods of industrial rationalisation, propagating the manufacturing techniques of American enterprise. Setting foot back in Britain, Cripps was 'bombarded' by loud protests in the press and Parliament. The present difficulties were great but interesting, he told his brother-in-law over lunch, and the attitudes of both the USA and the USSR unappealingly materialistic. The only recipe was 'the middle way & doing one's best'.[43]

Marshall Aid united all wings of the Parliamentary Labour Party, isolating a handful of crypto-Communists. One of them, John Platts-Mills, had already been expelled by his constituency party, with the blessing of Transport House. It is extraordinary that Bristol East, which had stood loyally by Cripps through thick and thin, came perilously close to disowning the Chancellor.

A 1930s hero of the Left, Cripps had never had his erratic past catch up with him. He freely spoke of it without regret.[44] During the war he had dallied in the middle ground, but this was obscured by the patched-up reconciliation with Labour in 1945. His speeches as President of the Board of Trade disconcerted party activists. The Cabinet clash over iron and steel nationalisation in 1947 revived the popular-front line-up of Cripps, Bevan and Strauss. Despite Plowden's contention that nationalising steel at such a moment was 'an act of, economic irresponsibility',[45] Cripps would not break with his earlier position. But when the NEC listed industrial insurance as a future target for public ownership, he put it to Morrison they should think twice before destroying an industry so important to the national balance of payments. This shifting of ground in domestic politics was matched by a growing general antagonism towards the Soviet Union – notwithstanding a trade agreement reached by Harold Wilson – which Cripps, denouncing Soviet support for 'fifth columnists' in the West, fully shared.

In the autumn of 1947, Bristol Trade Council delivered a ruling ordering members to refrain from making attacks on government policy – attacks inspired, according to the *Daily Herald*, by Communist infiltrators. A small but significant caucus in Bristol East had become disillusioned with Cripps ('there's something wrong when Tories cheer'), finding allies among those who felt their MP had neglected his constituency, although for understandable reasons. Mervyn Stockwood, an object of suspicion because of his 'non-proletarian' outlook, alerted Cripps to the danger in April 1948; Isobel wrote back that she only wished the local party 'could be as loyal to Stafford as he is to them'.[46]

The nationwide boundary redistribution of 1948 – the first for fully thirty years – awarded Bristol a sixth seat, Bristol North-East, taking over several wards from Bristol East, which was to form the lion's share of a new, more southerly, constituency of Bristol South-East. The new divisional party was due to meet to decide on Cripps's readoption. Harry Hennessy, the chairman, reproached Cripps for the wall of 'complete silence' between London and Bristol East, their only contact consisting of a quick handshake before Cripps was off to London again. Hennessy hoped Cripps would be able to attend, to clear the air of 'frustration' and 'disappointment'.

13.7.48

My dear Harry,

Very many thanks for your letter. I am so glad you wrote as you did. There is no trouble that I know of between me and the constituency. The real difficulty is that I am working 18 hours a day 7 days a week and that I just cannot fit in the visits I would like to make to Bristol to see you all. The load of work in trying to get the country straight is really tremendous and I feel that I must devote myself to it with all my energy if we are going to succeed. I will certainly do all I can to get down whenever it is possible but it is no good just breaking down over the effort. It might perhaps help if I were to send you a monthly letter telling you my activities and giving you some little picture of the situation. I would be glad to do this if you thought it would help. I am going to try and get down for the meeting on the 28th and I shall hope to be able to see you and have a chat then. If it can be fitted in perhaps you could let me come and have tea with you before the meeting. That is, subject to there being no crisis on, and no cabinet meeting'.[47]

The model rules of the Labour Party stipulated that, while all sitting Labour MPs had to be formally readopted, a constituency party wishing to sack its MP had to garner enough mandated votes to form a majority and ask the member to retire. Ted Rees (secretary of the Bristol Borough Labour Party) advised Cripps the day before that his seat was in danger.[48] With his wife, Cripps set off by car from London. After Rees had explained the constituency changes, the meeting discussed the parliamentary candidacy. A number attending claimed that delegates from the new wards had not been invited or had not had the chance to consider the matter. Cripps, in shirtsleeves, then spoke, saying he knew about local dissatisfaction and 'other domestic matters' and explaining why he could not pay frequent visits. If the Party wished him to stand, he expected all contentious matters would be dropped and the Party would work as a united team. His candidacy was carried by 15 votes to 14.[49] Cripps 'icily' insisted it was customary for a nomination to be unanimous.[50] If the new wards met and accepted him too, he would stand. The Crippses departed while the meeting was still in progress. Stockwood asserts that, had Cripps been outvoted, he (Cripps) would have counter-expelled the dissidents.

The problem, for the Chancellor thinking several steps ahead even of some ministerial colleagues, was that 'our people are slow to learn'.

He could already point, as he did in Paris, to several signs of economic advance, which he judged 'spectacular'.[51] Industrial production, including industrial goods, had leapt up by 15 per cent in twelve months. Agricultural output was rising. The export plan of September was on target. Crucially, exports of coal and steel had resumed. All of this had been achieved while holding down the internal price level, made possible by wage and dividend restraint. In September he praised industry for refraining from distributing profits. Businessmen who approached him for exemptions accepted his refusal. He attributed all this to the success of the planning policies that the government had implemented.

Encouraging as this was, there were two difficulties. Cripps had only retrieved lost ground, bringing the country back to the point in its recovery of early 1947. Since then the terms of trade had significantly worsened, with the buyer's market widening. Moreover, since everything had been thrown in and all resources fully utilised, the rise in output was unsustainable in the longer run. The fullest of full employment, combined with tight control of the factors of production and a clamping down on personal spending – how socialistic it now looks – meant squeezing the most out of the existing, highly regulated, economy, with little to spare. American aid – Britain took delivery of the first $310 million from the ECA in October – was propping up an economy which had yet to structurally adjust to the post-war challenge. Worst of all, increased exports were going in the main to the soft instead of hard (dollar) currency areas.

The Chancellor, who 'cannot be fundamentally unfriendly to the rest of the world, proclaimed the 'new stage' they were embarking on at the TUC annual conference.[52] Delegates were each given an economic dossier to digest. Exports were up and the trade gap had been substantially closed (by ERP), he told them, while the policy of restraint was holding – 93 per cent of companies declaring dividends in August had observed the standstill. Nevertheless, the country was still not paying its way. Increased production had largely been achieved by increased manpower. From now on, that source was all used up. Nor could help be got by taking more from profits. The cake was only so large, and if wages took a bigger slice, others would have a smaller one. To obtain a higher standard of living, the solution was to produce more, introducing new methods and new machinery. The TUC and the FBI needed to engage in 'parallel and co-ordinated action', under the auspices of the AACP. Existing policies were succeeding, judging by the latest results. But it followed that labour had to act with 'intelligence', continuing to embrace hard work and self-denial. If they persisted, the country would get through. Congress accorded the Chancellor and his wife a lengthy ovation, subsequently voting to turn down a statutory wages policy by a heavy margin.

Welcome economic news brought a precious political dividend. The Debate on the Address had been a subdued occasion until the Chancellor – none other than gloom incarnate[53] – stood up on 16 September. Announcing the halving of the balance-of-payments deficit and little or no net drawing on the gold and dollar reserves, he was showered with tributes from all quarters for his 'superb mastery of the White Paper', expounded with 'crystalline clearness', 'the best speaker to a brief who ever sat on the Treasury Bench'. The news was also a much needed tonic to his own side. 'I've just finished speaking here – a good party,' he dashed off in a note of jollity.[54] Jay, in the same debate, claimed the evidence 'proved' the value of the government's general management of the economy, inaugurated by the firm decisions on planning of October and November 1947.

Because of the sheer scale of public spending on current policies, however, 'the rich simply couldn't find the revenues'. Expenditure in fact was growing – a grand total of £470 million on food subsidies, £70 million for Bevan's National Health Service (which got off the ground in July 1948), and also funding of the Berlin airlift – and was set to rise further. Additionally, in response to the tension over Berlin, Britain had made its first moves since the war towards rearmament, by accelerating munitions production and postponing the release of conscripts, adding an extra £50–100 million to the defence bill. The Chancellor was confident of accommodating the increases, but could not entirely exclude the shrinkage of his Budget surplus.

This prospect made it imperative for Britain, while contributing to the promotion of European unity, to do its most to maintain and strengthen the Sterling Area, 'the only great multilateral trading system in the world'.[55] A frontal assault by the USA had been repulsed. Asked for guarantees by Cripps, Hoffman agreed he had no wish to see the Sterling Area broken up. Averell Harriman, assisting Hoffman (Cripps had met him in 1941 in Moscow – they did not get on), expressed admiration for the way Cripps had 'stuck to his guns'. The terms of ERP aid did, however, involve some loosening of exchange controls, owing to the proposed inception of an Intra-European Payments plan. The UK was still hoping to include the sterling deficits of the rest of the Sterling Area in its ERP account. The Truman administration countered by stipulating that Marshall Aid was not intended to be set aside to pay off sterling debts.

In September, Cripps visited Ottawa and Washington to state his case. A satisfactory compromise was reached on both issues, but only after Bevin had sent a telegram to Cripps entreating him to get the idea of Western Union 'back on the rails'.[56] Snyder made noises about overvalued European currencies. Talking with James Forrestal, the US Secretary of Defense, Cripps agreed that, with the stationing of American B-29 Superfortresses in Britain (from July 1948), 'Britain must be regarded as the main base for the deployment of American [air] power.'[57] In both capitals, Cripps nimbly fielded the enquiries of the press. When was Britain going to devalue? There was no possibility whatsoever, since devaluation would mean paying more for imports and receiving less for exports, 'which is the opposite of what we want to do'. How was Britain going to put up with his policies? 'They would grin and bear it.' Did he think the British people ungrateful for all he had done for them? 'Good gracious, no!'

Delivering his first speech as Chancellor at the annual Lord Mayor's Banquet, Cripps tried to discount the 'rather facile optimism' which had sprung up – partly in response to his own statements. The latest developments were encouraging, especially for the stability of sterling. Controls were working, but further abstinence was required. The outgoing governor of the Bank of England, Lord Catto, limited himself to some remarks about penal taxation. 'Hard responsibilities', noted the *Daily Telegraph*, 'have produced a more mellow and unprejudiced outlook in the Chancellor', who now chose to stress individual effort rather than socialist planning. Cripps tried but failed, however, to appoint an industrialist, Sir John Hanbury Williams, instead of the deputy governor, Cameron Cobbold, as the new governor.[58]

After only one year in office, Cripps had established an impressive personal ascendancy. He held on to the admiration of his officials and kept the trust of industry, was looked up to by a younger cohort of promising ministers, and was a tower of strength in the Cabinet, in the House and representing the country abroad – the 'astonishing Chancellor' handling all his duties with 'triumphant ease'.[59] Despite seeing the Prime Minister on a daily basis, however, his judgement of him had not altered. For Attlee to lead the party into the next election would be a calamity, Dalton (reappointed to the Cabinet as Chancellor of the Duchy of Lancaster) heard from Cripps. 'He still thought EB should be PM, but EB still said no.'[60] To another witness on his early morning walks, Cripps disclaimed any further political ambitions, although if the call were to come 'he would consider it his duty to accept'.[61] It was his wife, inviting trade-union MPs round to meet a more approachable husband, the *Daily Express* observed, who would not let up on her 'Cripps-for-Premier' campaign.[62]

THE LAST MAN

There is something epic about Sir Stafford Cripps. Some people may
not care for the look of the fellow. It is a tribute to the man's palpable
sincerity and dominance of character that we all of us, whatever our
political attitudes or personal reactions, implicitly believe him. He is
far too good for us.

Arthur Bryant, historian, in April 1949 [1]

The 'magical' upturn in Britain's prospects, *The Economist* intoned at the close
of 1948, 'is due overwhelmingly to one man – the Chancellor of the Exchequer,
Sir Stafford Cripps'.[2] He it was who had brought the country's external finances
back into balance. He it was who had advocated higher production and greater
exports. He, most of all, had ensured that the strong economy made for a
strong pound, the true measure of national prestige. Cripps and his advisers
had 'not only shaped the policies and tenaciously defended them, but had
provided the essential moral foundation', for the good of the whole community.
Cripps – according to other accolades – had performed as great a service to his
country as Churchill during the war.

Was he the economic saviour? By superimposing a regime of 'misery at all
costs' on to the normal pattern of economic motivation, he succeeded in
getting producers and consumers to behave other than in their immediate self-
interest.[3] It is questionable whether the effect – in planner's terminology – is
quantifiable. A climate of confidence grew up, encouraging business to invest,
freshened by the following wind of American dollars. Cripps's serene self-
belief, driven by an undercurrent of fanaticism, enhanced the impression of
an ability to work miracles. 'I am certain', Bracken told Churchill, 'that this
arrogant and ambitious man has an idea that as Britain's fortunes grow darker,
God, with the aid of some political intrigues, will call upon him to form a
coalition government.'[4]

Cripps's anxiety was that anyone should doubt him. He drew no distinction
between personal and public honesty, and endured stage-managed taunts of
'evasion' and 'lack of candour' by Tory backbenchers pursuing a vendetta
against him.[5] He lost his composure only once: barracked uninterruptedly

when winding up the second reading of the Iron and Steel Nationalisation Bill in November, he threatened to stop at nothing to get the industry into public hands, throwing the Commons into uproar. The State could cajole but was not free to compel, he argued in calmer moments. Recovery had to come from people themselves. Raising productivity required the highest moral standards. Otherwise the electorate 'would rot of its own corruption'. The nation had not as yet done all the government would wish of it.

This centrally planned conception of the public interest expressed the austere personal standards of Attlee and Cripps.[6] The crunch would come with the easing of shortages, the government then having to adapt to conditions of relative abundance.

Policy about rationing and controls was muddled. The government stood for planning but had, since 1945, been pledged to dismantle controls, though they were the instruments through which planning was carried out. Morrison had favoured the earliest possible decontrol. The emergencies of 1947 led instead to a tightened co-ordination of investment, imports and consumption. Little thought went into how the wartime apparatus of controls might be scrapped. For liberals like Plowden and Hall, 'planning should work towards its own abolition'.[7] The initiative to consider this came from civil servants, spurred on by the disinflationary success of the 1948 Budget to examine which if any controls were inhibiting the redeployment of resources,[8] with Bridges informing the Chancellor, who was 'in full agreement'. Hitherto the lifting of bread rationing and the raising of the fat or sweet ration had been announced without proper care, giving rise (Cripps worried) to the erroneous idea that the country's economic position was improving far more than was the case. He did not want people to think the system of controls was being 'materially weakened'. He asked other ministers to consult him before any changes were made, so that they could be combined in a single statement and 'put in the proper perspective'. When a request came in from the Ministry of Works to ease building-material controls, Jay satisfied him they could safely assent. The most spectacular instance was the Guy Fawkes Day 'bonfire' of controls by the Board of Trade, endorsed by the Chancellor. A second bonfire was set alight by Wilson in March 1949, ending textile, leather, paint and hardwood rationing, though on this occasion Wilson consulted only Attlee. Cripps raised it with Wilson at the weekly dinner of the production ministers. 'My general view', Jay reported back, 'is that we are now in danger of going too far in de-control' and that 'this is going to give the public an impression of general relaxation, making it more difficult to economise on dollar expenditure'[9] (paint and leather were imported from the Argentine, paid for in dollars).

How did ministers reconcile doing away with particular controls and the retention of the general goal of planning? What economic, as opposed to moral, curbs did Cripps consider would suffice? The paradox was quite apparent. Butler, a leading light of the Tory Opposition, good-naturedly teased the Chancellor in conversation about the second of Wilson's bonfires. 'Cripps was amused. "You do not realise how adaptable I am. I could become the champion of luxury and private enterprise overnight." '[10]

The paradox was commonly explained by the changing nature of planning, once it became clear that the policies of Cripps, based on the 'indivisibility' of fiscal and physical control, were paying off. Since the end of the war, full employment had been easier to maintain than anyone had expected. The Treasury surprised itself by how rapidly inflationary pressure was contained from late 1947 on, even with the economy operating at full pelt. Wilson justified giving up controls wherever no hardship to the consumer was likely. The Treasury was far more concerned about conserving dollars. What mattered was the machinery for determining priorities and enforcing 'indicative' co-ordination, not controls *per se* – the whole being watched over by an omniscient Chancellor.

The Long-Term Programme – the British tender to the OEEC in October 1948 – gave some indication of how the UK proposed to do away with external assistance by 1952. Britain intended to make 'resolute' use of the techniques of financial policy, the direct public control of the country's basic industries, and the allocating powers over imports, consumption and investment. Controls, while they restrained production and were being simplified as much as possible, would be retained so long as they were necessary to implement production plans. They were, in fact, an integral part of the attempt to boost productivity and close the trade gap while persisting with budgetary restraint.

This provisional programme – the product of the CEPS and the Economic Section – was constructed on the broad working assumptions that there would be no large-scale rearmament, no depression in the United States, an adequate provision of ERP aid, and closer European co-operation – sustained, Cripps added, by 'the most careful husbanding of foreign exchange earnings'. At a press conference to mark the publication of the Programme on 21 December, Cripps's *bête noire*, the lobby correspondent of the *Financial Times*, Paul Einzig, saw fit to ask him whether it was also based on the further assumption there would be no change in the terms of trade arising out of the devaluation of the pound. 'The introduction of the subject of devaluation', Cripps shot back, 'is merely a piece of gratuitous offensiveness.'[11]

From the point of view of economic strategy, the Programme embodied the framework of policy put into practice over the previous eighteen months. The thorniest problem was how far to go in reforming the OEEC, which, in scrutinising the national plans of Britain and the other participating countries, was being urged to move in a stronger political direction.

Whitehall was in the throes of a 'great debate' about Britain and Europe, struggling to define and decide on a future course for ministers. Confronted with the report of a study group on a European customs union in 1947, the Foreign Office had been warmly sympathetic, treating the free-trade opposition of the Treasury and the Board of Trade as anachronistic, even though the argument that an inward-looking customs union would do nothing to address the all-important dollar imbalance in the Western hemisphere had much force. Foreign Office Europeanism went only so far, however. Britain was committed to closer collaboration, but it had to be on the basis of intergovernmental co-operation, shorn of any supranational element, lest the UK was drawn into an ever tighter federal union. On balance, across all the departments, it was understood that it would be against the British interest for the Europeans to integrate their own economies (the likelihood seemed remote), shutting out the UK.

With the passing of time, attitudes modified. Bevin dropped what little enthusiasm for a united Europe he had, whereas the Treasury was tempted into launching an alternative to the customs-union concept, centred on the wider liberalisation of OEEC trade, which gained considerable European support. Cripps was ready to go even further. The OEEC exercise had obliged governments to survey their longer-term objectives. What if Britain were to seize the opportunity by spreading its planning ideas to cover the European continent? If the European economies could tap the resources of their colonies, better still. A 'Europeanised' Sterling Area, building on the non-dollar world with Europe, might help to head off American pressure on the pound and establish a lasting sterling-centred trade bloc.

In October 1948, Cripps had tried to dissuade Ludwig Erhard, head of the Bizonal Economic Council in western Germany, from giving up controls. He extolled the British way of planning to Paul-Henri Spaak, the Belgian Prime Minister, and drew from him an admission that the relatively free Belgian economy might benefit from a greater degree of *dirigisme*.[12] Cripps's suggestion was to run the OEEC Secretariat with a Committee of Five, served by high-level planning advisers answerable to their national delegations.[13] Plowden, noting the romantic streak in the Chancellor, had him 'all agog' and ready to go over to Paris, taking Plowden with him to embark on a Europe-wide plan.[14]

A joint Foreign Office–Treasury paper, which went to the EPC on 26 January 1949, laid down several historic-sounding propositions.[15] Britain had 'vital interests' in Europe, to which it should be prepared to provide a lead. Nevertheless, the government should never lose sight of the fact that, if war came, alliance with the United States (talks on the formation of NATO were secretly taking place) was the decisive consideration. It could make no sense to sacrifice the Commonwealth in order to throw in Britain's lot with Europe, especially in Europe were to go under. This being so, each proposal for closer European co-operation must be examined on its 'practical' merits. Cripps, leading off, said their plan for the future, strictly intergovernmental, structure of the OEEC had been worked out in concert by Bevin and him, and 'presented no difficulty'. In going through the paper, however, he leaned the other way, referring to the 'gamble' of having later to extricate themselves from Europe as well as the surrendering of some economic advantages, but stressing how, if European economic co-operation succeeded, Britain would 'gain considerably'. By joining in, furthermore, Britain would strengthen the hand of other planning governments in Europe. The Chancellor, it transpired, was willing to take the risk. His more forthcoming advice had some effect. After Bevin had expressed substantial Foreign Office reservations, Attlee, summing up, judged they could minimise the unpleasant features of European integration by confining themselves to the sphere of practical co-operation. The Cabinet endorsed the EPC recommendation at the end of February, provided the UK's economic recovery was not prejudiced.

Occupying his seat on the OEEC Executive Committee on 16 February, Cripps tabled the British proposal (with French backing) for the OEEC Secretariat. When Spaak produced an alternative draft, giving the OEEC more executive power, he was deftly outflanked by a revised British offer designed to meet the objections of the smaller European nations, ensuring the OEEC would have no independent decision-making autonomy. In a further tussle in March, Cripps arranged that Harriman could attend meetings of the Consultative Group only as an 'observer'; Harriman loudly complained about his 'humiliation' at the hands of the British Chancellor.[16]

Cripps's planning scheme had less of a run. It took Bridges, Hall and Plowden together to stop him, using the argument that adding a planning contingent to the British delegation would do for the time being. This did not dampen the Chancellor's spirit. Jean Monnet, High Commissioner of the French national plan, visited London in March, meeting both Cripps and Plowden. The Chancellor was 'beguiled' by Monnet's talk about the economic possibilities of a reviving Europe.[17] Monnet took away the impression that a special Franco-British understanding, sealed by swapping raw materials, was distinctly feasible.

Conceived by the UK as a countermeasure to a high-tariff 'little Europe', trade liberalisation had much in its favour. It would further Britain's economic recovery, fulfil the UK's European commitment, and help the UK to dominate non-dollar markets. It offered, in essence, a guarantee of Sterling Area trade, on which Cripps was pinning his all. There need be no incompatibility in tying up the Commonwealth with a European union, so long as Europe was not unduly protectionist. At the end of March, Cripps and Wilson informed the EPC of the idea of 'a general relaxation of import controls in Western Europe with a view to diverting US pressure for new European payments arrangements which would involve us in a loss of dollars'.[18] With this aim in mind, they were conducting a review of existing tariffs and quota restrictions, opening up

British industry to the efficiency gains of increased competition. It was a further sign of the Chancellor's move away from direct regulation.

What disturbed the British Treasury was the concerted effort, emanating from Washington and some European capitals, to talk down the pound. When, in November 1948, the Swedes had suggested discussing European exchange rates in the OEEC, the UK was quick to 'pour cold water'. Testimony by Snyder to the US Senate in February 1949 brought the issue into the open. 'Artificial' exchange rates were damaging European recovery and were the main reason why the dollar shortage persisted, in the US administration's opinion. Cripps maintained that the primary purpose of the OEEC was to aid international financial stability, as the Americans had always wanted. But, 'with the increasing strength of sterling, there were attempts in the United States to undermine it'.

The importance of extreme discretion sprang also from an anxiety not to jeopardise future ERP appropriations. Christopher Mayhew, the junior Foreign Office minister, painted a bright picture of Britain's completed 'recovery' before a United Nations meeting in February. His sin was compounded by the unguarded comments of another minister. The cries of triumph 'were a godsend to American opponents of Marshall aid, and the Foreign Affairs Committee of the US Senate immediately decided to reopen hearings on Britain's need for $940 million in the second year of ERP'.[19] Cripps had hurriedly to release a correcting statement. 'I admit when news of your fellow countrymen's speeches reached the ECA lots of blasphemous remarks were made,' Hoffman wrote to him. A 'magnificent performance' by Thomas Finletter, head of the ECA mission in Britain, calmed the (Republican) Senate.

Falling US prices pointed up the exchange-rate disparity, and the agitation for a realignment of sterling spread from the ECA to the US Treasury. Cripps finally broke cover. Asked whether devaluation was likely, 'he said "No" – and shut his mouth like a trap'. Morrison wanted to know from the Chancellor what preparations he was making in case of an American slump. Cripps replied by hand that he was aware of the problem but it was necessary not to talk about it, even in the Cabinet, as it might precipitate a flight from sterling.

For the whole of his time at the Exchequer, Cripps had had near-unanimous official advice counselling against devaluation. The Bank of England had been notably forthright, insisting that, since there was no ascertainable basis for deciding whether *any* rate of exchange was valid, it was wiser – according to Sir Otto Niemeyer, the Bank's key director – for the economy to adapt to the rate than for the rate to adapt to the economy. This was the thinking behind the Chancellor's pursuit of a 'strong pound', though he could also argue that it was morally wrong to betray the sacred trust of holders of sterling.

In the spring of 1949, the economic slowdown in America opened up the first breach among his civil servants. On 28 March, Hall told Plowden to tell

Cripps that he had changed his mind, not making the case for devaluation but arguing for having 'a good look' at what the case might be.[20] Exports, he reasoned, were at an all-time high, and the government would be lucky if they held up. All the measures they had taken – ring-fencing sterling, trying to boost home agriculture, food subsidies – indicated 'that we think the pound is over-valued at present, but that we hope that we can overcome this'. The high-pressure economy made him doubt it. Britain had over-full employment and wage inflation. The country had been constantly striving to attain a dollar balance, but, unless they were ready to be more economically self-sufficient, it was easier and more effective to devalue. Cleverly, he put the onus on those opposed to any inquiry. The old gold-standard remedy for a trade imbalance was a government-induced deflation (the Niemeyer approach). According to Lord Keynes's theories, 'which we are now following', it was up to those who said devaluation would not work to prove their point. Had it not been for Marshall Aid, they would in his opinion have had to devalue already.

Plowden was 'soon convinced'. Hall saw the Chancellor on 4 April, probing the extent of Cripps's understanding of his own policy not to sacrifice industry on the altar of finance. Cripps agreed to institute an official review. Hall 'came away feeling what a fine brain and what an integrated personality he has – one can say what one likes and get a good hearing and an intelligent reply. He is against it now but it is a first step: of course we shall not know even if there is a *prima facie* case until we have looked, though I myself believe that there is one.'[21]

The high but ultimately unsustainable level of exports – lending the illusion of an overall trade balance – was matched by the high expenditure and taxation of the domestic economy. Hall's submission to Cripps – that it would eventually be necessary to choose deflation or devaluation – brought nearer the day when the government would have to confront the consequences of its own spending programmes.

Cripps's second Budget accordingly took shape in the context of formidable financial constraints. His first, targeting the total economy, had contributed in large measure to the economic revival. Record exports had accompanied a halt in the upward movement of prices. The disquieting aspect, from autumn 1948 onwards, had been the rapid rise in expenditure, threatening to swallow up the increases in national production. Defence spending was only one item. The Ministry of Defence was asking for a further rise in the estimates for 1948–9, taking its outlay to £770 million. Cripps imposed an upper limit of £750 million, promising key services would not be affected in return for a defence review. When Alexander resisted, Cripps offered Treasury suggestions about where savings might be made. The largest rise, however, was spending on the National Health Service and on food subsidies. The Ministry of Health's own estimate for 1948–9 was £164 million – at least twice what had been anticipated. Bevan instituted an immediate review under his Permanent Secretary, while the Chancellor, directly and through intermediaries, tried to put a lid on the health budget. Bevan, now a member of the EPC, fought his corner. As for food subsidies, attempts to contain their rise was complicated by a festering row between Tom Williams (Agriculture) and John Strachey (Food), which Cripps had to smooth over.[22]

The Chancellor's briefs sounded the knell. The 'truly alarming' departmental estimates threw into doubt the whole economic strategy.[23] With the government's share of national income standing at around 40–45 per cent, Plowden was loath to further curtail individual choice. There was little hope of early tax relief, even for those on lowest incomes. The economy, equally, could not bear a heavier burden. Competitiveness was 'sluggish', many taxes acting as a brake on production rather than as a useful source of revenue. Policy put more reliance on exhortation than was either prudent or effective. Exports in some markets were flagging. Any rise in domestic prices was bound to bring up the question of the depreciation of the pound, exacerbating the problem of 'cheap sterling' (transacting at $3.20–$3.40, well below the official rate of $4.03) and reviving the spectre of a run on the pound. 'The bald fact', the Chancellor was informed, 'is that you cannot get more out of the economic system than it is capable of producing, and inflation is the reaction to attempts to do so.' No blame was attached to the Treasury; nor was it the fault of lack of financial control. Unless the higher estimates were substantially reduced, 'the Chancellor's Budgetary policy will be difficult if not impossible to maintain'.

The Treasury view was the Chancellor's view too. Already, in Washington, he had pointed out that if Britain 'indulged' in further social demands, it would wreck all hope of recovery.[24] Marquand reminded him of the hardships of pensioners. 'And I', Cripps countered, 'am thinking of the hardships of the taxpayers.'[25] After Dalton advocated a permanent capital levy, Cripps argued that a mandate for it should first be obtained from the voters. In 1949, as in 1948, he was searching for taxes he could abolish, not impose.

The arithmetic was against him. Judging by the Economic Section's calculations, the Budget surplus of 1948 had gone a long way to choking off the danger of inflation. But world inflationary pressure was still evident, and another, though much smaller, surplus would be needed to produce any further disinflationary effect. 'This', the Budget Committee reported, 'is the essential point around which the Budget centres.' Because the estimates were running so far ahead of revenue, where was the balance to come from?

Health Service expenditure and the food-subsidy bill (which the Treasury had long had in its sights) were obvious areas in which to economise. The Budget Committee withdrew to Roffey Park to argue it out. The size of the required Budget surplus was fixed at £150 million. Some officials wanted to make an example of health spending by charging for medicine. Raising national insurance was an alternative, but Jay blocked this, the Chancellor agreeing it was fairer to take the money out of general taxation. Eventually they settled on raising the lower rates of income tax by 6d in the pound, clawing back the easements of the year before. Jay fought a rearguard action over food subsidies, mindful of the explosive political effect of raising the price of necessities, especially as the Chancellor was insisting on renewal of the wage and price stabilisation policy. But Cripps was prevailed upon to carry out a promise of Dalton's to set a ceiling on subsidies.

While his officials made their way back to London, the Chancellor stayed on for a week's rest, having collapsed. His doctor, the psychiatrist T. M. Ling, persuaded him to give up smoking, arguing it was affecting his gastric condition, and to cut down on late nights. The break, if anything, made him worse, not better. For the first time in his eighteen-month ordeal, Cripps began talking of retirement.

In a preview of the Budget at Chequers, Attlee, Bevin and Morrison broadly approved. The increase in income tax was cut from 6d to 3d in the pound, and (at Bevin's request) the price of bread was increased instead of the price of meat. Importantly, Cripps obtained the authority to prepare a Treasury circular forbidding any Supplementary Estimates for 1949–50, except where major changes of policy necessitated them. Pre-Budget publication of the Economic Survey for 1949 celebrated the resounding success of the Budget surplus, adding to this the abandonment of longer-term planning targets and the onset of decontrol. It did not escape the notice of several commentators that the economic improvement 'has not been due to Socialist recipes, but to the reversion to a liberal cure'.[26]

Cripps spent the final weekend before the Budget at his home at Frith, going through his speech. He decided, after all, not to make any tax increases, contenting himself with a 'strong warning' that the social services were not 'free' as such but had to be paid for – in the main by the recipients. Even at this stage, Hall and Plowden were jumpy about the size of the surplus, worried they might be curbing domestic purchasing power by too much to be able to maintain exports.

At this exact moment, the Chancellor was presented with an American proposal for a review of European exchange rates by the International Monetary Fund. The threat to confidence this would entail, with orders drying up and purchasers holding off, was serious. 'We view this [IMF] prospect with horror,' the Treasury telegraphed to the UK ambassador in Washington, Oliver Franks. The government was ready at all times to discuss the matter, but it was imperative there should be no IMF resolution. If there was any leakage about this from Washington, 'we shall be quite unable to control the consequences'.[27]

The timing of the US move meant that Cripps had to submit his Budget – a Budget for sterling in all but name – to the Cabinet and Parliament with a nagging fear of instability. The Cabinet was difficult enough. Introducing the unprecedented Treasury circular on Supplementary Estimates, he unveiled his proposals in two parts, looking to obtain agreement with the strategy and the projected surplus before discussing individual tax changes. The tactic misfired. Ministers would not accept the Budget as a whole until they had seen what specific changes were likely.[28] Newspapers spoke of a 'battle' in the Cabinet, with the Chancellor insisting on clamping down on expenditure.[29] Dell remarks, however, that all the politically nasty decisions were deferred.[30] The Budget remained largely as it was, Cripps sent word to Woods (who was convalescing after an operation) as he put his Budget speech to bed at 12.30 a.m., and would get 'a very unfavourable reaction from "our folk" '. The parliamentary party meeting 'will not be a pleasant experience!!'.[31]

To the last, Cripps was distracted by events in Washington. Franks recommended putting aside any personal resentment, wishing to avoid 'lasting embitterment'. Cripps was inconsolable. At 2.40 p.m., only minutes before leaving the Treasury to deliver his Budget speech, he replied to Franks that the harm was already done and visible in the foreign-exchange markets as they talked (Wall Street prices for spot, ninety-day and six-month sterling had all fallen sharply). If the IMF resolution was tabled, the British representative was instructed to vote against. 'I regard the American attitude as deplorable. They are playing with fire.'[32]

On the stroke of 3.30 p.m., Cripps treated a thronged House to two-and-a-quarter hours of what Anthony Eden called 'condensed and brilliant oratory'. He reviewed the past year, contrasting the overall trade balance with a continuing dollar deficit. The Budget surplus of 1948 had provided an unexpectedly large yield, but this was offset by increasing expenditure, largely on defence and the social services. Redistribution had reached its limit, and would have to await the creation of new wealth, pending which new services were curbed. The age-old function of the Commons, he said, had been to protect the taxpayer from the demands of the executive – a function recently neglected. 'We must call a halt.' This brought him to particular measures – pegging food subsidies at £465 million, with increases on meat and cheese, making for a two-point rise in the cost of living; higher telephone charges; and a tax relief to industry for profits, which were 'frightfully high', ploughed back into re-equipment. The Treasury was issuing a circular forbidding any Supplementary Estimates, save as a result of a major policy change. Charges for the Health Service were, he hinted, a future possibility. Although he was dealing with matters of magnitude, the Chancellor, his voice 'sharp and resonant', justified one change after another 'by some high principle of rectitude',[33] lecturing the country that its new social obligations were not temporary but for all time. 'Labour people', according to 'Chips' Channon, seated on the other side of the chamber, 'snarled with anger.' In his evening broadcast, Cripps spoke of how he was longing to announce lower taxes and easier times, but could not shirk his responsibilities. 'It seems hard to you – and so it does to me.'[34]

His critics the following morning at the PLP meeting and in the second day's debate in the Commons were in near-rebellion. Cripps was a new 'Snowden'. The Budget was a victory for the Treasury in its 'war of attrition' against Labour's policies. Morrison made it clear that any challenge to the Chancellor was a challenge to the whole Cabinet; the Budget was a test of their capacity to govern, which they must not 'dodge' or they would have another 1931 on their hands.[35] Many in the government thought Cripps had blundered, however. Even Gaitskell and Jay suspected he had been leaned on by his officials. The party-political repercussions were not promising either. During March and April the Labour Party crept ahead of the Conservatives in the opinion polls for the first time since the fuel crisis, and there was strong public support for the Chancellor, whose policy was 'the only possible one in the circumstances'. This, however, did not translate into good local-election results, jolting party strategists.

American opinion was stirred. 'There has never been any risk of under-estimating the Chancellor's determination or boldness.' Nevertheless, 'his tough Budget had shocked the "ration-weary" British people', the *New York Times* commented. ('Those concerned may like to see these,' Cripps minuted.)[36] The crucial question, about which Cripps was scratching his thinning hair, was whether Americans, admiring the British from afar, would go on buying British goods, and in increasing quantities. Trade figures for the first quarter of 1949, released the day after the Budget, looked ominous. The Sterling Area was still in overall balance, but dollar earnings were falling. For the first time since August 1947 (when, after convertibility, the figures began to be closely monitored) the weekly dollar drain reappeared.[37]

The IMF squabble added impetus to the official review of the exchange-rate question, which the Bank was brought into. It also led to the Treasury examining a non-dollar currency bloc with the OEEC, from which gold and dollar payments would be excluded, permanently discriminating against the USA. Plowden and Hall, staying at the country home of Monnet, had four days of off-the-record talks about Anglo-French co-operation, including a common production scheme. The meeting was friendly, but Plowden was sceptical of Monnet's visionary approach. Cripps was more favourable, but Bevin, when the proposals were relayed to him, sat on them. Plowden was left to reply to Monnet that co-operation could not be pushed beyond a certain point. The outcome was that the Treasury and the Board of Trade made haste with the plan for wider trade liberalisation with the OEEC, protecting the integrity of the Sterling Area. In the House, Cripps accompanied another statement that 'there is no question of sterling being devalued' with a strengthening of the defences against 'cheap sterling', which 'twisted trade out of its normal channels' and was 'damaging' the position of the pound.

Once the Finance Bill was largely out of the way, the Crippses flew off to Rome for a two-week holiday. The first week was spent in conversation with members of the Italian government. It was also a chance for an audience with the Pope, to discuss forms of common worship by the Anglican and Roman Catholic Churches,[38] followed by a vegetarian banquet in the Vatican. At a large press conference on 30 April, the inevitable question cropped up. The *Financial Times* representative asked whether the devaluation of European currencies would be necessary in the near future. Cripps could not speak for other countries, but in the case of sterling it was 'neither necessary nor would it take place... It is in the general interest of Europe that sterling should be maintained as a stable and acceptable means of payment.' The Foreign Office was relieved that the conference passed off quietly.[39] The Office did not notice that Cripps had gone further – amounting to 'never' devaluing – than ever before, the whole of his exhausting personal effort to get Britain back on its feet being tied to an exchange parity over which he had scant control. All the foreign papers repeated the Chancellor's statement, and all of them considered devaluation likely sooner or later. Financial circles believed Cripps was sincere and serious, Einzig commented, but still he might be forced into it.

The Crippses then withdrew to the south of Italy, Cripps, not at all well, enjoying the sunshine and outdoor exercise, climbing the steep hillsides around Ravello. They did not get back until 17 May, when he was immediately acquainted with an 'unpleasantly large' dollar deficit for April, the news coinciding with more evidence of American belief in the certainty of devaluation of the pound.[40] Sterling suffered its 'worst break in years'.[41] Cripps acted promptly, delivering an unequivocal defence of the sterling parity. To go with this, he invited some forty editors of newspapers and magazines to his office in the Treasury to scotch speculation. 'In the strongest terms', he told them devaluation was not contemplated, but discussion of it was holding off customers for British goods.[42] On the floor of the House, he denied the UK was heading for a new crisis, though the dollar position was difficult. Finally, on 18 May, he saw Harriman and Finletter. Cripps 'started out by pointing out to [Harriman] the damage being done by all the gossip from Washington on devaluation and begged him to take any steps he could to stop it'.[43]

Hall by now was sure the overvalued pound was exposing sterling to international attack, showing up the 'bankruptcy' of present policies. The governor of the Bank, for his part, fearing sterling might be knocked off its perch, was reassured to find the Chancellor still strongly opposed to a rate change, Cripps explaining that his one fear was of a prolonged (and self-fulfilling) talking campaign.[44] The mere whisper of a rumour that Cripps had resigned sent gilt-edged (government) stocks tumbling.[45]

How unwell was the Chancellor? He had – excluding his stint in Moscow – held high office for seven continuous years.[46] Each post – Aircraft Production, the Board of Trade and the Treasury – was more demanding than the one before, not least because of his high sense of purpose. His sickness in India in 1946 was a premonition. It was Attlee, in the attempt to dislodge him from the prime ministership in 1947 – a battle by medical bulletin – who seemed the likelier to succumb to malady. Cripps's long-standing digestive trouble was well documented, though he did not give it a name and developed an ability to conceal when he was in pain. The rest of his family learned not to enquire. He was having difficulty eating and sleeping, but refused to take medication. Examined in early June 1949, he was found to be essentially fit and strong, but in need of complete rest and treatment lasting several weeks.

Cripps declined to go until he had entrenched the necessary measures, determined to use every means to buck market opinion, stave off American pressure, and rally the Labour Party, securing the position until his return. In the last resort, if all else failed, the government should put the issue of devaluation to the voters at an election. To those who had appreciated his open-mindedness, his refusal to reconsider was the obstinacy of an invalid.

One element – the scheme for liberalising OEEC trade – had gone through the EPC and the Cabinet. In the meantime two officials, Hall and Henry Wilson Smith, left for Washington to buy more time. At the party conference in Blackpool, opposition to the Budget was still evident. The chairman of the PLP, no less, moved a resolution calling for more to be done for the lower paid. All of the party stood for a higher standard of living, Cripps asserted, but it was not possible to go on increasing social spending and simultaneously reduce taxation. Delegates had to face the situation as it was, 'not as we should like it to be'. It was no answer to 'juggle' with money. Their 'virile democracy' needed higher production and higher efficiency, improving purchasing power, not depressing it. 'Our party has always insisted upon the supremacy of the moral value.'[47]

Reporters appreciated the odd artistry. Hugh Massingham of *The Observer* took a delight in watching Cripps moving along the seafront, 'with that strange springy walk that gave him the appearance of youth', past 'Stop-Me-and-Buy-One' and the larky postcards, on his way to deliver his conference sermon. 'Every mouth in the hall was open. They did not understand what he was saying but they hoped that it was doing them good. Then, in some bewilderment, they voted [on a show of hands] in favour of the wages freeze.'[48] The *Sunday Express* preferred to run a story about the Crippses' family fortune (actually Isobel's), showing how no family had been harder hit by the Chancellor's own policy of high taxation.

Returning to London, Isobel called round to see Attlee on 14 June, in some urgency, 'about Stafford'.[49] Her husband's deteriorating health meant he must go away for two months to Switzerland, hard though he found it to give up. The decision, she said, was unavoidable. He could rest and recover, and come back to give of his best again.

On 15 June, at the first meeting of the EPC since Blackpool, ministers faced the full force of the storm, the economic indicators 'all going wrong at once'. The trade gap had widened further, the reserves falling to £400 million, well below the safety level. Wilson Smith and Hall, reporting on their Washington discussions, revealed that Snyder was 'quite sold' on devaluation. Cripps was blunt. The danger was that within twelve months all the reserves would be gone, but with nothing behind them, threatening 'a complete collapse of sterling'.[50] When the meeting reconvened in the afternoon, he was authorised to stop all purchases in gold and dollars forthwith, anxious to take action before 5 July, when the next statement on the reserves was due to be made. Calmly he argued for an early general election. (If they had to devalue, Jay had admitted the month before, the cost of living would jump up, losing Labour the election.) Bevan also favoured one, as did Morgan Phillips, the party's general secretary. As they filed out, Attlee said to Dalton, '1931 all over again.' Dalton was reminded of the convertibility crisis of 1947. 'There are all the makings of a panic here.'

In great secrecy, Cripps notified the American ambassador of the accelerating gold and dollar drain – from £82 million in the first quarter to £150 million in the second – attributing it to widespread talk about a possible sterling devaluation and a diminution in US purchases from overseas.[51] Douglas passed the information on to Washington. The construction of an autarchic Sterling Area loomed larger, he reported – an attempt to 'insulate' the UK from US pressure, to the detriment of America. Devaluation 'will in our opinion be resisted to the end, principally because of a fear of a repetition of the 1931 debacle and because Cripps is convinced that devaluation by itself will not make any material contribution to a solution'. The unity shown at Blackpool suggested the government might elect to meet the crisis head on, possibly using the USA as a scapegoat.

Collecting the voices, Bridges submitted the results of the devaluation inquiry to Cripps in the form of individual memoranda, stressing that the Treasury and the Bank remained predominantly hostile to devaluing.[52] Eady was of the view that lowering the exchange rate was an unmistakable sign of weakness, rendering the currency 'worthless'. Cobbold's Bank findings were that any change in the rate would have to be accompanied by reductions in spending, a wages halt, tighter monetary policy, and a deflated Budget. Bridges himself wanted a £100 million cut in food subsidies. Only Wilson Smith, as a result of his talks in the USA, regarded devaluation as inevitable, though he was pessimistic about the consequences. Hall was equally adamant it would be a 'fantastic reversal of all we have striven for since 1931' if the government were to now go in for a substantial deflation. 'No government ought to do so.' ('I seem to be surrounded by invincible ignorance and prejudice,' he wrote in his diary.) Bridges, who came down on the side of the antis, reflected that most of them, with differing degrees of emphasis, 'are opposed to devaluation *now*' but did not rule out a forced decision at a later date, when other measures – such as a food subsidy cut – would be necessary to reduce the overload on the economy.

Cripps believed he could avoid either extreme by a gritty intensification of existing policy. He told this to the EPC. At the present rate, the reserves would all be gone by the new year. He proposed what he had always previously proposed: another austerity package, including a staggering cut of one-quarter in imports for the year to May 1950, co-ordinated with the rest of the Commonwealth. At the Chancellor's weekly dinner, Bevan called for 'something different from everlasting cuts'. The news that Cripps was not budging soon reached Douglas. Cripps intended to defend the currency by a sharp curtailment of imports from the dollar area, ready to 'stake his political position within the Cabinet and before the public on a refusal to change the present rate'.[53] Douglas went on to urge consultations with the British – Snyder was already coming to Paris – lent urgency by the announcement that the Chancellor had to go into a Swiss nursing home not later than 17 July.

Cripps's other plan – OEEC liberalisation with the Commonwealth – was bogged down. Any scheme to break the Sterling Area was completely unacceptable, he held – the government could not repeat the mistake of 1947. But what Harriman, Spaak and Maurice Petsche (the French Finance Minister) all saw in his OEEC plan was a permanent high-cost trading area allied to sterling, protected from the dollar world by high tariffs. By compromising, he hoped at least to get the Americans to underwrite the Sterling Area reserves. Harriman, guessing the UK was trying to 'high-pressure' the USA into accepting a closed, discriminatory Sterling Area-cum-OEEC, would not play. The British position could no longer be dealt with in terms of 'Crippsian rigidities'. 'Something must give and at the present time it is the British reserves.'[54]

Before leaving for Paris, Cripps spent the weekend in bed drawing up a memorandum for the Cabinet, setting out the lines of discussion with the Commonwealth finance ministers. To make his remedies stick, he swallowed some of the Bank's medicine. Despite the furious objections of Jay that the 'confidence' of the unions was infinitely more valuable, he adopted the ruling that excessive departmental spending be covered by an equivalent reduction in food subsidies.[55] This would add two more points to the cost of living, but could be contained by pulling out all stops to preserve the wage freeze. He did not go as far as advocacy of a rise in bank rate. 'The Chancellor is obviously torn,' Gaitskell noted of a 'hopelessly overworked' Cripps dashing between Paris, Brussels and London. 'Plowden has for long favoured devaluation; other parties in the Treasury favour deflation, but they all seem to want to cling to multilateralism and convertibility as our aim. Douglas [Jay] is opposed to this and has a continual struggle inside the Treasury for Stafford's soul.'[56]

The Paris meeting of the OEEC Council was deadlocked over an intra-European payments system. The arguing dragged on until 2 a.m., at which point Cripps set off back to London. Tired and drawn, he confronted a much enlarged EPC (Franks had flown over from Washington) at 11.30 a.m., delineating the three choices open to the government: the present policy of increasing industrial production while maintaining the social services and food subsidies; a policy of severe internal deflation; or the devaluation of sterling. Advocating the first, coupled with tighter control of spending, he referred to the disagreements among his advisers about devaluing, qualifying his preference:

> I do not believe that this is the right time to carry it out, whatever the ultimate decision may be. American opinion has certainly moved away from putting pressure upon us and I think they realise (or some of them do) the damage that has already been done. Anyway this is a matter we can discuss confidentially with them and if, as part of some great new and imaginative scheme to solve the world's dollar problems devaluation of sterling were to be proposed I would not necessarily be averse to including it as one item in such a plan. For the present however I am opposed to it.[57]

Present policy was all very well, but no one wanted a cut in food subsidies. It would, said Morrison, trigger off a parliamentary revolt. Bevan, Addison, Strachey and Dalton all raised objections, Dalton believing Cripps was the victim of a conspiracy by Bridges, Plowden and the Bank. Budgetary policy had no bearing on the balance of payments, he contended. Cripps, dismayed that the ex-Chancellor was not reciprocating the support he had given *him*, did not make a fight of it. When discussion resumed after lunch, the consensus was against any immediate devaluation of sterling. Morrison, tentatively backed by Attlee, explained that, while he did not favour it, it was in fact already taking place, in which case a planned (instead of a forced) devaluation was the least of evils. Bevin, feeling neither devaluation nor a food-subsidy cut would work, talked instead of settling the problem at the political level. For the first time, however, altering the rate of exchange had some support from inside the Cabinet.

Cripps's imminent statement to the Commons on the dollar position was character-testing. A flattering profile in the *Daily Mirror* had the Chancellor – 'the banker to the nation' – rising early even on a Sunday, cancelling all official engagements to prepare his speech, and timing himself as he read through it page by page before sending it off for typing.[57] Guided by the conclusions of the EPC, he did not intend referring to government spending or wage restraint. Cobbold advised him the speech would be bad for confidence. Cripps bluntly told him a deflationary policy was a political impossibility. Two newspapers reported that the Chancellor would rather resign than devalue. 'Sir Stafford's friends believe he would give up office rather than agree to it.'[59] Detailing the extent of gold and dollar losses to the House, he unveiled further import cuts, a standstill on all new dollar imports, and a reduction in the sugar ration. 'His Majesty's Government have not the slightest intention of devaluing the pound,' he answered a Tory questioner, banging the dispatch box to loud cheering from the government benches. At a press conference later in the day, he said he was putting his faith in British common sense. Was there not a case for less carrot and more stick? he was asked. 'You must ask the donkey.'

The EPC met again on 7 July, the day before Snyder's arrival, to flesh out what a 'general settlement' of the dollar problem might involve. The Chancellor presented one more position paper, 'The Choice Before Us'. A 'two-world' policy, amalgamating the Commonwealth and OEEC in a sheltered sterling bloc was one option, but a poor one, since it would cut across the Atlantic pact and lead to higher prices, lower living standards and unemployment at home. 'One-world' multilateralism, with the full convertibility of the pound, was equally out of the question – the British economy could not withstand the rigours of complete association with an open market. The suggested alternative was a 'constructive compromise' with the USA in which the UK would contain domestic spending and try to encourage the dollar trade (including some degree of convertibility with the dollar) in exchange for America relieving the pressure on the pound and other 'first aid' measures. If this seemed a high price to exact, Cripps looked to 'New Deal' America to soften its free-market doctrines with an injection of international planning.

His colleagues doubted how far the British and American systems – democratic socialism and unregulated capitalism – could reasonably combine. Attlee intervened, arguing that ideological differences between America and Britain were not as wide as sometimes supposed. The upshot was a recommendation for the Chancellor to use the position paper as a 'guide', introducing devaluation – 'a card to hold and not to play' – and convertibility at a late stage only if there had been prior American concessions. At the close of the EPC meeting, after Attlee had asked Bridges and Makins to leave the room, Cripps revealed he no longer trusted his officials in the Treasury and the Bank. They had, as he put it, more sympathy for the American viewpoint because of their strong belief in the virtues of a free economy.[60] Already, they were half-expecting the government to be defeated at the forthcoming election. Dalton advised Cripps to make more use of Jay in the US talks. Hall was disaffected. 'It is a tragedy that S.C. should be so ill at this time, it is almost impossible to get anywhere with him and he told P[lowden] that he felt suspicious of all his advisers and had to read all their stuff to see that they did not slip anything over on him that was flatly against his party beliefs.'[61]

The talks with Snyder and the Canadian Finance Minister, Douglas Abbott, lasted over the weekend of 9–10 July. Cripps and Bevin formed a common front, reiterating the UK's commitment to multilateral trading, admitting some British prices were too high, and suggesting remedial action only as part of a larger scheme to which the USA would have to contribute. Devaluation they did not regard as 'helpful', but it might be an element in that larger scheme. The sterling problem, as they saw it, was really a dollar crisis. Snyder's worst fears were confirmed. Cripps desired only to defend socialism, state planning and price supports for raw materials. There was no recognition of the need to shake out high costs or reduce restrictions. After Cripps had given an exposition of the drastic import cuts he was to announce to Parliament on 14 July, Snyder reserved his position, proposing trilateral discussions in the USA in August and September. When they came to the wording of the final communiqué, Cripps tried to include a sentence indicating that neither the USA nor Canada considered devaluation of the pound as the answer to Britain's difficulties. Snyder demurred. Cripps insisted that if nothing was said, people would infer he had been pressed to devalue. Snyder and Abbott had to give in, accepting the terse phrase that 'no suggestion was made that sterling be devalued'. Snyder left for home complaining of 'fundamental differences'.

The Chancellor's grip on policy was weakening, his 'greatest enemy' being time.[62] Jay had been brought in to even up the contest with 'reactionary' civil servants. Fearing for his own position, Plowden went to Cripps intending to stand down. Cripps reassured him by directing his criticisms at Cobbold. He handled the Commonwealth finance ministers' conference with his accustomed aplomb, securing agreement to an all-round 25 per cent cut in dollar imports. In setting out the details to the House on 14 July, he spoke slowly and eloquently but was plainly unwell – several times his voice faltered, and he dealt irritatedly with Churchill. The policy disarray, Gaitskell judged, was entirely due to the Chancellor's infirmity. 'It was quite clear from his vacillations that he was not really capable of thinking the problems out for himself; and the papers submitted were a hotch potch of official views – themselves divided on some issues – tempered by what Stafford thought his colleagues would feel.'[63]

Cripps's departure for Zurich for treatment of his digestive disorder was made public on 17 July, and was confirmed by Attlee in the House on the 18th.[64] He hoped, he mentioned to Cobbold, things would quieten down until the trip to Washington. In fact he wanted to fend off encirclement by the City, private industry and antagonistic counsellors:

16.7.49

Private and Confidential

My Dear Prime Minister,

I understand that some of the Ministers will be asking to see you and the Lord President about the question of an early election.

I have been very much impressed in the last few days with the growing political pressure both amongst certain circles in this country which have hitherto been constrained to cooperate with the Government, and from the United States and Canada where both the Governments are unsympathetic and critical of our policies. There is no doubt a sense of uncertainty as to whether we still have the support of the country for our economic policies and I feel that in this state of uncertainty we shall be and indeed are in a very weak bargaining position. It was symptomatic of this that a few days ago Abbott remarked to me, in the most friendly way, 'I wish your election was over it would be so much easier for you.' I am particularly worried about the recent news of American opinion in the Foreign Office telegrams, and there is really only one way to deal with this which is to have an early election after which we shall either receive a vote of confidence or be out!

I believe that from a narrow Party point of view it is much wiser to test the electorate now than leave it & we have a first-class excuse in the way the Tories have publicly challenged our economic policy in the debate on Thursday.

I fear that our discussions with the USA and Canada in September will be rendered fruitless if we are not by then at least in the position of having asked the People to support our views.

Yours,
Stafford[65]

The Labour government was under siege – a dock strike and the invoking of Emergency Powers, House of Lords obstruction of the Iron and Steel Bill, resistance to development councils, financial speculation against the pound and a press barrage. Cripps felt his economic policies were being directly attacked and that the 'willing co-operation' which had underpinned the country's recovery effort since 1945 was coming to an end, the market passing its verdict on the government's version of democratic planning. The only way out was to have an electoral showdown. A Labour victory would silence all talk of devaluation, and at the very least strengthen the government's hand for the Washington discussions. Quite how an election was to be fitted in – and in his own absence – he did not say.

His leave-taking occurred just as the first real shift of attitude began in Whitehall. At lunchtime on the day he was about to set off, Jay managed to see him in his room, announcing that Gaitskell and he had both come to the view that devaluation was now necessary. 'What – unilaterally?' the Chancellor asked incredulously.[66] He was, he confessed, 'a bit done in', his insides 'none too good'.[67] In the devilish circumstances, the dual role he had taken on in 1947 – to plan and to protect the currency – became too much for him.[68] Illness in leaders cannot be shown to influence particular decisions; it can explain paralysing *in*decision. 'Cripps was a marvellous man to work for,' Hall wistfully remarked many years later, 'but he was against devaluation. He was the last man to be persuaded.'[69]

23

PRICKLY CROWN

I have not slept.

Cripps in August 1949[1]

In Whitehall, in the wake of the planning reorganisation of 1947, everything – the Budget, consumption and investment, raw materials, the balance of payments, sterling and the OEEC, the whole structure of decision-making coordinated by a system of tailor-made committees topped off by the Economic Policy Committee – flowed through the Treasury. Within the Treasury, the main threads of policy were held by the Chancellor. For a year and a half he had carried an immense burden, until – crippled in body – he made his way to Switzerland. 'Like a burlesque juggler in the music halls, he walked off the stage, leaving the balls suspended in mid air.'[2]

The Chancellor gone, how long was his personal policy veto – no devaluation, no deflationary cuts and nothing but an election – likely to last? Continentals interpreted his Swiss respite as a 'diplomatic' illness, convenient for shuffling him out of the way. The Opposition joined in, Churchill depicting the Chancellor laid low by his own accumulating errors which others would have to clear up, the country 'rapidly approaching a grave and formidable event'.[3]

The Treasury was 'split from top to bottom', seething with disagreement.[4] Both courses – lowering sterling or cutting spending – carried great risks. Both, though technical in form, were highly political. Both camps attempted to win converts, confident the Chancellor would have the honesty, in spite of repeated denials, to change course. There are many inner histories of the devaluation crisis. None of them conveys the private drama of the Chancellor's public torment.

For the duration, Attlee put himself in charge of general Treasury policy, 'assisted' by Wilson, Gaitskell and Jay, the three most economically literate (and youngest) members of his administration. On 19 July, the day after the Chancellor's departure, he called a Cabinet 'Council of War' to consider the election date. He read out some of Cripps's letter arguing for an election before the Washington talks, believing Cripps had been 'very much wrought up' when he wrote it 'and hadn't thought it out'. Bevan spoke up for an election before the end of 1949, but Morrison was non-committal and Bevin hostile to any disruption of international policy. The one commonly agreed point was that, after the backlash of April 1949, they could not chance another one of the Chancellor's Budgets, which narrowed the choice down to the spring of 1950 at the latest. The dollar problem had to be squared up to, without a cut-and-run election and without jeopardising party unity.

Gaitskell and Jay had been won round to devaluation by the economist Nicholas Kaldor, a friend of Hall, the latter relieved that at long last opinions were altering. When they saw Wilson, he claimed to have held the same view for some time, but did not want to act ahead of the Washington summit. At their regular group dinner, Bevan and Strauss were 'easily' swung into line, Strachey having already been convinced by the EPC discussions on 1 July that they were trying to hold on to an unsustainable exchange rate. In a matter of days, all of Cripps's followers had deserted him.

Morrison, however, made the boldest foray on to Cripps's territory, arguing for vigorous reductions in government spending, drawing a 'close' relation between high expenditure and the dollar difficulty. Among officials, most of whom were still opposed to an early devaluation, the changes of mind by ministers allowed them the opportunity to break cover. Notwithstanding the 'delicacy' of his position, Bridges put to Attlee the advice that the Chancellor had not passed on to his colleagues: that the July measures were insufficient.[5] Officials now recognised the necessity of devaluation, but insisted it would have to go hand in hand with a reduction in government spending of the kind Morrison was recommending. Hall chipped in, suggesting a modest immediate cut was better than more drastic ones that would be necessary if they delayed. Attlee was unpersuaded, complaining to Dalton he was being served up with 'fallacious' arguments about the evil effects of public expenditure.

Attlee's three assistants saw Bridges, Wilson Smith and Hall on 25 July. Gaitskell took the initiative, eliciting from Bridges that all were agreed on altering the exchange rate, though Gaitskell thought devaluation in itself would suffice. To the surprise of Gaitskell and Jay, Wilson summed up by stressing how they could not make the move until Washington. The recruiting of Dalton to the devaluation camp, however, tilted the balance in the Cabinet decisively.

The next day a Treasury troika (Bridges, Plowden and Hall) handed a memorandum to Attlee, enclosing draft instructions for Washington. Devaluation was accepted, but only in conjunction with curbing public expenditure and an increase in short-term interest rates. Delay would rob the government of any control over events. For the talks to be a success, they must announce a package of cuts in advance. A hawkish Cobbold told Bridges he would 'refuse outright' to act on interest rates unless there was parallel action on public expenditure.[6]

Gathering without officials, Attlee, Morrison, Wilson, Gaitskell and Jay came to the shared view to devalue before Washington but after Cripps had returned, passing up using it as a bargaining counter but wanting the Chancellor – because of the 'great shock' – to broadcast the decision. At Cabinet, securing agreement in principle, Attlee got *carte blanche* to take all necessary steps, while Morrison's suggestion of a 5 per cent across-the-board cut in spending was written up in a formal directive. Jay and Gaitskell then drafted a proposed letter to the Chancellor. Arriving in Downing Street, they were intercepted by Bridges and Wilson Smith, who insisted on redrafting it to put the accent on delaying any announcement until the US talks were under way. When Gaitskell saw the rewording, he hit the roof, demanding the excision of lengthy references to cutting spending. 'All of us are now agreed, including our responsible officials, that this is a necessary step,' the letter read, if the reserves were not to fall to a dangerous, unmanageable level, and 'should not be delayed in order to await further decisions on Government expenditure.'[7] Devaluation should not, moreover, be 'traded' in for US concessions. It was deemed 'vital' that the Chancellor himself should be in the UK to explain the change of policy. Cobbold made one last throw, praising the achievements of the previous two years, purchased by the creation of an inflexible economic order of excessive controls and inadequate incentives.[8]

The courier of the sealed letter to Cripps was Wilson, who motored over to Zurich on 8 August after attending a trade meeting at Annecy (and also calling on Bevin), collecting the envelope from his private secretary, Max Brown, before turning up at the Bircher-Benner Klinik. Cripps, undergoing a new blood treatment to combat anaemia, was feeling 'mouldy' and was not sleeping well. Reading the contents through, he reacted badly, stunned by how quickly his position had crumbled. If they were going to devalue, it was 'more necessary than ever' to hold an election first.[9] Failing that, they should not devalue before Bevin and he left for Washington. It would be a piece of sharp practice, look panicky, and imply there had been a sharp worsening of the dollar drain. He particularly objected to the (toned-down) passage on cutting public spending, detecting the handiwork of Bridges. Since he understood 'there could be no question of taking the decision against his advice', he thought fixing the exact date could be settled on his return. 'The only change in his view', Wilson reported to Attlee, 'was that he was much more doubtful about the value of the step at all at first, but later appeared strongly to support it, given the right timing.' This put paid to the prompt action Gaitskell and Jay wanted.

Drafting the Washington briefs, Bridges, Wilson Smith and, latterly, Makins revived considerations about 'the need to restore confidence' by making large economies. Their anxiety that devaluation on its own would backfire was enough to make them reconsider devaluing at all. Gaitskell, rising to his full stature as 'Vice-Chancellor of the Exchequer', counter-attacked by writing a rival draft for comparison.[10] At this, Bridges caved in. Dalton, smiling on his protégé, was angered by the outbreak of official insubordination, after all the Cabinet's discussions and decisions. From that moment, Jay contends, the integrity of Gaitskell outshone the trimming of Wilson. He made up his mind, convinced the doubters, and supervised all the arrangements, establishing himself as Cripps's only possible successor.[11]

Cutting short his sick leave by one week – 'much improved' according to his doctor, Dagmar Liechti – Cripps landed at Northolt airport on 18 August, making straight for Chequers. On the 19th, Attlee, Bevin and Cripps assembled, along with Wilson and Gaitskell. Gaitskell talked them through a detailed memorandum expounding the economic case for devaluation 'at the earliest possible date', presuming to plump for a November election. The ensuing discussion went back and forth without any steering by Attlee. Cripps, 'quite out of touch' but eventually acquiescing, was still adamantly against any devaluation before Washington (though a date in mid-September meant the loss of two more months of gold and dollar reserves). This, Attlee accepted, had the force of a ruling. Hall, having felt it his duty to convert the politicians, was aghast that the one man who had affairs at his fingertips should go off and then become the principal obstructionist.[12] Cripps handed back his copy of the memorandum unread, retiring to Frith for a further week's rest.

On 29 August, the Cabinet met to confirm its earlier decision. Cobbold, bowing to the inevitable, saw the Chancellor shortly beforehand, suggesting a new rate as low as $2.75. Cripps, he recorded, 'does not think it will do much good but, now that it has been talked about so much and so widely for six months, he does not see much hope of getting away without it'.[13] The Chancellor, nevertheless, had no wish to tackle internal finance and had little expectation of positive American help. Cripps, side-stepping any argument about the mathematical costs and benefits, concentrated his case to the rest of the Cabinet on restoring the stability of the pound and on obtaining assurances from the Americans that they would not frustrate British plans by devaluing the dollar. The new rate was left open. Bevan entered the proviso that promises to the USA about the total size of government expenditure must be avoided. Anti-inflationary measures would be addressed only after the talks. That night, Cripps enjoyed his soundest sleep for many months, his fear of insomnia subsiding.[14]

Two days later, the Chancellor and the Foreign Secretary embarked for the United States on the cruise ship *Mauretania*. Plowden and Makins went with them. Wilson Smith and Hall flew on ahead by air. The ship had hardly left port before Cripps irritated Bevin by starting on their briefs.[15] Bevin withdrew to his cabin and, during the rough crossing, Cripps occupied himself pacing the deck, jogging his prescribed three miles to lose weight, and taking dips in the open-air pool. They docked in New York on the night of 6 September. A 'ragged' Cripps was still reluctant to devalue, and then by as little as possible, even to the point of thinking of asking the Americans what new rate they could suggest. The Chancellor, Plowden maintains, never did reconcile himself to the immorality of debasing the coinage. Afterwards, the press surged on to the liner. Bevin dealt with most questions, referring to a sheaf of notes. The Chancellor spoke only once, asked about the possibility of the devaluation of the pound, replying he was sticking by the statement he had recently made (on 6 July) to the House of Commons.[16]

Talks began at the State Department on 7 September, with Snyder, Hoffman and Dean Acheson (the US Secretary of State), Pearson (the Canadian Prime Minister) and Abbott, attended by crowds of advisers. Bevin and Cripps, according to Acheson, made a 'formidable pairing'.[17] During a largely 'futile' first day, the Americans turned down a number of British suggestions for correcting the dollar balance, such as waiving some provisions of the 1945 loan. Bevin clashed with Hoffman, who had been urging an even greater effort by British exporters to break into dollar markets, Bevin recollecting the tariff wall the USA had erected the last time Britain tried to do so in the 1920s.[18] Cripps 'swore' Britain would implement the import cuts he had negotiated with the Commonwealth. He did not notify the others of the British intention to devalue the pound until the second day (Cripps had been up at 5 a.m., jogging naked in the grounds of the British Embassy), once the conference room had been cleared. The disclosure had a swiftly beneficial effect, although Cripps was stung by Snyder's remarks that the British economy had serious faults; Bevin acted as the peacemaker. A decision on the new rate was left until 12 September, in a meeting at the Embassy. In England, Bevin had favoured $3.20; Cripps did not want to go below $3. Officials convinced them it was better to undershoot, plumping for $2.80. Bevin, on inquiring with Plowden, was told this would add only 1d to the price of a loaf of bread, which he would like to be whiter (Cripps approved only of brown bread).[19] Hall and Plowden meanwhile set to work drafting the Chancellor's broadcast, though a renewed run on the British reserves had begun.

A ten-point communiqué was issued at the close of the discussions. The jauntiness of the Chancellor, 'unmistakably laughing', was subsequently held against him.[20] But, in relaying the details of the talks back to London, the British delegation had every cause for optimism. Franks provided a shortlist. The USA was committed to remaking the economy of the Western world, with the UK as its principal partner. There was to be a partnership between the dollar and sterling areas, cemented by machinery for continuing consultation. The Americans also explicitly embraced the maintenance of employment and international trade as desirable objectives. The result, the British believed, was an 'Anglo-American accommodation', an economic counterpart to Bevin's American-guaranteed Atlantic pact.[21]

While the Foreign Secretary stayed on in Washington, Cripps returned by air on 16 September. The Cabinet assembled in secret session (arriving in various disguises) in the early evening of the next day to listen to a thin and drawn Chancellor give his account of the talks. Most of the meeting was taken up with rewording the proposed broadcast, removing any impression that devaluation was being done under American duress or as a result of the activities of currency speculators. Of other governments, only the Americans and the main Commonwealth countries had already been informed of the change of parity. The French were given twenty-four hours' notice.

As a courtesy, Cripps saw Churchill and Eden on the afternoon of 18 August. Retaining his composure, he told them of the impending move. Churchill wept, warmly recalled their wartime comradeship, and declared England was lucky to have leaders with the bravery to take such a decision, however unpalatable; he hoped to God if he had been in the same position he would have had the strength to do likewise. In the doorway, he turned back, adding 'But I shall make the utmost political capital out of it.'[22]

That evening the Chancellor addressed the nation. He had, he told listeners, just got back from the United States, having disclosed to the Americans a number of decisions. One was 'to reduce the dollar exchange value of the pound sterling'. Why was he taking a step contrary to what he had said in July? He cited two reasons. The first was loss of confidence in sterling and a consequent fall in the gold and dollar reserves, which had somehow to be stopped (a devaluation to $2.80 to the pound instantly wrote up the reserves by 42 per cent). The second was the effect this ebbing of confidence had on the UK's ability to earn dollars, hamstrung by overseas buyers going on 'strike'. It had been his policy to reduce costs and prices by expanding production, but the reserves were so low the government did not have enough time. 'Events have moved too fast.' The changed rate need not mean a rise in the cost of living. Wages and salaries would be unaffected, providing groups of workers did not attempt to improve their relative position. The only risk was of 'profiteering', which would nullify the change. Devaluation – a word omitted from the broadcast – was the 'most serious' step the government could take to solve an 'otherwise insoluble' problem: a step which protected the stability of sterling while avoiding heavy unemployment or an attack on the social services, a one-off opportunity to redouble their efforts and become self-supporting by the time Marshall Aid ended.

Despite what Plowden and Hall had recommended, he did not admit that devaluation was a setback. 'Bevin had told him never to apologise for your actions as a minister.'[23] To some extent he was shielded by Attlee, who let it be known that the decision to devalue had been taken while Cripps was away and could not subsequently be gone back on. Plowden, nevertheless, was in no doubt the Chancellor was left with 'a great sense of frustration and personal humiliation'.

The next day, a Monday, the Stock Exchange and the banks were closed by royal proclamation. Cripps held a press conference, accompanied by Wilson, Jay and Strachey. With 'superb skill and good humour',[24] he responded to dozens of questions, being even more than usually 'arrogant' in Einzig's view. He refused to accept the term 'devaluation' – the *Daily Herald* talked of 'revaluation' – and explained he had changed his mind only after coming back from Switzerland. He launched into a spirited justification of the Washington talks, claiming they would help towards the ultimate solution of the dollar shortage, the difficulty of which had been underestimated in 1945. 'We have been trying to deal with it by a series of temporary expedients which have led to a series of crises as each expedient has been exhausted. Now we have recognised that this is not enough.' The dollar and the pound were both world trading currencies; the stability of both was a precondition of world economic recovery. As to the domestic economy, there would be no cuts in defence or the social services. The general policy of the White Paper on incomes, costs and prices still held. Promotion of exports remained a priority – we 'have not completely lost our faith in private enterprise'.

His demeanour was not of a beaten man, but of a Chancellor proclaiming a victory. The *Manchester Guardian* remarked that:

> Anybody who imagines that Sir Stafford is betraying signs of embarrassment or guilt at having reversed his views on devaluation is wildly wrong. Those who have been seeing the Chancellor during the past few days have found his mood gay, almost jaunty. This may be due only to the relief that comes from making a hard and long-deferred decision. But it may be, too, that at last he sees a gleam of hope that one day, though yet far off, the dollar problem will be solved.[25]

Within hours, most other Sterling Area currencies had followed suit, devaluing by a similar amount (30 per cent) vis-à-vis the dollar. Some twenty-two countries realigned in all – reducing the effective devaluation of the pound to just under 10 per cent. The French, whose Finance Minister, Maurice Petsche, denounced the 'trade war rate' of $2.80, were particularly put out by British perfidy. An Italian paper ridiculed 'the congenital hypocrisy of the English puritan'.

British newspapers, with few exceptions, uniformly approved of the Chancellor's honourable dishonesty. He had told a 'necessary untruth', 'in no way unworthy of his office or of his own high reputation'.[26] He had uttered 'the lie politic', in the *Telegraph*'s opinion. W. J. Brown, directly linking the decision to the Chancellor's poor health, thought the divorcing of public professions and private preparations 'would have upset a stronger stomach than Sir Stafford's'.[27] The duty of all Chancellors, said the *Express*, was to sustain the currency 'by all and every means'. The *Mail* adopted a more pejorative tone, castigating

Cripps for having 'bamboozled' the country by asserting on at least nine occasions that he would 'never' devalue.[28] But the *Sunday Pictorial* captured the general view succinctly. 'Did Sir Stafford lie, both before and after his visit to America? The answer is "Yes". Could he have done otherwise and have still retained a clear conscience that he had done his duty? The answer is "No".'[29]

The tributes – Cripps disliked reading about himself in the papers at the best of times – were all double-edged. Parliament was unlikely to be so forgiving. At the request of the Opposition parties, the Cabinet consented to the recall of Parliament for a three-day inquest on the economic situation. An Opposition vote of no confidence in the government, or a vote censuring Cripps, was probable. The Chancellor's broadcast remarks about Tory calls for deflation were especially resented. Cripps and Bevan, deputed to speak in a general government debate for the first time since 1945, were inciting Attlee to meet the challenge by calling the election they had wanted in August. Devaluation must mean higher prices in the longer run. Cuts in spending would hit housebuilding. Above all, the trade unions had refused to publicly support devaluation, throwing the wage pause (just re-endorsed by the TUC) into confusion. The production ministers all still favoured an early election, but Cripps and Bevan had a further consideration – the disloyalty of officials. *Tribune* led with 'Let's Have an Election Now', denouncing top-ranking civil servants for recommending action opposed to the spirit of the government, manifested by the demand for cuts in the social services before the Washington talks. Bridges found the slight 'heartbreaking', and appealed to Cripps for a rebuttal. Cripps was 'disinclined to take any action'.[30]

Devaluation 'broke the halo' of the Chancellor's truth-telling.[31] Members of Parliament thronged the House to see him brought down to earth. Cripps, despite claims that his career was 'menaced, if not ended',[32] was far from considering his behaviour a resigning matter. Moving the government motion of approval, he took the House back twelve weeks to his statement of 6 July, when he had denied any intention of devaluing the pound – 'a completely accurate and deliberate statement' supported by the whole government. 'Even if we had then had some future intention of altering the exchange rate,' he added (looking up from his script), though in fact they had not, 'no responsible Minister could have done otherwise than deny such intention. To admit it would have been to have invited the speculators and profiteers to destroy our reserves.' On his return from Switzerland he had 'reviewed' the position with colleagues, as it became clear that 'adverse tendencies' were continuing, indeed worsening. Though the turnaround was rapid, the decline in overseas trade and the dollar drain, accentuated by a speculative assault on the pound, meant acting immediately. 'That could only be done by a reduction in the rate of exchange.' It was a matter for congratulation that there had not been any prior leakage.

He justified the new low rate, spoke of the co-operative spirit in Washington, and urged the country to persevere with the policy of restraint, without which the potential advantages of devaluation would be thrown away. The White Paper had to be strictly observed. Price controls would be 'rigorously administered'. Since lower income groups would be hardest hit, he exercised 'rough justice' by raising the tax on distributed profits. The government was to re-examine the whole field of expenditure, but food subsidies, defence and the social services were exempt. Other ministers had criticised the 'obscene plundering' and 'unpatriotic greed' of gold gamblers in the City. In spite of everything, he was still a believer in 'humanity', confident that people would forgo their own well-being for 'the greater good'.

Oliver Stanley, leading off for the Opposition, thought failure had turned the Chancellor's head. What had happened since July to make what was so repugnant then – devaluation – so imperative now? Could not the long, and expensive, interval between the decision and the actual announcement have been shortened? No Chancellor, he appreciated, 'could announce that he was going to devalue at some time in the future. To have done so would have courted complete disaster. The Chancellor of the Exchequer had no alternative but to deceive everybody, and he did it brilliantly but could not have liked doing it.'

Cripps rose to his feet, a 'baleful' expression on his face:

Will the Right Honourable Gentleman say when I deceived anybody?

MR STANLEY: I suppose the Chancellor assumes responsibility for the Treasury, who, when rumours arose only two days before devaluation, were asked by the press, said there had been no change in the Chancellor's policy.

SIR STAFFORD CRIPPS: I understand the person who answered the question did not know there had been any change.

MR STANLEY: Then I withdraw any suggestion that the Chancellor himself deceived us brilliantly. All he did was to allow those over whom he had authority to go on deceiving us brilliantly.

(Opposition cheers.)

The Chancellor's deception had not stopped, Stanley continued, as he had not come clean with the country about the effects of devaluation, the great mass of the public unlikely to be impressed by a government lurching from 'one temporary expedient after another'.

A succession of MPs opposite pressed the same point home. 'Probably for the first time in his life the Chancellor was deliberately dishonest with the nation. He hid the facts.' His 'Jesuitical' behaviour had done his office and himself untold harm. It was 'humbug' for the biggest-spending Chancellor in history to bluff the British people. The Deputy Speaker was puzzled that no one, on either side, raised any objection to the use of unparliamentary language.

The Conservative Party, emboldened by the course of the first day's debate, came forward with a motion of censure, charging the government with 'four years of financial mismanagement' culminating in devaluation, 'contrary to all the assurances given by the Chancellor of the Exchequer'. Churchill moved the motion himself, giving one of his liveliest speeches of the Parliament, overshadowed by reports that the Soviet Union had developed its own atomic bomb. Devaluation, he said, was a further and disastrous drawing on the lifeblood of Britain, carried out in the worst possible circumstances. This brought him, quickly, to a question 'much discussed in the country': the Chancellor's 'political honesty'.

How, people were asking, could a minister with all his knowledge and integrity turn completely around, 'like a squirrel in its cage' (he accompanied this by drawing circles with his hand), and do what he repeatedly said he would never do? It surprised him that the Chancellor had not felt he should not be the one to carry the opposite policy forward, now that he was 'woefully weakened in reputation'. The secret, however, had had to be kept, and he complimented both the Chancellor and the Foreign Secretary on 'the high art they displayed in the necessary process of deception' (great laughter). Although the Chancellor's personal honesty was not disputed, how would it be possible for anyone in future to accept with confidence any statements he made from the Treasury bench? He stood convicted of a lamentable lack of foresight. His usefulness, for all his abilities, had been impaired. ('No,' Cripps was heard to say, shaking his head.) Churchill, twisting the knife, found it hard to believe the Chancellor 'would have been content to stay in office if he thought his ordeal was likely to be a long one'. Speeches by Wilson and other Labour MPs, accusing Churchill and his party of helping to destroy world confidence in sterling by damaging questions and statements, did not carry the same flourish.

Cripps was mortified. Due to receive an honorary degree from Churchill, Chancellor of the University of Bristol, he wrote to the University to withdraw. 'In view of the Chancellor of Bristol University's observations about myself in the House of Commons last night it would obviously be impossibly embarrassing for him to have to confer a degree upon me next month.' Still acting closely with Bevan and feeling he could not 'go on' much longer, he stepped up the pressure on the Prime Minister to wind up the third and final day of debate by announcing a general election.

The Minister of Health, indulging in his irresistible sport of Tory-baiting, delivered an impassioned – and equally untechnical – retort to Churchill, mocking Churchill's own record as Chancellor (1925–9). The Labour benches were jubilant, Cripps slapping Bevan's back repeatedly after he had sat down. Attlee's winding-up was an anticlimax. Unhappy at having to do it, he defended Cripps from Churchill's 'bitter attack', insisting the Chancellor in July had been 'speaking the exact truth'. Unpatriotic comments did Britain harm abroad. The House dividing, the Opposition motion was defeated by 350 votes to 212. The government motion passed to a Tory abstention.

Why did Attlee spurn an election? Unsure of the Foreign Secretary's attitude, he was put off by the emotional state of the Chancellor, whose political astuteness he did not rate highly. The production ministers he dismissed as 'all the intellectuals'. Morrison, in the vanguard of the economy drive, blamed the Chancellor and the Minister of Health (because of the runaway cost of the Health Service) for the financial mayhem; they should be made to stay and clear it up.[33]

The Chancellor, showing no outward sign of distress, attended the annual Lord Mayor's Banquet, deriving satisfaction from the decision to devalue having caught people on the hop, though 'no one can suggest that it was a matter suddenly sprung upon an unsuspecting world'. Naming inflation as the greatest worry, he said economy measures would be settled upon 'soon'. The piles of correspondence in his postbag, much of it critical, registered his fall from grace.

On 4 October, Churchill wrote from Chartwell:

Dear Stafford,

I am sorry indeed that you feel my criticism of your political conduct should prevent you from accepting a degree from Bristol University, which it would have given me much pleasure to confer upon you.

If you will read the Official Report of what I said, you will see that your personal honour and private character were in no way impugned at any time by me. At the same time it is quite true that I consider your policy at the Exchequer in this crisis is open to criticism on public grounds. This would certainly not in my view make it embarrassing for us to meet together on an entirely non-Party occasion. We have done so frequently before, although our differences of outlook were extreme. If you feel that the darkening political scene in Britain renders it impossible for opponents to meet on non-Party occasions, I should regret it for many reasons.

Cripps sent a private and confidential letter in reply:

I have read through Hansard again and cannot agree with your version of your speech – nor is it consistent with a large number of letters that I have had from Conservatives and others upon the matter. The sentence starting at the bottom of Col. 167 and running on to the top of 168 ['like a squirrel in its cage'] is an accusation of lack of 'integrity'. The last sentence of the following paragraph accuses me of 'deception'. I am afraid I cannot personally separate what an individual says 'as Chancellor of the Exchequer' and as himself. If therefore I am called a liar it is of no consequence that it is hedged about by some fine distinctions!

This is not a question of political opponents meeting on non-party occasions – I do continuously meet my opponents most pleasantly and shall certainly not draw distinctions because of political views. Had you been in my own party it would not have made the slightest difference to my action.

It is merely the case that I do not wish to receive a degree or any other gift from a person who has publicly accused me of being 'void of integrity', 'a deceiver' and a liar.

'Dear Stafford,' Churchill responded on the 6th:

I have received your letter of October 5th. The sentence starting at the bottom of Column 167 and running on to the top of Column 168 is not an accusation of lack of integrity but of inconsistency. This is apparent from the next sentence, which contains the words '... however honest and necessary was his change of view...'

The word 'deception' is part of the phrase 'the necessary process of deception' and is preceded a few lines earlier by 'Of course we know that changes in currency cannot be announced beforehand. The secret had to be kept.' This is no more dishonest than what we all did so often in the war to guard the secrecy of military operations.

I have never accused you of being 'void of integrity', 'a deceiver' and 'a liar', as your last sentence states, and no such words were uttered or implied by me. In fact if anyone applied such terms to you I should be among the first to repudiate them.

I can only hope that you will reflect upon these matters in a calmer frame of mind.

Of course the charges which I made and adhere to against your financial administration and lack of foresight and lack of consistency, and the suggestion that your change of view might well have been accompanied by your resignation are serious. So also was your accusation against me, namely that I had pursued a policy 'which depended for its efficacy upon the massive extension of unemployment with the accompanying lowering of wage rates and so the impoverishment of the employed and the unemployed'. This seemed to me to be a very harsh statement, but as I was able to prove in the House that it was quite untrue, I did not let it rankle in my mind; nor should I have referred to it again but for this correspondence.

Since however, in view of my speech, you have taken the attitude you have chosen to do, you are quite right not to attend our function at Bristol University, much though we shall all regret your absence.

Dissatisfied, Cripps dispatched a final note on 7 October:

Dear Winston,

Thank you for your letter with the further explanation.

I will not prolong the argument. I can only judge the public interpretation put upon your statement (which is the important matter) by the reactions of the Press and the very numerous people who have spoken to me or written to me about it.

I am glad at any rate that we agree as to my action as regards the Bristol degree.

This exchange of letters[34] – unpublished until now – indicates how Churchill had so contrived to mix up two quite specific charges – the change of policy and the practising of deceit – as to call the Chancellor to account for dissembling. Such a charge, were it to be made to stick, would (with sterling still vulnerable) render Cripps powerless.

Other evidence bears out the Chancellor's anguish. 'Bevan said Cripps was in a very strained condition,' Dalton noted in his diary on 10 October. 'He now had a persecution mania, and was taking very hard charges of dishonourable conduct over devaluation.' Cripps lacked the thick skin or the aristocratic temperament needed in politics.[35] Jim Griffiths, the Minister of National Insurance, wrote (in 1969) that the Chancellor was to 'suffer agonies', and looked close to breaking down.[36] Cripps had had no real choice but to keep the secret, Jay averred. A Chancellor, even a Christian one – according to his private secretary, William Armstrong – cannot telegraph his punches.[37] First-hand witnesses all assumed it was having to do the deed which preyed on him. 'Devaluation was, in fact, quite unavoidable,' as Attlee later expressed it:

The pound was over-valued and we had extreme difficulty with the foreign exchange situation. I don't think anyone else could have done differently. But I am afraid Stafford did take it rather hard. He had a feeling that people were accusing him of something not quite honourable, particularly as he'd had to deny it right up to the last. He was rather a silly ass that way.[38]

Cripps's predicament has entered the collective memory of the House of Commons. In 1994, a minister in the John Major government, under questioning by a select committee, asserted that it was sometimes acceptable in exceptional circumstances to lie to Parliament, quoting the example of Cripps's denials of devaluation. A later Labour Chancellor than Cripps, James Callaghan, whom the minister also mentioned, had refused to 'do a Stafford Cripps' (i.e. mislead the House under oath), and demanded an apology.[39]

On the factual issue, the Chancellor, when he made his statement to the House on 6 July, had still been steadfastly opposed to devaluation. He was beginning, in the privacy of a Cabinet committee, to talk of it in the context of a 'wider settlement' with the United States, but construed in such a way that the Americans would have to pay to drag it out of him. At each stage thereafter – returning from Switzerland to meet at Chequers, just before putting the new policy to the Cabinet, even up to the moment when the *Mauretania* was anchoring in New York harbour – he accepted devaluation only with the greatest reluctance. Hence the exasperation of Hall and Plowden, that the Chancellor was far too unwell to think straight. He escaped with a single incriminating comment, to reporters in New York. It has been suggested that failure was too painful to own up to, even to himself.[40] This is doubtful. Cripps was indignant because, though conceding the need for disingenuousness, he did not believe that at any time he had in fact been guilty of it. He did not think he was in the wrong, and feared that further unjustified assaults on his character would undermine confidence in the new exchange rate.

A riddle remains. It is as if an essential piece is still missing. What?

Clues can be found in the correspondence with Churchill. Cripps complained about the press reaction to Churchill's comments, but the speech in fact received very little coverage, in comparison with the stinging discussion of the Chancellor's conduct the week beforehand. A remark of Churchill's about 'the darkening scene' was a reference to the Soviet explosion of an atomic device. Beaverbrook's *Daily Express*, in banner headlines the day before the debate, had announced that Britain was to make its own atomic bomb by producing plutonium. The same paper drew the inference from Churchill's speech that in order to 'bring Britain back to greatness' the Conservatives would 'free the pound' (let it float) and 'give Britain the bomb'.[41] Churchill had been briefed about British atomic research by Attlee in July. Bevin had stayed on in Washington to talk among other things about Anglo-American atomic collaboration. The possibility of Churchill (and Beaverbrook) throwing scruple aside and exposing the government's other 'deception' – concealed by the Treasury in the national accounts – was an unnerving one, especially for a Chancellor with moral qualms about a British atomic weapon.[42]

Gossip about the state of Cripps's health arose again in October, forcing him to release a statement saying stories of chronic insomnia were 'without foundation'. Isobel anxiously contacted friends, warning them of a pre-election campaign of personal vilification, 'in headlines "snippets", whispering and in every possible way',[43] accompanied by ironic reviews of an adulatory new biography of the Chancellor.[44] The public, the Central Office of Information found, were despondent – worried that the effect of devaluation on the cost of living had been understated. Following the announcement that there would be no autumn election (Cripps, Bevan and Wilson were in the minority), a weakened Chancellor was left to push through new spending cuts.

'Consequential' economies were needed to provide the leeway for taking advantage of devaluation by expanding exports; but they were also required to maintain intact the disinflationary Budget surplus, under threat from over-spending. Cripps had tied his hands by ruling out reducing spending on the three most glaring expenditure items: defence, the social services and food subsidies. A reduction of £300 million – with suggested ways to achieve this total – was recommended by Hall, annoying Dalton, who saw in it yet 'another flank attack by officials'. The Chancellor set himself an absolute minimum of £280 million in cuts; anything less and he would definitely resign. He was confronted, in committee and around the Cabinet table, by a flurry of counter-threats of resignation. Despite the Treasury *ukase* forbidding any Sup-plementary Estimates, Health Service spending was well over budget. Hall suggested a cut in housing and the introduction of charges for medical services. Bevan would not countenance either. Alexander gave way on a minor reduction in defence spending; with Bevin's stout support, he would not yield any further. The Treasury had its eyes on £30 million assigned to fertiliser subsidies. The Minister of Agriculture, Tom Williams, won a reprieve until February 1950. 'On this occasion, for the only time that I can recall, I saw signs of temper in Sir Stafford. He was a tired and sick man. I hope that his temper frayed because he had accepted unsound advice from his officials and not because of my opposition or stupidity.'[45]

Rather than resign or accept a lower figure, the Chancellor, in Hall's judge-ment, 'must win'. Cripps, according to Jay, was 'very messianic', refusing to 'appease' the trade unions and bewildered by the prospect of all his efforts as Chancellor going to waste.[46] Yet his predisposition for spending undercut his request for retrenchment. The desire not to give the Opposition what it wanted – another Labour government broken on the back of 'economy' – overcame ministerial obduracy. The Minister of Health accepted the principle of charging for prescriptions, little thinking it would ever be imposed,[47] hoping by this gesture to avoid a cut in new housebuilding. In the end he was made to agree to both. An extra £30 million was dragged out of the 'gorged' (Bevan's phrase) Ministry of Defence estimates.[48] The largest element was taken from projected capital investment, bringing total savings up to £270–280 million. The Bank of England at the same time was instructed to tighten credit policy. From the first, however, the Treasury had the greatest difficulty policing the reductions with unco-operative departments.

The other adjunct to the Washington talks was Britain's future association with the OEEC. The Foreign Office concluded from the new Anglo-American understanding that Britain would now be in a stronger position to stand apart from integrationist entanglements in Europe. The Americans still expected the UK to give encouragement to Western European union.[49] Britain itself, however, was not expected to participate fully. The UK's worldwide 'obligations', particularly to the Sterling Area, were re-emphasised. The devaluation crisis had demonstrated how much Britain relied on its Commonwealth and American connections.[50] The government was not to involve itself beyond the point at which it could, if it wished, safely withdraw.[51] On 1 November, the day after Hoffman had delivered a clarion call for a large single European market, Cripps issued a definitive statement of British intent to the OEEC Council, balancing the UK's role as banker to the Sterling Area with a categorical assurance that 'we are ready to help regional groupings within OEEC all we can'. Afterwards, Cripps put the UK's proposals for trade liberalisation before Hoffman. Responding to criticism, Bevin told Acheson and Robert Schuman, the French Foreign Minister, that the British electorate must not be forced to choose between the Commonwealth and Europe. The shock of devaluation had inflamed French distrust, and, although Monnet continued to make overtures to Hall about the symbolic swapping of British coal for French meat, Plowden was authorised to smother any idea of arrangements outside 'ordinary commercial exchanges'.[52] Before joining any linking up in an 'untried' customs union, Cripps told an American journalist, 'we need to see a good prospect that it will be a success, and in any event that it will not jeopardise the success of the Sterling Area'.[53]

The stability of sterling remained precarious. The reserves had increased in every week since devaluation. Exports had also gone up in October, though it was too early to establish whether this was because or in spite of their cheaper costs. But 'cheap sterling' transactions continued, casting doubt on the new parity. Some Tory MPs were troublesome. One, Robert Hudson, accused Cripps of manipulating the dollar market for electoral gain – an 'extraordinary' allegation which, Cripps told him, would be 'grossly improper'.[54] Cripps called in Churchill to point out the harm that his followers were inflicting, asserting that, whatever the outcome of the election, 'we – as a country – will stand or fall by the strength or weakness of our sterling currency'.[55] Churchill promised the Conservative Party would refrain from publicly discussing sterling until the results for the fourth quarter, in January. The press, principally *The Times* and the *Financial Times*, was contributing to 'nervousness'.[56] 'For the "Love of Mike"', Cripps had to caution John Edwards (Wilson's PPS), 'be careful on this topic – a word might do us millions of pounds worth of damage the position is so sensitive.'[57]

The 'remarkable restraint' of the trade unions was the key. At the time of devaluation, Cripps had favoured a six-month statutory wage, price and profits freeze. An early election might have given Labour a fresh mandate, disposing the unions to co-operate. In November, once this option was denied, the

Cabinet gave Cripps and Bevin the all-clear to approach the TUC General Council again. The General Council agreed to recommend a one-year extension of wage restraint, subject to the cost of living not increasing by more than 5 per cent. A TUC conference voted to accept, though by a much narrower margin than in 1949. The fear that the economy was likely to deteriorate throughout 1950 became a major factor in deciding when to dissolve Parliament. The Chancellor had already refused to have a pre-election Budget, lest he be upbraided for vote-catching.[58] On 7 December, when senior ministers met to decide on a date, he plainly stated he couldn't 'hold sterling beyond February'. Only Morrison wanted to wait until the summer.

Colleagues openly questioned whether Cripps was still directing operations. His plan for liberalising trade had never appealed to Jay. In early January, Gaitskell and Jay drafted a paper for the EPC arguing that economic controls were the distinguishing feature of socialist planning. Recognising inflation as an unavoidable accompaniment to full employment, they advocated the permanent retention of physical controls, rather than just budgetary measures, to counteract inflationary pressure. Cripps took it he was being snubbed. Others had to assure him that the paper was intended to prevent his officials from giving advice contrary to the government's aims.[59] Two weeks later, a group of Labour MPs published a pamphlet, *Keeping Left*, criticising the Treasury and the Bank of England for disloyalty. Bridges once again was disconcerted. 'I should like to assert very definitely and specifically', Cripps reprimanded one of the authors, 'that the policy in this matter has been definitely laid down by myself after full consideration and has been most faithfully carried out by my staff and the Bank of England.'[60] Cripps had once called the Bank 'my creature', but could not get the governor to comply with his directive on credit restriction. Bevan's staggering Supplementary Estimate of £90 million on the Health Service alarmed Cripps enough for him to worry that spending was 'out of control'.[61] With his OEEC duties thrown in, Attlee and Bevin both felt the Chancellor's burden was becoming too onerous for one man.[62]

It was a tribute to his will-power that Cripps, after preaching the virtues of controlling the human appetite at St Paul's Cathedral, was able to play a full part in the election campaign, right up to the eve of polling day on 23 February. He robustly defended his record as Chancellor and the five-year accomplishments of the Labour government, which had fulfilled all the promises made in 1945. Controls were necessary to direct policy so that people 'could not just do as they liked'. They were the essential concomitant of fair shares, doing away with the extremes of wealth and poverty. Austerity was popular. The country had recovered more rapidly from the war than any of its neighbours. Economic planning had pulled them through.[63] But he readily acknowledged the importance of Marshall Aid, which they hoped to dispense with by 1952.

The Chancellor's lack of candour was a central electioneering theme of the Opposition parties. Socialists had deceived the public by resorting to 'temporary expedients' like devaluation, 'squandering' the nation's resources. Cripps (said Churchill), his intellect 'precariously poised', had further egalitarianism in store. The Liberals charged him with hurrying into the election before voters began to 'feel the pinch'. Cripps denounced Churchill as a 'guttersnipe'.[64]

Most of the production ministers looked forward to Labour's re-election by an adequate majority. Cripps, expecting a vote of gratitude for the government from the British public, planned to retire from politics until he had made a full recovery. His new Bristol South-East seat, once the row with local party members had died down, was in no danger. The national result, however, was extremely close. Labour won a higher total vote than in 1945, but scraped home with a parliamentary majority of only six, diminished by Conservative tapping of suburban disillusionment with rationing.[65] The outcome, Cripps admitted to Rogers, was about as bad as it could be for the government – and for him personally.[66] Another election could not be long delayed. In the meantime, he would have to remain at his post. 'Edwin,' he told Plowden, 'I'm trapped.'[67]

HUSTLED

There is in every Chancellor of the Exchequer a Father Christmas struggling to get out, and this was very obvious in Stafford.

William Armstrong, Cripps's private secretary[1]

Attlee's bidding – 'we carry on' – went with the general Cabinet view that the new Labour administration, commanding such a bare majority, could not last longer than a few months. The Chancellor's third Budget was therefore fated to be a pre-election Budget after all, framed in the context of heightened demands from ministers and MPs for increased spending before Labour had to go to the country for a second time. Cripps 'felt isolated as almost all his colleagues could not understand why he needed such big surpluses and indeed did not understand modern Budgetary methods at all'.[2] He had the added help, however, of an understudy, Hugh Gaitskell, appointed Minister of State for Economic Affairs, the Treasury team – Cripps, Jay and Gaitskell – forming a phalanx of Wykehamists.

Budgetary policy continued to rest on a knife-edge judgement about the requisite amount of disinflation. The TUC had shown solidarity (weekly wage rates rose by only 2 per cent throughout 1949), but could make no guarantees about the future. Cripps's suggestion of a £50 million lump sum to share out in pay rises was rejected by Deakin.[3] The Budget Committee maintained that the economy was 'overloaded', singling out the Chancellor's over-lenient expenditure on the Health Service as a candidate for strong counter-measures. Bevan's Supplementary estimate on the Health Service had come in at £90 million. Cripps rescued the Minister of Health in the House on 14 March, but did so (Gaitskell had pressed him) by telling the Cabinet he still had charges in mind as the best way of keeping health spending below a financial ceiling. Bevan, threatening resignation, protested to Attlee about 'continual nibbling'.[4] Cripps found he could no longer quieten him. In a compromise brokered by Wilson, charges were again put off in exchange for the establishment of a Cabinet committee designed to monitor health spending and chaired by the Prime Minister. The ceiling for 1950–1 was fixed at £392 million, the Chancellor, after heated discussion, insisting there would be 'no excuse for exceeding the estimates in the coming twelve months'.[5] A lower ceiling for 1951–2, forcing Bevan to choose between cuts or charges, loomed. Otherwise, expenditure and revenue were largely unaltered. Though Hall estimated the inflationary gap at around £200 million, Jay thought it would be met by higher productivity. Even so, there was widespread Cabinet incomprehension about, in Lord Addison's words, 'extracting £600m a year from people, simply to prevent them spending it'.[6] The result was an aiming at overall fiscal balance, the doubling of petrol duty being compensated for by a reduction in the lower rates of income tax.[7] Heartening evidence of the fruits of devaluation – a recouping of all the reserves lost in the run-up to devaluing, coupled with higher dollar exports – pointed to a timely transformation of the external setting.

In his low-key Budget statement on 18 April, Cripps did two things. Denying that democratic planning had been all but abandoned, he described the annual financial Budget as 'the most powerful instrument for influencing economic policy which is available to the government', superseding – by implication – manpower or other physical controls. In place of central direction, he still cleaved to persuasion, seeming not to regard high taxation as coercive. The attainment of full employment without inflation spoke for itself.[8] He would have dearly loved – secondly – to relieve the tax load. The country had, however, adopted as much social spending as it could 'possibly afford'. Were he now to relax budgetary restraint by tax remissions, 'we should be like those bees, which seeing the honey stored in their hive for the winter, gave up their work and indulged themselves upon their apparent but much needed surplus, with fatal results in the ensuing cold weather'. The government must never forget 'that in our generosity it is not our money we are giving away, but that of somebody else'.

At the end of April, Cripps wrote to Attlee to serve notice of his retirement. 'Now that the Budget is over and through I feel that the time has come to let you know that I cannot continue very much longer at my job, and that I shall have to relinquish it by the end of this summer at the latest.'[9] It was an awkward moment. Gaitskell, without being assigned to a particular sphere of responsibility, had not yet won his spurs. He had, nonetheless, taken up a tougher stance than the Chancellor on several foreign economic issues, unsettling officials.

One of these was the OEEC. Cripps, still favouring trade liberalisation, dug in his heels when he saw just how far-reaching American proposals for the elimination of import restrictions and the creation of a European payments union actually were. They amounted to a 'fifty year programme', he averred.[10] When, in January, the ECA tied one-quarter of future ERP aid to progress on liberalisation, Cripps complained of 'dollar dictation'. Labour would not reshape its 'planned economy' to fall in with the freer economies of Western Europe.[11] Writing to Hoffman after the election to tell him (contrary to his plans) 'I'm still here', Cripps asked the Americans not to 'hustle' the UK into accepting a more integrated Europe.[12] Gaitskell, along with Jay, was even more wary than the Chancellor about prematurely discarding the country's economic defences against an American slump. The gold and dollar reserves were simply too unstable to run such risks. These clashes took the edge off what ministers had assumed to be the harmonious Washington accord of September 1949.

Quite imperceptibly, the initiative had passed to the Europeans.[13] Out of the blue on 9 May, with American foreknowledge, the French Foreign Minister, Robert Schuman, announced over the radio a plan to place French and German coal and steel production under a 'common authority', binding Germany to a Westernised orientation. Britain was invited to participate, but Monnet, originator of the plan, intended it to be a supranational concern with or without the UK (and its veto). Bevin and Cripps, at first sight, were worried that the idea displayed a 'regrettable tendency' to depart from the conception of an 'Atlantic community' in the direction of 'European federalism'.[14] Monnet came to London and spoke with Cripps on 15 May. Cripps heard him out, seeking clarification on a number of points. He asked him point blank whether France would proceed even in Britain's absence. Monnet said he hoped with all his heart Britain would join in, but if it did not they would press ahead regardless – being realists, the British would come in once they saw it was a success.[15] To Plowden's great surprise, Cripps dived in and agreed the UK should negotiate. Plowden had to interject that this was only the Chancellor's personal view. It is unlikely that Cripps was just 'letting his guest down lightly'.[16] At the EPC the next day, Cripps clearly put the burden of proof on the need for the Foreign Office to be satisfied about the political implications. Nobody was prepared, however, to commit Britain to the principle of Schuman's plan in advance of an investigation of its – hitherto obscure – details, which officials were instructed to pursue. As Hall explained to one of Monnet's party, ministers were held back by 'hazy fears'.[17]

Cripps, at the end of his tether, then left to stay at the home of Petsche, near Briançon in the French Alps. He had a brief conversation with waiting French journalists. 'I very much hope we will be associated [sic] with it [the Schuman plan],' he declared, 'for it is an excellent initiative for Europe. The thing is serious, and we must work without respite with France to arrive at a favourable result. From the economic point of view such a plan is completely desirable.'[18]

On 1 June, Schuman, cutting short any extensive examination of his 'piece of paper', put the British government on the spot by insisting on a firm decision either way by eight o'clock the following evening. The Cabinet – minus Attlee (also on holiday in France), Bevin (who was in hospital) and Cripps – rejected Schuman's ultimatum. Although the three most senior and centrally involved ministers were absent, the decision was perfectly consistent with the EPC ruling not to unconditionally commit the UK until the scheme had been fully elaborated – and indeed of the conclusions of January and October 1949 not to pass the point of no return. Britain, the Foreign Office maintained, had as yet neither accepted nor rejected the plan. Cripps, meeting Eric Roll (a member of the UK's OEEC delegation) in Briançon, expressed concern that the UK was being too 'mesmerised' by words.[19] He travelled up to Paris with Roll to discuss the European payments union, unofficially talking with Petsche about 'practical' Anglo-French alternatives to the Schuman plan – a plan about which Petsche had misgivings.[20] The Foreign Office, thinking it was far too soon to be making any counter-offer, was not pleased by his escapades. (Cripps told Dalton he had always found the Foreign Office 'difficult' to deal with.) The starkly anti-European sentiments of a Labour Party policy statement on 'European Unity', published on 13 June when he was back in London, also upset him.

Attlee opened and Cripps wound up the two-day debate in Parliament about the Schuman plan at the end of June. The Opposition reprimanded the government for not agreeing to participate, even if it turned out Britain might later have to withdraw. Cripps made a trenchant, largely economic, reply. Britain manufactured, in nationalised and about-to-be-nationalised undertakings, one-half of the coal and one-third of the steel of Western Europe. How could it agree to surrender control over these vital industries to a higher power that was 'responsible to nobody' to dispose of them as it wished? Cripps still hoped to table some counter-proposals, wanting to be in a position (he tried prompting Bevin) to 'help' Schuman and others 'if they indicate they would like our help'. But the British government had already agreed not to do so while the plan was under discussion, and in the end the right moment never came.[21]

Britain's rejection of the Schuman plan has been invested with a tragic quality by some historians. Bevin and Cripps were exhausted and infirm. Britain responded out of injured pride, instead of weighing up the alternatives. Britain stood aside, smugly (and wrongly) assuming the plan would never get off the ground. Had Cripps been Foreign Secretary – it is contended[22] – the outcome would have been wholly different. This is to exaggerate. The Cabinet was caught out, but the arguments against participating accorded with existing policy towards Europe. Ministerial differences were tactical, about whether British interests were best protected by taking part in any talks. Cripps, Gaitskell attests, was attracted by the idea of replacing Bevin at the Foreign Office, when it looked as if Bevin could not carry on.[23] The last thing he contemplated was 'pooling sovereignty' with Continental enthusiasts. He welcomed the advantages of greater efficiency, but his suspicion of private enterprise (a European cartel in iron and steel, closing British factories) was far too deeply rooted. He expressed this conviction at the Labour Party Executive's weekend seminar in

May, putting the stress on preserving Britain's national economic gains in a hostile environment.

> The theme of the [next election] programme should be the need to gain independence by 1952. But we must realise that there is nothing socialist about this. The Tories express the same desire. What is really essential is full employment. The problem is not solved. We are in danger all the time. The bases of our present planning methods are precariously holding the position, but the private sector is continually succeeding in jeopardising our whole economic recovery. It was private enterprise which forced the devaluation crisis.[24]

His defensiveness stemmed from an extreme anxiety to protect the home market and home employment which the government had worked so painfully to build up.[25]

The Schuman plan was quickly overtaken in British eyes, in any case, by the North Korean invasion of South Korea, and the headlong reinforcement of Western military security. In late July, Cripps recommended to the Cabinet a supplementary defence estimate of £100 million, subsequently extended into a four-year programme adding up to £3,400 million, to be partly covered by 'free' American dollars.[26] The sum was held to be the most the UK could manage without causing undue disruption to domestic recovery. Only one minister dissented – Bevan, objecting to the abandonment of defeating communism by social and economic example. Health Service expenditure, already on course for overspending in the new financial year, came under renewed scrutiny. Cripps and Gaitskell brought up again the issue of charges, this time on hospital stays. Bevan, roused by 'unjustifiable needling', ceased to attend the Chancellor's weekly dinners, their long 'personal association' marred, he felt, by Cripps's inability to appreciate how much the principle of a free Health Service meant to him. If charges were imposed, he made it clear, his resignation would 'automatically follow'.[27] About the growing rift between Bevan and Gaitskell, Cripps fatalistically 'shrugged his shoulders'.

While Gaitskell – who moved into the Chancellor's office – flew to the United States to haggle over the burden-sharing on defence, Cripps took off for a long summer break, largely at home in Gloucestershire, uncertain he would even return to the Treasury (he volunteered to have his salary docked). Then he went off to Switzerland. In early October, he wrote to Attlee informing him of the Bircher-Benner Klinik's opinion that 'unless I now go off for a prolonged rest I shall probably do irreparable harm to my health'.[28] Accordingly he proposed to resign from office and, in spite of the government's narrow majority, from the House of Commons. He was profoundly tired in mind and body. His back was troubling him. His teeth no longer fitted. When he briefly went back to the Treasury to tidy his desk, callers were shocked by his bony, skeletal appearance. 'They put up such superb reports', he said, passing his hand over the official papers in front of him, 'you have to read them two or three times to find the snags. And now I'm so weary I just want to accept what they say. When that happens it's time to go.'[29]

There remained the problem of his successor. At one time Cripps had leaned Bevan's way. Bevan may even have believed the Chancellorship had been promised to him.[30] However, the crucial loss of so much of the Labour Party's middle-class electoral support was – according to Cripps – Bevan's fault.[31] Differences over health spending severed their close relationship. Both Attlee and Cripps thought Gaitskell had been deputising well and should (at the early age of forty-four, and even though not yet a full member of the Cabinet) be given his chance. Bevin could not be spared, Attlee explained to the King, and the only other possible candidate was Wilson, 'but he is very young & I should prefer to leave him where he is'.[32] Fred Lee asked Cripps (in Switzerland) who would be taking over. 'I suppose it will be Hugh,' Cripps had sighed. Lee pressed him: 'I wonder how Nye [Bevan] will react to that?' Cripps paused, and then answered, 'I am much too tired to cope with that sort of problem, Fred – you younger people will have to see it through.'[33] Bevan's reaction was witnessed by Woodrow Wyatt. Bevan 'reddened furiously', leaving the room muttering it was all wrong.[34] The full-blown clash between Gaitskell (dismayed by the dearth of friendship at the top of politics) and Bevan over the 1951 Budget was just six months away.

On 19 October – he had cast his last vote in the House, on a Tory challenge to the nationalisation of road transport, the day before – Cripps announced his departure to a surprised Bristol South-East Labour Party, his resignation being accepted 'with sorrow' by the Executive Committee. 'My trouble is a tired heart. After twelve years I am just exhausted. I knew it was a danger a year ago, but I felt it necessary to keep on under the circumstances.'[35] At the same time an exchange of letters with the Prime Minister was released, Attlee emphasising how 'we are all indebted to you for the great work you have done'. On the 20th, the two companions had an hour and a half's conversation. 'In all the years I have known him it was the first time we ever talked frankly and openly to each other,' Cripps confided to Wyatt.[36]

He bowed out to a chorus of acclaim, to this day, the one and only post-war Chancellor to depart at the time of his own choosing and with his reputation still in one piece. The latest figures – the complete closing of the dollar gap for the first half of 1950, and the value of exports exceeding the value of imports for the first time since 1929 – capped his attainments. He was the man who had carried the biggest burden 'of any other Englishman in peacetime', 'his illness caused by having pushed his frail frame too hard and too long in the service of things he believes in'.[37] Bevin was the Labour government's greatest natural force, Cripps its outstanding intellect,[38] who 'made himself, or was made by circumstances, more than merely the Chancellor of the Exchequer',[39] the nation's 'Minister of Recovery'.[40] If devaluation was a black spot, it was because he was 'harshly judged by his own high standards'.[41] To Dalton's chagrin, Cripps was widely commended for banishing the 'horrors' of his predecessor. In fact, the *Observer* noted, Cripps conceded more on tax than he levied, the really decisive change in budgetary restraint coming towards the end of Dalton's stewardship. But it was his name and his habits – 'rising at four, walking at seven, eating garden roughage at eight, sticking at his desk until nightfall'[42] – that had become synonymous with austerity. The retirement of this 'gent' – this 'goose', a character of calculated complexity[43], his peculiar 'self-invented' quality all his own[44] – marked the ending of the Crippsian epoch.

On the same day, Cripps handed in his seals of office to George VI. Aside from his stalwart service, Cripps had done the royal family many kindnesses, including releasing extra coupons for Princess Elizabeth's wedding dress. The audience was hurtful. '[The King] just said goodbye and talked of nothing in particular. He didn't once thank me for all I had done for the country.'[45]

25

CHEERIO

Our hearts go out to the noble woman, his devoted wife, who through these long months of agony, mocked by false dawns, has been his greatest comfort on earth.

Churchill, in April 1952

Cripps, who had 'almost reached the limit allowed by nature',[1] journeyed back to Switzerland with Isobel in November. Using a tomograph, the Klinik eventually identified the cause of his back pain – the early stages of a painful tubercular infection of the spine, spondylitis, requiring prolonged rest and treatment. He was rendered immobile, encased in a plaster shell, and given a course of streptomycin. Part of the necessary cure was to cut him off from all newspapers, telephone calls and visitors. His son and daughters were the only regular guests. In January, after a complicating attack of pleurisy, he was transported 250 miles by a special hospital train to a sanatorium at Leysin, in the Swiss Alps, to benefit from the healing effects of the Alpine sun. By April, back in the Klinik in Zurich, there had been no improvement, and Isobel issued a sombre message revealing that the situation was 'serious' and that her husband did not have 'a great reserve of strength'. Of politics in Britain he knew little. Gaitskell's first Budget success 'pleased' him (this was before Bevan's resignation in protest at the imposition of health charges), but he was not told about the death of Bevin – the other pillar of the 1945 government – on 14 April, 'as it would be too great a shock for him'.[2] However, he did receive, among hundreds of letters, an inscribed copy of Churchill's latest volume of his war memoirs, dealing with Cripps's return from Russia in 1942.[3]

In early May, though free from his plaster casing, he and Isobel learned the shattering diagnosis that he was suffering from 'a rare and dangerous disease', 'incurable from the ordinary medical standpoint',[4] according to specialists in Lausanne – in truth a rare form of cancer of the bone marrow. He was too weak to be operated upon. His life was in danger. Mervyn Stockwood was sent for to administer the last rites of the dying, stooping over Cripps's bed to trace a cross in oil (oil blessed by the Archbishop of Canterbury) on his forehead.

Stockwood brought back to England last messages to some of Cripps's closest friends.

Miraculously, Cripps rallied. He was able to sit up, move around with the help of an iron corset and crutches, and even walk again unaided, tutored by an expert in the Alexander technique. He was persuaded to eat enough nourishing food to build up his strength. (Though deficient in protein, he would not agree to eat meat, having been upset to discover it in his meals in one hospital.) He went out for drives around the Swiss countryside. At the beginning of September, a special test indicated no traces of the former bone-marrow cancer. His condition was 'highly satisfactory'. 'Isn't it wonderful?' Isobel rejoiced.[5] 'There is a factor here which I do not understand,' Dr Dagmar Liechti commented.[6]

Eleven weeks after rising from his bed, 'all treatments [for his tubercular infection] completed',[7] they flew back to England on 5 October, the former Chancellor hollow-cheeked and snowy-haired, thanking everyone for their prayers for his well-being. Apart from going to vote at his local polling station, he took no part in the general election called by Attlee, confining himself to his 'Happy Valley' in Frith. Gaitskell called in late November:

> He has certainly had a most appalling experience. He has suffered from three grave illnesses at the same time: T.B. abscess in the spine; tumours in the stomach and a wasting bone disease. All these are said to have cleared up but left him appallingly weak. The Doctors in Lausanne, Isobel told me, gave him up for lost. But at Zurich they never gave up and somehow or other pulled him through. One gets no clear idea of how this happened, and I rather imagine that they both look on it as a kind of miracle.[8]

Cripps had already arranged – in October – to return to the Klinik for a check-up in the new year. His doctors, knowing the possibility of complete recovery was slight, hoped his familiar home surroundings would strengthen his will to resist. He had an inevitable relapse. Violent sweating began to disturb his sleeping again. With difficulty, on 3 January 1952 he was taken by stretcher to an aerodrome near to his home and flown to Switzerland by air ambulance. The pain returned, he could manage only small amounts of food at a time, and he was hardly able to speak, having to resolve (Isobel wrote) something 'deep within himself'. In spite of X-ray treatment, the cancer – which specialists established as a malignant disease of the endocrine system – spread slowly through his body, attacking surrounding tissue and settling in the liver and lungs. 'His heart and circulation are beginning to feel the strain as the disease spreads to various parts of the body,' Dr Liechti reported.

On the morning of 21 April, Cripps 'drifted into a state of deep and painless unconsciousness'. He improved in the afternoon, but 'passed peacefully away' that evening, three days short of his sixty-third birthday, Isobel at his side, the inspirer and director of Britain's post-war recovery finally belonging to history.

NOTES AND REFERENCES

PREFACE

1. M. Sissons and P. French, eds., *Age of Austerity, 1945–1951* (London, Hodder & Stoughton, 1963; Penguin, London, 1965).
2. *Sunday Telegraph*, 13 October 1963.
3. B. Pimlott, *Labour and the Left in the 1930s* (Cambridge University Press, Cambridge, 1977); G. Gorodetsky, *Stafford Cripps' Mission to Moscow, 1940–1942* (Cambridge University Press, Cambridge, 1984): R. J. Moore, *Churchill, Cripps and India, 1939–1945* (Clarendon, Oxford, 1979).
4. C. Bryant, *Stafford Cripps – the First Modern Chancellor* (Hodder & Stoughton, London, 1997).
5. Elizabeth Bowen, on Angus Calder's *The People's War*, in *The Spectator*, 20 September 1969.
6. Hugh Gaitskell, in *The Wykehamist*, 25 June 1952.

Chapter 1: DAD

1. Quotation from the *Memoir* of Theresa Cripps compiled by Alfred Cripps in 1893.
2. *The Times Literary Supplement*, 9 December 1949.
3. *Evening Post* (Bristol), 20 January 1949.
4. Georgie Meinertzhagen, one of Theresa's sisters, in a letter to Beatrice Potter, quoted in B. Caine, *Destined to be Wives – the Sisters of Beatrice Webb* (Clarendon, Oxford, 1986), p. 74.
5. An English Heritage plaque was unveiled at the house by Bishop Mervyn Stockwood, Michael Foot and Lord Longford on the centenary of Cripps's birth in 1989.
6. F. Cripps, *Life's a Gamble* (Odhams, London, 1957), p. 22.
7. The Parliamentary Bar is composed of barristers who deal with private-bill legislation, representing the private interests promoting or opposing particular bills. One of Alfred's brothers was a partner in Dyson & Co., a leading firm of parliamentary agents, and he was able to put a great deal of casework in Alfred's direction.
8. *Local Men of Mark* (South Bucks Standard, High Wycombe, 1891), pp. 84–5.
9. S. and B. Webb, *Indian Diary*, ed. N. G. Jayal (Oxford University Press, London, 1990), p. 71.
10. *Stroud News*, 26 May 1893.
11. *South Bucks Standard*, 2 June 1893.
12. The diphtheria bacterium was not fully understood until a series of pathbreaking experiments in 1888–90. An antitoxin did not come into general use until 1894. In the crucial interval, in 1892 and 1893, there was a particularly severe increase in London in the incidence of, and death from, diphtheria (C. Creighton, *A History of Epidemics in Britain: Vol. 2* (Frank Cass, London, 2nd edn, 1965), pp. 741–2).
13. Before their marriage, Theresa used to hold seances at Standish. After her own father's death in 1892, she wrote and

published a spiritualist pamphlet, *Message to Earth*, expressing her views on religion and her 'faith in the hope that shines beyond the grave'.

14. Quoted in E. Estorick, *Stafford Cripps – a Biography* (Heinemann, London, 1949), p. 30.

15. K. Courtney's diary, Vol. 27, entry dated 7 August 1893.

16. A. Cripps, *Memoir*.

17. J. Bowlby, *Child Care and the Growth of Love* (Penguin, London, 2nd edn, 1965), p. 192.

18. L. Iremonger, *The Fiery Chariot: A Study of British Prime Ministers and the Search for Love* (Secker & Warburg, London, 1970); H. Berrington, review article in *The British Journal of Political Science*, July 1974, pp. 345–69.

19. The familial interconnections and mutual values of the nineteenth-century 'intellectual aristocracy' – among them the Macaulays, Trevelyans, Potters and Crippses – were examined by Noel Annan in J. H. Plumb, ed., *Studies in Social History* (Longmans, London, 1955), pp. 243–87.

20. He told one biographer (Estorick) that if his mother had had a tracheotomy she would have lived, since Dr Cripps, Alfred's brother, was only a mile away on the day she died – apparently a mistaken view, although the delay in Dr Cripps's arriving from London testifies to the inaccessibility of Parmoor.

21. *The Times*, 22 June 1943.

22. W. Wyatt, *Daily Herald*, 31 October 1949.

23. F. Cripps, *Life's a Gamble*, p. 23.

24. See the comments quoted by Leonard and Ruth Cripps in Estorick, *Stafford Cripps*, pp. 32–3.

25. P. Strauss, *Cripps – Advocate and Rebel* (Gollancz, London, 1943), p. 24.

26. *Gloucestershire Journal*, 30 June 1945.

27. Strauss, *Cripps*, p. 24.

28. Leonard had gone to Radley earlier that same year. His 'one secret regret', his wife later wrote, 'was that he had not been sent to Winchester as were his brothers. Doubtless his father had his reasons; he may have thought that Stafford would have been too close on Leonard's heels' (B. Cripps, *Leonard Cripps* (privately published, 1960), p. 43).

29. Memoir by Lord Charnwood in H. M. Burge, *Discourses and Letters of H. M. Burge*, ed. Lord Charnwood (Chatto & Windus, London, 1930).

30. C. Dilke, *Dr Moberley's Mint-Mark: A Study of Winchester College* (Heinemann, London, 1965), especially Chapter 1.

31. It was a bad notion, for example, for a 'man' who had been in the school less than two years to use the verb 'think', or for one there less than four years to sport a speckled straw hat.

32. E. Estorick, in *Leader*, 17 September 1949.

33. Sir G. Schuster, *Private Work and Public Causes – a Personal Record 1881–1978* (D. Brown, Cowbridge, 1979), p. 5.

34. K. Muggeridge, *Beatrice Webb: A Life* (Secker & Warburg, London, 1967), p. 12.

35. W. B. Croft, in *The Wykehamist*, September 1905.

36. C. Cooke, *The Life of Richard Stafford Cripps* (Hodder & Stoughton, London, 1957), pp. 58–9.

37. Cripps to Kate Courtney, 15 May 1918 (Courtney papers). Courtney was fond of reciting Browning to his nieces on Beachy Head, 'sometimes in a howling gale' (M. Muggeridge, *The Green Stick* (Collins, Glasgow, 1972), p. 158).

38. Letter to Sir Alfred Egerton, 25 April 1948 (Egerton diary).

39. A. P. Herbert, *A. P. H. – His Life and Times* (Heinemann, London, 1970), p. 21.

40. The recommendation of the Royal Commission on Local Taxation, on which Sir Alfred had sat.

41. *Bucks Free Press*, 25 April 1952.

42. *The Wykehamist*, November 1908.

43. N. Annan, *Our Age – Portrait of a Generation* (Weidenfeld & Nicolson, London, 1990), pp. 43–4. The ideal training, as Annan remarks, for civil servants and proconsuls – and lawyers.

44. 'But I was becoming a Wykehamist. All that is conveyed by this word can be understood only by people who are Wykehamists' (Lord Grey, quoted in G. M. Trevelyan, *Grey of Fallodon* (Longmans, London, 1937), p. 12).

45. T. E. Hulme, *Speculations* (Routledge, London, 1949), pp. 50–1. Another authority places greater emphasis upon Cripps's 'idiosyncracy' rather than on any 'common conditioning' (A. F. Thompson, 'Winchester and the Labour Party – Three Gentlemanly Rebels', in R. Custance, ed., *Winchester College – Sixth-Centenary Essays* (Oxford University Press, London, 1982), p. 503).

46. Strauss, *Cripps*, p. 27.

47. Estorick, *Stafford Cripps*, p. 39.

48. See the obituary of Cripps in *Justice of the Peace and Local Government Review*, 3 May 1952.

49. Ramsay achieved the unique feat of finding a whole family of five rare inert gases – helium, argon, neon, krypton and xenon – which extended the periodic table of chemical elements and eventually led to developments in atomic theory. His chief dream, the unlocking of radioactivity, was the work of future scientists.

50. Ramsay papers, Vol. 14/2, letter of 2 February 1908.

51. *Picture Post*, 10 May 1952.

52. The Hon. Lady Egerton, *Sir Alfred Egerton FRS 1886–1959 – a Memoir with Papers* (privately published, London, 1963), p. 15.

53. B. Webb, *The Diary of Beatrice Webb: Vol. 3, 1905–1924*, ed. N. and J. MacKenzie (Virago, London, 1984), p. 131, entry dated 20 December 1909.

Cripps, in his youth, found Aunt Bo a rather forbidding figure.

54. Charles Alfred Cripps was knighted in 1908.

55. While a student at Oxford, Seddon used to have his laundry sent to Geneva.

56. *South Bucks Standard*, 7 September 1906.

57. An echo of Disraeli's claim, to have been locally 'bred if not born', at Wycombe in the 1820s.

58. L. J. Mayes, *The History of the Borough of High Wycombe – from 1880 to the Present Day* (Routledge & Kegan Paul, London, 1960), pp. 38–41.

59. *South Bucks Standard*, 28 January 1910.

60. Stafford had been in charge of the advertising side of the paper for the previous five years. He later told Estorick that he was 'almost entirely politically unconscious … neither aware of democracy nor of politics in any real sense' and participating in an election 'in the same way that I engaged in any other sport or social event'.

61. Estorick, *Stafford Cripps*, pp. 42–3.

62. See 'Mr Can – the Story of James Crossley Eno', in *Beecham's Group Journal*, winter 1961.

63. W. A. Campbell, 'James Crossley Eno', in D. J. Jeremy, ed., *The Dictionary of Business Biography: Vol. 2* (Butterworth, London, 1984), pp. 293–4.

64. *Middlesex and Buckinghamshire Advertiser*, 15 July 1911.

65. Sir M. Wheeler, *Still Digging* (Michael Joseph, London, 1955), pp. 30–1.

66. His UCL student record does not list a B.Sc., but does refer to an M.Sc., in chemistry – students took many different classes and subjects, and some combinations qualified them for a higher degree.

67. Probate Calendar in the Principal Registry of the Family Division, Somerset House.

68. A. Cripps, *Spice of Life* (privately printed, no date), pp. 18–19.

Chapter 2: A CHEMIST'S WAR

1. Quoted by E. Estorick in *Leader,* 1 October 1949.
2. Some put the figure even higher. Colin Cooke, with a sight of Sir Alfred's fee book, said that he was earning over £25,000 *a year* by the early 1900s.
3. Colefax had read natural science at Cambridge, and spoke German fluently. He was also a Conservative MP from January to December 1910, after which, at his wife's urging, he gave up any political ambition. (K. McLeod, *A Passion for Friendship – Sibyl Colefax and Her Circle* (Michael Joseph, London, 1991)).
4. T. H. O'Dell, *Inventions and Official Secrecy – a History of Secret Patents in the United Kingdom* (Clarendon, Oxford, 1994), p. 69.
5. *Bowden Wire Ld v. Bowden Brake Company Ld,* in June 1913, in a dispute over the Bowden control mechanism for motorcycles. The case was lost.
6. V. Bonham Carter, *Winston Churchill as I Knew Him* (Eyre & Spottiswoode, London, 1965), p. 208.
7. Sir Alfred would not touch the £400 salary for MPs, introduced in 1913, arguing that a man should sit in the House out of 'public duty', without 'the private factor' entering into it.
8. Earl of Crawford, *The Crawford Papers* (Manchester University Press, Manchester, 1984), entry dated 7 November 1940.
9. *South Bucks Standard,* 8 January 1914.
10. F. Cripps, *Life's a Gamble* (Odhams, London, 1957), p. 96.
11. G. Greenwood, in *The Millgate,* December 1931, pp. 131–2.
12. Some 40 per cent of those volunteering in the opening months of the war were rejected on health grounds (B. Waites, *A Class Society at War – England 1914–18* (Berg, Leamington Spa, 1987), p. 188).
13. British Red Cross Society, *Reports by the Joint War Committee, 1914–1919* (British Red Cross Society, 1921), p. 287. Cripps was subsequently awarded the 1914 Star, the first campaign medal of the Great War, which was given to those who had served in France between August and November 1914.
14. K. Courtney's diary, Vol. 36, entry dated 8 January 1915.
15. *History of the Ministry of Munitions: Vol. 1, Industrial Mobilisation 1914–1915* (HMSO, London, 1921).
16. H. F. Moulton, *The Life of Lord Moulton* (Nisbet & Co, London, 1922).
17. Ramsay attributed German barbarism to a very high incidence of syphilis among Germans (L. Badash, 'British and American Views of the German Menace in World War One', *Notes and Records of the Royal Society,* Vol. 34 (1979), pp. 91–121).
18. G. Hartcup, *The War of Invention – Scientific Developments, 1914–18* (Brassey's, London, 1988), p. 44.
19. The following details come from Cripps's personal Ministry of Munitions file (MUN 7/8), far-sightedly preserved at the Public Record Office.
20. The factory was visited by a Ministry of Munitions inspector in December 1916 (for which see the report in MUN 5/158, 1122.7/2).
21. Quotation from *H. M. Factory Queen's Ferry – Its History and Development from May 1915 to November 1919* (Queen's Ferry, no date).
22. Corbett to Henriques (both of the Explosives Supply Department of the Ministry of Munitions), 4 May 1916 (MUN 7/8).
23. Henriques to Corbett, 6 May 1916 (MUN 7/8).
24. Waring to Corbett, 15 July 1916 (MUN 7/8).
25. *History of the Ministry of Munitions: Vol. 8, Control of Industrial Capacity and Equipment* (HMSO, London, 1922), p. 79.
26. Medical report by R. Streatfield, 30 August 1917 (MUN 7/8).

27. S. C. Truelove, 'Ulcerative colitis', in D. Weatherall, J. Ledingham and D. Warrell, eds., *The Oxford Textbook of Medicine* (Oxford University Press, Oxford, 2nd edn, 1987), pp. 12.126–32.

28. Cripps to the Staff Bureau of the Board of Agriculture, 28 September 1917 (MUN 7/8).

29. Weaver to Corbett, 20 October 1917 (MUN 7/8).

30. Interview with Lionel Elvin, who recalls Cripps telling him this after he (Cripps) had faced a stormy public meeting in the 1930s.

31. Lord Parmoor, 'Do Well and Right and Let the World Sink', University College, London, Union Society Oration (March 1915).

32. Lord Parmoor to Lord Courtney, 7 October 1916 (Courtney papers, Vol. 143).

33. Note to the second edition of M. Hobhouse, *I Appeal Unto Caesar* (1917), p. xvi.

34. Lord Parmoor, 'Lord Lansdowne and the League of Nations', *Contemporary Review*, January 1918, pp. 8–13.

35. G. R. Crosby, *Disarmament and Peace in British Politics 1914–1919* (Harvard University Press, Cambridge, Mass., 1957), pp. 65–6.

36. The Hon. Lady Egerton, *Sir Alfred Egerton FRS 1886–1959 – a Memoir with Papers* (privately published, London, 1963), p. 26.

37. Lord Parmoor, 'Force and Christian Ethics', in *Contemporary Review*, December 1920, pp. 809–15.

38. Lord Parmoor, letter to *The Times* on 'Distress in Europe', 7 February 1919.

39. Cripps to Lady Courtney, 15 May 1918 (Courtney papers, Vol. 12, No. 41).

40. P. Strauss, *Cripps – Advocate and Rebel* (Gollancz, London, 1943), p. 35.

41. Cripps to Lady Courtney, 1 December 1918 (Courtney papers, Vol. 12, No. 143).

Chapter 3 : HOLY TRINITY

1. The Queensferry plant was closed down and its equipment sold off at war's end.

2. *Illustrated Official Journal (Patents)*, Reports of Patent, Design, and Trade Mark Cases, 25 February 1920, pp. 1–7.

3. *Financial Times*, 16 February 1920.

4. '. . . all this mystification about the component parts of "Eno's Fruit Salts" is somewhat ridiculous. The formula is 53% bicarbonate of sodium and the rest tartaric acid,' a Foreign Office official noted unsympathetically in February 1920 (PRO/FO 371/4475).

5. Sir L. Weaver, 'A Victorian Apostle of Health', in *A Birthday and Some Memories 1868–1928* (J. C. Eno Ltd, London, 1928), p. 25.

6. G. Lazell, *From Pills to Penicillin – the Beecham Story* (Heinemann, London, 1975), pp. 93–4.

7. *Illustrated Official Journal (Patents)*, Reports of Patent, Design, and Trade Mark Cases, 24 August 1921, pp. 277–94.

8. *The Times*, 10 August 1920.

9. The Hon. Richard Stafford Cripps, Certificate of Candidate for Ballot, 21 June 1922 (The Library, The Athenaeum).

10. Arbitration Proceedings, Eastern Pamphlet No. 232 (Colonial Office Library).

11. *Truth*, 29 November 1922 and 24 January 1923.

12. Viscount Maugham, *At the End of the Day* (Heinemann, London, 1954), p. 74.

13. Eighteenth day of proceedings, 15 July 1924, p. 858 (PRO CO717/37).

14. Summons for a Special Case, High Court, Chancery Division, ninth day, 1 July 1925, p. 403 (PRO CO717/45).

15. *Morning Post*, 2 December 1925.

16. Maugham, *At the End of the Day*, pp. 14–15.

17. Leonard Cripps, in *Sunday Dispatch*, 10 April 1949.

18. *Railway Gazette*, 30 May 1924.

19. LCC minutes, 6 February 1923, p. 134.

20. Proceedings of the Railway Rates Tribunal, fifth day, 5 March 1923, p. 143.

21. W. A. Robson, *Justice and Administrative Law – a Study of the British Constitution* (Macmillan, London, 1928), p. 100.

22. Proceedings of the Railway Rates Tribunal, minutes of evidence, 14 January 1926, pp. 987–8.

23. The Trade and Engineering Supplement of *The Times*, 26 February 1926.

24. *Daily Telegraph* (Derby), 24 October 1930.

25. LCC minutes, 26 July 1927, p. 253.

26. G. Rentoul, *This is My Case* (Hutchinson, London, 1944), p. 46.

27. Cripps to Kennie (?), 13 February 1926 (Cripps papers, 590).

28. Sir Lionel Heald, in *Picture Post*, 10 May 1952.

29. E. Plowden, *An Industrialist in the Treasury* (Deutsch, London, 1989), p. 20.

30. Lord Radcliffe, quoted in Lord Birkenhead's *Walter Monckton* (Weidenfeld & Nicolson, London, 1969), p. 76.

31. R. Stevens, *Law and Politics – the House of Lords as a Judicial Body* (Weidenfeld & Nicolson, London, 1979), pp. 184–185 and Part 2.

32. G. Swinford, *History of Filkins* (privately published, 1958). Swinford was the mason, carpenter and builder employed by Cripps at Goodfellows.

33. *Witney Gazette*, 31 January 1920.

34. John Cripps, reported in *Daily Express*, 17 February 1950.

35. C. Williams Ellis, *Sir Lawrence Weaver* (Bles, London, 1933), p. 83.

36. F. Tyler, *Cripps – a Portrait and a Prospect* (Harrap, London, 1942), p. 12.

37. J. W. Robertson Scott, *'We' and Me* (W. H. Allen, London, 1956), p. 191.

38. Comment by Burge, quoted in H. M. Burge, *Discourses and Letters of H. M. Burge*, ed. Lord Charnwood (Chatto & Windus, London, 1930), p. 292.

39. *The Times*, 16 August 1922.

40. Cripps, 'In Memoriam: Hubert Murray Burge', in *Goodwill*, July 1925, p. 2.

41. Cripps, in *Goodwill*, November 1922, p. 235.

42. From Burge's 'Christians and the Peace of the World', in *Contemporary Review*, July 1923.

43. Cripps, quoted in *Witney Gazette*, 1 December 1922.

44. Burge to Elizabeth Haldane, 22 December 1923 (Haldane papers).

45. Burge to Cripps, 26 November 1922, quoted in E. Estorick, *Stafford Cripps – a Biography* (Heinemann, London, 1949), p. 67.

46. H. Gaitskell, *The Diary of Hugh Gaitskell 1945–1956*, ed. P. M. Williams (Cape, London, 1983), p. 94n.

47. 2nd Lord Parmoor, *Parmoor and the Cripps Family* (privately published, no date), p. 15.

48. [1st] Lord Parmoor, *A Retrospect* (Heinemann, London, 1936), pp. 193–4.

49. Burge to Elizabeth Haldane, 15 January 1924 (Haldane papers, 6028).

50. Estorick, *Stafford Cripps*, p. 71.

51. The Attorney-General had intended prosecuting J. R. Campbell, editor of the *Worker's Weekly*, for incitement to mutiny, but then withdrew the prosecution amid accusations of political interference.

52. L. Chester, S. Fay and H. Young, *The Zinoviev Letter* (Heinemann, London, 1967), p. 141. The letter, purportedly written by Gregory Zinoviev, president of the (Communist) Third International, called for the stirring up of the British proletariat and the secret creation of Communist cells in the British armed forces. The original of the letter never came to light.

53. *Church of England Newspaper*, 10 April 1925; *Manchester Guardian*, 10 July 1925. Parmoor hoped there was no truth in the story, adding that 'no attack was made on the religious life of the community by the Labour Party'.

54. Cripps, 'In Memoriam: Hubert Murray Burge', in *Goodwill*, July 1925, pp. 2–4.
55. Obituary in *Manchester Guardian*, 12 June 1925.
56. Lionel Heald, who worked in Cripps's chambers from 1922 to 1929, in *Picture Post*, 10 May 1952.
57. Foreword to *The Alliance*, midsummer 1926.
58. R. Ingrams, *God's Apology – a Chronicle of Three Friends* (Deutsch, London, 1977), p. 15.
59. Cripps to George Bell (the Dean of Canterbury), 16 May 1927 (Bell papers, 196/241–2).
60. [1st] Lord Parmoor, 'Geneva and League Policy', in *Contemporary Review*, September 1927, pp. 422–30.
61. *The Times*, 25 November 1927.
62. Viscount Cecil, *A Great Experiment – an Autobiography* (Cape, London, 1941), pp. 158–9.
63. C. Norwood, *Christian World*, 26 May 1927.
64. Interview with Barbara Drake (Estorick papers).

Chapter 4 : GOING OVER

1. H. M. Burge, *Discourses and Letters of H. M. Burge*, ed. Lord Charnwood (Chatto & Windus, London, 1930), p. 44.
2. 'The Naphthol AS Case' (ICHO/H15/0158(i), ICI archive).
3. Quoted in W. J. Reader, *Imperial Chemical Industries, Vol. 2* (Oxford University Press, London, 1975), p. 190.
4. P. Strauss, *Cripps – Advocate and Rebel* (Gollancz, London, 1943), p. 42.
5. Quoted by G. Greenwood, in *The Millgate*, December 1931, p. 134.
6. H. Morrison, *An Autobiography* (Odhams, London, 1960), pp. 114–15.
7. H. Laski, *Daily Herald*, 17 January 1931.
8. Interview with Pritt (Morrison papers, Donoughue and Jones archive).
9. Sir P. Hastings, 'Sir Stafford Cripps', radio broadcast on 25 March 1942 (BBC Written Archives Centre), p. 2.
10. 'William Allen Jowitt', in E. T. Williams and C. S. Nichols, eds., *The Dictionary of National Biography 1961–1970* (Oxford University Press, Oxford, 1981), p. 562.
11. J. C. Eno Company Return, June 1928 (Company No. 163774, Companies House).
12. *Sunday Express*, 12 June 1949.
13. In an unsigned contribution in *The Countryman*, July 1929, p. 280.
14. Morrison, *An Autobiography*, p. 115.
15. Morrison to Cripps, 1 May 1929 (Cripps papers, 590).
16. D. N. Pritt, *The Autobiography of D. N. Pritt: Vol. 1, From Right to Left* (Lawrence & Wishart, London, 1965), p. 98.
17. M. Stockwood, 'Cripps – Statesman and Christian', in *Church of England Newspaper*, 3 November 1950.
18. Interview with Isobel Cripps, courtesy of Professor George Jones.
19. R. B. Stucke, ed., *Woolwich Labour Party – Fifty Years 1903–1953* (Woolwich, 1953).
20. Woolwich Labour Party minutes, 23 July 1929 (Reel 3, 1924–1931).
21. E. Estorick, *Stafford Cripps – a Biography* (Heinemann, London, 1949), p. 79.
22. *Kentish Independent*, 4 April 1930.
23. *The Times*, 26 October 1929.
24. Shepherd to Cripps, 5 November 1929 (Cripps papers, 590).
25. Green to Bearfoot (*sic*), 21 November 1929 (Woolwich Labour Party archive). Will Crooks won a famous Labour victory in a by-election in Woolwich in 1903.
26. *Kentish Independent*, 3 January 1930.
27. *The Pioneer*, March 1930.
28. Quoted by G. Greenwood, in *The Millgate*, December 1931, p. 132.
29. *Daily Express*, 20 October 1950.
30. *Kentish Independent*, 6 June 1930.
31. Cripps to Barefoot, 10 January 1931 (Cripps papers, 712).
32. Melville to MacDonald, 6 October 1930

(MacDonald papers, PRO 30/69/676).

33. Pritt, *Autobiography: Vol. 1*, p. 27.

34. H. Montgomery Hyde, *Norman Birkett: The Life of Lord Birkett of Ulverston* (Hamish Hamilton, 1964), p. 270.

35. *News Chronicle*, 7 November 1935.

36. See page 74.

37. Duff to Stamfordham, 20 October 1930 (Royal Archives RA PS/GV/K 2283/6).

38. Macdonald to Morrison, 22 October 1930 (MacDonald papers, PRO 30/69/676).

39. Letters of congratulation (Cripps papers, 712).

40. C. Cooke, *The Life of Richard Stafford Cripps* (Hodder & Stoughton, London, 1957), p. 103. The Macmillan Committee on Finance and Industry had just been set up by the Chancellor of the Exchequer, Philip Snowden.

41. Bobler to Cripps, 4 November 1930 (Cripps papers, 712).

42. King George V's diary, entry dated 27 October 1930 (Royal Archives).

43. Unpublished autobiography of Herbert Rogers, agent of Bristol East Labour party, p. 64.

Chapter 5: BRISTOL EAST

1. B. Webb, *The Diary of Beatrice Webb: Vol. 4, 1924–1943*, ed. N. and J. MacKenzie (Virago, London, 1985), p. 235.

2. *Empire News*, 29 October 1930.

3. *Bristol Times*, 27 October 1930.

4. H. Laski, 'The Victor of Bristol', in *Daily Herald*, 17 January 1931.

5. J. Edwards, *The Law Officers of the Crown* (Sweet & Maxwell, London, 1964), p. 306, quoting comments by Cripps in a House of Commons debate in June 1937.

6. *Goodwill*, January 1931.

7. Dickinson to Cripps, 25 October 1930 (Cripps papers, 712).

8. L. Manning, *A Life for Education* (Gollancz, London, 1970), Chapter 7.

9. Minutes of the Special Executive Committee meeting, 13 December 1930 (BELP archive, 40488/M/3/2).

10. Minutes of the Special General Council meeting, 13 December 1930 (BELP archive, 40488/M/3/2).

11. E. Estorick, *Stafford Cripps – a Biography* (Heinemann, London, 1949), p. 82.

12. *Picture Post*, 10 May 1952.

13. *Bristol Labour Weekly*, 20 December 1930.

14. S. Bryher, *An Account of the Labour and Socialist Movement in Bristol* (Bristol Socialist Society, Bristol, 1931), Part 2.

15. B. Whitfield, *A Brief History of Bristol South-East Labour Party 1918–1950* (Bristol, 1979).

16. H. Tout, *The Standard of Living in Bristol* (University of Bristol, 1938), based on a social survey of 1937.

17. H. Rogers, 'How East Bristol Makes Members', *Labour Organiser*, May 1931, pp. 84–5.

18. Cripps to G. R. Shepherd, 20 January 1931 (Cripps papers, 578).

19. Jowitt to Cripps, undated (Cripps papers, 1263).

20. Parmoor to Cripps, 13 January 1931 (Cripps papers, 688).

21. F. Tyler, *Cripps – a Portrait and a Prospect* (Harrap, London, 1942), p. 18.

22. Cripps to MacDonald, 18 January 1931 (MacDonald papers, PRO 30/69/1176).

23. J. R. Clynes, *Memoirs* (Hutchinson, London, 1937), p. 256.

24. By-election notebook (Cripps papers, 689x).

25. *Western Daily Press*, 2 March 1931.

Chapter 6: 1931

1. W. A. Harriman and E. Abel, *Special Envoy to Churchill and Stalin 1941–1946* (Hutchinson, London, 1976), p. 95.

2. R. Boothby, in his obituary of Cripps in *News of the World*, 27 April 1952.

3. Sir H. Slessor, 'Changes in Legal Status', in *Sixty Years of Trade Unionism 1868–*

1928 (Trades Union Congress, London, 1928), p. 39.

4. Jowitt to Citrine and MacDonald, 2 December 1930 (TUC MSS. 292, 46. 52).

5. Some lawyers, including Sir John Simon, the leading Liberal, held the general strike to have been illegal *at the time* (Sir J. Simon, *Three Speeches on the General Strike* (Macmillan, London, 1926)).

6. TUC General Council minutes, 20/15, 28 January 1931.

7. *Daily Herald*, 29 January 1931.

8. *Daily Telegraph*, 29 January 1931.

9. R. Macdonald's diary, entry dated 28 January 1931 (PRO 30/69/1753).

10. *The Times*, 2 February 1931.

11. *The Times*, 3, 4, 5 and 6 February 1931.

12. *Morning Post*, 6 February 1931.

13. TUC Trade Union Bill Sub-Committee minutes, 25 February 1931.

14. Cripps was unable to make a donation to the Fabian Society in 1931 because the drop in his earnings, combined with higher taxation, 'more than wipes out everything I earn' (Cripps to F. W. Galton (secretary of the Fabian Society), 10 June 1931 (Fabian Society records, A7/1).

15. Easton Lodge meeting on the reform of Parliament, 21 March 1931 (SSIP papers, J2/3).

16. B. Webb's unpublished diary, 8 March 1931.

17. Both recalled in *Recorder*, 20 November 1948.

18. PRO T172/1149.

19. P. J. Grigg, *Prejudice and Judgment* (Cape, London, 1948), p. 247. Grigg was the then chairman of the Inland Revenue.

20. Ibid., p. 250.

21. Snowden to Cripps, 30 April 1931 (PRO T172/1449).

22. F. Pethick-Lawrence, *Fate Has Been Kind* (Hutchinson, London, 1943), pp. 159–61.

23. *New Statesman*, 23 May 1931.

24. Wedgwood to Snowden, undated but 11 June 1931 (PRO T172/1449).

25. *Christian World*, 14 May 1931 (written by Joe Johnstone, prominent parliamentary correspondent of the *Yorkshire Post*).

26. *Evening World* (Bristol), 12 June 1931.

27. MacDonald papers, PRO 30/69/259.

28. MacDonald to Snowden, 12 June 1931 (PRO 30/69/1311).

29. Note by Cripps in the Samuel papers, A/76/1–2.

30. R. MacDonald's diary, entry dated 16 June 1931 (PRO 30/69/1753).

31. MacDonald to Snowden, 16 June 1931 (PRO 30/69/1311).

32. D. Marquand, *Ramsey MacDonald* (Cape, London, 1977), p. 601.

33. C. Cross, *Philip Snowden* (Barrie & Rockliff, London, 1966), p. 272.

34. *Daily Herald*, 29 June 1931.

35. *The Times*, 21 July 1931.

36. Chaired by Sir George May, the Committee had been set up in March, charged with recommending 'forthwith all possible reductions in National Expenditure'.

37. *Evening World* (Bristol), 26 August 1931; *Evening Times* (Bristol), 26 August 1931.

38. M. Cole, *The Life of G. D. H. Cole* (Macmillan, London, 1971), p. 189.

39. From a letter quoted in T. N. Graham, *The Life of the Rt Hon. Willie Graham* (Hutchinson, London, 1948), p. 198.

40. K. Martin, *Editor – a Volume of Autobiography 1931–1945* (Hutchinson, London, 1968), p. 44.

41. Tweed to Miss Stevenson, 31 August 1931 (Lloyd George papers, HLRO Hist. Coll. 192, G 28/2/3).

42. S. Webb (Lord Passfield), 'What Happened in 1931: A Record', in *Political Quarterly*, January–March 1932; H. Nicolson, *King George the Fifth – His Life and Reign* (Constable, London, 1952), p. 458n; [1st] Lord Parmoor, *A Retrospect* (Heinemann, London, 1936), p. 312.

43. R. Bassett, *1931 – Political Crisis* (Macmillan, London, 1958), Appendix V; see also S. and B. Webb, *The Letters*

of Sidney and Beatrice Webb: Vol. 3,
Pilgrimage, 1912–47, ed. N. MacKenzie
(Cambridge University Press,
Cambridge, 1978), pp. 362–3.

44. *Sunday Times*, 4 October 1931.
45. B. Webb's unpublished diary, entry
    dated 10 October 1931.
46. K. Martin, *Harold Laski – a Biographical
    Memoir* (Cape, London, 1969), p. 77.
47. E. Bevin and G. D. H. Cole, *The Crisis –
    What it is, How it Arose, What to Do*
    (New Statesman, London, 1931), pp. 37–
    40.
48. *Daily Mail* (Hull), 9 October 1931.
49. *The Times*, 14 October 1931.
50. *Manchester Guardian*, 17 October 1931.
51. *Daily Mail*, 20 October 1931.
52. E. Ellis ('Your Father assured me your
    seat was quite safe') to Cripps, undated
    (Cripps papers, 600).
53. *Morning Post*, 20 October 1931.
54. Cripps to Adams, 12 October 1931
    (Cripps papers, 600).
55. *Evening Times* (Bristol), 20 October
    1931.
56. *Times and Mirror* (Bristol), 24 October
    1931.
57. Rogers to Cripps, 13 November 1931
    (Cripps papers, 603).
58. Cripps to Henderson, 29 October 1931
    (Cripps papers, 600).
59. Marley to Cripps, 31 October 1931
    (Cripps papers, 600).
60. Lawrence to Cripps, undated (Cripps
    papers, 600).
61. *New Statesman*, 31 October 1931.
62. G. R. Shepherd to Rogers, 17 November
    1931 (BELP archive, 39035/60). 'This
    [Post Office] scare, coupled with our
    own proposal for banking, the
    particulars of which we had not got over
    to the electors, proved to be too much
    for those who have hitherto supported
    the Party without too many fixed
    principles.'
63. *Reynold's News*, 27 December 1931.
64. R. MacDonald's diary, entry dated 12
    November 1931 (PRO 30/69/1753).

Chapter 7 : RED SQUIRE

1. *Manchester Guardian*, 5 November 1934.
2. *Week-End Review*, 28 May 1932.
3. G. Lansbury, *British Weekly*, 5 October
   1933.
4. Cited in C. Cooke, *The Life of Richard
   Stafford Cripps* (Hodder & Stoughton,
   London, 1957), p. 147.
5. B. Webb's unpublished diary, 7 March
   1932.
6. Notes for speech of 3 March 1932 (Cripps
   papers, 516). The economist Silvio Gesell
   proposed that the money note issue
   should depreciate in value over a year by
   a fixed rate, robbing money-holders of
   the privilege of charging interest.
7. *Forward*, 26 June 1932.
8. V. Adams ['Watchman'], *Right
   Honourable Gentlemen* (Hamish
   Hamilton, London, 1939), pp. 202–3.
9. R. Postgate, *The Life of George Lansbury*
   (Longmans, London, 1951), p. 281.
10. H. Fyfe, *My Seven Selves* (Allen &
    Unwin, London, 1935), p. 243.
11. M. Reckitt, *As It Happened* (Dent,
    London, 1941), p. 125.
12. Cripps to E. A. Radice, 15 September
    1932 (SSIP papers, J4/3).
13. Cripps, in *New Statesman*, 3 September
    1932.
14. Cripps, in *New Clarion*, 13 August 1932.
15. M. A. Hamilton, *Arthur Henderson*
    (Heinemann, London, 1938), p. 419.
16. M. Cole, 'William Mellor' in J. Bellamy
    and J. Saville, eds., *The Dictionary of
    Labour Biography: Vol. 4* (Macmillan,
    London, 1977), p. 125.
17. H. Dalton, *The Fateful Years – Memoirs
    1931–1945* (Muller, London, 1957), p. 24.
18. Cripps to Pethick-Lawrence, 2
    November 1932 (Pethick-Lawrence
    papers, P-LS48).
19. *Daily Herald*, 21 November 1932.
20. Letter of 3 January 1933 (Cripps papers,
    570).
21. B. Webb's unpublished diary, entry
    dated 3 October 1932.
22. The League had seventy branches by

March 1932, made up of about 2000 members, but was mainly London-based and predominantly middle class (P. Seyd, 'Factionalism within the Labour Party: The Socialist League, 1932–1937', in A. Briggs and J. Saville, eds., *Essays in Labour History 1918–1939* (Croom Helm, London, 1977)).

23. *Left Review*, December 1934, p. 63.
24. 'Will Capitalism Crash?', *New Leader*, 18 March 1932.
25. A. Beattie, ed., *English Party Politics: Vol. 2* (Weidenfeld & Nicolson, London, 1970), p. 237.
26. S. Cripps, *Can Socialism Come by Constitutional Means?* (Socialist League, 1934), p. 14.
27. Bevin to Lansbury, 8 March 1933 (Lansbury papers, Vol. 28).
28. *Daily Herald*, 12 April 1933.
29. *Daily Express*, 8 May 1933.
30. A. Williams, *Labour and Russia – the Attitude of the Labour Party to the USSR, 1924–34* (Manchester University Press, Manchester, 1989), p. 151.
31. *Daily Herald*, 13 June 1932.
32. *New Clarion*, 25 March 1933.
33. Ibid., 1 April 1933.
34. Cripps to Strachey, 7 April 1933 (Cripps papers, 570).
35. Laski to Justice Holmes, 13 May 1933, in O. W. Holmes and H. Laski, *The Holmes-Laski Letters 1916–1935*, ed. M. de W. Howe (Oxford University Press, London, 1953), p. 1439.
36. S. Cripps, *Are You a Worker? Where the Middle Class Stands* (Socialist League, 1935).
37. Dalton, *The Fateful Years*, p. 42.
38. *The People*, 14 February 1954.
39. The *Manchester Guardian*, on 7 June 1933, had arrived at the same verdict, asserting that 'Sir Stafford Cripps, if he continues, is more likely to be the architect of a British Fascism, based on the fears of a frightened middle class, than Sir Oswald Mosley.'
40. Lord Citrine, *Men and Work – an Autobiography* (Hutchinson, London, 1964), pp. 293–301.
41. *The Times*, 28 August 1933.
42. C. Headlam, 'Labour and the Constitution', in *Quarterly Review*, April 1934, pp. 350–66.
43. *News Chronicle*, 31 August 1933.
44. *Daily Herald*, 11 September 1933.
45. B. Webb's unpublished diary, entry dated 2 June 1933.
46. Lansbury to J. Middleton, 22 November 1933 (Middleton papers, MID 56/68).
47. Cripps to K. Zilliacus, 20 November 1933 (Cripps papers, 515). Zilliacus had been carrying on a long correspondence with Cripps, and other Labour leaders, from his post with the League of Nations Secretariat.
48. Earlier in 1933, Cripps had successfully defended a certain Nguyen Ai Hoc, an alleged Soviet agent, from deportation from Hong Kong for 'plotting the destruction of a British Crown Colony'. Hoc later took the name Ho Chi Minh (W. Burchett, *North of the Seventeenth Parallel* (People's Publishing House, Delhi, 1956), pp. 17–18).
49. Attlee to Cripps, 30 December 1933 (Attlee papers, Countess Attlee).
50. Cripps to Attlee, 30 December 1933.
51. *Morning Post*, 5 January 1934.
52. *Daily Telegraph*, 8 January 1934.
53. R. Rhodes James, *Anthony Eden* (Weidenfeld & Nicolson, London, 1986), p. 130.
54. T. Nairn, *The Enchanted Glass – Britain and its Monarchy* (Radius, London, 1988), pp. 340–1.
55. 25 November 1933.
56. *Sunday Dispatch*, 28 January 1934.
57. Sir R. B. Lockhart, *The Diaries of Sir Robert Bruce Lockhart*, ed. K. Young (Macmillan, London, 1973), p. 284, entry dated 17 January 1934.
58. Cripps papers, 553.
59. R. Pound, *Their Moods and Mine* (Chapman & Hall, London, 1937).
60. T. Stannage, *Baldwin Thwarts the*

Opposition – the British General Election of 1935 (Croom Helm, London, 1980), p. 43.

61. Sunday Dispatch, 4 February 1934.

62. Isobel Cripps to Lansbury, 10 January 1934 (Lansbury papers, Vol. 15).

63. The Times, 15 January 1934.

64. Evening World (Bristol), 15 January 1934.

65. Ibid., 17 January 1934.

66. Rogers to Cripps, 17 January 1934 (BELP archive, 39035/74).

67. H. Dalton, The Political Diary of Hugh Dalton 1918–1940, 1945–1960, ed. B. Pimlott (Cape, London, 1986), pp. 181–2, entry dated 19 January 1934.

68. Isobel Cripps to Rogers, 22 January 1934 (BELP archive, 39035/74).

69. Evening World (Bristol), 27 January 1934.

70. Daily Herald, 29 January 1934.

71. Seyd, 'Factionalism within the Labour Party', p. 218.

72. B. Webb's unpublished diary, entry dated 3 May 1934.

73. Manchester Guardian, 17 September 1934.

74. Ibid., 3 October 1934.

75. Cripps to F. Hardie, 8 October 1934 (Hardie papers, C. 459).

76. 22 October 1934.

77. Cripps to Strachey, 16 October 1934 (Cripps papers, 553).

78. Shawcross, H., Life Sentence – the Memoirs of Hartley Shawcross (Constable, London, 1995), p. 31.

79. A. Horner, Incorrigible Rebel (MacGibbon & Kee, London, 1960), p. 144.

80. Morrison to Cripps, 15 November 1934 (Cripps papers, 1148).

81. Middleton to Lansbury, 7 January 1935 (Middleton papers, MID 46/65).

82. Daily Mail, 23 February 1935.

83. Dalton, Political Diary, p. 187, entry dated 13 February 1935.

84. R. Bassett, Democracy and Foreign Policy: A Case History – the Sino-Japanese Dispute 1931–1933 (Longmans, London, 1952), p. 545. In the relevant debate of February 1933, Cripps referred to economic sanctions against Japan as 'the last resort'.

85. Rogers to Cripps, 13 June 1935 (BELP archive, 39035/75).

86. I. Maisky, Memoirs of a Soviet Ambassador 1938–1943 (Hutchinson, London, 1967), p. 35.

87. Dalton, The Fateful Years, p. 66.

88. A. Bullock, The Life and Times of Ernest Bevin: Vol. 1, Trade Union Leader 1881–1940 (Heinemann, London, 1960), p. 562n.

89. News Chronicle, 16 September 1935.

90. The Times, 23 September 1935.

91. Dalton to Martin, 24 September 1935, printed in K. Martin, Editor – a Volume of Autobiography, 1931–1945 (Hutchinson, London, 1968), pp. 173–4.

92. Cripps to Martin, 25 September 1935 (Martin papers, SxMs11).

93. M. A. Hamilton, Remembering My Good Friends (Cape, London, 1944).

94. Postgate, The Life of George Lansbury, p. 303.

95. Labour Party Annual Conference Report 1935, p. 180.

96. Lionel Elvin, interview.

97. The People, 14 February 1954.

98. M. R. Gordon, Conflict and Consensus in Labour's Foreign Policy 1914–1965 (Harvard University Press, Cambridge, Mass., 1969), p. 25.

99. When Toby Weaver told Cripps he was taking up a post as a local education officer, at an annual salary of £400, Cripps said, 'I earned that much yesterday afternoon in refreshers.'

100. Sir A. Mackintosh, Echoes of Big Ben (Jarrold's, London, 1945), p. 133.

Chapter 8: REJECT

1. N. Davenport, Memoirs of a City Radical (Weidenfeld & Nicolson, London, 1974), p. 97.

2. *Oxford Times*, 6 December 1935.

3. *Daily Telegraph*, 30 November 1935. Also S. and B. Webb, *The Letters of Sidney and Beatrice Webb: Vol. 3, Pilgrimage, 1912–47*, ed. N. MacKenzie (Cambridge University Press, Cambridge, 1978), p. 401, letter dated 16 September 1934.

4. In December, Hoare agreed with Laval, the French Foreign Minister, to dismember Abyssinia in Italy's favour. Baldwin supported and then (in response to public clamour) disowned the pact, replacing Hoare with Eden. Sanctions against Italy were never imposed. The episode ended the League of Nations as an effective international institution. Attlee told Baldwin he had thrown away the people's (and Labour's) trust and 'will not get it again'.

5. N. Annan, *Our Age – Portrait of a Generation* (Weidenfeld & Nicolson, London, 1990), pp. 187–94.

6. J. Strachey, *The Strangled Cry* (Bodley Head, London, 1962), p. 218.

7. J. Lewis, *The Left Book Club* (Gollancz, London, 1970), p. 15.

8. B. Webb's unpublished diary, entry dated 2 February 1936.

9. Middleton to Murphy, 6 February 1936 (Labour Party archives, LP/SL/35/17).

10. J. T. Murphy, *New Horizons* (John Lane, London, 1940), p. 318.

11. *Forward*, 3 October 1936.

12. *News Chronicle*, 2 October 1936.

13. Quoted in K. Martin, *Harold Laski – a Biographical Memoir* (Cape, London, 1969), p. 98.

14. K. Harris, *Attlee* (Weidenfeld & Nicolson, London, 1982), p. 127.

15. *The Socialist*, November 1936.

16. *Daily Herald*, 23 November 1936.

17. Ibid., 21 November 1936.

18. *Manchester Guardian*, 19 November 1936.

19. Pritt to Cripps, 20 November 1936 (Cripps papers, 501).

20. *Morning Post*, 26 November 1936.

21. Cripps to Middleton, 26 November 1936 (Cripps papers, 501).

22. B. Inglis, *Abdication* (Hodder & Stoughton, London, 1966), p. 258.

23. *News Chronicle*, 7 December 1936.

24. M. Foot in E. Thomas (ed.), *Tribune 21* (Macdonald, London, 1958), p. 7.

25. J. Paton, *Left Turn! The Autobiography of John Paton* (Secker & Warburg, London, 1936), p. 427.

26. D. Blaazer, *The Popular Front and the Progressive Tradition* (Cambridge University Press, Cambridge, 1992), p. 171.

27. J. McNair, *James Maxton – the Beloved Rebel* (Allen & Unwin, London, 1955), pp. 262–3.

28. K. Morgan, *Harry Pollitt* (Manchester University Press, Manchester, 1993), p. 92.

29. 'Basis of Unity Campaign – Confidential' (Estorick archive).

30. B. Pimlott, *Labour and the Left in the 1930s* (Cambridge University Press, Cambridge, 1977).

31. Letter extract dated 13 December 1936 (Labour Party archives, LP/SL/35/29).

32. *The Tribune*, 1 January 1937.

33. *Party Loyalty – an Appeal to the Movement*, 12 January 1937.

34. Letter in *New Statesman*, 30 January 1937.

35. *Daily Herald*, 22 February 1937.

36. On one occasion Cripps, Brockway and Willie Gallagher of the CP were booked to address a unity rally in Southampton. They travelled down on the same train from Waterloo, but in separate compartments (R. Eatwell, 'The Cripps Expulsion – Sir Stafford Cripps and the Labour Party, 1937–1939' (unpublished typescripts 1972)).

37. A. Bullock, *The Life and Times of Ernest Bevin: Vol. 1, Trade Union Leader 1881–1940* (Heinemann, London, 1960), p. 596.

38. Rogers to Cripps, 26 February 1937 (Cripps papers, 515).

39. Cripps to Rogers, 6 March 1937 (Cripps papers, 514).

40. *The Tribune*, 12 March 1937.

41. The first Air Ministry production order for Supermarine to construct 310 Spitfires – to be completed by 1939 – was placed in June 1936.
42. *The Times*, 15 March 1937.
43. I. Colvin, *Vansittart in Office* (Gollancz, London, 1965), p. 134.
44. During the 1945 general election, a Conservative candidate said Cripps, before the war, 'went about telling aeroplane workers to down tools'. 'If it had come off', Cripps retorted, 'we might have avoided war altogether by allying with the Soviet Union.'
45. McNair, *James Maxton*, p. 264.
46. *News Chronicle*, 8 April and 10 April 1937.
47. *Daily Herald*, 26 April 1937.
48. *The Tribune*, 21 May 1937.
49. Cripps to Elvin, 9 June 1937 (Cripps papers, 514).
50. Both citations are taken from J. Jupp, *The Radical Left in Britain 1931–1941* (Cass, London, 1982), p. 224, n. 20.
51. Blaazer, *The Popular Front and the Progressive Tradition*, Chapter 6.
52. B. Webb's unpublished diary, entry dated 18 April 1937.
53. Foot in Thomas (ed.), *Tribune 21*, p. 7.
54. *The Tribune*, 24 September 1937.
55. Cripps to W. Cole, 28 July 1937 (Cripps papers, 503).
56. *The Times*, 7 October 1937.
57. *Manchester Guardian*, 8 October 1937.
58. A. J. P. Taylor, *The Troublemakers – Dissent over Foreign Policy 1792–1939* (Hamish Hamilton, London, 1957), p. 167.
59. *World Review of Reviews*, July 1936.
60. *Daily Herald*, 29 November 1937.
61. Ibid., 9 December 1937.
62. Ibid., 10 December 1937.
63. *Manchester Guardian*, 18 March 1938.
64. Ibid., 11 March 1938.
65. Cripps to Gollan, 15 March 1938 (Cripps papers, 543).
66. Pimlott, *Labour and the Left in the 1930s*, pp. 153–4.
67. *The Tribune*, 15 April 1938.
68. *Reynold's News*, 17 April 1938.
69. Martin, *Harold Laski*, p. 112.
70. Letter quoted in M. Jones, *Michael Foot* (Gollancz, London, 1994), pp. 62–3. *The Tribune* lost £13,000 in all in 1938.
71. B. Castle, *Fighting All the Way* (Macmillan, London, 1993), p. 87.
72. Foot to Cripps, undated (Cripps papers, 566).
73. *The Tribune*, 27 May 1938.
74. Brailsford to Foot, in M. Jones, *Michael Foot*, p. 62.
75. C. Cooke, *The Life of Richard Stafford Cripps* (Hodder & Stoughton, London, 1957), p. 227.
76. *The Times*, 6 October 1938.
77. *Manchester Guardian*, 31 October 1938.
78. H. Dalton, *The Fateful Years – Memoirs 1931–1945* (Muller, London, 1957), pp. 200–3.
79. R. Eatwell, 'Munich, Public Opinion and Popular Front', in *Journal of Contemporary History*, Vol. 6 (1971), p. 134.
80. Bartlett in the *News Chronicle*, 24 January 1942. See also his *And Now, Tomorrow* (Chatto & Windus, London, 1960), pp. 85–6.
81. *The Tribune*, 2 December 1938.
82. Cripps to G. Shepherd, 4 November 1938 (Cripps papers, 504).
83. Cripps to Kneeshaw, 6 December 1938 (Cripps papers, 507).
84. Kneeshaw to Cripps, 8 December 1938 (Cripps papers, 507).
85. Cripps to Kneeshaw, 9 December 1938 (Cripps papers, 507).
86. Dalton, *The Fateful Years*, p. 212.
87. D. N. Pritt, *The Autobiography of D. N. Pritt: Vol. 1, From Right to Left* (Lawrence & Wishart, London, 1965), pp. 103–5.
88. *Daily Telegraph*, 16 January 1939.
89. *Daily Herald*, 25 January 1939.
90. F. Williams, *Ernest Bevin* (Hutchinson, London, 1952), p. 211.
91. Cripps papers, 506.
92. B. Webb, *The Diary of Beatrice Webb: Vol. 4, 1924–1943*, ed. N. and J.

MacKenzie (Virago, London, 1985), pp. 430–1, entry dated 20 March 1939.

93. *Daily Herald*, 26 January 1939.

94. *Daily Mail*, 3 February 1939.

95. F. Cripps, *Evening Standard*, 30 May 1939.

96. *Daily Herald*, 18 January 1939.

97. *News Chronicle*, 1 February 1939.

98. Cripps to B. Drake, 20 March 1939 (Cripps papers, 566).

99. H. Dalton, *The Political Diary of Hugh Dalton 1918–1940, 1945–1960*, ed. B. Pimlott (Cape, London, 1986), p. 265.

100. *The Chronicle*, 25 February 1939.

101. *Forward*, 25 February 1939.

102. *New Statesman*, 11 March 1939.

103. *News Chronicle*, 13 March 1939.

104. Tweed to Lloyd George, 16 March 1939 (Lloyd George papers, HLRO Hist. Coll. 192, G/28/2/12).

105. M. Postan, in W. T. Rodgers, ed., *Hugh Gaitskell 1906–1963* (Thames and Hudson, London, 1964), p. 63.

106. *News Chronicle*, 27 February 1939.

107. E. Estorick, *Stafford Cripps – a Biography* (Heinemann, London, 1949), p. 166.

108. R. Acland, ed., *Why I am a Democrat – a Symposium* (Gollancz, London, 1939), p. 90.

109. J. Mahon, *Harry Pollitt – a Biography* (Lawrence & Wishart, London, 1976), pp. 235–6.

110. An argument advanced by R. Eatwell in his *The 1945–1951 Labour Governments* (Batsford, London, 1979), pp. 28–9.

111. *Law Journal*, 14 March 1942.

112. Eatwell, 'The Cripps Expulsion', p. 23.

113. *The Times*, 30 May 1939.

114. N. Mitchison, *You May Well Ask – a Memoir 1920–1940* (Gollancz, London, 1979), pp. 204–5.

115. *News Chronicle*, 12 June 1939.

116. Cripps to Brailsford, 5 June 1939 (Cripps papers, 510).

117. *Sunday Referee*, 4 June 1939.

118. Cripps to B. Webb, 23 June 1939 (Webb papers, PASSFIELD II/4/1).

119. Lord Swinton, *Sixty Years of Power* (Hutchinson, London, 1966), p. 123.

120. Chuter Ede's diary, entry dated 2 May 1942.

121. 'Watchman', *Right Honourable Gentlemen* (Hamish Hamilton, London, 1939), p. 203. 'Watchman' was the Tory backbencher Vyvyan Adams.

122. T. Willis, *Whatever Happened to Tom Mix?* (Cassell, London, 1970), p. 183.

123. E. Thurtle (Lansbury's son-in-law), *An Onlooker* (Chaterson, London, 1945), p. 127.

124. Acland, ed., *Why I am a Democrat*, p. 71.

125. A. Rossi, *The Russo-German Alliance – August 1939–June 1941* (Chapman & Hall, London, 1950), p. 8.

126. Cited by R. Lamb in *The Drift to War* (W. H. Allen, London, 1989), p. 312.

127. Cripps's diary, quoted in Cooke, *The Life of Richard Stafford Cripps*, p. 242.

128. V. Maisky, *Memoirs of a Soviet Ambassador 1938–1943* (Hutchinson, London, 1967), p. 37.

129. F. King and G. Matthews, eds., *About Turn – the British Communist Party and the Outbreak of the Second World War* (Lawrence & Wishart, London, 1990), p. 198.

130. Cripps to Pollitt, 12 October 1939 (Labour Party archives, CP/IND/POLL/2/7).

131. 'Why Blame Russia?' (Cripps papers, 566).

132. J. Stuart, *Within the Fringe – an Autobiography* (Bodley Head, London, 1967), p. 119.

133. Lloyd George to Cripps, 24 November 1939 (Lloyd George papers, G/5/6/5). The secret weapon turned out to be magnetic mines for use against the British fleet.

134. *The Tribune*, 6 October 1939.

135. Cripps to Laski, 28 September 1939 (Laski papers, DLA/15).

136. Cripps to M. Burton, 7 November 1939 (Cripps papers, 566).

Chapter 9: GLOBETROTTING

1. *The Countryman,* January 1940.
2. G. Gorodetsky, *Stafford Cripps' Mission to Moscow 1940–42* (Cambridge University Press, Cambridge, 1984), p. 12.
3. R. J. Moore, *Churchill, Cripps and India 1939–1945* (Clarendon, Oxford, 1979), p. 8.
4. Ibid., p. 10n.
5. *The Times,* 1 December 1939.
6. B. Jones, *The Russia Complex – the British Labour Party and the Soviet Union* (Manchester University Press, Manchester, 1977), p. 47.
7. B. Morris, *The Roots of Appeasement* (Cass, London, 1991), p. 46.
8. Moore, *Churchill, Cripps and India,* p. 15.
9. C. Thorne, *Allies of a Kind – the United States, Britain and the War against Japan 1941–1945* (Hamish Hamilton, London, 1978), pp. 193–4.
10. Gorodetsky, *Stafford Cripps' Mission to Moscow,* pp. 22–3.
11. Cripps to Lansbury, 24 April 1940 (Lansbury papers, Vol. 17, 229).
12. Sir Geoffrey Wilson, interview.

Chapter 10: LEFT SPEAKING TO LEFT

1. PRO/CAB 127/75.
2. A view, arrived at from opposite directions, by P. Addison, *The Road to 1945* (Cape, London, 1975) and M. Cowling, *The Impact of Hitler* (Cambridge University Press, Cambridge, 1975).
3. R. Butt, *The Power of Parliament* (Constable, London, 1967), p. 167.
4. G. Orwell, *The Collected Essays, Journalism and Letters: Vol. 2, 1940–1943* (Penguin, London, 1968), pp. 398–9; E. Estorick, *Stafford Cripps – a Biography* (Heinemann, London, 1949), p. 239.
5. Cripps to Lloyd George, 5 May 1940 (Lloyd George papers, G/3/6/6).
6. *Daily Mail,* 6 May 1940.

7. J. Colville, *The Fringes of Power: Downing Street Diaries 1939–1955* (Hodder & Stoughton, London, 1985), p. 137.
8. Sir E. Spears, *Assignment to Catastrophe: Vol. 1, Prelude to Dunkirk* (Heinemann, London, 1954), pp. 125–6.
9. D. N. Pritt, *The Autobiography of D. N. Pritt: Vol. 1, From Right to Left* (Lawrence & Wishart, London, 1965), p. 235.
10. Sir R. B. Lockhart, *The Diaries of Sir Robert Bruce Lockhart,* ed. K. Young (Macmillan, London, 1973), pp. 57–8.
11. C. Attlee, *Granada Historical Records Interview* (Panther, London, 1967), p. 24.
12. Sargent to Butler, 2 June 1940; Butler to Sargent, 4 June 1940 (PRO/FO 371/24847).
13. C. Cooke, *The Life of Richard Stafford Cripps* (Hodder & Stoughton, London, 1957), p. 266.
14. Churchill to Cripps, 21 June 1940 (PRO/FO 371/24847).
15. Sir G. Rendel, *The Sword and the Olive* (Murray, London, 1957), pp. 169–70.
16. A. Cadogan, *The Diaries of Alexander Cadogan, O.M., 1938–1945,* ed. D. Dilks (Cassell, London, 1971), pp. 318–19, entry dated 1 August 1940.
17. G. Bilainkin, *Maisky: Ten Years Ambassador* (Allen & Unwin, London, 1944), p. 322.
18. Cripps to Monckton, 2 September 1940 (Monckton papers, 3/71).
19. Maclean to Butler, 6 September 1940 (PRO/FO 371/24841).
20. Hill to Monckton, 12 November 1940 (Monckton papers 3/71).
21. Cripps to Monckton, 25 November 1940 (Monckton papers, 3/71).
22. R. J. Sontag and J. S. Beddie, eds., *Nazi–Soviet Relations 1939–1941* (Department of State, Washington DC, 1948), pp. 166–8.
23. J. M. Gwyer and J. R. M. Butler, *Grand Strategy: Vol. 2* (HMSO, London, 1964), pp. 50–1.

24. R. Cecil, *Hitler's Decision to Invade Russia, 1941* (Davis-Poynter, London, 1975), p. 81. Hitler thought Cripps was a half-caste with Jewish blood in his family, a puritan, 'a man without roots' (H. Trevor-Roper, ed., *Hitler's Table Talk 1941–1944* (Weidenfeld & Nicolson, London, 1953), pp. 368–9, 545).

25. B. H. Liddell-Hart, *A History of the Second World War* (Cassell, London, 1970), p. 144.

26. Colville, *The Fringes of Power*, pp. 367–8.

27. H. Hanak, 'Sir Stafford Cripps as British Ambassador in Moscow, May 1940 to June 1941', in *English Historical Review*, Vol. 370 (1979), p. 68.

28. Cripps to Rogers, 10 December 1940 (BELP archive).

29. Sir W. Churchill, *The Second World War: Vol. 3, The Grand Alliance* (Cassell, London, 1950), pp. 289–92.

30. Ibid., p. 290.

31. On the first day of the German invasion of the Soviet Union, the Soviet air force lost over 1200 aircraft.

32. Churchill to Eden and Beaverbrook, 14 October 1941 (PRO/PREM 3/403/7).

33. Gwyer and Butler, *Grand Strategy: Vol. 2*, p. 81.

34. E. L. Woodward, *British Foreign Policy in the Second World War, Vol. 1* (HMSO, London, 1970).

35. F. Hinsley et al., *British Intelligence in the Second World War: Vol. 1* (HMSO, London, 1979), pp. 452–3. 'Ultra' was the British cover name for the deciphered signals of the 'Enigma' encoding machine used for secure communications by the German armed forces.

36. G. Gorodetsky, *Stafford Cripps' Mission to Moscow, 1940–1942* (Cambridge University Press, Cambridge, 1984), and his 'Churchill's Warning to Stalin: A Reappraisal', in *Historical Journal*, Vol. 29 (1986), pp. 979–90.

37. Hinsley et al., *British Intelligence in the Second World War: Vol 1*, p. 430.

38. Cripps to Churchill, 6 April 1941 (PRO/FO 371/29544).

39. A. Rossi, *The Russo-German Alliance – August 1939–June 1941* (Chapman & Hall, London, 1950), p. 203. Stalin received eight-four separate warnings, all of them recorded. 'Don't you see,' he told General Zhukov, 'they are trying to frighten us with the Germans and to frighten the Germans with us, setting us one against the other?' (G. Zhukov, *Marshal of the Soviet Union G. Zhukov: Reminiscences and Reflections: Vol. 1*, trans. V. Schneierson (Central Books, London, 1985), p. 268). According to one Soviet historian, Schulenberg himself told the Soviet ambassador to Berlin of the exact date of the German attack; Stalin called it 'disinformation' (*The Independent*, 23 June 1989). A German soldier who went over to the Soviets to warn of an attack was shot by order of Stalin. Soviet suspicions were so intense that the Russians even thought the Yugoslav ambassador, Milovan Gavrilovich, was playing a double game, recruited by the Soviet Secret Service but reporting to Cripps (A. Sudoplatov, *Special Tasks* (Little, Brown, London, 1994), p. 119).

40. A. Werth, *Russia at War 1941–1945* (Barrie & Rockliff, London, 1964), pp. 276–7.

41. *The Guardian*, 12 September 1995.

42. G. Roberts, *The Unholy Alliance* (I. B. Tauris, London, 1989), p. 208.

43. *Documents on German Foreign Policy* (US Government Print Office, Washington DC, 1948), April 1941, pp. 604–5.

44. W. L. Shirer, *The Rise and Fall of the Third Reich* (Pan, London, 1960), p. 1009.

45. The German High Command did not settle on an invasion date until the very end of April.

46. Sontag and Beddie, eds., *Nazi–Soviet Relations 1939–1941*, pp. 330–2.

47. H. C. Cassidy, *Moscow Dateline*

(Cassell, London, 1943), p. 20.

48. In a final talk with Vyshinsky, Cripps had said he would not return to Moscow if a new Soviet–German agreement was reached in the meantime.

49. Cripps to Rogers, 3 May 1941 (Rogers papers).

50. I. Deutscher, *Stalin: A Political Biography* (Oxford University Press, London, 1949), pp. 455–6.

51. *Khruschev's Secret Speech* (Manchester Guardian, Manchester, 1956), pp. 18–19.

52. Ibid., p. 19.

53. V. Rothwell, *Britain and the Cold War 1941–1947* (Cape, London, 1982), pp. 78–9.

54. I. Maisky, *Memoirs of a Soviet Ambassador 1939–1943* (Hutchinson, London, 1967), p. 156.

55. *Keesing's Contemporary Archive*, 21–8 June 1941.

56. *Christian Science Monitor*, 4 April 1942.

57. G. Dawson (editor of *The Times*) to Halifax, 22 June 1941 (Dawson papers, The Times Archive).

58. E.g. Sir Archibald Sinclair in A. J. P. Taylor, ed., *W. P. Crozier: Off the Record – Political Interviews 1932–1944* (Hutchinson, London, 1973), p. 231. See G. Gorodetsky, *Stafford Cripps' Mission to Moscow*, pp. 170–1.

59. *Daily Express*, 25 June 1941.

60. Cooke, *The Life of Richard Stafford Cripps*, p. 271.

61. D. Volkogonov, *Stalin* (Weidenfeld & Nicolson, London, 1991), p. 406.

62. Ibid., pp. 412–13.

63. G. Hill to Monckton, 2 August 1941 (Monckton papers, 6).

64. *Forward*, 9 August 1941.

65. Cripps to Eden, 15 September 1941 (Beaverbrook papers, BBK D/90).

66. C. L. Sulzberger, *A Long Row of Candles* (Macdonald, London, 1969), p. 183.

67. Eden 'complained vociferously about Stafford Cripps who, he says, changes his opinion every few minutes and wants to teach him (Eden) how to manage Foreign Affairs' (Colville, *The Fringes of Power*, pp. 485–6, entry dated 30 June 1941).

68. Churchill to Eden and Beaverbrook, 1 November 1941 (Beaverbrook papers, D93).

69. Sir W. Citrine's diary, 22 October 1941 (Citrine papers, 1/32).

70. A. J. P. Taylor, *Beaverbrook* (Penguin, London, 1972), pp. 638–9.

71. H. Hanak, 'Sir Stafford Cripps as Ambassador in Moscow June 1941–January 1942', in *English Historical Review*, Vol. 383 (1982), p. 344.

Chapter 11: THE ASTRAKHAN CAP

1. W. S. Churchill, *The Second World War: Vol. 4, The Hinge of Fate* (Cassell, London, 1951), p. 77.

2. W. A. Harriman and E. Abel, *Special Envoy to Churchill and Stalin 1941–1946* (Hutchinson, London, 1976), p. 128.

3. Quoted in D. Carlton, *Anthony Eden* (Allen Lane, London, 1981), p. 201.

4. J. Charmley, *Churchill and the End of Glory* (Hodder & Stoughton, London, 1993), p. 484, quoting from Eden's diary, entry dated 14 November 1941.

5. R. Barrington-Ward's diary, entry dated 26 January 1942.

6. A. J. P. Taylor, *Beaverbrook* (Penguin, London, 1972), p. 652.

7. R. Cockett, *David Astor and the* Observer (Deutsch, London, 1991), Chapters 3 and 4.

8. E. Ellis, *T. J.: A Life of Dr Thomas Jones C. H.* (University of Wales, Cardiff, 1992), p. 453.

9. *Manchester Guardian*, 2 March 1942.

10. *Daily Herald*, 3 February 1942.

11. BBC Sound Archive, accession numbers 9CL0003980 and 9CL0003981.

12. M. Foot, *Debts of Honour* (Pan, London, 1980), p. 93, recalling the reaction of the National Liberal MP Leslie Hore-Belisha.

13. Mass Observation file reports 1111 (24

February 1942), 1166 (23 March 1942) and 1264 (17 May 1942).

14. *Evening Standard*, 11 February 1942. From the response to this article, Beaverbrook assumed (wrongly) that the Cripps wave was passing.

15. A Liberal MP and Crippsite convert, Edgar Granville, 'had said Cripps brought Russia into the war and was very angry when Florence Horsburgh [a Tory] said that Hitler brought the Russians in' (Chuter Ede's diary, entry dated 15 February 1942).

16. Martin to V. Markham, 11 February 1942 (Markham papers, 5/20).

17. A. Koestler, *The Yogi and the Commissar* (Cape, London, 1945), p. 221.

18. Estorick archive.

19. M. Stockwood, *Chanctonbury Ring – the Autobiography of Mervyn Stockwood* (Hodder & Stoughton, London, 1982), p. 59.

20. V. Bonham Carter's diary, entry dated 24 February 1945.

21. H. Hanak, 'Sir Stafford Cripps as Ambassador in Moscow June 1941– January 1942', in *English Historical Review*, Vol. 383 (1982), p. 343.

22. D. Day, *The Great Betrayal – Britain, Australia and the Onset of the Pacific War 1939–1942* (Angus & Robertson, London, 1988).

23. Churchill had suffered a heart attack in January 1942. It was kept secret.

24. S. Bruce, 'Sir Stafford Cripps', 16 February 1942 (Australian Archives, file M100).

25. D. Day, 'Churchill and his War Rivals', in *History Today*, April 1991, p. 18.

26. A. Cadogan, *The Diaries of Alexander Cadogan, O.M., 1938–1945*, ed. D. Dilks (Cassell, London, 1971), p. 435.

27. C. King, *With Malice Towards None: A War Diary* (Sidgwick and Jackson, London, 1970), p. 173–4, reporting Hore-Belisha, entry dated 10 April 1942.

28. Carlton, *Anthony Eden*, p. 204, quoting Oliver Harvey's diary, entry dated 25 February 1942.

29. A. J. P. Taylor, ed., *W. P. Crozier: Off the Record – Political Interviews 1932–1944* (Hutchinson, London, 1973), p. 293, entry dated 20 February 1942.

30. *Daily Express*, 26 February 1942.

31. *News Chronicle*, 26 February 1942.

32. Chuter Ede's diary, entry dated 25 February 1942.

33. V. Bonham Carter's diary, entry dated 6 March 1942.

Chapter 12: THE OFFER

1. Quoted in P. S. Gupta, *Imperialism and the British Labour Movement 1914–1964* (Macmillan, London, 1975), p. 270n.

2. *Daily Express*, 7 February 1942.

3. R. J. Moore, *Churchill, Cripps and India, 1939–1945* (Clarendon, Oxford, 1979), p. 65.

4. L. S. Amery, *The Empire at Bay – the Leo Amery Diaries 1929–1945*, ed. J. Barnes and D. Nicholson (Hutchinson, London, 1988), pp. 785–6, entry dated 8 March 1942.

5. R. J. Moore, 'The Mystery of the Cripps Mission', in *Journal of Commonwealth Political Studies*, Vol. 11 (1973), p. 199.

6. N. Mansergh, ed., *The Transfer of Power 1942–1947: Vol. 1, The Cripps Mission, January to April 1942* (HMSO, London, 1970).

7. *The Times Literary Supplement*, 1 January 1971; E. Stokes, 'Cripps in India', in *Historical Journal*, Vol. 14 (1971), pp. 427–34.

8. Halifax to the King, 15 March 1942 (Royal Archives, RA PS/GVI/C 053/USA/07).

9. *The Observer*, 15 March 1942.

10. *Foreign Relations of the United States [FRUS], 1942: Vol. 1, The British Commonwealth* (US Government Print Office, Washington DC, 1960), p. 661.

11. Spry was a Canadian national, a former broadcaster and executive with the Standard Oil Company; Owen wrote for *The Times* and was a member of Cripps's 'brains trust'; Turnbull was

Amery's India Office private secretary.

12. In fact Bose, having escaped to Berlin in 1941, had been in the care of the German Foreign Office, liaising with Adam von Trott, the Crippses' family friend. (Cripps probably was not aware of this at the time of his Indian mission.)

13. W. J. West, ed., *Orwell – The War Broadcasts* (Duckworth, London, 1985), p. 33.

14. C. Allen, ed., *Plain Tales from the Raj* (Century, London, 1975), p. 80.

15. H. V. Hodson, *The Great Divide: Britain–India–Pakistan* (Hutchinson, London, 1969), p. 98.

16. Amery to Linlithgow, in Mansergh, ed., *The Transfer of Power: Vol 1*, p. 481.

17. Hodson, *The Great Divide*, p. 103.

18. Mansergh, ed., *The Transfer of Power: Vol. 1*, pp. 484–5.

19. Though a moderate, Rajagopalachari had only recently been released from prison for his part in the non-co-operation campaign.

20. G. N. Molesworth, *Curfew on Olympus* (Asia Publishing House, Bombay, 1965), p. 219.

21. A. Moorehead, *African Trilogy* (Hamish Hamilton, London, 1944), p. 276.

22. Ibid., p. 277.

23. R. Coupland, *The Cripps Mission* (Oxford University Press, London, 1942), p. 33.

24. J. Glendevon, *The Viceroy at Bay – Lord Linlithgow in India 1936–1943* (Collins, London, 1971), p. 231.

25. Mansergh, ed., *The Transfer of Power: Vol. 1*, pp. 614–15.

26. Johnson, a lawyer, had been US Assistant Secretary of War in 1937 to 1940.

27. Johnson to Roosevelt, 4 April 1942 (*FRUS, 1942: Vol. 1*, p. 627).

28. Linlithgow to Churchill and Amery in Mansergh, ed., *The Transfer of Power: Vol 1*, pp. 653–5.

29. Graham Spry's diary, entry dated 7 April 1942.

30. Ibid., 8 April 1942.

31. Ibid., 9 April 1942.

32. Johnson to Roosevelt, 11 April 1942 (*FRUS, 1942: Vol. 1*, p. 631).

33. *FRUS, 1942: Vol. 1*, p. 659.

34. B. Shiva Rao, 'India 1935–47', in C. Philips and M. Wainwright, *The Partition of India – Problems and Perspectives 1935–1947* (Allen & Unwin, London, 1970), p. 436.

35. Churchill to Cripps, in Mansergh, ed., *The Transfer of Power: Vol 1*, p. 739.

36. M. Edwardes, *The Last Years of British India* (Penguin, London, 1967), p. 90.

37. *Indian Information*, 15 June 1942.

38. R. J. Moore, *Escape from Empire: The Attlee Government and the Indian Problem* (Clarendon, Oxford, 1983), p. 72.

39. *FRUS, 1942: Vol. 1*, p. 661.

40. C. Thorne, *Allies of a Kind – the United States, Britain and the War against Japan 1941–1945* (Hamish Hamilton, London, 1978), p. 236.

41. *The Times*, 13 April 1942.

42. B. Webb's unpublished diary, entry dated 6 April 1942.

43. P. Gordon Walker, *Patrick Gordon Walker – Political Diaries 1932–1971*, ed. R. Pearce (Historians' Press, London, 1991), p. 110, entry dated 25 April 1942.

44. C. King, *With Malice Towards None: A War Diary* (Sidgwick and Jackson, London, 1970), p. 177, entry dated 30 April 1942.

Chapter 13 : TAR

1. Sir A. Eden, *Memoirs: The Reckoning* (Cassell, London, 1965), p. 343, diary entry dated 2 October 1942.

2. P. Gordon Walker, *Patrick Gordon Walker – Political Diaries 1932–1971*, ed. R. Pearce (Historians' Press, London, 1991), pp. 111–12.

3. Sir Edward Bridges, interview (Estorick archive).

4. See D. Saward, *Bomber Harris* (Buchan & Enright, London, 1984), pp. 244–5.

5. Cripps to Churchill, 20 March 1942 (PRO/PRE 3/291/6). 'I do not wonder everything was so pleasant,' Churchill replied, 'considering you seem to have accepted everything they said...'

6. K. von Klemperer, *German Resistance Against Hitler – the Search for Allies Abroad* (Clarendon, Oxford, 1992), p. 218.

7. G. Bell (Bishop of Chichester), 'The Church and the Resistance Movement', in W.-D. Zimmermann and R. G. Smith, eds., *I Knew Dietrich Bonhoeffer* (Fontana, London, 1966), p. 208.

8. Churchill to Lord Cherwell, 10 March 1942, reprinted in W. S. Churchill, *The Second World War: Vol. 4, The Hinge of Fate* (Cassell, London, 1951), p. 679.

9. H. Nicolson, *Diaries and Letters 1939–1945*, ed. N. Nicolson (Collins, London, 1967), p. 223, entry dated 3 May 1942.

10. Palmer to Cripps, 30 April 1942 (PRO/CAB/127/79).

11. P. Goodhart, *The 1922* (Macmillan, London, 1973), pp. 114–20.

12. *Reynold's News*, 13 June 1942.

13. R. A. Butler papers, July 1942 (Butler MSS RAB G14 fs. 58–60).

14. D. Eccles, *By Safe Hand – Letters 1939–1942* (Bodley Head, London, 1985), p. 364.

15. H. Dalton, *The Political Diary of Hugh Dalton 1918–1940, 1945–1960*, ed. B. Pimlott (Cape, London, 1986), p. 480, entry dated 24 August 1942.

16. Lord Moran, *Winston Churchill: The Struggle for Survival 1940–1965* (Sphere, London, 1968), p. 59.

17. Lord Chandos, *Memoirs* (Bodley Head, London, 1962), p. 313.

18. C. King, *With Malice Towards None: A War Diary* (Sidgwick & Jackson, London, 1970), pp. 181–2, entry dated 9 July 1942.

19. Cripps to Jones, 22 July 1942 (Thomas Jones archive, Class W, Vol. 3, No. 18).

20. M. MacDonald, *Titans and Others* (Collins, London, 1972), pp. 109–10.

21. D. McLachlan, *In the Editor's Chair* (Weidenfeld & Nicolson, London, 1971), p. 199.

22. Cripps to Churchill, 'War Situation: Immediate Needs', 30 July 1942 (PRO/CAB127/67).

23. H. Massingham in M. Cummings, *These Uproarious Years – a Pictorial Post-War History by Cummings* (MacGibbon & Kee, London, 1954), p. 10.

24. Quoted in P. Addison, *The Road to 1945* (Cape, London, 1975), p. 208–9.

25. H. Dalton, *The Second World War Diary of Hugh Dalton 1940–1945*, ed. B. Pimlott (Cape, London, 1986), pp. 479–80.

26. Churchill to Cripps, 2 September 1942 (PRO/CAB/21/1349).

27. Moran, *Winston Churchill*, p. 93.

28. I. Maisky, *Memoirs of a Soviet Ambassador 1938–1943* (Hutchinson, London, 1967), p. 329.

29. PRO/PREM 4/63/2.

30. Gordon Walker, *Political Diaries*, pp. 110–13.

31. King, *With Malice Towards None*, p. 189, entry dated 8 September 1942.

32. R. Barrington-Ward's diary, entry dated 11 September 1942.

33. PRO/CAB 65/27, War Cabinet minutes, 9 September 1942.

34. Cripps to Churchill, 21 September 1942 (PRO/CAB 127/85).

35. Sir L. Rowan, in Sir J. Wheeler-Bennett, ed., *Action This Day* (Macmillan, London, 1968), p. 263.

36. Eden, *Memoirs*, p. 342.

37. N. Davenport, *Memoirs of a City Radical* (Weidenfeld & Nicolson, London, 1974), pp. 139–40.

38. After Churchill's successful talks with Stalin, Stanley Bruce, the Australian High Commissioner, informed Cripps he would not have his support if Cripps were to try to dislodge the Prime Minister.

39. Gordon Walker, *Political Diaries*, p. 116, entry dated 1 October 1942.

40. R. Barrington-Ward's diary, entry dated 2 October 1942.

41. R. Overy, *Why the Allies Won* (Cape, London, 1995), p. 268.

42. Jones to Markham, 6 October 1942 (Thomas Jones archive, Class T, Vol. 7, No. 66).

43. Addison, *The Road to 1945*, p. 210.

44. King, *With Malice Towards None*, p. 195, entry dated 21 October 1942.

45. M. Edelman, The Mirror – *A Political History* (Hamish Hamilton, London, 1966), pp. 134–5.

46. B. Webb's unpublished diary, entry dated 26 October 1942.

47. Addison, *The Road to 1945*, p. 216.

48. *The Times*, 6 November 1942.

49. Cripps to Churchill, 11 November 1942 (PRO/PREM 4/63/2).

50. Jones to Markham, 20 November 1942 (Thomas Jones archive, Class T, Vol. 7, No. 67).

51. King, *With Malice Towards None*, p. 201, entry dated 4 December 1942.

52. *Daily Herald*, 24 November 1942.

53. Lionel Elvin, interview.

54. In a November poll, only 17 per cent could put a name to the Lord Privy Seal unprompted.

55. Jennie Lee, *World Review*, January 1943.

56. *News Chronicle*, 24 November 1942.

Chapter 14 : MAP

1. V. Bonham Carter's diary, entry dated 6 January 1943.

2. Cripps to J. Martin, 26 November 1942 (PRO/CAB 127/87).

3. M. M. Postan, *British War Production* (HMSO, London, 1952), p. 303.

4. C. King, *With Malice Towards None: A War Diary* (Sidgwick & Jackson, London, 1970), pp. 201–2, entry dated 4 December 1942.

5. Cripps to Churchill, 4 January 1943 (PRO/AVIA 9/44).

6. E. Devons, *Planning in Practice – Essays in Aircraft Planning in Wartime* (Cambridge University Press, Cambridge, 1950). Devons was director-general of planning in the MAP from 1941 to 1945.

7. S. Freeman, *Production under Fire* (C. J. Fallon, Dublin, 1967), pp. 60–1.

8. Sir R. Watson-Watt, *Three Steps to Victory* (Odhams, London, 1957), pp. 448–9.

9. T. Jones to V. Markham, 3 December 1942 (Thomas Jones archive, Class T, Vol. 7, No. 69).

10. Sir J. Slessor, *The Central Blue* (Cassell, London, 1956), p. 483. During Beaverbrook's time, Freeman had been displaced by newcomers.

11. Sir G. Schuster, 'Richard Stafford Cripps', in *Biographical Memoirs of Fellows of the Royal Society* (Royal Society, London, 1955), p. 13.

12. Sir Wilfred Freeman, interview (Estorick archive).

13. *Daily Worker*, 28 December 1942.

14. Morning meeting, 4 February 1943 (PRO/AVIA 15/2151).

15. C. H. Barnes, *Shorts Aircrafts since 1900* (Putnam, London, 1967), p. 29.

16. PRO/PREm 4/34/5.

17. Cripps to Lyttleton, 3 February 1943 (PRO/AVIA 9/44).

18. S. Roskill, *The War at Sea 1939–1945: Vol. 2* (HMSO, London, 1956).

19. W. S. Chalmers, *Max Horton and the Western Approaches* (Hodder & Stoughton, London, 1954), pp. 175–7.

20. PRO/PREM 3/414/1.

21. Sir B. Lovell in *The Times*, 13 March 1987.

22. R. V. Jones, *Most Secret War* (Hamish Hamilton, London, 1978), p. 440.

23. Cecilia Sebestyien, interview.

24. See F. Hinsley et al., *British Intelligence in the Second World War: Vol. 3* (HMSO, London, 1989).

25. Morning meeting, 9 September 1943 (PRO/AVIA 15/2153).

26. N. Davenport, *Memoirs of a City Radical* (Weidenfeld & Nicolson, London, 1974), p. 140.

27. Sir F. Whittle, *Jet – the Story of a Pioneer*

(Muller, London, 1953), p. 263.

28. J. E. Morpurgo, *Barnes Wallis* (Longmans, London, 1972), pp. 180–1.

29. S. Brooke, *Labour's War – the Labour Party During the Second World War* (Clarendon, Oxford, 1992).

30. H. Dalton, *The Second World War Diary of Hugh Dalton 1940–1945*, ed. B. Pimlott (Cape, London, 1986), p. 736, entry dated 14 April 1944.

31. Cripps to Attlee, 20 November 1943 (PRO/CAB 118/23).

32. C. King, in L. Gourlay, ed., *The Beaverbrook I Knew* (Quartet, London, 1984), p. 40.

33. T. Jones to E. Jones, 28 September 1943 (Thomas Jones archive, Class X, Vol. 10, Nos. 129–31.

34. A. J. P. Taylor, *Beaverbrook* (Penguin, London, 1972), pp. 699–700.

35. Rogers to Cripps, 25 April 1944 (Rogers papers).

36. Stockwood to I. Cripps, 10 October 1944 (Cripps papers, 623).

37. Sir R. Fedden, *Britain's Air Survival* (Cassell, London, 1957), pp. 76–9.

38. Sir Harold Scott, *Your Obedient Servant* (Deutsch, London, 1959), p. 168. Cripps was good at 'picking winners' to finance – the jet engine, the Massey Ferguson tractor and the Land Rover.

39. 'Government and Science in Great Britain', in *Nature*, 6 February 1943.

40. W. T. Gunston, *By Jupiter! The Life of Sir Roy Fedden* (Royal Aeronautical Society, London, 1978), p. 124.

41. *Sunday Times*, 1 November 1943.

42. Isobel Cripps's foreword to A. Williams Ellis, *Women in War Factories* (Gollancz, London, 1943).

43. *Manchester Guardian*, 6 November 1944.

44. T. Jones to V. Markham, 6 October 1942 (Thomas Jones archive, Class T, Vol. 7, No. 66).

45. *Daily Herald*, 19 August 1944.

46. *Daily Telegraph*, 9 August 1943.

47. *Manchester Guardian*, 18 December 1944.

48. Canon L. J. Collins, *Faith Under Fire* (Frewin, London, 1966), p. 89.

49. D. Irving, *The Destruction of Dresden* (William Kimber, London, 1963), pp. 53–4.

50. Bruce-Gardner to Cripps, 1 January 1945 (PRO/CAB 127/127).

51. M. Gowing, *Independence and Deterrence – Britain and Atomic Energy 1945–1952* (Macmillan, London, 1974), p. 5.

52. L. S. Amery, *The Empire at Bay – the Leo Amery Diaries 1929–1945*, ed. J. Barnes and D. Nicholson (Hutchinson, London, 1988), p. 1042, entry dated 15 May 1945.

53. R. Barrington-Ward's diary, entry dated 3 October 1944.

54. C. Barnett, *The Audit of War – the Illusion and Reality of Britain as a Great Nation* (Macmillan, London, 1986).

55. J. Jewkes, *Ordeal by Planning* (Macmillan, London, 1948), p. 14.

56. The thesis of J. Vaizey's *In Breach of Promise* (Weidenfeld & Nicolson, London, 1983).

57. Devons, *Planning in Practice*, p. 150.

58. D. Edgerton, *England and the Aeroplane* (Macmillan, Basingstoke, 1991), pp. 79–82.

59. C. Oakley, *Men at Work* (Hodder & Stoughton, London, 1945).

60. 'Government and the Major Industries', Cabinet memorandum by Cripps of 8 March 1944, quoted in H. Mercer, N. Rollings and J. Tomlinson, eds., *Labour Governments and Private Industry – the Experience of 1945–1951* (Edinburgh University Press, Edinburgh, 1992), p. 94.

Chapter 15 : GESTAPO

1. B. de Jouvenel, *Problems of Socialist England* (Batchworth, London, 1949), p. 161.

2. *News Review*, 15 March 1945.

3. Minutes of the NEC Elections Sub-

Committee of the Labour Party, 1 August 1944.

4. R. Barrington-Ward's diary, 13 September 1944.

5. Bristol East Labour Party General Council minutes, 1 October 1944 (BELP archive, 39035/19).

6. H. Dalton, *The Political Diary of Hugh Dalton 1918–1940, 1945–1960*, ed. B. Pimlott (Cape, London, 1986), pp. 516–17.

7. Rogers to Cripps, 10 October 1944 (Rogers papers).

8. D. N. Pritt, *The Autobiography of D. N. Pritt: Vol. 2, Brasshats and Bureaucrats* (Lawrence & Wishart, London, 1966), pp. 22–3.

9. C. King, *With Malice Towards None: A War Diary* (Sidgwick & Jackson, London, 1970), p. 282, entry dated 9 December 1944.

10. Labour Party Annual Conference Report 1945, p. 95.

11. *Daily Express*, 15 November 1947.

12. Sir A. Eden, *Memoirs: The Reckoning* (Cassell, London, 1965), p. 539.

13. R. B. McCallum and A. Readman, *The British General Election of 1945* (Oxford University Press, London, 1947), p. 142.

14. J. Colville, *Footprints in Time* (Collins, London, 1976), Chapter 36.

15. R. Cockett, *Thinking the Unthinkable – Think-Tanks and the Economic Counter-Revolution 1931–1983* (HarperCollins, London, 1994), p. 94.

16. *Daily Telegraph*, 9 June 1945.

17. Cripps to BELP General Council, 28 May 1945 (Cripps papers, 548).

18. *Dewsbury Reporter*, 23 June 1945.

19. *Newcastle Journal*, 16 June 1945.

20. *South Wales Evening Post*, 2 July 1945.

21. Letter of 28 March 1945 (Cripps papers, 548).

22. Letter of 21 June 1945 (Cripps papers, 548).

23. I. Cripps to A. Jarvis, 11 July 1945 (Jarvis papers).

24. John Freeman, interview.

25. *Picture Post*, 23 June 1945.

26. *Evening World* (Bristol), 26 July 1945.

27. M. Stockwood, *Chanctonbury Ring – the Autobiography of Mervyn Stockwood* (Hodder & Stoughton, London, 1982), pp. 65–6.

28. F. Williams, *The People*, 28 February 1954.

29. H. Rogers, unpublished autobiography, pp. 21–2.

30. Stockwood, *Chanctonbury Ring*, p. 66.

31. Chuter Ede's diary, entry dated 28 May 1945.

32. Lord Woolton, *Memoirs* (Cassell, London, 1959), p. 300.

33. Cripps to J. Collins, 30 July 1945 (Collins papers, MS 3288).

Chapter 16 : POST-WAR

1. Reprinted in A. Jarvis, ed., *Democracy Alive* (Sidgwick & Jackson, London, 1946), p. 71.

2. *World Report*, 4 March 1947.

3. Cripps to Attlee, 2 August 1945 (Attlee papers, 59, Bodleian).

4. Freeman to Cripps, 28 July 1945 (Cripps papers, 549).

5. *News Chronicle*, 1 August 1945.

6. H. Grisewood, *One Thing at a Time* (Hutchinson, London, 1968), pp. 152–3.

7. Sir F. Lee, *The Board of Trade* (Athlone Press, London, 1958).

8. R. Barrington-Ward's diary, entry dated 22 August 1945.

9. 'The Work of the Board of Trade', 7 August 1945 (PRO/BT 13/220A); finally revised on 29 August 1945.

10. Sir R. Streat, *Lancashire and Whitehall: The Diary of Sir Raymond Streat: Vol. 2, 1939–1957* ed. M. Dupree (Manchester University Press, Manchester, 1987), p. 271, entry dated 2 August 1945.

11. *The Tribune*, 17 August 1945.

12. D. Collins, *Partners in Protest – Life with Canon Collins* (Gollancz, London, 1992), p. 139.

13. Cripps to Frankfurter, 15 August 1945 (PRO/CAB 127/126).

14. L. S. Pressnell, *External Economic Policy since the War* (HMSO, London, 1986).
15. The Americans submitted a list of bases they wanted on assorted British islands in the Atlantic and Pacific.
16. D. Moggridge, *Maynard Keynes: An Economist's Biography* (Routledge, London, 1992), p. 264.
17. B. Castle, *Fighting All the Way* (Macmillan, London, 1993), pp. 139–40.
18. A. Cairncross, ed., *Anglo-American Economic Collaboration in War and Peace 1942–1949* (Clarendon, Oxford, 1982), p. 79.
19. J. E. Meade, *The Collected Papers of James Meade: Vol. 4, The Cabinet Office Diary 1944–1946*, ed. S. Howson and D. Moggridge (Unwin Hyman, London, 1990), p. 115, entry dated 26 August 1945.
20. 'Economic Planning', meeting of 20 August 1945 (T273/298).
21. Woods to Martin, 30 November 1945 (PRO/T273/298).
22. President's morning meeting, 17 January 1946 (PRO/BT 13/220A).
23. Ministerial Committee on Economic Planning, 21 January 1946 (PRO/CAB 134/503).
24. S. S. Wilson, interview (Donoughue and Jones archive).
25. P. Pagnamenta and R. Overy, *All Our Working Lives* (BBC, London, 1984), pp. 40–1.
26. *Financial Times*, 10 January 1946.
27. Cabinet minutes, 4 September 1945 (PRP/CAB 128/1).
28. Streat, *Lancashire and Whitehall*, p. 284, entry dated 9 September 1945.
29. Sir G. Schuster, *Private Work and Public Causes – a Personal Record 1881–1978* (D. Brown, Cowbridge, 1979), p. 141.
30. Cripps to Woods, 22 October 1945 (PRO/BT 13/220A).
31. W. Plowden, *The Motor Car and Politics in Britain* (Penguin, London, 1971), p. 321.
32. *News Chronicle*, 13 February 1946.
33. *The Observer*, 3 February 1946.
34. *Daily Telegraph*, 1 December 1945.
35. *Reynold's News*, 27 October 1946.
36. *Daily Mail*, 17 November 1945.
37. *The Observer*, 17 February 1946.
38. 'Consumer Needs and Public Relations', 20 August 1945 (PRO/BT13/220A).
39. George Blaker, interview.
40. J. Bellamy and J. Saville, eds., *The Dictionary of Labour Biography: Vol. 9* (Macmillan, London, 1993), p. 268.
41. E. Estorick, *Stafford Cripps – a Biography* (Heinemann, London, 1949), p. 320.
42. *Daily Mail*, 23 February 1946.
43. Ibid., 28 February 1946.
44. Cripps to Woods, 11 April 1946 (BT91/1).
45. Charles Bruce-Gardner, interview (Estorick archive).

Chapter 17 : THE AWARD

1. Quoted in H. V. Hodson, *The Great Divide: Britain–India–Pakistan* (Hutchinson, London, 1969).
2. H. Dalton, *High Tide and After – Memoirs 1945–1960* (Muller, London, 1962), p. 105, diary extract dated 9 March 1946.
3. Cripps to Pethick-Lawrence, December 1945 (Pethick-Lawrence papers, PL563).
4. Gandhi to Cripps, 12 January 1946 (Pethick-Lawrence papers, P-L 566).
5. Cripps to R. Casey, 1 March 1946 (PRO/CAB127/122).
6. C. King's unpublished diary, entry dated 9 May 1947.
7. N. Mansergh, ed., *The Transfer of Power 1942–1947: Vol. 7, The Cabinet Mission, 23 March–29 June 1946* (HMSO, London 1977).
8. W. Wyatt, *Confessions of an Optimist* (Collins, London, 1985), p. 140.
9. S. Hamid, *Disastrous Twilight* (Cooper, London, 1986), entry dated 10 April 1946. Hamid was the private secretary of Auchinleck, the Commander-in-Chief.
10. A. P. Wavell, *Wavell: The Viceroy's Journal*, ed. P. Moon (Oxford

University Press, London, 1973), p. 269, entry dated 11 May 1946.

11. Hodson, *The Great Divide*, Chapter 11.
12. Cripps to Gandhi, 26 May 1946 (PRO/CAB 127/128).
13. Gandhi to Cripps, 27 May 1946 (PRO/CAB 127/128).
14. Gandhi to Cripps, 13 June 1946 (PRO/CAB 127/128).
15. Mansergh, ed., *The Transfer of Power: Vol. 7*, pp. 785–6.
16. Wavell, *The Viceroy's Journal*, p. 299, entry dated 21 June 1946.
17. Mansergh, ed., *The Transfer of Power: Vol. 7*, pp. 1038–40 and 1042–3.
18. Sir E. Wakefield, *Past Imperative* (Chatto & Windus, London, 1966), p. 212.
19. V. Brittain, *Pethick-Lawrence – a Portrait* (Allen & Unwin, London, 1963), p. 175.
20. Hodson, *The Great Divide*, p. 211.
21. *Leader*, 6 July 1946.
22. A. Campbell-Johnson, *Mission with Mountbatten* (Hale, London, 1951), p. 219.
23. Discussion between Pethick-Lawrence and Cripps, 27 September 1946, in Mansergh, ed., *The Transfer of Power: Vol. 7*, pp. 613–15.
24. Lord Listowel, 'The Whitehall Dimension of the Transfer of Power', in *Indo-British Review*, 1979, Parts 3 and 4, p. 23.

Chapter 18: TELLING THE PEOPLE

1. Brendan Bracken, in *Financial Times*, 13 December 1946.
2. Sir J. H. Woods, 'Administrative Problems of Trade', in *Public Administration*, summer 1948, p. 87.
3. Speech to the National Joint Advisory Council for Industry, 30 October 1946 (PRO/BT 64/2221).
4. Cripps to Attlee and Bevin, 17 September 1946 (PRO/CAB 21/2277).
5. W. Plowden, *The Motor Car and Politics in Britain* (Penguin, London, 1971), pp. 321–2.
6. T. Driberg, *Swaff: The Life and Times of Hannen Swaffer* (Macdonald & Jane's, London, 1974), p. 224.
7. P. Addison, *The Road to 1945* (Cape, London, 1975), p. 262.
8. N. Brook to Sir E. Bridges, 4 September 1946 (PRO/CAB 21/1701).
9. C. King, *Strictly Personal* (Weidenfeld & Nicolson, London, 1969), p. 119.
10. F. Williams, *A Prime Minister Remembers: The War and Post-War Memoirs of the Rt Hon. Earl Attlee* (Heinemann, London, 1961), p. 223.
11. *The Times*, 14 September 1946.
12. Ibid., 30 September 1982.
13. Attlee to the Chiefs of Staff, 26 September 1946 (PRO/PREM 8/345).
14. A. Cairncross, *Years of Recovery – British Economic Policy 1945–1951* (Methuen, London, 1985), p. 63.
15. PRO/BT 64/2227.
16. *The Statist*, 28 December 1946.
17. *News Chronicle*, 28 October 1946.
18. Sir R. Streat, *Lancashire and Whitehall: The Diary of Sir Raymond Streat: Vol. 2, 1939–1957* ed. M. Dupree (Manchester University Press, Manchester, 1987), p. 373, entry dated 1 November 1946.
19. Dame A. Meynell, *Public Servant, Private Woman – an Autobiography* (Gollancz, London, 1988), p. 245.
20. Sir Edward Bridges, interview (Estorick archive).
21. J. E. Meade, *The Collected Papers of James Meade: Vol. 4, The Cabinet Office Diary 1944–1946*, ed. S. Howson and D. Moggridge (Unwin Hyman, London, 1990), p. 294.
22. Sir John Henry Woods, interview (Estorick archive).
23. *The Times*, 28 November 1946.
24. *Daily Mail*, 19 December 1946.
25. N. Owen, ' "Responsibility without Power" – the Attlee Governments and the End of British Rule in India', in N. Tiratsoo, ed., *The Attlee Years* (Pinter, London, 1991), pp. 175–6.

26. P. Ziegler, *Mountbatten* (Book Club Associates, Swindon, 1985), pp. 355–6.
27. *Daily Telegraph*, 11 October 1946.
28. Cripps to Attlee, 13 November 1946 (PRO/PREM 8/729).
29. Cabinet minutes, 19 November 1946 (PRO/CAB 129/14).
30. Cripps to Shinwell, 24 December 1946 (Shinwell papers 3/2).
31. A. J. Robertson, *The Bleak Midwinter 1947* (Manchester University Press, Manchester, 1987), p. 76.
32. D. Jay, *Change and Fortune* (Hutchinson, London, 1980), p. 152.
33. *The Economist*, 25 January 1947.
34. Sir N. Kipping, *Summing Up* (Hutchinson, London, 1972), p. 17.
35. Morning meeting, 18 February 1947 (PRO/BT 13/220A).
36. *Manchester Guardian*, 8 February 1947.
37. *The Observer*, 16 February 1947.
38. Cripps to Shinwell, 15 February 1947 (Shinwell papers, 3/2).
39. Williams, *A Prime Minister Remembers*, p. 221.
40. L. Hannah, *Electricity Before Nationalisation* (Macmillan, London, 1979), p. 317.
41. Cairncross, *Years of Recovery*, p. 380.
42. 'Draft Economic Survey', 8 January 1947 (PRO/CAB 134/503).
43. Cabinet minutes and associated papers, 16 and 17 January 1947 (PRO/PREM 8/646).
44. Marquand to Cripps, 16 February 1947 (PRO/CAB 124/1079).
45. *Empire News*, 23 February 1947.
46. *Evening Post* (Bristol), 31 March 1947.
47. *World Report*, 4 March 1947.
48. Sir G. Russell, *Designer's Trade* (Allen & Unwin, London, 1968) pp. 218–19.
49. Mass Observation report no. 2476, 'Trends in Attitudes to Government Leaders', April 1947.
50. *Financial Times*, 17 March 1947.
51. *The Times*, 11 March 1947.
52. Cripps to Attlee, 18 March 1947 (Attlee papers, 50, Bodleian).
53. *News Chronicle*, 10 April 1947.
54. W. Crofts, *Coercion or Persuasion – Propaganda in Britain after 1945* (Routledge, London, 1989), p. 39.
55. *Public Opinion*, June/July 1985, quoting a Gallup survey of May 1947.
56. S. C. Leslie, 'The Work of the Economic Information Unit', in *Public Administration*, spring 1950.
57. *Daily Mail*, 3 April 1947.
58. H. Dalton, *High Tide and After – Memoirs 1945–1960* (Muller, London, 1962), p. 237.
59. Bevin, quoted in *The Observer*, 30 March 1947.
60. Clayton believed Britain had agreed, in return for American assistance in 1945, to abandon Imperial Preference. Discovering Cripps was only prepared to negotiate it away over a long period in conjunction with US tariff reductions, Clayton momentarily thought of scrapping the loan agreement (E. Garwood, *Will Clayton – A Short Biography* (University of Texas Press, Austin, 1958), p. 26).
61. 'Marshall Proposals – Alternative Action in Event of Breakdown', July 1947 (PRO/T229/136).
62. *The Observer*, 29 June 1947.
63. *Manchester Guardian*, 12 June 1947.
64. Ibid., 16 June 1947.

Chapter 19 : CLEM

1. I. Cripps to A. Jarvis, 17 July 1947 (Jarvis papers).
2. *Foreign Relations of the United States [FRUS], 1947: Vol. 3* (US Government Print Office, Washington DC, 1971), p. 277.
3. *Christian Life and Times*, July 1947.
4. Collins to A. Sampson, 27 January 1947 (Collins papers, MS 3299 f. 176).
5. Sir Max Brown, interview.
6. K. Martin, *Harold Laski – a Biographical Memoir* (Cape, London, 1969), p. 181.
7. F. Williams, *The Triple Challenge* (Heinemann, London, 1948), p. 83.

8. W. Wyatt, *Confessions of an Optimist* (Collins, London, 1985), p. 143. Cripps, however, warned John Belcher, his Parliamentary Secretary, about his drinking. Belcher was brought down by his friendship with 'the contact man' and wheeler-dealer Sidney Stanley.

9. Sir R. B. Lockhart, *The Diaries of Sir Robert Bruce Lockhart*, ed. K. Young (Macmillan, London, 1973) p. 588, entry dated 12 March 1947.

10. *FRUS, 1947: Vol. 3*, p. 969.

11. *New Statesman*, 27 March 1954.

12. From a letter of January 1947, quoted by S. Ghosh in his *Gandhi's Emissary* (Cresset Press, London, 1967), pp. 46–7.

13. Dame Isobel Cripps, interview (Donoughue and Jones archive).

14. *The Times*, 8 August 1947.

15. D. Jay, *Change and Fortune* (Hutchinson, London, 1980), pp. 176–7.

16. *The Tribune*, 15 August 1947.

17. *Sunday Express*, 17 August 1947.

18. *Daily Mail*, 15 August 1947. The 'report' of 'a week ago'.

19. J. Lee, *My Life With Nye* (Penguin, London, 1980), p. 176.

20. Royal Commission on the Press, minutes of evidence, 29 April 1948, pp. 9–10.

21. G. Wakeford, in *Fleet Street – the Inside Story of Journalism* (Macdonald, London, 1966), p. 152.

22. H. Dalton, *The Political Diary of Hugh Dalton 1918–1940, 1945–1960*, ed. B. Pimlott (Cape, London, 1986), pp. 409–10.

23. C. Mayhew (the junior Foreign Office Minister), interview (Donoughue and Jones archive).

24. *Daily Mail*, 20 August 1947.

25. Ibid., 21 August 1947.

26. *FRUS, 1947: Vol. 3*, p. 978.

27. R. J. Moore, *Escape From Empire: the Attlee Government and the Indian Problem* (Clarendon, Oxford, 1983), p. 348.

28. Ghosh, *Gandhi's Emissary*, p. 220.

29. I. Cripps to Jones, 18 August 1947 (Thomas Jones archive, WW32/8).

30. Jones to Markham, 28 August 1947 (Thomas Jones archive, Class T, Vol. 8, No. 62).

31. I. Cripps to Jones, 29 August 1947 (Thomas Jones archive, WW32/9).

32. Plowden to Bridges, 31 July 1947 (PRO/T 229/208).

33. E. Plowden, *An Industrialist in the Treasury* (Deutsch, London, 1989), p. 18.

34. *The Times*, 5 September 1947.

35. H. Dalton's unpublished diary, entry dated 5 September 1947 *et seq.*

36. Morrison to Cripps, 8 September 1947 (copy at BLPES).

37. Cripps to Morrison, 8 September 1947 (copy at BLPES).

38. Morrison to Cripps, 8 September 1947 (copy at BLPES).

39. PRO/BT 11/3386.

40. Cripps, Clem Leslie (head of the EIU) thought, was a slave to paper plans, lacking Morrison's nose for the politically possible.

41. Cabinet minutes, 9 September 1947 (PRO/CAB 128/10).

42. H. Dalton's unpublished diary, entry dated 9 September 1947.

43. *Evening Standard*, 12 February 1962.

44. I. Cripps to A. Jarvis, 30 September 1947 (Jarvis papers).

45. P. Gordon Walker to Morrison, 23 September 1947 (Gordon Walker papers, GNWR 1/6).

46. K. Harris, *Attlee* (Weidenfeld & Nicolson, London, 1982), p. 408.

47. *FRUS, 1947: Vol. 3*, p. 979.

48. Sir George Schuster, in *The Observer*, 14 September 1947.

49. *Daily Mail*, 13 September 1947.

50. *The Listener*, 18 September 1947.

51. *Daily Mail*, 13 September 1947.

52. Sir R. Streat, *Lancashire and Whitehall: The Diary of Sir Raymond Streat: Vol. 2, 1939–1957* ed. M. Dupree (Manchester University Press, Manchester, 1987), p. 410, entry dated 11 September 1947.

53. B. Donoughue and G. Jones, *Herbert*

Morrison – Portrait of a Politician (Weidenfeld and Nicolson, London, 1973), p. 424.

54. *The Times*, 30 September 1947.
55. Cripps to Dalton, 30 October 1947 (Dalton papers).

Chapter 20 : SIX WEEKS

1. Harold Macmillan, in *The Listener*, 25 September 1969.
2. *Sunday Times*, 5 October 1947.
3. PRO/CAB 21/1702.
4. PRO/CAB 21/2218.
5. 'Cabinet Business and Procedure', 18 October 1947, Cabinet memorandum CP (47) 288.
6. R. Hall, *The Robert Hall Diaries 1947–1953*, ed. A. Cairncross (Unwin Hyman, London, 1989), p. 10, entry dated 7 October 1947. To Gaitskell, Cripps said, 'I cannot really do this job, you see, unless I am PM' (H. Gaitskell, *The Diary of Hugh Gaitskell 1945–1956*, ed. P. M. Williams (Cape, London, 1983), p. 46, entry dated 14 November 1947).
7. *Manchester Guardian*, 29 October 1947.
8. D. Jay, in The Fabian Society, *The Road to Recovery* (Allan Wingate, London, 1948), p. 24.
9. *Sunday Times*, 5 October 1947.
10. E. Watkins, *The Cautious Revolution* (Secker & Warburg, London, 1951), p. 38.
11. 'The Dollar Problem in 1948', 16 October 1947, Cabinet memorandum (PRO/CAB 129/21).
12. Sir G. Schuster, 'Richard Stafford Cripps', in *Biographical Memoirs of Fellows of the Royal Society* (Royal Society, London, 1955), p. 12.
13. *Daily Mail*, 25 October 1947.
14. *Evening Standard*, 30 October 1947.
15. I. Mikardo, *Backbencher* (Weidenfeld & Nicolson, London, 1988), p. 96.
16. *Daily Telegraph*, 16 October 1947.
17. Note attached to the report of the Investments Programme Committee, October 1947 (PRO/T 229/66).
18. D. Marquand, *The Unprincipled Society* (Fontana, London, 1988), p. 43.
19. 'The Framework of Economic Planning', 10 November 1947 (PRO/T 229/417).
20. *The Wykehamist*, 25 June 1952.
21. PRO/T 229/208.
22. V. L. Allen, *Trade Union Leadership – Based on a Study of Arthur Deakin* (Longmans, London, 1957), p. 123.
23. Gaitskell, *Diary*, p. 45, entry dated 14 November 1947.
24. J. Margach, *The Abuse of Power* (W. H. Allen, London, 1978), p. 99; *Evening Standard*, March 7 1985.
25. F. Williams, *Nothing So Strange* (Cassell, London, 1970), p. 226.
26. Quoted in H. Dalton, *High Tide and After – Memoirs 1945–1960* (Muller, London, 1962), p. 286.
27. E. Powell, in *Sunday Telegraph*, 17 March 1985.
28. *The People*, 9 November 1947.
29. Cripps to Lady H. Wilson, 14 December 1947 (PRO/CAB 127/153).

Chapter 21 : CHANCELLOR

1. J. C. R. Dow, *The Management of the British Economy 1945–1960* (Cambridge University Press, Cambridge, 1964), p. 33. The Permanent Secretary at the Ministry of Fuel and Power continued to grumble about 'economists' interfering with the Ministry's steel allocating.
2. B. Riley to Cripps, 1 December 1947 (Curtis papers, 118 (1947)).
3. Cited in A. Cairncross, *Years of Recovery – British Economic Policy 1945–1951* (Methuen, London, 1985), p. 140.
4. A. Robinson, 'The Economic Problems of the Transition from War to Peace: 1945–1949', in *Cambridge Journal of Economics*, Vol. 10 (1986), p. 174.
5. 'Marshall Aid – Undertakings on UK Internal Finance', 29 December 1947 (PRO/CAB 134/215).

6. Dalton denied any political differences. They had disagreed in the past, about Cripps's vegetarianism. But there had been 'no two ministers who have more continuously agreed than Sir Stafford and myself' (*The Times*, 29 November 1947).

7. Lord Cockfield, interview.

8. Chancellor's notes for lobby correspondents, 21 February 1948 (PRO/T 229/46).

9. Bevan, though he respected Cripps, knew him to be pliable. Cripps's leniency with Bevan meant, the Opposition charged, that Bevan 'torpedoed' the curtailing of investment. Bevan floored his critics opposite by demanding to know exactly what they would cut.

10. See S. Newton, 'The Sterling Crisis of 1947 and the British Response to the Marshall Plan', in *English Historical Review*, August 1984, pp. 391–408.

11. Cripps to Snyder, 17 January 1948 (PRO/PREM 8/879).

12. J. Fforde, *The Bank of England and the Public Policy 1944–1958* (Cambridge University Press, Cambridge, 1992), p. 279.

13. Bevin and Attlee with the TUC General Council, 17 November 1947 (PRO/T 171/395).

14. Cripps to Bridges and Plowden, 23 November 1947 (PRO/T 171/395).

15. V. L. Allen, *Trade Unions and the Government* (Longmans, London, 1960), p. 285.

16. PRO/PREM 8/903.

17. K. Middlemas, *Power, Competition and the State: Vol. 1, Britain in Search of Balance 1940–1961* (Macmillan, London, 1986), p. 159.

18. See J. Hinton's comments in *Contemporary Record*, summer 1994, pp. 181–3.

19. B. Headey, *British Cabinet Ministers* (Allen & Unwin, London, 1974), p. 143 (based on interviews with former civil servants).

20. *The Spectator*, 30 June 1990.

21. J. Lees-Milne, *Midway on the Waves* (Faber, London, 1985), p. 28, entry dated 18 February 1948.

22. *Daily Mail*, 13 March 1948.

23. H. Gaitskell, *The Diary of Hugh Gaitskell 1945–1956*, ed. P. M. Williams (Cape, London, 1983), p. 56, entry dated 16 February 1948.

24. J. Mackintosh, *The British Cabinet* (Stevens & Sons, London, 1962), p. 466.

25. E. A. G. Robinson, *Economic Planning in the United Kingdom – Some Lessons* (Cambridge University Press, London, 1967), p. 21.

26. Cairncross, *Years of Recovery*, p. 420.

27. Plowden to Cripps, 31 March 1948 (PRO/T 171/395).

28. R. Hall, *The Robert Hall Diaries 1947–1953*, ed. A. Cairncross (Unwin Hyman, London, 1989), p. 21, entry dated 24 March 1948.

29. A. Wildavsky, *The Private Government of Public Money* (Macmillan, London, 1974), p. 352.

30. F. Lee's unpublished autobiography.

31. Speech at the Albert Hall, 25 April 1948, quoted in Cripps's *God in Our Work* (Nelson, London, 1949), p. 50.

32. D. Jay, in A. Thompson, *The Day Before Yesterday* (Sidgwick & Jackson, London, 1971), p. 62.

33. H. L. 'Etang, 'The Health of Statesmen and Affairs of Nations', in *The Practitioner*, January 1958.

34. Cripps to Attlee, 19 March 1948 (PRO/T 172/2128).

35. M. Beloff, *New Dimensions in Foreign Policy* (Allen & Unwin, London, 1961), p. 42.

36. A. Sampson, *The Anatomy of Britain* (Hodder & Stoughton, London, 1962), p. 330.

37. Sir O. Franks, *The Movement Towards Unity in Europe* (University of Texas, 1989), p. 8.

38. *Foreign Relations of the United States, 1948: Vol. 3* (US Government Print Office, Washington DC, 1971), p. 1079.

39. Cripps's draft memorandum, 3 March 1948 (PRP/CAB 21/2244).
40. *New York Times*, 19 March 1948, cited in PRO/T 236/1892.
41. Note by F. Roberts of talk between Bevin and Attlee, 25 June 1948 (PRO/FO 800/460).
42. K. Burk, 'Britain and the Marshall Plan', in C. Wrigley, ed., *Warfare, Diplomacy and Politics* (Hamish Hamilton, London, 1986), p. 219.
43. Sir Alfred Egerton's diary, 13 July 1948.
44. Lord Roll, interview.
45. Plowden to Cripps, 24 May 1948 (PRO/CAB 21/2244).
46. M. Stockwood, *Chanctonbury Ring – the Autobiography of Mervyn Stockwood* (Hodder & Stoughton, London, 1982), p. 72.
47. Cripps to H. Hennessy, 13 July 1948 (Cripps papers, 623).
48. H. Dalton, *The Political Diary of Hugh Dalton 1918–1940, 1945–1960*, ed. B. Pimlott (Cape, London, 1986), p. 517.
49. Minutes of the Bristol South-East Divisional Labour Party, 28 July 1948 (BELP 40488/M/3/3).
50. *Leader*, 31 December 1949.
51. Visit of the Chancellor to Paris, July 1948 (PRO/T 232/27).
52. *The Times*, 8 September 1948.
53. *Manchester Guardian*, 17 September 1948.
54. Cripps to A. Newton, 16 September 1948 (letter in the possession of Adela Newton's daughter).
55. Cripps's speech to the 1944 Association, 7 July 1948 (Labour Party archives).
56. Bevin to Cripps, 29 September 1948 (PRO/FO 371/71937).
57. W. Millis, ed., *The Forrestal Diaries: The Inner History of the Cold War* (Viking, New York, 1951), p. 491.
58. H. Dalton, *High Tide and After – Memoirs 1945–1960* (Muller, London, 1962), pp. 287–8.
59. *Manchester Guardian*, 9 October 1948.
60. Dalton, *Political Diary*, p. 439, entry dated 11 September 1948.
61. Canon L. J. Collins, *Faith under Fire* (Frewin, London, 1966), p. 105.
62. *Daily Express*, 23 October 1948.

Chapter 22 : THE LAST MAN

1. *Illustrated News*, 23 April 1949.
2. *The Economist*, 28 December 1948.
3. A. Shonfield, *British Economic Policy since the War* (Penguin, London, 1958), p. 166.
4. C. Lysaght, *Brendan Bracken* (Allen Lane, London, 1979), p. 281.
5. F. Lee's unpublished autobiography, p. 30.
6. A. Budd, *The Politics of Economic Planning* (Fontana, London, 1978), p. 76.
7. E. Dell, *The Chancellors* (HarperCollins, London, 1996), p. 109.
8. PRO/T 223/90.
9. Jay to Cripps, 17 March 1949 (PRO/T 229/266).
10. H. Nicolson, *Diaries and Letters 1945–1962*, ed. N. Nicolson (Fontana, London, 1970), p. 166, entry dated 15 March 1949.
11. *Daily Graphic*, 22 December 1948.
12. 'Although a policy of austerity had been forced on him by events, Cripps insisted it had been freely chosen and he wanted me to acknowledge it was fundamentally right' (P.-H. Spaak, *The Continuing Battle* (Weidenfeld & Nicolson, London, 1971), p. 192).
13. 'The Future Structure of the OEEC', 16 January 1949 (PRO/T 273/351).
14. R. Hall, *The Robert Hall Diaries 1947–1953*, ed. A. Cairncross (Unwin Hyman, London, 1989), p. 48, entry dated 13 January 1949.
15. EPC minutes, 26 January 1949 (PRO/CAB 134/220).
16. M. Hogan, *The Marshall Plan – America, Britain and the Reconstruction of Western Europe 1947–1952* (Cambridge University Press, Cambridge, 1987), pp. 218–21.
17. E. Plowden, in M. Charlton, *The Price*

of Victory (BBC, London, 1983), pp. 82–3.

18. H. Pelling, *Britain and the Marshall Plan* (Macmillan, London, 1987), p. 70.

19. *Annual Register* (Royal Institute of International Affairs, London, 1949), pp. 17–18.

20. Hall to Plowden, 28 March 1949 (PRO/T 236/2398).

21. Hall, *Diaries*, p. 56, entry dated 6 April 1949.

22. Cripps had just limited Strachey's expenditure on the East African 'Groundnuts' scheme to £50 million (A. Wood, *The Groundnut Affair* (Bodley Head, London, 1950)).

23. PRO/T 171/397.

24. D. N. Pritt, *The Labour Government 1945–1951* (Lawrence & Wishart, London, 1963), p. 310.

25. D. Marquand, 'Sir Stafford Cripps', in M. Sissons and P. French, eds., *Age of Austerity, 1945–1951* (Penguin, London, 1965), p. 191.

26. R. F. Harrod, in *Soundings*, May 1949, p. 5.

27. 1 April 1949 (PRO/T 236/2398).

28. H. Wilson, *The Labour Government 1964–1970* (Penguin, London, 1974), p. 127.

29. *Daily Mail*, 7 April 1949.

30. Dell, *The Chancellors*, p. 112.

31. Cripps to Woods, 6 April 1949 (Woods papers).

32. Cripps to Franks, 6 April 1949 (PRO/T 236/2398).

33. *Manchester Guardian*, 7 April 1949.

34. Chancellor's script (PRO/T 171/399).

35. *Daily Telegraph*, 8 April 1949.

36. PRO/CAB 127/122.

37. PRO/T 273/369.

38. B. Trend to Collins, 3 May 1949 (Collins papers, 3290/147).

39. PRO/FO 371/79333.

40. H. Wilson Smith, 17 May 1949 (PRO/T232/88).

41. *New York Times*, 18 May 1949.

42. Ibid., 19 May 1949.

43. Chancellor's note, 27 May 1949 (PRO/T 232/88).

44. J. Fforde, *The Bank of England and Public Policy 1941–1958* (Cambridge University Press, Cambridge, 1992), p. 287.

45. *Daily Graphic*, 3 June 1949.

46. With only an interval of a few weeks during Churchill's interim coalition in the summer of 1945.

47. *The Times*, 8 June 1949.

48. H. Massingham, in *Aspect*, February 1963. In the late 1940s, Massingham 'knew as much of what went on in the Cabinet as the Cabinet did'. Who were his sources? One of them, according to Massingham's opposite number on the *Sunday Times*, James Margach, was Lady Cripps (J. Margach, *The Anatomy of Power* (W. H. Allen, London, 1979), p. 146). They were spotted taking tea together at The Ritz. One of Massingham's novels, *The Best Days*, which was published in Budget week in 1949, described the fall from grace of a country vicar, blinded by Gladstonian pride into visiting a prostitute, complete with references to God, love, economics, Winchester, and Eno's Fruit Salts. Massingham kept a diary of his contacts, promising to tell all 'when the lawyers were no longer on the prowl'. He died in 1972. The diaries have disappeared.

49. I. Cripps to Attlee, 13 June 1949 (Attlee papers, Countess Attlee).

50. H. Dalton's unpublished diary, 15 June 1949.

51. *Foreign Relations of the United States [FRUS], 1949: Vol. 4* (US Government Print Office, Washington DC, 1971), pp. 784–7.

52. A. Cairncross and B. Eichengreen, *Sterling in Decline* (Blackwell, Oxford, 1983), pp. 121–2; P. Hennessy, *Never Again – Britain 1945–1951* (Cape, London, 1992), p. 371.

53. *FRUS, 1949: Vol. 4*, pp. 787–90.

54. Ibid., pp. 792–3.

55. Jay to Cripps, 30 June 1949 (PRO/T 172/2038).
56. H. Gaitskell, *The Diary of Hugh Gaitskell 1945–1956*, ed. P. M. Williams (Cape, London, 1983), p. 116, entry dated 28 June 1949.
57. EPC (49) 72 (PRO/CAB 134/222).
58. *Daily Mirror*, 4 July 1949.
59. *Daily Express*, 6 July 1949.
60. H. Dalton's unpublished diary, 19 July 1949.
61. Hall, *Diaries*, pp. 63–4, entry dated 8 July 1949.
62. *Daily Mirror*, 15 July 1949.
63. Gaitskell, *Diary*, p. 126, entry dated 3 August 1949.
64. *The Times*, 18 July 1949.
65. Cripps to Attlee, 16 July 1949 (PRO/PREM 8/1027).
66. D. Jay, *Change and Fortune* (Hutchinson, London, 1980), p. 187.
67. Cripps to A. Newton, 16 July 1949 (Newton letters).
68. B. Trend, interview (courtesy of Professor K. O. Morgan).
69. *The Times*, 3 January 1980.

Chapter 23 : **PRICKLY CROWN**

1. H. Gaitskell, *The Diary of Hugh Gaitskell 1945–1956*, ed. P. M. Williams (Cape, London, 1983), p. 138, entry dated 21 September 1949.
2. *Daily Mail*, 20 September 1949.
3. *The Times*, 25 July 1949.
4. Sir E. Plowden, in *Contemporary Record*, winter 1991, p. 494.
5. Bridges to Attlee, 23 July 1949 (PRO/PREM 8/1178 part 1).
6. J. Fforde, *The Bank of England and Public Policy 1941–1958* (Cambridge University Press, Cambridge, 1992), p. 294n.
7. Attlee to Cripps, 5 August 1949 (PRO/PREM 8/1178 part 1).
8. Cobbold to Attlee, 3 August (PRO/PREM 8/976).
9. Wilson to Attlee, 8 August 1949 (PRO/PREM 8/1178 part 1).
10. P. M. Williams, *Hugh Gaitskell – a Political Biography* (Cape, London, 1979), pp. 195–203.
11. D. Jay, in W. T. Rodgers, ed., *Hugh Gaitskell 1906–1963* (Thames and Hudson, London, 1964), p. 95. But see B. Pimlott's *Harold Wilson* (HarperCollins, London, 1992), Chapter 8.
12. R. Hall, *The Robert Hall Diaries 1947–1953*, ed. A. Cairncross (Unwin Hyman, London, 1989), p. 71, entry dated 26 August 1949.
13. Fforde, *The Bank of England and Public Policy*, p. 298.
14. Cripps to D. Liechti, 30 August 1949 (Liechti papers).
15. Sir R. Barclay, *Ernest Bevin and the Foreign Office* (Latimer, London, 1975), p. 64.
16. *New York Times*, 7 September 1949.
17. D. Acheson, *Sketches from Life* (Hamish Hamilton, London, 1961), p. 23.
18. D. Acheson, *Present At The Creation* (Hamish Hamilton, London, 1971), p. 324.
19. *The Times*, 4 January 1980.
20. *The Spectator*, 30 September 1949.
21. S. Newton, 'The 1949 Sterling Crisis and the British Policy towards European Integration', in *Review of International Studies*, July 1985, pp. 169–82.
22. W. Wyatt, *Turn Again, Westminster* (Deutsch, London, 1973), pp. 179–80.
23. E. Plowden, *An Industrialist in the Treasury* (Deutsch, London, 1989), pp. 64–5.
24. *The Times*, 20 September 1949.
25. *Manchester Guardian*, 20 September 1949.
26. Ibid., 21 September 1949.
27. *Evening Standard*, 21 September 1949.
28. *Daily Mail*, 20 September 1949.
29. *Sunday Pictorial*, 25 September 1949.
30. PRO/T 273/232.
31. M. A. Hamilton, 'Sir Stafford Cripps – a Personal Sketch', in *Britain Today*, January 1951, p. 19.
32. *Daily Mail*, 29 September 1949.

33. H. Dalton's unpublished diary, 29 September 1949.
34. PRO/CAB 127/122.
35. H. Dalton, *The Political Diary of Hugh Dalton 1918–1940, 1945–1960*, ed. B. Pimlott (Cape, London, 1986), p. 459.
36. J. Griffiths, *Pages From Memory* (Dent, London, 1969), p. 195.
37. *The Listener*, 9 May 1968.
38. F. Williams, *A Prime Minister Remembers: The War and Post-War Memoirs of the Rt Hon. Earl Attlee* (Heinemann, London, 1961), p. 227.
39. *The Times*, 9 and 10 March 1994.
40. Lord Salter, *Memoirs of a Public Servant* (Faber, London, 1961), p. 291.
41. *Daily Express*, 29 September 1949.
42. 'It is one of the disasters of civilisation, unfortunately, that that discovery [the splitting of the atom] was ever perfected' (*Western Daily Press*, 1 November 1948).
43. I. Cripps to C. Haslett, 10 October 1949 (Haslett papers).
44. E. Estorick, *Stafford Cripps – a Biography* (Heinemann, London, 1949).
45. Lord Williams, *Digging For Britain*, Hutchinson, London, 1965), pp. 170–1.
46. Dalton, *Political Diary*, p. 458, entry dated 10 October 1949.
47. J. Campbell, *Nye Bevan and the Mirage of British Socialism* (Weidenfeld & Nicolson, London, 1987), pp. 182–5.
48. C. Webster, *The Health Services Since the War* (HMSO, London, 1988), pp. 143–5.
49. M. Hogan, *The Marshall Plan – America, Britain and the Reconstruction of Western Europe 1947–1952* (Cambridge University Press, Cambridge, 1987), p. 276.
50. J. Young, *Britain, France and the Unity of Europe 1945–1951* (Leicester University Press, Leicester, 1984), p. 127.
51. PRO/CAB 129/37(1).
52. M. Charlton, *The Price of Victory* (BBC, London, 1983), pp. 86–8.
53. Quoted in E. Watkins, *The Cautious Revolution* (Secker & Warburg, London, 1951), p. 33.
54. Cripps–Hudson correspondence, November 1949 (PRO/CAB 127/131).
55. Cripps to Churchill, 12 December 1949 (PRO/T 172/2039).
56. *The Times*, 28 November 1949.
57. Cripps to L. Edwards, 1 December 1949 (PRO/T 172/2121).
58. D. Jay, *Socialism in the New Society* (Longmans, London, 1962), p. 378.
59. Dalton, *Political Diary*, p. 465, entry dated 24 January 1950.
60. Cripps to R. Acland, 18 January 1950 (PRO/T 273/235).
61. Cripps to Attlee, 2 February 1950 (PRO/T 172/2121).
62. Attlee to Bevin, 7 January 1950 (PRO/T 273/140).
63. *Manchester Guardian*, 6 February 1950.
64. *Daily Telegraph*, 16 February 1950.
65. I. Zweiniger-Bargielowska, 'Rationing, Austerity and the Conservative Party Recovery after 1945', in *Historical Journal*, March 1994, pp. 173–95.
66. Cripps to Rogers, 25 February 1950 (BELP).
67. Plowden, *An Industrialist in the Treasury*, p. 105.

Chapter 24 : HUSTLED

1. *The Listener*, 9 May 1968.
2. R. Hall, *The Robert Hall Diaries 1947–1953*, ed. A. Cairncross (Unwin Hyman, London, 1989), p. 106, entry dated 1 March 1950.
3. H. A. Clegg, *A History of British Trade Unions since 1889: Vol. 3, 1934–1951* (Clarendon, Oxford, 1994), p. 389–92.
4. M. Foot, *Aneurin Bevan: Vol. 2, 1945–1960* (Davis-Poynter, London, 1973), p. 292.
5. C.Webster, *The Health Services since the War* (HMSO, London, 1988), p. 156.
6. Quoted in K. O. Morgan, *Labour in Power 1945–1951* (Oxford University Press, London, 1984), p. 407n.
7. A. Cairncross and N. Watts, *The*

Economic Section – a Study in Economic Advising (Routledge, London, 1989), pp. 250–2.

8. In a Cabinet paper in March, Cripps set out his Budget rationale of managing demand – striving for an equilibrium between investment and savings – at greater length. K. O. Morgan has called it his 'economic testament' (*Labour in Power*, p. 407n).

9. E. Dell, *The Chancellors* (HarperCollins, London, 1996), p. 133.

10. A. Milward, *The Reconstruction of Western Europe 1945–1951* (Methuen, London, 1984), p. 304.

11. M. Hogan, *The Marshall Plan – America, Britain and the Reconstruction of Western Europe 1947–1952* (Cambridge University Press, Cambridge, 1987), pp. 302–3.

12. Cripps to Hoffman, 7 March 1950 (PRO/T 172/2121).

13. R. Bullen, 'An Idea Enters Diplomacy: The Schuman Plan, May 1950', in R. Bullen et al., eds., *Ideas into Politics* (Croom Helm, London, 1984), pp. 193–204.

14. *Documents on British Policy Overseas, Series 2 – the Schuman Plan* (HMSO, London, 1986), Document 3, p. 7.

15. J. Monnet, *Mémoires* (Fayard, Paris, 1976), p. 363.

16. R. T. Griffiths, in *Reviews in History*, July 1996.

17. P. Uri, in *Le Monde*, 9 May 1975.

18. *Le Monde*, 30 May 1950.

19. *Documents on British Policy Overseas, Series 2 – the Schuman Plan*, Document 93, p. 164.

20. E. Roll, *Crowded Hours* (Faber, London, 1985), pp. 82–3.

21. G. Warner, 'The Labour Governments and the Unity of Western Europe, 1945–51', in R. Ovendale, ed., *The Foreign Policy of the British Labour Governments 1945–1951* (Leicester University Press, Leicester, 1984), p. 74.

22. E. Dell, *The Schuman Plan and the British Abdication of Leadership in Europe* (Clarendon, Oxford, 1995), Conclusion.

23. H. Gaitskell, *The Diary of Hugh Gaitskell 1945–1956*, ed. P. M. Williams (Cape, London, 1983), p. 187, entry dated 26 May 1950.

24. Morgan Phillips papers, GS26/3, 20–21 May 1950.

25. Milward, *The Reconstruction of Western Europe*, pp. 405–6.

26. A. Bullock, *The Life and Times of Ernest Bevin: Vol. 3, Foreign Secretary 1945–1951* (Heinemann, London, 1983), p. 799.

27. Foot, *Aneurin Bevan: Vol. 2*, pp. 296–7.

28. F. Williams, *A Prime Minister Remembers: The War and Post-War Memoirs of the Rt Hon. Earl Attlee* (Heinemann, London, 1961), pp. 244–5.

29. F. Williams, *Nothing So Strange* (Cassell, London, 1970), p. 280.

30. D. Jay, *Change and Fortune* (Hutchinson, London, 1980), p. 202.

31. In a speech in July 1948, Bevan caused a sensation by calling Tories 'lower than vermin'. He was quoting Disraeli, but the press neglected to say so.

32. Attlee to the King, 17 October 1950 (Windsor archives, 350/14).

33. F. Lee's unpublished autobiography, p. 53.

34. W. Wyatt, *Turn Again, Westminster* (Deutsch, London, 1973), p. 147.

35. *Evening World* (Bristol), 20 October 1950.

36. *New Statesman*, 13 October 1967.

37. *Daily Express*, 18 October 1950.

38. *Manchester Guardian*, 20 October 1950.

39. *Financial Times*, 20 October 1950.

40. *Daily Herald*, 20 October 1950.

41. *Manchester Guardian*, 20 October 1950.

42. *Church of England Newspaper*, 21 October 1950.

43. *Financial Times*, 23 October 1950.

44. *Sunday Chronicle*, 22 October 1950.

45. W. Wyatt, *To the Point* (Weidenfeld & Nicolson, London, 1981), p. 121.

Chapter 25 : CHEERIO

1. *Sunday Express,* 19 November 1950.
2. I. Cripps to C. Haslett, 20 April 1951 (Haslett papers).
3. *Daily Mirror,* 18 May 1951.
4. *Sunday Chronicle,* 23 September 1951.
5. I. Cripps to C. Haslett, 7 September 1951 (Haslett papers).
6. *Sunday Chronicle,* 23 September 1951.
7. *News Chronicle,* 25 August 1951.
8. H. Gaitskell, *The Diary of Hugh Gaitskell 1945–1956,* ed. P. M. Williams (Cape, London, 1983), p. 309, entry dated 23 November 1951.

BIBLIOGRAPHY

1. PRIMARY SOURCES

(a) Official papers

(i) Public Records Office

Board of Trade
Cabinet minutes and papers
Colonial Office Arbitration Proceedings
Stafford Cripps's private office papers
Foreign Office
Ramsay MacDonald diary and papers
Ministry of Aircraft Production
Ministry of Munitions
Ministry of Transport
Prime Minister
Treasury
War Cabinet minutes

(ii) Others

The Athenaeum
BBC Sound Archives (including BBC radio transcript *The Apostle of Austerity* (February 1987))
BBC Written Archives Centre
The British Red Cross Society
Companies House
Fabian Society (British Library of Political and Economic Science (BLPES))
London County Council Minutes (Greater London Record Office)
Royal Archives (Windsor)
Proceedings of the Railway Rates Tribunal (BLPES)
Society for Socialist Information and Propaganda (BLPES)
Trades Union Congress (Modern Records Centre, Warwick)

(b) Official Publications

All England Law Reports
Annual Register (Royal Institute of International Affairs, London, 1949)
British Red Cross Society, *Reports by the Joint War Committee, 1914–1919* (British Red Cross Society, 1921)
Documents on British Policy Overseas (HMSO, London, various dates)

353

Documents on German Foreign Policy (US Government Print Office, Washington DC, various dates)

Foreign Relations of the United States (US Government Print Office, Washington DC, various dates)

History of the Ministry of Munitions: Vol. 1, Industrial Mobilisation 1914–1915; Vol. 8, Control of Industrial Capacity and Equipment (HMSO, London, 1921, 1922)

H. M. Factory Queen's Ferry – Its History and Development (Queen's Ferry, no date)

Illustrated Official Journal (Patents)

Labour Party Annual Conference Reports

Mansergh, N., ed., *The Transfer of Power 1942–1947: Vol. 1, The Cripps Mission, January to April 1942; Vol. 7, The Cabinet Mission, 23 March–29 June 1946* (HMSO, London, 1970, 1977)

Parliamentary Debates (Hansard)

Royal Commission on the Press 1947–1949 (HMSO, London, 1949)

(c) Unpublished private papers

Clement Attlee (Anne, Countess Attlee)

——(Bodleian Library)

R. Barrington-Ward (Mark Barrington Ward)

Lord Beaverbrook (House of Lords)

Bishop George Bell (Lambeth Palace Library)

Violet Bonham Carter (the Bonham Carter family)

Stanley Bruce (Australian Archives)

R. A. Butler (Trinity College, Cambridge)

Sir Walter Citrine (BLPES)

L. John Collins (Lambeth Palace Library)

Kate Courtney (BLPES)

Stafford Cripps (Nuffield College, Oxford)

Lionel Curtis (Bodleian Library)

Hugh Dalton (BLPES)

Geoffrey Dawson (The Times Archive)

Bernard Donoughue and George Jones (BLPES)

James Chuter Ede (British Library)

Sir Alfred Egerton (The Royal Society)

Eric Estorick (Michael Estorick)

H. V. Evatt (Flinders University, Australia)

Patrick Gordon Walker (Churchill College, Cambridge)

Elizabeth Haldane (National Library of Scotland)

Frank Hardie (Bodleian Library)

Caroline Haslett (Institute of Electrical Engineers)

Alan Jarvis (University of Toronto)

Cecil King (Boston University)

Thomas Jones (National Library of Wales)

George Lansbury (BLPES)

Harold Laski (University of Hull)

Fred Lee (Pam Flint)

Dagmar Liechti (Bircher-Benner Klinik)

David Lloyd George (House of Lords)

Violet Markham (BLPES)
Kingsley Martin (University of Sussex)
Jim Middleton (Ruskin College, Oxford)
Walter Monckton (Bodleian Library)
Herbert Morrison (Nuffield College, Oxford)
——(Donoughue and Jones, BLPES)
Adela Newton (Rosemary Hoare)
Frederick Pethick-Lawrence (Trinity College, Cambridge)
Morgan Phillips (Labour Party)
Sir William Ramsay (University College, London)
Herbert Rogers (Irving Rogers)
Herbert Samuel (House of Lords)
Emmanuel Shinwell (BLPES)
Graham Spry (National Archives of Canada)
Beatrice Webb (BLPES)
Sir John Henry Woods (Mary Woods)

(d) Other archives

Bristol East Labour Party (BELP) (Bristol Record Office)
Imperial Chemical Industries (London)
The Labour Party (National Museum of Labour History)
Mass Observation (University of Sussex)
Woolwich Labour Party (Blackheath Local History Library)

(e) Published diaries

Amery, L. S., *The Empire at Bay – the Leo Amery Diaries 1929–1945*, ed. J. Barnes and D. Nicholson (Hutchinson, London, 1988)
Cadogan, A., *The Diaries of Alexander Cadogan, O.M., 1938–1945*, ed. D. Dilks (Cassell, London, 1971)
Colville, J., *The Fringes of Power: Downing Street Diaries 1939–1955* (Hodder & Stoughton, London, 1985)
Crawford, D. Lindsay, Earl of, *The Crawford Papers* (Manchester University Press, Manchester, 1984)
Dalton, H., *The Political Diary of Hugh Dalton 1918–1940, 1945–1960*, ed. B. Pimlott (Cape, London, 1986)
——*The Second World War Diary of Hugh Dalton 1940–1945*, ed. B. Pimlott (Cape, London, 1986)
Gaitskell, H., *The Diary of Hugh Gaitskell 1945–1956*, ed. P. M. Williams (Cape, London, 1983)
Gordon Walker, P., *Patrick Gordon Walker – Political Diaries 1932–1971*, ed. R. Pearce (Historians' Press, London, 1991)
Hall, R., *The Robert Hall Diaries 1947–1953*, ed. A. Cairncross (Unwin Hyman, London, 1989)
Hamid, S., *Disastrous Twilight* (Cooper, London, 1986)
Holmes, O. W., and Laski, H., *The Holmes–Laski Letters 1916–1935*, ed. M. de W. Howe (Oxford University Press, London, 1953)
King, C., *With Malice Towards None: A War Diary* (Sidgwick & Jackson, London, 1970)

Lockhart, Sir R. B., *The Diaries of Sir Robert Bruce Lockhart*, ed. K. Young (Macmillan, London, 1973)

Meade, J. E., *The Collected Papers of James Meade: Vol. 4, The Cabinet Office Diary 1944–1946*, ed. S. Howson and D. Moggridge (Unwin Hyman, London, 1990)

Millis, W., ed., *The Forrestal Diaries: The Inner History of the Cold War* (Viking, New York, 1951)

Moorehead, A., *African Trilogy* (Hamish Hamilton, London, 1944)

Nicolson, H., *Diaries and Letters 1939–1945*, ed. N. Nicolson (Collins, London, 1967)

——*Diaries and Letters 1945–1962*, ed. N. Nicolson (Fontana, London, 1970)

Streat, Sir R., *Lancashire and Whitehall: The Diary of Sir Raymond Streat: Vol. 2, 1939–1957* ed. M. Dupree (Manchester University Press, Manchester, 1987)

Wavell, A. P., *Wavell: The Viceroy's Journal*, ed. P. Moon (Oxford University Press, London, 1973)

Webb, B., *The Diary of Beatrice Webb: Vol. 3, 1905–1924; Vol. 4, 1924–1943*, ed. N. and J. MacKenzie (Virago, London, 1984, 1985)

Webb, S. and B., *Indian Diary*, ed. N. G. Jayal (Oxford University Press, London, 1990)

——*The Letters of Sidney and Beatrice Webb: Vol. 3, Pilgrimage, 1912–1947*, ed. N. MacKenzie (Cambridge University Press, Cambridge, 1978)

2. SECONDARY SOURCES

(a) Books

Acheson, D., *Sketches From Life* (Hamish Hamilton, London, 1961)

——*Present at the Creation* (Hamish Hamilton, London, 1971)

Acland, R., ed., *Why I am a Democrat – a Symposium* (Gollancz, London, 1939)

Adams, V. ['Watchman'], *Right Honourable Gentlemen* (Hamish Hamilton, London, 1939)

Addison, P., *The Road to 1945* (Cape, London, 1975)

——*Now The War Is Over – a Social History of Britain 1945–1951* (BBC, London, 1985)

Allen, C., ed., *Plain Tales from the Raj* (Century, London, 1975)

Allen, V. L., *Trade Union Leadership – Based on a Study of Arthur Deakin* (Longmans, London, 1957)

——*Trade Unions and the Government* (Longmans, London, 1960)

Angell, N., *The Autobiography of Norman Angell* (Hamish Hamilton, London, 1951)

Annan, N., *Our Age – Portrait of a Generation* (Weidenfeld & Nicolson, London, 1990)

Attlee, C., *As It Happened* (Heinemann, London, 1954)

——*Granada Historical Records Interview* (Panther, London, 1967)

Barclay, Sir R., *Ernest Bevin and the Foreign Office* (Latimer, London, 1975)

Barnes, C. H., *Shorts Aircrafts since 1900* (Putnam, London, 1967)

Barnett, C., *The Audit of War – the Illusion and Reality of Britain as a Great Nation* (Macmillan, London, 1986)

——*The Lost Victory – British Dreams, British Realities 1945–1950* (Macmillan, London, 1995)

Bartlett, V., *And Now, Tomorrow* (Chatto & Windus, London, 1960)

Bassett, R., *Democracy and Foreign Policy: A Case History – the Sino-Japanese Dispute 1931–1933* (Longmans, London, 1952)

——*1931 – Political Crisis* (Macmillan, London, 1958)

Beattie, A., ed., *English Party Politics: Vol. 2* (Weidenfeld & Nicolson, London, 1970)

Beckett, F., *The Enemy Within – the Rise and Fall of the British Communist Party* (Murray, London, 1995)

Bellamy, J., and Saville, J., eds., *The Dictionary of Labour Biography: Vols. 4 and 9* (Macmillan, London, 1977, 1993)

Beloff, M., *New Dimensions in Foreign Policy* (Allen & Unwin, London, 1961)

Beveridge, Lord, *Power and Influence* (Hodder & Stoughton, London, 1953)

Bevin, E., and Cole, G. D. H., *The Crisis – What it is, How it Arose, What to Do* (New Statesman, London, 1931)

Bilainkin, G., Maisky: *Ten Years Ambassador* (Allen & Unwin, London, 1944)

Birkenhead, Lord, *Walter Monckton* (Weidenfeld & Nicolson, London, 1969)

A Birthday and Some Memories 1868–1928 (J. C. Eno Ltd, London, 1928)

Blaazer, D., *The Popular Front and the Progressive Tradition* (Cambridge University Press, Cambridge, 1992)

Bonham Carter, V., *Winston Churchill as I Knew Him* (Eyre & Spottiswoode, London, 1965)

Bowlby, J., *Child Care and the Growth of Love* (Penguin, London, 2nd edn, 1965)

Briggs, A., and Saville, J., eds., *Essays in Labour History 1918–1939* (Croom Helm, London, 1977)

Brittain, V., *Pethick-Lawrence – a Portrait* (Allen & Unwin, London, 1963)

Brooke, S., *Labour's War – the Labour Party during the Second World War* (Clarendon, Oxford, 1992)

Bryant, A., *Stanley Baldwin – a Tribute* (Hamish Hamilton, London, 1937)

Bryant, C., *Stafford Cripps – the First Modern Chancellor* (Hodder & Stoughton, London, 1997)

Bryher, S., *An Account of the Labour and Socialist Movement in Bristol* (Bristol Socialist Society, Bristol, 1931)

Budd, A., *The Politics of Economic Planning* (Fontana, London, 1978)

Bullen, R. et al., eds., *Ideas into Politics* (Croom Helm, London, 1984)

Bullock, A., *The Life and Times of Ernest Bevin: Vol. 1, Trade Union Leader 1881–1940; Vol. 2, Minister of Labour 1940–1945; Vol. 3, Foreign Secretary 1945–1951* (Heinemann, London, 1960, 1967, 1983)

Burchett, W., *North of the Seventeenth Parallel* (People's Publishing House, Delhi, 1956)

Burge, H. M., *Discourses and Letters of H. M. Burge*, ed. Lord Charnwood (Chatto & Windus, London, 1930)

Butt, R., *The Power of Parliament* (Constable, London, 1967)

Caine, B., *Destined to be Wives – the Sisters of Beatrice Webb* (Clarendon, Oxford, 1986)

Cairncross, A., ed., *Anglo-American Economic Collaboration in War and Peace 1942–1949* (Clarendon, Oxford, 1982)

——*Years of Recovery – British Economic Policy 1945–1951* (Methuen, London, 1985)

——and Eichengreen, B., *Sterling in Decline* (Blackwell, Oxford, 1983)

——and Watts, N., *The Economic Section – a Study in Economic Advising* (Routledge, London, 1989)

Calder, A., *The People's War – Britain 1939–1945* (Cape, London, 1969)

Campbell, J., *Nye Bevan and the Mirage of British Socialism* (Weidenfeld & Nicolson, London, 1987)

Campbell-Johnson, A., *Mission with Mountbatten* (Hale, London, 1951)

Carlton, D., *Anthony Eden* (Allen Lane, London, 1981)

Cassidy, H. C., *Moscow Dateline* (Cassell, London, 1943)

Castle, B., *Fighting All the Way* (Macmillan, London, 1993)

Cecil, R., *Hitler's Decision to Invade Russia, 1941* (Davis-Poynter, London, 1975)

Cecil, Viscount, *A Great Experiment – an Autobiography* (Cape, London, 1941)

Chalmers, W. S., *Max Horton and the Western Approaches* (Hodder & Stoughton, London, 1954)

Chandos, Lord, *Memoirs* (Bodley Head, London, 1962)

Charlton, M., *The Price of Victory* (BBC, London, 1983)

Charmley, J., *Churchill and the End of Glory* (Hodder & Stoughton, London, 1993)

Chester, L., Fay, S., and Young H., *The Zinoviev Letter* (Heinemann, London, 1967)

Churchill, W. S., *The Second World War: Vol. 3, The Grand Alliance; Vol. 4, The Hinge of Fate* (Cassell, London, 1950, 1951)

Citrine, Lord, *Men and Work – an Autobiography* (Hutchinson, London, 1964)

Clegg, H. A., *A History of British Trade Unions since 1889: Vol. 3, 1934–1951* (Clarendon, Oxford, 1994)

Clynes, J. R., *Memoirs* (Hutchinson, London, 1937)

Cockett, R., *David Astor and the* Observer (Deutsch, London, 1991)

——*Thinking the Unthinkable – Think-Tanks and the Economic Counter-Revolution 1931–1983* (HarperCollins, London, 1994)

Cole, G. D. H., *The People's Front* (Gollancz, London, 1937)

Cole, M., *The Life of G. D. H. Cole* (Macmillan, London, 1971)

Collins, D., *Partners in Protest – Life with Canon Collins* (Gollancz, London, 1992)

Collins, Canon L. J., *Faith under Fire* (Frewin, London, 1966)

Colville, J., *Footprints in Time* (Collins, London, 1976)

Colvin, I., *Vansittart in Office* (Gollancz, London, 1965)

Cooke, C., *The Life of Richard Stafford Cripps* (Hodder & Stoughton, London, 1957)

Coupland, R., *The Cripps Mission* (Oxford University Press, London, 1942)

Cowling, M., *The Impact of Hitler* (Cambridge University Press, Cambridge, 1975)

Creighton, C., *A History of Epidemics in Britain: Vol. 2* (Frank Cass, London, 2nd edn, 1965)

Cripps, A., *Memoir* (privately published, 1893)

——*Spice of Life* (privately published, no date)

Cripps, B., *Leonard Cripps* (privately published, 1960)

Cripps, F., *Life's a Gamble* (Odhams, London, 1957)

Cripps, S., *Can Socialism Come by Constitutional Means?* (Socialist League, 1934)

——*Are You a Worker? Where the Middle Class Stands* (Socialist League, 1935)

——*The Struggle for Peace* (Gollancz, London, 1936)

——*God in Our Work* (Nelson, London, 1949)

Crofts, W., *Coercion or Persuasion – Propaganda in Britain after 1945* (Routledge, London, 1989)

Crosby, G. R., *Disarmament and Peace in British Politics 1914–1919* (Harvard University Press, Cambridge, Mass., 1957)

Cross, C., *Philip Snowden* (Barrie & Rockliff, London, 1966)

Cummings, M., *These Uproarious Years – a Pictorial Post-War History by Cummings* (MacGibbon & Kee, London, 1954)

Custance, R., ed., *Winchester College – Sixth-Centenary Essays* (Oxford University Press, London, 1982)

Dalton, H., *The Fateful Years – Memoirs 1931–1945* (Muller, London, 1957)

——*High Tide and After – Memoirs 1945–1960* (Muller, London, 1962)

Davenport, N., *Memoirs of a City Radical* (Weidenfeld & Nicolson, London, 1974)

Day, D., *The Great Betrayal – Britain, Australia and the Onset of the Pacific War 1939–1942* (Angus & Robertson, London, 1988)

Dell, E., *The Schuman Plan and the British Abdication of Leadership in Europe* (Clarendon, Oxford, 1995)

——*The Chancellors* (HarperCollins, London, 1996)

Deutscher, I., *Stalin: A Political Biography* (Oxford University Press, London, 1949)

Devons, E., *Planning in Practice – Essays in Aircraft Planning in Wartime* (Cambridge University Press, Cambridge, 1950)

Dilke, C., *Dr Moberley's Mint-Mark: A Study of Winchester College* (Heinemann, London, 1965)

Donoughue, B., and Jones, G., *Herbert Morrison – Portrait of a Politician* (Weidenfeld & Nicolson, London, 1973)

Dow, J. C. R., *The Management of the British Economy 1945–1960* (Cambridge University Press, Cambridge, 1964)

Driberg, T., *Swaff: The Life and Times of Hannen Swaffer* (Macdonald & Jane's, London, 1974)

Eatwell, R., *The 1945–1951 Labour Governments* (Batsford, London, 1979)

Eccles, D., *By Safe Hand – Letters 1939–1942* (Bodley Head, London, 1985)

Edelman, M., The Mirror – *a Political History* (Hamish Hamilton, London, 1966)

Eden, Sir A., *Memoirs: The Reckoning* (Cassell, London, 1965)

Edgerton, D., *England and the Aeroplane* (Macmillan, Basingstoke, 1991)

Egerton, The Hon. Lady, *Sir Alfred Egerton FRS 1886–1959 – a Memoir with Papers* (privately published, London, 1963)

Edwardes, M., *The Last Years of British India* (Penguin, London, 1967)

Edwards, J., *The Law Officers of the Crown* (Sweet & Maxwell, London, 1964)

Ellis, E., *T. J.: A Life of Dr Thomas Jones C. H.* (University of Wales, Cardiff, 1992)

Estorick, E., *Stafford Cripps – a Biography* (Heinemann, London, 1949)

Fabian Society, *The Road to Recovery* (Allan Wingate, London, 1948)

Fedden, Sir R., *Britain's Air Survival* (Cassell, London, 1957)

Fforde, J., *The Bank of England and Public Policy 1941–1958* (Cambridge University Press, Cambridge, 1992)

Findlay, A., and Mills, W., eds., *British Chemists* (Chemical Society, London, 1947)

Fleet-Street – the Inside Story of Journalism (Macdonald, London, 1966)

Foot, M., *Aneurin Bevan: Vol. 1, 1897–1945* (MacGibbon & Kee, London, 1962); *Vol. 2, 1945–1960* (Davis-Poynter, London, 1973)

——*Debts of Honour* (Pan, London, 1980)

Franks, O., *The Movement towards Unity in Europe* (University of Texas, 1989)

Freeman, S., *Production under Fire* (C. J. Fallon, Dublin, 1967)

Fyfe, H., *My Seven Selves* (Allen & Unwin, London, 1935)

Gardner, R. N., *Sterling–Dollar Diplomacy* (Clarendon, Oxford, 1956)

Garwood, E., *Will Clayton – a Short Biography* (University of Texas Press, Austin, 1958)

Ghosh, S., *Gandhi's Emissary* (Cresset Press, London, 1967)

Glendevon, J., *The Viceroy at Bay – Lord Linlithgow in India 1936–1943* (Collins, London, 1971)

Gollancz, V., *Reminiscences of Affection* (Gollancz, London, 1968)

Goodhart, P., *The 1922* (Macmillan, London, 1973)

Gordon, M. R., *Conflict and Consensus in Labour's Foreign Policy 1914–1965* (Harvard University Press, Cambridge, Mass., 1969)

Gorodetsky, G., *Stafford Cripps' Mission to Moscow, 1940–1942* (Cambridge University Press, Cambridge, 1984)

Gourlay, L., ed., *The Beaverbrook I Knew* (Quartet, London, 1984)

Gowing, M., *Independence and Deterrence – Britain and Atomic Energy 1945–1952* (Macmillan, London, 1974)

Graham, T. N., *The Life of the Rt Hon. Willie Graham* (Hutchinson, London, 1948)

Griffiths, J., *Pages from Memory* (Dent, London, 1969)

Grigg, P. J., *Prejudice and Judgment* (Cape, London, 1948)

Grisewood, H., *One Thing at a Time* (Hutchinson, London, 1968)

Gunston, W. T., *By Jupiter! The Life of Sir Roy Fedden* (Royal Aeronautical Society, London, 1978)

Gupta, P. S., *Imperialism and the British Labour Movement 1914–1964* (Macmillan, London, 1975)

Gwyer, J. M., and Butler, J. R. M., *Grand Strategy: Vol. 2* (HMSO, London, 1964)

Hamilton, M. A., *Arthur Henderson* (Heinemann, London, 1938)

——*Remembering My Good Friends* (Cape, London, 1944)

Hannah, L., *Electricity before Nationalisation* (Macmillan, London, 1979)

Hannington, W., *Unemployed Struggles 1919–1936* (Lawrence & Wishart, London, 1936)

Hartcup, G., *The War of Invention – Scientific Developments 1914–1918* (Brassey's, London, 1988)

Harriman, W. A., and Abel, E., *Special Envoy to Churchill and Stalin 1941–1946* (Hutchinson, London, 1976)

Harris, K., *Attlee* (Weidenfeld & Nicolson, London, 1982)

Headey, B., *British Cabinet Ministers* (Allen & Unwin, London, 1974)

Hennessy, P., *Never Again – Britain 1945–1951* (Cape, London, 1992)

Herbert, A. P., *Independent Member* (Methuen, London, 1950)

——*A. P. H. – His Life and Times* (Heinemann, London, 1970)

Hinsley, F., et al., *British Intelligence in the Second World War: Vols. 1 and 3* (HMSO, London, 1979, 1989)

Hodson, H. V., *The Great Divide: Britain–India–Pakistan* (Hutchinson, London, 1969)

Hogan, M., *The Marshall Plan – America, Britain and the Reconstruction of Western Europe 1947–1952* (Cambridge University Press, Cambridge, 1987)

Horner, A., *Incorrigible Rebel* (MacGibbon & Kee, London, 1960)

Hulme, T. E., *Speculations* (Routledge, London, 1949)

Hunter, L., *The Road to Brighton Pier* (Arthur Barker, London, 1959)

Hyde, H. Montgomery, *Norman Birkett: The Life of Lord Birkett of Ulverston* (Hamish Hamilton, 1964)

Inglis, B., *Abdication* (Hodder & Stoughton, London, 1966)

Ingrams, R., *God's Apology – a Chronicle of Three Friends* (Deutsch, London, 1977)

Iremonger, F. A., *William Temple Archbishop of Canterbury – His Life and Letters* (Oxford University Press, London, 1948)

Iremonger, L., *The Fiery Chariot: A Study of British Prime Ministers and the Search for Love* (Secker & Warburg, London, 1970)

Irving, D., *The Destruction of Dresden* (William Kimber, London, 1963)

Jarvis, A., ed., *Democracy Alive* (Sidgwick & Jackson, London, 1946)

Jay, D., *Socialism in the New Society* (Longmans, London, 1962)

——*Change and Fortune* (Hutchinson, London, 1980)

Jeremy, D. J., *The Dictionary of Business Biography: Vol. 2* (Butterworth, London, 1984)

Jewkes, J., *Ordeal by Planning* (Macmillan, London, 1948)

Jones, B., *The Russia Complex – the British Labour Party and the Soviet Union* (Manchester University Press, Manchester, 1977)

Jones, M., *Michael Foot* (Gollancz, London, 1994)

Jones, R. V., *Most Secret War* (Hamish Hamilton, London, 1978)

Jouvenel, B. de, *Problems of Socialist England* (Batchworth, London, 1949)

Jupp, J., *The Radical Left in Britain 1931–1941* (Cass London, 1982)

Khrushchev's Secret Speech (Manchester Guardian, Manchester, 1956)

King, C., *Strictly Personal* (Weidenfeld & Nicolson, London, 1969)

King, F., and Matthews, G., eds., *About Turn – the British Communist Party and the Outbreak of the Second World War* (Lawrence & Wishart, London, 1990)

Kipping, Sir N., *Summing Up* (Hutchinson, London, 1972)

Klemperer, K. von, *German Resistance Against Hitler – the Search for Allies Abroad* (Clarendon, Oxford, 1992)

Koestler, A., *The Yogi and the Commissar* (Cape, London, 1945)

Lamb, R., *The Drift to War* (W. H. Allen, London, 1989)

Lazell, G., *From Pills to Penicillin – the Beecham Story* (Heinemann, London, 1975)

Lee, Sir F., *The Board of Trade* (Athlone Press, London, 1958)

Lee, J., *My Life With Nye* (Penguin, London, 1980)

Lees-Milne, J., *Midway on the Waves* (Faber, London, 1985)

Lewis, J., *The Left Book Club* (Gollancz, London, 1970)

Liddell-Hart, B., *A History of the Second World War* (Cassell, London, 1970)

Local Men of Mark (South Bucks Standard, High Wycombe, 1891)

Lysaght, C., *Brendan Bracken* (Allen Lane, London, 1979)

McCallum, R. B., *Public Opinion and the Last Peace* (Oxford University Press, London, 1944)

——and Readman, A., *The British General Election of 1945* (Oxford University Press, London, 1947)

MacDonald, M., *Titans and Others* (Collins, London, 1972)

Mackintosh, Sir A., *Echoes of Big Ben* (Jarrold's, London, 1945)

Mackintosh, J., *The British Cabinet* (Stevens & Sons, London, 1962)

McLachlan, D., *In the Editor's Chair* (Weidenfeld & Nicolson, London, 1971)

McLaine, I., *Ministry of Morale – Home Front Morale and the Ministry of Information in World War Two* (Allen & Unwin, London, 1979)

McLeod, K., *A Passion for Friendship – Sibyl Colefax and Her Circle* (Michael Joseph, London, 1991)

McNair, J., *James Maxton – the Beloved Rebel* (Allen & Unwin, London, 1955)

Mahon, J., *Harry Pollitt – a Biography* (Lawrence & Wishart, London, 1976)

Maisky, I., *Memoirs of a Soviet Ambassador 1938–1943* (Hutchinson, London, 1967)

Manning, L., *A Life for Education* (Gollancz, London, 1970)

Margach, J., *The Abuse of Power* (W. H. Allen, London, 1978)

——*The Anatomy of Power* (W. H. Allen, London, 1979)

Marquand, D., *Ramsay MacDonald* (Cape, London, 1977)

——*The Unprincipled Society* (Fontana, London, 1988)

Martin, K., *Harold Laski – a Biographical Memoir* (Cape, London, 1969)

——*Editor – a Volume of Autobiography 1931–1945* (Hutchinson, London, 1968)

Maugham, Viscount, *At the End of the Day* (Heinemann, London, 1954)

Mayes, L. J., *The History of the Borough of High Wycombe – from 1880 to the Present Day* (Routledge & Kegan Paul, London, 1960)

Mercer, H., Rollings, N., and Tomlinson, J., eds., *Labour Governments and Private Industry – the Experience of 1945–1951* (Edinburgh University Press, Edinburgh, 1992)

Meynell, Dame A., *Public Servant, Private Woman – an Autobiography* (Gollancz, London, 1988)

Middlemas, K., *Power, Competition and the State: Vol. 1, Britain in Search of Balance 1940–1961* (Macmillan, London, 1986)

Mikardo, I., *Backbencher* (Weidenfeld & Nicolson, London, 1988)

Milward, A., *The Reconstruction of Western Europe 1945–1951* (Methuen, London, 1984)

Mitchison, N., *You May Well Ask – a Memoir 1920–1940* (Gollancz, London, 1979)

Moggridge, D., *Maynard Keynes: An Economist's Biography* (Routledge, London, 1992)

Molesworth, G. N., *Curfew on Olympus* (Asia Publishing House, Bombay, 1965)

Monnet, J., *Mémoires* (Fayard, Paris, 1976)

Moore, R. J., *Churchill, Cripps and India, 1939–1945* (Clarendon, Oxford, 1979)

——*Escape from Empire: the Attlee Government and the Indian Problem* (Clarendon, Oxford, 1983)

Moran, Lord, *Winston Churchill: The Struggle for Survival 1940–1965* (Sphere, London, 1968)

Morgan, K., *Harry Pollitt* (Manchester University Press, Manchester, 1993)

Morgan, K. O., *Labour in Power 1945–1951* (Oxford University Press, London, 1984)

——*Labour People* (Oxford University Press, London, 1987)

Morpurgo, J. E., *Barnes Wallis* (Longmans, London, 1972)

Morris, B., *The Roots of Appeasement* (Cass, London, 1991)

Morrison, H., *An Autobiography* (Odhams, London, 1960)

Moulton, H. F., *The Life of Lord Moulton* (Nisbet & Co, London, 1922)

Muggeridge, K., *Beatrice Webb: A Life* (Secker & Warburg, London, 1967)

Muggeridge, M., *The Green Stick* (Collins, Glasgow, 1972)

Murphy, J. T., *New Horizons* (John Lane, London, 1940)

Nairn, T., *The Enchanted Glass – Britain and its Monarchy* (Radius, London, 1988)

Nicolson, H., *King George the Fifth – His Life and Reign* (Constable, London, 1952)

Oakley, C., *Men at Work* (Hodder & Stoughton, London, 1945)

O'Dell, T. H., *Inventions and Official Secrecy – a History of Secret Patents in the United Kingdom* (Clarendon, Oxford, 1994)

Orwell, G., *The Collected Essays, Journalism and Letters: Vol. 2, 1940–1943* (Penguin, London, 1968)

Ovendale, R., ed., *The Foreign Policy of the British Labour Governments 1945–1951* (Leicester University Press, Leicester, 1984)

Overy, R., *Why the Allies Won* (Cape, London, 1995)

Pagnamenta, P. and Overy, R., *All Our Working Lives* (BBC, London, 1984)

Parmoor, [1st] Lord, *Do Well and Right and Let the World Sink* (University College, London, 1915)

——*A Retrospect* (Heinemann, London, 1936)

Parmoor, 2nd Lord, *Parmoor and the Cripps Family* (privately published, no date)

Paton, J., *Left Turn! The Autobiography of John Paton* (Secker & Warburg, London, 1936)

Pelling, H., *The Labour Governments 1945–1951* (Macmillan, London, 1984)

——*Britain and the Marshall Plan* (Macmillan, London, 1987)

Pethick-Lawrence, F., *Fate Has Been Kind* (Hutchinson, London, 1943)

Philips, C., and Wainwright, M., eds., *The Partition of India -Problems and Perspectives 1935–1947* (Allen & Unwin, London, 1970)

Pimlott, B., *Labour and the Left in the 1930s* (Cambridge University Press, Cambridge, 1977)

——*Hugh Dalton* (Cape, London, 1985)

——*Harold Wilson* (HarperCollins, London, 1992)

Plowden, E., *An Industrialist in the Treasury* (Deutsch, London, 1989)

Plowden, W., *The Motor Car and Politics in Britain* (Penguin, London, 1971)

Plumb, J. H., ed., *Studies in Social History* (Longmans, London, 1955)

Postan, M. M., *British War Production* (HMSO, London, 1952)

Postgate, R., *The Life of George Lansbury* (Longmans, London, 1951)

Pound, R., *Their Moods and Mine* (Chapman & Hall, London, 1937)

Pressnell, L. S., *External Economic Policy since the War* (HMSO, London, 1986)

Pritt, D. N., *The Labour Government 1945–1951* (Lawrence & Wishart, London, 1963)

——*The Autobiography of D. N. Pritt: Vol. 1, From Right to Left; Vol. 2, Brasshats and Bureaucrats* (Lawrence & Wishart, London, 1965, 1966)

Reader, W. J., *Imperial Chemical Industries: Vol. 2* (Oxford University Press, London, 1975)

Reckitt, M., *As It Happened* (Dent, London, 1941)

Rendel, Sir G., *The Sword and the Olive* (Murray, London, 1957)

Rentoul, G., *This is My Case* (Hutchinson, London, 1944)

Rhodes James, R., *Anthony Eden* (Weidenfeld & Nicolson, London, 1986)

Roberts, G., *The Unholy Alliance* (I. B. Tauris, London, 1989)

Robertson, A. J., *The Bleak Midwinter 1947* (Manchester University Press, Manchester, 1987)

Robertson Scott, J. W., *'We' and Me* (W. H. Allen, London, 1956)

Robinson, E. A. G., *Economic Planning in the United Kingdom – Some Lessons* (Cambridge University Press, London, 1967)

Robson, W. A., *Justice and Administrative Law – a Study of the British Constitution* (Macmillan, London, 1928)

Rodgers, W. T., ed., *Hugh Gaitskell 1906–1963* (Thames and Hudson, London, 1964)

Roll, E., *Crowded Hours* (Faber, London, 1985)

Roskill, S., *The War at Sea 1939–1945: Vol. 2* (HMSO, London, 1956)

Rossi, A., *The Russo-German Alliance – August 1939–June 1941* (Chapman & Hall, London, 1950)

Rothwell, V., *Britain and the Cold War 1941–1947* (Cape, London, 1982)

Russell, Sir G., *Designer's Trade* (Allen & Unwin, London, 1968)

Salter, Lord, *Memoirs of a Public Servant* (Faber, London, 1961)

Sampson, A., *The Anatomy of Britain* (Hodder & Stoughton, London, 1962)

Saward, D., *Bomber Harris* (Buchan & Enright, London, 1984)

Schuster, Sir G., 'Richard Stafford Cripps', in *Biographical Memoirs of Fellows of the Royal Society* (Royal Society, London, 1955)

——*Private Work and Public Causes – a Personal Record 1881–1978* (D. Brown, Cowbridge, 1979)

Scott, Sir H., *Your Obedient Servant* (Deutsch, London, 1959)

Shawcross, H., *Life Sentence – the Memoirs of Hartley Shawcross* (Constable, London, 1995)

Shirer, W. L., *The Rise and Fall of the Third Reich* (Pan, London, 1960)

Shonfield, A., *British Economic Policy since the War* (Penguin, London, 1958)

Simon, Sir J., *Three Speeches on the General Strike* (Macmillan, London, 1926)

Sissons, M., and French, P., eds., *Age of Austerity* (Penguin, London, 1965)

Sixty Years of Trade Unionism 1868–1928 (Trades Union Congress, London, 1928)

Slessor, Sir J., *The Central Blue* (Cassel, London, 1956)

Sontag, R. J., and Beddie, J. S., eds., *Nazi–Soviet Relations 1939–1941* (Department of State, Washington DC, 1948)

Spaak, P.-H., *The Continuing Battle* (Weidenfeld & Nicolson, London, 1971)

Spears, Sir E., *Assignment to Catastrophe: Vol. 1, Prelude to Dunkirk* (Heinemann, London, 1954)

Stannage, T., *Baldwin Thwarts the Opposition – the British General Election of 1935* (Croom Helm, London, 1980)

Stevens, R., *Law and Politics – the House of Lords as a Judicial Body* (Weidenfeld & Nicolson, London, 1979)

Stockwood, M., *Chanctonbury Ring – the Autobiography of Mervyn Stockwood* (Hodder & Stoughton, London, 1982)

Strachey, J., *The Strangled Cry* (Bodley Head, London, 1962)

Strauss, P., *Cripps – Advocate and Rebel* (Gollancz, London, 1943)

Stuart, J., *Within the Fringe – an Autobiography* (Bodley Head, London, 1967)

Stucke, R. B., ed., *Woolwich Labour Party – Fifty Years 1903–1953* (Woolwich, 1953)

Sudoplatov, A., *Special Tasks* (Little, Brown, London, 1994)

Sulzberger, C. L., *A Long Row of Candles* (Macdonald, London, 1969)

Swinford, G., *History of Filkins* (privately published, 1958)

Swinton, Lord, *Sixty Years of Power* (Hutchinson, London, 1966)

Taylor, A. J. P., *The Troublemakers – Dissent over Foreign Policy 1792–1939* (Hamish Hamilton, London, 1957)

——*Beaverbrook* (Penguin, London, 1972)

——, ed., *W. P. Crozier: Off the Record – Political Interviews 1932–1944* (Hutchinson, London, 1973)

Thomas, E., ed., *Tribune 21* (Macdonald, London, 1958)

Thomas, H., *John Strachey* (Eyre, Methuen, London, 1973)

Thompson, A., *The Day Before Yesterday* (Sidgwick & Jackson, London, 1971)

Thorne, C., *Allies of a Kind – the United States, Britain and the War against Japan 1941–1945* (Hamish Hamilton, London, 1978)

Thorpe, A., *The British General Election of 1931* (Clarendon, Oxford, 1991)

Thurtle, E., *An Onlooker* (Chaterson, London, 1945)

Tiratsoo, N., ed., *The Attlee Years* (Pinter, London, 1991)

Tout, H., *The Standard of Living in Bristol* (University of Bristol, 1938)

Trevelyan, G. M., *Grey of Fallodon* (Longmans, London, 1937)

Trevor-Roper, H., ed., *Hitler's Table Talk 1941–1944* (Weidenfeld & Nicolson, London, 1953)

Tyler, F., *Cripps – a Portrait and a Prospect* (Harrap, London, 1942)

Vaizey, J., *In Breach of Promise* (Weidenfeld & Nicolson, London, 1983)

Volkogonov, D., *Stalin* (Weidenfeld & Nicolson, London, 1991)

Waites, B., *A Class Society at War – England 1914–18* (Berg, Leamington Spa, 1987)

Wakefield, Sir E., *Past Imperative* (Chatto & Windus, London, 1966)

Watkins, E., *The Cautious Revolution* (Secker & Warburg, London, 1951)

Watson-Watt, Sir R., *Three Steps to Victory* (Odhams, London, 1957)

Weatherall, D., Ledingham, J., and Warrell, D., eds., *The Oxford Textbook of Medicine* (Oxford University Press, Oxford, 2nd edn, 1987)

Webster, C., *The Health Services since the War* (HMSO, London, 1988)

Werth, A., *Russia at War 1941–1945* (Barrie & Rockliff, London, 1964)

West, W. J., ed., *Orwell – the War Broadcasts* (Duckworth, London, 1985)

Wheeler, Sir M., *Still Digging* (Michael Joseph, London, 1955)

Wheeler-Bennett, Sir J., ed., *Action This Day* (Macmillan, London, 1968)

Whitfield, B., *A Brief History of Bristol South-East Labour Party 1918–1950* (Bristol, 1979)

Whittle, Sir F., *Jet – the Story of a Pioneer* (Muller, London, 1953)

Wildavsky, A., *The Private Government of Public Money* (Macmillan, London, 1974)

Williams, A., *Labour and Russia – the Attitude of the Labour Party to the USSR 1924–34* (Manchester University Press, Manchester, 1989)

Williams, E. T., and Nichols, C. S., eds., *The Dictionary of National Biography 1961–1970* (Oxford University Press, Oxford, 1981)

Williams, F., *The Triple Challenge* (Heinemann, London, 1948)

——*Ernest Bevin* (Hutchinson, London, 1952)

——*A Prime Minister Remembers: The War and Post-War Memoirs of the Rt Hon. Earl Attlee* (Heinemann, London, 1961)

——*Nothing So Strange* (Cassell, London, 1970)

Williams, Lord, *Digging for Britain* (Hutchinson, London, 1965)

Williams, P. M., *Hugh Gaitskell – a Political Biography* (Cape, London, 1979)

Williams Ellis, A., *Women in War Factories* (Gollancz, London, 1943)

Williams Ellis, C., *Sir Lawrence Weaver* (Bles, London, 1933)

Williamson, P., *National Crisis and National Government, 1926–1932* (Cambridge University Press, Cambridge, 1992)

Willis, T., *Whatever Happened to Tom Mix?* (Cassell, London, 1970)

Wilson, H., *The Labour Government 1964–1970* (Penguin, London, 1974)

Wood, A., *The Groundnut Affair* (Bodley Head, London, 1950)

Woodward, E. L., *British Foreign Policy in the Second World War: Vol. 1* (HMSO, London, 1970)

Woolton, Lord, *Memoirs* (Cassell, London, 1959)

Wrigley, C., ed., *Warfare, Diplomacy and Politics* (Hamish Hamilton, London, 1986)

Wyatt, W., *Turn Again, Westminster* (Deutsch, London, 1973)

——*To the Point* (Weidenfeld & Nicolson, London, 1981)

——*Confessions of an Optimist* (Collins, London, 1985)

Young, J., *Britain, France and the Unity of Europe 1945–1951* (Leicester University Press, Leicester, 1984)

Zhukov, G., *Marshal of the Soviet Union G. Zhukov: Reminiscences and Reflections: Vol. 1*, trans. V. Schneierson (Central Books, London, 1985)

Ziegler, P., *Mountbatten* (Book Club Associates, Swindon, 1985)

Zimmerman, W.-D., and Smith, R. G., eds., *I Knew Dietrich Bonhoeffer* (Fontana, London, 1966)

(b) Articles and essays

Badash, L., 'British and American Views of the German Menace in World War One', *Notes and Records of the Royal Society*, Vol. 34 (1979), pp. 91–121

Berrington, H., review article in *The British Journal of Political Science*, July 1974, pp. 345–69

Day, D., 'Churchill and his War Rivals', in *History Today*, April 1991, pp. 15–21

Eatwell, R., 'Munich, Public Opinion and Popular Front', in *Journal of Contemporary History*, Vol. 6 (1971), pp. 122–139

——'The Cripps Expulsion – Sir Stafford Cripps and the Labour party, 1937–1939' (unpublished typescript, 1972)

Gorodetsky, G., 'Churchill's Warning to Stalin: A Reappraisal', in *Historical Journal*, Vol. 29 (1986), pp. 979–90

Hamilton, M. A., 'Sir Stafford Cripps – a Personal Sketch', in *Britain Today*, January 1951, pp. 15–19

Hanak, H., 'Sir Stafford Cripps as British Ambassador in Moscow, May 1940 to June 1941', in *English Historical Review*, Vol. 370 (1979), pp. 48–70

——'Sir Stafford Cripps as Ambassador in Moscow June 1941–January 1942', in *English Historical Review*, Vol. 383 (1982), pp. 332–44

Headlam, C., 'Labour and the Constitution', in *Quarterly Review*, April 1934, pp. 350–66

Leslie, S. C., 'The Work of the Economic Information Unit', in *Public Administration*, spring 1950, pp. 17–26

L'Etang, H., 'The Health of Statesmen and Affairs of Nations', in *The Practitioner*, January 1958, pp. 113–18

Listowel, Lord, 'The Whitehall Dimension of the Transfer of Power', in *Indo-British Review*, 1979, Parts 3 and 4, pp. 22–31

Moore, R. J., 'The Mystery of the Cripps Mission', in *Journal of Commonwealth Political Studies*, Vol. 11 (1973), pp. 195–213

Newton, S., 'The Sterling Crisis of 1947 and the British Response to the Marshall Plan', in *English Historical Review*, August 1984, pp. 391–408

——'The 1949 Sterling Crisis and the British Policy towards European Integration', in *Review of International Studies*, July 1985, pp. 169–82

Parmoor, [1st] Lord, 'Lord Lansdowne and the League of Nations', *Contemporary Review*, January 1918, pp. 8–13

——'Force and Christian Ethics', in *Contemporary Review*, December 1920, pp. 809–15

——'Geneva and League Policy', in *Contemporary Review*, September 1927, pp. 422–30

Robinson, A., 'The Economic Problems of the Transition from War to Peace: 1945–1949', in *Cambridge Journal of Economics*, Vol. 10 (1986), pp. 165–85

Stokes, E., 'Cripps in India', in *Historical Journal*, Vol. 14 (1971), pp. 427–34

Webb, S. (Lord Passfield), 'What Happened in 1931: A Record', in *Political Quarterly*, January–March 1932

Wichert, S., 'The British Left and Appeasement: Political Tactics or Alternative Policies', in W. Mommsen and L. Kettenacker, eds., *The Fascist Challenge and the Policy of Appeasement* (Allen & Unwin, London, 1983)

Woods, Sir J. H., 'Administrative Problems of Trade', in *Public Administration*, summer 1948, pp. 85–91

Zweiniger-Bargielowska, I., 'Rationing, Austerity and the Conservative Party Recovery after 1945', in *Historical Journal*, March 1994, pp. 173–95

(c) Newspapers and journals

The Alliance, Aspect, the *Beechams' Group Journal*, the *Bristol Labour Weekly, Britain Today*, the *British Weekly*, the *Bucks Free Press, Christian Life and Times*, the *Christian Science Monitor*, the *Christian World*, the *Church of England Newspaper*, the *Contemporary Record*, the *Contemporary Review, The Countryman*, the *Daily Express*, the *Daily Graphic*, the *Daily Herald*, the *Daily Mail* (Hull), the *Daily Mail* (London), the *Daily Telegraph* (Derby), the *Daily Telegraph* (London), the *Daily Worker*, the *Dewsbury Reporter, The Economist, Empire News*, the *Evening Post* (Bristol), the *Evening Standard* (London), the *Evening Times* (Bristol), the *Evening World* (Bristol), the *Financial Times, Forward*, the *Gloucestershire Journal, Goodwill – a Journal of International Friendship, The Guardian*, the *Illustrated London News, The Independent, Justice of the Peace*, the *Kentish Independent*, the *Labour Organiser*, the *Law Journal, Leader*, the *Left Review, The Listener*, the *Manchester Guardian*, the *Middlesex and Buckinghamshire Advertiser, The Millgate, Le Monde*, the *Morning Post, Nature*, the *Newcastle Journal*, the *New Clarion*, the *New Leader*, the *News Chronicle, News Review*, the *New Statesman and Nation*, the *News of the World*, the *New York Times, The Observer*, the *Oxford Times, The People, Picture Post, The Pioneer, Public Opinion*, the *Quarterly Review*, the *Railway Gazette, Recorder, Reynold's News, Reviews in History, The Socialist, Soundings*, the *South Bucks Standard*, the *South Wales Evening Post, The Spectator, The Statist*, the *Stroud News*, the *Sunday Chronicle*, the *Sunday Dispatch*, the *Sunday Express*, the *Sunday Pictorial*, the *Sunday Referee*, the *Sunday Telegraph*, the *Sunday Times, The Times, The Times Literary Supplement*, the *Times and Mirror* (Bristol), *The Tribune, Truth*, the *Week-End Review*, the *Western Daily Press*, the *Wilts and Gloucestershire Standard*, the *Witney Gazette, World Report*, the *World Review of Reviews, The Wykehamist*

INDEX